Ranking Economic Performance and Efficiency in the Global Market:

Emerging Research and Opportunities

Benjamen Franklen Gussen
University of Southern Queensland, Australia & Australian Law and Economics Association, Australia

A volume in the Advances in Finance, Accounting, and Economics (AFAE) Book Series

IGI Global
DISSEMINATOR OF KNOWLEDGE

Published in the United States of America by
IGI Global
Business Science Reference (an imprint of IGI Global)
701 E. Chocolate Avenue
Hershey PA, USA 17033
Tel: 717-533-8845
Fax: 717-533-8661
E-mail: cust@igi-global.com
Web site: http://www.igi-global.com

Library of Congress Cataloging-in-Publication Data

Names: Gussen, Benjamen Franklen, 1968- author.
Title: Ranking economic performance and efficiency in the global market : emerging research and opportunities / by Benjamen Franklen Gussen.
Description: Hershey : Business Science Reference, [2017]
Identifiers: LCCN 2017010689| ISBN 9781522527565 (hardcover) | ISBN 9781522527572 (ebook)
Subjects: LCSH: Economic indicators. | Industrial efficiency.
Classification: LCC HB135 .G87 2017 | DDC 330.9--dc23 LC record available at https://lccn.loc.gov/2017010689

This book is published in the IGI Global book series Advances in Finance, Accounting, and Economics (AFAE) (ISSN: 2327-5677; eISSN: 2327-5685)

British Cataloguing in Publication Data
A Cataloguing in Publication record for this book is available from the British Library.

For electronic access to this publication, please contact: eresources@igi-global.com.

Advances in Finance, Accounting, and Economics (AFAE) Book Series

ISSN:2327-5677
EISSN:2327-5685

MISSION

In our changing economic and business environment, it is important to consider the financial changes occurring internationally as well as within individual organizations and business environments. Understanding these changes as well as the factors that influence them is crucial in preparing for our financial future and ensuring economic sustainability and growth.

The **Advances in Finance, Accounting, and Economics (AFAE)** book series aims to publish comprehensive and informative titles in all areas of economics and economic theory, finance, and accounting to assist in advancing the available knowledge and providing for further research development in these dynamic fields.

COVERAGE

- Finance
- Corporate finance
- Development Economics
- Environmental and Social Accounting
- Behavioral Economics
- Ethics in Accounting and Finance
- Investments and Derivatives
- International trade
- Economic Indices and Quantitative Economic Methods
- Finance and Accounting in SMEs

IGI Global is currently accepting manuscripts for publication within this series. To submit a proposal for a volume in this series, please contact our Acquisition Editors at Acquisitions@igi-global.com or visit: http://www.igi-global.com/publish/.

The Advances in Finance, Accounting, and Economics (AFAE) Book Series (ISSN 2327-5677) is published by IGI Global, 701 E. Chocolate Avenue, Hershey, PA 17033-1240, USA, www.igi-global.com. This series is composed of titles available for purchase individually; each title is edited to be contextually exclusive from any other title within the series. For pricing and ordering information please visit http://www.igi-global.com/book-series/advances-finance-accounting-economics/73685. Postmaster: Send all address changes to above address.

Titles in this Series

For a list of additional titles in this series, please visit:
https://www.igi-global.com/book-series/advances-finance-accounting-economics/73685

Technological Integration as a Catalyst for Industrial Development and Economic Growth
Bryan Christiansen (PryMarke, LLC, USA) and Ülkü Yüksel (The University of Sydney Business School, Australia)
Business Science Reference • © 2017 • 272pp • H/C (ISBN: 9781522523192) • US $185.00

Handbook of Research on Economic, Financial, and Industrial Impacts on Infrastructure...
Ramesh Chandra Das (Katwa College, India)
Business Science Reference • © 2017 • 466pp • H/C (ISBN: 9781522523611) • US $230.00

Handbook of Research on Policies and Practices for Sustainable Economic Growth...
George M. Korres (University of Aegean, Greece) Elias Kourliouros (University of Aegean, Greece) and Maria P. Michailidis (University of Nicosia, Cyprus)
Business Science Reference • © 2017 • 440pp • H/C (ISBN: 9781522524588) • US $255.00

NFC Payment Systems and the New Era of Transaction Processing
Vibha Kaw Raina (Birla Institute of Technology, India)
Business Science Reference • © 2017 • 193pp • H/C (ISBN: 9781522523062) • US $155.00

Social, Health, and Environmental Infrastructures for Economic Growth
Ramesh Chandra Das (Katwa College, India)
Business Science Reference • © 2017 • 355pp • H/C (ISBN: 9781522523642) • US $200.00

Method of Systems Potential (MSP) Applications in Economics...
Grigorii Pushnoi (Independent Researcher, Russia)
Business Science Reference • © 2017 • 162pp • H/C (ISBN: 9781522521709) • US $135.00

Outward Foreign Direct Investment (FDI) in Emerging Market Economies
Tomasz Dorożyński (University of Lodz, Poland) and Anetta Kuna-Marszałek (University of Lodz, Poland)
Business Science Reference • © 2017 • 377pp • H/C (ISBN: 9781522523451) • US $210.00

For an enitre list of titles in this series, please visit:
https://www.igi-global.com/book-series/advances-finance-accounting-economics/73685

IGI Global
DISSEMINATOR OF KNOWLEDGE

701 East Chocolate Avenue, Hershey, PA 17033, USA
Tel: 717-533-8845 x100 • Fax: 717-533-8661
E-Mail: cust@igi-global.com • www.igi-global.com

Table of Contents

Preface

Soaked in blood were roses of white,

Little reminders of the Red Queen's might.

Cracked grounds and cloudless skies,

Echoed by those whom lost their lives.

Towering castles made of flesh,

Veins and arteries made a mesh,

Of which skeleton guards went to protect,

Nothing could stop a card that's undead.

Winds of dust and burning heat,

Lead to where you and the queen might meet.

The Red Queen, 2012 poem by DiamondDustMirror (The White Rabbit)

'Canada.' It is without much hesitation that most readers would give this answer to the question: 'Which country is economically more efficient, Canada or East Timor?' Similarly, the reader would not have any difficulty accepting that Japan is more efficient than San Marino, or that France is more efficient than Qatar. There is an ingrained expectation as to efficiency that we tend to take at face value——usually as an extension of 'economic development' or even 'economic complexity.' While this monograph acknowledges an overlap between efficiency, development, and complexity, it challenges efficiency 'stereotypes' by looking at economic efficiency through the lens of 'jurisdictional footprints.' Unlike geographical areas, these footprints indicate the spatial extent of a given country's monopoly over lawmaking. Figure 1 provides an efficiency classification of world countries. According to this map, there are only 'islands' of economic efficiency. The world is dominated by countries that are either economically inefficient or highly inefficient.

As a teenager, I used to stare at the (political) world map for hours on end. With its mosaic of colors, it was simply fascinating, and my passion for it became a life-long obsession. I delved into the map's 'life cycles.' The more I thought about how the map changed over time, the more I became convinced that countries are living organisms, each with its unique 'DNA' and traits. What became really intriguing was the idea of isolating the 'DNA' responsible for their prosperity and longevity. I became convinced that there were certain traits that helped predict the growth and collapse of countries——not in isolation, but within the world-system that produced them in the first place. I hence set out to identify traits of 'evolutionary fitness.' This eventually led to a rethinking of economic efficiency, in other words, the ability of countries to produce a given level of goods and services with the minimum amount of inputs. It became evident that efficient countries dominated their world-systems, and that the path to such efficiency was determined by these countries' ability to absorb and accumulate capital.

Figure 1. The world economic efficiency map

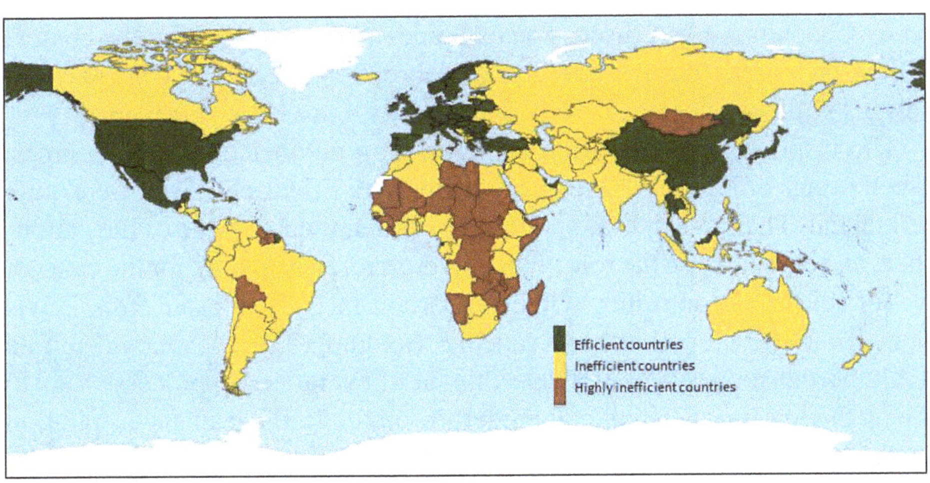

This book is hence about rethinking economic efficiency and its determinants. Broadly, the approach can be situated within the economic analysis of the law (law-and-economics), especially the normative strand of constitutional economics. The methodology, however, is heterodox. The theoretical underpinnings are based on an application of the laws of thermodynamics to the economic process, and more specifically, on interpreting the former as an energy transformation process. The resulting model is used to analyze the 'efficiency signature' of world countries for the period from 1990 to 2015, with emphasis on the world's largest economies (the G-20), and the United States in particular.

The purpose of this book is two-fold. The first is descriptive: to rank all world countries according to their economic efficiency. Some of the rankings challenge existing conceptions. For example, countries like Australia and Canada were found to be economically inefficient, notwithstanding their high per capita and HDI rankings. This is a direct result from their large jurisdictional footprints. Other countries that are also large by area, such as the United States and China, were found to be efficient. The difference is in how these efficient countries were able to 'perforate' their footprints with 'attractors' that enabled them to achieve efficiency. The second purpose is normative: to furnish specific insights into the determinants of economic efficiency. From Chapter 4 onwards, the emphasis is on this second objective. The analysis explores how countries can reduce their jurisdictional footprints to the end of improving their economic efficiency. In particular, the principle of hypotaxis and the legal personality of cities are enlisted to explore (economically efficient) constitutional designs. An analytical model that builds on universal constructs such as symmetry and scale is introduced to rationalize the normative signals gained from the descriptive part of the book (Chapters 1-5). A discussion of Spinozistic sovereignty in the context of the Dutch Republic furnishes further elaboration on efficient constitutional designs in the 21st century (see Conclusion).

The inspiration for the book comes from a number of diverse sources. The writings of Leopold Kohr, Jane Jacobs, and Friedrich Hayek were quite influential. Their analysis of spontaneous order, their critique of the nation-state, and emphasis on the role of cities were a reference point for the concept of 'jurisdictional footprints.' Other important influences came from Lewis Mumford, Peter Kropotkin, and Kenneth E. Boulding. These scholars identified the importance of 'scale' as a determinant of evolutionary processes. As to the methodology used in the 'ψ model' (Chapter 2), the primary inspiration came from Nicholas Georgescu-Roegen, who models the economic process as an energy-transformation process governed by the laws of thermodynamics. Henry Paynter was also inspirational, especially his 'bond graphs,' which allowed for modeling the interactions between different energy systems. Baruch Spinoza, and his understanding of sovereignty, also form a substantial influence on this tome. In the context of the Dutch Republic (1581-1795), Spinoza identified a nexus between the way polities are constituted, and their economic prosperity. His analysis remains relevant today. The normative part of this book builds on his insights.

The book has a number of distinct parts. Chapters 1 and 2 are highly theoretical and present the underpinnings for the mathematical models used to ascertain economic efficiency. Chapter 1 analyzes evolution to the end of furnishing a general theory of economic change. This analysis is applicable to both organisms and organizations. The general theory presented here is based on four analytical constructs: symmetry, scale, complexity, and collapse. Complexity is modeled as a force, similar to gravitation, while evolution is understood as a condition exhibiting an increase in morphological complexity. In the final analysis, economic change is linked to the structure of the political state. Pathologies of economic change, including morphostasis (in other words reaching a stage where growth and development are anemic due to the system's form and structure becoming static), necessitate a rethinking of political organization. Polycentricity and the principle of hypotaxis, with a praxis inspired by sovereign cities, are identified as imperative for the continuous evolution of societies, and hence their economies. In this future, nation-states become hypotactic. Charter cities replace nation-states on the 'international' stage. Chapter 2 builds on this theoretical framework by developing the 'ψ model.' The chapter furnishes a new metric for economic efficiency based on interpreting economies as energy transformation processes. Economic efficiency is attained through efficiencies in the transformation of (energy) inputs to (energy) outputs. Using per-unit (normalized) variables, an analytical model is constructed where the expected output from a Cantillonian production function (with only land and population as inputs) is compared to the actual GDP output. The data used for the 'ψ model' is readily available for free from a variety of databases. Readers should be able to easily verify the results in Chapters 3-5.

Readers can skip Chapters 1 and 2 and go directly to the findings in Chapters 3-5 and their appendices. Chapter 3 represents high-level results from the ψ model. The model classifies countries into sinks and sources, the former being countries for which the actual output is greater than that expected by the model. In Chapter 4, the ψ model is applied to study the composition of G-20 countries, where we find sinks and sources. The list of the highest-ranking sinks suggests smaller geopolitical footprints are more conducive to higher levels of economic efficiency. This in turn suggests that the effectiveness of economic policies, such as immigration, would be contingent on the size of these footprints. While small footprints are necessary for high economic efficiency, they are not sufficient. Future research needs to identify a set of conditions that are both necessary and sufficient for such efficiency. Chapter 5 continues the application of the analytical framework developed in Chapter 2, but this time at a sub-national level. The chapter looks at the 50 US states and the District of Columbia to investigate their relative efficiencies over time. The findings confirm the normative signals gained from the previous two chapters. Detailed analysis of the findings in each chapter can be found in the appendices at the end of the book. The *Appendix to Chapter 3* provides the 'efficiency signatures' for all world countries in 2015, for the period from 1990 to 2015. The *Appendix to Chapter 4* provides detailed analysis of each of the 19 countries in the G-20, while the *Appendix to Chapter 5* provides an analysis of each of the 50 US States and the District of Columbia.

Chapters 6 and 7 help the reader gain further understanding of the evolutionary role that 'jurisdictional footprints' play in enhancing economic efficiency. In particular, Chapter 6 presents the 'complexity ansatz,' a non-mathematical model to analyze the evolutionary fitness of polities. The chapter starts from the observation that there is no shortage of crises in the ecological (e.g. climate change), economic (e.g. the Global Financial Crisis), and socio-political spheres (e.g. the Arab Spring). While such crises are not new to the human saga, both the magnitude and frequency of these crises seem to be intensifying. The usual prognosis follows the public/private dichotomy, suggesting more or less government intervention (and the closely related variants of more integration and regime change). However, there are 'islands' of alternative analyses where crises result from scale distortion (organizational structures of states, markets, and firms that are too large or too small) and scale entanglement (strong rather than weak ties between different scales such as the local, national and global). The chapter attempts to synthesize this scale problematization into one coherent school of thought. To this end, the chapter introduces the 'complexity ansatz,' which links complexity to symmetry (breaking), scale and collapse. The chapter traces this ansatz in the writings of Friedrich Hayek, Leopold Kohr and Jane Jacobs (HKJ). The thesis is that the moribund nation-state needs to be relegated to a hypotactic role to evade its collapse. The chapter suggests that loosely coupled (fiscally and monetarily) autonomous city-regions should be the 'eyes' of socio-economic action. Chapter 7 builds on this normative signal by arguing that sovereignty, as envisaged by Spinoza, is the logical foundation for economically efficient constitutional designs. Constitutional constructs such as sovereignty weave an evolutionary dialectic between different organizational scales (the local, national, and global). This dialectic continues to wreak havoc at the local scale and can be interrupted only through explicit constitutional constraints on the size of jurisdictions. The chapter argues for more emphasis on constitutional orders in the spirit of Spinoza's understanding of sovereignty. This entails preference for hypotactic polities in which sovereignty is shared between different cities rather states where capital cities dominate.

I began writing this monograph in March 2016. Most of the chapters were written before the US presidential elections that year. In the aftermath of the Trump presidency, however, the normative signals in this book became even more relevant. On 27 January 2017, President Trump signed Executive Order 13769, titled 'Protecting the Nation from Foreign Terrorist Entry into the United States.' Aside from the legal challenges mounted against this order, a number of cities were prompted to reaffirm their status as a 'sanctuary city.' For example, on 29 January 2017, the Mayor of Chicago, Rahm Emanuel, affirmed the status of Chicago as a city that welcomes undocumented refugees and immigrants. The city became a 'de jure' sanctuary city in 2012 when the City Council passed the Welcoming City Ordinance (§ 2-173). The ordinance protects the residents' rights to access city services regardless of immigration status and prevents police officers from arresting individuals based on their immigration status alone (§ 2-173-042). Affirming such sanctuary status, whether in law or practice, is a form of affirming sovereignty, which can be traced back to the Kingdom of Israel, and the six cities of refuge named in the Torah, which included the first capital of Israel: Shechem. Moreover, while it could be argued that the rationale for these rights was based on atonement rather than protection, their very existence suggests a (*Jarlsberg*-like) 'perforation' of jurisdictional footprints, in a manner similar to the normative observation made in relation to attaining economic efficiency. 'Sanctuary cities' are one dimension in the more general proposition for 'charter cities,' where federal lawmaking becomes hypotactic (or subsidiary) to the basic laws of these cities. It is submitted that the ability of the Trump administration to 'Make America Great Again' rests on understanding the nexus between economic efficiency and the notion of 'jurisdictional perforation,' at the sub-national level. Accelerating the economic 'miracle' of less efficient States (see Chapter 5) requires a degree of hypotaxis that can stimulate the creation of more 'global cities' within such States.

Before I leave the readers to embark on their journey, I take their leave to thank the following people, who played an important role in bringing this book to fruition. The company of my mother through hard times, if only in spirit, was an important psychological factor. For her sacrifices throughout her life, she cannot be less than a full partner in my success. I also acknowledge the love and dedication that my wife and stepdaughters have given me throughout the writing and editing process. I gratefully acknowledge Professor Klaus Bosselmann, Associate Professor Marjan van den Belt, and Dr. Joel Colon-Rios for their valuable comments on earlier drafts of this book. Last but not least, I am indebted to the anonymous referees. Their feedback has been invaluable.

While lingering for the visitors,

B. F. Gussen
University of Southern Queensland, Australia
19 June 2017

Introduction

In the book of Exodus, we read about Jethro, Moses' father-in-law and the appointment of judges (Exodus: 18). The story goes as follows. Jethro objected to Moses' approach in managing the affair of the Israelites. Moses wanted to be the sole source of the law and how it applied. Jethro saw the long-term instability inherent in this approach. He advised his son-in-law to adopt what could be called today 'subsidiarity' (D'onorio, 1995, pp. 13-14). Moses hence chose capable men and made them leaders. These judges now decided the law for the people, save for difficult cases which were still brought to Moses. Now the law was able to evolve—to allow for local variation. This book maps this Mosaic approach unto the efficiency and sustainability of the world-economy. This is done by developing an analytical model that sets economic evolution as this Mosaic Law that needs to be dispensed to the people, and that the people need to adhere to for their salvation. Sustainability is Moses. However, just like Moses, it cannot overcome what Leopold Kohr, a rather obscure Austrian economist, called 'the problem of scale.' In the words of Kohr's most famous protégé, Ernst F. Schumacher, this problem can be described as follows: '[s] mall scale operations, no matter how numerous, are always less likely to be harmful to the natural environment [*qua* sustainability] than large-scale ones' (Schumacher, 1999, p. 22). Kohr spoke of a 'characteristic scale' (Kohr, 1978). In the context of the Israelites, Jethro's advice was about adherence to this scale. Even if we dispense with our Mosaic analogy in entirety, as discussed in the following chapters, we still end up facing a problem of scale.

To sustain and increase economic efficiency, we need to govern at the 'characteristic scale.' This entails devolving decision-making to local communities while providing a constitutional space—as in legal space within the constitution— that recognizes local decision-making (as a body politic). This approach requires a 'world-system' based on (global) cities rather than nation-states. Countries that have a large 'jurisdictional footprint,' such as the

United States, Canada, and Australia, need to provide this form of hypotaxis to continue their economic evolution in the future.

The rest of the book unpacks how global cities update Jethro's advice in the context of world-systems. The book elaborates the problem and the solution, and possible future development.

THE PROBLEM WITH ECONOMIES TODAY

In a nutshell, world-economies have largely eschewed their evolutionary kernel: localism. This resulted in a decrease in economic efficiency and reduced the stability of the world-system. In this monograph, localism is defined as:

An umbrella term which refers to the devolution of power and/or functions and/or resources away from central control and towards front-line managers, local democratic structures, local institutions and local communities, within an agreed framework of minimum standards. (Evans et al., 2013, p. 401)

Localism has been marginalized in the current responses to crises including the ecological crisis (Gussen, 2012). Probably, the reader can point out some exceptions to this general trend. Notwithstanding, even the most iconic of all environmental law instruments favors national and supranational intervention over localism. Take for example the *Earth Charter*, the flagship in the discourse on the response to the current ecological crisis. The *Charter* is mostly tilted in favor of nation-states rather than the local autonomy without which any response to the crisis would at best be a 'placebo effect' (Gussen, 2012, p. 182). We were led to believe in the virtues of current social, economic, and political integration through three 'technologies.' First, through the fiction of 'indigenous people,' which marginalizes local communities in search of self-organisation. Second, through 'universal human rights,' with their emphasis on individual rather than collective (communal) rights. Third, through the illusion of the 'complexity imperative' where the complex nature of our world dictates coordination at the global rather than the local level. We now accept globalization, which is only one particular modality of integration, as the only valid form of combating crises. There is an apparent insistence on the hegemony of a global response. One that is orchestrated by global institutions. All communities have to do is to implement the global vision bestowed on them by such institutions.

What is wrong with this picture? In one word, complexity. Elsewhere I have explained the nature of the complexity of ecological systems and the importance of self-organization (Gussen, 2015a; Gussen, 2015b). Let me elaborate through Joseph Tainter, a leading scholar on the collapse of complex societies. He finds that, historically, increasing complexity has limited the 'system capacity' of nations to resolve their problems and to adapt to their environment (Tainter, 1995, p. 400; Tainter, 2006). Tainter's argument is one of diminishing returns to complexity. Although Tainter does not use the term self-organizing, he correctly identifies the transition to self-organization and the ensuing decentralization of decision-making.

Tainter's depiction of complex societies is one where there is either resistance to self-organisation, which leads to collapse (e.g. the Roman Empire), or where self-organisation is enabled, hence evading potential collapse (e.g. the Byzantine Empire). A better way to understand the difference is to think of two types of complexity: one based on hierarchical organization (simple complexity), the other based on rhizomatic organization (emergent complexity) (Deleuze & Guattari, 1980). Rhizomatic causality is not chronological and does not look at the origin of things (inputs) but at their conclusions (outputs). For example, in the case of democracy, rhizomatic causality would look at outputs such as happiness, the rule of law, and economic growth, rather than the inputs of electoral processes, political parties, and civil rights. A rhizomatic interpretation favors a non-hierarchical polity based on non-linear self-organization and decentralization. Growing degrees of economic integration (globalization) and the ensuing modulation of local-global power relations is putting more emphasis than ever before on clarifying our understanding of the democratic ideal and its operation from within the nation-state. In fact, some argue that "globalization is the self-organizing process of constructing a world socio-economic community" (Voets & Biggiero, 2000; Schmitter, 1999). This level of economic integration is resulting from a paradigm shift away from the 'international model' and to a 'transnational model' (Voets & Biggiero, 2000; Mateos et al., 2002). Today, to cope with increasing complexity, there needs to be a move away from hierarchical organization, and towards growing degrees of self-organisation. Tainter provides one way of looking at the transition. Another way of explaining the same transition is the concept of a rhizome (above).

THE SOLUTION

Hypotaxis (also known as subsidiarity or spheres of sovereignty) is a response to the 'problem of scale' (see Chapter V). It is a fitness trait that prevents highly complex systems from collapsing. Sustainability cannot occur without hypotaxis, while hypotaxis guarantees sustainability. The dialectic between hypotaxis and sustainability becomes apparent when we understand hypotaxis as self-organization and sustainability as an emergent property. Emergence cannot occur in highly complex systems (such as polities) without self-organization (Gussen, 2015a; Gussen, 2015c). Hypotaxis is a modality of localism where the emphasis is on local communities. Hypotaxis is about embedding the decision-making process at the local level and ensuring that central government is subsidiary to local government (Gussen, 2014a; Gussen, 2014b). A related concept is 'solidarity' or 'social cohesion' (Wildt, 1999). It is defined as "a union of interests, purposes, or sympathies among members of a group; [the] fellowship of responsibilities and interests" (Gutierrez, 2005). Hypotaxis is the mechanism that bridges 'solidarity' (a local concept) and 'sustainability' (a global concept) (Gussen, 2015a; Gussen, 2015c).

The nation-state is a highly complex system within which cities function as 'attractors' (see glossary section). The collapse of such systems would ensue if there were a strong coupling between attractors (such coupling obtains in administrative rather than global cities). Only hypotaxis can make this eventuality improbable. Understanding the 'emergent properties' of sustainability and the 'self-organizing' properties of hypotaxis entails a shift in (policy) emphasis towards the latter. A historical reconstruction of the concepts of sustainability and hypotaxis elucidates their interdependence and suggests future global governance structures based on a hypotaxis where cities take the lead on (economic) sustainability (Gussen, 2013a; Gussen, 2013b).

Today, the contiguous-and-non-perforated-state principle is being challenged by new conceptions of the state as well as its sovereignty (Kurrild-Klitgaard, 2002, 146). There is an ongoing shift towards seeing the state as constituted on a non-contiguous basis. Using the analogy with the idea of a 'polycentric' legal order implying a multiplicity of independent centers of decision making (Hayek, 1983; Bell, 1991), there is no extensive evaluation of the need for, or merit of, an analogous 'polycentric' constitutional order (Barnett, 1998). Here the emphasis would be on maximizing constitutional options rather than deciding among constraints *per se*. Instead, usually, the assumption is made that "there is a state or a commonwealth, without exploring the question of which domain [a scalar construct] this commonwealth or state should actually occupy, and in relation to what other public bodies" (Backhaus, 1999, 281).

Such non-contiguous states are at the center of Spinoza's discourse (Spinoza, 1951; Balibar et al., 1989; Prokhovnik, 2004; Prokhovnik, 2001; Prokhovnik, 1997; Gross, 1996; Havercroft, 2010). Because his 'sovereignty' is closer to hypotaxis than to federalism, it is more receptive to city power and city autonomy (Blank, 2010, 549). The sharing of sovereignty (through subsidiarity) among cities hence finds explicit endorsement in his scholarship (Gussen, 2013b). Spinoza separates the constitutional and operational levels of collective decision-making, thus paving the way for the possibility of shared sovereignty. Shared sovereignty is also the approach followed in constitutional economics (Buchanan and Tullock, 1962). For Spinoza, who allied himself with the Dutch republican movement, under hypotaxis, sovereignty is not repugnant to principles of provincial autonomy. Spinozistic 'sovereignty' provides a model:

In which powers are shared between sovereign bodies . . . which reaffirm their separateness . . . . In federal systems such as the United States or in Australia, legislative, judicial and executive powers are distributed between federal and different state governments . . . under [Spinozistic sovereignty], however, 'confederal' powers . . . were extremely closely restricted . . . . Rather than attempting to harmonize differences [it upholds] the constructiveness of difference . . . . (Prokhovnik, 2007, p. 228).

It could be in fact argued that "Spinoza's notion of sovereignty is crucially designed as an instrument to defend the constitutional tradition, and not as an instrument to unify and strengthen the state. Its purpose is to check the development of centralized government, not to promote it" (Prokhovnik, 2001, p. 297).

James Buchanan echoes Spinoza. He explains his idea for European 'federalism' (better understood as subsidiarity) as "diversity among separate co-operative communities, of shared sovereignty, of effective devolution of political authority and, perhaps most importantly, of the *limits on* such authority" (Buchanan, 1990, pp. 3-4) (italics in the original, underlining added). Buchanan envisaged a "federal union within which members of separate units cooperate ..." and share sovereignty, where constitutional requirements guarantee free trade, and with a monetary constitution based on competing national currencies (Buchanan, 1990, p. 18).

In the following chapters, I elucidate this rationale through an analytical model that ranks world economies based on their efficiency. This model suggests a nexus between the 'jurisdictional footprint' of a given country, and its economic evolution (i.e. its ability to absorb and accumulate capital). Generally, countries with small footprints evolve (towards increased economic complexity). Large countries, on the other hand, require a 'perforation' of their jurisdiction through what came to be known as global cities (the Anglo-American approach), or through industrial clusters (the German approach), or through special economic and administrative zones (the Chinese approach). Economic evolution requires continued cellular division in the form of the production of new global cities or industrial clusters/zones.

CODETTA

The world-system needs to move to an Olympic future, as opposed to a 'World Cup' one. Let me explain. In an Olympics, for example, Rio 2016, one city hosts a multitude of games. All happening in one place, under the auspices of one city. The city becomes a showcase for the whole world. In a 'World Cup' instead, for example, the 2015 Rugby World Cup, a whole nation organizes games for one sport across its geographic extent. In the case of the 2015 World Cup, England hosted the tournament in no less than eleven cities. The 'World Cup' was showcasing England rather than any of these cities *per se*. Some would argue that it would not be efficient for one city to host a Rugby world cup, as it would not have enough stadia to have all games played on a tight schedule (usually 30 days). However, London alone has at least 15 venues (including Wembley, Twickenham, Emirates, Stamford, White Hart Lane, and the Olympic Stadium). Such global cities are capable of hosting a 'World Cup'—alone.

The key point is that the existing nation-state 'world-system' has weakened the economic evolution of these states. Much of the work being done under the nation-state paradigm is 'cosmetic.' What is needed instead is a brave departure towards a 'world-system' dominated by hypotaxis on the city-region scale (a city and its hinterland). Economic evolution would diffuse through this 'world-system' from one global city to another (just like technology). In this future, self-organization at the city-scale helps ensure (economic) sustainability. In this future, global cities replace democracy as the benchmark for progress.

REFERENCES

Backhaus, J. G. (1999). Subsidiarity. In J. G. Backhaus (Ed.), *The Elgar companion to law and economics* (2nd ed., pp. 280–286). Northampton, Mass.: Edward Elgar. doi:10.4337/9781843768692.00020

Balibar, E., Stolze, T., & Giancotti, E. (1989). Spinoza, the anti-Orwell: the fear of the masses. *Rethinking Marxism: A Journal of Economics. Cultura e Scuola*, *2*(3), 104–139.

Barnett, R. E. (1998). *The structure of liberty: Justice and the rule of law.* Oxford: Clarendon Press.

Bell, T. W. (1991). Polycentric law. *Humane Studies Review, 7*(1). Retrieved from http://osf1.gmu.edu/~ihs/w91issues.html

Blank, Y. (2010). Federalism, subsidiarity, and the role of local governments in an age of global multilevel governance. *The Fordham Urban Law Journal*, *37*(2), 509–558.

Buchanan, J., & Tullock, G. (1962). *The calculus of consent: Logical foundations of constitutional democracy*. Ann Arbor: University of Michigan Press. doi:10.3998/mpub.7687

Buchanan, J. A. (1990). *Europe's constitutional future*. London: Institute of Economic Affairs.

D'Onorio, J.-B. (1995). *La subsidiarité: De la théorie à la pratique*. Paris: Téqui.

Deleuze, G., & Guattari, F. (1980). *A thousand plateaus*. London: Continuum.

Evans, M., Marsh, D., & Stoker, G. (2013). Understanding localism. *Policy Studies*, *34*(4), 401–407. doi:10.1080/01442872.2013.822699

Gross, G. M. (1996). Spinoza and the federal polity. *Publius*, *26*(1), 117–136. doi:10.1093/oxfordjournals.pubjof.a029830

Gussen, B. F. (2012). The marginalisation of localism in current responses to the ecological crisis. *New Zealand Journal of Environmental Law*, *16*, 167–201.

Gussen, B. F. (2013a). On the problem of scale: Hayek, Kohr, Jacobs and the reinvention of the political state. *Constitutional Political Economy*, *24*(1), 19–42. doi:10.1007/s10602-012-9130-7

Gussen, B. F. (2013b). On the Problem of Scale: Spinozistic Sovereignty as the Logical Foundation of Constitutional Economics. *The Journal of Philosophical Economics*, *7*(1). Retrieved from http://www.jpe.ro/pdf.php?id=4997

Gussen, B. F. (2014a). The evolutionary economic implications of constitutional designs: Lessons from the constitutional morphogenesis of New England and New Zealand. *Perspectives on Federalism, 6*(2), E319 - E346. Retrieved from http://www.on-federalism.eu/attachments/004_Volume%206%20-%20 issue%202%20-%202014.pdf

Gussen, B. F. (2014b). Subsidiarity as a constitutional principle in New Zealand. *New Zealand Journal of Public and International Law*, *12*(1), 123–144.

Gussen, B. F. (2015a). Is subsidiarity a *conditio sine qua non* for sustainability? *Policy Studies*, *36*(4), 384–398. doi:10.1080/01442872.2015.1073244

Gussen, B. F. (2015b). The state is the fiduciary of the people. *Public Law*, *3*, 440–457.

Gussen, B. F. (2015c). On the problem of scale: The inextricable link between environmental and constitutional laws'. *New Zealand Journal of Public and International Law*, *13*(1), 39–63.

Gutierrez, L. (2005). Solidarity, subsidiarity, and sustainability. *Solidarity and Sustainability, 1*(8). Retrieved from http://www.pelicanweb.org/solisust08.html

Havercroft, J. (2010). The fickle multitude: Spinoza and the problem of global democracy. *Constellations (Oxford, England)*, *17*(1), 120–136. doi:10.1111/j.1467-8675.2009.00560.x

Hayek, F. A. (1983). *Law legislation and liberty: A new statement of the liberal principles of justice and political economy* (Vol. 2). Chicago: The University of Chicago Press.

Kohr, L. (1977). *The Overdeveloped Nations: the diseconomies of scale.* New York: Schocken Books.

Kurrild-Klitgaard, P. (2002). Opting-out: The constitutional economics of exit. *Journal of Economics and Sociology*, *61*(1), 123–158. doi:10.1111/1536-7150.00154

Mateos, R., Olmedo, E., Sancho, M., & Valderas, J. M. (2004). From linearity to complexity: Towards a new economics. *Complexity International,* 10. Retrieved from https://www.researchgate.net/publication/242781616_From_linearity_to_complexity_Towards_a_new_economics

Prokhovnik, R. (1997). From democracy to aristocracy: Spinoza, reason and politics. *History of European Ideas*, *23*(2-4), 105–115. doi:10.1016/S0191-6599(96)00012-5

Prokhovnik, R. (2001). Spinozas conception of sovereignty. *History of European Ideas*, *27*(3), 289–306. doi:10.1016/S0191-6599(01)00051-1

Prokhovnik, R. (2004). *Spinoza and republicanism.* New York: Palgrave Macmillan. doi:10.1057/9780230000902

Prokhovnik, R. (2007). *Sovereignties: Contemporary theory and practice.* New York: Palgrave Macmillan. doi:10.1057/9780230593527

Schmitter, P. C. (1999). The future of democracy: Could it be a matter of scale? *Social Research*, *66*(3), 933–958.

Schumacher, E. F. (1999). *Small is beautiful*. Vancouver: Hartley & Marks Publishers. (Original work published 1973)

Spinoza, B. (1951). *A theologico-political treatis and a political treatise.* New York: Dover Publications.

Tainter, J. (1995). Sustainability of complex societies. *Futures*, *27*(4), 397–407. doi:10.1016/0016-3287(95)00016-P

Tainter, J. (2006). Social complexity and sustainability. *Ecological Complexity*, *3*(2), 91–103. doi:10.1016/j.ecocom.2005.07.004

Voets, H., & Biggiero, L. (2000). Globalization and self-organization: The consequences of decentralization for industrial organization. *International Review of Sociology*, *10*(1), 73–82. doi:10.1080/713673987

Wildt, A. (1999). Solidarity: Its history and contemporary definition. In K. Bayertz (Ed.), *Solidarity* (pp. 209–220). New York: Springer. doi:10.1007/978-94-015-9245-1_11

Chapter 1
Morphogenesis

ABSTRACT

This chapter analyzes evolution to the end of furnishing a general theory of economic change. The analysis is applicable to both organisms and organizations. The general theory presented here is based on four analytical constructs: symmetry, scale, complexity, and collapse. Complexity is modeled as a force, similar to gravitation. Evolution is understood as a condition exhibiting an increase in morphological complexity. In the final analysis, economic change is linked to the structure of the political state. Pathologies of economic change, including morphostasis (in other words reaching a stage where growth and development are anemic due to the system's form and structure becoming static), necessitate a rethinking of political organization. Polycentricity and the principle of subsidiarity, with a praxis inspired by sovereign cities, are imperative for the continuous evolution of societies, and hence economies. In this future, nation-states become subsidiary. Sovereign cities replace nation-states on the 'international' stage.

INTRODUCTION[1]

I rank our growing preference for automated sameness over a personal touch as one of the greatest ills of our age. (Gould, 2009)

The proposition in this chapter is that an evolutionary understanding of economics produces specific normative signals as to the structure of the political state. More precisely, the evolution of economies requires a political

DOI: 10.4018/978-1-5225-2756-5.ch001

structure around cities that interact freely with each other (on a global scale). This proposition flows from an analogy between organisms and organizations, and an understanding of the evolutionary process through the theory of complexity.

I follow in the footsteps of Adam Smith, Alfred Marshall, W. Brian Arthur and other prominent economists in modeling economic change through biological metaphors (Callejas, 2007). In particular, constructs from evolutionary biology provide policy signals apt for the complexity inherent in economic processes and economic change, especially when the latter is embedded in their wider social context. While other economists have frowned upon the use of metaphors, notably Joseph Schumpeter, metaphors are in line with the breakdown of the reductionist paradigm and the rise of complexity in its place (Hodgson, 1999, pp. 60 and 67). Given the general theory of morphogenesis presented in this chapter, which represents evolution as a process leading to greater complexity, it would be apposite to rely on metaphors if only to help explain the workings of this model.[2]

There are more similarities than differences between social organizations and organisms to justify considering the former as analogous to a biological organism (Waldrop, 1992, p. 179). Both organizations and organisms are behavior systems (Boulding, 1981, p. 169). Both biological and human systems self-organize towards higher complexity (Saviotti & Pyka, 2008; Carroll, 2001). This complexity is reflected in the richness of self-organizing interactions between independent (and hence heterogeneous) agents. These behavior systems are not only complex and self-organizing but also adaptive: they try to turn events around them into their advantage. This process of adaptation is the trademark of evolution. However, like every analogy, ours has its limitations (Knudsen, 2002, p. 446; Hayek, 1990, p. 291). In particular, human systems, unlike biological ones, are capable of mutating at negligible time spans (Gould, 2007). Human evolution shifts to attributes that are easier and faster to adapt. Humans evolve along a pathway that maximizes the options of behavior for the least cost to adapt (see below).[3] Options are related to rules. Rules could be defined as the *enforced* prescriptions concerning what actions are required, prohibited, or permitted (Commons, 1924; Ostrom, 1980).[4] Options, on the other hand, are *enforceable* rather than *enforced* prescriptions (Ross, 1976).[5] Note that this objective of maximizing options is analogous to biological evolution in that it induces larger variety (I elaborate on this point later). Take for example the local varieties of beak designs that Darwin recorded in finches on the Galapagos Islands. Human behavior attempts to provide similar variety in designs that are suited to their local environments. An example of this variety is studied below in the context of the history of the Australian electric power grid. Notwithstanding these differences, both behavior systems could be understood through the process of exchange (Boulding, 1984; Archer, 2013).[6] The analogy is strengthened when we study life and evolution looking for macro trends that exist in both organisms and organizations. To be precise, our analogy entails understating organizations as possessing the quality of life and changing through the process of evolution. A common denominator is seen in a trend towards larger, more varied and more complex structures. These points are delineated in the following sections.[7]

The chapter is organized as follows: the next section expounds the meaning of evolution as it applies to the Australian electric power grid. Later, I introduce a general theory of morphogenesis that explains evolution in terms of symmetry, scale, and complexity. I then continue the analysis by examining the problems flowing from the current architecture of economic organization under the nation-state. The chapter ends with some concluding remarks.

A HISTORY OF THE ELECTRIC GRID IN AUSTRALIA

To motivate our discussion of evolution, I introduce a brief history of the electric power grid in Australia. Australia is one of the three great Anglo-American federations that I analyze in more detail in later chapters (the United States and Canada being the other two). However, the history of the Australian grid is no different from most other countries, except for the vast areas and the relatively low-density population covered by the grid. The analysis that follows is hence general in nature and applies in other contexts. The 'evolution' of the grid can be seen in Figure 1 which provides a comparison between the high voltage transmission systems over a span of seventy years (from 1927 to 1997).[8] In this narrative, the focus is on the change in the structure of the grid and the geographic distribution of technologies used to generate electricity. This example will motivate our discussion on the nature of evolution.

Since the creation of the Australian Commonwealth in 1901, the Australian Constitution was silent on the subject of electricity supply. This allowed each of the six states making the Commonwealth to legislate independently for its own grid (Brady, 1996). In New South Wales, Queensland and Western Australia ownership was vested in local authorities. However, there was also competition from private utilities, resulting in piecemeal allocation of

Figure 1. The growth of the Australian electric grid from 1927 to 1997
Source: Brady (1996).

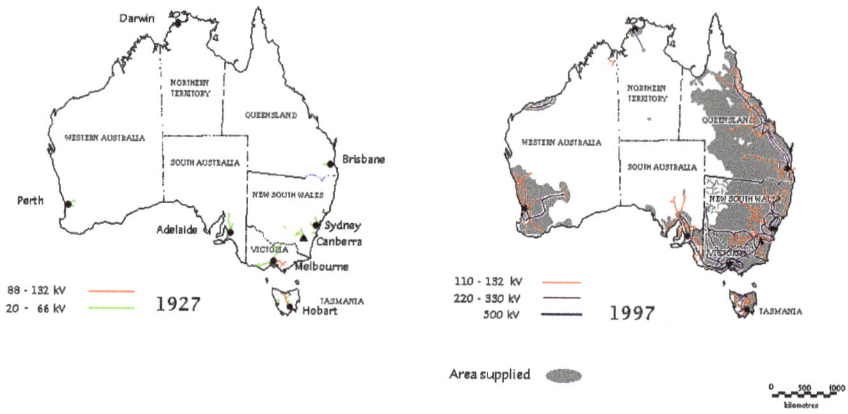

franchise areas. In the other states (Victoria, Tasmania, and South Australia) ownership was more in the hands of the private sector.

From the beginning, there were indigenous varieties in the favored fuel for electricity generation. Figure 2 shows this geographic distribution of large generators in Australia by technology.[9] Notice the clustering of similar types of generators in some geographic regions. In Victoria, around Melbourne, we see a clustering of coal-fired electricity generation where there are vast (brown) coal deposits in the Latrobe Valley. In Tasmania, we see a clustering of hydroelectric generators where they avail themselves from the capacity of the Great Lake and other hydro resources. In South and Western Australia, the emphasis is more on the vast oil and gas fields (not shown in Figure 2).

Today the generation mix has become more diverse.[10] In Queensland, the maximum installed capacity of coal-powered stations is around 8,500 MW. However, there is now a capacity of 3,500 MW from gas turbine stations, 200 MW from reciprocating engines, 650 MW from hydroelectric stations, 10 MW from wind farms, and 350 MW from biomass. This is not to mention an increasing uptake of photovoltaic cells. Note that the oldest of these technologies uses fossil fuels. Among the most recent are wind farms and biomass. A similar picture can be seen in the other states. In Tasmania for example, we see 250 MW from gas-fired steam turbines, 315 MW from gas turbines, 5 MW from reciprocating engines, and 2300 MW from hydroelectric stations. In Western Australia steam turbines fired by coal account for 2300 MW, while 65 MW come from gas turbines. Steam turbines powered by gas account for 400 MW. Reciprocating gas stations account for 110 MW. Only

Figure 2. Large electricity generators in the National Electricity Market
Sources: the Australian Energy Market Operator (AEMO), the Australian Energy Regulator (AER).

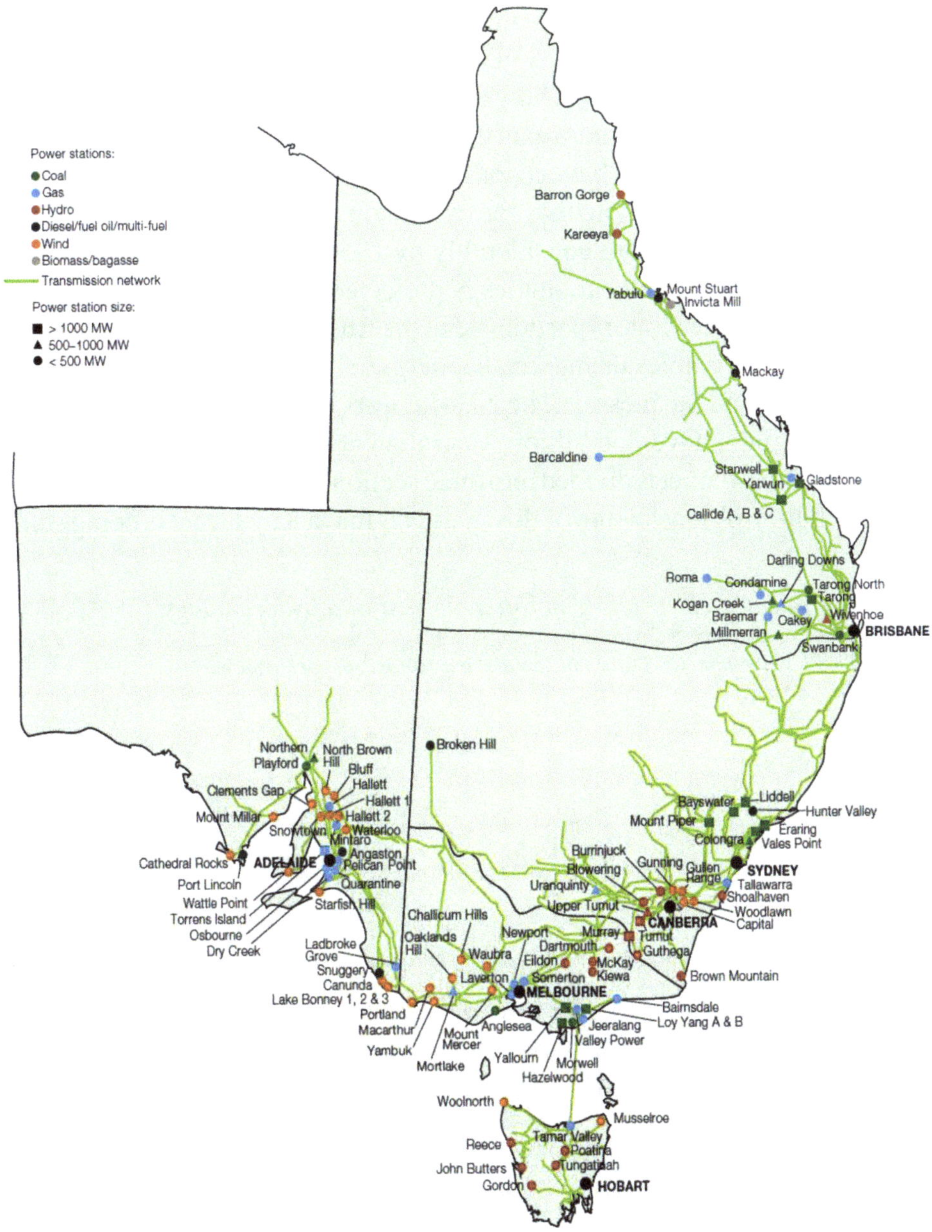

30 MW come from hydroelectric, and wind farms provide 400 MW. Biofuel provides only 5 MW, while solar photovoltaic stations provide 10MW.

The same picture of 'increase in variety' can be seen moving forward. Current projections for electricity generation, in Gigawatt-Year (GWYr), are shown in Figure 3 below.[11] Note how over time new technologies are expected to join the mix. For example, solar thermal is expected to gain momentum in the next few years, and have a considerable share by 2050. On the other hand, we can also see a potential for extinction. For example, black coal is expected to shrink its share considerably by 2050.

This mix of different technologies is projected to be produced by various generators. These generators participate in the Australian National Electricity Market (NEM), a wholesale market that helps deliver electricity to almost 10 million homes and businesses. The NEM covers all Australian states except Western Australia. Over ten billion Australian dollars are traded annually in this market. The market is divided into three sections: generation, transmission, and distribution. A key feature of this market is the fact that what is being sold,

Figure 3. Projected electricity generation in Australia by technology
Source: Hayward & Graham, 2012.
Legend: PV Photo Voltaic, CCS Carbon Capture and Storage, pf pulverized fuel

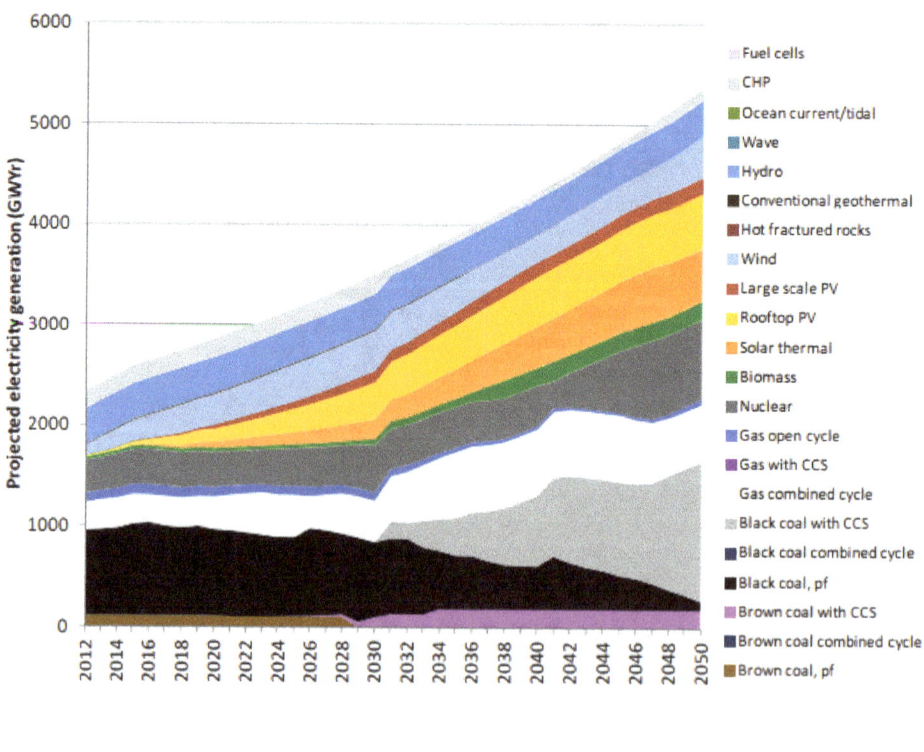

namely electricity, cannot be stored efficiently, and hence needs to be sold in real time (as it is generated). Efficiency in this market requires the coordination of generation and distribution over the transmission network. Competition in the upstream (generation) and the downstream (distribution) is intended to deliver efficient outcomes. However, given the highly-integrated nature of the power market, sometimes, these efficient outcomes would be delivered by cooperation between the upstream and downstream operations rather than through competition. The role of the Australian Electricity Market Operator (AEMO), the Electricity Suppliers Association of Australia (ESAA), and the Australian Electricity Regulator (AER) is to ensure the cooperation between upstream and downstream organizations leads to the envisaged efficiencies.

This brief introduction to the history of the Australian electric grid will be revisited in the following sections to elaborate on the meaning of evolution.

A GENERAL THEORY OF MORPHOGENESIS

Our analysis so far leads to the evolutionary process shown in Figure 4.[12] The process is built on four core concepts: symmetry, scale, complexity, and collapse. Evolution suggests a difference in temporal rhythm and temporal clock from institution to institution and from organism to organism (Hayden, 1987). Symmetry breaking leads to *anagenesis* (i.e. change within species), but also to speciation (new species). A break is shown in the line leading to collapse (or extinction) to indicate that this eventuality occurs at time scales too remote to be treated with the four preceding stages. Each concept has a technical meaning. Their treatment here is not extensive—only their essential features are summarized.

DEFINITIONS

Symmetry (σ)

Symmetry exists where change leaves some aspects of a system unchanged. Symmetry is immunity to a possible change. [13] Generally, symmetry implies that certain degrees of freedom are absent——to enable a state of equilibrium (de Wit and Smith, 1986). The degrees of freedom refer to the number of ways the system can possess energy. More complex systems have more degrees of

Figure 4. The five stages of evolution

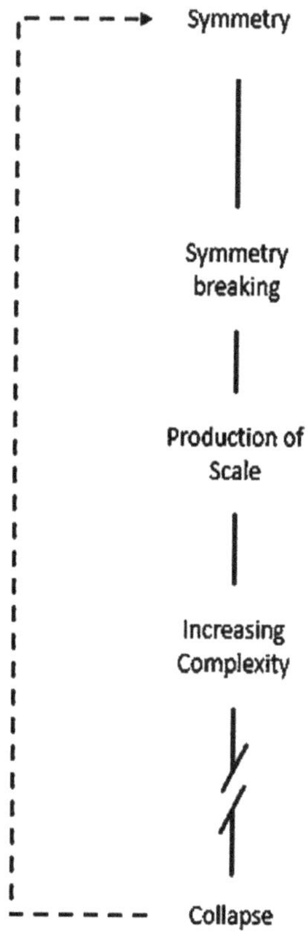

freedom. In this sense, symmetry is analogous to entropy (S) (see below). In particular, we think of homogeneity as symmetry. Symmetry is broken due to instabilities in the local surroundings. More precisely, symmetry is broken when undifferentiated (identical) degrees of freedom become differentiated.

Symmetry breaking does not mean that all symmetry is lost. There would be still a new symmetry but different from the one before. The process of symmetry breaking is represented by the change of symmetry with respect to degrees of freedom $\left(\tau\right)$:

$$\text{Symmetry breaking: } \frac{d\sigma}{d\tau} \neq 0 \tag{1}$$

where τ represents a tensor of the degrees of freedom in the system (i.e. the organism or organization), including time.[14]

Entropy (S)

Entropy is taken to be analogous to symmetry. More precisely, it is a condition that maximizes symmetry:[15]

$$S : \frac{d\sigma}{d\tau} \to 0 \tag{2}$$

It follows that negentropy $\left(J\right)$ is a condition on symmetry such that:

$$J : \frac{d^2\sigma}{d\tau^2} \to 0 \tag{3}$$

By entropy, we mean the disorder registered by a given system. This disorder is proportional to the degrees of freedom of the system (Brissaud, 2005). The more freedom, the more entropy. For an isolated system (i.e. a system subject only to its own gravity), this means that entropy is maximized as the system is isolated from environmental forces (that contribute to complexity) and hence maximizes its symmetry. Note that this also means that entropy is proportional to the symmetry inherent in the system. As symmetry is broken, entropy is reduced, or to put it differently, negative entropy (or negentropy) is increased. Negentropy is increased due to symmetry breaking.

Scale (μ)

Scale is the set of relationships between constituent parts and their change over degrees of freedom. Symmetry is an ontological concept, i.e. related to existence, while scale is *predominantly* an epistemological one related to our knowledge of symmetry. Scale relates to the proportionality (relationship) of parts (to themselves and to their environment) as perceived by an observer. Scale is said to be produced as a result of symmetry breaking (i.e. negative entropy). To produce scale, we first need to introduce asymmetry. We compensate for the loss of symmetry by increased interaction between the resulting different agent types.

Given that symmetry relates to a generalized concept of distance, scale can be defined as a generalized momentum:

$$\mu \triangleq \kappa \frac{d\sigma_{\kappa}}{d\tau} + d\kappa \frac{d\sigma_{d\kappa}}{d\tau} \tag{4}$$

where κ refers to the quantum of matter in the system (e.g. the number of agents).[16] Quantum (κ) can be thought of as a form of generalized mass. There are two symmetries in the definition. The first σ_{κ} is in relation to the symmetry of the existing quantum. The second symmetry is $\sigma_{d\kappa}$ and refers to the symmetry in the change of the existing quantum, which allows for growth in the population of existing matter (agents) in the system.

To see why scale is defined as a generalized momentum we only need to consider the nature of the relationship between symmetry and distance. A generalized concept of distance is a metric for a set of states of a system. A null distance represents equivalence between two states, and hence symmetry (Rosen, 2008). For example, think of the bilateral symmetry of the human body. We are able to recognize this symmetry due to the similar distance that points on the human body have from the plane that cuts the body into two identical halves.

One form of producing scale is where strong links between elements (or subsystems) emerge. This is a form of 'impatient' production of scale that results in $\frac{d^2\mu}{d\tau^2} \to \infty$. Such tight 'coupling' in dynamical systems results in chaotic behavior. This is the kind of coupling emphasized in evolutionary economics today, where options are reduced through competition. Instead of allowing for local variety between different attractors (which are points in phase space towards which the system evolves), a tight coupling destroys these attractors but one. On the other hand, if systems are neither too tightly nor too loosely coupled, that is to say there is symmetry in the production of scale (or in other words there is no acceleration in the production of scale), they will have complex attractors. These attractors have local characteristics that differ from one another as they have limited access to one another (Marion, 1999, p. 155).

Morphology

Morphology is defined as the study of forms and structures that give rise to scale. For our purposes, morphology is used interchangeably with scale. We therefore also attribute to morphology the study of relationships between entities constituting the quantum in the system. Note that morphogenesis is the process that leads to a particular scale (form and structure) in a given organism or organization. Morphological analysis is a technique that identifies the dimensions of complexity over a number of constructs and analyzes the resulting structures from a variation in each dimension.[17]

Complexity (π)

Complexity is simply the operational ramification of scale production. Complexity, and the produced scale on which it operates, using energy throughput, compensates for lost symmetry. Complexity is the change over time and space of the relational field we call scale. Complexity to scale is what force is to momentum. Complexity is the force required to bring an organism (or organization) up to a certain operational level, given its scale. In other words, by breaking symmetry, or freezing some degrees of freedom, a system gains structure. As the dialectic between symmetry and symmetry breaking continues, the system becomes fractal: it evolves a structure at every (observational) scale. This structure manifests itself in spatial and temporal complexity. Because of the need for energy throughput, the notion of complexity is more meaningful when describing living forms.[18]

Complexity is defined as follows:

$$\pi \triangleq \frac{d\mu}{d\tau} = \kappa \frac{d^2\sigma_{\kappa}}{d\tau^2} + \left(\frac{d\sigma_{\kappa}}{d\tau} - \frac{d\sigma_{d\kappa}}{d\tau} \right) \frac{d\kappa}{d\tau} \tag{5}$$

Note that complexity exists even if there is no change in quantum (κ). The level of complexity depends not only on the quantum in the system (e.g. number of constituent parts), but also on the rates at which symmetry and quantum are changing. Where quantum is constant (no growth), complexity is proportional to the curvature of symmetry. A key feature of complex systems is decentralized structures as opposed to the centralized and hierarchical structures found in simple systems (Hanusch & Pyka 2007, p. 278). Morphological complexity, which is the key product of evolution (see below), exhibits itself in a variety of structures and forms that share a common origin. Complexity is closer to a Lamarckian explanation of evolution than a Darwinian one. In Darwinian selection, the replicator set cannot be changed, while in a Lamarckian selection, the set is modified by environmental stimuli (from interactors) (Knudsen, 2002, p. 449). In (emergent) complexity, the macrostructure affects the local scale and vice versa (Allen, 2001, p. 313).[19]

PROPOSITIONS

Proposition 1: Evolution is a process of change that leads to increased morphological complexity. Evolution is a process of change where:[20]

$$\frac{d\pi}{d\tau} = \frac{d^2\mu}{d\tau^2} > 0 \tag{6}$$

This condition accounts for an increase in morphological complexity.

For us to understand evolution, we need to understand development. To understand development, we need to understand the trail left by development, namely morphology. Morphology is focused on the analysis of form and structure. Form is an envelope that describes spatial qualities such as size. Structure is about scale: the relationships between entities which define physiology or functionality.[21] A form could be the product of many structures, but a structure is more likely to have only one form. Form could linger even after structure has changed. Emphasis on form as a proxy for functionality risks assuming the stability of forms. Morphology, on the other hand, puts emphasis on scale.

In economics, evolution has been defined in a number of ways. Boulding defines evolution in relation to ecosystems as "ongoing ecological interaction, of populations of species of all kinds which affect each other, under conditions of constantly changing parameters" (Boulding, 1981, p. 23). Witt defines evolution as the "self-transformation over time of a system under investigation" (Witt, 1993, p. 91). Dopfer and Potts define evolution as the ongoing endogenous process of emergent novelty, re-coordination and change in the knowledge base of the economic order through the origination of new ideas (Dopfer & Potts, 2014, p. ix). The objective is to understand the dynamic process behind *the spread* of observed change, rather than the origin of this change (which is simply explained by chance). The classical formulation of this dynamic process is where economic agents are faced with two alternative modes of behavior (two options) (Matthews, 1984, p. 91; Arthur, 1989, p. 117): A and B. The issue under investigation is the process that may cause

A to become *generally* adopted. If the economic agent is rational and fully informed, she would use the process of optimization to maximize utility: she would adopt A because of her rational foresight (or learning) that enables her to discern the relative merits of A over B *ex ante*. If however rationality is bounded or there is no full information, agents would maximize survival through competitive selection (or survivor selection) where some choose A and some choose B. Over time, those who selected option B would be eliminated in the ensuing competition. The optimization under competitive selection is indirect. This second approach has developed into an analogy with biology that informs the process of economic 'natural selection.'

Looking back at our electric grid example it seems that there is more to evolution than mere competitive selection. Figure 3 projects an increased variety of options for generating electricity. Change is not governed by choice between two *existing* options, but by adding new options to an existing set. Evolution seems to correspond to the following operation: $\{A,B\}\xrightarrow{time}\{A,B,C\}$, while there is also the possibility of extinction as we saw with black coal (in Figure 3), which also suggests the inverse operation: $\{A,B,C\}\xrightarrow{time}\{A,B\}$. It is this last operation that economic literature is mostly interested in. On the balance, however, we could see from our power grid example that the general trend is for more options to be added to already existing ones. The combined representation would be as follows: $\{A,B,C\}\xrightarrow{time}\{A,B,D,E\}$. Hence while some options become extinct, other options become operational. The resultant being a net increase in options.

For us to better understand evolution, we need first to look at what life is. If we are to describe the economy as a living organism, this would suggest that economies exhibit the following signs of life (Whitfield, 1998, pp. 48-50):

- **Reproduction:** Where living organisms make copies of themselves.
- **Growth:** Where organisms produce new living cells.
- **Nutrition:** Where organisms convert raw material into their own substances.
- **Respiration:** Where energy from the environment operates the process of nutrition.
- **Excretion:** Where living organisms remove waste that cannot be processed any further.
- **Senses:** Where organisms gather information to obtain nutrients.

To illustrate, we will use the electricity industry as an example. In this industry, organisms are represented by electricity generators. They make copies of themselves through new entrants to the market. This can be seen in Figure 2 where generators using the same type of technology cluster in a small geographical region. This asexual production is driven by the learning process that occurs over time and allows new generators to enter the industry. These companies produce new cells in the form of newly added capacity (turbines), new power plants, and new connections to the transmission grid. They convert raw materials to the substances they would use in their products (for example coal, gas, or wind are converted into electricity), obtain energy to enable the conversion process (for example using coal to run steam turbines which are then used to produce electricity), and produce waste in the form of greenhouse gases. As to senses (and locomotion), companies pick up information about the state of their environment throughout the planning process, from short-term to long-term planning.

When we look at evolution, we can detect a gradient where unicellular organisms (less than one millimeter in diameter) evolve to the rich variety of life-forms we have today. Evolution resulted in a stunning diversity of life, with over nine million living species (Camilo et al., 2011). The change can be discerned as one of production of scale where organisms became larger and more complex,[22] and more diverse (Bonner, 1988; Gould, 1996; McShea, 1994). The increase in size creates the potential for different cell types, which in turn leads to morphological complexity (Carroll, 2001), something we can also discern in Figure 1 in the context of the Australia electric grid. The variety we see today in the design of power plants, the fuel type, the nameplate capacity, and so on, resembles the diversity in living species (both in adaptation and speciation). For example, the structural variation in the beaks of the Galapagos finches (studied by Darwin). It is the increase over time in the (structural) variety that suggests the occurrence of evolution. This variety is linked to adaptation to local conditions (i.e. environment). In the Australian power grid, new technologies were adapted to existing fuel types in different geographic locations. Going back to the Galapagos finches, we see different beak designs adapted to obtaining the type of food available on each island. Finches who feed on the flowers of cactus trees have long and pointed beaks more fitted for picking seeds out of cactus fruit, while finches who feed on seeds found on the ground have shorter and stouter beaks. This suggests that evolution is about tweaking structures to meet *local* needs. In the evolutionary process, the environment puts certain demands on species to change. Evolution is about the creation of options that serve to meet indigenous needs. Evolution is about the creation of options, or as Niklas Luhmann puts it, evolution is about "normalizing the improbable." (Luhmann, 1979, p. 162). Evolution "involves increasing the rate of movement, interdependencies, lack of time of varying degrees and risks which are conditioned by and increased reciprocally with the remedies which relate to them" (Luhmann, 1979, p. 162).

The analogy between evolutionary economics and evolutionary biology requires an analytical regime grounded in complexity theory.[23] The tendency to increase options explains the dynamics inherent in social (and economic) change through the construct of emergence, which leads directly to complexity theory. Complexity theory, through emergence, explains the mechanisms leading to order and disorder (which through entropy leads eventually to symmetry).[24] Emergence leads to higher scales which have arisen from—— but are not predictable at, lower scales (Lawson, 1997, p. 176). Complexity enables order for a low cost and a short time span. Complexity will not eliminate the possibility of extinction but will increase the rates of adaptability to support a given level of scale. Evolution is the path that organisms take towards the increased complexity of more elaborately-structured organisms. During emergence, an interaction of biological and cultural evolution leads to higher levels of self-organization where organisms coevolve: they adapt to each other. Free markets are a prime example of where structures emerge. The ability of buyers and sellers to interact freely changes the structure of a given market in ways that were not intended or envisaged in the first place (Kirman & Vriend, 2001). In the context of the Australian electric grid, the structure of transmission networks, and the production of more generation capacity was coevolving with public purposes. For example, in Queensland, the first generation of electricity was in the capital and largest city—Brisbane—to provide a lighting system in the city center (Dunn, 1985). The grid coevolved with the social and economic structures in the same locale.

While the evolutionary approach in economics suggests that it seeks to account for the development of the structure of economies (Metcalfe, 2008, p. 24), the understanding of evolution under this approach seems to be purely statistical. In economics, evolution is understood as a general (uncoordinated) selection theory, largely based on Darwinian natural selection and modeled using biological constructs such as genotypes (replicators) and phenotypes (interactors) (Dawkins, 1976). Evolutionary economics is largely based on the Darwinian model of struggle resulting in the survival of the fittest. For Darwin nature is savage. Each creature is locked in a struggle for survival that leads inevitably to (violent) death. Survivors were the best adapted to their environment. On the hands of Adam Smith, this became the idea of perfection through competition. To be precise, it was the ideas first formulated by Adam Smith and Thomas Robert Malthus that had a lasting impact on Charles Darwin (Claeys, 2000; Coase, 1998; Gordon, 1989). The Darwinist analogy in evolutionary economics limits evolution to combinatorial novelty that reduces the process of evolution to statistical probabilities within a closed system, hardly able to exhibit any signs of life. Evolution results from novel connections between existing predefined and fixed agents. This is a short-term view of evolution. In the long run, under Lamarckian progressive evolution of complexity, new agents are added to the mix (Boden, 1990; Wilkins, 2001).

The analogy propounded in this chapter is, therefore, a critique of the orthodox view of evolution, which emphasizes competition over cooperation. Given the huge species variety that we have today, evolution cannot be based on keen competition alone. All habitats contain a community of species living and evolving side by side. The individuals of these species interact with one another by competing for resources. It is in this context that a change in one species may stimulate an alteration in another. Such interlocked evolution can be seen in parasitism or symbiosis. In the former, the parasite damages the host, while in the latter, survival chances are improved for both partner species. Coevolution is based on this dialectic of competition and cooperation.[25] There is no need to assume that humans cooperate to gain a mutual benefit. Humans could be selfish and still choose to cooperate. Power imbalances are one reason why a weaker group chooses to cooperate with a stronger one. Stronger groups also have a selfish motive to cooperate: they force the weaker group to adapt and hence externalize the cost of change, while still reaping the benefits of that change (Kropotkin, 1904; Axelrod, 1984; Goodwin, 1994; Waldrop, 1992; Bookchin, 1982).

While Darwinian evolution (through natural selection and adaptation) suggests that all states of a dynamical system are potential equilibria, morphological fields have attractors to which the system settles.[26] These attractors are structures that are intrinsically robust. According to Darwin, evolution is a *gradual* historical process where the logical unity of biological forms comes from historical continuity and diversity comes from functional necessity. This meant that any form is possible and the only principle is survival through adaptation. Darwinian evolution is not helpful when it comes to morphological analysis. In contrast, complexity theory explains evolution as an increase in morphological complexity, where evolution is abrupt, analogous to a jerk (the derivative of force with time or the change in acceleration).

In addition, complexity brings into the analysis the idea of self-organization.[27] Self-organization provides dynamism not evident under Darwinian evolution. In other words, complexity leads to a non-equilibrium understanding of evolution where the emphasis is on transformation and change. This emphasis can be seen in the work of Brian Arthur and positive feedback loops that lead away from equilibrium (Arthur, 1989; Arthur, 1994). These positive feedback loops are associated with cooperation, while negative ones are associated with competition. In the Australia electric grid example, we see this in Figure 2, which shows the clustering of power generators using the same technology. A model of economic change based on self-organization means that there are no externalities since all parts of the system would constantly be changing. Complexity theory would also open the door for modeling the economy as an ecosystem where resilience, hierarchy theory, and the theory of dissipative structures help explain economic change. Ordinary complexity involves structure and self-organization (implying some teleology) where behavior can be explained by mechanistic models with functional growth and survival. In such ordinary complexity, competition and cooperation are complementary. In emergent complexity, there is an oscillation between competition and cooperation. This leads to a level of consciousness and morality that cannot be explained mechanistically and functionally. In emergent complexity, mechanical models are only temporary representations of structure. The focus of the analysis should instead be on the evolution of the structure of such systems, i.e. on morphogenesis. Morphology (structure and form) and physiology (functionality) are interrelated; the question is one of emphasis. Machines, given their static structure, are more about functionality, while organisms of emergent complexity are more about morphology (Lewin, 1992; Goodwin, 1994; Inayatullah, 1994; Helling, 1994; Arthur, 1994; Funtowicz & Ravetz, 1994; Allen, 1994).

Proposition 2: the change of energy (W) in the system could be represented as

$$\delta W = \pi d\sigma \tag{7}$$

where δ emphasizes that the energy is path-dependent and hence can only be differentiated inexactly. This suggests that an organism can do work only if complexity is non-zero and symmetry is changing.

The idea that economies are 'alive' leads to another proposition. The structure of any organism, including economies, is the culmination of its evolutionary history, a history of speciation (emergence of new species or technologies), adaptation (change within the same species), and extinction. Enter the concepts of negative entropy and energy.

Energy and negative entropy (or potential) are necessary for the evolutionary process, both in organizations and organisms (Boulding, 1981). In the words of Erwin Schrodinger "evolution is the segregation of entropy" (Schrodinger, 1967, p. 79). Evolution is about the creation of "extraordinary little islands of order" in the organism at the cost of disorder elsewhere (Boulding, 1981, p. 151). In fact, the second law of thermodynamics could be stated in terms of potential (negative entropy) as follows: evolution occurs because there is potential for it to occur. In other words, evolution occurs due to a process of symmetry breaking, which as discussed in the following section, would inevitably lead to the production of scale, and higher levels of complexity. This also suggests that evolution occurs only in open systems where there is a throughput of energy. The process of reproduction moving from a genotype (e.g. a fertilized egg) to the phenotype (the organism) requires an energy throughput that leads to this growth process. However, the law of entropy is one of diminishing return. Evolution cannot continue indefinitely (at any scale), unless potential (negative entropy) is continuously replenished, for example through new technology and new resources. Eventually, however, it is not unlikely that the diminishing potential would lead to a global death (extinction), both in organizations and organisms (see below).

In summary, evolution requires energy potential and leads to emergence that is registered through an increase in the behavioral options (variety) available at any given analytical scale. For example, an evolved economy would be able to avail itself of a number of technological revolutions simultaneously: the agricultural revolution, the Industrial Revolution, and the information revolution (albeit at different intensities). It follows that evolution is not about (natural) selection. It is about progress towards higher levels of scale (and hence complexity).[28] We have already seen this trend in Figure 1 above where the Australian electric grid, just like a living organism, spread over a larger area, exhibiting more technological variety in generating electricity, and as a consequence more complexity in the operation of the National Electricity Market (NEM).

Proposition 3: Collapse is a process that results from sustaining the following condition:

$$\delta W = \pi d\sigma = 0 \quad (8)$$

As to collapse, insights can be gleaned from the reliability theory of aging and longevity. According to this theory, redundancy is at the center of evading collapse, both for machines and organisms (Gavrilov & Gavrilova, 2004). From another angle, collapse can be seen as a relief from the complexity condition. A system with a high level of complexity will usually have more than one (complex) attractor. The interaction (coupling) of these attractors leads to a restoration of the symmetry that was originally 'lost.' Hence, after several stages of symmetry breaking, the symmetry is 'resurrected' by a series of symmetry creating collisions of chaotic attractors. This symmetry creation destroys the (spatial and temporal) structure gained earlier through symmetry breaking.

Complex attractors are especially useful for understanding how collapse can be mitigated, as these attractors are largely immune to cascading damage (Marion, 1999). The collapse of complex systems is, therefore, a function of the level of coupling between the subsystems or elements of any given system. The higher the coupling between the elements, the wider will be the effect of any sudden changes on the system as a whole (hence collapse is globalized). With no coupling between the elements, there will be no system of course. However, in between these extremes, there is a region where a low level of coupling will localize the effects of collapse and provide a more robust system.[29]

HISTOPATHOLOGY OF ECONOMIC CHANGE

While morphology looks at the form and structure of organisms in general, histogenesis looks at the formation of tissues from undifferentiated cells. For an organism, tissues constitute a meso scale between individual cells and organs (i.e. subsystems that perform a specific function). In contrast, physiogenesis looks at the role of such organs. To understand the problems facing economic change, we need to look at a histopathology that seeks to understand organizations at a meso level (the city), and a cytopathology, which studies diseases on the cellular (individual) level. This chapter focuses exclusively on histogenesis, taking the city to be the characteristic level for our analysis.

When economic change is analyzed as morphogenesis, the emphasis is placed on structure (Schumacher, 1977; Schumacher, 1999). One of the most dominant structures is that of the political state, with political borders being one of the key structural elements of the state. The bigger the country, the greater is the need for internal structure to support its size (Mumford, 1967; Schumacher, 1999). An emphasis on structure leads in turn to an emphasis on scale, and to a lesser extent on its manifestation as form. Scale "is extremely crucial today, in political, social, and economic affairs just as in almost everything else" (Schumacher, 1999, p. 49). Just like language, scale (*qua* space and time) conditions action. In the medieval period, it signified importance. Between the 14th and 17th centuries, with the development of capitalism and the discovery of the laws of perspective, the scalar hierarchy of values was replaced by a system of magnitude. Through a long sequence of abstractions, scale was transformed from a signifier of importance to a proxy for relationships. Unfortunately, this abstraction progressed to a stage where it threatened the life of real organisms. These scalar changes brought about the 'human machine,' which required a 'priesthood' for the reliable organization of knowledge (natural and supra-natural), and a 'bureaucracy' for an elaborate structure for giving and carrying out orders. There was now an almost universally institutionalized concern with punctuality and regularity (Mumford, 1972).

An understanding of evolution as competition *and* cooperation leads to a critique of the necessity of a strong central government, particularly as advocated by Thomas Hobbes. Hobbes starts his analysis from two contradictory positions: while he sees men as virtual machines, he also sees them in constant conflict until they surrender to an external sovereign. Surrender is analogous to the behavior of automata, which are machines. For Hobbes, life is a power struggle. This understanding later resulted in the Malthus-Darwin struggle for existence, which emphasizes competition to the point of extermination. Hobbes' *Leviathan* turns men into machines, hence removing to a sovereign all decision-making powers. *Leviathan* reveals the ultimate tendency of despotic governments, namely automatism. This automatism signaled the rise of the machine. For the greatest part of human history, tools were simply an extension of the human organism.

They did not exist independently. However, through their semiautomatic functioning, they came to be regarded as having an independent existence. Hobbes' emphasis on power translated into the need for a centralized state to establish law and order. The goal of this power system is progress measured in quantitative units, leading to a perpetual effort to increase size, but not necessarily structure. Technology made every part of this system undergo rapid change, but the system as a whole became rigid (with low variety). Under this Hobbesian existence, the purpose of life is quantitative increase to ensure domination (Hobbes, 2011; Kropotkin, 1904; Gould, 2007; Mumford, 1934; Mumford, 1970). This Hobbesian model lacks any moral content. It has no anthropological concerns. It is limited to biological needs. Only through limiting humanity's existence to biological needs would totalitarian states be possible (Bookchin, 1982; Schumacher, 1977). The triumph of order over freedom is exhibited in the idea of 'mechanomorphism,' or the scientific approach, where a mechanistic explanation of organic behavior is seen as sufficient. The problem with economics is that it imitates science in being 'mechanomorphic.' Hobbes' 'zoomorphism,' where animal attributes are passed to human beings, led to distortion greater than the 'anthropomorphism' it reacted against. The character of systems changes not only because of scale production but also because they reach morphostasis. In essence, the production of scale leads to a distortion of the structural proportionality that defines the system. While technological change extends the size limits for social organizations, for example, improved communication or transportation systems, such mechanical aids are not enough. There is also need to change the internal structure to push the envelope of change. This is achieved by new methods of specialization (the division of labor). Increasing form (size) would be an evolutionary stable strategy only if accompanied by an increasing complexity of structure (Boulding, 1971; Mumford, 1970; Boulding, 1984).[30]

The etiquette of history is scalar change. A vivid example of this etiquette can be seen in the transformation from medieval to baroque institutions, a shift from localism to centralism, from the absolutism of God to the absolutism of the temporal sovereign and the nation-state.

The nation-state is anti-evolutionary. It prevents any evolutionary praxis. Through its uniform 'jurisdictional footprint' (*qua* contiguous territory), it limits all available options but one. This worship of national history (à la Fichte) is a perversion driven by a mechanistic model of human relationships which is intended to exclude and dominate. The same mechanism can be traced throughout the 19th century in a Malthusian gradient that saw an imperialist struggle between nation-states occult class struggle, and by doing so preserving the status quo of economic and power distribution. The nation-state was the harbinger of a very specific pathology: the 'ancien régime' syndrome. Internal contradictions, the birthmark of civilization, were suppressed rather than resolved. Novelty and diversity are now suffocated by the nation-state. The homogenization of society suppressed social problems to ensure the creation of a state that favored the expansion of a market economy. In the process, the modality of capitalism adopted by the nation-state ensured destroying governance structures at the local level. The rise of the nation-state led to the death of the city, through a transformation that is recorded through history as a change in scale (Mumford, 1934; Mumford, 1944; Mumford, 1961; Funtowicz & Ravetz, 1994; Kropotkin, 1975; Boulding, 1971; Bookchin, 1982; Bookchin, 1987).

Before the nation-state, governance was based on sovereign cities rather provinces and nations. The nation-state replaced the *polis* and its politics (a grass-root organization embedded in localism) with statecraft to the end of highly centralized structures. The centralization brought about by the nation-state can be traced back to the French Revolution of 1794. City-based governance before the revolution can be seen in Italian city-states (or *communa*). However, these communes did not last long, as they created economic and political differentiation, setting *popologrosso* versus *popolomagro*. The rich merchants hence favored the rise of the nation-state to lessen local resistance to free trade. As a result, city sovereignty was lost, and the role of cities was reduced to one of slavery to the nation-state.

Cities are a viable alternative to the nation-state. The city is an emergent complex system, the hub for economic activity (Chen, 2003), and hence a natural candidate for designation as an attractor. Historically, the city was the state itself. It was sovereign. However, it was not a centralized state. It was organized as a federation of villages with common interests and aimed to achieve peace. The origin of the city arises from villages attaining a critical mass. The rise of cities is a product of 'cultic practices' rather than technological discoveries. The self-jurisdiction of the city developed out of the jurisdiction in the marketplace. The earliest cities were ideological creations of highly mutualistic communities.

Tinkering with ancient morphogenetic principles such as structural proportions led to the histopathology we see today. The demise of the sovereign city was not only due to limiting cooperation to a small association that distinguished between immigrants and earlier settlers, but more importantly to neglecting agriculture in favor of industry and trade. It was Roman law that eventually brought down the medieval city with the idea that salvation must be sought in a strongly centralized state. The state proceeded to weed out internal structure (of subsidiarity), in favor of narrow-minded individualism (as a cytopathology). The state brought about standardization, mass production, and the factory system. The same role of the state can be seen in legislation passed in England in 1809 marking the end of small-scale manufacturing. Such laws not only emphasized quantitative growth but denied a just distribution system. There is now tension between current economic theories and localism. The former are never submitted to the test of experiment. Now, monotechnics created for economic expansion and military superiority has taken the place of a polytechnics, based on the needs of living organisms (i.e. their ecologies) (Goodwin, 1994; Kropotkin, 1904; Mumford, 1970).

Schumacher links the size of the 'jurisdictional footprint' with the theory of 'economies of scale' and modern technologies. He looks back at his native Germany and compares its economic fortunes under the Bismarck Reich with those of German-speaking Swiss and Austrian citizens, finding that the latter were no worse economically. He goes on to give a hypothetical where Denmark was annexed by Bismarck, and then queries whether Copenhagen would be under that scenario anything more than a provincial city (Schumacher, 1999, pp. 46-47, 53).

Over time, the power over other men that flowed from mechanomorphism resulted in a reversal where the organic [began] to dominate the machine. There was now a qualitative change towards social interests, due to a tendency to attain 'smallness within bigness' once the size of organizations (including polities) reaches a 'great size.' During the 19th century, there was a significant increase in self-governance. Regional entities suppressed by mechanomorphic technics are resurrected on every continent, both culturally and politically. The Scottish and Catalan separatist movements evidence this gradient. The most effective form of organization is where society is 'polylithic' rather than 'monolithic,' with many centers of power and an overall organization with limited power to underwrite the system. The ideal of capitalism is based on a 'polylithic' society, as opposed to a 'monolithic' one. The latter epitomizes communism. In 'small-scale' organizations, private ownership is natural. Conversely, in medium-scale organizations, private ownership is unnecessary, as 'voluntary surrender of privilege' is not likely to occur where there is a large number of anonymous members. In large-scale organizations, private ownership is irrational. Nationalism is a response to the irrationality of private ownership in large 'jurisdictional footprints,' which accentuates the danger of over-centralization. Capitalism is about small scale. When wedded to large-scale organization, capitalism faces the same fate of communism (à la Marx). Large scale organizations suffer a breakdown of communication before reaching the size of the Soviet Union. Russia, China, India, and the USA, *inter alia*, are destined to face a similar collapse albeit under different time scales (Mumford, 1934; Mumford, 1970; Schumacher, 1999; Boulding, 1984; Boulding, 1971). In particular, the rise of large organizations does not destroy small ones, due to the *Principle of Interstices*: holes can be occupied by organizations of smaller sizes. Small-scale organizations are resilient. Even under a system of keen competition, the middle-sized farm can compete with the large (Mumford, 1938; Mumford, 1967; Bookchin, 1987; Boulding, 1971; Kropotkin, 1901; Kropotkin, 1904).

The solution lies in municipal freedom, which is the basis for political freedom. Free cities act as 'peripheral niches' which become 'supernovas' of evolutionary change. Today 'regionalism' (the development of regions within a country) is the most pressing issue for countries with large jurisdictional footprints (like the United States, Canada, and Australia). For such regionalism to be successful, emphasis should shift to 'intermediate technology' geared towards local production and local use. Economic development is the process of transition from one type of organization of society to another at a higher level of complexity. Economic regionalism leads to a balanced economy, where technic is spread not by transport (as it was in the 19th century), but by local development. The greatest benefit of economic regionalism is that different development practices could be experimented with and compared. Emphasis would be on qualitative riches rather than quantitative abundance. Such emphasis would bring an economy of 'plenitude.' The best examples of plenitude exist in quite 'primitive' communities (Bookchin, 1987; Gould, 2007; Schumacher, 1999; Boulding, 1971; Mumford, 1934; Mumford, 1970).

CODA

This chapter furnishes a general theory of morphology that explains evolution in terms of complexity. Evolution leads to increased diversity and variety. In relation to the nation-state, this suggests the need for polycentricity. Our analysis suggests a problematization of scale, where the rise of the nation-state portends a structural collapse. Evading such collapse would require restructuring inter-communal relations away from the epistemological privilege attached to the nation-state. Moving from large to small polities does not necessarily mean secession. Instead, the decision-making process needs to be embedded in the affected localities. This could be achieved by borrowing from one of the pages of the Middle Ages, by resurrecting the idea of charter cities.[31] While I do not go into any detail as to what would be the best locality to carry out the burden of autonomy, nor do I delineate the legal architecture that would lead to propelling such localities into taking over much of the role currently played by nation-states, the following chapters will be dedicated to carrying out these tasks.

REFERENCES

AER. (2014). *State of the energy market 2014. Australian Energy Regulator*. Canberra: Competition and Consumer Commission.

Aligica, P. D., & Tarko, V. (2012). Polycentricity: From Polanyi to Ostrom, and beyond. *Governance: An International Journal of Policy, Administration and Institutions*, *25*(2), 237–262. doi:10.1111/j.1468-0491.2011.01550.x

Allen, P. M. (1994). Coherence, chaos and evolution in the social context. *Futures*, *26*(6), 583–597. doi:10.1016/0016-3287(94)90030-2

Allen, P. M. (2001). Knowledge, ignorance, and evolution in complex systems. In J. Foster & J. S. Metcalfe (Eds.), *Frontiers of evolutionary economics* (pp. 313–350). Cheltenham: Edward Elgar. doi:10.4337/9781843762911.00024

Allen, P. M. (2005). Understanding social and economic systems as evolutionary complex systems. In K. Dopfer (Ed.), *The Evolutionary foundations of economics* (pp. 431–458). Cambridge: Cambridge University Press. doi:10.1017/CBO9780511492297.013

Amabile, T. M., Kramer, S. J., Bonabeau, E., Bingham, A., Litan, R. E., Klein, J., & Ross, C. (2010). Breakthrough ideas for 2010. *Harvard Business Review*, *88*(1/2), 41.

Archer, M. S. (2013). Social morphogenesis and the prospect of morphogenetic society. In M. S. Archer (Ed.), *Social Morphogenesis* (pp. 1–22). New York: Springer. doi:10.1007/978-94-007-6128-5_1

Arthur, W. B. (1989). Competing technologies, increasing returns, and lock-in by historical events. *The Economic Journal*, *99*(394), 116. doi:10.2307/2234208

Arthur, W. B. (1994). *Increasing returns and path dependence in the economy*. Ann Arbor: Michigan University Press. doi:10.3998/mpub.10029

Axelrod, R. (1984). *The evolution of cooperation*. New York: Basic Books.

Boden, M. (1990). *The creative mind: Myths and mechanisms*. London: Weidenfeld and Nicolson.

Bonner, J. T. (1988). *The evolution of complexity by means of natural selection*. Princeton: Princeton University Press.

Bookchin, M. (1982). *The ecology of freedom: The emergence and dissolution of hierarchy*. Palo Alto: California Cheshire Books.

Bookchin, M. (1987). *The rise of urbanization and the decline of citizenship*. San Francisco: Sierra Club Books.

Boulding, K. (1968). *Beyond economics*. Ann Arbor: University of Michigan Press.

Boulding, K. (1971). *Collected Papers* (Vol. I and II). Boulder, Colo.: Colorado Associated University Press.

Boulding, K. (1981). *Evolutionary economics*. London: Sage Publications.

Boulding, K. (1984). *The organizational revolution: A study in the ethics of economic organization*. Westport, Conn.: Greenwood Press. (Original work published 1953)

Brading, K., & Castellani, E. (Eds.). (2003). *Symmetries in physics: Philosophical reflections*. Cambridge: Cambridge University Press. doi:10.1017/CBO9780511535369

Brady, F. (Ed.). (1996) *A dictionary on electricity: Contribution on Australia* (unpublished). CIGRE and AHEF. Retrieved from http://www.ewh.ieee.org/r10/nsw/subpages/history/electricity_in_australia.pdf

Brissaud, J.-B. (2005). The meaning of entropy. *Entropy*, *7*(1), 68–96. doi:10.3390/e7010068

Callejas, D. G. (2007). Biology and economics: Metaphors that economists usually take from Biology. *Ecos de Economía*, *24*, 153–164.

Camilo, M., Tittensor, D. P., Adl, S., Simpson, A. G. B., & Worm, B. (2011). How many species are there on earth and in the ocean? *PLoS Biology*, *9*(8). doi:10.1371/journal.pbio.1001127 PMID:21886479

Carroll, S. B. (2001). Chance and necessity: The evolution of morphological complexity and diversity. *Nature*, *409*(6823), 1102–1109. doi:10.1038/35059227 PMID:11234024

Chen, Y. G. (2003). Self-organization and self-organizing cities. *City Planning Review*, *27*(10), 17–22.

Claeys, G. (2000). The survival of the fittest and the origins of social Darwinism. *Journal of the History of Ideas*, *61*(2), 223–240. doi:10.1353/jhi.2000.0014

Coase, R. (1998). The new institutional economics. *The American Economic Review*, *88*(2), 72–74.

Commons, J. R. (1924). *Legal foundations of capitalism*. New York: Macmillan.

Dawkins, R. (1976). *The selfish gene*. Oxford: Oxford University Press.

de Wit, B., & Smith, J. (1986). *Field theory in particle physics*. Amsterdam: North-Holland.

Dopfer, K., & Potts, J. (2014). Introduction: Evolutionary Microeconomics. In K. Dopfer & J. Potts (Eds.), *The new evolutionary economics* (Vol. 1, pp. ix–xiii).

Dunn, C. (1985). *The History of Electricity in Queensland: An outline of the history of electricity and its progress in Queensland 1882-1984. Bundaberg*. Col Dunn publisher.

Elsner, W. (2010). The process and a simple logic of meso. Emergence and the Co-evolution of Institutions and Group Size. *Journal of Evolutionary Economics*, *20*(3), 445–477. doi:10.1007/s00191-009-0158-4

ESAA. (1996). *Electricity Australia*. Electricity Supply Association of Australia.

Føllesdal, A. (1998). Survey article: Subsidiarity. *Journal of Political Philosophy*, *6*(2), 190–218. doi:10.1111/1467-9760.00052

Funtowicz, S., & Ravetz, J. R. (1994). Emergent Complex Systems. *Futures*, *26*(6), 568–582. doi:10.1016/0016-3287(94)90029-9

Gavrilov, L., & Gavrilova, N. (2004). Why We Fall Apart. *IEEE Spectrum*, *41*(9), 30–35. doi:10.1109/MSPEC.2004.1330807

Geisendorf, S. (2009). The Economic Concept of Evolution: Self-organization or Universal Darwinism. *Journal of Economic Methodology*, *16*(4), 377–391. doi:10.1080/13501780903337347

Gibson, A. J. (1927). *Power Development in Australia*. A report to the Commonwealth Government.

Goodwin, B. (1994). *How the leopard changed its spots: The evolution of complexity*. London: Weidenfeld &Nicolson.

Gordon, S. (1989). Darwin and political economy: The connection reconsidered. *Journal of the History of Biology*, *22*(3), 437–459. doi:10.1007/BF00401577

Gould, S. (2007). *The theory of options: A new theory of the evolution of human behavior*. Boca Raton, FL: Universal Publishers. (Original work published 2000)

Gould, S. J. (1996). *Full house*. New York: Harmony Books. doi:10.4159/harvard.9780674063396

Gould, S. J. (2009). Preface. In R. Milner (Ed.), *Darwin's universe* (pp. 2–3). Berkeley: University of California Press.

Granovetter, M. S. (1973). The strength of weak ties. *American Journal of Sociology*, *78*(6), 1360–1380. doi:10.1086/225469

Granovetter, M. S. (1983). The strength of weak ties: A network theory revisited. *Sociological Theory*, *1*, 201. doi:10.2307/202051

Granovetter, M. S. (1985). Economic action and social structure: The problem of embeddedness. *American Journal of Sociology*, *91*(3), 481–510. doi:10.1086/228311

Gussen, B. F. (2013a). On the problem of scale: Spinozistic sovereignty as the logical foundation of constitutional economics. *The Journal of Philosophical Economics*, *7*(1). Retrieved from http://www.jpe.ro/?id=autor&p=1851

Gussen, B. F. (2013b). On the problem of scale: Hayek, Kohr, Jacobs and the reinvention of the political state. *Constitutional Political Economy*, *24*(1), 19–42. doi:10.1007/s10602-012-9130-7

Gussen, B. F. (2015). On the problem of scale: A general theory of morphogenesis and normative policy signals for economic evolution. *Evolutionary and Institutional Economics Review*, *12*(1), 81–104. doi:10.1007/s40844-015-0001-6

Hanusch, H., & Pyka, A. (2007). Principles of neo-Schumpeterian economics. *Cambridge Journal of Economics*, *31*(2), 275–289. doi:10.1093/cje/bel018

Hayden, F. G. (1987). Evolution of time constructs and their impact on socioeconomic planning. *Journal of Economic Issues*, *21*(3), 1281–1312. doi:10.1080/00213624.1987.11504704

Hayek, F. (1990). *New studies in philosophies, politics, economics and the history of ideas*. London: Routledge.

Hayward, J., & Graham, P. (2012). *Australian electricity generation technology cost projections: Application of a global and local learning model*. Canberra: CSIRO.

Helling, C. S. (1994). Simplifying the complex: The paradigms of ecological function and structure. *Futures*, *26*(6), 598–609. doi:10.1016/0016-3287(94)90031-0

Heylighen, F. (2009). Complexity and self-organization. In M. J. Bates & M. N. Maack (Eds.), *Encyclopedia of Library and Information Sciences* (3rd ed., pp. 1215–1224). New York: Taylor & Francis. doi:10.1081/E-ELIS3-120043869

Hobbes, T. (2011). *Leviathan*. Seattle, WA: Pacific Publishing Studio. (Original work published 1651)

Hodgson, G. M. (1999). *Evolution and institutions*. Cheltenham, England: Edward Elgar.

Holt, R., Rosser, J. B. Jr, & Colander, D. (2011). The complexity era in economics. *Review of Economic Policy*, *23*(3), 357–369. doi:10.1080/09538259.2011.583820

Inayatullah, S. (1994). Life, the universe and emergence. *Futures*, *26*(6), 683–696. doi:10.1016/0016-3287(94)90037-X

Kirman, A. P., & Vriend, N. J. (2001). Evolving market structure: An ACE model of price dispersion and loyalty. *Journal of Economic Dynamics & Control*, *25*(3-4), 459–502. doi:10.1016/S0165-1889(00)00033-6

Knudsen, T. (2002). Economic selection theory. *Journal of Evolutionary Economics*, *12*(4), 443–470. doi:10.1007/s00191-002-0126-8

Kropotkin, P. (1901). *Fields, factories and workshops or industry combined with agriculture and brain Work with manual work*. New York: GP Putman's Sons.

Kropotkin, P. (1904). *Mutual aid: A factor of evolution.* London: William Heinemann.

Kropotkin, P. (1975). *The Essential Kropotkin.* New York: Liveright.

Lawson, T. (1997). *Economics and reality.* London: Routledge. doi:10.4324/9780203195390

Lewin, R. (1992). *Life at the edge of chaos.* New York: Collier Books.

Luhmann, N. (1979). *Trust and Power.* New York: John Wiley & Sons.

Marion, R. (1999). *The edge of organization: Chaos and complexity theories of formal social systems.* London: Sage Publications.

Martin, R. (1999). The new geographical turn in economics: Some critical reflections. *Cambridge Journal of Economics, 23*(1), 65–91. doi:10.1093/cje/23.1.65

Martin, R., & Sunley, P. (2001). Rethinking the economic in economic geography: Broadening our vision or losing our focus. *Antipode, 33*(2), 148–161. doi:10.1111/1467-8330.00173

Matthews, R. C. O. (1984). Darwinism and economic change. In D. A. Collard, N. H. Dimsdale, C. L. Gilbert, D. R. Helm, M. F. G. Scott, & A. K. Sen (Eds.), *Economic Theory and Hicksian Themes* (pp. 91–117). Oxford: Clarendon Press.

McShea, D. W. (1994). Mechanisms of large-scale evolutionary trends. *Evolution; International Journal of Organic Evolution, 48*(6), 1747–1763. doi:10.1111/j.1558-5646.1994.tb02211.x PMID:28565153

Metcalfe, J. S. (2008). Accounting for economic evolution: Fitness and the population method. *Journal of Bioeconomics, 10*(1), 23–49. doi:10.1007/s10818-008-9029-6

Mumford, L. (1934). *Technics and civilization.* London: Routledge & Kegan Paul.

Mumford, L. (1938). *The culture of cities.* New York: Harcourt, Brace and Company.

Mumford, L. (1944). *The condition of man.* New York: Harcourt, Brace and Company.

Mumford, L. (1961). *The city in history: Its origins, its Transformations, and its prospects*. New York: Harcourt, Brace & World.

Mumford, L. (1967). *The myth of the machine* (Vol. 1). New York: Harcourt Brace Jovanovich.

Mumford, L. (1970). *The myth of the machine* (Vol. 2). New York: Harcourt Brace Jovanovich.

Mumford, L. (1972). *The transformations of man*. New York: Harper & Row. (Original work published 1956)

North, D. (1990). *Institutions, institutional change and economic performance*. Cambridge: Cambridge University Press. doi:10.1017/CBO9780511808678

Ostrom, V. (1980). Artisanship and artefact. *Public Administration Review*, *40*(4), 309–317. doi:10.2307/3110256

Philo, C., & Parr, H. (2000). Institutional geographies: Introductory remarks. *Geoforum*, *31*(4), 513–521. doi:10.1016/S0016-7185(00)00018-X

Porpora, D. V. (2013). Morphogenesis and social change. In M. S. Archer (Ed.), *Social Morphogenesis* (pp. 25–37). New York: Springer. doi:10.1007/978-94-007-6128-5_2

Potts, J. (2007). Evolutionary institutional economics. *Journal of Economic Issues*, *41*(2), 341–351. doi:10.1080/00213624.2007.11507020

Prigogine, I., Nicolis, G., & Babloyantz, A. (1972a). Thermodynamics of evolution. *Physics Today*, *25*(11), 23–28. doi:10.1063/1.3071090

Prigogine, I., Nicolis, G., & Babloyantz, A. (1972b). Thermodynamics of evolution. *Physics Today*, *25*(12), 38–44. doi:10.1063/1.3071140

Rosen, J. (2008). *Symmetry rules: How science and nature are founded on symmetry*. Berlin: Springer. doi:10.1007/978-3-540-75973-7

Ross, S. A. (1976). Options and efficiency. *The Quarterly Journal of Economics*, *90*(1), 75–89. doi:10.2307/1886087

Saviotti, P., & Pyka, A. (2008). Product variety, competition and economic growth. *Journal of Evolutionary Economics*, *18*, 167–182. doi:10.1007/s00191-007-0077-1

Schrodinger, E. (1967). *What is life?* Cambridge: Cambridge University Press.

Schumacher, E. F. (1977). A guide for the perplexed. London: Cape.

Schumacher, E. F. (1999). *Small is beautiful: Economics as if people mattered.* Vancouver: Hartley & Marks.

Voets, H. J. L., & Biggiero, L. (2000). Globalization and self-organization: The consequences of decentralization for industrial organization. *International Review of Sociology, 10*(1), 73–82. doi:10.1080/713673987

Waldrop, M. M. (1992). *Complexity: The emerging science at the edge of order and chaos.* New York: Simon & Schuster.

White, C. (2013). Morphogenesis, continuity and change in the international political system. In M. S. Archer (Ed.), *Social Morphogenesis* (pp. 85–101). New York: Springer.

Whitfield, P. (1998). *Evolution: The greatest story ever told.* London: Marshall Publishing.

Wilkins, J. S. (2001). The appearance of Lamarckism in the evolution of culture. In J. Laurent, & J. Nightingale (Eds.), Darwinism and evolutionary economics. Cheltenham, UK: Edward Elgar. doi:10.4337/9781843762942.00016

Witt, U. (1993). Emergence and dissemination of innovations: Some principles of evolutionary economics. In R. Day & P. Chen (Eds.), *Nonlinear Dynamics and Evolutionary Economics* (pp. 91–100). Oxford: Oxford University Press.

Wood, A., & Valler, D. (2001). Turn again? Rethinking institutions and the governance of local and regional economies. *Environment & Planning A, 33*(7), 1139–1144. doi:10.1068/a3472

Zwicky, F. (1969). *Discovery, invention, research.* New York: Macmillan.

ENDNOTES

1 This chapter is based on a paper that was first published in the *Evolutionary and Institutional Economics Review*. See Gussen (2015).

2 For other theories of evolution see for example Prigogine et al (1972a, 1972b).

3 The model presented in this chapter is neo-Lamarckian. It attempts to explain evolution without 'random variation' and 'natural selection.'

4 Note that 'institutions' in economics are understood as the 'basic rules of the game.' See North (1990). In this chapter I expand the definition to include options (of rules) rather than enforced rules only.

5 Both rules and options can be seen as part of institutions. This paper emphasizes the complex causational chain between the structure of such institutions and the localization of economic activities. On this point see also Martin (1999); Philo and Parr (2000); Martin and Sunley (2001); Wood and Valler (2001). Emphasis is on Original Institutional Economics (à la Veblen) were an institution is "a process of changing structure" rather than a "structure of changing process" as under New Institutional Economics (Potts 2007, p. 343).

6 See Boulding (1984 [1953], pp. xix, xxix, and xxxi). This, therefore, provides a link to constitutional economics through the extension of this exchange regime to politics.

7 This, therefore, provides a link to constitutional economics through the extension of this exchange regime to politics.

8 Adopted from Brady (1996), Figure 1. The 1927 map is based on data from A. J. Gibson (1927), while the 1997 map is based on data from the Electricity Supply Association of Australia (ESAA, 1996).

9 Australian Energy Regulator (AER, 2014), Figure 4.

10 Data from the Australian Energy Market Operator (AEMO). Retrieved from https://www.aemo.com.au.

11 Adopted from Hayward and Graham (2012), Figure 6.

12 See Chapter VI and Gussen (2013b) for the background of this model.

13 For a general introduction to symmetry, see Rosen (2008) and Brading and Castellani (2003).

14 Tensors include scalars and vectors but could also have higher dimensionality.

15 Entropy attempts to achieve absolute symmetry where there is a total lack of differentiation.

16 I use quantum in its physical sense, as the physical entity involved in the interactions defining a given system.

17 See for example Zwicky (1969).

18 But this does not mean that these living forms have to be carbon-based. See the discussion on the signs of life in the following section.

19 We can think of this along the lines of the first law of thermodynamics.

20 This means that evolution progresses through "jerks" rather than gradually as proposed by Darwin.

21 Structure is taken to mean relationships rather than rules, and hence maintaining the ontological divide between structure and agency. See Porpora (2013: 26).

22 A formal definition of scale and complexity is furnished in the previous section.

23 On the application of complexity in economics see Holt et al. (2011).

24 Through Evolutionary Institutional Economics we can interpret the emergence of structure as institutionalization. See Elsner (2010, p. 450).

25 One of the prime examples of the interaction of competition and cooperation in economics is the Prisoners' Dilemma.

26 Compare to the discussion of structural attractors in Allen (2005).

27 For the role of self-organisation as a principle of economic evolution see Geisendorf (2009). Friedrich Hayek was one of the main economists to stress the role of self-organisation albeit at the group rather than the group level. See also Heylighen (2009).

28 See the next section. See also Gussen (2013b).

29 The work by Mark Granovetter is useful here to explain further the nature of coupling. See Granovetter (1973); Granovetter (1983); Granovetter (1985).

30 Also Refer to Boulding's five principles of morphology (structural organisation) that illustrate how growth creates form and how form limits growth (Boulding, 1968, p. 81).

31 See also Amabile et al. (2010) for a discussion of Paul Romer's idea of charter cities.

Chapter 2
The Model

ABSTRACT

This chapter introduces the ψ model, the analytical model used to investigate the economic efficiency of countries. The chapter provides an explanation of this model through the second law of thermodynamics, the concept of 'complex energy,' and the principle of equipartition (from statistical mechanics). To eliminate the need for using energy units, and to enable the conversion between different input and outputs, the engineering concept of per-unit is also introduced.

INTRODUCTION

Hands being the Father, as Lands are the Mother and Womb of Wealth. (Petty, 1899, II, p. 377), cited in Georgescu-Roegen (1971, p. 280, fn 9)

As explained by Georgescu-Roegen, 'thermodynamics is largely a physics of economic value' (1971, p. 276). Thermodynamics, which could be traced back to Sadi Carnot (1890) and his 19th-century study of steam engines, developed from an economic problem, namely, the efficiency of steam engines. Carnot was interested in identifying the conditions under which one could obtain the highest output of mechanical work from a given input of free heat. Thermodynamics explains why the things that are useful also have an economic value. In other words, all economic value can be reduced to a common denominator: low

DOI: 10.4018/978-1-5225-2756-5.ch002

entropy. The etymology of the word 'entropy' comes from the prefix 'en' for 'inside,' and the Greek root 'tropē,' which means 'transformation.' The term was coined by Rudolf Clausius (1850) to describe the amount of lost energy in an irreversible process.[1] For our purposes, we define entropy as the extent of 'spread out' of energy in the system. Entropy is the amount of energy not available for the economic process. Low entropy suggests more free energy (available to do work), and less bounded energy. Low entropy is a necessary condition for the existence of economic value. The second law of thermodynamics, or the entropy law, states that isolated systems tend to maximize their entropy. In other words, while total energy remains constant (the first law of thermodynamics), the distribution of this energy becomes more even. The economic transformation is not automatic, as in the material domain, but depends on the actions of human beings. The economic process is distinguished by its purposive activity and its objective of 'enjoyment of life.' In summary, the economic process requires low entropy or free energy that is available for transforming inputs, such as land and people, to output, such as goods and services.

Georgescu-Roegen suggests that "the economic process is entropic: it neither creates nor consumes matter or energy, but only transforms low [entropy] into high entropy" (1971, p. 281). Based on this conclusion, he created a simple model of the economic process (1971, Chapters IX and X). The model includes three main inputs: land, labor, and capital. Using this model, Georgescu-Roegen explains the influence of entropy on (economic) development (1971, p. 292). It was this approach to modeling the economic process that inspired the ψ model.

The ψ model represents the economic process as a special case of energy transformation processes. The model has two inputs: land and population.[2] The model uses one output, which represents all goods and services produced within a given country. The model accounts for differences between the total input energy and output energy through 'capital,' which is interpreted as a proxy for the efficiency of the energy transformation process over time. The energy conversion efficiency (η) is allowed to be greater than 1 through a process of accumulation from different time periods, and different space points——although this applies to microstates only. The total efficiency at the macro state, given our assumptions in relation to the 'original condition' (see below), is equal to 1. Capital could be interpreted as a third energy input, although it is of a different type. As detailed in the next section, capital is modeled as 'apparent energy,' while land and people are modeled as 'real energy.'

Previous work on complex adaptive systems by Prigogine (1978) and others recognized that economic systems are not in 'classical' thermodynamic equilibrium. This realization allowed for a new conception of the entropy law. In the 1990s, the nexus between entropy and the economic process was updated through a new understanding of the law of entropy:

We examine the thermodynamic evolution of various evolving systems ... The reformulated second law suggests that as systems are moved away from equilibrium they will take advantage of all available means to resist externally implied gradients ... We argue that as ecosystems grow and develop, they should increase their total dissipation, develop more complex structures with more energy flow, increase their cycling activity, develop greater diversity and generate more hierarchic levels, all to abet energy degradation. Species which survive in ecosystems are those that funnel energy into their own production and reproduction and contribute to autocatalytic processes which increase the total dissipation of the ecosystem. In short, ecosystems develop in ways which systematically increases their ability to degrade the incoming solar energy. We believe that our thermodynamic paradigm makes it possible for the study of ecosystems to be developed from a descriptive science into a predictive science founded on the most basic principles of physics. (Schneider & Kay, 1994, 25)

It is useful here to expand on the idea of autocatalysis. An autocatalytic process is one where an output is also an input that acts as a catalyst. The process is nonlinear, and this results in a reduction in the entropy of the system through the creation of spontaneous order. Biodiveristy can be considered as an autocatalytic system (Gatti et al., 2017). Because of the entropy law, this also means that the process exports entropy to its surroundings. Autocatalysis has already been applied to the economic process:

Biological organisms are ... autocatalytic networks of chemical transformations, which continually reconstruct both themselves and their physical containers ... This chemical perspective can be applied to ... products and firms through the following analogy. Skills, like chemical reactions, are rules that transform products into other products. Products, like chemicals, are transformed by skills. Firms, like organisms, are containers of skills that transform products. Trade, like food, passes around through exchange networks, renewing skills and thereby firms in the process ... Economic "life" exists if an autocatalytic network of interlinked skills and products can emerge and renew itself in the face of continual turnover and "death" in its component skills and products. (Padgett, McMahan, & Zhong, 2012, pp. 70-71)

The autocatalysis analogy suggests a form of feedback loops in the economic process. In our model, we use this insight to inform not only the way 'capital' is utilized within a given national economy but also the way it is exchanged within the world-system.

While Georgescu-Roegen (1971) used classical conceptions of the entropy law as applied to economic analysis, a more qualitative approach is required to analyze long-run development in systems that are far from thermodynamic equilibrium (FFE). Georgescu-Roegen employed Schumpeter's distinction between growth and development (1971, p. 294), and Lotka's endo- and exo-somatic instruments (1971, p. 307), to argue that the evolution of FFE economic systems is a qualitative process (of structural change). It follows that:

In an economic environment, it could be postulated that there is an attractor, in the space of institutional arrangements towards which the acquisition of knowledge drives economic systems because the production of new knowledge maximizes the throughput of energy. (Rainer, Foster, & Potts, 2006, p. 355)

The concept of attractor has a particular role in complex systems. We model attractors in the world-economy as 'global cities' (Sassen, 1991, 2006) that enable national economies to absorb and store capital. In later chapters, we present some propositions as to the role that global cities play in the economic efficiency of countries and the world-system.

Rainer et al. (2006) formalized the concept of economic evolution as the development of structural complexity to harness available energy from the environment to avert degradation gradients. In Chapter I, we expanded the link between evolution and complexity through a formal model that elucidates the results from the model presented in this chapter. In Chapter I, evolution is presented as a process that leads to greater complexity. In the final analysis, economic efficiency is linked to the structure of the political state. Pathologies, including *morphostasis* (where growth and development are anemic due to the system's form and structure becoming static), necessitate a rethinking of political organization. Polycentricity and the principle of hypotaxis,[3] with a praxis inspired by sovereign cities (Gussen, 2013), are imperative for the continuous evolution of societies, and hence economies. In this future, nation-states become subsidiary, and sovereign cities replace nation-states on the 'international' stage.

THE CLASSICAL PRINCIPLE OF ENERGY EQUIPARTITION

The equipartition principle, which was first proposed by John James Waterston (1846) and later developed by Ludwig Boltzmann (1871), states that in (thermal) equilibrium, energy is shared equally among all its various forms (Tolman, 1918). The system maximizes its entropy by distributing the available energy evenly amongst all the accessible modes of motion. In terms of irreversibilities, the principle suggests that achieving a thermodynamic optimum would require designing less irreversible systems. This can be done by distributing the irreversibilities to minimize the production of entropy, based on nonequilibrium thermodynamics (Demirel, 2007, p. 176).

The principle of equipartition helps explain why more complex systems have more internal energy compared to less complex systems. The equipartition principle suggests that more advanced economies have more capacity to store capital (internal energy) than less advanced systems. To put it differently, energy is shared equally amongst all accessible degrees of freedom of a system. The more complex the system, the more degrees of freedom it has. Note that the degrees of freedom refer to the number of ways a component (a molecule or a country) of the system can possess energy. The total of these energies, other than those associated with land and population, are referred to collectively as 'capital.' In later chapters, I link the Economic Complexity Index (ECI), developed by Hausmann et al. (2011), with the ability of more complex economies to store capital.

The principle deals with the distribution of the mean of the energy of a dynamical system in thermal equilibrium due to quadratic terms in the Hamiltonian (see below). More precisely, it confirms that any canonical variable x entering the Hamiltonian through an additive term proportional to x^2 has a thermal mean energy equal to $\frac{kT}{2}$, where T is the temperature, and k is the Boltzmann constant (Lima & Plastino, 2000). Note, however, that the equipartition of energy is not a necessary consequence of the Hamiltonian. It has been derived from these equations "merely because energy has, quite unnecessarily, always been taken as a homogenous quadratic function of the generalized coordinates." (Toleman, 1918, p. 262). Toleman (1918) provides a generalized equipartition law which reduces to the special quadratic case. For developing the ψ model, we will continue to consider the special, and simpler, case of the quadratic form of energy.

The Hamiltonian is the set of equations that describe the evolution (motion) equations of a physical system (Taylor, 2005). The equations describe the scalar function $H(q,p,t)$, where p is the generalized momentum, and q is the generalized position. The system is described by the trajectory $r=(q,p)$, and the initial condition $r(0)=r_0$. The evolution equations are given by:

$$\begin{aligned}\frac{dp}{dt}&=-\frac{\partial H}{\partial q}\\ \frac{dq}{dt}&=+\frac{\partial H}{\partial p}\end{aligned} \tag{1}$$

For example, a one-dimensional harmonic oscillator has a Hamiltonian given by:

$$H=\frac{p^2}{2m}+\frac{kx^2}{2} \tag{2}$$

where, k is the spring constant, and m is the inertial mass. The same observation on the relationship of quadratic terms to the expression of energy will guide the development of the ψ model in relation to the inputs to, and the output from, the economic process. In particular, we use land and population as the canonical variables of the energy inputs to the economic process. Similarly, we use the GDP as the canonical variable of the energy output from the economic process.

While the principle of equipartition was one of the most significant results of classical mechanics, experimental findings did not always agree with its predictions (Tolman, 1918). There are some limitations of the equipartition principle. The first is 'ergodicity.' The principle holds only for ergodic systems (in thermal equilibrium). The word 'ergodic' comes the Greek roots 'ergon' (work) and 'hodos' (way). In thermodynamics, the 'ergodicity hypothesis' states that for a given dynamic system, all accessible microstates are equiprobable in the long run. Ergodicity is taken to mean long-run predictability—that at any future date the outcome is statistically determined from past and current data. Where ergodicity breaks down, the system becomes path-dependent (Horst, 2008). A system of *coupled* harmonic oscillators is an example of a non-ergodic system because energy is not transferred between different modes (Reichl, 1998, pp. 326–333). In economic systems, oscillations are exhibited through (business) cycles of varying length. While these cycles were discovered in the 19th century, classical economists such as Adam Smith and David Ricardo denied the possibility of their existence on a global scale. It was only recently that these cycles were modeled as part of the oscillations of a complex system (Schweitzer; 2002; Markose, 2005). They are usually modeled as second-degree differential equations (Antonov, 2010). Mishchenko (2014) explains the dynamics of these cycles as follows:

In mainstream economic theory, business cycles are associated with the fluctuations in aggregate demand coupled with so called accelerator and multiplier effects. Accelerator effect is the tendency of businesses to increase their investment spendings [sic] beyond usual levels in growing economies and to lower that in shrinking economies. Multiplier effect is the tendency of increased investment spendings [sic] to additionally stimulate [the] economy as the result of the money turnover. The multiplier-accelerator model, if represented in a mathematical form, does give rise to oscillatory patterns in the fluctuations of aggregate demand; however, for that it relies on economically ''irrational'' tendency of businesses to continue expanding their investments even in already oversaturated but still growing economy, as embodied by the accelerator effect, and leaves without explanation the nature of the initial fluctuation that gives rise to subsequent oscillations. A completely different perspective on business cycles have [sic] been assumed by the more recent real business cycles theory. The real business cycles theory supposes that business cycles always have an exogenous cause such as disruptive new technologies, geo-economical changes, political crises, wars, etc. and, in that sense, are just a response to the changes in real markets' conditions. Credit/debt cycles theory, on the other hand, attributes business cycles to the dynamics of over-borrowing by businesses during the times of economic booms, followed by economic slowdown and, finally, a debt crisis and a recession. Political cycles theory attributes business cycles directly to political manipulations and improper government interventions. Some of the oldest views on business cycles in Marxian economics associate business cycles with the intrinsic property of businesses to lose profitability and fail with time, translating into recessions accompanied by mass unemployment, wealth inequality and economical restructuring aimed at recovering profitability. (Mishchenko, 2014, e87820: 1)

While these oscillations are integral to the economic process (Zarnowitz 1996; Mokyr 2003; Bannock and Baxter 2009; Barber 2009), the ψ model does not account, at least directly, for these oscillations. The rationale for ignoring oscillations is the 'original position' we take the world-economy to be in at the beginning of the economic (transformation) process. In essence, in the 'original position,' the model imagines a world with no countries. There is only one macro state: the world-economy. Because of this assumption, the model ignores the existence of economic oscillations at the global scale. As we will see later (in Chapters III and IV), oscillations emerge within the partitioned world-economy, both at the country scale, and the global scale.

The failure of the equipartition principle under oscillations is linked to another failure. The principle does not hold when 'quantum effects' are not insignificant. In other words, when the thermal energy is smaller than the quantum energy spacing in a particular degree of freedom, this degree of freedom is 'frozen out.' The energy associated with a 'frozen out' degree of freedom is less than that predicted by the equipartition principle. The quantum failure of the principle of equipartition was identified by Albert Einstein:

[I]n his 1905 paper on the light quantum, Einstein ... pointed out that TEE [The Theory of Equipartition], together with standard assumptions of radiation theory, leads necessarily to ... sharp contradiction with the experiments. In 1907, in his celebrated paper on the specific heats of solid bodies, he made a decisive step in the direction of casting serious doubts on the validity of TEE for elementary structures whose energy spectrum one had, as it appeared, to quantize. (Bergia & Navarro, 1997, 184)

The principle of equipartition applies only to classical systems. In other words, the larger the densities in the economic system, and the lower the absolute economic temperature, the less justified is the use of this principle. Population density and output density (measured as GDP per square kilometer) are taken as proxies for (country-specific) economic density. Economic temperature is interpreted as the ability of the economy to absorb capital (Sella, 1915; Erreygers, 2001, pp. 160-163). Hence, in the ψ model, we do not have any equipartition failure in the 'original position' as we assume that the world-system has a uniform (per-unit) density of 1, and that the total capital at that juncture is equal to zero (initial condition). During the evolution of the world-economy, capital 'tears' out. Some degrees of freedom become frozen, and not all countries are able to absorb capital. We now see an exchange of capital. This is the basis for distinguishing between sources, or countries that cannot absorb capital (and hence export it to the world-system), and sinks, which are countries that can absorb capital from the world-system. Capital can now have both negative and positive signs. Notwithstanding, the total capital in the world-system at any given time is always equal to zero (the first law of thcrmodynamics).

THE POWER POSTULATE

Power is defined as the rate at which energy is transferred. The formulae for power involve the product of two time-dependent variables. Take for example the formula for the instantaneous power in electric networks: $\mathbb{P}(t) = v(t)^T i(t)$. This is a matrix formula that gives the scalar power as a function of time, and relates it to the output of an inner product between two column vectors, namely the instantaneous voltage vector $v(t)$, and the instantaneous current vector $i(t)$. Another formula for instantaneous power is that of the discrete mechanical domain: $\mathbb{P}(t) = f(t)^T v(t)$. The power in this case is the inner product of the instantaneous force vector $f(t)$, and the instantaneous velocity vector $v(t)$. This observation on the nature of the power formula spans the gamut of physical systems, and in fact, constitutes a basis for integrating the analysis of different energy systems (Paynter, 1961).

The variables in the above formulas belong to two types. The first, known as the flow (f), is built from the time derivative of the so-called 'configuration-like variable' of the system, for example the generalized coordinates in discrete mechanical systems, or the electric charge in electrical networks (Toni, 1977). For discrete systems, we will call the configuration 'generalized displacement' (q) so that it agrees with the existing nomenclature. The second type, known as an effort (e) or the source-like variable is built from the partial derivative of the energy of the domain under consideration with respect to the configuration. Mathematically, this translates to:

$$\mathbb{P}(t) \triangleq \frac{dE}{dt} = \frac{\partial E}{\partial q}\frac{dq}{dt} = e(t)^T f(t) \qquad (3)$$

or

$$\mathbb{P}(t) \triangleq \frac{dE}{dt} = \frac{\partial E}{\partial p}\frac{dp}{dt} = f(t)^T e(t) \tag{4}$$

where (p) is the generalized momentum. Note that each formula is associated with a specific kind of energy. It is convenient to also define the integral of the effort with respect to time as the generalized momentum. This generalization provides a unified approach to the analysis and synthesis of any dynamical system. A table that summarizes the relation between the fundamental variables and conventional variables for some discrete domains is provided in van Dixhoorn (1982).

Using tensors, we can write a more generalized formula for the scalar power (Π) as follows:

$$\Pi = e_{\alpha\beta\gamma\ldots} f^{\alpha\beta\gamma\ldots} \tag{5}$$

The above generalization can allow us to write any energy expression as a quadratic equation in an effort or a flow variable:

$$\mathcal{E} \propto e^2 \tag{6}$$

or

$$\mathcal{E} \propto f^2 \tag{7}$$

where $\mathcal{E}$ is the energy stored in an element. For example, the energy stored in an electric capacitor can be written as

$$\mathcal{E} = \frac{1}{2}CV^2 \propto V^2 \tag{8}$$

where C is the capacitance, and V is the voltage (an effort variable). Similarly,

$$\mathcal{E} = \frac{1}{2}LI^2 \propto I^2 \tag{9}$$

where L is the inductance, and I is the electric current (a flow variable). Similar energy equations can be seen in every domain. For example, in classical mechanics, kinetic energy is given by:

$$\mathcal{E} = \frac{1}{2}mv^2 \propto v^2 \tag{10}$$

where m is the mass, and v is the speed. This rationale of quadratic equations guides the arguments below in developing a model based on energy-equivalent expressions for economic efficiency.

COMPLEX ENERGY

The concept of complex energy was first introduced by Landau and Lifshitz (1977), and already has applications in quantum physics (Bender, 2005). I use complex energy to model 'capital.' It is also of interest because it helps explain quantum behavior using classical mechanics, or complex classical mechanics to be precise (Bender, Brody, & Hook, 2008). Given a classical Hamiltonian $H(x,p)$, the path $x(t)$ of a particle is fully determined by Hamilton's equations of motion (1) together with the initial conditions $x(0)$ and $p(0)$. The energy E is invariant under the Hamiltonian. In classical mechanics, the initial conditions are usually taken to be real so that the energy E is real and, in addition, particle trajectories are restricted to the real-x axis. Allowing the initial conditions to take complex values, which is an interpretation of the Heisenberg uncertainty principle, and allowing the energy to be complex, results in quantum like dynamics.

Let us go back to modeling 'capital' using complex energy. A useful analogy can be made with electrical impedance Z, which is a measure of the opposition an electrical circuit gives to the passage of an electrical current when voltage is applied. The term 'impedance' was coined in 1886 by Oliver Heaviside (1886; 1970, II, pp. 39 - 44). But it was Arthur Kennelly (1893) who first represented impedance as a complex number.

In Cartesian form, impedance is represented as:

$$Z = R + jX \tag{11}$$

where the real part is the electrical resistance R, and the imaginary part is the electrical reactance X. The latter represents the opposition of an electrical circuit to a change in the electrical current or voltage. It represents either an inductance or a capacitance. The impedance of an inductance is $Z_L = jX_L$, while that of a capacitance is $Z_c = -jX_c$. In these equations, $j = \sqrt{-1}$ (the complex operator). The ψ model interprets capital as the energy from a combination of a reactance that is capacitive $\left(X_c\right)$ and a reactance that is inductive $\left(X_L\right)$, within an electrical circuit that represents the world-economy. In other words, capital in equation (7), is represented by an imaginary power of form $j\left(X_L - X_c\right)$. This means that the (imaginary) energy resulting from this power can be either positive or negative. While we call this energy 'imaginary,' due to the fact that the flow variable has an imaginary value, the energy itself takes only (positive or negative) real values. In the 'original position,' the inductive and capacitive reactances are equal: $X_L = X_c$. This phenomenon occurs at a characteristic frequency, and is known as resonance. At this characteristic frequency, the world-system oscillates violently to a point where breaking the equality through the introduction of compartments (countries) could stabilize the system. The total energy from capital at the world scale remains equal to zero.

Electric alternating current (or AC) power provides a useful analogy for modeling capital as imaginary or reactive power. The total power in an electric circuit with a load that has resistive, capacitive, and inductive elements can be represented by complex (apparent) power $\left(\mathbb{S}\right)$, which is measured in units of volt-amperes or VA, as follows:

$$\mathbb{S}\left(t\right) \triangleq \mathbb{P}\left(t\right) + j\mathbb{Q}\left(t\right) \tag{12}$$

Real power $\left(\mathbb{P}\right)$ is measured in Watts, while the imaginary (or reactive) part $\left(\mathbb{Q}\right)$ is measured in Vars.

The interpretation of the imaginary part relates to the stability of the electrical network. If not controlled, reactive power could push the voltage level outside acceptable limits. Reactive power is called imaginary because it is not consumed by a resistor since the latter does not store energy, the way a capacitor or inductor do. This idea of 'storage' is what motivates interpreting 'capital' as a form of reactive energy. Admittedly, this is different from the way we have been accustomed to using the concept of capital in economics. Here we interpret capital as a storage mechanism that is essential to the stability of the economic system.

The complex power $(\mathbb{S})$ can be written in terms of energy as follows:

$$\int \mathbb{S}(t)\,dt \triangleq \int \mathbb{P}(t)\,dt + j\int \mathbb{Q}(t)\,dt \tag{13}$$

Later on, we associate these quantities with real and imaginary inputs as follows:

$$\int \mathbb{P}(t)\,dt = \tilde{E}_1 + \tilde{E}_2 \tag{14}$$

where $\tilde{E}_1$ represents the total energy from land, while $\tilde{E}_2$ represents the total energy from people.

The imaginary component is given by:

$$\int \mathbb{Q}(t)\,dt = \tilde{E}_3 = 0 \tag{15}$$

In other words, the total capital, at the scale of the world-system, is equal to zero. This does not mean, however, that there is no 'imaginary power' flows between the country compartments (the molecules) of the world-system. More on this point in the following sections.

Note that, at the world-system scale, we can write:

$$\left|\int \mathbb{S}(t)\,dt\right| = \tilde{E}_1 + \tilde{E}_2 \tag{16}$$

PER-UNIT SYSTEMS

The ψ model represents economic efficiency as thermodynamic efficiency in the energy transformation process we refer to as the economy (Bryant, 1982; Georgescu-Roegen, 1986). Economic efficiency is measured as thermodynamic loss, or in mathematical terms, as η, where:

$$\eta = \ln\left(\frac{Output\ Energy}{Input\ Energy}\right) = \ln\left(\frac{E_{out}}{E_{in}}\right) \tag{17}$$

We also employ the concept of complex energy (above), where the output is the resultant of real as well as imaginary input. The input is composed of real (land and people), and imaginary (capital) components. The latter emerges from the first two (Bender, 2005; Bender, 2007; Dorey, Dunning, & Tateo, 2007; Hockey, 2012).

We assume that the world-economy as a whole is an isolated system (i.e. as a system that does not exchange any energy with its surroundings). This approximation allows not only predicting the expected world energy output but also allows predicting a state of internal equilibrium. We also assume that the world-economy follows a production function where three energy inputs (land, people, and capital) are converted into one energy output, namely goods and services as measured by Gross Domestic Product (GDP). See Figure 1. Land and labor are represented as primary inputs, while capital is modeled as an autocatalytic positive feedback loop that results from the evolution of the world-economy (towards more complexity).

Here we have the total (energy) input into the world-economy $\left(E_1, E_2, E_3\right)$ transformed into an output $\left(E_y\right)$ measured by total world GDP (as the sum of the GDP of all world economies). E_1 and E_2 are proxy energy flow from

Figure 1. The world-economy as a living organism that transforms input energies into output

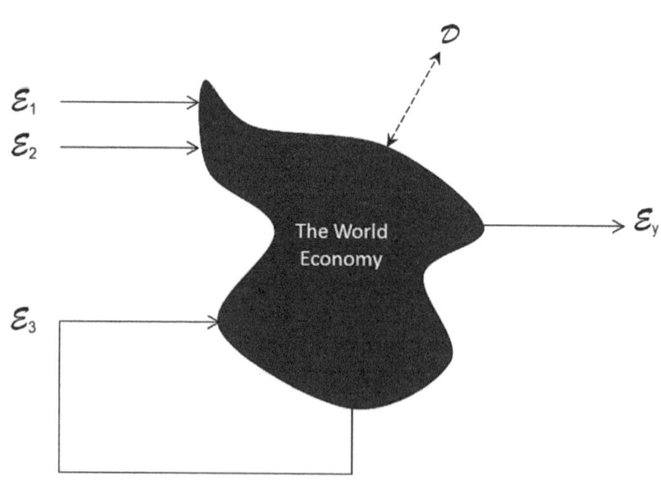

land and labor respectively. Energy inputs other than land and people are taken to represent various forms of capital which are treated as factors of production in addition to land and labor.

We start from an 'original position' where there is no 'jurisdictional compartmentalization'—there are no countries. This corresponds to pre-civilization (subsistence) societies (Ingold, Riches, & Woodburn, 1991). It is assumed that in the 'original position' the world-economy is a 'physiocracy' or at least pre-neoclassical (imbued with natural laws, including thermodynamics) (Neill, 1949): All inputs other than land and labor are reactive, as opposed to real. They go towards balancing the energy exchange ('dissipation') resulting from the conversion of inputs into outputs. Similar to the 'original position' in Rawls (1971), I use a 'veil of ignorance' where energy from people and energy from land are treated as homogenous. Heterogeneity enters the model through the reactive (derivative) input (i.e. capital) as shown in Figure 1.

The total world GDP output is obtained from all energy inputs, real as well as imaginary. The numeric difference between exchange (*D*) and capital $\left(E_3\right)$, i.e. energy inputs other than area $\left(E_1\right)$ and people $\left(E_2\right)$, is defined as the efficiency residual $\left(\epsilon\right)$:

$$E_y = E_1 + E_2 + \underbrace{\left[E_3 - D\right]}_{=\int} \tag{18}$$

Or rearranging:

$$\eta_{World} = \ln\left(\frac{E_y}{E_1 + E_2}\right) = \ln\left(1 + \frac{\int}{E_1 + E_2}\right) \tag{19}$$

Because we assumed that the world-economy is an isolated system, it will tend to an equilibrium where the total energy output is equal to the total input from land and labor, while the reactive residual (measured as the difference between exchange and capital) is equal to zero. In equilibrium, we have zero efficiency where the expected output (from the model) is equal to actual output and the efficiency residual is equal to zero:

$$\eta_{World} = 0 \tag{20}$$

This zero-efficiency is resultant: it results from over- and under- efficiency canceling each other out on the global scale (a 'zero-sum' outcome). At lower scales, on the scale of countries, efficiency could be above or below this zero-efficiency. Efficiencies greater than η_{World} result from positive capital inflow that allow more energy inputs to be converted into energy output, and the accumulation of capital through the feedback loop shown in Figure 1. According to the model, there are countries that have greater efficiency than η_{World} and others that have lower efficiencies. On aggregate however, these differences average out to a zero efficiency.

Now we allow for the existence of separate jurisdictions represented by political states. We assign a portion of each input to each country. Hence, each country receives a percentage of the world area (including territorial seas) and population. Each country is expected to transform its inputs into a portion of the total world output. We then measure the difference (the residual) between this expected (original position) output and the actual GDP output as a proportion of the world-economy. For example, in 2015 the US had a population of around 319 million, an area of around 10,000,000 square kilometers, and a GDP of around USD 17000 billion. The model translates these into per-unit amounts as part of the total world population, area and GDP. The per-unit values are as follows: 0.02640 population (out of a total world population of 1), 0.1199 area (out of a total world area of 1), and 0.9841 GDP (out of a total world GDP of 2).

The 'original position' is imposed on this compartmentalized world. We hence expect the aggregate efficiency residual for all countries to equal zero (normalized mean), as it did in the 'original position.' Individual countries will, however, have positive or negative residuals indicative of their level of economic efficiency. In other words, the reactive energy associated with capital will be exhibited in the performance of individual countries. However, the world aggregate (of all reactive energy) is equal to zero, just as it were in the 'original position.'

The following section delineates the logical nexus between the economy and energy transformations. I present the motivation for the choice of variables and their units of measurement and introduce the workings of the model through the production function and our measure of economic efficiency. Chapter IV applies the model to G-20 countries. Later on, we contemplate the common characteristics of more-developed countries and conclude with a synopsis of findings and propositions for further research.

THE ECONOMY AS AN ENERGY TRANSFORMATION PROCESS

The starting point is the proposition that the economy can be modeled as an evolutionary process governed by the second law of thermodynamics (Georgescu-Roegen, 1971). The introduction of 'complex energy' into our model also suggests an analogy between economies and biological organisms. The economy is modeled as a living organism that maximizes 'energy flux' but minimizes "the amount of specific dissipation as heat" (Raine, Foster, & Potts, 2006, p. 357). We, therefore, conceive economies as dissipative structures that come into existence as "energy throughput devices" (Raine et al., 2006, p. 355). The world-economy is modeled as an isolated system made of open sub-systems that represent national economies. These economies grow in such a way that equalizes energy densities on the scale of the world as a whole (Annila & Salthe, 2009, p. 608). Based on this formulation, economic growth is inevitably "coupled with increasing consumption of energy" (Annila & Salthe, 2009, p. 623). Based on this prediction, our ψ model expects developed countries to exhibit a high level of capital (apparent energy) absorption and accumulation.

The model also requires 'de-coupling' land (area) from capital (contra the approach taken by neoclassical economics) as factors of production, which would admit real input in the form of land (and labor), and imaginary input in the form of capital. Economies are systems of 'energy transduction' (Annila & Salthe, 2009, p. 608), as illustrated in Figure 1 (above). Economies are 'energy systems' of energy flows that start with nature and culminate in GDP and waste (Alam, 2009, pp. 171-172). The creation of wealth itself is seen as a direct result of energy conversion (Kümmel, 2011, p. 246), especially through the conversion of real energy into apparent energy.

I model the world-economy as an 'energy transformer' composed of sub-transformers representing all world nations. In 2015 we had a world-economy composed of $\left(n=\right)$ 196 sub-transformers (political states), each converting free energy $\left(E_i\right)$ inputs into one output, with some energy being released from the transformation process as dissipation $\left(D\right)$, which in the isolated world-system would be available for exchange as apparent energy (capital). We assume that the partition of the world-economy into unequal jurisdictions (in their input endowments), would not result in energy loss (as a result of the partition). We therefore expect the world-economy as a whole (with no partitions in the form of polities or countries) to follow the theorem of energy equipartition (and hence ergodicity) where the same amount of energy is utilized from each of the energy inputs.[4] The equipartition hypothesis is borrowed from statistical mechanics, where energy is equally distributed among the number of degrees of freedom of a given system. The theorem could be thought of as a version of the second law of thermodynamics which states that isolated systems tend to maximize their entropy. In our model, equipartition means that the land-energy and population-energy inputs into the world-economy are equal. By accepting the equipartition theorem we are assuming that the world-economy *as a whole* represents a system in equilibrium. Note that the equipartition theorem applies only when the relevant degrees of freedom (energy inputs in our model) can be freely 'excited.' This means that the input energy is going to be distributed evenly only through two degrees of freedom, namely land and people. Capital (as apparent energy) is not freely excited as it has to be derived from later time periods. Moreover, there may be certain degrees of freedom that are 'frozen' due to differentiations in land and people, or due to the nature of governance structures and policies implemented in a certain polity. Frozen degrees of freedom do not make any contribution to the output or to dissipation.

Furthermore, while we expect a Pythagorean relationship to hold between the inputs and the outputs to the world-economy, the same is not expected to hold for individual countries. In other words, "living systems will maximize energy flux but minimize the amount of specific dissipation as heat" (Raine et al., 2006, p. 357), and "more mature ecosystems will re-radiate a lower amount of energy than less developed ecosystems by creating dissipative structures …" (Raine et al., 2006, p. 356). More developed economies will have less energy dissipation $\left(D\right)$ and can harness capital (apparent energy).

The next two sections develop the ψ model based on the energy formulation presented above. The model uses energy storage through a quadratic form of energy inputs and uses *per-unit* (normalized) variables to give effect to the equipartition hypothesis.

GENERALIZED PER-UNIT ENERGY VARIABLES

We use the power postulate to find the mathematical form of the input and output energies. The energy transformation exhibited by each country's economic system is mediated by the flow of power (i.e. the rate of change

Table 1. Efforts and flows for a number of systems

System	Effort (e)	Flow (f)
Mechanical	Force (F)	Velocity (v)
	Torque (τ)	Angular velocity (ω)
Thermal	Temperature (T)	Entropy change rate (ds / dt)
	Pressure (P)	Volume change rate (dV / dt)
Chemical	Chemical potential (μ)	Mole flow rate (dN / dt)
	Enthalpy (h)	Mass flow rate (dm / dt)
Electrical	Voltage (V)	Current (i)
Hydraulic	Pressure (P)	Volume flow rate (dQ / dt)

Adopted from Borutzky (2010) Table 2.4, p. 27.

of energy over time). This power flow is expressed as the product of two types of conjugate variables: efforts and flows. For example, in a mechanical system, force represents the effort variable, while velocity represents the flow variable. In a thermal system, the effort is represented by temperature, while flow is represented by the entropy rate of change. See Table 1 for efforts and flows in a number of other systems.

There are two storage elements designated by the symbols C and I (which stands for capacitance and inductance respectively). In translational mechanics, the C-store is represented by a spring, while the I-store is represented by a rigid body. In rotational mechanics the, C-store represents a torsion spring, while the I-store takes the form of a flywheel. In the electromagnetic domain, the C-store represents capacitors while the I-store represents coils. In thermodynamics, there is only a C-store (the I-store has no representation), which takes the form of a lump of material (Borutzky, 2010, p. 46).

Similarly, the energy input into economic systems is modeled as the real energy stored in systems of generalized momenta and generalized displacement.

In particular, we represent the energy associated with capital as a C-store. Land is assumed to be related to an effort variable that resembles 'force' acting on an area. The force can be represented as the product of pressure and area. Given our assumption of equal energy density, we take the pressure to be the same at every polity (country). This gives a direct relation between force (the effort variable) and area.

The use of these storage elements enables us to express the energy inputs in Figure 1 as quadratic functions in endowment variables (inputs to the production function):[5]

$$E_i = \frac{1}{2}a\left(x_i\right)^2, i \in \left[1,2\right] \tag{21}$$

where x_i is the effort (or flow) variable associated with energy source E_i. The constant a represents the storage element. Given that this element represents the total (real) energy used by the world-economy, and given the equipartition theorem, we take the storage capacity for all inputs to be identical. This 'quadratic degree of freedom' form suggests that land and labor are quadratic and independent degrees of freedom. This result also confirms the discussion in relation to the equipartition hypothesis and its applicability to area and people.

We also introduce a *per-unit* system to express the energies associated with the world-economy.[6] This *per-unit* system normalizes quantities to a common base and allows the elimination of (measurement) units associated with efforts and flows, and hence enables the comparison between inputs from different energies and between inputs and outputs. By using *per-unit* or normalized variables, we can compare the input energy from land (measured in length-squared), and the input energy from people (measure in headcount), with the output energy from GDP (measured in currency). In *per-unit,* the world receives one unit of area energy, and one unit of people energy, and combines these to produce two units of output energy. Unlike the inputs of land and people, the output energy is complex——imaginary to be specific. It has an apparent component representing all forms of capital other than land and people. On a global scale, this apparent component is set equal to zero, given our assertions as to the condition of the world in the 'original position.' It is the ability to harness this apparent energy that splits nation-states into efficient and inefficient entities.

A *per-unit* variable $\left(\tilde{x}_{ij}\right)$ is one that is expressed as a fraction of a base quantity. These *per-unit* variables represent a percentage of the total existing in the world-economy. The energy input to each of n countries (in 2015, $n = 196$) can hence be represented as:

$$\tilde{E}_{ij} = \frac{a\left(x_{ij}\right)^2}{\sum_{j=1}^{n} a\left(x_{ij}\right)^2} = \left(\frac{x_{ij}}{\sqrt{\sum_{i=1}^{n}\left(x_{ij}\right)^2}}\right)^2 = \left(\tilde{x}_{ij}\right)^2, \forall i \in [1,2] \tag{22}$$

Based on the above, the sum of all the energy from input i would be equal to one:

$$\tilde{E}_{i} = \sum_{j=1}^{n} \tilde{E}_{ij} = \sum_{j=1}^{n} \left(\tilde{x}_{ij}\right)^2 \equiv \left(\tilde{x}_{i}\right)^2 = 1, \forall i \in [1,2] \tag{23}$$

In other words, we follow the equipartition hypothesis where the total energy input to the world-economy from m different degrees of freedom is equal to one *per-unit* for each input. The total energy stored in each of the input degrees of freedom is therefore the same for all inputs.

PRODUCTION FUNCTION[7]

I assume that economic output (as measured by GDP) is decomposed into two components. The first, the expected output, is the output associated with two energy sources: land $\left(\tilde{x}_{1j}\right)$ and people $\left(\tilde{x}_{2j}\right)$. We hence adopt a production function similar to that proposed by Cantillon (1755, 2010). Cantillon suggests that the price and intrinsic value of goods and services is the measure of land and labor which enter into their production. This does not mean of course that we exclude all other possible inputs. We simply isolate land and labor as the two most important inputs for the production function, while we lump the other inputs (and dissipation) into a residual (apparent) term. For simplicity, we assume land and people are homogenous across all countries, and that all population in any given country contributes equally to its economic output.[8] Augmentation of land and people is assumed to enter the ψ model through other energy inputs. Hence, land 'improvements' and knowledge enter the model through the residual component.

This second component of economic output, the residual, is treated as apparent energy and is composed of all other energy inputs and the exchange (dissipation) resulting from the energy transformation process (and negative differentiation in land and people). We expect the residual to equal to zero for the world-economy as a whole, although non-zero residuals would be expected for each individual country.

Based on the above formulation of each country's economy, the model can be expressed as follows (see Figure 1):

$$Output\ Energy\ for\ country\ j = Input\ Energy\ for\ j - Dissipation\ from\ j\ ,$$

or

$$Output\ Energy\ for\ country\ j = \tilde{E}_{1j} + \tilde{E}_{2j} + \tilde{E}_{3j} - \tilde{D}_{j}, \forall j \in \left[1, n\right] \tag{24}$$

Energy input $\tilde{E}_{1j}$ is from land, while $\tilde{E}_{2j}$ is the energy input from people. For simplicity, I have dropped the time index from equation (24). Note however that the output energy is at the end of any given period, while the input energies are at the beginning, with dissipation taking place throughout the period. We assume that reported land and population figures for any given year correspond to the beginning of the period, while the output corresponds to the end of that period.

We define the Cantillonian expected output energy as follows:

$$Expected\ output\ energy\ for\ state\ j = \tilde{\mathrm{E}}_{1j} + \tilde{\mathrm{E}}_{2j} = \left(\tilde{x}_{1j}\right)^2 + \left(\tilde{x}_{2j}\right)^2 \tag{25}$$

This expectation is based on our assertion that the energy residual for the world-economy as a whole is equal to zero (see below). Other energy inputs derive from the primary inputs of land and people. Such inputs are derivative forms of capital and represent reactive or imaginary forms of energy.

The *per-unit* output energy can now be written as:

$$\frac{\left(y_j\right)^2}{\sum_{j=1}^{n}\left(y_j\right)^2} = \frac{\left(x_{1j}\right)^2}{\sum_{j=1}^{n}\left(x_{1j}\right)^2} + \frac{\left(x_{2j}\right)^2}{\sum_{j=1}^{n}\left(x_{2j}\right)^2} + \left(\tilde{E}_{3j} - \tilde{D}_j\right) \tag{26}$$

where the last term is defined as the (apparent) energy residual:

$$\textit{Energy residual for country } j = \left(\tilde{E}_{3j} - \tilde{D}_j\right) \tag{27}$$

We can hence rewrite the expected output for the whole world-economy as:

$$\left(y_j\right)^2 = \left(\tilde{x}_1\right)^2 + \left(\tilde{x}_2\right)^2 + \sum_{j=1}^{n}\left(\tilde{E}_{3j} - \tilde{D}_j\right) \tag{28}$$

and we choose our *per-unit* variable for the world output, $\left(\tilde{y}\right)^2$, such that the world residual evaluates to zero:

$$\sum_{j=1}^{n}\left(\tilde{E}_{ij} - \tilde{D}_j\right) = \left(\tilde{y}\right)^2 - \left(\tilde{x}_1\right)^2 + \left(\tilde{x}_2\right)^2 = 2 - 1 - 1 = 0 \tag{29}$$

Based on the energy residual, I proceed to define a measure of economic development (as efficiency in energy transformations) where world countries are divided into two groups: more-developed (efficient) and less-developed (inefficient) countries. Economic development is defined narrowly, as wealth creation resulting from efficiencies in the use of (reactive) energy inputs (over and above those from land and population). We define psi $\left(\psi_j\right)$ as the economic efficiency of country j:

$$\psi_j = \ln\left[\frac{\tilde{E}_{yj}}{E\left(\tilde{E}_{yj}\right)}\right] \tag{30}$$

where $E\left(\tilde{E}_{yj}\right)$ is the expected per-unit output from the ψ model, and $\tilde{E}_{yj}$ is the actual per-unit output. Economic efficiency is measured as the ratio of observable economic output to the economic output as predicted by the model. Country j is efficient if it has a positive ψ_j. This measure is indicative of qualitative and quantitative changes in the economy. More-developed countries, for which ψ is positive, are referred to as sinks, given that they exceed their expected (Cantillonian) output, and less-developed countries, for which ψ is negative, are referred to as sources. A large positive ψ is indicative of (productive) efficiency where there is less dissipation, and abundance of energy input, other than land and people (refer to Figure 1).[9] A positive ψ is indicative of a country's ability to absorb capital from the world-system, and to store and use this capital. Changes in the ψ measure are expressed in percentage points, or simply in points.

The next chapter provides the results for world countries for the 25-year period from 1990 to 2015.

CODA

This chapter develops the ψ model for measuring the economic efficiency of world economies. The model is built on a simple proposition: the economy is an energy transformation system with two inputs and one output. The inputs are land and people, while the output is the goods and services produced by the economy (as captured by GDP). The difference between the output and input energies is interpreted as 'capital.' In the original position, under a Rawlsian veil of ignorance, and before the creation of countries, there was no capital and inputs were treated as homogenous. Moreover, output and input energies were equal. Once we introduce counties and their jurisdictional footprints, capital is exchanged between countries. Countries that export capital have negative efficiency. These are referred to as source countries. On the other hand, countries that are able to absorb and accumulate capital are referred to as sink countries.

Inputs and outputs are converted into energy equivalent values using the power postulate. Based on this postulate, energy has a quadratic form in inputs and outputs. Inputs and outputs are calculated as per-unit variables, that is to say, they are normalized to one. The total (world) land input is equal to one unit. Similarly, the total (world) population input is equal to one unit.

Therefore, the model assumes the equipartition of energy between the two inputs. The total energy output is equal to two units (on the world scale).

The model attributes differences in land and population to capital. Capital is modelled as a zero-sum variable that represents an autocatalytic process in every economy. The total capital at the world scale remains equal to zero as in the original position (in order to satisfy the first law of thermodynamics). Capital is hence modeled as an imaginary (or apparent) form of energy. This means that capital affects the stability (and hence efficiency) of a given economy, but does not add to the real energy provided by land and people.

REFERENCES

Alam, M. S. (2009). Bringing energy back into the economy. *The Review of Radical Political Economics*, *41*(2), 170–185. doi:10.1177/0486613409331423

Aligica, P. D., & Tarko, V. (2012). Polycentricity: From Polanyi to Ostrom, and beyond. *Governance: An International Journal of Policy, Administration and Institutions*, *25*(2), 237–262. doi:10.1111/j.1468-0491.2011.01550.x

Annila, A., & Salthe, S. (2009). Economies evolve by energy dispersal. *Entropy*, *11*(4), 606–633. doi:10.3390/e11040606

Antonov, A. A. (2010). Economic Oscillating Systems. *Am. J. Sci. Ind. Res.*, *1*(2), 359–363.

Bannock, G. & Baxter, R. (2009). *The Palgrave encyclopedia of world economic history: Since 1750*. Basingstoke, UK: Palgrave Macmillan.

Barber, W. J. (2009). *A History of Economic Thought*. Middletown, Conn.: Wesleyan University Press.

Battese, G. E., & Coelli, T. J. (1995). A model for technical inefficiency effects in a stochastic frontier production function for panel data. *Empirical Economics*, *20*(2), 325–332. doi:10.1007/BF01205442

Bender, C. M. (2005). Introduction to *PT*-symmetric quantum theory. *Contemporary Physics*, *46*(4), 277–292. doi:10.1080/00107500072632

Bender, C. M. (2007). Making sense of non-Hermitian Hamiltonians. *Reports on Progress in Physics*, *70*(6), 947–1018. doi:10.1088/0034-4885/70/6/R03

Bender, C. M., Brody, D. C., & Hook, D. W. (2008). Quantum effects in classical systems having complex energy. *J. Phys. A: Math. Theor., 41*(35). doi:10.1088/1751-8113/41/35/352003

Bergia, S., & Navarro, L. (1997). Early quantum concepts and the theorem of equipartition of energy in Einstein's work (1905-1925). *Physis-Firenze, 34*(1), 183–224.

Boltzmann, L. (1871). Über das Wärmegleichgewicht zwischen mehratomigen Gasmolekülen. *Wiener Berichte, 63*, 397–418.

Borutzky, W. (2010). *Bond Graph methodology*. London: Springer-Verlag. doi:10.1007/978-1-84882-882-7

Bryant, J. (1982). A thermodynamic approach to economics. *Energy Economics, 4*(1), 36–50. doi:10.1016/0140-9883(82)90042-1

Cantillon, R. (1755). Abhandlung über die natur des handels im allgemeinen (H. Hayek, Trans. 1931 ed.). Jena, Germany: Verlag von Gustav Fischer.

Cantillon, R. (2010). *An Essay on Economic Theory (Large Print Edition): An English translation of the author's Essai sur la Nature du Commerce en Général*. CreateSpace Independent Publishing Platform.

Carnot, S. (1890). *Reflections on the Motive Power of Heat. Thurston, Robert Henry (editor and translator)*. New York: J. Wiley & Sons.

Clausius, R. (1850). *On the Motive Power of Heat, and on the Laws which can be deduced from it for the Theory of Heat. Poggendorff's Annalen der Physick, LXXIX, 368, 500*. Dover Reprint.

Demirel, Y. (2007). *Nonequilibrium Thermodynamics: Transport and Rate Processes in Physcial, Chemical and Bilogical Systems* (2nd ed.). Amsterdam: Elsevier.

Dorey, P., Dunning, C., & Tateo, R. (2007). The ODE/IM Correspondence. *Journal of Physics A. Mathematical and Theoretical, 40*(32), R205–R283. doi:10.1088/1751-8113/40/32/R01

Erreygers, G. (Ed.). (2001). *Economics and Interdisciplinary Exchange*. New York: Routledge.

Føllesdal, A. (1998). Survey article: Subsidiarity. *Journal of Political Philosophy*, *6*(2), 190–218. doi:10.1111/1467-9760.00052

Gatti, R. C., Hordijk, W., & Kauffman, S. (2017). Biodiversity is Autocatalytic. *Ecological Modelling*, *346*, 70–76. doi:10.1016/j.ecolmodel.2016.12.003

Georgescu-Roegen, N. (1971). *The entropy law and the economic process*. Cambridge, Mass.: Harvard University Press. doi:10.4159/harvard.9780674281653

Georgescu-Roegen, N. (1986). The entropy law and the economic process in retrospect. *Eastern Economic Journal*, *12*(1), 3–25.

Gussen, B. F. (2013). On the problem of scale: Spinozistic sovereignty as the logical foundation of constitutional economics. *Journal of Philosophical Economics, 7*(1). Retrieved from http://www.jpe.ro/?id=autor&p=1851

Hausmann, R., Hidalgo, C. A., Bustos, S., Coscia, M., Chung, S., & Jimenez, J. … Yıldırım, M. A. (2011). The Atlas of Economic Complexity. Cambridge: MIT Press.

Heaviside, O. (1886). Electromagnetic induction and its propagation. *The Electrician*, *XXV*, 469.

Heaviside, O. (1970). *Electrical Papers (in two volumes). American Mathematical Society (AMS)*. Providence, RI: Chelsea Publishing.

Hockey, M. (2012). *The God Equation*. Hyperreality Books.

Horst, U. (2008). Ergodicity and nonergodicity in economics. In S. N. Durlauf & L. E. Blume (Eds.), *The new Palgrave dictionary of economics* (2nd ed.). New York: Palgrave Macmillan. doi:10.1057/978-1-349-95121-5_2498-1

Ingold, T., Riches, E., & Woodburn, J. (Eds.). (1991). *Hunters and gatherers*. London: Bloomsbury Academic.

Kennelly, A. E. (1893). Kennelly on impedance. In *Proceedings of the 76th meeting of the American Institute of Electrical Engineers (AIEE)* (pp. 175-232).

Kümmel, R. (2011). *The second law of economics: energy, entropy, and the origins of wealth*. New York: Springer Science.

Laundau, L., & Lifshiz, E. (1977). Quantum mechanics: non-relativistic theory (3rd ed., trans. J.B. Sykes & J.S. Bell.). Oxford: Pergamon Press.

Lima, J. A. S., & Plastino, A. R. (2000). On the classical energy equipartition theorem. *Brazilian Journal of Physics*, *30*(1), 178–180. doi:10.1590/S0103-97332000000100019

Markose, S. M. (2005). Computability and Evolutionary Complexity: Markets as Complex Adaptive Systems (CAS). *The Economic Journal*, *115*(504), F159–F192. doi:10.1111/j.1468-0297.2005.01000.x

Mishchenko, Y. (2014). Oscillations in Rational Economies. *PLoS ONE*, *9*(2), e87820. doi:10.1371/journal.pone.0087820 PMID:24505319

Mokyr, J. (Ed.). (2003). *The Oxford Encyclopedia of Economic History*. Oxford: Oxford University Press.

Neill, T. P. (1949). The Physiocrats concept of economics. *The Quarterly Journal of Economics*, *63*(4), 532–553. doi:10.2307/1882137

Padgett, J. F., McMahan, P., & Zhong, X. (2012). Economic production as chemistry II. In J. F. Padgett & W. W. Powell (Eds.), *The emergence of organizations and markets* (pp. 70–91). Princeton University Press.

Pathria, R. K., & Beale, P. D. (2011). Statistical mechanics (3rd ed.). Burlington, MA: Butterworth-Heinemann (Elsevier).

Paynter, H. M. (1961). *Analysis and design of engineering systems*. Boston: MIT Press.

Petty, W. (1899). *The economic writings of Sir William Petty* (C. H. Hull, Ed.). Cambridge.

Prigogine, I. (1978). Time, structure and fluctuations. *Science*, *201*(4358), 777–784. doi:10.1126/science.201.4358.777 PMID:17738519

Raine, A., Foster, J., & Potts, J. (2006). The new entropy law and the economic process. *Ecological Complexity*, *3*(4), 354–360. doi:10.1016/j.ecocom.2007.02.009

Rawls, J. A. (1971). *A Theory of Justice*. Cambridge, Mass.: Belknap Press.

Reichl, L. E. (1998). *A Modern Course in Statistical Physics* (2nd ed.). New York: Wiley-Interscience.

Sassen, S. (1991). *The global city: New York, London, Tokyo*. Princeton: Princeton University Press.

Sassen, S. (2006). *Cities in a world economy*. Thousand Oaks, CA: Pine Forge Press.

Schneider, E., & Kay, J. (1994). Life as a manifestation of the second law of thermodynamics. *Mathematical and Computer Modelling*, *19*(6-8), 25–48. doi:10.1016/0895-7177(94)90188-0

Schweitzer, F. (Ed.). (2002). *Modeling Complexity in Economic and Social Systems*. Singapore: World Scientific. doi:10.1142/4994

Sella, E. (1915). La Concorrenza: Sistema e Critica dei Sistemi [Competition: Systems and Criticism of Systems] (2 volumes). Torino.

Stevenson, W. D. (1982). *Elements of power system analysis*. New York: McGraw-Hill.

Taylor, J. R. (2005). *Classical mechanics*. Sausalito, Calif.: University Science Books.

Tolman, R. (1918). A general theory of energy partition with applications to quantum theory. *Physical Review*, *11*(4), 261–275. doi:10.1103/PhysRev.11.261

Toni, E. (1977). The reason for analogies in physics. In F. H. Branin & K. Huseyin (Eds.), *Problem Analysis in Science and Engineering* (pp. 463–514). New York: Academic Press. doi:10.1016/B978-0-12-125550-3.50018-1

van Dixhoorn, J. (1982). Bond graphs and the challenge of a unified modelling theory of physical systems. In F. E. Cellier (Ed.), *Progress in Modeling and Simulation* (pp. 207–245). New York: Academic Press.

Waterston, J. J. (1846). On the physics of media that are composed of free and elastic molecules in a state of motion. Edinburgh: Oliver & Boyd.

Zarnowitz, V. (1996). *Business cycles. Theory, history, indicators, and forecasting (abstract only)*. Chicago: University of Chicago Press.

ENDNOTES

1 An irreversible process is one where the system is not at equilibrium throughout the process. In contrast, a reversible process can be restored to the initial state from the final state without producing any changes in the thermodynamic properties of the universe. This is possible because the process is in thermodynamic equilibrium with its surroundings. There is no change in the entropy of the system. Note however that perfectly reversible processes are impossible, as it would take an infinite amount of time for the reversible process to finish. Natural processes are generally irreversible. During these processes entropy is increased decisively and cannot be returned to its initial value.

2 The rationale for the homogeneity that the model imposes on these resources will become apparent later in the chapter.

3 See e.g. Aligica & Tarko (2012), and Føllesdal (1998).

4 For a discussion of energy equipartition see Pathria & Beale (2011). For a classical work on this hypothesis, see Tolman (1918).

5 Note the similarity between this expression and those for the energy stored in electrical inductance and capacitance. The same expression can be seen, *inter alia*, in kinetic energy.

6 For background information see for example Stevenson (1982).

7 See Chapter 10 of Cantillon (2010).

8 This is similar to assumptions made for *per capita* comparisons between countries.

9 For the relationship between economic development and economic (production) efficiency, see for example Battese and Coelli (1995).

Chapter 3
The World

ABSTRACT

We will now look at the general results from the ψ model (developed in Chapter II). The chapter examines the overlap between the world-systems theory classification of core and periphery countries and the ψ model classification of sink (economically efficient) and source (economically inefficient) countries. Core countries exhibit not only economic complexity but also complex institutions. However, some of these countries, such as Australia and Canada, are not economically efficient, mainly due to their large footprint and low population density. On the other hand, some semi-periphery countries, such as South Korea and Turkey, are economically efficient according to the model.

INTRODUCTION

In Chapter II, we defined economic efficiency at country j as follows:

$$\psi_j = \ln\left[\frac{\tilde{E}_{yj}}{E\left(\tilde{E}_{yj}\right)}\right] \tag{1}$$

The model argues that countries are entrusted with a portion of the world's area and population, and are expected to transform these energies into an output in the form of goods and services. This expectation provides a normative signal where a minimum, or a floor, is established as a proportion of the 'world-system' output (see below). For countries to exceed the minimum

DOI: 10.4018/978-1-5225-2756-5.ch003

output, they have to utilize capital, which they have to absorb from the 'world-system,' and accumulate within their economies. Countries that can do so are said to be efficient. This efficiency is linked to economic complexity and suggests a corresponding level of economic growth and development. These countries are called 'sink' countries because of their ability to attract and absorb capital. On the other hand, countries that are unable to employ capital in their economic process are called 'sources,' because they release their capital to the sink countries. These source countries are below the floor output and hence are classified as inefficient.

The 'world-systems' theory is a useful framework for understanding the ψ model. First, the chapter introduces the theory and its application with the 'global cities hypothesis.' Later the chapter looks at the overlap between this theory and the results from the model. The analysis unveils economic weakness in countries considered to be at the core of the existing world-system, while others that are considered at the periphery show robust economic efficiency.

The concept of 'world-systems' was introduced by Immanuel Wallerstein in the 1970s to provide a new analytical framework that is not limited to the nation-state (Wallerstein, 1974, 2007). Wallerstein defines a world-system as follows:

A world-system is not the system of the world, but a system that is a world and that can be, most often has been, located in an area less than the entire globe. World-systems analysis argues that the unities of social reality within which we operate, whose rules constrain us, are for the most part such world-systems (other than the now-extinct small minisystems [sic] that once existed on the earth). World-systems analysis argues that there have been thus far only two varieties of world-systems: world-economies and world-empires. A world-empire (such as the Roman Empire, Han China) is a large bureaucratic structure with a single political center and an [Axial Division of Labor,][1] but multiple cultures. A world-economy is a large axial division of labor with multiple political centers and multiple cultures. In English, the hyphen is essential to indicate these concepts. "World system" without a hyphen suggests that there has been only one world-system in the history of the world. "World economy" without a hyphen is a concept used by most economists to describe the trade relations among states, not an integrated system of production. (Wallerstein, 2004, pp. 98-99)

World-systems can be analyzed using 'global cities' (Sassen, 2001, 2005, 2006) rather than nation-states. The 'world-system' incorporates 'global cities' (i.e. privileged cities that have a global economic status driven by innovation) that steer political and economic processes on a global scale (Knox, 1995, p. 6). The 'global cities' hypothesis was introduced by John Friedmann in the 1980s. He argued that cities articulate larger regional, national, and international economies (Friedmann, 1986). The hypothesis represents the political economy of the global urban system (Simon, 1995, p. 132). World cities are large, urbanized regions that are defined by dense patterns of interaction rather than by political-administrative boundaries. Global cities have a direct effect on global affairs. Such cities exhibit a level of infrastructure concentration that enables them to influence global processes. Such cities function as the "organizing nodes of a global economic system" (Friedmann, 1995, p. 25),[2] defined by dense patterns of interaction between people, goods, and information (Keeling, 1995). Such cities are linked in a single network (Smith & Timberlake, 1995, p. 80 and 88), sometimes referred to as a 'world system,' which sharpens the competition between them (Taylor, 1995; Wallerstein, 1974). The spatial dispersion of economic activities and global integration has contributed to the strategic role of these cities in the current world system.

Taylor compares these cities with the nation-state in the following terms:

If we are to return to a 'states versus cities' situation such as obtained before the seventeenth century, we can speculate on the basic differences the return of an autonomous city politics may mean for our world. From a Longue duée perspective the most intriguing potential for change comes in terms of the limits to economic growth: the earth is not large enough for capitalism as an ever-expanding system. But the modern state has evolved as an economic growth machine, and mainstream politicians of all states see their prime purpose as boosting their country's gross national product (GNP). The state is tied to 'development.' It is hard to imagine any 'national' politician winning office on a promise of no growth or even slow growth. But city politicians in select areas have done just that.

In the mini-boom of the mid- to late- 1980s some prosperous localities were becoming conscious of the disadvantages of continuous economic growth on their quality of life. Concern for such 'over-development' was a sort of aggregate 'not in my back yard [sic]' response to the continuously dynamic, changing nature of capitalism. Now such anti-growth political movements were certainly not anti-capitalist in any general sense capital accumulation would have to continue to support their good life but it did not have to occur in their communities. Since capital accumulation cannot go on infinitely on our finite earth [sic] and states are growth machines, it follows that in these selfish affluent city-based movements we may be seeing the beginnings of the long-awaited challenge to capitalism as a system. Without growth there can be no capitalism, the world city hierarchy might just be the structure through which a sustainable non-capitalist development is created that protects the affluent at the expense of the rest (Taylor 1993b). (Taylor, 1995, p. 60)

Our approach to the 'global cities' hypothesis is based on the mechanism through which capital is absorbed and accumulated. In Chapter IV, a direct link is made between the existence of such cities in large countries——large in terms of area——and the ability of such countries to maintain their status as sink countries. In other words, while a small 'jurisdictional footprint' is a necessary condition for economic efficiency, it is not a sufficient one. Larger countries can reduce their jurisdictional footprint through global cities within their jurisdiction. These cities act as (complex) attractors of capital. They enable these countries to produce an output above the minimum required by the ψ model.

The 'connectivity' we see today between 'global cities' under processes of globalization has been the norm under 'world-systems' throughout history. For example, the world-system that existed between 1250 and 1350 was an archipelago of 'world cities' (Abu-Lughod, 1989, p. 353). An earlier example at the beginning of the Common Era was the system where cities in the Roman Empire, the Han Empire, and India dominated world commerce; although this system had a much lower level of interaction between these constituent parts. An important insight from this world system archipelago is its cyclical emergence and collapse, largely through fluctuations in population levels (due to pandemics, wars, or even 'social engineering') where emphasis swings between rural and urban centers, or between immigrant and indigenous populations. World-systems rise when economic integration increases, sometimes driven by military might, and collapse when connections along older pathways increase, although collapse does not necessarily return the world to the *status quo ante*.

Amalgamation is a stepping stone for understanding the correlation between economic growth and (global) city governance structures. A case in point is the amalgamation of Auckland, New Zealand. In 2009, a Royal Commission on Auckland Governance made the case for change in the local governance structure (Salmon, Bazley, & Shand, 2009b, p. 3). The Commission's report reviews the economic literature on economic growth, both at the national and city-region levels (Salmon, Bazley, & Shand, 2009a). In particular, the Commission summarizes the research by (Quigley, 1998) on the economic factors provided by cities. These could be divided into scale economies (e.g. larger plant sizes and larger parks and libraries), shared inputs (e.g. legal and accounting services and recreational facilities including theatres and restaurants), transaction costs (e.g. matching in labour markets, and in large shopping malls), and statistical economies (e.g. lower unemployment and lower inventory levels) (Salmon et al., 2009a, p. 113). The Commission also refers to the seminal work by Fujita, Krugman, and Venables (2001) who identified both centripetal and centrifugal forces of economic activity arising from agglomeration. The commission also looked at the work by David Maré (2008) who distinguishes between the effects of localization, which refers to congregations of similar firms, and urbanization, which refers to diversity (congregations of different firms). These effects, however, usually work simultaneously in a given locale.

While amalgamation does not necessarily lead to innovation, a relatively recent review concludes that the literature is not definitive, in particular, due to definitional issues around cities and innovation (Shearmur, 2012). Such problems could be attenuated by focusing on a subset of cities, i.e. global cities. Focusing on subsets of innovation could also be informative. The difficulty is that global cities are an 'ideal type.' However, we can use a proxy construct, namely 'polycentricity' (Aligica & Tarko, 2012), as it applies to existing levels of governance, and extrapolate its effect on innovation to that of 'charter cities.' For example, in the context of the United States, Derek Kauneckis showed that an increasingly proactive role for the States in setting the research agenda (as opposed to being implementation instruments of a national research agenda) is having positive effects on innovation (Kauneckis, 2009).

More broadly, we need to invoke an analogy between global cities and competitive markets. The latter, as Adam Smith reminds us, align the interests of private and public agents. In particular, global cities allow for the creation of competing legal systems.[3] Under this analogy, innovation is enhanced by the existence of competitive markets. For example, Elinor Ostrom, citing W. Ross Ashby, argues that "any governance system that is designed to regulate complex biological systems [such as cities] must have as much variety in the actions that it can take as there exists in the systems being regulated." (Ostrom, 1998, p. 150). Ostrom elaborates that "[a]mong the institutions that humans utilize for generating highly desirable future goods are open, competitive markets. [These markets] … create incentives for innovation and entrepreneurship." (Ostrom, 1998, p. 150). This competition becomes more difficult when public goods are offered, but not impossible. If voters have perfect mobility and perfect information, they will move from one city (local community) to another to maximize their personal utility (Tiebout, 1956). Allowing cities to differentiate their public goods to attract more residents allows not only for efficiency gains but also for innovation.

Besides governance structures, there are other factors affecting the economic performance of cities. The scholarship of Michael Storper is useful here (Storper, 2013). Storper identifies institutions as such factors. While institutions include legal systems, they go beyond. They include firms, markets, and social conventions. Michael Porter joins in the emphasis on innovation——in particular in the regions. He also emphasizes the role of (industry) clusters (Porter, 2003). This chimes with Putnam who emphasizes culture as a predictor of economic development (Putnam, Leonardi, & Nonetti, 1994). Putnam made the conjecture that 'social capital' is a function of autonomous governance at the local level, especially as exemplified by free city-states in the Middle Ages (Guiso, Sapienza, & Zingales, 2008). Another insight comes from the literature on the resilience (resistance to recessions) of regional and local economies. For example, Martin et al. suggest a complex array of factors (Martin, Sunley, Gardiner, & Tyler, 2016). These include industrial and business structures (e.g. firm size and ownership, debt structure and financial strength, and supply chains), financial arrangements with national governments, equity market conditions, and labor market conditions (e.g. skill profiles, gender profile, and mobility). Martin et al. also identify governance structures as one of the factors of resilience, which also include national and local policies, and international regulatory arrangements.

Global cities are the nuclei of innovation worldwide (Bettencourt & West, 2011; Beugelsdijk, 2007; Chakrabarti, 2013; de Groot, Poot, & Smit, 2007; Glaeser, 1998, 2011; Mumford, 1961). The Innovation Cities Global Index (ICGI) measures the potential of cities as innovation economies and ranks 445 cities worldwide on innovation (2thinknow, 2014, p. 23). In the 2015 version, the top five cities were (in descending order): London, San Francisco, Vienna, Boston, and Seoul. The top five complex economies, according to the Economic Complexity Index, or ECI (Hausmann et al., 2014), had the following cities in the top 100: Japan (Tokyo 10, Osaka 32, Kyoto 36, and Kobe 66), Germany (Munich 12, Berlin 14, Hamburg 31, Stuttgart 24, Frankfurt 37, Leipzig 34, Düsseldorf 55, Cologne 59, Dresden 89, Karlsruhe 80, Hannover 92), Switzerland (Zürich 72, Geneva 82), South Korea (Seoul 5), and Sweden (Stockholm 17). In comparison, Australia, a country that is classified as a source country by the ψ model, had only Sydney (18), Melbourne (33), and Brisbane (57). The other state capitals are ranked low: Adelaide (186), Perth (156), Canberra (190), and Hobart (292), with Darwin not even making it to the list. Canada, another source country, had Toronto (11), Vancouver (35), Montréal (41), Québec (62), and Calgary (87). The other main cities were ranked as follows: Edmonton (108), Ottawa (261), Winnipeg (274), Halifax (302), London (305), Hamilton (313), Kitchener (335), Fredericton- St John (343), and Moncton (350). While Canada has more cities in the list, they are mostly lower ranked than those in more complex economies, such as Germany and Japan.

Another useful way of looking at global cities is through the Globalization and World Cities Research (GaWC) Network, which is one of the oldest rankings of such cities (Taylor, 2001). Looking at Australia, we find Sydney (Alpha +), Melbourne (Alpha -), Brisbane (Beta), Perth (Beta -), and Adelaide (Gamma +). Compare this to the United Kingdom which has London (Alpha ++), Manchester (Beta), Birmingham and Edinburgh (Beta -), Bristol (Gamma +), and Glasgow and Belfast (Gamma); the United States with New York City (Alpha ++), Chicago and Los Angeles (Alpha), San Francisco, Washington DC, Miami, Boston, and Atlanta (Alpha -), Dallas, Philadelphia and Houston (Beta +), Minneapolis, Cleveland, Seattle, Detroit, Denver, San Diego (Beta -), Baltimore, St Louis, Charlotte, Tampa (Gamma +), San Juan, Raleigh, San Jose, Cincinnati, Milwaukee (Gamma), and Columbus, Orlando, Kansas City, and Portland (Gamma -). Canada, however, fairs even worse than Australia with only three cities making the rankings: Toronto (Alpha), Montréal (Beta +), and Calgary (Beta -).

At first glance, it seems 'Alpa' cities have little in common. To elucidate their similarities we need to delineate how the GaWC model ranks cities. The model is a city-centric flow model, as opposed to one based on the boundaries of nation-states. It ranks cities based on their 'advanced producer services,' using an interlocking network model (Taylor, 2001). These 'advanced producer services' include accounting, advertising, finance, insurance, and law applied in transnational contexts. In particular, the model interprets cities as nodes, but not as primary actors. The model evaluates the presence of 'advanced producer service' firms in cities, and the size of this presence. In other words (Beaverstock, Smith, & Taylor, 2000, cited in Taylor 2001 pp. 182-183). In the words of Saskia Sassen, global cities have "a particular component in their economic base" which gives them a "specific role in the current phase of the world economy" (Sassen 1991, p. 126; cited in Taylor, 2001, p. 183). The model uses indirect measures of flows to compute a city's network connectivity, which is a measure of a city's integration into the world city network. These connectivity measures are then used to classify cities into levels of world city network integration. Alpha++ cities stand out as clearly more integrated than all other cities and constitute their own high level of integration. Alpha+ cities are highly integrated cities that complement Alpha ++ cities, largely filling in advanced service needs for Asia-Pacific. Alpha & Alpha- cities are very important world cities that link major economic regions and states into the world-economy. There are also Beta cities, which are instrumental in linking their region or state into the world-economy, and Gamma cities that either link smaller regions or states into the world-economy, or world cities whose major global capacity is not in advanced producer services.

While Alpha cities function within national jurisdiction frameworks, from a historical perspective, nation-states are not necessary for the creation of Alpha cities. Probably, the Hanseatic League is the quintessential example (Harreld, 2015). Historically, territorial states were the League's nemesis. From the 16th century, and the ascendancy of the Westphalian model of sovereignty, leading to the Peace of Westphalia in 1648, the League succumbed to the political authority of nation-states——the last formal meeting of the League taking place in 1669 (Dollinger, 2000). Moreover, while Alpha cities *used* to function within national frameworks, this is no more the case. The contemporary city is no longer 'installed' in a territory. The city is diverging from its historical model as part of a larger 'national' framework. Today, cities are about the flows (of activities made in the world and hence perennially on the move, of non-resident, migrant population) that seem to be exponentially growing in all directions. Perulli (2012) illustrates the point with statistics on the number of migrants worldwide, and how they concentrate in global cities. Global cities are transcending the limitations imposed by the nation-state and its constructs of citizenship and sovereignty. Ideas such as the 'fatherland' and the '*Heimat*' (homeland) are being replaced by an economic calculus of efficiency.

Global cities can come about either by evolution or revolution. Cities such as Singapore and Hong Kong are classified as Alpha + cities and share a specific characteristic. They did not need to go through the long evolutionary path of other Alpha + cities like Paris and Beijing. They achieved their status within one or maybe two generations. Notwithstanding, all Alpha + cities enjoyed——and some continue to enjoy——a clear privileged position: that of the *capital* city. For example, Sydney and Dubai are capitals of their (subnational) states. A key fact to highlight from the GaWC ranking is the very high scores that city-states have achieved. For example, Hong Kong,

Singapore, and Dubai are all Alpha + cities. In the following chapters, this link between city-states and global cities is analyzed further to ascertain the type of empowerment that could lead to global cities.

Keeping in mind the role of global cities in economic performance, we now proceed to analyze the data for the period from 1990 to 2015 (inclusive). For 2015, out of 196 countries, only 70 have positive ψ (around 36 percent of world countries). These 'sink' countries are shown in Table 1, while the 'source' countries are shown in Table 2 (below). This chapter will next discuss capital exchange in the world-system from 1990 to 2015. Later, the chapter analyzes the results in relation to sink and source countries.

However, first, let us look at some of the general results from the model. The distribution of ψ values for all countries is shown in Figure 1. The largest positive ψ is 8.19 and goes to the Holy See (Vatican City), while the lowest negative ψ is -9.45 and belongs to the Central African Republic. The next largest (positive) ψ belongs to Monaco at 6.33. On the other hand, large negative ψ values are more persistent, as shown in Figure 1, panel (b). Note that the totals of positive ψ and negative ψ values are *not* equal to zero. This is true for all years. This negative total score compares to a ψ score of zero for the non-compartmentalized world-system. However, as discussed below, there is an evolutionary trend towards more efficiency.

Throughout the observation period, the total of negative ψ values is always greater than the total of positive ψ values, which again suggests that the current world-system is economically inefficient. The evolution of world-system efficiency is shown in Figure 2.

The figure shows the natural logarithm of the ratio of the total negative ψ, in absolute value, to the total positive ψ:

Figure 1. Distribution of ψ values for sink (Panel (a)) and source countries in (Panel (b))

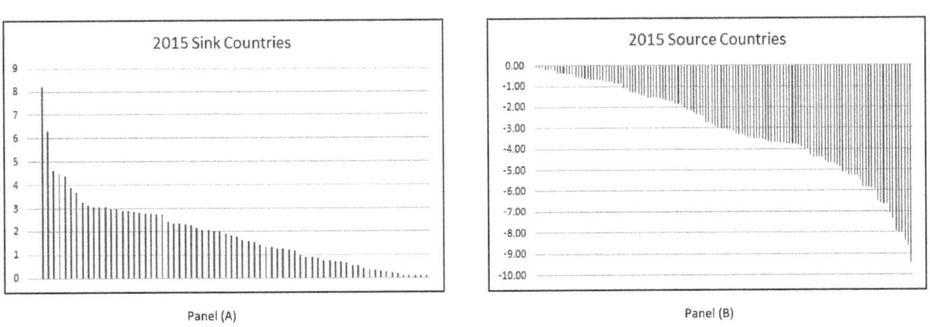

Figure 2. World-system efficiency from 1990 to 2015

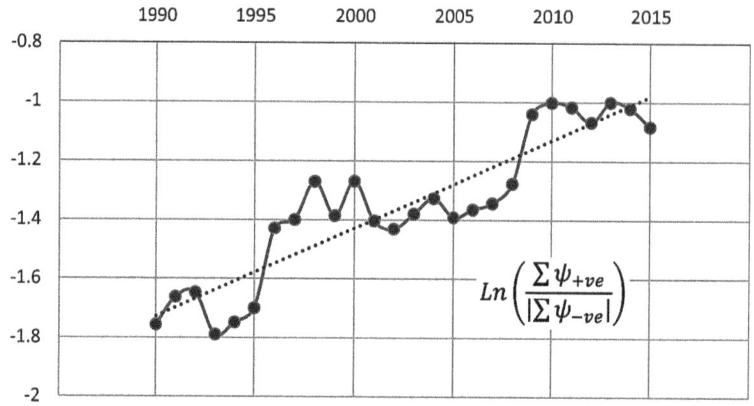

$$Ln\left(\frac{\sum\psi_{+ve}}{\left|\sum\psi_{-ve}\right|}\right) \quad (2)$$

While the world-system efficiency is negative, it also registers a positive trend over the observation period. Note, however, the cyclical nature of the change in efficiency, and in particular the decrease in this efficiency before major economic crises, such as the Asian Financial Crisis (AFC) of 1997, and the Global Financial Crisis (GFC) of 2008. As can be seen in Figure 2, there was a trough in the period from 1993 to 1995, and then later on from 2005 to 2008. These troughs were followed by an increase in world-system efficiency in the aftermath of these crises. From this perspective, economic crises function as a response to inefficiencies in world economies. This could be a normative signal for predicting the advent of such crises in the future. More on this point later in this chapter.

Most sink countries, i.e. efficient countries, have a score less than 4 (half of the maximum score), while many sources have scores more than half of the minimum $\left(\psi = -9.45\right)$. The ten most efficient sink countries, and the ten least efficient source countries are listed in Table 1.

Similarly, the ten least efficient sink countries and the ten most efficient source countries are shown in Table 2. It is reasonable to classify these countries as borderline countries that 'hover' around the minimum output required by the ψ model. Given measurement inaccuracies, we can interpret a band of 'sufficiency' or 'equilibrium' around the output floor. This is especially so

Table 1. Top ten 'sink' and bottom ten 'source' countries

Sink	Value	Source	Value
1 Vatican city	8.19	117 Chad	-6.62
2 Monaco	6.33	118 Namibia	-6.63
3 Qatar	4.65	119 Zimbabwe	-7.09
4 Liechtenstein	4.52	120 Mali	-7.36
5 Luxembourg	4.40	121 Congo, Democratic Republic of the	-7.92
6 Singapore	3.92	122 Mongolia	-8.00
7 Kuwait	3.72	123 Niger	-8.01
8 Switzerland	3.24	124 Somalia	-8.38
9 Netherlands	3.12	125 Mauritania	-8.63
10 Belgium	3.06	126 Central African Republic	-9.45

Table 2. Bottom ten 'sink' and top ten 'source' countries in 2015

Sink	Value	Source	Value
61 Panama	0.24	1 Jamaica	-0.07
62 Equatorial Guinea	0.21	2 Macedonia	-0.08
63 Dominican Republic	0.16	3 Finland	-0.10
64 Azerbaijan	0.10	4 Maldives	-0.17
65 Cuba	0.10	5 Latvia	-0.18
66 Serbia	0.09	6 Albania	-0.18
67 China, Peoples' Republic	0.07	7 El Salvador	-0.26
68 Estonia	0.07	8 Tonga	-0.36
69 Thailand	0.05	9 New Zealand	-0.37
70 Belarus	0.03	10 Iran	-0.39

in relation to measurement using GDP (PPP) figures, as many countries have a sizable 'black economy' that does not get recorded as part of the GDP.

As seen in Table 2, values of the top and bottom countries range from 0.24 (Panama) to - 0.39 (Iran). These countries can be interpreted as 'equilibrium' economies in that they are close to the normative floor, and hence do not contribute substantially to world-system capital flows. We will normalize this band around the floor by making it symmetrical, with ± 0.5 around the ψ floor $\left(\psi = 0\right)$. This translates to roughly 6 percent of the maximum ψ score for sink countries, and 5 percent of the minimum ψ score for source countries. We can track this equilibrium band from 1990 to 2015. Table 3 shows the results for five-year intervals from 1990 to 2015.

Table 3 suggests that the band has expanded significantly from 1990 to 2015. This is confirmed by the positive trend in Figure 3. In 1990, there were

Table 3. The equilibrium band for the years 1990, 1995, 2000, 2005, 2010, and 2015

1990	
Trinidad and Tobago	0.4767
Greece	0.2349
Cyprus	0.0357
Seychelles	0.0141
Korea, South	-0.1154
Portugal	-0.1251
Bahamas, The	-0.2351
Bulgaria	-0.2962
Cuba	-0.3923

1995	
Poland	0.4996
Trinidad and Tobago	0.3602
Saint Kitts and Nevis	0.1108
New Zealand	0.0715
Bulgaria	0.0543
Bahamas, The	0.0322
Turkey	-0.1321
Macedonia	-0.2717
Yugoslavia	-0.3176
Grenada	-0.3304
Bosnia and Herzegovina	-0.3666

2000	
Syria	0.3444
Saint Kitts and Nevis	0.3270
Finland	0.2295
Palau	0.2038
Turkey	0.1997
Mexico	0.0519
Dominican Republic	0.0341
Romania	-0.0225
Lebanon	-0.0725
Costa Rica	-0.1239
Croatia	-0.2080
Indonesia	-0.2122
New Zealand	-0.2572
Saint Lucia	-0.2814
Fiji	-0.3174
Sri Lanka	-0.3333
Chile	-0.4275
Jamaica	-0.4513

2005	
Seychelles	0.4952
Kiribati	0.4080
Costa Rica	0.3804
Malaysia	0.2916
Thailand	0.2813
Finland	0.2500
Mexico	0.0285
Romania	0.0127
Dominican Republic	-0.0413
Bulgaria	-0.0511
Estonia	-0.0681
Bahamas, The	-0.0793
Turkey	-0.1174
Macedonia	-0.1557
South Africa	-0.1912
Saint Lucia	-0.2087
Latvia	-0.2322
Palau	-0.2846
New Zealand	-0.3074
Tunisia	-0.3482
Grenada	-0.3487
Bosnia and Herzegovina	-0.3684
Nauru	-0.4017
Lebanon	-0.4088
El Salvador	-0.4218
Dominica	-0.4635
China, Peoples' Republic	-0.4722

2010	
Costa Rica	0.4904
Finland	0.3734
Estonia	0.3700
Dominica	0.3215
Latvia	0.2907
Cuba	0.2703
Azerbaijan	0.2127
Dominican Republic	0.1990
Thailand	0.1215
Jamaica	0.0636
Macedonia	0.0310
Malawi	-0.0232
Belarus	-0.0504
Iran	-0.1127
New Zealand	-0.1791
Panama	-0.2065
El Salvador	-0.3044
Montenegro	-0.3218
Ukraine	-0.4349

2015	
Romania	0.4189
Costa Rica	0.3781
Bulgaria	0.3312
Mexico	0.2905
Panama	0.2449
Equatorial Guinea	0.2073
Dominican Republic	0.1575
Azerbaijan	0.1000
Cuba	0.0956
Serbia	0.0874
China, Peoples' Republic	0.0686
Estonia	0.0663
Thailand	0.0512
Belarus	0.0293
Jamaica	-0.0677
Macedonia	-0.0825
Finland	-0.1015
Maldives	-0.1733
Latvia	-0.1812
Albania	-0.1834
El Salvador	-0.2567
Tonga	-0.3640
New Zealand	-0.3656
Iran	-0.3888
Kosovo	-0.3982
Tunisia	-0.4390
Marshall Islands	-0.4814

Figure 3. Number of countries in the equilibrium band from 1990 to 2015

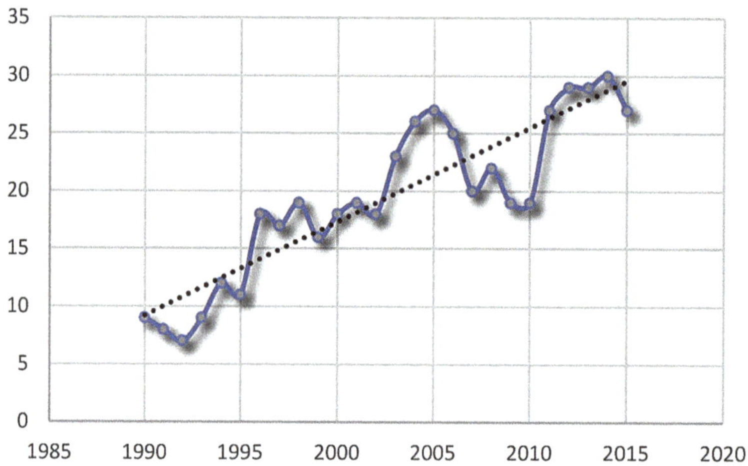

nine countries in the band (five percent of world countries). By 2015, the number of countries in the band grew to 27 (14 percent of world countries). Note, however, that the composition of this band changes over time. Some countries have featured in this band consistently. For example, New Zealand and the Dominican Republic. Other countries, such as South Korea, were able to move out from this band upwards. Others, such as Palau, slipped downwards into source countries.

Some of the findings from the model are not intuitive. For example, according to the model, a country like Bahrain $\left(\psi_{2015} = 2.26\right)$ is more efficient than Spain $\left(\psi_{2015} = 2.03\right)$. Seychelles $\left(\psi_{2015} = 2.12\right)$ is more efficient than Greece $\left(\psi_{2015} = 1.58\right)$. Canada $\left(\psi_{2015} = -2.75\right)$ and Australia $\left(\psi_{2015} = -3.05\right)$ turn out to be less efficient than Timor-Leste $\left(\psi_{2015} = 1.25\right)$. Such propositions require a rethinking of the essence of economic efficiency. To elucidate the underlying rationale for these discrepancies let us take a closer look at Australia. The key development issues with Australia can be highlighted by the following comparison. This comparison is admittedly limited by different histories, different geographies, and different anthropologies, but is still useful to understand the discrepancies. In 990 CE, Europe had one city of 10,000 inhabitants for every twenty or thirty states. In 1490 CE, one such city existed for every one or two states. By 1890, the average state in Europe had about 60 cities of 10,000 inhabitants or more (Tilly, 1992, p. 51). In comparison, in Queensland, which has an area larger than France, Germany, and Italy combined, there are less than 25 such cities——today. The whole Australian continent has roughly around 114 cities of 10,000 inhabitants or more, less than what two average European states had more than a century ago.[4] Of course, Australia is a very young country relative to the old continent. Europe enjoyed a trajectory of development over millennia. But that fact on its own does not explain the disparity between the economic efficiency in Australia and Europe, especially given the emergence of efficient countries such as Singapore and even China, in the span of the 20th century.

To understand these non-intuitive results, we need to look at the effect of 'jurisdictional footprints' on economic efficiency. For our purposes, we define 'jurisdiction' as the state monopoly on legislation, and hence on creating the legal frameworks that drive economic activity. The ψ model suggests that efficiency requires an output above a minimum defined by the portion of input energies (land and people) bestowed on a given country. In countries with large territories there are areas that are highly developed, such as urban areas. But there are also large areas where there is hardly any development. When we take this unevenness into consideration, it is difficult for larger territories to be as (uniformly) developed as smaller jurisdictions. However, larger countries, such as the United States, are able to achieve economic efficiency through their 'global cities,' such as New York or Los Angeles, which act as attractors of capital from other parts of the world-system. Other countries, such as China, opt for special economic zones. A third approach can also be seen in Europe where countries like Germany and Italy absorb capital through industrial clusters. Hence, while the ability to absorb capital is enhanced through smaller 'jurisdictional footprints,' large footprints can also absorb capital through attractors such as global cities, economic zones, and industrial clusters. In the next chapter, we take a closer look at these (large) countries, and the connection between their economic efficiency and the existence of attractors within their jurisdictions.

To illustrate the difference between ψ efficiency and other proxies for economic performance,[5] we compare the economies of the United Kingdom and the United States. The ψ measure suggests that the United Kingdom is more efficient than the United States. In other words, the model suggests that the UK economy is more complex, and hence more developed than that of the US. Economic prosperity is related to economic complexity, especially as measured by the Economic Complexity Index (ECI). In the 2014 ranking, the United Kingdom was ranked at 10, the United States at 14, Canada at 39, New Zealand at 49, and Australia at 82 (Hausmann et al., 2014). According to the Economic Complexity Index (ECI) country rankings of 2014, the UK had a score of 1.48 compared to a United States score of 1.36 (Hausmann et al., 2014). Moreover, the export tree maps for the UK and the US suggest that the two economies are relatively similar in terms of economic complexity, one is ranked 10th while the other 14th in the world. Figure 4, however, suggests that this small difference in their ECI score has resulted in considerable increase in efficiency in the UK economy vis-à-vis the US economy.

Other measures of economic performance could lead to conclusions different from those given by the ψ model. To illustrate this point, let us

Figure 4. The difference between ψ and per capita scores for the US and UK

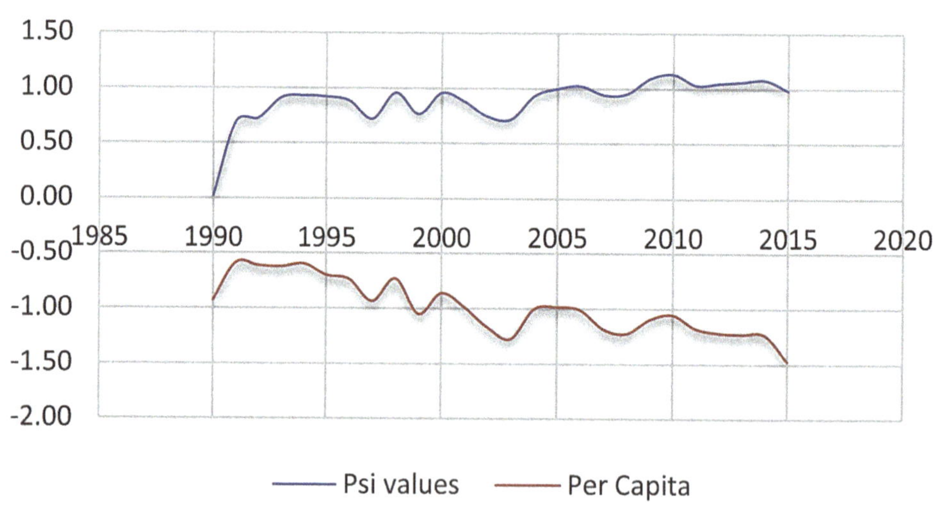

Table 4. A comparison between the United States and the United Kingdom on ψ efficiency and on per capita income

ψ	1990	1991	1992	1993	1994	1995	1996	1997	1998	1999	2000	2001	2002	2003	2004	2005	2006	2007	2008	2009	2010	2011	2012	2013	2014	2015
United Kingdom	2.30	3.02	3.15	3.17	3.16	3.22	3.06	3.06	3.19	3.00	3.09	3.05	2.98	2.99	3.04	3.09	3.10	2.94	2.90	3.23	3.22	3.08	3.04	3.00	2.98	2.89
United States	2.28	2.33	2.43	2.25	2.23	2.30	2.17	2.34	2.23	2.24	2.13	2.17	2.24	2.27	2.11	2.10	2.08	2.00	1.94	2.13	2.09	2.05	1.99	1.94	1.90	1.91
Difference	**0.02**	**0.69**	**0.72**	**0.91**	**0.93**	**0.92**	**0.88**	**0.72**	**0.96**	**0.76**	**0.96**	**0.88**	**0.74**	**0.72**	**0.93**	**1.00**	**1.02**	**0.94**	**0.95**	**1.09**	**1.13**	**1.03**	**1.05**	**1.06**	**1.08**	**0.99**
Per Capita																										
	1990	1991	1992	1993	1994	1995	1996	1997	1998	1999	2000	2001	2002	2003	2004	2005	2006	2007	2008	2009	2010	2011	2012	2013	2014	2015
United Kingdom	8,897	13,270	14,758	15,463	15,831	15,836	16,814	17,952	19,451	19,501	21,010	21,039	21,627	22,751	25,316	27,609	29,781	29,698	31,262	34,458	35,999	33,682	35,089	36,481	37,858	37,651
United States	18,182	19,171	20,908	21,712	21,827	22,822	24,184	27,301	26,758	30,002	29,636	30,886	33,284	35,511	35,369	37,471	39,901	41,549	43,501	45,421	46,548	45,450	47,259	48,750	50,210	52,369
Difference	**-0.93**	**-0.59**	**-0.61**	**-0.62**	**-0.60**	**-0.70**	**-0.74**	**-0.93**	**-0.73**	**-1.05**	**-0.86**	**-0.98**	**-1.17**	**-1.28**	**-1.01**	**-0.99**	**-1.01**	**-1.19**	**-1.22**	**-1.10**	**-1.05**	**-1.18**	**-1.22**	**-1.23**	**-1.24**	**-1.47**

continue with our comparison of the UK and the US economies. Table 4 shows how UK ψ values are not only higher that their US counterparts, but that the gap between the two economies has been increasing. A 1990 difference of 0.02 in ψ values increased to 0.99 by 2015. Using *per capita* values, however, we find that the US is economically doing better than the UK, with a widening gap between the two countries. See Figure 4 (above). The *per capita* measure seems to suggest that economically the UK is doing worse than the US, while the ψ measure suggests that the UK is doing better than the US. Moreover, the ψ measure shows a widening gap between the UK and the US, where the UK is becoming relatively more efficient. The *per capita* measure shows a widening gap in the opposite direction. This comparison goes to show that the ψ measure gives a different perspective on economic performance compare to *per capita* figures.

The ψ measure also evaluates economic growth. Here it is important to explain the difference between efficiency and productivity. Efficiency in our model is about using less inputs (land and people) to produce more output (products and services), through the absorption of capital from the world-economy, and accumulating this capital over time. This is a form of 'technical efficiency' that is identical to the general understanding of productivity. The ψ score could hence be understood as a form of total factor productivity (TFP) in the sense that it is the portion of the output not explained by the amount of input (land and people) used in the model (Hulten, 2001). In this sense, TFP explains the role of capital in the change of ψ scores from the ψ floor, both in positive (above floor output) and negative (below floor output) terms. This also provides a link between our model and others in the literature, such as the Solow model (1956). The ψ measure provides a link between efficiency, productivity, and economic growth. For example, the cumulative increase in ψ for the UK from 1990 to 2015 is 2.89 – 2.30 = 0.59, while the cumulative increase in the US ψ is 1.91 – 2.28 = -0.37. The only period that the US has seen any economic growth over the last twenty-five years was between 1990 to 1992. On the other hand, the UK saw economic growth from 1990 to 1995 and again from 2002 to 2006.

GLOBAL EXCHANGE

In Chapter II we indicated that in the 'original position,' capital was equal to zero, given the resonance resulting from capital's equal inductive and capacitive reactances (in the original position). The motivation for this assumption is that initially there were only two forms of energy: area and people. Time was needed for capital to evolve, for example, in the form of accumulated knowledge. Capital was able to evolve through the 'invention' of 'jurisdiction,' namely the monopoly over the allocation of land and labor for the production of goods and services. The introduction of countries to the model created a 'capital exchange.' Now some countries are able, through their jurisdictional differentiation, rather than a sorting of the two inputs (land and labor), to absorb capital from the world-system. At the country level, capital's reactances are not equal anymore, although this does not get rid of world-system oscillation as shown in Figure 5. This is the motivation for modeling capital as a form of reactive or 'imaginary' power. While capital affects the 'stability' of the world-system, it does not add, at least directly, to its total (real) energy. The total capital at the world-system level continues to be equal to zero.

Figure 5. The variation in the ψ sink envelope at the global scale

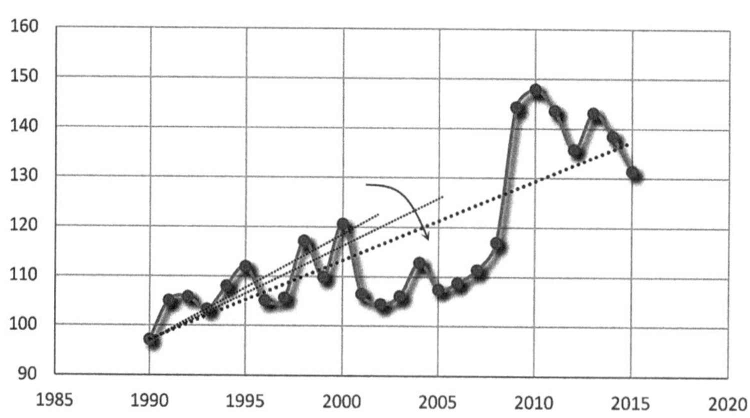

Figure 5 shows the value of the ψ envelope for sink countries. The envelope is the sum of all positive ψ values for every year in the covered period (1990-2015). There are two points to highlight in relation to Figure 5. First is the secular trend(s). The second is the ψ cycle.

The ψ envelope indicates that the efficiency of the world-system has been increasing. There is a positive long-term trend, which in agreement with the overall picture in Figure 2. The trend is defined by the cyclical changes in ψ. The latter can be decomposed into three phases. The first phase was from 1990 to 1995. This registered a higher trend compared to the second trend from 1996 to 2001. The third secular movement, with the lowest slope, can be seen in the period from 2002 to 2015. These three periods suggest that, in the long run, the improvement in the economic efficiency of the world-system is slowing down. The current world-system is 'saturating.' The same can be said about the world's economic productivity and growth. In 1990, there were 170 world countries in the model. By 2001, the number of countries grew to 192. In 2015, there were 196 countries. Hence, while there was an 11 percent increase in the number of countries in the second period, there was only a two percent increase in the third period. Notwithstanding, the decrease in the slope of secular variation in the second and the third periods is of similar magnitude. The explanation for this decrease comes instead from the capital oscillations at the world-system scale. The decrease in efficiency (in the long run) is affected by the oscillation in the ψ envelope (for sink countries). These oscillations start small at the beginning of the observation period, but become substantial at the end of the period. For example, the years 1993 and 1996 registered a 'dip' in world's efficiency, although the amplitude for the dip is less than the peak seen in the first cycle (from 1990 to 1993). The wavelength of the first wave is three years, $\lambda = 3$, which suggests a cycle similar in duration to a minor cycle (Kitchin, 1923). This cycle repeated itself from 1994 to 1996. There was then another cycle from 1997 to 2001. This third cycle is still similar in duration to a Kitchin cycle, although it now exhibits a 'dip' in the ψ envelope. This dip became much deeper in the fourth cycle from 2001 to 2015. The peak amplitude is now three times that seen in the previous cycles. Moreover, the wavelength is now five times that seen from 1990 to 2000. What can explain this increase in oscillation? To answer this question, we turn to freshwater economics, and in particular to the Chicago school.

The ψ envelope for sink countries seems to be in agreement with the Real Business Cycle (RBC) theory (Young, 2013). The ψ envelope explains global oscillations as variations in efficiency (productivity). Real business cycles are produced through oscillations in capital, i.e. the 'imaginary power' in the ψ model. This is analogous to the effect of reactive power in electrical circuits. The cycle is an efficient response to the economic environment. The RBC could explain the trough from 2001 to 2007 through the admission of China to the World Trade Organization (WTO). The increase in world trade through Chinese exports has reduced the overall productivity of sink countries. This RBC explanation is particularly useful in explaining the peak in 2010 which suggests that the Global Financial Crisis (GFC) (Cette, Fernald, & Mojon, 2015; Crotty, 2009; Nanto, 2009; Summers, 2000) led to increasing the gap between sink and source countries. For example, Cette et al.

> *... discuss the pre-GFC slowdown in productivity growth ... [G]rowth had a brief resurgence in the second half of the 1990s and early 2000s. But productivity growth slowed markedly prior to the GFC. We update estimates ... [that link] this rise and fall to the production and use of information technology (IT). A large literature argues that IT can have a broad-based and pervasive effect through its role as a general purpose technology (GPT) that fosters complementary innovations, such as business reorganization. But the transformative nature of these reorganizations is, plausibly, limited. For example, once retailing was reorganized to take advantage of faster information processing, the gains may have become more incremental. (Cette, Fernald, & Mojon, 2015, p. 2)*

As shown in Figure 5, the trough from 2001 to 2007 is relatively flat. There was a jump in 2004, but only in 2008 did the ψ envelope begin to reach for a new peak. The GFC had the positive effect of increasing the efficiency of sink countries. In effect, the GFC increased the gap between sink and source countries. It rewarded those who were already efficient, and punished those who were inefficient.[6] As seen in Figure 5, the effect of this 'GFC wave' (from 2000 to 2015) on the world-system seems to have ended. However, the productivity and growth effects from the crisis will come with a lag. During this lagging phase, we will see a reduction in the ψ envelope while the positive effects from the GFC propagate through the world-system.

There is likely to be a new cycle, which given the amplitude of the 'GFC wave,' suggests that the next cycle's effect on the world-system might be quite different. *Ceteris paribus*, if the amplification that we saw from 1990 to 2015 continues, the next wave could have a much longer and much larger effect. The trough is likely to last twice as long as the GFC wave. The next trough is likely to go for over a decade, probably as long as 15 years, up until 2030.

During this phase, sink countries draw closer to the equilibrium band, and capital absorption is much lower. World productivity will be lower during this stage. Unless there is a different approach to world trade and economic integration, away from a WTO system dominated by China, another crisis might result in a complete or partial collapse of the current world-system. We have already seen a similar collapse in the 13th century where before the West rose, China had to weaken. This was a necessary precondition to the rise of capitalism as we know it today. The East "had already substantially 'fallen' before the Portuguese men-of-war appeared in the Indian Ocean" (Abu-Lughod, 1989, p. 260). If the rise of China continues over the next decade or so, there is likely to be a partial collapse of the world-system. The current world-system was possible only because of a weak China. The next ψ peak could hence see the economic collapse of some sink countries. This understanding of the oscillations of the ψ envelope echo's Thomas Barfield's (1992) argument that, between 209 BCE and the 20th century, there has always been a correlation between a strong China and strong empires on the steppes, except in the 13th century.

Note that if there is an attenuation of the role of China as envisaged by Peter Navarro (2006; Navarro & Autry, 2011), and as likely to be pursued by the Trump administration, we will still have a collapse of the current world-system. Now, however, Asia gives way to a rising West.[7] Under this scenario, we still see (at least) a partial collapse but in the other direction. It seems that either way we will witness the emergence of a new world-system. Winners in this new system are those that recognize the positive role played by 'global cities' as explained further in the next Chapter.

Let us now move on to analyze the ψ envelope for the source countries. The values for this envelope are shown in Figure 6.

Figure 6 shows a general improvement in source economies. From 1990 to 1995 the total ψ was in the range of -600 to -500. However, since 1995,

Figure 6. The Variation in the ψ source envelope at the global scale

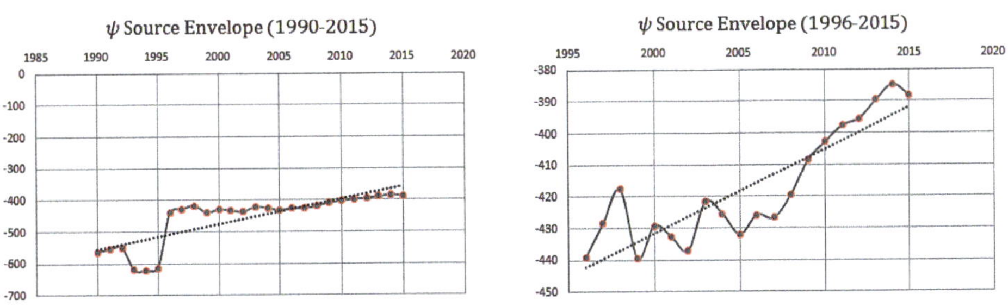

the total ψ seems to be closer to -400. If we remove the values from 1990 to 1995, we can see a cyclical behavior similar to that in Figure 5, although with a lower amplitude. Source countries exhibit a worsening of their inefficiencies prior to the GFC, and an improvement afterwards. These countries also exhibit the effect of the Asian Financial Crisis (AFC) in the mid 1990s. The negative effects of this crisis seem to have been stronger in source countries relative to sink countries, although contamination was eventually inevitable given the large foreign exchange reserves that some source countries opted for as a hedge against further crises, and how this fueled the demand for financial assets in the United States, which in effect set up the stage for the GFC.

The next section of this chapter looks in some more detail at the composition of sink and source countries (in 2015).

SINK COUNTRIES

According to the model, the most efficient countries are those with the largest ψ values. As seen in Table 5, the positive ψ values range from 8.19 (Vatican

Table 5. Countries with positive ψ (sink countries) in 2015

	ψ		ψ		ψ
1 **Vatican city**	8.19	24 France	2.42	47 Poland	1.54
2 Andorra	2.81	25 Germany	2.97	48 Portugal	1.63
3 Antigua and Barbuda	1.32	26 Greece	1.58	49 Qatar	4.65
4 Austria	2.86	27 Grenada	0.88	50 Romania	0.42
5 Azerbaijan	0.10	28 Hungary	1.32	51 Saint Kitts and Nevis	1.42
6 Bahamas, The	0.54	29 Ireland	2.35	52 Saint Lucia	0.84
7 Bahrain	2.26	30 Israel	2.78	53 Saint Vincent and the Grenadines	0.71
8 Barbados	2.06	31 Italy	2.34	54 San Marino	3.05
9 Belarus	0.03	32 Japan	2.88	55 Serbia	0.09
10 Belgium	3.06	33 Korea, South	2.77	56 Seychelles	2.12
11 Brunei	3.00	34 Kuwait	3.72	57 Singapore	3.92
12 Bulgaria	0.33	35 Lebanon	1.16	58 Slovakia	1.76
13 China, Peoples' Republic	0.07	36 Liechtenstein	4.52	59 Slovenia	2.02
14 Costa Rica	0.38	37 Lithuania	0.64	60 Spain	2.03
15 Croatia	0.87	38 Luxembourg	4.40	61 Sweden	0.68
16 Cuba	0.10	39 Malaysia	0.97	62 Switzerland	3.24
17 Cyprus	1.27	40 Malta	2.30	63 Taiwan (Republic of China)	3.05
18 Czech Republic	2.05	41 Mauritius	1.21	64 Thailand	0.05
19 Denmark	2.72	42 Mexico	0.29	65 Timor-Leste	1.25
20 Dominica	0.52	43 Monaco	6.33	66 Trinidad and Tobago	1.82
21 Dominican Republic	0.16	44 Netherlands	3.12	67 Turkey	0.71
22 Equatorial Guinea	0.21	45 Norway	0.72	68 United Arab Emirates	2.72
23 Estonia	0.07	46 Panama	0.24	69 United Kingdom	2.89
				70 United States	1.91

City) to as low as 0.03 (Belarus). Some of these countries, such as Belarus, China, and Thailand, should be considered as borderline countries.

According to the model, the most efficient 'country' in the world is the Holy See, with a score of eight. The next largest ψ score belongs to Monaco (6.3). These polities are followed by Qatar (4.7), Liechtenstein (4.5), and Luxembourg (4.4). According to the model, these countries are the most efficient in the world.

Sink countries can be divided into three tiers. Sink countries in the equilibrium band are outside these tiers. As shown in Table 6, the largest tiers are Tiers 2 and 3, which are also of a similar size, rough 35 percent of all sink countries per tier. In comparison, in Tier 1, we find only five countries (seven percent of all sinks). In terms of the world-system classification, however, only Luxembourg is classified as a core country (see above). On the other hand, some sink countries in Tier 2 (such as Andorra and Malta) and Tier 3 (such as Cyprus or Lebanon) are not considered as core countries. This comparison is a reminder of the differences between the ψ model and the 'world-system' theory.

However, some of the results are counter-intuitive. Qatar comes out as more efficient than countries like the United Kingdom and the United States. According to the model, a country like Barbados is (slightly) more efficient than Spain, while San Marino is (slightly) more efficient than Germany. How can we explain these results?

Table 6. The classification of sink countries into three tiers

Tier 1

1	**Vatican city**	8.1914
2	Monaco	6.3304
3	Qatar	4.6463
4	Liechtenstein	4.5205
5	Luxembourg	4.4038

Tier 2

6	Singapore	3.9198
7	Kuwait	3.7214
8	Switzerland	3.2428
9	Netherlands	3.1225
10	Belgium	3.0572
11	Taiwan (Republic of China)	3.0510
12	San Marino	3.0482
13	Brunei	2.9965
14	Germany	2.9658
15	United Kingdom	2.8909
16	Japan	2.8809
17	Austria	2.8616
18	Andorra	2.8134
19	Israel	2.7751
20	Korea, South	2.7736
21	Denmark	2.7219
22	United Arab Emirates	2.7207
23	France	2.4231
24	Ireland	2.3501
25	Italy	2.3407
26	Malta	2.3011
27	Bahrain	2.2645
28	Seychelles	2.1207
29	Barbados	2.0610
30	Czech Republic	2.0501
31	Spain	2.0293
32	Slovenia	2.0234

Tier 3

33	United States	1.9055
34	Trinidad and Tobago	1.8160
35	Slovakia	1.7585
36	Portugal	1.6307
37	Greece	1.5814
38	Poland	1.5361
39	Saint Kitts and Nevis	1.4185
40	Hungary	1.3238
41	Antigua and Barbuda	1.3223
42	Cyprus	1.2681
43	Timor-Leste	1.2539
44	Mauritius	1.2075
45	Lebanon	1.1592
46	Malaysia	0.9665
47	Grenada	0.8788
48	Croatia	0.8738
49	Saint Lucia	0.8364
50	Norway	0.7173
51	Turkey	0.7124
52	Saint Vincent and the Grenadines	0.7080
53	Sweden	0.6827
54	Lithuania	0.6357
55	Bahamas, The	0.5437
56	Dominica	0.5184

Let us start from the top of the ladder. Why is Vatican City ranked so high? What could justify such a result? The starting point is to remind ourselves of the meaning of efficiency under the model. Efficiency is related to the ability to exceed the expected (floor) output. Each country is provided with a portion of the two types of real energy inputs (land and people) and is expected to contribute at least the sum of these energies to the output (assuming a frictionless world in the 'original position'). Sink countries that diverge significantly from model predictions exhibit a 'quantum-like' effect where the equipartition principle does not hold. The Vatican is given a very small portion of world input energies, with its area of 0.44 square kilometers, and population of only 1000. In per-unit energies, these figures translate into 1.84E-13 and 3.59E-17. Each of these input energies adds up to 1 per-unit for the whole world-system. Nevertheless, the Vatican is also able to absorb more capital from the world-economy. The Holy See is supported by financial contributions from more than 1.2 billion Roman Catholics around the world (Peter's Pence). In addition to tourism, these contributions accounted for over USD 450 million in 2008. This translates to 6.65E-10 of the world-system per-unit energy output, where the total world-system output adds up to 2 per-units (from the two energy inputs).

The next highest ψ score belongs to Monaco. Monaco has an area of 2 square kilometers (4.97E-15), and a population just under 40,000 (2.42E-10). Its area is four times larger than Vatican City, and its population is 40 times larger. Nevertheless, Monaco scores 6, compared to Vatican City's 8. Monaco's economy (with an output of 1.36E-7) is based on gambling, banking, and tourism; its economy is hence not very different from that of Vatican City. They both encourage a form of 'donation' as a large component of their revenue. The third country on the list is however quite different from Vatican City and Monaco. Qatar is over 5000 times the size of Monaco (1.67E-07), and its population is 60 times larger (1.17E-6). It receives an efficiency score of 4.7. Unlike the top two countries, Qatar's economy (at 1.39E-4) is based on natural resources.

Most of the sink countries are smaller than 120,000 square kilometers in area, which is the median area of world countries. Notable exceptions include Germany, the United Kingdom, and the United States. However, area alone does not give an indication of efficiency. As we will see in the next section, small countries can also be inefficient. In Chapter IV, we will take a closer look at large sink countries, when we look at G-20 countries.

It is useful to compare the area of the top five sink countries with the top three 'global cities.' The concept of 'global' or 'world cities' was introduced by John Friedmann (1986) and later refined by others, including Saskia Sassen (2005). She locates the emergence of global cities in the following context:

[Each phase in the long] history of the world economy raises specific questions about the particular conditions that make it possible. One of the key properties of the current phase is the ascendance of information technologies and the associated increase in the mobility and liquidity of capital. There have long been cross-border economic processes—flows of capital, labor, goods, raw materials, tourists. But to a large extent these took place within the inter-state system, where the key articulators were national states. The international economic system was ensconced largely in this inter-state system. This has changed rather dramatically over the last decade as a result of privatization, deregulation, the opening up of national economies to foreign firms, and the growing participation of national economic actors in global markets.

It is in this context that we see a re-scaling of what are the strategic territories that articulate the new system. With the partial unbundling or at least weakening of the national as a spatial unit due to privatization and deregulation and the associated strengthening of globalization come conditions for the ascendance of other spatial units or scales. Among these are the sub-national, notably cities and regions; cross-border regions encompassing two or more sub-national entities; and supra-national entities, i.e. global digitalized markets and free trade blocs. The dynamics and processes that get territorialized at these diverse scales can in principle be regional, national or global. (Sassen, 2005, p. 27)

Sassen introduces the 'global city model' to "recognize the anchoring of multiple cross-border dynamics in a network of places, prominent among which are cities, particularly global cities or those with global city functions" (2005, p. 36). These cities are "the terrain where a multiplicity of globalization processes assume concrete, localized forms. These localized forms are, in good part, what globalization is about" (2005, p. 40). Later on, Sassen (2001) discusses three leading examples of this type of city, namely New York, London, and Tokyo. She explains the role of these specific cities in the world-economy as follows:

The widely accepted notion that density and agglomeration will become obsolete because global telecommunications advances allow for maximum population and resource dispersal is poorly conceived. It is, I argue, precisely because of the territorial dispersal facilitated by telecommunication that agglomeration of certain centralizing activities has sharply increased. This is not a mere continuation of old patterns of agglomeration; there is a new logic for concentration. In Weberian terms, there is a new system of "coordination," one which focuses on the development of specific geographic control sites in the international economic order. (Sassen, 2001, p. 5)

Global cities play a key role in the ψ model. They explain the ability of cities to absorb and accumulate capital from the world-system.

As shown in Table 7, the top five sink countries are analogous to city-states. Compared to New York, London, and Tokyo, they exhibit similar densities. Table 7 shows the (2015) area, population and density of these three cities compared to the top five sink counties.

As can be seen in Table 7, (metropolitan) New York City is larger in area than each of the top five sink countries. Its population is also larger than all of these countries——combined. However, the top five sink countries exhibit higher population and output densities. There are similarities between the agglomeration effects seen in these global cities and the economic efficiency registered in top sink counties. All top 10 sink countries adhere to this pattern. However, not all sink countries are similar to global cities. Larger sink countries, which collectively constitute the G-20 group, have areas too large to be considered analogous to global cities. However, as will be discussed

Table 7. The metropolitan area of the three leading cities compared to the top five sink countries

Global City	Area (km^2) (I)	Population (II)	GDP (Billion USD) (III)	Density (II/I)	Density (III/I)
New York City	34,490	23,723,696	1,330	689	0.04
London	8,382	13,879,757	670	1656	0.08
Tokyo	13,572	37,800,000	1,900	2785	0.21
Sink Country	**Area (km^2) (I)**	**Population (II)**	**GDP (Billion USD) (III)**	**Density (II/I)**	**Density (III/I)**
Vatican City	0.44	1000	0.31	2272	0.7
Monaco	2.00	38,800	3	19400	1.5
Qatar	11,586	2,383,705	334	206	0.029
Liechtenstein	160	37,340	5	233	0.03
Luxembourg	2,586	576,249	58	223	0.02

in Chapter IV, these countries can be modeled as networks of global cities (or other forms of agglomeration, such as economic zones and industrial clusters). This understanding helps explain why some G-20 countries are sinks, and others are sources.

Sink countries overlap with core countries under the world-systems theory classification. The latter are countries that exhibit not only economic complexity but also complex (state) constitutions. The core countries according to (Chase-Dunn, Kawano, & Brewer, 2000) and Babones (2005) are shown in Table 8.

While there is an overlap between economic efficiency and the 'core' designation, there are also significant differences. In particular, Australia and Canada are seen as core countries, although the ψ model suggests that they do not have the economic efficiency to be able to absorb enough capital from the world-system (given their share of world area and population). On the other hand, some countries are designated as semi-periphery countries. These countries are defined as industrializing countries that have characteristics between core and periphery countries. Notable semi-periphery countries include China, India and Iran (Babones, 2005; Chase-Dunn et al., 2000).

Table 8. Core countries and their ψ scores

Country	ψ	Country	ψ
Australia	-3.05	Italy	2.34
Austria	2.86	Japan	2.88
Belgium	3.06	Luxembourg	4.4
Canada	-2.75	Netherlands	3.12
Denmark	2.72	New Zealand	-0.37
Finland	-0.1	Norway	0.72
France	2.42	Singapore	3.92
Germany	2.97	Portugal	1.63
Greece	1.58	Spain	2.03
Hong Kong	n/a	Sweden	0.68
Iceland	-3.08	Switzerland	3.24
Ireland	2.35	Taiwan	3.05
Israel	2.78	United Kingdom	2.89
		United States	1.91

South Korea and Turkey are also classified as semi-periphery countries. In our model, however, the former countries (except China) are source counties, while the latter are sink countries. There is therefore similar overlap between the semi-periphery classification and the ψ model.

SOURCE COUNTRIES

The ψ model lists 126 countries as source countries in 2015. These countries are listed in Table 9. These sources represent 64 percent of total world countries. These countries were unable to absorb and accumulate enough capital from the world-system. Instead, they transfer their capital to sink countries. While many of these economies have been sources since the beginning of the observation period (1990), others, such as New Zealand $\left(\psi_{2015} = -0.37\right)$, slipped into the list only recently. In fact, 10 percent of the 2015 list, including New Zealand, is in the equilibrium band (see above). These countries are 'breaking even,' and could be interpreted as analogous to 'semi-periphery' countries (in terms of the world-system theory). They also include European countries such as Finland $\left(\psi_{2015} = -0.10\right)$ and Macedonia $\left(\psi_{2015} = -0.08\right)$.

The worst performing source countries are in Africa. Moreover, 40 percent of source countries are in that continent. If we add the countries of the Arabian Peninsula and the Levant to a 'Greater Africa,' the percentage goes up to 44 percent. The rest of the source countries are spread out across Central and South America, Asia, and Oceania. Some are in Europe, such as Bosnia and Herzegovina ($\psi_{2015} = -0.67$) and Kosovo $\left(\psi_{2015} = -0.40\right)$, although these states came into the list as new countries emerging from protracted civil wars. Others, however, such as Libya, have been consistently a source country since the 1990s, which could be partly explained by the United States sanctions on Libya since the 1980s. The country continues to feature a high negative ψ as a result of the Libyan Civil War.

In the terminology of world-systems, *most* of these countries are periphery countries. Their main role in the world-economy is to export cheap labor and raw materials to core countries (and import high-profit consumption goods). These countries are less developed than semi-periphery and core countries. According to the ψ model, these countries exhibit poor absorption and accumulation of capital. While they exist at the periphery of world trade,

Table 9. Countries with negative ψ (source countries) in 2015

	ψ		ψ		ψ
1 Afghanistan	-4.69	43 Guinea	-5.27	85 Niger	-8.01
2 Albania	-0.18	44 Guinea-Bissau	-5.12	86 Nigeria	-2.43
3 Algeria	-3.26	45 Guyana	-5.93	87 Oman	-1.34
4 Angola	-3.50	46 Haiti	-3.75	88 Pakistan	-2.23
5 Argentina	-1.57	47 Honduras	-1.86	89 Palau	-0.58
6 Armenia	-0.86	48 Iceland	-3.08	90 Papua New Guinea	-5.28
7 Australia	-3.05	49 India	-1.54	91 Paraguay	-3.37
8 Bangladesh	-2.96	50 Indonesia	-1.27	92 Peru	-1.70
9 Belize	-3.01	51 Iran	-0.39	93 Philippines	-1.46
10 Benin	-3.77	52 Iraq	-0.85	94 Russia	-2.74
11 Bhutan	-3.03	53 Jamaica	-0.07	95 Rwanda	-3.75
12 Bolivia	-4.82	54 Jordan	-1.31	96 Samoa	-1.54
13 Bosnia and Herzegovina	-0.67	55 Kazakhstan	-3.79	97 Sao Tome and Principe	-2.83
14 Botswana	-4.64	56 Kenya	-3.74	98 Saudi Arabia	-0.67
15 Brazil	-1.60	57 Kiribati	-0.75	99 Senegal	-3.57
16 Burkina Faso	-4.29	58 Korea, North	-3.45	100 Sierra Leone	-3.91
17 Burundi	-5.50	59 Kosovo	-0.40	101 Solomon Islands	-4.39
18 Cambodia	-2.92	60 Kyrgyzstan	-4.38	102 Somalia	-8.38
19 Cameroon	-3.74	61 Laos	-3.98	103 South Africa	-0.67
20 Canada	-2.75	62 Latvia	-0.18	104 South Sudan	-6.58
21 Cape Verde	-1.95	63 Lesotho	-3.48	105 Sri Lanka	-0.71
22 Central African Republic	-9.45	64 Liberia	-6.50	106 Sudan	-5.09
23 Chad	-6.62	65 Libya	-5.31	107 Suriname	-5.24
24 Chile	-0.69	66 Macedonia	-0.08	108 Swaziland	-1.86
25 Colombia	-0.80	67 Madagascar	-5.81	109 Syria	-1.46
26 Comoros	-3.99	68 Malawi	-4.78	110 Tajikistan	-3.48
27 Congo, Democratic Republic of the	-7.92	69 Maldives	-0.17	111 Tanzania	-4.37
28 Congo, Republic of the	-4.64	70 Mali	-7.36	112 Togo	-4.56
29 Cote d'Ivoire	-3.67	71 Marshall Islands	-0.48	113 Tonga	-0.36
30 Djibouti	-3.64	72 Mauritania	-8.63	114 Tunisia	-0.44
31 Ecuador	-0.62	73 Micronesia, Federated States of	-0.56	115 Turkmenistan	-3.34
32 Egypt	-1.09	74 Moldova	-2.03	116 Tuvalu	-1.70
33 El Salvador	-0.26	75 Mongolia	-8.00	117 Uganda	-3.66
34 Eritrea	-5.88	76 Montenegro	-0.58	118 Ukraine	-0.87
35 Ethiopia	-4.38	77 Morocco	-1.53	119 Uruguay	-1.31
36 Fiji	-2.17	78 Mozambique	-5.83	120 Uzbekistan	-2.34
37 Finland	-0.10	79 Myanmar	-3.45	121 Vanuatu	-3.53
38 Gabon	-3.33	80 Namibia	-6.63	122 Venezuela	-0.76
39 Gambia, The	-3.14	81 Nauru	-0.63	123 Vietnam	-1.66
40 Georgia	-1.55	82 Nepal	-3.79	124 Yemen	-3.66
41 Ghana	-2.13	83 New Zealand	-0.37	125 Zambia	-5.80
42 Guatemala	-1.10	84 Nicaragua	-2.38	126 Zimbabwe	-7.09

their designation as periphery could also be the result of weak institutions and unstable governance systems. As we discuss in Chapter IV, these countries lack mechanisms to absorb capital from the world-system. Even where some of these countries have global cities, such as in Australia and Canada, they do not have enough cities to score a positive ψ, give the large land proportion that they have been 'assigned.'

Some of the results in Table 9 are surprising. For example, countries such as Australia and Canada are listed as source countries. We also find the following G-20 countries: Argentina, Brazil, India, Indonesia, Russia, Saudi Arabia, and South Africa. In the next chapter, we take a closer look at the composition of G-20 countries (their classification into sinks and sources) and the secular variation in their ψ scores. At this juncture I will simply point out the fact that some source countries are thought of as major economies, although according to the ψ model they do not exhibit an ability to absorb and accumulate capital from the world-economy. In other words, they are not able to achieve the ψ floor (for output in terms of goods and services).

According to the ψ model, see Figure 2, in terms of the world-system theory, core and periphery countries converged from 2001 and up to the GFC in 2007. This can be seen in the reduction of the relative magnitude between the total positive ψ envelope, $\sum \psi_{+ve}$, and the (absolute value of) total negative ψ envelope, $\left|\sum \psi_{-ve}\right|$.

One particular point to highlight is the common denominator between source countries. Most have no global cities. Those who do, have only one or a few. Hence, while Australia and Canada have some global cities, given the area of these countries, they still cannot absorb enough capital (through these cities) to move into sink countries. The same diagnosis accounts for the weak economic performance seen in some sink countries such as China—— although China relies more on special economic zones for attracting capital. The diagnosis is probably more persuasive when we compare the United States (a sink country) to China (a source country). The two countries have relatively the same total area, but China has three times the population in the US. Notwithstanding, China has only two Alpha + cities (Shanghai and Beijing), one Beta + (Guangzhou), one Beta – (Shenzhen), and one Gamma – (Tianjin). We can also add Hong Kong (Alpha +). In total, the United States has thirty cities ranked Gamma and above, to China's six (including Hong Kong). This difference is the main indicator of the relative power between the US and China and the reason behind their economic efficiency (or inefficiency). In a nutshell, "The main phases in the economic development of the United States are clearly reflected in the growth of its great cities" (Dickinson, 2007, p. 205). In the next chapter, we expand on this proposition in a detailed analysis of G-20 countries and their global cities.

CODA

The chapter introduces a world-system where countries compete for capital. It is this capital that decides which countries become economically efficient or inefficient. According to the model, sink countries are becoming more efficient, and source countries are becoming more inefficient. In other words, the gap between sink countries and source countries is widening. At the same time, more and more countries can meet the efficiency floor predicted by the model. These countries exhibit an 'original position' efficiency. In 2015, there were 70 sink countries and 126 source countries. Most world countries are inefficient.

Countries with highest efficiency scores exhibit similar traits to those found in global cities. In particular, they have small jurisdictional footprints, and high population densities. A country like Monaco, second in economic efficiency only to the Holy See, has a footprint of around 2 square kilometers and a density of around 19,400. In comparison, New York City has a footprint of 34,490 square kilometers and a density of 689. These countries (and cities) exhibit what could be thought of as 'quantum effects' that allow them to exceed the expected energy output—by a large amount.

REFERENCES

Abu-Lughod, J. L. (1989). *Before European hegemony: The world system A.D. 1250-1350.* Oxford: Oxford University Press.

Aligica, P. D., & Tarko, V. (2012). Polycentricity: From Polanyi to Ostrom, and beyond. *Governance: An International Journal of Policy, Administration and Institutions*, *25*(2), 237–262. doi:10.1111/j.1468-0491.2011.01550.x

Babones, S. J. (2005). The country-level income structure of the world-economy. *Journal of World-systems Research*, *11*(I), 29–55. doi:10.5195/JWSR.2005.392

Barfield, T. (1992). *The perilous frontier: Nomadic empires and China, 221 BC to AD 1757.* New York: Wiley-Blackwell.

Beaverstock, J. V., Smith, R. G., & Taylor, P. J. (2000). World city network: A new metageography? *Annals of the Association of American Geographers*, *90*(1), 123–134. doi:10.1111/0004-5608.00188

Bettencourt, L. M. A., & West, G. B. (2011). Bigger cities do more with less: New science reveals why cities become more productive and efficient as they grow. *Scientific American*, *305*(3), 52–53. doi:10.1038/scientificamerican0911-52 PMID:21870443

Beugelsdijk, S. (2007). Trust, institutions and the generally speaking question: A reply to Uslaner. *Cambridge Journal of Economics*, *32*(4), 633–638. doi:10.1093/cje/bem060

Cette, G., Fernald, J., & Mojon, B. (2015). The pre-global-financial-crisis slowdown in productivity: Working Paper. Retrieved from http://ec.europa.eu/economy_finance/events/2015

Chakrabarti, V. (2013). *A country of cities: A manifesto for an urban America*. New York: Metropolis Books.

Chase-Dunn, C., Kawano, Y., & Brewer, B. D. (2000). Trade globalization since 1795: Waves of integration in the world-system. *American Sociological Review*, *65*(1), 77–95. doi:10.2307/2657290

Crotty, J. (2009). Structural causes of the global financial crisis: A critical assessment of the new financial architecture. *Cambridge Journal of Economics*, *33*(4), 563–580. doi:10.1093/cje/bep023

de Groot, H. L. F., Poot, J., & Smit, M. J. (2007). Agglomeration, innovation and regional development: Theoretical perspectives and meta-analysis. In R. Capello & P. Nijkamp (Eds.), *Handbook of Regional Growth and Development Theories* (pp. 256–281). Cheltenham, England: Edward Elgar Publishing. doi:10.2139/ssrn.1021942

Dickinson, R. E. (2007). *City, region and regionalism: A geographical contribution to human ecology*. New York: Routledge. (Original work published 1947)

Dollinger, P. (2000). *The German Hansa*. New York: Routledge.

Friedmann, J. (1986). The world city hypothesis. *Development and Change*, *17*(1), 69–83. doi:10.1111/j.1467-7660.1986.tb00231.x

Friedmann, J. (1995). Were we stand: A decade of world city research. In P. L. Knox & P. J. Taylor (Eds.), *World cities in a world-system* (pp. 21–47). Cambridge: Cambridge University Press. doi:10.1017/CBO9780511522192.003

Fujita, M., Krugman, P., & Venables, A. J. (2001). *The spacial economy: cities, regions, and international trade*. Cambridge, Mass.: MIT Press.

Glaeser, E. (1998). Are cities dying. *Economic Inquiry*, *36*, 429–443. doi:10.1111/j.1465-7295.1998.tb01724.x

Glaeser, E. (2011). *Triumph of the city*. New York: Penguin Press.

Guiso, L., Sapienza, P., & Zingales, L. (2008). *Long term persistence (Working Paper 14278)*. National Bureau of Economic Research. Retrieved from http://www.nber.org/papers/w14278

Harreld, D. J. (2015). *A companion to the Hanseatic league*. Leiden: Brill. doi:10.1163/9789004284760

Hausmann, R., Hidalgo, C. A., Bustos, S., Coscia, M., Chung, S., Jimenez, J., & Yildirim, M. A. et al. (2014). *The atlas of economic complexity*. Cambridge: MIT Press.

Hulten, C. R. (2001). Total factor productivity: A short biography. In C. R. Hulten, E. R. Dean, & M. J. Harper (Eds.), *New developments in productivity analysis* (pp. 1–54). Chicago: University of Chicago Press. doi:10.7208/chicago/9780226360645.003.0001

Kauneckis, D. (2009). The Polycentricity of Innovation: Explaining variation in the new role of the states in science and technology policy. *Paper presented at the Workshop on the Workshop (WOW4)*, Bloomington, IN.

Keeling, D. J. (1995). Transport and the world city paradigm. In P. Knox & P. Taylor (Eds.), *World cities in a world-system* (pp. 115–131). Cambridge: Cambridge University Press. doi:10.1017/CBO9780511522192.008

King, A. D. (1995). Re-presenting world cities: Cultural theory/social practice. In P. L. Knox & P. J. Taylor (Eds.), *World cities in a world-system* (pp. 215–231). Cambridge: Cambridge University Press. doi:10.1017/CBO9780511522192.013

Kitchin, J. (1923). Cycles and trends in economic factors. *The Review of Economics and Statistics*, *5*(1), 10–16. doi:10.2307/1927031

Knox, P. L. (1995). World cities in a world system. In P. L. Knox & P. J. Taylor (Eds.), *World Cities in a World System* (pp. 3–20). Cambridge: University Press Cambridge. doi:10.1017/CBO9780511522192.002

Maré, D. C. (2008). *Labour productivity in Auckland firms*. Auckland: Motu Economic and Public Policy Research.

Martin, R., Sunley, P., Gardiner, B., & Tyler, P. (2016). How regions react to recessions: Resilience and the role of economic structure. *Regional Studies, 50*(4), 561–585. doi:10.1080/00343404.2015.1136410

Morris, I. (2011). *Why the West rules – For now*. London: Profile Books.

Mumford, L. (1961). *The city in history: its origins, its transformations, and its prospects*. New York: Harcourt, Brace & World.

Nanto, D. K. (2009). *The global financial crisis: Analysis and policy implications*. New York: Diane Publishing.

Navarro, P. (2006). *The coming China wars: Where they will be fought and how they will be won*. Upper Saddle River, N.J.: FT Press.

Navarro, P., & Autry, G. (2011). *Death by China: Confronting the dragon-a global call to action*. Upper Saddle River, N.J.: Prentice Hall.

Ostrom, E. (1998). Scales, polycentricity, and incentives: Designing complexity. In L. D. Guruswamy & J. A. McNeely (Eds.), *Protection of global biodiversity: Converging strategies* (pp. 149–167). Durham: Duke University Press.

Perulli, P. (2012). The ontology of global city-region: A critique of statehood. *GaWC Research Bulletin, 415*. Retrieved from http://www.lboro.ac.uk/gawc/rb/rb415.html

Porter, M. (2003). The economic performance of regions. *Regional Studies, 37*(6-7), 545–546. doi:10.1080/0034340032000108688

Putnam, R. D., Leonardi, R., & Nonetti, R. Y. (1994). *Making democracy work: Civic traditions in modern Italy*. Princeton: Princeton University Press.

Quigley, J. M. (1998). Urban diversity and economic growth. *The Journal of Economic Perspectives, 12*(2), 127–138. doi:10.1257/jep.12.2.127

Salmon, P., Bazley, M., & Shand, D. (2009a). *Royal commission on Auckland governance report* (Vol. 4). Auckland: Royal Commission on Auckland Governance.

Salmon, P., Bazley, M., & Shand, D. (2009b). *Royal commission on Auckland Governance report* (Vol. 2). Auckland: Royal Commission on Auckland Governance.

Sassen, S. (1991). *The global city: New York, London, Tokyo*. Princeton: Princeton University Press.

Sassen, S. (2001). *The global city: New York, London, Tokyo* (2nd ed.). Princeton: Princeton University Press. doi:10.1515/9781400847488

Sassen, S. (2005). The global city: Introducing a concept. *The Brown Journal of World Affairs*, *11*(2), 27–43.

Sassen, S. (2006). *Cities in a world economy*. Thousand Oaks, Calif.: Pine Forge Press.

Shearmur, R. (2012). Are cities the font of innovation? A critical review of the literature on cities and innovation. *Cities (London, England)*, *29*, S9–S18. doi:10.1016/j.cities.2012.06.008

Simon, D. (1995). The world city hypothesis: Reflections from the periphery. In P. L. Knox & P. J. Taylor (Eds.), *World cities in a world-system* (pp. 132–155). Cambridge: Cambridge University Press. doi:10.1017/CBO9780511522192.009

Smith, D. A., & Timberlake, M. (1995). Conceptualising and mapping the structure of the world systems city system. *Urban Studies (Edinburgh, Scotland)*, *32*(2), 287–302. doi:10.1080/00420989550013086

Solow, R. (1956). A contribution to the theory of economic growth. *The Quarterly Journal of Economics*, *70*(1), 65–94. doi:10.2307/1884513

Storper, M. (2013). *Keys to the city: How economics, institutions, social interaction, and politics shape development*. Princeton: Princeton University Press.

Summers, L. H. (2000). International financial crises: Causes, prevention, and cures. *The American Economic Review*, *90*(2), 1–16. doi:10.1257/aer.90.2.1 PMID:18459243

Taylor, P. J. (1995). World cities and territorial states: The rise and fall of their mutuality. In P. L. Knox & P. J. Taylor (Eds.), *World cities in a world-system* (pp. 48–62). Cambridge: Cambridge University Press. doi:10.1017/CBO9780511522192.004

Taylor, P. J. (2001). Specification of the world city network. *Geographical Analysis, 33*(2), 181-194. Retrieved from http://www.lboro.ac.uk/gawc/rb/rb23.html

2. thinknow. (2014). *Innovation Cities Analysis Report.* Retrieved from http://report.innovation-cities.com

Thorn, R. S. (1968). Per capita income as a measure of economic development. *Zeitschrift für Nationalökonomie, 28*(2), 206–216. doi:10.1007/BF01320103

Tiebout, C. M. (1956). A Pure Theory of Local Expenditure. *Journal of Political Economy, 64*(5), 416–424. doi:10.1086/257839

Tilly, C. (1992). *Coercion, Capital and European States, A.D. 990-1992.* Cambridge, MA: Blackwell.

Wallerstein, I. (1974). *The modern world-system I: Capitalist agriculture and the origins of the European world-economy in the sixteenth century.* New York: Academic Press.

Wallerstein, I. (2004). World-systems analysis. In G. Modelski (Ed.), *World system history.* Oxford: EOLSS Publishers.

Wallerstein, I. (2007). *World-systems analysis: An introduction.* Durham, N.C.: Duke University Press.

Young, W. (2013). *Real business cycle models in economics.* New York: Routledge.

ENDNOTES

1 Axial Division of Labor is "A term used in articulating the argument that what holds the capitalist world-economy intact is an invisible axis binding together core-like and peripheral processes" (Wallerstein, 2004, p. 91).

2 The term 'world city' or 'weltstadt' can in fact be traced back to the Johann Wolfgang von Goethe who used it to refer to the cultural eminence of Paris and Rome. See (King, 1995, p. 219).

3 In later chapters this point is elucidated with a discussion of 'charter cities.'

4 For data on city populations refer to the Australian Bureau of Statistics (ABS) 2011 census.

5 For a discussion of the use of *per capita* income as a measure of economic development see Thorn (1968).

6 However, the GFC did not have any statistically significant effect on the number of countries in the equilibrium band. These countries seem to be the least affected by the GFC.

7 For the interaction between East and West, see also Morris (2011).

Chapter 4
G-20 Countries

ABSTRACT

This chapter applies the ψ model to the G-20 countries. The model suggests that the group is not homogenous. Some G-20 countries are economically efficient, while others are not. The jurisdictional footprints of these countries help explain the efficiency differences. The chapter introduces an evolutionary construct, the Red Queen Effect (RQE) to further explain the evolutionary stability of the world-system. The chapter also provides a brief analysis of the efficiency relativities of European countries.

INTRODUCTION

The ψ model reveals important differences in the economic performance of the countries of the Group of Twenty (G-20). While the group was officially formed in 1999, the Group's performance is analyzed based on member states' level of economic efficiency from 1990.[1] Table 1 provides a snapshot of the scores at the beginning and at the end of the observation period.[2]

Figures in parentheses are for negative scores. A detailed analysis of the economic signature of each country can be found in the appendix to this chapter.

The differences in the ψ scores do not only suggest a quantitative difference. When analyzed over the observation period (from 1990 to 2015), they indicate qualitative differences as well. One important observation when comparing the sink and source groups within the G-20 is in relation to the size of the

DOI: 10.4018/978-1-5225-2756-5.ch004

Table 1. The G-20 countries divided into two groups of sources and sinks

G-20 Sink Countries				G-20 Source Countries			
Country	**ψ 1990**	**ψ 2015**	**Difference**	**Country**	**ψ 1990**	**ψ 2015**	**Difference**
China	(4.94)	0.07	5.01	Argentina	(3.22)	(1.57)	1.65
France	4.02	2.42	(1.60)	Australia	(2.99)	(3.05)	(0.06)
Germany	3.21	2.97	(0.24)	Brazil	(3.09)	(1.60)	1.49
Italy	1.62	2.34	0.72	Canada	(2.49)	(2.75)	(0.26)
Japan	3.42	2.88	(0.54)	India	(4.50)	(1.54)	2.96
Mexico	(2.05)	0.29	2.34	Indonesia	(3.82)	(1.27)	2.55
South Korea	(0.11)	2.77	2.88	Russia	(0.52)	(2.74)	(3.26)
Turkey	(2.51)	0.71	3.22	Saudi Arabia	(2.11)	(0.66)	1.45
United Kingdom	2.30	2.89	0.59	South Africa	(2.26)	(0.67)	1.59
United States	2.28	1.91	(0.37)				

geopolitical footprint exhibited by each group. Notice how source countries are much larger than those in the sink group, with the notable exception of China and the United States, which are discussed further in the appendix. The interesting question is whether there is a relationship between the ψ efficiency score and the size of jurisdictional footprints (as area). This is what we will explore in this chapter.

The ψ model divides the G-20 into sink countries and source countries. In 2015 there were ten sinks and nine sources.[3] In 1990, the total sum of all ψ scores of these 19 countries was $\sum \psi_{1990} = -17.78$, compared to a 2015 score of $\sum \psi_{2015} = 3.39$. Over the twenty-five-year period from 1990 to 2015, four countries changed their status from source to sink. In descending order (in terms of improvement), these countries are: China, Turkey, South Korea, and Mexico. These countries exhibit substantial increases in their ψ scores. On the other hands, so far, no sink country switched its classification into a source. However, from among the other six sink countries in 2015, we find four that have reduced their ψ score over the observation period. In descending order, these countries are: Germany, the United States, Japan, and France. Only Italy and the United Kingdom were able to improve their sink status between 1990 and 2015. France stands out as the worst performing sink country, losing almost 40 percent of its ψ score during the observation period.

On the other hands, China stands out as the best performing source country, improving its score by over 100 percent (from 1990 to 2015).

As to the nine source countries, six were able to improve their ψ score during the observation period. These countries are: India, Indonesia, Argentina, Brazil, South Africa, and Saudi Arabia. The other three sources, namely Russia, Canada and Australia, exhibited a worsening of their ψ score, with Russia being the worst performer out of all G-20 countries. Note, however, that the ψ values for Russia from 1990 to 1992 are in fact the scores for the former Soviet Union. If we substitute an estimate for these years, we get $\psi_{1990} = 2.68$, which would suggest that Russia's efficiency was stable over the observation period. Note that these countries (Russia, Canada, and Australia) are rich in natural resources, which the model accounts for indirectly, i.e. as improvements going into the economic transformation process through capital. But even with these improvements, the actual (observed) output is much lower than that predicted by the model.

Out of all G-20 countries, seven have deteriorating efficiency scores. Out of this group, Russia and France have deteriorated the most. On the other hand, twelve countries have registered improvement in their scores. The best performers in this group are China, Turkey, and India.

Many countries in the sink group exhibit the 'Red Queen Effect' (RQE) (Valen, 1973), where they seem to run in the same position, not able to register considerable improvement in their efficiency measure vis-à-vis other countries in the world-system.[4] Valen used this analogy to explain the effect of a new evolutionary rule, where "[t]he effective environment of the members of any homogeneous group of organisms deteriorates at a stochastically constant rate" (1973, p. 16). Valen explains the hypothesis in the following terms:

We can think of the Red Queen's Hypothesis in terms of an unorthodox game theory. To a good approximation, each species is part of a zero-sum game against other species. Which adversary is most important for a species may vary from time to time, and for some or even most species no one adversary may ever be paramount. Furthermore, no species can ever win, and new adversaries grinningly replace the losers …

From this overlook we see dynamic equilibria on an immense scale, determining much of the course of evolution by their self-perpetuating fluctuations. (Valen, 1973, p. 21)

The hypothesis suggests that countries need to 'run' (evolve) to stay in 'the same place' (remain extant). In the case of Russia, Australia, and Canada this seems to be true. The ψ scores for these countries exhibit a long-term trend equal to zero, or with a small gradient.[5] They seem to face a 'glass ceiling' where their economic efficiency is limited by a certain maximum (negative) ψ score.

THE TIERS

Based on the analysis above, G-20 countries can be grouped into six tiers based on their (Red Queen) ψ scores.

Tier 1: France (although showing signs of deterioration), Germany, Italy (although showing strong deterioration since 2010), Japan (with signs of deterioration), South Korea (but only since 2011), and the United Kingdom. These countries exhibit economic efficiency around $\psi = 3$. However, only Germany and the United Kingdom seem to have an RQE. However, South Korea is also likely to show similar stability in the next decade. France, Italy, and Japan on the other hand seem to be heading to lower levels of efficiency.

Tier 2: The United States, which exhibit a $\psi = 2.00$. Like France, Italy, and Japan, the US has been experiencing a reduction in its efficiency since 1990.

Tier 3: China (since 2014), Mexico, and Turkey. These countries hover around $\psi = 0$. Only Turkey seems to have settled into an RQE. China is set to continue to increase its efficiency, while Mexico seems to continue to return to the zero score.

Tier 4: Indonesia, Saudi Arabia, and South Africa. These inefficient countries exhibit an RQE around $\psi = -1.00$, although Saudi Arabia seems to increase its efficiency to a new plateau (always under zero).

Tier 5: Argentina, Brazil, and India. These countries have an RQE around $\psi = -2.00$.

Tier 6: Australia, Canada, and Russia with an RQE at $\psi = -3.00$.

What is of interest to us is how these countries breakdown into tiers based on their jurisdictional footprint. We can identify two approaches to economic efficiency. The first is where the country has a small jurisdictional footprint relative to other G-20 countries. All countries in the first tier seem to follow this approach. France, Germany, Italy, and the United Kingdom have per-unit energy-equivalent areas as follows: 5.2E-04, 1.6E-04, 1.1E-04, and 7.4E-05. They are all in the order of E-04 and E-05. Japan and South Korea are of the order of E-04 and E-05 as well. However, the footprint is only part of the explanation. Compare Tier 1 to the countries in the last tier (Tier 6). These countries have per-unit energy-equivalent areas as follows. Australia: 7.5E-02, Canada: 1.2E-01, and Russia: 3.6E-01. These countries have footprints in the order of E-01 and E-02. Tier 5 countries also exhibit footprints in the order of E-02 and E-03. In Tier 2 we find the United States with an area equivalent of 1.2E-01, and in Tier 3 we find China with a footprint of 1.1E-01. These are very large countries in terms of area, but are still able to be at higher Tiers. To understand why this is so we need to look at the second approach to economic efficiency.

Under the second approach, we find large jurisdictional footprints that are 'perforated' by (capital) attractors. These attractors could be global cities such as in the United States, or Special Economic Zones (SEZs) as in China. Countries in Tiers 4, 5, and 6, which have large footprints, are not able to create enough attractors to absorb enough capital to be efficient. Chapter V looks at the role of these attractors in absorbing capital within countries with large jurisdictional footprints.

EUROPE

It is useful to zero-in on the economic efficiency of European countries to see how they compare to the ones in the G-20. The European countries in the G-20 group are: France, Germany, Italy, Turkey, and the United Kingdom. The economic efficiency of these countries relative to other European countries is shown in Figure 1. These countries exhibit a range of $\psi_{2015} \in [-3.1, 8.2]$. The lowest score belongs to Iceland. While the highest score belongs to the Holy See.

The continent exhibits four tiers of economic efficiency. The lowest tier has only one country: Iceland $(\psi_{2015} = -3.1)$, but would also include Russia $(\psi_{2015} = -2.7)$ if added to the geographic definition. The third tier has an efficiency range of $\psi_{2015} \in [-2.0, -0.4]$, and has the following countries: Armenia $(\psi_{2015} = -0.9)$, Bosnia and Herzegovina $(\psi_{2015} = -0.7)$, Georgia

Figure 1. Efficiency ranking of European countries; the legend represents ψ scores.

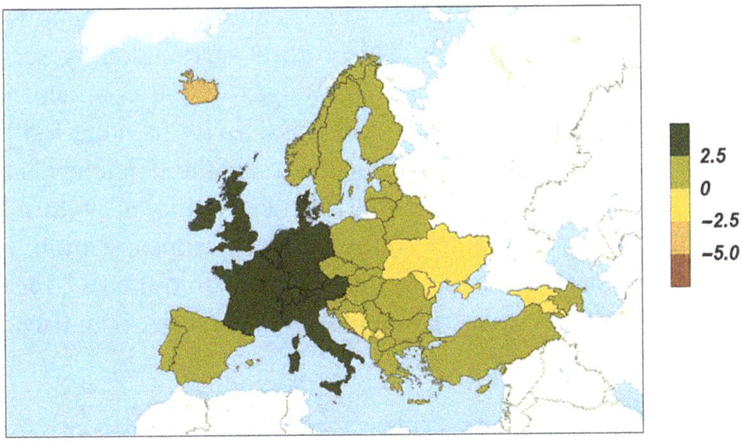

($\psi_{2015} = -1.5$), Kosovo ($\psi_{2015} = -0.4$), Moldova ($\psi_{2015} = -2.0$), Montenegro ($\psi_{2015} = -0.6$), and the Ukraine ($\psi_{2015} = -0.9$). All counties in this tier are in Eastern Europe.

The second tier has an efficiency range of $\psi_{2015} \in [-0.2, 2.0]$. The tier covers the following countries: Albania ($\psi_{2015} = -0.2$), Azerbaijan ($\psi_{2015} = 0.1$), Belarus ($\psi_{2015} = 0.00$), Bulgaria ($\psi_{2015} = 0.3$), Croatia ($\psi_{2015} = 0.9$), Cyprus ($\psi_{2015} = 1.3$), Czech Republic ($\psi_{2015} = 2.0$), Estonia ($\psi_{2015} = 0.1$), Finland ($\psi_{2015} = -0.1$), Greece ($\psi_{2015} = 1.6$), Hungary ($\psi_{2015} = 1.3$), Latvia ($\psi_{2015} = -0.2$), Lithuania ($\psi_{2015} = 0.6$), Macedonia ($\psi_{2015} = -0.1$), Norway ($\psi_{2015} = 0.7$), Poland ($\psi_{2015} = 1.5$), Portugal ($\psi_{2015} = 1.6$), Romania ($\psi_{2015} = 0.4$), Serbia ($\psi_{2015} = 0.1$), Slovakia ($\psi_{2015} = 1.8$), Slovenia ($\psi_{2015} = 2.0$), Spain ($\psi_{2015} = 2.0$), and Turkey ($\psi_{2015} = 0.7$).

The first tier, comprising the most economically efficient countries in Europe has a range of $\psi_{2015} \in [2.3, 8.2]$, and comprises the following countries: Andorra ($\psi_{2015} = 2.8$), Austria ($\psi_{2015} = 2.9$), Belgium ($\psi_{2015} = 3.1$), Denmark ($\psi_{2015} = 2.7$), France ($\psi_{2015} = 2.4$), Germany ($\psi_{2015} = 3.0$), the Holy See ($\psi_{2015} = 8.2$), Ireland ($\psi_{2015} = 2.4$), Italy ($\psi_{2015} = 2.3$), Lichtenstein ($\psi_{2015} = 4.5$), Luxembourg ($\psi_{2015} = 4.4$), Malta ($\psi_{2015} = 2.3$), Monaco ($\psi_{2015} = 6.3$), the Netherlands ($\psi_{2015} = 3.1$), San Marino ($\psi_{2015} = 3.0$), and Switzerland ($\psi_{2015} = 3.2$).

The efficiency map of Europe shows a high-efficiency core (shown in Figure 1 in dark green) that stretches from Ireland and the United Kingdom in the north, to Italy in the south. This core is surrounded by second tier countries, and third tier countries at the edges of the continent. Iceland with its remote geographic location, and Russia with its huge footprint (in addition to geographic isolation) make up the rest of the efficiency landscape. It seems that there is hence a form of efficiency 'radiation' within Europe, which is being enhanced by the workings of the European Union. It would be reasonable to expect that as third tier countries join the EU, they would be elevated to second tier countries, while some first tier countries join the efficiency core.

WORLD-SYSTEM STABILITY

The analysis in this chapter can help us understand the stability of the current world-system, namely, the system created by the WTO in 1995. Given that the G-20 represents the largest economies in the world—accounting for more than 85 percent of the gross world product—the world-system stability depends on the *efficiency relativities* of these countries, i.e. their relative positions regarding efficiency. In other words, the world-system stability is defined by the RQE that these countries exhibit during the observation period. If these economies cannot maintain their efficiency vis-à-vis other world countries, there would be a structural shift and a transition to a new world-system. Based on our earlier analysis, most of the G-20 countries seem to exhibit an RQE. The exceptions being China, France, Italy, Japan, Mexico, Saudi Arabia, and the US. These countries exhibit either an increase in efficiency (China and to a lesser extent Saudi Arabia) or a decrease in efficiency relative to the rest of the world. Given the size of these economies, it would be reasonable to suggest that the world-system is already is in a phase of transition to a new equilibrium (of efficiency relativities). This is, of course, assuming that the world-economy will continue to evolve along the WTO path it has been traveling on since 1995. There are however potential geopolitical developments, such as closer political integration in the EU, or protectionist trade policies (such as those proposed by populist governments), that could result in a different equilibrium. Regardless of which equilibrium is reached, the current world-system is already in a transition phase. There will necessarily be winners and losers.

CODA

This chapter introduced the Red Queen Effect (RQE). This effect represents the evolutionary stability of the world-system. Based on the analysis, the world-system is already in a phase of transition towards a new equilibrium. The composition of G-20 countries suggests that economic efficiency could be achieved either by opting for smaller jurisdictional footprints, or by perforating existing large footprints with (capital) attractors such as global cities and Special Economic Zones (SEZs). The chapter also provides a brief analysis of the efficiency relativities of European countries. Europe has a high efficiency core represented by the 1973 European Community countries and Switzerland.

The next chapter unpacks the evolution of efficiency in the United States at the subnational level. The efficiency of each of the 50 States (and the District of Columbia) is analyzed throughout the period from 1990 to 2015. The analysis provides more insights into the role of jurisdictional footprints and attractors in enhancing economic efficiency.

REFERENCES

Carrol, L. (1872). *Through the looking glass and what Alice found there*. London: Macmillan.

Valen, L. V. (1973). A new evolutionary law. *Evolutionary Theory*, *1*, 1–30.

ENDNOTES

1 I exclude the European Union as it does not represent a sovereign country.

2 Some surprising results emerge from the model. For instance, Australia's ψ value is close to Brazil's, which sounds odd, given the difference in their *per-capita* incomes. The ψ model offers a perspective that is different from traditional economic performance measures. See also the comparison between the United Kingdom and the United States in Chapter III.

3 In relation to energy surplus and deficit. See the definition of sink and source countries in Chapter I.

4 The 'Red Queen' hypothesis explains that for an evolutionary system, perpetual development is needed just in order to maintain its fitness relative to the systems it is co-evolving with. According to this hypothesis organisms are in a perpetual struggle to keep up with one another. The name comes from Lewis Carroll's *Through the Looking Glass* (Carrol, 1872). When Alice decides to see the garden by climbing the hill, as she follows what appears to be a straight path, she finds that it leads her back to the house. When she tries to speed up, she crashes into the house. In this world, forward movement takes Alice back to her starting point (Red Queen dynamics), and rapid movement causes abrupt stops (extinction). Eventually, the Red Queen leads Alice directly to the top of the hill. At the top of the hill, the Red Queen begins to run, faster and faster. Alice runs after the Red Queen but is further perplexed to find that neither one seems to be moving. When they stop running, they are in the same place. The Red Queen tells Alice that "it takes all the running you can do to stay in the same place" (Carrol, 1872, Chapter 2).

5 For Canada, the 'Red Queen' starts from 2000. For Russia, the 'Red Queen' can be seen from 2004.

Chapter 5
The United States

ABSTRACT

This chapter applies the ψ model to the United States of America. By assuming that the US is a 'world-system,' we can measure the economic efficiency of each state (and the District of Columbia). The model predicts an output floor based on the inputs of land and people as per-unit energy-equivalents. This expected output is then compared to the actual Gross State Product (GSP) as a per-unit energy-equivalent. States that are economically efficient register a positive residual, and hence a positive ψ score. However, given potential measurement inaccuracies, states with low negative scores are also added to this efficient tier.

INTRODUCTION

Figure 1 shows the 'efficient' US states in dark green. These states are considered 'sinks' in that they are able to absorb and accumulate capital. The rest (the 'sources') are shown in a (decreasing efficiency) gradient from light green to yellow, and finally dark red.

Table 1 provides the actual scores for the four tiers in Figure 1. A detailed analysis of the 50 states and the District of Columbia can be found in the appendix to this chapter.

The highest-ranking states are divided into two tiers, each having the same number of states (with the District of Columbia going to the first tier). According to the model, in 2015, there were only seven states with positive scores. However, there are another six states that received scores very close

DOI: 10.4018/978-1-5225-2756-5.ch005

Figure 1. A 2015 efficiency map of the US states; highest efficiency scores are in dark green.

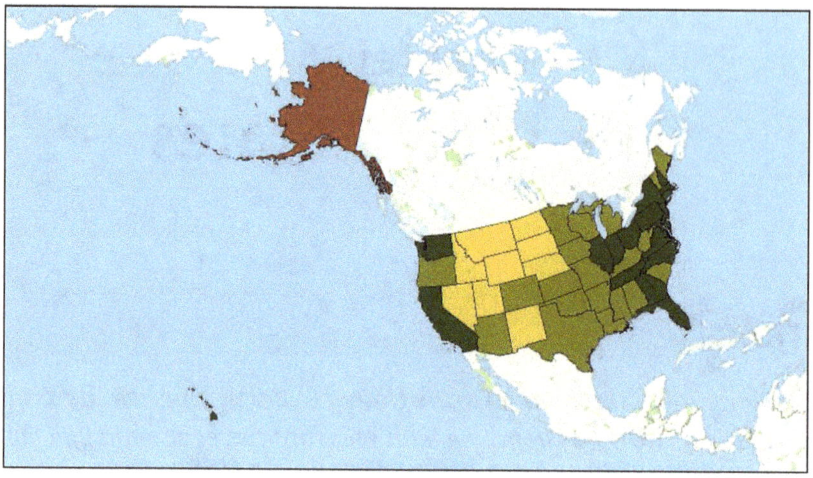

Table 1. A breakdown of the four efficiency tiers in Figure 1

Dark Green		Light Green		Yellow		Dark Red	
1 District of Columbia	0.97	22 Texas	(0.58)	42 Utah	(2.27)	51 Alaska	(8.31)
2 Connecticut	0.55	23 Wisconsin	(0.69)	43 Nebraska	(2.40)		
3 Massachusetts	0.42	24 South Carolina	(0.75)	44 Nevada	(2.66)		
4 New Jersey	0.39	25 Michigan	(0.76)	45 Idaho	(3.34)		
5 Maryland	0.31	26 Louisiana	(0.80)	46 New Mexico	(3.52)		
6 New York	0.28	27 Minnesota	(0.84)	47 North Dakota	(3.61)		
7 Rhode Island	0.04	28 Missouri	(0.86)	48 South Dakota	(3.93)		
8 Virginia	(0.03)	29 Vermont	(0.88)	49 Wyoming	(4.91)		
9 California	(0.04)	30 Kentucky	(0.88)	50 Montana	(5.14)		
10 Pennsylvania	(0.07)	31 Alabama	(0.98)				
11 Illinois	(0.07)	32 Iowa	(1.12)				
12 Delaware	(0.08)	33 Colorado	(1.16)				
13 New Hampshire	(0.08)	34 West Virginia	(1.20)				
14 Florida	(0.26)	35 Oklahoma	(1.28)				
15 Hawaii	(0.32)	36 Arizona	(1.45)				
16 Ohio	(0.32)	37 Mississippi	(1.51)				
17 Washington	(0.43)	38 Arkansas	(1.60)				
18 Indiana	(0.50)	39 Oregon	(1.81)				
19 North Carolina	(0.52)	40 Kansas	(1.84)				
20 Tennessee	(0.53)	41 Maine	(1.87)				
21 Georgia	(0.56)						

to zero. States with 'equilibrium' band scores $\left(-0.5 \leq \psi \leq 0.5\right)$ were also added to this tier. The total number of states in this tier is 20. Note how most of these states are on the East Coast. The rest (California and Washington) are on the West Coast. Most of these states are also the oldest. Twelve of the thirteen original colonies are in the first tier: Connecticut, Massachusetts, New Jersey, Maryland, New York, Rhode Island, Virginia, Pennsylvania, Delaware, New Hampshire, North Carolina and Georgia are original US colonies. Only South Carolina is in the second tier. The rest of the first tier is composed of states that are geographically close to these original states. The three exceptions are West Virginia, Kentucky, and South Carolina, which are juxtaposed to the original states but do not make it to the first-tier.

The next tier, shown in light green in Figure 1, has 20 states. These second-tier states are all inefficient, exhibiting scores within the range $-0.58 \leq \psi \leq -1.87$. They spread further west—all the way to the Pacific Ocean (Oregon), but with an inland gap constituting third-tier states (shown in yellow in Figure 1). Hawaii, California, and Washington are in tier one. West Virginia, Kentucky, and South Carolina are all in this second tier. The best-performing state in this tier is Texas. The worst-performing is Maine.

Third tier states have efficiency scores of negative two and below. These states, shown in yellow in Figure 1, are all inland——none have access to coasts. In contrast, all first-tier states (except Tennessee) have access either to the Atlantic Ocean, the Pacific Ocean, or the Laurentian Great Lakes. This tier exhibits a wider inefficiency band, from scores of negative two to negative five $\left(-2.27 \leq \psi \leq -5.14\right)$.

The last tier, shown in dark red in Figure 1, has only one state, Alaska, which registers an efficiency score of $\psi = -8.31$, compared to the lowest score of $\psi = -5.14$ in the second tier, which belongs to Montana.

CONNECTICUT VS. CALIFORNIA

Let us go over the main characteristics of the states in each tier. Let us start with the third and fourth tiers (shown in yellow and dark red in Figure 1). The first observation is that these states have large jurisdictional footprints. The smallest state in the third-tier is North Dakota with an area of 183,108 square kilometers. The largest is Montana with 380,800 square kilometers. The average footprint is 250,547 square kilometers. Alaska, in the fourth tier, has an area of 1,717,856 which is greater than the combined area of Germany, France, Italy, and Spain. The second observation about the states in tiers three and four is that they have low population densities. The highest density is that of Utah (14 per square kilometer), and the lowest is that of Wyoming (2.3 per square kilometer). The average population density in the third tier is 6.85, while Alaska has a density of 0.5 per square kilometer. The third observation is that none of these states have global cities. Utah has a highly sufficient city (Salt Lake City), and Nevada has a sufficiency city (Las Vegas). The rest have cities that depend on other global cities for services (such as banking and accounting). States in the third and fourth tiers have large jurisdictional footprints, with low population density, and no global cities.

Let us now look at the states in the first tier. Note that high population densities characterize states in this tier. Figure 2 shows the population density distribution of US states.

Let us look at the top ten in Table 1. The District of Columbia comes on top with a footprint of only 177 square kilometers, and a 2015 population density of 4,300 per square kilometer. The 20 states in this tier have an average density of 164 per square kilometer, and an average footprint of 100,633 square kilometers. The largest footprint belongs to California (423,970), while the smallest belongs to Rhode Island (3,144 square kilometers). The highest density is in New Jersey (467 per square kilometer) while the lowest is in

Figure 2. Population density (per km²) in the United States using 2015 data

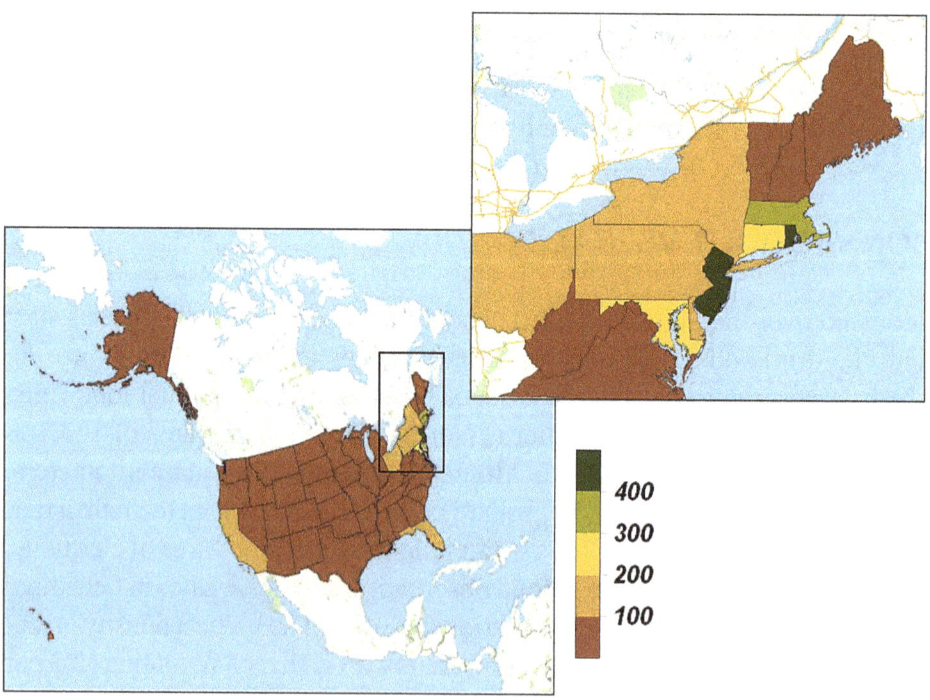

Washington (40 per square kilometer). This tier illustrates two approaches to economic efficiency. The first, what could be called the 'Connecticut approach,' is where you start with a small jurisdictional footprint and use a distributed urban system (and industrial clusters) to absorb capital. The second approach, which could be referred to as the 'California approach,' is where you start with a large jurisdictional footprint but bolster the effects of agglomeration through global cities. In other words, the 'California approach' requires 'perforating' jurisdictional footprints with global cities. These cities provide very high population density within areas smaller than 25,000 square kilometers. Let us unpack each approach in some more detail.

There are two paths to economic efficiency. The first approach relies on a small jurisdictional footprint, similar to the Holy See, Luxembourg, Lichtenstein, and Qatar (see Chapter III). These policies have a footprint at the global-city scale, or smaller. This scale is measured using New York City as a benchmark (25,000 square kilometers). In the US first tier, we find that the District of Columbia, Connecticut, Massachusetts, New Jersey, Rhode Island, Delaware, and New Hampshire are all below this scale, while Maryland (32,133 square kilometers) and Hawaii (28,311 square kilometers) are just above. In total nine jurisdictions follow the 'Connecticut approach.' These entities are characterized by high population densities: between 57 in New Hampshire and 467 in New Jersey (per square kilometer). Moreover, out of all nine jurisdictions, only three have global cities: the District of Columbia (Washington, D. C: Alpha -), Massachusetts (Boston: Alpha -), and Maryland (Baltimore: Gamma +). The 'Connecticut approach' is similar to the approach seen in Germany and Italy. These jurisdictions rely more on distributed urban systems with industrial clusters, rather than global cities. However, in essence, given the footprints of the nine US jurisdictions, they in fact function as global cities themselves. They use their small area to generate agglomeration effects similar to those seen in global cities (Glaeser, 2011, 2010). The 'Connecticut approach' requires evolution over centuries.

On the other hand, we have the California approach——the revolutionary approach. This approach is adopted by the other 12 states in the first tier. These states have much larger footprints that are perforated by global cities: New York (New York City: Alpha ++), California (Los Angeles: Alpha, San Diego: Beta -, San Jose: Gamma, San Francisco: Alpha -), Pennsylvania (Philadelphia: Beta +), Illinois (Chicago: Alpha), Florida (Miami: Alpha -, Tampa: Gamma +, Orlando: Gamma -), Ohio (Columbus: Gamma -, Cleveland: Beta -, Cincinnati: Gamma), Washington (Seattle: Beta -), North Carolina (Charlotte: Gamma +, Raleigh: Gamma), and Georgia (Atlanta: Alpha -).

The exceptions are Tennessee, which has an efficiency city (Nashville); and Virginia, which has a high-efficiency city (Richmond). In this second path to economic efficiency, we start from a large jurisdictional footprint with low population density and perforate that footprint with global cities (so that it looks like a cross section of *Jarlsberg* cheese). These global cities replicate the 'Connecticut approach' in that they produce small footprints with high population densities. We can hence think of the 'California approach' as a network of smaller jurisdictions following the 'Connecticut approach.'

The ability to induce economic efficiency is, therefore, a function of small jurisdictional footprints. These footprints could be independent polities (such as Lichtenstein), or subnational units of a larger polity (such as New York City). Such units transform these larger polities into (networks of) 'islands' of economic efficiency. These 'islands' could be either global cities, industrial clusters, or special economic zones.

When we take a closer look at the second tier in Table 6.1, we find that it has an average population density and an average footprint between the first and third tiers. The 20 states in this tier have an average density of 31 per square kilometer and an average area of 188,666 square kilometers. The largest footprint belongs to Texas (696,241 square kilometers), while the smallest belongs to Vermont (24,923 square kilometers). The highest density is in Michigan (67 per square kilometer), while the lowest is in Kansas (13.5 per square kilometer). When we look at the global cities in this tier, we find the following ten cities: Texas (Houston: Beta +, Dallas: Beta +), Wisconsin (Milwaukee: Gamma), Michigan (Detroit: Beta -), Minnesota (Minneapolis: Beta -), Missouri (Kansas City: Gamma -, Saint Louis: Gamma +), Colorado (Denver: Beta -), Arizona (Phoenix: Gamma +), and Oregon (Portland: Gamma -). Louisiana has a sufficiency city (New Orleans). There are no Alpha cities in this tier. Moreover, the total number of global cities in the tier is only half that in the first tier.

Out of all the states in the second tier, only Vermont has a footprint at the global-city scale. Vermont differs from the 'Connecticut' states (in the first tier) in that it has a low population density. In 2015, Vermont's density was 26, compared to 324 in Massachusetts, 467 in New Jersey, 239 in Maryland, and 57 in New Hampshire (all figures per square kilometer). A state like Vermont needs larger density for it to be able to function as a global city.

Table 2 summarizes the findings. Higher economic efficiency is a function of small jurisdictional footprints with large population densities. The quintessential example of such footprints is the global city.

Table 2. A summary of the comparison between the four efficiency tiers in Figure 1

Tier	Average Population Density per km² (2015)	Average Jurisdictional Footprint	Number of Global Cities in the Tier
First	163	103,529	20
Second	31	188,666	10
Third	7	250,547	0
Fourth	< 1	1,717,856	0

Can we take these findings and provide a normative signal for economic efficiency. How can a country like the United States become more efficient? Is it just a matter of investment and immigration into new global cities? Is it about splitting existing states into smaller jurisdictions? The next section refines our findings through the prism of 'legal personality,' and how this personality affects the nature of cities and their role within the world-system. The second question on the number of states is discussed through contrasting the option of small-scale statehood with that of (local government) amalgamation (see below).

THE LEGAL PERSONALITY OF CITIES

This section takes a closer look at the legal personality of cities throughout the past, up to the present, and further beyond. By legal personality I mean the "device by which the law creates or recognizes units to which it ascribes certain powers and capacities" (Paton 1973, p. 393). Such units could either be natural human beings or artificial entities. A legal person can include a body politic and a body corporate. The assertion is that throughout history, cities oscillated between strong and weak personalities. Strong personalities dominated when higher orders of political organization were undergoing crises, while weak personalities dominated under the reverse conditions. To understand these different personalities better, we need to take a detour to introduce, if only briefly, the legal theories behind them. These theories are usually discussed in the context of corporations, but apply equally to cities, especially in an analysis of international legal personality, as the latter continues to be understood as a body corporate (Derham, 1958; Hager, 1988; Hallis, 1930; Klabbers, 2005; Maitland, 1900; Nijman, 2004). Some theories focus on the reality of city legal personality, while others concentrate on the source of legal personality. For our purposes, the former theories are of particular interest, and two theories among these are pertinent to our analysis.

Under the positivist 'fiction theory,' championed by Friedrich Carl von Savigny, John Salmond, Edward Coke, and William Blackstone, the legal personality of cities is fictional. Nevertheless, this personality is different from that of its inhabitants, which means that changes in the population would not alter the legal personality of the city. The property of the city is not (in law) the property of its inhabitants. On the other hand, the 'Realist Theory,' a natural rights theory that found favor with Johannes Althusius and Otto von Gierke, asserts that cities are 'social organisms' with a real (psychological rather than physical) existence—an existence separate from its inhabitants. This assertion later came to be known as the 'Cooley-Eaton-McQuillin thesis' which denied "the existence of absolute state supremacy over cities" (Frug, 1980, pp. 1113-1115). The 'realist' theory envisages the possibility of cities' strong personality, while the 'fiction' theory suggests a weaker version.

To give the analysis some informative structure, I map the status of cities along a two-dimensional continuum of (1) economic independence, and (2) political independence. Together, economic and political independence represent a proxy for jurisdiction, i.e. "a government's general power to exercise authority over all persons and things within its territory; especially, a state's power to create interests that will be recognised under common-law principles as valid in other states" (Jurisdiction, 2004, p. 867). Hence cities are distinguished from towns and villages not by their size, but by possessing privileges of self-governance (Friedrichs, 1981, p. 109)——nor does the size of a given city has any bearing on its importance or influence (Friedrichs, 1981, p. 124). The city, in essence, participates consciously in the making of history (Mumford, 1961, p. 576), or as put by Oswald Spengler, a city has a soul (1969, p. 66). According to Max Weber (Weber, 1969, p. 38), the city ideal-type displays autonomous legal, economic and political systems were (small scale) democracy represents a viable alternative to (large scale) bureaucracy. This continuum reflects not only the fact that there are potentially as many legal personalities for cities as there are cities, but that there are different ideal-types for different cities. To simplify the analysis further, and without any loss of generality, we can digitize the continuum into three models: the territorial city, the charter city, and the sovereign (fully autonomous) city. This analytical framework is shown in Figure 3. The success of cities under all three models depends more or less upon their ability to exercise control over their economic surplus (Griffeth & Thomas, 1981, p. xvi).[1] In fact, there were chiefly three ways for cities to succeed in the world-system of

Figure 3. The analytical framework showing three types of cities

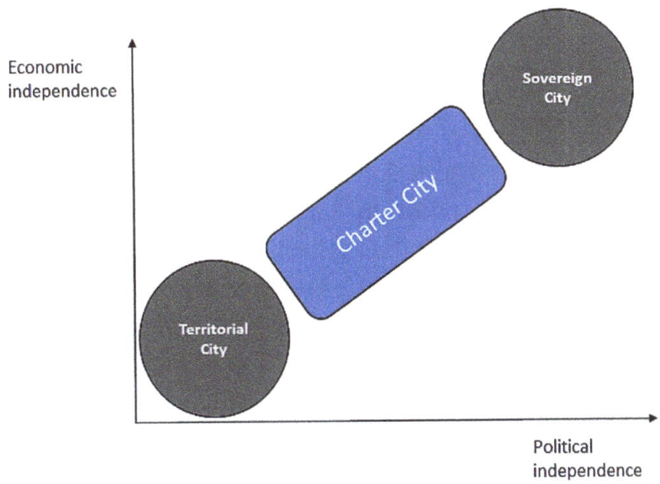

their time (Abu-Lughod, 1989, pp. 129-130). Cities could be trade sites, for example, Troyes and Provins historically, and Singapore and Hong Kong in our time. Alternatively, cities could become powerful industrial exporters, for example, the textile towns of Flanders, or today the oil-rich emirates of the Persian Gulf. The third option is where they can function as commercial shippers transferring goods between different markets, for example, Genoa and Venice.

Moreover, one can discern an (evolutionary) oscillation from the sovereign city, the default mode of organization, to the charter city, and eventually to the territorial city. The shift can be explained to a large extent by understanding the *mutuality* between cities and territorial nation-states. Nation-states brought about a new scale of war in which cities became politically dependent on these states. Losing this political independence shifted city-states to the status of charter cities. However, this was only a transient phase from which territorial states proceeded to extinguish the economic independence of their cities through the fiction of 'national consciousness.' The stripping of political independence can be seen in the military advantage that France and Spain had in the Italian wars of the 1490s, while the loss of economic independence can be seen in the first half of the 17th century in the destruction of German cities in the Thirty Years' War. Even when the state was organized around mercantilism (rather than 'pure' military concerns) as the favored mechanism for economic growth, the territorial city was the favored model. This was clear in the Dutch Republic and the rise of Amsterdam as a global city (Taylor, 1995, pp. 50-52) (see also Chapter VII). By the time of the Industrial Revolution, the transformation of cities to creatures of the state——to territorial cities where growth is driven externally——was complete (Sennett, 1969, p. 4).

However, the cycle does not stop there. It continues through a phase where we see another rise of city-states. A harbinger of this process can be seen in the 20th century where the number of polities doubled (Taylor, 1995, p. 56). Countries in Europe, including Great Britain, are being increasingly challenged by subnational identities (Marx, 1997). There is now not only a growing interdependence between the global and the local scales, but even their fusion into a 'glocal' dimension (Beauregard, 1995, p. 239). Moreover, the original 'security' function of territorial nation-states is becoming redundant due to an increasingly influential international law.

In a clear departure from the historical trend where cities were created not by governments but by their citizens,[2] most legal systems today treat cities as creatures of state and statute (the Dillon doctrine)—as implementation agencies of national and supra-national agendas. In most legal frameworks today, cities do not have any 'natural' or 'inherent' powers (Frug, 1980, pp. 1062-1063, 1109). They are governed more as bureaucracies than democracies. For example, in the United States cities are treated as administrative subdivisions of their states (Frug, 1999, pp. 3-7). Unlike states, they are not "general lawmaking bodies" (Frug, 1980, p. 1065). Even though there have been attempts in the 19th and 20th century to model American cities after European 'free' cities. When large American cities faced an urban crisis driven by unprecedented growth, they looked to the old continent for inspiration. Comparative analysis of the legal frameworks governing cities in the US and Europe resulted in constitutional amendments where many states granted their cities 'home rule' (Frug & Barron, 2006, p. 6), although denied them planning powers commensurate to those seen in Europe, and hence the 'home rule' given to American cities did not alleviate the powerlessness of American cities. The most liberal plans for home rule reserved to the state power that would be most injurious to the city, such as police power and the power to regulate elections and local finances (Brooks, 1915, p. 239).

Throughout the 1980s and 1990s, in many jurisdictions but most notably in the United Kingdom and New Zealand, there was another central government intervention that saw local governments, especially metropolitan authorities, become even more powerless. Any political devolution focused almost exclusively on regional autonomy, such as in the case of Scotland (Caulfield & Larsen, 2002). In Australia, local governments were reduced to property servicing functions, although economic pressures brought about larger units of local government through amalgamation. The same mega city amalgamations can also be seen in Canada and New Zealand (Caulfield & Larsen, 2002). Just like statehood, amalgamation is based on efficiency gains arising from economies of scale, economies of scope, and network effects (agglomeration effects). The fusion of numerous local government areas into one strong 'regional' government helps streamline economic activity through an integrated approach to infrastructure development (Dollery, 2009). Amalgamation is a cost-saving measure. On the other hand, amalgamation is related to governance structures that are not constitutionally recognized. Hence, unlike the statehood option (i.e. the creation of constitutionally recognized states), amalgamation has been happening very much on an 'ongoing basis.' Statehood provides not only cost-savings analogous to those from amalgamation but also productivity gains from legal systems tailor-made for the economic and social makeup of a given city-region. This point can be illustrated by Hamburg (a Beta + city) and Vienna (an Alpha - city).

The fact that Hamburg is both a city and a state represented institutionally on the German Senate or *Bundesrat* has given the city the ability to legislate for its economic needs. Hamburg develops its own economic policy. In particular (Hamburg, 2011):

Hamburg was one of the first states to cultivate its own strengths through a proactive cluster policy while at the same time developing the most important fields for future growth. We now support eight successful cluster initiatives. They clearly delineate where the city-state has special skills, making it a magnet for mobile capital, top professionals, all kinds of skilled workers and business enterprises.

Hamburg's clustering policy allows for innovation via "inter-ministerial bundling of various policy areas, e.g. economic, labour, science and education policies" (Hamburg, 2011, p. 5). Moreover, Hamburg coordinates inter-state economic policy. For example, in 2011, together with Lower Saxony and Schleswig-Holstein, they launched the 'North German Maritime Cluster Management.' The initiative focuses on state-specific requirements across a wide range of competencies, including shipping, shipping lines, port facilities, marine technology, education, research and maritime services. Hamburg's ability to organize such initiatives and to coordinate with other states is a function of its status as a federal state, and the legislative margin afforded to states within the German federation. Note also that in Germany, over 40 percent of the tax revenue comes from 'shared taxes' where both the federal and state governments receive revenue. Salient among these taxes is the personal income tax.

The other point on social considerations comes from Vienna but has parallels in other jurisdictions. The idea is that urban areas are more likely to vote for social (welfare) policies compared to their rural counterparts (the 'Red Vienna' phenomenon). Vienna is not only Austria's capital city, but also one of its nine states (or federal provinces), and a charter city in its own right. Vienna's special position within the (Federal) Republic of Austria means that it is the capital, a federal state, and a municipality with a legal status as a charter city.

The city began in the 1st century CE, as a Roman military base. By the 11th century, given its geographic location on the Danube, it grew into a European trading hub, achieving the status of a city and a staple port (a right which was essential for the economic development of river cities) by the 13th century. Nevertheless, it remained in the shadow of Prague (under the Luxembourg emperors) until the 15th century, when Vienna became the capital of the Holy Roman Empire. Later on, in the 16th century, Vienna remained a capital city, this time for the Habsburg emperors. However, the Habsburgs took away the city's self-governance rights through a process that saw the execution of three of its mayors (Parsons, 2009, p. 13). After World War II and the Austrian State Treaty of 1955, which eventually established Austria's neutrality, Vienna emerged as not only the capital of Austria, but as the seat of many international organizations, including the United Nations (the third seat after New York and Geneva), and OPEC. After a second wave of modernization that came to the city at the end of the 20th century (Redak, Novy, & Becker, 2005), Vienna is now consistently ranked as one of the most livable cities in the world (Mercer, 2015).

Vienna's statehood within Austria was granted by the *Federal Constitution* of 1920 and is in force since January 1922, where the mayor of the city is also the governor of the state (*Landeshauptmann*). The city-state has an area of around 414,000 square kilometers and a total population of just under two million. Its population density is around 4,300 per square kilometer. While the city's statehood was the culmination of a long period of *de facto* autonomy before World War I, the formal status entitled the city to its own legislative body and executive government. It also entitles the city to direct representation in the Federal Assembly (or Chamber of Provinces), which serves as Austria's second chamber of federal legislation. This representation is analogous to the one that Hamburg has in the *Bundesrat*. The establishment of Vienna as a state seems to have been incentivized by a divorce of convenience between

Vienna and Lower Austria (*Niederösterreich*) (one of the other nine states), for which Vienna served as a capital. This was a convenient divorce given the agrarian nature of Lower Austria, and the *hydrocephalus* nature of Vienna (referring to its high unemployment rate after World War I). The former was squarely conservative, while the latter in the camp of the Christian social movement (Parsons, 2009, p. 13). The governance structures of Vienna at the state and municipal levels have hence been historically associated with 'Red Vienna,' in reference to a rich history of social welfare policies (Redak et al., 2005). Note that the social and Christian democratic movements register similar domination of politics in Hamburg.

The municipality of Vienna has three bodies: the City Council, the City Government or Senate, and the Mayor. The city has 23 districts (*Wiener Gemeindebezirke*) which evolved from the 19th century due to the expansion of the city to include surrounding villages and communities. Each of these districts has a political head (*Bezirksvorsteher*), and a district assembly (*Bezirksvertretung*). Nicholas Parsons describes the city as an "agglutination of villages (known as *Vororte*, and lying outside the *Gürtel* or Ring Road) and suburbs with distinctive identities (*Vorstädte*), lying between the Gürtel and the Ringstrasse" (Parsons, 2009, p. xvii).

Being the capital city, Vienna houses the federal parliament, the head of state, the federal government, and the highest courts. It is no surprise then that Vienna is Austria's largest city and cultural and economic hub. In fact, Vienna accounts for over a quarter of Austria's GDP. This capital-city status would suggest ties with economic, political and military power brokers. However, since the 1920s, the city-state has won the nickname 'Red Vienna,' as it consistently voted for social welfare reforms. Even before World War I, Viennese politics were dominated by Christian and democratic social political parties. In particular, the Social Democratic Party (*Sozialdemokratische Partei Österreichs*, SP), previously (from 1888 to 1945) the Social Democratic Workers' Party of Austria (*Sozialdemokratische Arbeiterpartei Österreichs*, SDAPÖ), and a member of the Labour and Socialist International from 1923-1940, has been able to hold a majority of seats in the Vienna city council and govern alone for most of the 20th century. 'Red Vienna' became a socialist enclave within a conservative nation (Pelinka, 2005).

In summary, statehood would allow urban agglomerations to have more tailor-made economic policies to the end of elevating them to 'alpha' cities. Statehood would also allow for more stability in governance. Because rural areas vote almost always for conservative candidates, separating urban amalgamations would allow for more stable, more strategic, policy options, including those relating to the economy.

Current local government law envisages state administrative control over city-regions regardless of their varying capacities and competencies. For example, local government law in the United States simply decentralizes power by moving its location without reshaping the nature of the relationship between central and local governments (Frug, 1999, p. 10). To be precise, there has been real limits to local (financial) autonomy as evidenced by increasing fiscal dependence on central governments and less policy discretion over resources (Caulfield & Larsen, 2002). The legal conception today is that "cities are governmental bodies with delegated powers created and limited by the authority of state governments" (Frug, 1980). Cities have only powers delegated to them by state governments, and even these powers have traditionally been severely limited by the courts. In fact, the US Supreme Court has excessively emphasized the absolute power states have over cities.[3] The rationale for this approach stems from two main arguments. The first enlists the complexity of today's world, with its large-scale organizations, to evidence the impossibility of decentralizing power to cities. A related second argument sets up the sovereign city as a selfish entity that cannot be trusted to exercise unsupervised power. City power is feared for it strangles capitalism by a maze of local regulations, and frustrates national political objectives by parochial agendas. City discretion invokes images of corruption and even foolishness. Both arguments allude to a necessity of the powerlessness of cities—a necessity that Tocqueville, Marx, and Hegel identified as a cornerstone of government policies in the democratic era (Arendt, 1965, pp. 113-115).

Both arguments are flawed. The first for misunderstanding the nature of the complexity involved (Gussen, 2012), the second for conflating the concept of legal empowerment (as a form of bounded autonomy) with that of sovereignty (Golub, 2006, 2010). Increasing people's control over their lives is not tantamount to prohibiting control from other stakeholders. This conflation harks back to an already archaic formulation of sovereignty where it exhibits an abstract absolute, or to a formulation that envisages a division of sovereignty (as under federalism), rather than a sharing of sovereignty (as under *hypotaxis,* see below). As discussed in Gussen (2013), sovereignty is a *relational* construct that envisages sharing sovereignty, which in turn means organizing jurisdictions on a small scale. On the other hand, ensuring city-regions are the primary unit of political organization also forces cities to take regional considerations into account.

It was 20th-century liberalism that brought about the current powerlessness of cities. Liberalism, with its model of the world as dualities, saw participatory democracy on a small scale like the city-region as unworkable. Cities with real power were intermediate structures between the state and the individual. Through legal doctrine, liberalism proceeded to eliminate this intermediate structure and replace it with powerless, coercive instruments of the state (Frug, 1980, pp. 1074-1080).

The 'connectivity' we see today between 'world cities' under processes of globalization has been the norm for 'world systems' throughout history. For example, the world-system that existed between 1250 and 1350 was an 'archipelago' of 'world cities' (Abu-Lughod, 1989, p. 353). An earlier example at the beginning of the Common Era was the system where cities in the Roman Empire, the Han Empire, and India dominated world commerce, although this system had a much lower level of interaction between these constituent parts. An important insight from this world-system 'archipelago' is its cyclical emergence and collapse, largely through fluctuations in population levels (due to pandemics, wars, or even 'social engineering') where emphasis swings between rural and urban centers, or between immigrant and indigenous populations. World systems rise when economic integration increases, sometimes driven by military might; and collapse when connections along older pathways increase—— although collapse does not necessarily return the world to the *status quo ante*.

In 1915 one scholar commenting on the unsatisfactory governance structures for cities within US states was inspired by the German federal system to ask the following question: "Why should we not look forward to the entire separation of metropolitan cities such as New York, Chicago, and Philadelphia from state ties, and their erection into free city commonwealths within our federal system?" adding that "Hamburg, Bremen and Lübeck ... are splendid examples of municipal progress and self-development in freedom" (Brooks, 1915, pp. 230-231). While his proposal would have been deemed unconstitutional, if only because it would have been perceived to advocate secession, the real issue—not addressed by this scholar—is how to design a governance structure that would pave the way to such constitutional reality. Instead of statehood, such cities could be given their *sui generis* status as charter cities. Not in the way this term is understood in California today, but as it has been used historically, for example, in cities like Philadelphia.

City power is again on the ascendancy. Today we can discern a move towards empowering cities on two fronts: one is domestic, where there is constitutional recognition of city-regions as co-equal to federal and state governments through the development of what is known as the 'doctrine of usurpation of jurisdiction' (Humby, 2012). This approach emphasizes *the principle of hypotaxis* (see below) where general competence powers are extended to city-regions (Caulfield & Larsen, 2002). The second front is international, where there is an emerging field of law that acknowledges city-regions as independent international actors. While international law has long had an *indirect* impact on cities, now there is an emerging trend where cities are becoming distinct international actors almost co-equal to their nation-states. International law is enlarging the nation-state club that dominated its institutions since their emergence, to admit city-regions, mainly through regulating the relationship between cities and their nation-states.

The traditional approach for creating legal frameworks to govern city-regions, namely local government law, has been through domestic instruments. The main objective of such rules, under the classic doctrine of state responsibility, was to prevent exposing (sovereign) nation-states to liability under international law for the conduct of their subnational governments (that are not directly obligated to comply with international law). Traditionally, international law bestowed a legal personality only on sovereign nation-states (with a few exceptions). A key requirement for recognition being that the political entity has no government above it. This resulted in strict domestic regulation of subnational governments (Frug & Barron, 2006, p. 18).

The traditional approach where local government is an administrative division of the state is now being replaced by an approach, driven largely by globalization, where international institutions redefine the scope of domestic frameworks. This has come to be known as 'International Local Government Law,' a hitherto uncodified interdisciplinary field that draws on comparative urban governance (which focuses on domestic rules) as well as on the 'world cities' hypothesis which highlights the impact of economic forces in shaping 'world-systems' (Frug & Barron, 2006, p. 2).[4] Unlike these other disciplines, however, international local government law emphasizes the dual legal nature of city-regions as both subnational governments and as independent international actors. This emerging field would determine both, who should regulate the legal framework for city-regions and the nature of that framework. Examples of this approach include decisions by international arbitration tribunals regulating cities' land use. This international framework envisages (at least tentatively) empowering cities "principally as a mechanism for promoting private economic development" (Frug & Barron, 2006, p. 4).

International instruments such as the United Nations International Covenant on Civil and Political Rights (ICCPR) and the International Convention on

Economic, Social and Cultural Rights (ICESCR), *inter alia*, are altering the relationship between cities and nation-states. City-regions are becoming "nodal points for radially distinct governance projects that have their common goal to transform cities from mere subdivisions of sovereign states into legally empowered entities, able to advance goals and values that are different from their states" (Blank, 2005-2006, p. 899).

In summary, this section argues that the 'creation' of global cities does not need time on an evolutionary scale. Such cities can be created in one generation, provided these cities are given political and economic independence. The envisaged level of autonomy can be bestowed through charters, not very different from the one Charles II of England granted to William Penn in 1681 for what later became the city of Philadelphia. The next section outlines the constitutional vehicle for delivering such charters in the 21st century.

THE PRINCIPLE OF HYPOTAXIS[5]

The origins of the principle of hypotaxis could be traced back to ancient Greece (Brennan, 2014), if not even all the way back to the Sumerian city-states (Gussen, 2013; Gussen, 2014; Gussen, 2015a, 2015b, 2015c). Hypotaxis entails the following decision rule: as much freedom as possible, as much state as necessary (Dölken, 2013, p. 3). Put differently, the principle envisages so much expertise in the ever-smaller social units as possible, and as much competence for ever larger social units as necessary (Dölken, 2013, pp. 3-4). Hypotaxis is hence an analytical principle to decide the optimal size for political, legal, and social organization, although it has a legal presumption in favor of smaller community units (Dölken, 2013, p. 8). Some suggest however that the fundamental purpose of the principle is "to reinforce the right of local government to take the first legislative action" (Bayer, 2003, p. 1459). These different representations of hypotaxis are reconcilable when the principle is understood as both a principle for constitutional design and a principle of sharing power between various entities.

The rationale for the principle is both economic and ethical. The core of hypotaxis is a heuristic (economic) efficiency rule (Portuese, 2010). From an 'institutional economics' perspective, hypotaxis can be reconstituted as the following decision rule (Dölken, 2013): an institution is to be established if and only if the cost of their construction is lower than the benefits associated with it. The fact that can be inferred from this rule is that there is an optimal size for political organization and that hypotaxis is the principle that attempts to define that size.

Notwithstanding a number of different renditions of the principle, it is dominated by a 'state-centric' approach (Føllesdal, 2014a), due to the current world-system that is difficult to combine plausibly with non-Westphalian renditions of sovereignty——such as that of Baruch Spinoza (Gussen, 2013) (see Chapter VII). The main renditions of hypotaxis can be represented vis-à-vis state authority as shown in Figure 4. Here an 'organizational units' represents a pre-existing social structure that mediates between the individual and higher orders of organization. These higher orders include the family, the church, and the city. In other words, the renditions that are most in favor of *individual* freedom (under a nation-state) are those further to the left in Figure 4. As we move from left to right (in Figure 4), the rendition becomes more territorial—here hypotaxis does not only defend non-territorial entities such as the individual, the family, or the church, but more importantly territorial organisations such as cities or regions (at the subnational level), and even supra-national organisations such as the European Union. For an elaboration of these versions, and their advantages and disadvantages, refer to Føllesdal (2013). One point worth emphasizing about hypotaxis is that it conflicts with the welfare state (Zimmermann, 2014). The principle envisages a plurality of orders that consists of different realms of governance, which is pragmatically a 'red line' under the welfare state.

The principle of hypotaxis is related to a number of similar principles. Salient among these is the principle of subsidiarity in modern Catholic social doctrine. Another related structural principle is known as 'spheres of sovereignty,' which comes from Calvinist teachings as opposed to the Catholic origins of (modern) subsidiarity. Some suggest that the two principles are complementary (Zimmermann, 2014). Others point to their differences,

Figure 4. Main renditions of hypotaxis relative to increasing authority of the political state

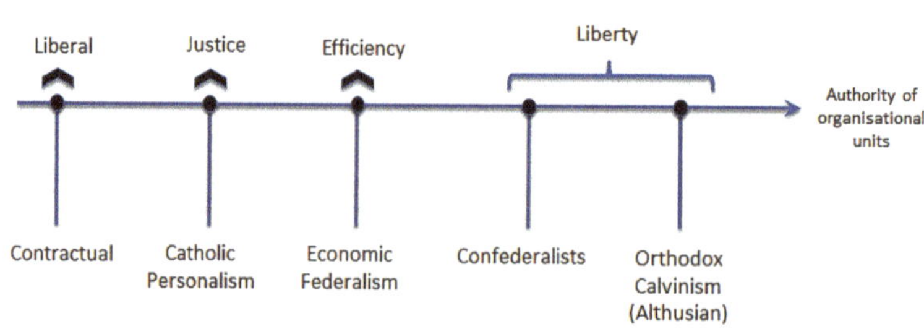

especially that subsidiarity is about hierarchy, while spheres of sovereignty are about process (Evans, 2012, p. 90). It is also constructive to contrast hypotaxis with the principle of 'competence catalogs.' The latter is predicated on two doctrines: supremacy and preemption (Kirchner, 1997, p. 76). Another related principle is the 'auxilium principle' which interprets hypotaxis as only one of the modes through which there is 'auxilium' between the individual and nested levels of government. Other modes include the 'fiduciary principle' (Gussen, 2015c). Others have also used the concept of auxilium, but in a different context, namely to distinguish between hypotaxis which applies to a social whole, and an auxilium principle that applies between different social wholes (Ermercke, 1976). If we superimpose the concept of sovereignty on the 'social whole' we can integrate these principles as seen in Figure 5.

Within a given sphere of sovereignty (from the Calvinist conception), we can discern the operation of the principles of subsidiarity (the Catholic conception) and solidarity,[6] within what Ermercke (1976) calls a social whole (*sozialen Ganzen*). Under this construction, the state is seen as a moral organism (whole) analogous to a physical organism (e.g. the human body).

Some also suggest that there are only minor differences between hypotaxis (especially its subsidiarity rendition) and federalism (Evans, 2012, p. 126). Jordan and Jeppesen (2000, p. 66) suggest that hypotaxis is the defining feature of federalism. However, hypotaxis should be seen as a principle that encompasses federalism. In other words, federalism is a subset of hypotaxis.

Figure 5. The relationship between subsidiarity, spheres of sovereignty and auxilium

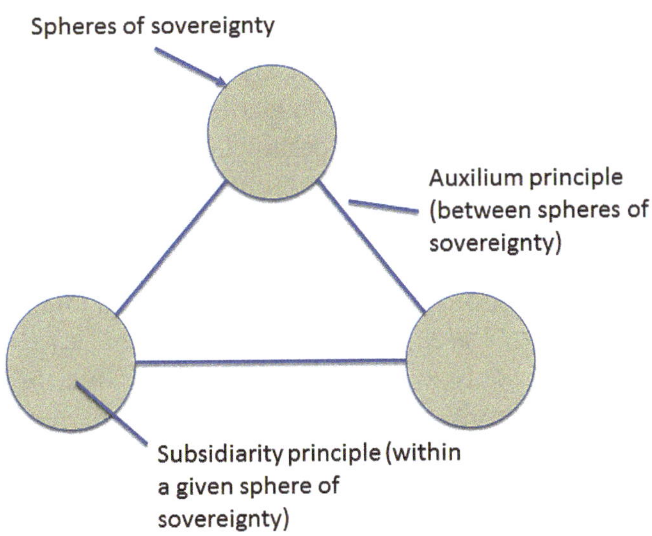

Federalism is about dividing powers, which is only one modality through which we can share powers as stipulated for by the principle of hypotaxis (Gussen, 2013; Gussen, 2014; Gussen, 2015b).

It is the ethical rationale that differentiates hypotaxis from centralization. Hypotaxis is understood as legal decentralization (Portuese, 2010), but is intended to ensure a moral principle guaranteeing free will to everyone, namely human dignity (Martinez de Anguita, Martín, & Clare, 2013). It is the equity criterion that differentiates hypotaxis from decentralization. In a sense, hypotaxis integrates efficiency and equity in a way similar to that championed by Albert Einstein in his special and general relativity theories. Instead of using space and time as separate constructs, Einstein understood them as dimensions of the same construct. Similarly, Hypotaxis represents efficiency and equity as one construct: efficiency-equity. Hypotaxis ensures that the calculus of efficiency is always weaved into that of equity. This approach is hugely different from what we have come to be accustomed to under traditional approaches to law-and-economics, and to neo-classical economics generally.

The principle of hypotaxis is both, a *prima facie* rule of intuitive thinking (the heuristic principle), and a methodological principle of critical thinking (the methodological principle) (Dölken, 2013). Hypotaxis has three core functions (Føllesdal, 2013): (1) to regulate the allocation of powers within political or legal order, (2) to structure the debate on the distribution of powers between various organisational scales (local, national, and global), and (3) to serve as a normative 'constitutional principle' to justify state authority. Melé suggests nine attributes to hypotaxis (Melé, 2005, pp. 300-301): (1) the principle arises from the concept that humans are endowed with reason and freedom; (2) the principle has a close ethical content; (3) hypotaxis has to be considered with other ethical principles: solidarity, authority, and participation; (4) hypotaxis has to be applied considering all the relevant circumstances in a situation;[7] (5) the principle stipulates that whatever could be done by an inferior social group should not be absorbed by a superior organisational group; (6) the principle also states that initiatives by individuals and groups must contribute to the good of the whole community; (7) under hypotaxis, people and inferior social groups should do as much as they can; (8) while superior entities have a duty to favour the initiatives of inferior groups; and last, (9) the principle requires that if an individual or an inferior group cannot perform a necessary activity, even if provided with appropriate help, then the superior group can and ought to carry out the activity.

The principle of hypotaxis, *qua* subsidiarity, has been one of the legal, political and philosophical pillars of the European Union since the 1990s (Jordan & Jeppesen, 2000; Evans, 2012, p. 115). The economic rationale, in particular, is seen to flow through the 2007 Lisbon Treaty (Føllesdal, 2014b). Under Article 5(3) of the Treaty of the European Union (TEU), subsidiarity is interconnected to two other principles: (1) The principle of proportionality, and (2) the principle of attributed EU competencies (De Búrca, 1998). After the Amsterdam Treaty, the legal test applied by the European Court of Justice (ECJ) is 'comparative efficiency,' and has two criteria: (1) efficiency scale or effects, and (2) closeness to the citizen. However, the Amsterdam Protocol stressed that subsidiarity in the EU context does not affect the existence of powers, but their exercise (De Búrca, 1998, p. 219). In essence, after Amsterdam, the European Court of Justice (ECJ) changed its methodology from one of teleology of integration to one of teleology of subsidiarity. The purpose of ECJ intervention is subsidiarity rather than integration *per se.* Note, however, that there remain issues with using subsidiarity as a basis for judicial review (de Sadeleer, 2012; Evans, 2012).

The principle of hypotaxis provides the economic and ethical rationale for bestowing charters on cities. As a legal principle, hypotaxis informs the coordination between vertical levels of government. The principle could enable the US Federal Government to legislate for new charters given to cities on the verge of becoming global cities, and given to global cities who are hoping to improve their rankings. Take Salt Lake City as an example. The city is currently classified as a 'sufficiency city.' To move Salt Lake City into a Gamma classification, what is needed is not more investment or immigration. What is needed is changing the legal personality of the city to a charter city, with a wide autonomy on economic and political matters. This change enables the city to reach a global status. The evolutionary alternative could prove to be too late given the fast-paced changes in the world-system today.

CODA

For the United States to increase its economic efficiency, it needs to perforate the jurisdictional footprints of existing states by empowering cities. The historical perspective (on the legal personality of cities) helps explain what I mean by an 'empowered' city. The best definition of empowerment is the 'global city,' namely a city that has a direct effect on global affairs (Sassen, 2001). Such cities exhibit a level of infrastructure concentration that enables them to influence global processes (Sassen, 1995, p. 63). This is the best definition (of empowerment) because it allows for a multi-disciplinary approach to 'empowering' cities, rather than the already largely discredited neo-classical approach of growth theory. Such cities are also known as 'world cities' that function as the "organizing nodes of a global economic system" (Friedmann 1995, p. 25),[8] defined by dense patterns of interaction between people, goods, and information (Keeling 1995, p. 115). Such cities are always linked in a single network (Smith & Timberlake 1995, pp. 80 and 88),[9] sometimes referred to as a 'world-system,' which sharpens the competition between them (Friedmann 1995, p. 32). The spatial dispersion of economic activities and the global integration has contributed to the strategic role of these cities in the current world-system (Sassen 1997, p. 19).

The principle of hypotaxis can empower American cities. By using this principle as a guiding constitutional principle for the relations between vertical levels of government, and by giving cities (constitutional) charters, the US can accelerate the creation of more attractors, especially in states identified as economically inefficient. In the next chapter, this hypotactic vision is delineated for political state in the 21st century.

REFERENCES

Abu-Lughod, J. L. (1989). *Before European hegemony: The world system A.D. 1250-1350*. Oxford: Oxfrod University Press.

Arendt, H. (1965). *On revolution*. New York: Penguin Books.

Bayer, J. (2003). Re-balancing state and federal power: Toward a political principle of subsidiarity in the United States. *The American University Law Review*, *53*, 1421–1472.

Beauregard, R. A. (1995). Theorizing the global-local connection. In P. L. Knox & P. J. Taylor (Eds.), *World cites in a world system* (pp. 232–248). Cambridge: Cambridge University Press. doi:10.1017/CBO9780511522192.014

Blank, Y. (2005-2006). The city and the world. *Columbia Journal of Transnational Law*, *44*, 875–939.

Brennan, P. M. (2014). Subsidiarity in the tradition of catholic social doctrine. In M. Evans & A. Zimmermann (Eds.), *Global perspectives on subsidiarity* (pp. 29–47). Dordrecht: Springer. doi:10.1007/978-94-017-8810-6_3

Brooks, R. C. (1915). Metropolitan free cities. *Political Science Quarterly, 30*(2), 222–234. doi:10.2307/2141920

Caulfield, J., & Larsen, H. O. (Eds.). (2002). *Local government at the millenium*. Opladen: Springer. doi:10.1007/978-3-663-10679-1

De Búrca, G. (1998). The principle of subsidiarity and the Court of Justice as an institutional actor. *Journal of Common Market Studies, 36*(2), 217–235. doi:10.1111/1468-5965.00107

de Sadeleer, N. (2012). Principle of subsidiarity and the EU environmental policy. *Journal for European Environmental & Planning Law, 9*(2), 63–70. doi:10.1163/187601012X632256

Derham, D. P. (1958). Theories of legal personality. In L. C. Webb (Ed.), *Legal personality and political pluralism* (pp. 1–19). Melbourne: Melbourne University Press.

Dölken, C. (2013). Subsidiarität und institutionenökonomik. Zu einer sozialtheoretischen und –ethischen präzisierung des subsidiaritätsprinzips. *Jahrbuch für Christliche Sozialwissenschaften, 54*. Online-Supplement. Retrieved from http://www.unimuenster.de/Ejournals/index.php/jcsw/article/view/656/pdf

Dollery, B. (2009). *Local government amalgamation. Centre for Local Government, School of Business, Economics and Public Policy*. University of New England.

Ermercke, G. (1976). Subsidiarität und auxiliarität in staat und kirche. *Jahrbuch für Christliche Sozialwissenschaften, 17*, 81–90.

Evans, M. (2012). *The use of the principle of subsidiarity in the reformation of Australia's federal system of govenment (PhD)*. Perth: Curtin University.

Føllesdal, A. (2013). The Principle of subsidiarity as a constitutional principle in international law. *Global Constitutionalism, 2*(1), 37–62. doi:10.1017/S2045381712000123

Føllesdal, A. (2014a). *Competing conceptions of subsidiarity. Nomos LV: Federalism and Subsidiarity* (pp. 214–230). New York: New York University Press. doi:10.18574/nyu/9781479868858.003.0007

Føllesdal, A. (2014b). Subsidiarity and the global order. In A. Zimmerman & M. Evans (Eds.), *Global perspectives on subsidiarity* (pp. 207–220). Dordrecht: Springer. doi:10.1007/978-94-017-8810-6_11

Friedmann, J. (1995). Where we stand: A decade of world city research. In P. L. Knox & P. J. Taylor (Eds.), *World cities in a world system* (pp. 21–48). Cambridge: Cambridge University Press. doi:10.1017/CBO9780511522192.003

Friedrichs, C. R. (1981). The Swiss and German city-states. In R. Griffeth & C. G. Thomas (Eds.), *The city-state in five cultures* (pp. 109–142). Santa Barbra, CA: ABC Clio.

Frug, G. E. (1980). The city as a legal concept. *Harvard Law Review*, *93*(6), 1057–1154. doi:10.2307/1340702

Frug, G. E. (1999). *City making: Building communities without building walls*. Princeton: Princeton University Press.

Frug, G. E., & Barron, D. J. (2006). International local government law. *The Urban Lawer*, *38*(1), 1–62.

Glaeser, E. (Ed.). (2010). *Agglomeration economics*. Chicago: University of Chicago. doi:10.7208/chicago/9780226297927.001.0001

Glaeser, E. (2011). *Triumph of the city*. New York: Penguin Press.

Golub, S. (2006). *The legal empowerment alternative. Promoting the rule of law abroad: In search of knowledge*. Washington, DC: Carnegie Endowment for International Peace.

Golub, S. (2010). What is legal empowerment? An introduction. In *Legal Empowerment: Practitioners' Perspectives* (pp. 9–18).

Griffeth, R., & Thomas, C. G. (Eds.). (1981). *The city-state in five cultures*. Santa Barbra, CA: ABC Clio.

Gussen, B. F. (2012). The marginalisation of localism in the current response to the ecological crisis. *New Zealand Journal of Environmental Law*, *16*, 167–201.

Gussen, B. F. (2013). On the problem of scale: Spinozistic sovereignty as the logical foundation of constitutional economics. *The Journal of Philosophical Economics*, *7*(1), 1–19.

Gussen, B. F. (2014). Subsidiarity as a constitutional principle in New Zealand. *New Zealand Journal of Public and International Law*, *12*(1), 123–144.

Gussen, B. F. (2015a). Is subsidiarity a *conditio sine qua non* for sustainability? *Policy Studies*, *36*(4), 384–398. doi:10.1080/01442872.2015.1073244

Gussen, B. F. (2015b). On the problem of scale: The inextricable link between environmental and constitutional laws. *New Zealand Journal of Public and International Law*, *13*(1), 39.

Gussen, B. F. (2015c). The state is the fiduciary of the people. *Public Law*, *3*, 440.

Hager, M. M. (1988). Bodies politic: The progressive history of organizational real entity theory. *U. Pitt. L. Rev.*, *50*, 575.

Hallis, F. (1930). *Corporate personality: A study of jurisprudence*. Oxford: Oxford University Press.

Hamburg. (2011). *Hamburg's cluster policy: Reaching the top together*. Hamburg Ministry of Economics, Transport and Innovation.

Humby, T. (2012). Maccsand: Intergovernmental relations and the doctrine of usurpation. *South African Public Law Journal*, *27*(2), 628–638.

Jordan, A., & Jeppesen, T. (2000). EU environmental policy: Adapting to the principle of subsidiarity? *European Environment*, *10*(2), 64–74. doi:10.1002/(SICI)1099-0976(200003/04)10:2<64::AID-EET219>3.0.CO;2-Z

Jurisdiction. In (2004). *Black's law dictionary* (8th ed.). New York: West Publishing.

Keeling, D. J. (1995). Transport and the world city paradigm. In P. L. Knox & P. J. Taylor (Eds.), *World cities in a world system* (pp. 115–131). Cambridge: Cambridge University Press. doi:10.1017/CBO9780511522192.008

King, A. D. (1995). Re-presenting world cities: Cultural theory/social practice. In P. L. Knox & P. J. Taylor (Eds.), *World cities in a world-system* (pp. 215–231). Cambridge: Cambridge University Press. doi:10.1017/CBO9780511522192.013

Kirchner, C. (1997). Competence catalogues and the principle of subsidiarity in a European constitution. *Constitutional Political Economy*, *8*(1), 71–87. doi:10.1023/A:1009042106028

Klabbers, J. (2005). The concept of legal personality. *Ius Gentium*, *11*, 35–66.

Maitland, F. M. (1900). *Introduction to Gierke's political theories of the Middle Ages*. Cambridge: Cambridge University Press.

Martinez de Anguita, P., Martín, M. Á., & Clare, A. (2013). Environmental subsidiarity as a guiding principle for forestry governance: Application to payment for ecosystem services and REDD+ architecture. *Journal of Agricultural & Environmental Ethics*, *27*(4), 617–631. doi:10.1007/s10806-013-9481-8

Marx, G. T. (1997). The declining significance of traditional borders. In P. Droege (Ed.), *Intelligent environments: Spatial aspects of the Information Revolution* (pp. 484–493). Amsterdam: Elsevier. doi:10.1016/B978-044482332-8/50027-5

Melé, D. (2005). Exploring the principle of subsidiarity in organisational forms. *Journal of Business Ethics*, *60*(3), 293–305. doi:10.1007/s10551-005-0136-1

Mercer. (2015). *Mercer 2015 quality of living rannkings*. Retrieved March 7, 2017, from http://www.uk.mercer.com/newsroom/2015-quality-of-living-survey.html

Mumford, L. (1961). *The city in histroy: Its origins, its transformations, and its prospects*. London: Harcourt.

Nijman, J. E. (2004). *The concept of international legal personality: An inquiry into the history and theory of international law*. The Hague: TMC Asser Press. doi:10.1007/978-90-6704-701-2

Ottino, J. M. (2003). Complex Systems. *American Institute of Chemical Engineers*, *49*(2), 292–299. doi:10.1002/aic.690490202

Parsons, N. (2009). *Vienna: A cultural history*. Oxford: Oxford University Press.

Paton, G. W. (1973). A textbook of jurisprudence (G. W. Paton & D. P. Derham Eds., 4th ed.). Oxford: Oxford University Press.

Pelinka, P. (2005). *Eine kurze geschichte der SPÖ. Ereignisse, persönlichkeiten, jahreszahlen*. Vienna: Ueberreuter.

Portuese, A. (2010). The principle of subsidiarity as a principle of economic efficiency. *Columbia Journal of European Law*, *17*, 231.

Redak, V., Novy, A., & Becker, J. (2005). Modernizing or polarizing Vienna? In F. Moulaert, A. Rodriguez, & E. Swyngedouw (Eds.), *The globalized city: Economic restructuring and social polarization in European cities* (pp. 167–180). Oxford: Oxford University Press.

Sassen, S. (1995). On concentration and centrality in the global city. In P. L. Knox & P. J. Taylor (Eds.), *World cities in a world system* (pp. 63–75). Cambridge: Cambridge University Press. doi:10.1017/CBO9780511522192.005

Sassen, S. (1997). The new centrality: The impact of telematics and globalization. In P. Droege (Ed.), *Intelligent environments: Spatial aspects of the information revolution* (pp. 19–27). Amsterdam: Elsevier. doi:10.1016/B978-044482332-8/50004-4

Sassen, S. (2001). *The global city: New York, London, Tokyo*. Princeton: University Press Princeton. doi:10.1515/9781400847488

Sennett, R. (Ed.). (1969). *Classic essays on the culture of cities*. Englewood Cliffs, NJ: Prentice-Hall.

Smith, D. A., & Timberlake, M. (1995). Cities in global matrices: Toward mapping the world-system's city system. In P. L. Knox & P. J. Taylor (Eds.), *World cities in a world-system* (pp. 79–97). Cambridge: Cambridge University Press. doi:10.1017/CBO9780511522192.006

Spengler, O. (1969). The soul of the city. In R. Sennett (Ed.), *Classic essays on the culture of cities* (pp. 61–88). Englewood Cliffs, NJ: Prentice-Hall.

Taylor, P. (1995). World cities and territorial states: The rise and fall of their mutuality. In P. L. Knox & P. J. Taylor (Eds.), *World cites in a world system* (pp. 48–62). Cambridge: Cambridge University Press. doi:10.1017/CBO9780511522192.004

Weber, M. (1969). The nature of the city. In R. Sennett (Ed.), *Classic essays on the culture of cities* (pp. 23–46). Englewood Cliffs, NJ: Prentice-Hall.

Zimmermann, A. (2014). Subsidiarity and a free society. *Policy*, *30*(4), 15–18.

ENDNOTES

1 This was a necessary but not sufficient condition. Other conditions such as location and resource endowment would have also mattered.

2 Although some were created by proto-governments or groups of elites that were akin to governments.

3 See for example *Hunter v City of Pittsburgh* (1907) 207 US 161, 178-179, cited in Frug (1999, p. 17).

4 Although Frug and Barron suggest that international local government law "should not be evaluated in terms of whether the world is enhancing or limiting local power. The focus instead should be on the kinds of cities that international local government law is trying to create" (Frug & Barron, 2006, pp. 3, 60-61), this author argues that international local government law enables city-regions to become *independent* international actors (as stated by Frug and Barron on page 2), which would make sense only if we empower them to act in such capacity. This author suggests that international local government law does in fact empower city-regions rather than simply making cities creatures of international statutes rather than domestic ones.

5 This is a legal version of the rules of grammar that govern the modalities of coordination among clauses within grammatically complex sentences.

6 Solidarity operates 'horizontally', that is to say it applies within a sphere of sovereignty and between groups at the same organisational scale (e.g. between inferior groups). It requires horizontal coordination among groups. In contrast, subsidiarity is about vertical coordination between groups that belong to different organisational scales.

7 In essence, hypotaxis is a principle of reflection rather than a mechanical rule.

8 The term 'world city' or 'weltstadt' can in fact be traced back to the Johann Wolfgang von Goethe who used it to refer to the cultural eminence of Paris and Rome. See King (1995, p. 219).

9 A network is a system of nodes with connecting links. The network that cities form has a particular type of topology called 'scale-free topology' which refers to the distribution principle of how many links there are per any given node in the network. These networks follow a power law distribution and hence are scale invariant. See Ottino (2003, p. 296).

Chapter 6
The Political State

ABSTRACT

This chapter advocates for a paradigm shift. Its main critique problematizes the scale invariance that permeates economics (both orthodox and heterodox). Just like Newtonian gravitation, economics assumes that the relationships defining any given system, both internally and in relation to the environment, do not change when that system undergoes any dilation. In other words, no matter how large or small the system becomes, economics assumes that the laws governing its dynamics do not change. One example comes from using homogeneous production functions to ensure the scale invariance of growth models. In contrast, in physics, we know that there is a characteristic scale dictated by constants such as the speed of light or the Planck length. As objects reach that limit, the Newtonian model would no longer be valid. Economics due to its scale-invariance, furnishes public policy prescriptions that engender such scale distortions.

INTRODUCTION

An earlier version of this chapter appeared in *Constitutional Political Economy*. See Gussen (2013). The observation that economics is scale-invariant is not new.[2] Anecdotally, James Buchanan, the father of constitutional political economy, used to invite his students to reflect on what would happen to a fly if we were to increase its size ten times. Would it still be able to fly? This problematization of scale invariance, however, has not been generalized. This

DOI: 10.4018/978-1-5225-2756-5.ch006

chapter takes the above 'imperial' critique and applies it to the political state. As discussed below, this leads to advocacy for local autonomy, especially through the resurrection of free city-regions. The chapter is hence part of the literature on localism and urban economics, with a constitutional anchor. In this sense, it belongs to (normative) constitutional political economy.

The chapter's main thesis is that societal crises are manifestations of 'the problem of scale.' Through scale distortion or scale entanglement or both, society's cyclical fluctuations inevitably result in collapse. 'Scale distortion' is when the relative size of societies (dynamic systems generally) grows to a critical level that precipitates crisis. This is related to population and jurisdiction growth. 'Scale entanglement' is what results from strong modalities of integration (including innovation). Globalization—at least the top-down approach espoused by nation-states—is the archetype of such entanglement. To prevent this outcome, scale has to be corrected downwards. This can be done only if the state is reinvented as subsidiary to autonomous city-regions of limited jurisdictional footprint.

There are six parts to this chapter. The first furnishes an ansatz explaining the problem of scale. The next three parts follow closely the ansatz in section one. Section two zeros in on the link between symmetry breaking and the production of scale. Section three focuses on the second link between the production of scale and complexity, while section four establishes the link between increased complexity and collapse. Section five elaborates on the central idea that autonomous city-regions, characterized by small jurisdictional footprints, mitigate the possibility of collapse. Section six provides some concluding remarks.

A DIAGNOSTIC ANSATZ

This section introduces the 'complexity ansatz,' a framework that integrates different analytical constructs into a smaller set of only four variables, namely symmetry (breaking), scale, complexity, and collapse. Figure 1 is a vignette constituting the problem of scale. The ansatz is built on four core concepts: symmetry, scale, complexity and collapse. Each concept has a technical meaning and their essential features are described following.

'Symmetry' is simply "immunity to a possible change" (Rosen, 1995, p. 2); it is the essence of equilibrium. Symmetry freezes degrees of freedom.

Figure 1. The complexity ansatz

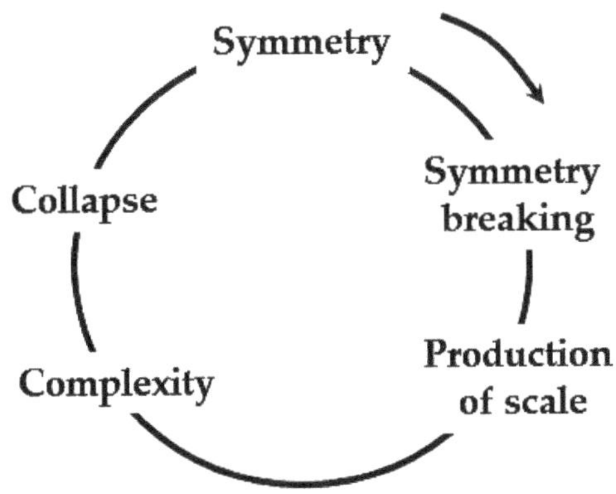

For example, "local symmetry … implies that certain degrees of freedom are absent" (de Wit and Smith, 1986, p. 590). More generally, 'homogeneity' denotes symmetry. Often 'homogeneity' is a form of local symmetry in that it can occur in a system that does not exhibit global symmetry.

When systems have symmetry, "there is a good chance that the symmetry may break. When it does, very tiny asymmetries play a crucial role in selecting the actual outcome from a range of potential outcomes" (Stewart and Golubitsky, 1992, p. 17). Symmetry is broken due to instabilities. When symmetry (*qua* equilibrium) is 'lost' due to instabilities, random fluctuations can trigger a symmetry-breaking 'bifurcation.' If the instabilities are endogenous to the system, symmetry breaking is said to be spontaneous—a natural sequence of internal instability. If instabilities are exogenous, symmetry breaking is said to be induced (from the environment). The division of labor is the symmetry-breaking anchor in the writings of Friedrich Hayek, Leopold Kohr and Jane Jacobs (HKJ). However, this does not mean that it is the only symmetry-breaking mechanism in economics.[3]

While symmetry is an ontological concept (related to existence), 'scale' is predominantly an epistemological phantasmagoria (related to our knowledge of symmetry and more generally to information).[4] Symmetry is independent of our knowledge of it (through an observer). In contrast, scale depends on the way an observer can describe spatial and temporal relationships among distinct entities. Scale is the proportionality (relationship) of parts (to themselves and to their environment) as perceived by an observer and is produced through symmetry breaking. We elucidate this interpretation of scale using the discourse in HKJ.

Symmetry breaking in the form of division of labor creates another dimension to society: interaction among different types of agents. This interaction gives society (system) an (holistic) identity. 'Complexity' arises from this interaction. In this sense, complexity is simply the operational ramification of scale production. Complexity to scale is what force is to momentum: scale is the relational field; complexity is the change of that field with (space) time.

However, to produce scale, asymmetry first needs to be introduced. It follows that by breaking symmetry—for example, through the division of labor—we are 'compensating' for the loss of symmetry by increased interaction among the resulting different agent types. Complexity, and the produced scale on which it operates, is simply compensating for lost symmetry. In other words, by breaking symmetry, or unfreezing some degrees of freedom, a system gains structure. As the dialectic between symmetry and symmetry breaking continues, the system becomes fractal: it evolves a structure at every scale. This structure manifests itself in spatial and temporal complexity.

What is essential for our discussion is the impact of how scale is produced on the nature of temporal complexity and, eventually, on the tendency of systems to collapse. Strong links that emerge among elements (or subsystems) are one form of scale production. Such tight coupling in dynamical systems results in chaotic behavior. Alternatively, if systems are coupled neither too tightly nor too loosely they will have 'complex attractors' that enhance their robustness (Marion 1999).

As to collapsc, important insights can be gleaned from the reliability theory of ageing and longevity. In this theory, 'redundancy exhaustion' is at the center of collapse, both for machines and organisms (Gavrilov and Gavrilova 2004). From another angle, collapse signifies relief from the complexity condition. A system with a high level of complexity will usually have more than one attractor. The interaction (coupling) of these attractors leads to a restoration of the symmetry that was originally 'lost.' Hence, after several stages of symmetry breaking, the symmetry is 'resurrected' by a series of symmetry-creating collisions of chaotic attractors. This symmetry creation destroys the (spatial and/or temporal) structure gained earlier through symmetry breaking.

Complex attractors are especially useful for understanding how collapse can be mitigated, as these attractors are largely immune to cascading damage (Marion, 1999, p. 157–158). Collapse in complex systems is a function of the level of coupling among subsystems or elements. The higher the level of coupling among the elements, the wider the effect of any sudden changes on the system as a whole (hence, collapse is globalized). Of course, with no coupling among the elements, there is no system; however, between these extremes, there is a region where a low level of coupling will localize the effects of collapse and provide a more robust system.[5] The key insight is that (Marion, 1999, p. 158–159):

When major cascading damage occurs [i.e. global collapse], we often look for outside causal forces, or we attribute the damage to simple causal events. According to Complexity Theory, cascading damage is more often the result of normal internal dynamics [i.e. ageing process] (Emphasis added).

We have now completed the introduction on symmetry, scale, complexity and collapse. The remainder of this Chapter will examine the writings of HKJ in relation to complexity to ascertain whether there are germinal arguments in support of the complexity ansatz outlined.

SYMMETRY BREAKING AND THE PRODUCTION OF SCALE

HKJ do not refer to 'symmetry' or 'symmetry breaking', but it can be shown that they discuss these concepts indirectly.

Hayekian Discourse

Hayek (1967, p. 25) defines 'complexity' in the following terms:

There seems to exist a fairly easy and adequate way to measure the degree of complexity of different kinds of abstract patterns. The minimum number of elements of which an instance of the pattern must consist in order to exhibit all the characteristic attributes of the class of patterns in question appears to provide an unambiguous criterion.

Earlier in the same chapter, 'The Theory of Complex Phenomena,' Hayek treats 'regularity,' 'recurring pattern,' and 'order' as synonyms. Moreover, he makes a link between 'patterns' and mathematics, in particular, geometry

(Hayek, 1967, p. 23–24). For Hayek, hierarchy is also associated with 'classes of patterns of a highly abstract character.' In everyday parlance, 'pattern' and 'symmetry' are used almost interchangeably (Stewart and Golubitsky, 1992, p. 2). Mathematicians use 'pattern' informally and reserve 'symmetry' for the more precise technical concept. Hayek seems also to use 'pattern' as a substitute for 'symmetry.' This is more evident when he links 'recurring pattern,' 'regularity,' and 'order.' In particular, Hayek seems to allude to temporal symmetry—the regularity that recurs through time.

Hayek's discourse on complexity in terms of order is synonymous with symmetry. He elaborates that from order 'we may learn from our acquaintance with some spatial or temporal section of the whole to form correct expectations concerning the rest' (Hayek, 1983, p. 35–36).[6] Hayek's 'order' and 'pattern' are hence synonymous with 'symmetry.' Moreover, Hayek's use of 'recurring patterns' as well as 'structure' suggests that he was alive to both temporal and spatial symmetry, respectively.

With regard to symmetry breaking, we need to look at the two types of 'order' that Hayek entertains. One is exogenous, producing made symmetry; the other is endogenous, resulting in spontaneous symmetry. These orders result from interaction between symmetry and symmetry breaking. The 'spontaneous' ('made') nature of 'spontaneous order' ('made order') signifies a form of symmetry breaking that is endogenous (exogenous) to the system, and that results in a new symmetry group. Another key mechanism through which symmetry is broken in Hayekian complexity is through interaction between these two types of order. This is where exogenous symmetry breaking induces endogenous symmetry breaking and vice versa (Hayek, 1983, p. 45).

Hayekian symmetry breaking can also be seen in the process of adaptation to the environment through abstraction (Hayek, 1978, pp. 48–49). Adaptation (symmetry breaking) results in abstraction ('second order' symmetry) in a cyclical form of causation. Here, abstraction is an endogenous mechanism that allows evolution to emerge in the form of new behavior patterns. Abstraction is also a form of information management, filtering out enough information to produce scale. The genesis of the scale in its epistemological nature is where this abstraction process leads to a certain perspective from which (Kantian) scale is born. The same scale matures into a materialist (Marxist) existence evidenced in patterns of behavior, but will inevitably suffer a Kohresque death (as will be discussed further on). Scale production, which is addressed next, emanates from this form of abstraction.

For Hayekian complexity to fit into the ansatz, his definition of complexity must be linked to a form of scale production. Let us look again at Hayek's definition of complexity (Hayek, 1967, p. 25). Two things can be argued here. First, Hayek sees scale manifesting itself in the (relative) size of the system. This is straightforward in Hayek's identification of 'the number of its elements' as part of the criterion for the degree of complexity. The second argument hinges on realizing that Hayek is employing the language of systems theory.[7] This suggests another manifestation of scale in Hayekian complexity, in that the scale of a system is manifested in the interaction among its elements. For Hayek, scale is in the form of the size of systems (number of elements) as well as the relationships among these elements; both are reducible to a quantum of information describing relative size and interaction.

In summary, Hayekian complexity is predicated on symmetry and symmetry breaking as well as on a 'size' and 'relationship' (informational) interpretation of scale.

Kohresque Discourse

Symmetry and symmetry breaking as well as the concept of scale, can be gleaned from Kohr's elaboration on Aristotle's conviviality theory, in which there is an inherent tension between the *summum bonum* condition (good life) and the scale of the state (Kohr, 1978, p. 14). The larger the state and the more interdependent its functional parts are, the less likely it will attain the objective of good life.

The homogeneity of the original society is Kohr's idea of 'symmetry.' The size of such a society was small: less than 100 members. From this size handicap, we can see some congruence between Hayek's treatment of what he called 'primitive societies', and the Kohresque 'homogenous society'. Of course, Hayek reserved 'society' for spontaneous order, while relegating small societies such as the 'tribe' to an organized form of order (Hayek, 1983, p. 47). This still allows a form of symmetry breaking when a tribe structure is established. In contrast, Kohr's homogenous societies are a pre-tribal formation. They are in the original state, still lacking any symmetry breaking.[8]

The original Kohresque position, then, is a homogenous society with hardly any functional differentiation. It is here that a symmetry breaking takes place in the form of division of labor or specialization. For Kohr, this symmetry breaking (through specialization) will repeat at each stage where the society attains a larger size.

According to Kohr, the first symmetry breaking resulted in the emergence of an official who was more probably an inn- (or gathering place-) keeper rather than a president. However, the function of inn keeping is a full-time task that requires a new 'social contract' regulating how the innkeeper will provide for him or herself. Now this society's expenditures and revenues start to drift apart. The expenditure relates to the innkeeper's activities, while the revenue originates from members of the group. Kohr estimates that for a society to carry out such a function, it requires an optimal size of around 100 people.

In Kohr's discourse, scale is largely a Malthusian construct: the size or population (density) of society is the signifier for scale. As the symmetry-breaking process (more specialization) is repeated, the society attains a higher scale (Kohr, 1978, p. 15–19). However, as for Hayek, the fact that symmetry breaking results in an integrated whole that we refer to as 'society' means that the produced scale in the form of size will inevitably have a complementary interpretation in the form of relationships among the specialized members of society. Hence, when society was small and homogenous, there was little need for enduring relationships among members. However, once symmetry breaking starts, these members become interdependent. It is this dynamic that provides a full picture of Kohresque scale.

Kohr provides a scalar interpretation of history. For Kohr, changes in social size and interrelationships are the primary cause of historic change and human evolution. While there are other forces that influence historical development, Kohr suggests that these 'exercise a significant role only in societies of sub-critical or optimum dimensions' (Kohr, 1978, p. 10). 'Scale' in Kohr's discourse represents a dichotomy between 'critical size' and 'optimal size.'

The problematised scale is that of 'critical size'. When critical size is reached, governments are not able to predict market behavior (Kohr, 1978, p. 9). This encourages governments to attempt direct control of these markets, even though such control would be inutile in alleviating the problems faced by society. For whole economic systems, the critical size 'sets in when social overgrowth begins to curtail the choice between alternatives, leaving only socialism viable, *and even this only for a little while longer*' (Kohr, 1978, p. 9; emphasis added). However, Kohr explains that the optimum limit of society is not a rigid magnitude. Optimal scale is rather analogous to an elastic ribbon. The width of the ribbon 'permits considerable stretching before it reaches the outer limit at which optimum size turns into critical size' (Kohr, 1978, p. 20–21).

Jacobsian Discourse

For Jacobs, symmetry is approached through the concept of 'generality'. Jacobs provides a gloss for Kohr's transition from conviviality to exchange by suggesting an intermediate phase of (institutionalized) 'sharing' (Jacobs, 2000, p. 27) which would not be necessary in early society, unless there was functional differentiation. In this sense, Jacobs' ideation of symmetry is closely related to Kohr's, as both see symmetry *qua* homogeneity. However, while Kohr's homogeneity is functional-based on the role assigned to members, Jacobs' homogeneity seems closer to Hayek's 'order'. Jacobsian symmetry is predicated on institutionalized social practices. For Jacobs, symmetry is process-based.

In Jacobs' discourse, symmetry breaking takes the form of 'differentiation' (Jacobs, 2000, p. 27). She identifies 'sharing' as a phase that preceded trading, since the latter 'emerged' from the former. This emergence registers a form of symmetry breaking leading to scale production: trading is based on exchange, which would not obtain unless there is 'differentiation.' This differentiation is the result of heterogeneity (symmetry breaking) replacing homogeneity (symmetry).

However, Jacobs, like Kohr, is also able to see the dialectic between symmetry and symmetry breaking. Hence, while trading is the result of symmetry breaking, it also functions as a form of symmetry from which further symmetry breaking can result. Jacobs also sees the link between this symmetry breaking process and Hayekian rules, both formally—'in the development of legal codes involving contracts, ownership, and liabilities'—and in 'social codes involving long-distance cooperation and relationships with strangers' (Jacobs, 2000, p. 27).

This symmetry breaking is also seen in her analysis of 'economic development.' In elaborating on 'development' as differentiation emerging from generality, Jacobs offers the solar system as an example of a continued process of symmetry breaking in the form of emerging differentiation resulting in production of scale that is now the solar system (Jacobs, 2000, p. 16). This is again the same understanding we saw in Kohr's discourse on the evolution of societies.

For Jacobs, the specific context of economic development is synonymous with 'innovation' as a form of symmetry breaking through a process of trial and error (Jacobs, 1984, p. 155)—a form of differentiation that moves from homogeneity to heterogeneity. However, according to Jacobs, this form of symmetry breaking has very specific characteristics. She emphasizes 'embeddedness' or the 'indigenous nature' of true economic development. Here, we see a sign of scale problematisation in Jacobsian discourse. She gives Imperial Iran and Russia as instances when this indigenous nature was not taken into account (Jacobs, 1984, p. 135 and 139–140).

In summary, Jacobs illustrates how with every symmetry breaking, a new group of generalities emerges (symmetry groups). The interpretation of Jacobsian symmetry is tied to the concept of generality, while symmetry breaking is 'qualitative change', which, when discussed in the context of economic development, relates to the ideas of differentiation and improvisation (innovation).

Jacobs, then, was alive to the dialectic between symmetry and symmetry breaking. However, while Kohr is largely focused on scale distortion (scale manifesting itself in the form of number of elements and size), Jacobs emphasizes the problem of scale entanglement (in the interaction of elements in the form of city-regions). Hayek, alternatively, seems to account explicitly for the potential of both scale distortion and entanglement—at least as stated in his definition of complexity—although he stops short of developing these into a problematisation of scale.

Jacobsian scale has its genesis in her criticism of the national scale, which is the ideological scale (Herod, 2011, p. 7), as the anchor for economic analysis. Jacobsian problematisation of scale manifests itself in the detrimental effect of nation-centered economic development and economic expansion. Jacobs suggests that neoclassical economics proceeds on the (mercantilist) false assumption that the national economy provides the fundamental data for macroeconomic analysis (Jacobs, 1984, p. 29). Citing a continuum of crises, especially on the path to economic development, a recent manifestation of which could include the Global Financial Crisis, Jacobs argues that national governments have failed on the economic front. She adds that this failure suggests a growing irrelevance of the nation state when it comes to economic activity (Jacobs, 1984, p. 32).

The most important observation relating to scale is that economic development as symmetry breaking occurs at the local (urban) scale: it is embedded in cities and their hinterlands. Economic development is a form of local (rather than global) symmetry breaking. This is the Jacobsian (evolutionary) meso (scale) (Jacobs, 2000, p. 32).

Jacobs suggests that the production of scale is exhibited in the process of bifurcation, which in turn produces complexity through feedback loops (Jacobs, 2000, p. 103). The production of scale in Jacobsian discourse is vivid in her analysis of economic expansion. Jacobs explains that "Development is qualitative change. Expansion is quantitative change. The two are closely linked, but they aren't the same thing" (Jacobs, 2000, p. 37).

In a way similar to her questioning of national aggregates, Jacobs is critical of the long-held belief in exports as the main drivers of economic expansion. Jacobs uses an energy calculus to explain the spurious nature of the exports-led rationale (Jacobs, 2000, pp. 51–56). For Jacobs, economic analysis should not be focused on exports and their possible 'multiplier effect' but on imports, which leads to identifying the practical link between economic development and economic expansion as economic diversity (Jacobs, 2000, p. 63). Based on the energy-flow hypothesis, the neoclassical approach is fundamentally flawed. The production of scale flows from 'diversity', which is linked to economic development as a form of localized symmetry breaking (Jacobs, 2000, p. 106).

Summary Schema

Figure 2 summarizes the way symmetry, symmetry breaking and the production of scale are discussed in the works of HKJ. The links should be interpreted as circular causations among scale production, symmetry breaking and symmetry.

For Hayek, symmetry is signified by pattern and order. Spontaneous and made orders relate to endogenous and exogenous symmetry breaking, respectively. Hayekian symmetry breaking is discussed using the terms 'adaptation' and 'abstraction'. Moreover, the interaction between spontaneous and made orders also induces symmetry breaking. Hayekian scale represents both the size of a given system calculated as its number of elements as well as interaction (relationships) among these elements.

Kohr sees symmetry in homogeneity and generality. Specialization and the division of labor result in symmetry breaking. Kohr's scale, while registering a relational construct, is largely related to (localized) size, especially (society's) population density.

Symmetry and generality are synonymous for Jacobs. Economic development (in the form of innovation and qualitative change) leads, through

Figure 2. Signifiers of symmetry, symmetry breaking, and scale in the discourse of HKJ

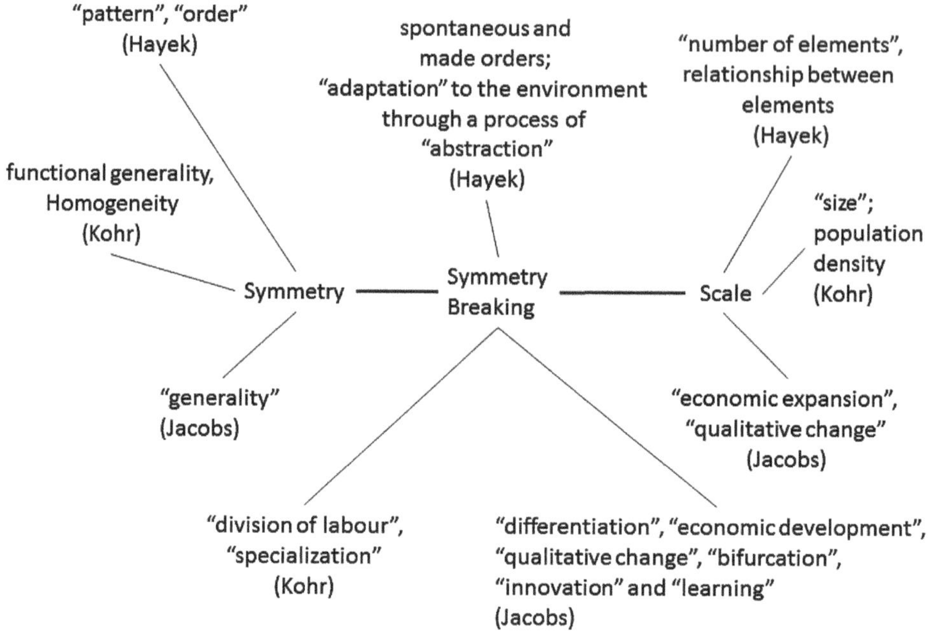

bifurcation, to symmetry breaking. Scale production is seen in economic expansion and quantitative change.

THE PRODUCTION OF SCALE AND COMPLEXITY

This section elaborates on the way HKJ discuss complexity and how their formulations are related to the production of scale. It is argued that all three see the production of scale as a condition for complexity to emerge.

Hayekian Complexity

As previously discussed, Hayek's definition of complexity is a function of scale where scale represents relationships (of elements to each other and to their environment). For Hayek, this formulation of complexity as a function of scale is 'adequate' or sufficient for an 'unambiguous criterion.' The central concept in Hayek's complexity discourse is that of order, which we identified as symmetry. Hayek distinguishes two types of order. The first is described as 'taxis': an 'organization' that is 'made' or 'artificial.' This type is created only by exogenous forces and is epitomized in 'government' as 'a directed social order.' In particular, 'the organization of society as a whole' refers to 'what we now describe as socialism' (Hayek, 1983, p. 54). According to Hayek, such order is 'relatively *simple* or at least necessarily confined to such moderate degrees of complexity as the maker can still survey' (Hayek, 1983, p. 38; emphasis in the original).

The way Hayek positions his two types of order on the dimension of complexity directly links to scale. Hayek argues that there can be spontaneous orders that are not complex, but there cannot be very complex orders that are not spontaneous (Hayek, 1983, pp. 38–43). Here, spontaneous order is a necessary condition for attaining a high degree of complexity. Hayek links the high degree of complexity with the way spontaneous orders form: through endogenous adaptation that leads to abstraction in the form of 'certain rules' in response to exogenous 'immediate environment' stimuli. Linking this to our earlier discussion, we can see the nexus between scale and complexity through this abstraction process.

When Hayek's high complexity is examined, only spontaneous order can be seen. The high complexity of such order is the result of elements adapting to their immediate environment (within the system) independent of purpose. A primary example of this high complexity is 'the structure of the modern society'. In any given society, micro-level entities such as families and companies, which are organizations, are integrated into 'a more comprehensive' (macro-level) spontaneous order (Hayek, 1983, p. 46). Here, we see a clear nexus between the production of scale and complexity. It is the emergence of the macro-level spontaneous order from an ensemble of micro-level made orders that creates complexity.

We have seen earlier how Hayek makes a connection between the concepts of 'abstraction' and 'adaptation.' In relation to spontaneous order, the elements of such an order will often adapt to the environment through a process of abstraction. Through evolution (Darwinian natural selection), 'a repertory of action type adapted to standard features of the environment. Organisms become capable of ever greater varieties of actions' (Hayek, 1978, p. 42). Hayek also asserts that 'the formation of a new abstraction seems never to be the outcome of a conscious process, not something at which the mind can deliberately aim, but always a discovery of something which *already* guides its operation' (Hayek, 1978, p. 46; emphasis in the original). Hayek explains the role of abstraction in the emergence of new behavior in the following terms (Hayek, 1978, pp. 48–49):

It is the determination of particular actions by various combinations of abstract properties that makes it possible for a causally determined structure of actions to produce actions it has never produced before and, therefore, to produce altogether new behavior not commonly expected from what it usually described as a 'mechanism'. Even a relatively limited repertory of abstract rules that can thus be combined into particular actions will be capable of 'creating' an almost infinite variety of particular actions.

Previously, we said abstraction is the first step in the production of scale. We also said that scale is born Kantian: as an epistemological construct. Abstraction is 'never ... the outcome of a conscious process'. Thus, Hayekian scale results from an unconscious 'spontaneous' symmetry breaking through the process of abstraction. This then leads to 'ever greater varieties of actions,' which then becomes synonymous with complexity.

Kohresque Complexity

While Kohr does not define complexity directly, like Hayek, he links scale and complexity. For Kohr, complexity is due to scale production in the form of 'overgrowth,' more so than "the nature of ... things" (Kohr, 1978, pp. 5 and 63). His complexity is manifested in "increasing ferocity of cyclical fluctuations" that engenders crises resulting in increasing government intervention. He opines (Kohr, 1978, p. 165):

The problem is that when a field has grown too large, its natural tendency is, as in the case of a state having reached critical size, to diffuse and to fringe, creating thereby simultaneously a demand for integration and the very condition making it impossible.

For a given system, Kohr suggests that the increase of scale beyond optimum size vitiates the relationship among its elements to the point that the system disintegrates—it is "not fused into an organic whole" (Kohr, 1978, p. 165). Compared with Hayek, for whom complexity is the result of integration of made order into spontaneous order, Kohr's complexity does not arise so much from the act of integration as from the impossibility of such integration. In this regard, Kohr is closer to understanding complexity as the manifestation of tension between two opposing fields: evolution, which vies for more differentiation and diversity, and gravitation, which strives for more integration (symmetry in the form of homogeneity).

Kohr employs scale primarily in the context of 'social size,' which is the product of the "number of population, population density, the degree of its administrative integration, and the velocity of its movements" (Kohr, 1978, p. 8). In due course, the internal pressures of numerically larger societies are bound to produce, first, greater density, then greater integration and, finally, greater velocity. These stages correspond to the production of scale (greater density), complexity (greater integration) and collapse (greater velocity leading to cyclical fluctuations and distorted feedback).

'Social size' is then a function of density, a relative quality linking the magnitude of the number of a given population to the jurisdiction in which they live. Being a quantity of relative magnitude, density is a spatial attribute of scale. The same can be said of integration, being the 'entanglement' of different levels of spatial scale— for example the local urban scale and the national or global scale. However, Kohr's concept of social size is also a function of temporal scale in the form of the velocity of a population's movement.

For Kohr, the problems associated with complexity accelerate when a system reaches its critical scale, which he describes as "that mysterious social volume at which [war] breaks out spontaneously irrespective of the ideology, religion, leadership, culture, or economic system of the countries involved" (Kohr, 1978, p. 7).[9] At this scale, "the survival requirements of society begin to increase at a faster rate than its productivity" (Kohr, 1978, p. 5). More and more output will now have to be diverted to 'social use' rather than to raising 'personal living standards'.

Kohr emphasizes that the harmony of proportions (which is the essence of scale) is vital in a self-regulatory system. It follows that balancing forces must be large in number and small in power. For Kohr, when this harmony is lost, a regulatory force must be introduced from outside—namely, through government. However, it is not sufficient that government is recalled. At the same time, its powers must be increased "to such an extent that none of the economic colossi surviving the competitive struggle can challenge its decisions" (Kohr, 1978, p. 55). Thus, the purely economic sequence leading excessively large political units to inevitable socialism seems quite clear. For Kohr, an economic system is determined by scale; if a community is too small or too large, the only economic system is socialism (Kohr, 1978, p. 51).

Kohr suggests that the socialization of uber-societies (societies at the critical size) is driven by four forces: military necessity, economic opportunity, physical density and rationalization. This socialization process distorts societal identity by taking away society's freedom to invent its own collective personality.[10] The key assertion is that "Anything that is irrational qualifies as a tool for strengthening the social fabric [to produce yet further scale]" (Kohr, 1978, p. 133). This identity distortion can be seen in the economic development of such societies where identity and the economic activities it produces are based on emotion rather than rationality. At the critical scale, forging a united and separate identity is essential to the functioning of the state. It is the mechanism through which the last stage of socialization, the fourth force, rationalization, takes place. Kohr summarizes the irrationality creation process as (Kohr, 1978, p. 144):

Thus, an examination of the group-building process will always reveal the same basic method: the protective application of a succession of bandages of manifestly irrational rituals, symbols, practices, gestures, costumes, sports, modes of behaviour and speech, to a fiercely irrational elemental nucleus—the conviction that membership in one's own group is the main source of human dignity, difference, and superiority.

To summarize, Kohr sees complexity resulting from the production of scale and its impossible demand for integration. Kohr identifies socialism and irrationality as integration technologies. Both require as a necessary and sufficient condition the production of scale in the form of increased population density or size of society.

Jacobsian Complexity

Jacobs' conception of complexity is closer to Hayekian than Kohresque complexity as far as her use of systems theory is concerned. In particular, Jacobs builds on an analogy between ecological and economic systems. She suggests economies (and the societies they are based on) are a form of organism. For Jacobs, complexity is a collapse-evading technology manifested in feedback loops and bifurcations (Jacobs, 2000, p. 103). Put differently, Jacobs sees the dialectic between symmetry and symmetry breaking as the process that generates complexity (Jacobs, 2000, p. 17).

To explain the emergence of complexity through symmetry breaking and production of scale, Jacobs gives the example of an embryonic human being (Jacobs, 2000, p. 17). A repeated process of symmetry breaking creates scale in the form of "diverse and complicated tissues and organs" from "a microscopically small fertilized egg." This is in line with our earlier discussion of how the dialectic between symmetry and symmetry breaking leads to the production of scale. The fact that complexity has emerged from this form of circular causation is further captured by Jacobs' emphasis on 'co-development' (Jacobs, 2000, p. 19).

For Jacobs, the process of import replacing is the evolutionary defining moment in the transition from a settlement to a city (Jacobs, 1984, p. 41). Jacobs also suggests a quantum nonlinear approach to such evolution (Jacobs, 1984, pp. 41 & 42). Thus, in essence, economic growth from the perspective of import replacing at the city level "is by no means all net growth" (Jacobs, 1984, p. 42). In large cities, import-replacing plays a compensatory (rather than a growth) role. Jacobs identifies three causes for this form of depreciation: first, former customer cities 'take to replacing imports themselves,' second, some well-established enterprises leave the city and move to distant places and, third, some older enterprises become obsolete.

Cities and potential cities have two fundamental economic needs. Cities need trade with one another. Large nations can serve this need because they can "eliminate gratuitous barriers in their domestic trade" (Jacobs, 1984, p. 208). Nations can provide jurisdictional arbitrage so cities can trade with each other within a nation's boundary. However, nation states hurt the second need, as, just like the players in a team, cities need to keep their competitive skills 'up to scratch' individually—nations distort this need owing to feedback flaws (Jacobs, 1984, pp. 208–209).

Thus, Jacobsian complexity is based on the idea of diversity in ecosystems governed by a bifurcation process leading to feedback loops. The production of scale is the result of interaction between symmetry and symmetry breaking, which, in turn, gives rise to complexity (diversity).

Summary Schema

Figure 3 provides a synopsis of the analysis so far. The middle part of the complexity ansatz, connecting scale to complexity, is evident in the discourse of HKJ. In their conceptualization of scale as the size of a system, Hayek and Kohr suggest increase in scale must result in higher complexity. Jacobs identifies complexity as the outcome of a bifurcation process that alters dynamic relationships among system's elements through (positive and negative) feedback loops. Kohr's analysis is more attentive to the problem of scale in two respects. First, he sees complexity-reducing options open for government intervention. Second, he identifies crisis under high complexity in the cyclical fluctuations (business cycles) produced by critical size. Jacobs' analysis explains the entanglement resulting from the production of scale.

Figure 3. Signifiers of complexity in the discourse of HKJ

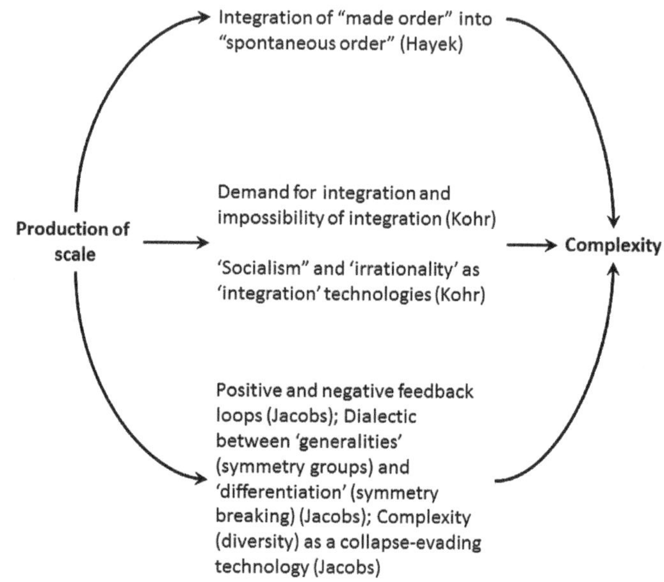

The concept of 'integration' in one form or another seems to be the common denominator for HKJ's complexity discourse. However, Kohr asserts the impossibility of such integration. Jacobs (as will be discussed below) also registered this impossibility in what she refers to as 'transactions of decline.' Figure 3 shows the tension between the demand for and impossibility of integration, which leads to complexity. Of course, integration is predicated on relationships among elements of a given system and the relationship of the system (the whole) to its environment. This then leads to a direct link between the production of scale and complexity.

However, did HKJ envisage crisis or 'aging' (and eventual collapse) as an inevitable product of high complexity? This is what is investigated next.

COMPLEXITY AND COLLAPSE

This section traces the concept of collapse in HKJ due to complexity. It is argued that all three make the link between complexity and collapse, although each place different emphasis on the consequences of collapse. Kohr and Jacobs seem more concerned about the terminal nature of collapse than Hayek.

Hayekian Collapse

Hayekian collapse can be studied through his trade cycle theory. Hayek's discourse can be described as an unlimited self-generating theory (of the spontaneous order). According to this interpretation, there is no terminal phase in the trade cycle. Hayek introduces this concept of collapse only indirectly (Hayek, 1983, p. 51; emphasis added):

The spontaneous order arises from each element balancing all the various factors operating on it and by adjusting all its various actions to each other, a balance which will be destroyed if some of the actions are determined by another agency on the basis of different knowledge and in the service of different ends.

Of course, destruction can be a form of symmetry breaking—another aspect of an aging process. For collapse (*qua* death) to occur, a form of symmetry creation rather than symmetry breaking needs to be discerned. Again, the issue is dependent on scale. Death requires 'global' symmetry breaking—in other words, a breaking that annihilates localized symmetry breaking (localized structures) and leaves only temporal and/or structural symmetry. For Hayek, this symmetry creation can come in the form of government intervention (through monetary policy) but is also endogenous to the nature of cyclical fluctuations (Hayek, 1933, pp. 184–185). Hayekian collapse is in the nature of the imbalance brought about through government intervention in the revision of spontaneous order rules (Hayek, 1983, p. 51). When the 'agency' determining the rules is endogenous to the spontaneous order, Hayek sees credit banking (as part of the economic system) as a mechanism leading to collapse. Collapse is brought about through the bust phase of cyclical fluctuations (trade cycles).

Hayekian collapse is summoned through cyclical fluctuations. This can be seen in his analysis of trade cycles and their origin in the form of national currencies and monetary policy (Hayek, 1933, pp. 139–141). Starting from a position of equilibrium (symmetry),[11] "the economic system always reacts to such changes by its well-known method of adaptation, i.e. by the formation of a new equilibrium" (Hayek, 1933, p. 43). Here, Hayek is referring to the dialectic between symmetry and symmetry breaking that results in the production of scale. Hayek emphasizes that collapse in the form of symmetry creation comes about as an 'inevitable reaction' (Hayek, 1933, pp. 182–183). Collapse manifests itself in the creation of some form of lag in the dialectic between symmetry and symmetry breaking. Instead of 'immediate adjustment', there will be a 'sticky' phase that postpones the inevitable reaction of symmetry creation (new equilibrium).

According to Hayek, the factor that brings about cyclical fluctuations is money (Hayek, 1933, pp. 44–45). Money brings about (Hayek, 1933, p. 123):

Certain deviations in individual price-relations occurring because changes in the volume of money appear at certain individual points ... Every disturbance of the equilibrium of prices leads necessarily to shifts in the structure of production, which must therefore be regarded as consequences of monetary change.

For Hayek, trade cycles are fueled by monetary policy, but there would be no monetary policy under a system of concurrent currencies. It is then the existence of a single national currency that abets cyclical fluctuations, which, in turn, results in collapse (Hayek, 1976, pp. 17 and 75).

Again, it should be emphasized that Hayekian collapse is not terminal. He identifies collapse as a recurring phase within trade cycles, exhibited in the bust phase leading to depression and unemployment. For Hayek, society (being a spontaneous order) is self-organizing and self-generating. As such, it never reaches a terminal stage due to endogenous dynamics. Terminal collapse for Hayek would only come (if ever) through the exogenous intervention of government, especially as made order imparting on spontaneous order.

Kohresque Collapse

Unlike Hayek, Kohr is very explicit about the inevitability of terminal collapse (although Kohr uses the word 'collapse' to mean implosion) (Kohr, 1986, p. 98). Kohr is more worried about 'organic' or endogenous collapse from within the Hayekian spontaneous order. Kohr suggests that an uncontrolled 'spontaneous order' at the critical scale leads to business cycles that in turn precipitate government intervention (Kohr, 1978, p. 65). Kohr breaks away from Hayek's unlimited self-generating theories by acknowledging depression as a terminal stage. Kohr then suggests that the business (trade) cycles brought about by the critical scale necessitate at least a compensatory intervention by government. However, what is useful for Kohr is not intervention to counter trade cycles but intervention to counter scale cycles. Kohr asserts that the identification of scale cycles (manifested in size) as distinct from business cycles resolves the theoretical 'basic error of the limited self-generating theories whose rationalizations dealt such a mortal blow to the defensibility of capitalism' (Kohr, 1978, p. 67).

However, like Hayek, Kohr is also skeptical of the ability of control systems in the form of socialism (and mixed systems of socialism) to mitigate cyclical fluctuations caused by complexity (Kohr, 1978, p. 68). Growth beyond the optimum size increases societal complexities faster than humanity's ability to manage them. In these post-optimum societies, the political function already curtails individual freedom to the point that it ceases to be compatible with *summum bonum*. The second stage in these societies is where culture is frozen: creative talent is now diverted to prevent society from collapse. In essence, the (individual) spirit of these societies becomes moribund. Society is now transformed to a welfare society, a military society and a divine society. The third stage is where growth is not through the biological way of splitting, duplicating and multiplying, but rather through the "cancerous way of expansion and integration" (Kohr, 1978, p. 32). The fourth and final stage is where the convivial function (the *raison d'être* of society) is paralyzed by the increasing internal pressures of oversize and external pressures from equally large rival societies.

This post-optimum society now exists in the collective rather than having individual members. This is the stage signaling the emergence of uber-society, or society's society, where a "new concept of optimum size which, unlike the individualistic optimum, can no longer be outgrown" (Kohr, 1978, p. 24). This is the genesis of the insatiable growth preached by neoclassical economics. Kohr prophesizes that this uber-society at the limit gyrates towards 'a mankind-embracing world state' (Kohr, 1978, p. 22).

Jacobsian Collapse

Jacobs states that "[a]ll dynamic systems are in danger of succumbing to instability, which is why they constantly need self-correction. If and when a dynamic system decisively loses stability, it either collapses into inertia or disintegrates" (Jacobs, 2000, p. 85). For Jacobs, the "essence of dynamic stability is constant self-correction" (Jacobs, 2000, p. 84), where 'dynamic stability' is defined as 'energetic steadiness' (Jacobs, 2000, p. 84). Jacobs argues that "Diversity [complexity] protects ecosystems against total devastation by diseases and abnormal weather that demolish one-crop plantations" (Jacobs, 2000, p. 83). For Jacobs, (positive and negative) feedback loops create the complexity of ecosystems. Such loops are also related to self-organization (Jacobs, 2000, p. 103), which, using Hayekian constructs, leads to spontaneous order. In this sense, complexity emerges from endogenous control signals (relationships) that guide the spontaneous order.

The genesis of Jacobsian collapse is in her critique of nations as economic units. She elaborates by identifying the economically unstable nature of nations (Jacobs, 1984, p. 208). For Jacobs, collapse comes because of faulty feedback loops that create instability through 'bizarre and unbalanced' effects from scale entanglement. In particular, Jacobsian collapse becomes clearer in terms of 'vicious circles': "Positive-feedback ... can intensify ... destructive situations ... Then we call the loops 'vicious circles'" (Jacobs, 2000, pp. 95–96). For Jacobs, "A vicious circle's limit is not an achieved dynamic equilibrium but collapse" (Jacobs, 2000, p. 101). Vicious circles are 'dead-ends' (Jacobs, 2000, p. 96), or, as Kohr would put it, they are terminal. However, if not disturbed, they die out: "[while] vicious circles are damaging [they are] self-terminating" (Jacobs, 2000, p. 99). Jacobs emphasizes the role of government in subsidizing vicious circles through 'transactions of decline' (Jacobs, 2000, p. 100).

The subsidization of vicious circles can be seen in government interference with economic expansion. According to Jacobs, the forces of economic expansion (a signifier of the production of scale) grow 'out of sync' due to scale entanglement (Jacobs, 1984, p. 47). Jacobs also provides three other related collapse mechanisms. These mechanisms are all forms of faulty feedback signals, the second of which is the faulty feedback of national currency (Jacobs, 1984, pp. 156–162; Jacobs, 2000, p. 12). Currencies are intended as feedback mechanisms on a local scale—the city-region.

Having national or European Union (EU)-style single currencies can never improve the economy of such city-regions.

Jacobs' third collapse mechanism identifies how nation states distort business cycles. Jacobs links business cycles to the idea of 'emergence adaptations' (which does not fall far from Hayekian adaptation). These adaptations address temporary instability. They are in response to instabilities that are only temporary but may be devastating (Jacobs, 2000, p. 115). Jacobs agrees with Hayek and Kohr that business cycles cannot be eliminated by government intervention (Jacobs, 2000, p. 118). For Jacobs, nation states amplify business cycles through the synchronizing effect of national currencies (Jacobs, 1984, p. 210–211).

In the fourth mechanism leading to collapse, Jacobs identifies what she refers to as 'transactions of decline' that are intended to prop up the Kohresque critical size (Jacobs, 1984, p. 198). These transactions of decline fall into three main groups. They are similar to the three socialization processes discussed by Kohr. The first policy is to engage in prolonged military production (Jacobs, 1984, p. 190). The second is what came to be known as the 'welfare state' (Jacobs, 1984, pp. 191–193).[12] The third is that of investments promoting trade between advanced and backward economies (Jacobs, 1984, p. 196). Jacobs concludes that "Transactions of decline, no matter which guise they take, are not remedies for stagnation and don't address causes of poverty, yet [they] are precisely what national governments have become well fitted to deliver" (Jacobs, 1984, p. 204).

Jacobs uses an analogy with earth's crust to discuss how transactions of decline lead to collapse through discontinuities *qua* 'bifurcations', adding that "What all bifurcations have in common is that they are not first causes, but responses to prior accruing instabilities and stresses" (Jacobs, 1984, p. 208). However, just like the outcome of a psychosis—something Kohr discusses in the context of group irrationality—nations continue to implement transactions of decline in the face of deep depression. Jacobs cites a group of Princeton political scientists who identified increased load and decreased capability as the causes for political disintegration "of sovereign political units—nations, empires, [and] confederations" (Jacobs, 1984, p. 212). Loads include: prolonged military commitments, substantial increase in political participation on the part of populations, regions or social strata that previously had been politically passive, and political awareness of ethnic or linguistic differences (Jacobs, 1984, p. 212).[13]

Jacobs then contemplates a Kohresque solution as a theoretical possibility to transactions of decline[14]: "the division of the single sovereignty into a family of smaller sovereignties … not after things had reached a stage of breakdown and disintegration, but long before while things were still going reasonably well" (Jacobs, 1984, pp. 214–215).

Summary Schema

Figure 4 summarizes collapse according to HKJ. All exhibit the logic of faulty feedback. The faultiness is endogenously induced by the scale calculus. Then, the government exogenously compounds these problems. Unless localized scale correction is implemented, global collapse must ensue.

Figure 4. Signifiers of collapse in the discourse of HKJ

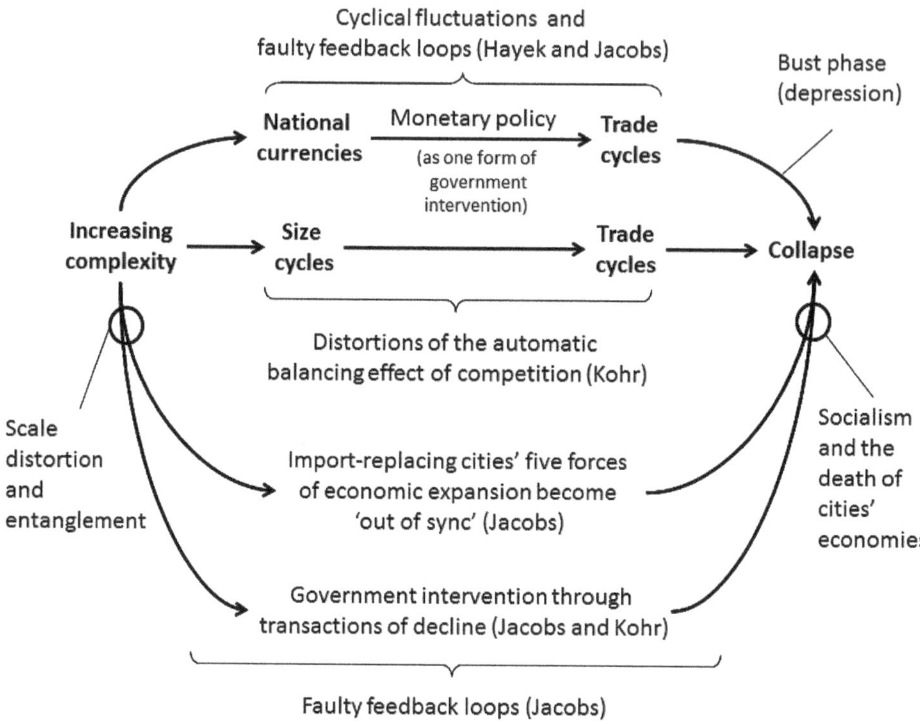

EVADING COLLAPSE

The main result of our analysis on complexity is that properly coupled systems (not too loose, not too tight) produce complex attractors. These attractors are capable of change but are immune to cascade collapse. In this part, we examine whether this is apparent in the discourse of HKJ. The twin concepts of 'jurisdictional footprint' and 'jurisdictional arbitrage' are also introduced to guide the discussion.

The Hayekian Solution

Spanning the process leading from symmetry breaking to collapse (and symmetry generation), Hayek comes to his central conclusion: "To maintain that we must deliberately plan modern society because it has become so complex is … paradoxical, and the result of a complete misunderstanding" (Hayek, 1983, pp. 50–51). The best solution is to allow the private sector to control the economic system (endogenously). This, even if it could result in faulty outcomes, is still preferred to the stagnation that government intervention brings.

For Hayek, scale reduction is not a viable option. He seems to set up a straw man whenever he gives short shrift to the idea of scale reduction. For example, for Hayek, only tribes or clans qualify as made orders (Hayek, 1983, p. 47). More evidence of this inclination comes from his thesis on concurrent currencies. He asks whether, when there is competition between currencies, having local currencies would offer any benefit over and above that of having national currencies. His answer is no (Hayek, 1976, p. 86). At any rate, Hayek does not suggest a break up of sovereign states into smaller ones as a solution to assuage trade cycles or the effects of inflation and unemployment. Hayekian competition is always predicated on the existence of nation-states within which the private sector should inherit ever more state monopolies.

The Kohresque Solution

Kohr suggests the logical method for evading collapse is to decentralize, devolve and dissolve existing nation-states into a "loosely linked free-trading system based on common but regional markets composed of … self-manageable small units" (Kohr, 1978, p. 125). In defending his advocacy for *Kleinstaaterei* (proliferation of small states), Kohr presents three arguments (Kohr, 1978, pp. 108–111). First, he suggests that in autarky the domestic market of 'moderately sized countries' will be large enough for optimum plant size. Second, under trade, Kohr emphasizes the distinction between economic and political integration, which means that the size of a country is not the size of its markets. Third, Kohr points out to the higher bargaining power of small countries.

Kohr is therefore critical of the EU. He argues that the development of the EU is not unprecedented; its success is not due to the act of 'union' either. Kohr explains that the claimed success of the EU is due to historical factors not predicated on the union experiment itself. All these factors can be traced to the rejuvenation of Europe post World War II. When this dissipates, the effects of critical scale will take hold. Based on this analysis, Kohr makes the ominous prediction that "there is no reason to assume that the [EU] should last." While the EU continues to grow, "it is simply the swelling of a balloon" (Kohr, 1978, p. 123).

The Jacobsian Solution

For Jacobs, the logic for sovereign locality is in our ability to evade collapse. In advocating a return to locality, Jacobs continues her criticism of the idea of 'nation,' hinting at the imperativeness of local autonomy (Jacobs, 1984, pp. 162–163). Jacobs explains that "a chief advantage of … [such a division] would be [the] multiplication of currencies" (Jacobs, 1984, p. 215). However (Jacobs, 1984, p. 216):

There is no magic in mere smallness or division of sovereignties per se … [this] is no substitute for the volatile trade backward cities must develop with one another if they are to develop. Nor is it any substitute for the necessity of vigorous cities remaining creative.

The conclusion Jacobs reaches is that there are no remedies at a city's or a nation's command, short of separation in the pattern of, for example, Singapore (Jacobs, 1984, pp. 180–181).

CODA

[T]he preferred form of [the political] state is a polycentric aristocratic republic … sovereignty … was seen to reside in a considerable number of self-governing cities … (Prokhovnik 2001: 300; emphasis added).

The above quote on Spinoza's preferred form for the political state (see Chapter 8) summarizes the thesis in this Chapter as supported by a meta-analysis of HKJ. The findings are given in Table 1.

Table 1. Summary of HKJ analysis

System	Symmetry (Breaking)	Scale	Complexity	Collapse
Hayek	Abstraction (adaptation)	Elements & their relationships	Integration of orders	Cyclical fluctuations
Kohr	Homogeneity (specialization)	Size & population density	Impossibility of integration	Distorted balancing
Jacobs	Generality (differentiation)	Quantitative change	Collapse-evading technology	Out of sync expansion

Table 1 suggests that HKJ have identical positions, albeit with different emphasis on certain parts of the complexity ansatz. They all start their analyses delineating different aspects of symmetry and symmetry breaking. They also see the production of scale as ensuing from this starting point. Complexity is seen as a collapse-evading technology pandering to policymakers' myopic insistence on integration (induced by economics' scale-invariance hangover) and the impossibility of the same.

Complexity theory, through the diagnostic ansatz introduced in this paper (as illustrated in the writings of HKJ—especially those of Kohr and Jacobs) suggests societies should be reorganized as 'sovereign' city-regions that mimic the functionality of complex attractors. This provides the only insurance against global collapse.

We have seen (from the analysis in the previous three parts) that Hayek focused mainly on the middle part of the ansatz, namely on scale and complexity. Hayek hardly discusses collapse in his writings, save for his intuition that interference of the made order (e.g. government's monetary policy) with the spontaneous order (the economic system) will result in trade cycles (of which the bust phase is interpreted as collapse).

Kohr and Jacobs formulate their solutions as a choice between Kleinstaaterei and the Tower of Babel syndrome (the existence of colossal states such as Brazil, Russia, India, China, the United States and the EU). For both, only political separation can end stagnation.

Kohr and Jacobs saw their proposals as impractical as nation states would have to cease to exist completely. Hence, Kohr's Chapter 11 in The Breakdown of Nations (Kohr, 1986) has only one word—'no'—in response to the question about whether his call for Kleinstaaterei will ever become a reality. Similarly, in Cities and the Wealth of Nations, Jacobs is clear that her proposition for the division of sovereignty is 'theoretical only' (Jacobs, 1984, p. 216). It is respectfully submitted that a proposition to keep the nation-state structure in parallel to the proposed sovereign city-regions (albeit in a subsidiary role) would overcome many of the practical difficulties envisaged by Kohr and Jacobs. Such an approach leads to the idea of city regions as complex attractors within a wider political system.

The best example of such a setup is the European Union. The current sovereign debt and Euro crisis is amenable to the analysis presented in this paper. This crisis is the result of a problem of scale that can be resolved only through a structural change—through resurrecting Europe's 'civic-ness.' The vision advocated by this paper is, à la Spinoza, for an EU 'driven' by free cities reminiscent of those in Italy or Germany in the early 2nd millennium.

Given that cities are complex attractors, their tight coupling through national governance or further European integration results in instability and collapse. Only loose coupling 'slows' complexity (*qua* aging process). This mode of coupling is done through resurrecting sovereign city-regions within the larger political system of the EU. As a result, nation states are relegated to a hypotactic role.

REFERENCES

Caldwell, B. (2004). *Hayek's challenge*. Chicago: University of Chicago Press.

de Wit, B., & Smith, J. (1986). *Field theory in particle physics*. Amsterdam: North-Holland.

Engels, F. (1972). *The origin of the family, private property, and the state*. New York: Pathfinder Press.

Everstine, G. C. (1987). Symmetry. In H. Kardestuncer & D. H. Norrie (Eds.), Finite element handbook (Vol. Part 4, Section 3.3, p. 4.183). New York: McGraw-Hill Company.

Gavrilov, L., & Gavrilova, N. (2004). Why we fall apart. *IEEE Spectrum*, *41*(9), 30. doi:10.1109/MSPEC.2004.1330807

Granovetter, M. S. (1973). The strength of weak ties. *American Journal of Sociology*, *78*(6), 1360–1380. doi:10.1086/225469

Granovetter, M. S. (1983). The strength of weak ties: A network theory revisited. *Sociological Theory*, *1*, 201–233. doi:10.2307/202051

Granovetter, M. S. (1985). Economic action and social structure: The problem of embeddedness. *American Journal of Sociology*, *91*(3), 481–510. doi:10.1086/228311

Gussen, B. F. (2013). On the problem of scale: Hayek, Kohr, Jacobs and the reinvention of the political state. *Constitutional Political Economy*, *24*(1), 19–42. doi:10.1007/s10602-012-9130-7

Hayek, F. A. (1933). *Monetary theory and the trade cycle*. London: Jonathan Cape.

Hayek, F. A. (1967). *Studies in philosophy, politics and economics*. London: Routledge & Kegan Paul.

Hayek, F. A. (1976). *Denationalisation of money*. London: Institute of Economic Affairs.

Hayek, F. A. (1978). *New studies in philosophy, politics, economics and the history of ideas*. London: Routledge & Kegan Paul. doi:10.7208/chicago/9780226321288.001.0001

Hayek, F. A. (1983). *Law, legislation and liberty: A new statement of the liberal principles of justice and political economy* (Vol. 1). Chicago: The University of Chicago Press.

Herod, A. (2011). *Scale*. London: Routledge.

Jacobs, J. (1984). *Cities and the wealth of nations*. Ringwood, Australia: Penguin Books.

Jacobs, J. (2000). *The nature of economies*. New York: The Modern Library.

Kohr, L. (1978). *The overdeveloped nations: The diseconomies of scale*. New York: Schoken Books.

Kohr, L. (1986). *The breakdown of nations*. New York: Routledge Kegan & Paul.

Marion, R. (1999). *The edge of organization: Chaos and complexity theories of formal social systems*. London: Sage Publications.

Prokhovnik, R. (2001). Spinozas conception of sovereignty. *History of European Ideas*, *27*(3), 289–306. doi:10.1016/S0191-6599(01)00051-1

Rosen, J. (1995). *Symmetry in science*. New York: Springer.

Sato, R., & Ramachandran, R. (1990). *Conservation laws and symmetry: Applications to economics and finance*. Boston: Kluwer. doi:10.1007/978-94-017-1145-6

Sato, R., & Ramachandran, R. (1998). *Symmetry and economic invariance: An introduction*. Norwell, Massachusetts: Kluwer. doi:10.1007/978-1-4615-5513-1

Stewart, I., & Golubitsky, M. (1992). *Fearful symmetry: Is god a geometer?* Oxford: Blackwell. Publishers.

Zajdenweber, D. (1997). Scale invariance in economy and finance. In B. Dubrulle, F. Graner, & D. Sornette (Eds.), *Scale invariance and beyond* (pp. 185–194). Berlin: EDP Sciences and Springer. doi:10.1007/978-3-662-09799-1_14

ENDNOTES

1 See for example Zajdenweber (1997).

2 As a starting point, see Sato and Ramachandran (1990; 1998).

3 For a non-mathematical introduction to scale see Herod (2011).

4 The work by Mark Granovetter is useful here to explain further the nature of coupling. See Granovetter (1973), Granovetter (1983), and Granovetter (1985).

5 More generally, symmetry is used to simplify the analysis of complex problems. See Everstine (1987).

6 There is evidence of intellectual cooperation between Hayek and Ludwig von Bertalanffy, the father of General Systems Theory. Hayek influenced von Bertalanffy's Theory. See, for example, Caldwell (2004).

7 The comparison between Hayek and Kohr on the original society can be enriched by injecting some of the insights from Engels (1972) on the origin of the state.

8 Kohr uses spontaneous in the normal sense: to indicate that the causal link is endogenous.

9 This is the usual process of production of scale where degrees of freedom are frozen (hence symmetry breaking) at lower scales to allow for the 'macro' to emerge.

10 For Hayek 'equilibrium' means "the general interdependence of all economic quantities, which has been most perfectly expressed by the Lausanne School of theoretical economics" (Hayek, 1933, p. 42).

11 An interesting variation on this theme came recently under the GFC where governments bailed out collapsing private enterprises.

12 One can link this to the adoption of the MMP (Mixed Member Proportional) representation system from a mature Germany to a coming-of-age New Zealand, and how the same can be detrimental to the latter.

13 Albeit based on city-regions instead of Kohresque *Kleinstaaterei*.

Chapter 7
Spinoza

ABSTRACT

This chapter argues that sovereignty, as envisaged by Spinoza, is the logical foundation for constituting polities in the 21st century. Constitutional constructs such as sovereignty weave an evolutionary dialectic between different organizational scales (the local, national, and global). This dialectic continues to wreak havoc at the local scale, and can be interrupted only through explicit constitutional constraints on the size of jurisdictions. The chapter argues for more emphasis on constitutional orders in the spirit of Spinoza's understanding of sovereignty. This entails preference for federal policies in which sovereignty is shared between different cities rather states where once capital cities dominate.

INTRODUCTION

An earlier version of this chapter appeared in the *Journal of Philosophical Economics*. See Gussen (2013). In *The Calculus of Consent*, Buchanan and Tullock (1962) state that the political ideas of Baruch Spinoza, "in many respects … may be taken as the most appropriate chosen classical precursor to [constitutional economics]" (p. 313). Notwithstanding this endorsement,

DOI: 10.4018/978-1-5225-2756-5.ch007

the authors do not investigate Spinoza's rendition of sovereignty. Instead, they point out that:

Spinoza's influence on our own ideas has been limited to his general and indirect effects on the Western intellectual tradition. In a specific sense, we have carefully reviewed Spinoza only after the completion of an initial draft of the main body of this book [The Calculus of Consent]. (Buchanan & Tullock, 1962, p. 313)

In *The Calculus*, one of the foundational works in constitutional economics, the word 'sovereignty' appears only four times; two of these appearances are in the appendices, and not as the subject of analysis but as a reference point for the models therein. A similar marginalization of sovereignty can be seen in recent works. For example, in a monograph entitled *The Calculus of Consent and Constitutional Design* (Dougherty, 2011), the word 'sovereignty' appears only once—in the introduction. This is problematic not only because sovereignty is closely related to the evolution of the state, but because, through the temples of constitutional order, sovereignty became the shaman of all economic activity (Beard, 1935).

Sovereignty is a fundamental pillar of the capitalist world-economy. Mercantilism led to the first constitutional rationalization of the exercise of sovereign power as a practice of government (Foucault, 1991). Later, the nation-state, through its legislative monopoly, became indispensable to the conduct of economic enterprise. Probably the strongest evidence of the link between sovereignty and economics comes from the idea of legal tender and the historical evolution of (national) territorial currencies. The same can be said about the rise of central banks and their influence, through sovereignty, on economic activity. Some would argue that the tendency to grant independence to central banks and the creation of non-national currencies such as the euro signify the increasing irrelevance of sovereignty (Helleiner, 2003). However, a quick glance at the European sovereign debt crisis (which continues to unfold since 2009) shows why such logic is wanting. In fact, the current drive within the European Union for economic integration (through the euro) is matched with a similar political integration (Halleberg, 2011). If anything, this suggests a resilient link between economics and politics. Even the analysis of what some theorists perceive as the 'decline' of sovereignty is also framed in reference to economic systems, in which the 'decline' of sovereignty today is seen as a "sign of the acute crisis of capitalism as an historical system" (Wallerstein, 1999, p. 33).

The link between economics and sovereignty suggests that the latter should be at the heart of economic analysis. This is more so in the case of constitutional economics, given its focus on the analogy between markets and politics. It is difficult to see how constitutional economics can treat the subject of choice among constraints without an examination of as fundamental a constitutional concept as sovereignty. Observing that sovereignty is becoming less and less relevant in a world with increasing economic integration not only misses the point of the choice among constraints, but also amounts to a misunderstanding of the concept of sovereignty itself. Historically, sovereignty has been, and continues to be, a response mechanism to forms of *universitas*, the current exemplar of which is globalization.[2]

Admittedly, just as with most political concepts, sovereignty is intrinsically controversial (Walker, 1990). Nevertheless, sovereignty has a common denominator that makes it a viable explanatory variable. This denominator is seen in a (political) power struggle between three scales: the local, the national, and the global. Within the European context, sovereignty grew from the impulse towards independence following protracted tensions between medieval kings and external powers in the form of popes and emperors (Hinsely, 1966). From the 16th century and up to the 1920s, power was transferred from local to national levels of governance, and then, through globalization, from national to global governance. The weakening of the role of the nation-state since World War I led to a reversal of this transfer.

This chapter attempts to elucidate the role of sovereignty within constitutional economics. In particular, an investigation is made into the nature of Spinozistic sovereignty and how it moves beyond an analysis of power relations, and into providing a normative discourse on the form of the state. To this end, the second section of the chapter furnishes a brief introduction to sovereignty. The third section expands on sovereignty under the analogy between markets and politics. The fourth section elaborates on Spinoza's understanding of sovereignty, especially his preferred structure for the state. The chapter ends with some concluding remarks.

SOVEREIGNTY BETWEEN ABSOLUTENESS AND DIVERSITY

The literature on sovereignty provides a plethora of classes and categories.[3] Only a few of these are explored in some detail here. The aim is to clarify the links between constitutionalism and sovereignty and trace the concept's transformation from absolute sovereignty to a divided sovereignty. A key feature of sovereignty is power exchange. This exchange leads to a specific structure of the state. For example, Hobbesian sovereignty leads to a unitary state, whereas that of Spinoza favors a federal polity.

Etymologically, the word 'sovereign' derives from the popular Latin for 'above' (superānus), as in 'more powerful (Sovereign, 2004). The issues that arose in the early history of sovereignty were centred on the legitimization of this power by investigating its source and extent. However, sovereignty on the most part is a legal concept (Macdonald & Nielsson, 1995). It is the power to make binding law in a particular territory. Within the European context, sovereignty grew from the impulse towards independence following protracted tensions between medieval kings and external powers (popes and emperors). The genesis of sovereignty lies in claims to local supremacy. It is this point that will be developed further by examining the link between sovereignty and constitutionalism.

Constitutionalism, especially in the context of states, is integral to sovereignty. Sovereignty is 'constitutional independence,' 'a claim to the exclusive right to make rules' (Smith et al., 1999, p. 2), and hence 'the first bulwark of constitutional government—as it implies the right to say no to outsiders' (Rabkin, 2005, p. 69). The starting point is to interpret the concept of constitution widely as the fundamental law principles from which the state draws its authority. Under this interpretation, constitutionalism can result either from a (revolutionary) contractarian approach, or through an evolutionary approach based on norms and conventions. Constitutionalism moderates the absoluteness of the sovereign's power, making its exercise subject to authorization, while supplying internal sovereignty through legitimacy. Sovereignty is inseparable from constitutionalism.

The pedigree of the link between sovereignty and constitutionalism can be traced through the long history of the contractarian approach.[4] Aristotle (2013) states that the constitution is the government, and the government is the sovereign in the state. This constitutional link to sovereignty is also seen in medieval Europe (Beard, 1935). In the history of sovereignty leading up to the European revolutionary upheavals in the 16th and 17th centuries, there is almost universal agreement that the foundation of sovereign power comes from an original contract (Merriam, 1900), either between the government and the people (Althusius, 1965), or between the people among themselves followed by a further agreement between people and government (Pufendorf), or a single contract in which the sovereign and the state are created simultaneously

(Hobbes and Rousseau). Early formulations of sovereignty focused on deriving the power of the sovereign from the people as a whole, whereas later formulations reverted to individual 'natural rights.'

The sovereign state came to be conceived of as a territorial jurisdiction at the national scale (Jackson, 1999). It was not until the rise of the federal states, as exemplified by the United States that a shift occurred in the analysis towards a possible divisibility of sovereignty. Hence, for Bodin (1955), who developed a political theory to serve as a fortification against anti-nationalism, sovereignty is always in service of a nation. Bodin signaled the advent of sovereignty's absolutism, which reached its zenith in the seventeenth century with the Leviathan of Thomas Hobbes (1982). This absolutism meant that sovereignty could not be shared or divided. Absolutist sovereignty had intellectual opposition in the form of the Monarchomachs, epitomized by Johannes Althusius (1965), who revived the Middle Ages (democratic) trust-based theories of sovereignty. This approach was also dominated by a contractarian approach—again emphasizing the nexus between sovereignty and constitutionalism. More recently, Habermas (1996) elaborated on the idea that sovereignty is the people, underscoring the importance of involving 'the people' actively in rational decisions that guide sovereigns.

To the absolutist and trust-based theories of sovereignty is added a Germanic 'natural rights' strand, which led to the articulation of theories by Samuel Pufendorf, John Locke, and Christian Wolff, among others. Under these theories, sovereignty's absoluteness was watered down to mere supremacy, either in the person of a monarch, in the case of Germany, or through a (fiduciary) legislature, in the case of England. In France, however, the 'natural rights' discourse, especially that of Jean-Jacques Rousseau (2010), was committed to a sovereignty that was absolute, infallible, and inalienable. In the 1794 French Revolution, sovereignty resided in the nation. Similarly, after the July 1830 Revolution, sovereignty emanated from the reason (intelligence) of the collective (community) as a whole. Now, it was the nation that was recognized as sovereign, not the monarch, nor reason in the absolute. By the time of the 1848 Revolution, the idea of sovereignty of the nation had gained general acceptance (Merriam, 1900).

The German States exhibited a similar evolution, in which the seat of sovereignty was also shifted from the people to the state. However, the German tradition emphasized the need for an organic law—a constitution—binding the sovereign. The state, as a Platonic organism, was promoted as the new bearer of sovereignty. Here, the state was a product of evolution rather than revolution. This organic conception of the state follows a tradition extending from the Greeks through the Middle Ages, and registering acceptance in the theories of Althusius, Hobbes, and Pufendorf.

However, Buchanan and Tullock reject the organic conception of the state. They point out that '[o]nly some organic conception of society can postulate the emergence of a mystical general will that is derived independent of the decisionmaking process in which the political choices made by the separate individuals are controlling' (Buchanan & Tullock, 1962, p. 12). This rejection negates the possibility of treating the state as a legal person and hence closes the door on the jurisprudential dimension of the state, at least as discussed by Max Weber (1981). The organic-state tradition is diagonal to the Roman approach, in which the state never appeared as a distinct personality, 'but always the sum of the Roman citizens' (Merriam, 1900, p. 109). This is also the Wicksellian ideation at the crux of constitutional economics—that the state is the sum of its citizens: 'If utility is zero for each individual member of the community, the total utility for the community cannot be other than zero' (Wicksell, 1994, p. 77).

Historically, a shift in theoretical emphasis was triggered by the growth of state federations, especially in the Swiss, German, and American contexts. The emphasis was now on division of sovereignty. A salient example is the 1789 United States Constitution, in which sovereignty was divided between the states and federal government. In the Federalist Papers, James Madison elaborated on the theoretical foundations of the possibility of a divided sovereignty in which the states were sovereign as long as their sovereignty was not affected by the constitution (Hamilton et al., 1852). The idea of divided sovereignty later found its way to Europe through Tocqueville (1856), although he was of the opinion that a divided sovereignty would be impractical in Europe given the presence of the great military monarchies of Europe. Similarly, John C. Calhoun (1853), in what could be considered an overture to the American Civil War, attacked the doctrine of divided sovereignty because it was contrary to the logical basis of secession. After the American Civil War, the nationalist movement gained the upper hand. The writings of Francis Lieber (1861), who found the location of an organic sovereignty in the nation, capture the essence of their drive. The same logic was followed by Jameson, Brownson, Hurd, Mulford, and Pomeroy (Merriam, 1900).

The above brief history of sovereignty illustrates the origin of the state as a response to crises, at least in the European context. The evolution of the concept of sovereignty goes hand in hand with the civil wars of the sixteenth and seventeenth centuries. The key point is the tension between absolute (i.e.

undivided) and divided sovereignty, and the dominance of the former strand since the eighteenth century.

THE ANALOGY BETWEEN MARKETS AND POLITICS

This section examines how sovereignty is positioned relative to a core premise in constitutional economics, namely, the analogy between markets and politics. This analysis suggests that sovereignty under constitutional economics would have the characteristics of being relational (contractarian) and divided. As delineated in the next section, both characteristics dominate Spinoza's conception of sovereignty. Without any constitutional safeguards in place, this relational basis continues to fray as sovereignty, predominantly through its economic rationale, amplifies the jurisdiction of the state.

To bring sovereignty into the exchange process inherent in markets, we need a relational definition. In constitutional economics, the market, as an evolutionary selection process, was extended to politics, by using an exchange paradigm to describe cooperative interactions (Buchanan, 1991, 1993). This exchange analogy carries 'relational' tones in which '[b]oth the economic relation and the political relation represent co-operation' (Buchanan & Tullock, 1962, p. 19).[5]

Baruch Spinoza provides a relational definition of sovereignty. Sovereignty à la Spinoza is an abstract notion (albeit not ahistorical one) of 'the relationship between rulers and ruled for the exercise of political power [and] the independent status of the body politic on the international stage' (Prokhovnik 2001, p. 291). Under this understanding, sovereignty 'is not a substantive quality to be possessed but rather a condition of political interactions, embedded in [relations] that ground association' (Smith 2011, p. 426). Through this relational definition, sovereignty becomes the exchange taking place at the input to the process in which the state transforms power into authority. It is the source from which the state makes binding law in a particular territory.

A relational definition of sovereignty imports a small-scale organization of the state.[6] A stark difference exists between economic exchanges in large 'modern' societies and those registered in so-called 'primitive' societies (societies of relatively small size and lacking in technological and economic development). In these societies, economic transactions cannot be understood apart from 'relational' social obligations. For the analogy to work, a 'relational' level commensurate with that of politics is required, one in which participants take the interests of other participants (especially their long-term interests) into account. In contrast, the 'theory of markets postulates only that the relationship be economic, that the interest of [the other party] in the exchange be excluded from consideration' (Buchanan and Tullock 1962, 16). Politics is seen to exhibit efficiency similar to that of voluntary markets in which unanimity around the political process can judge the efficiency of collective action. This analogy suggests that 'the average individual acts on the basis of the same over-all [sic] scale when he participates in market activity and political activity' (Buchanan & Tullock, 1962, p. 18). In this sense, there is a continuum between economic and political 'exchanges.'

Constitutional economics emphasizes cooperative forms of interaction through a contractarian approach in which legitimacy is assured through the agreement of all parties concerned. In contrast, politics—'orthodox' politics, to be precise—has a non-cooperative, 'conflictual' perspective, focusing on the distribution of value among winners and losers. However, in constitutional economics there would be no net losers. This last point has been critiqued on the grounds that 'the analogy between politics and markets made by constitutional economists is theoretically weak and clouds rather than enhances our understanding of political economy. Politics has very little in common with non-coercive, voluntary exchange in the marketplace' (Block & DiLorenzo, 2000, p. 567). Note, however, that the theoretical approach to the state as a voluntary institution can be traced to Aristotle's conviviality theory of the origin of the state, especially as delineated by Kohr (1978). The conflict-based origin of the state (notwithstanding its long tradition through the scholarship of Bodin, Hume, Turgot, and Nietzsche, among others) conflates the origin of the state with its operation beyond the constitutional phase. A sustained 'production of scale' phase (which increases the size of the political community) will result in such conflict. This is when the state continues to grow in size (larger territory, larger population, and larger government). However, that does not mean that the origin of the state is conflictual. The Hobbesian state of nature, in which he opined that conflict was the raison d'être for the state, was the product of Hobbes's own *Zeitgeist*. At the constitutional level, politics would also lend itself to a cooperative analytical framework: 'The market and the State are both devices through which co-operation is organized and made possible' (Buchanan & Tullock, 1962, p. 19).

Reconciling markets and politics as cooperative at the constitutional phase formulates the core issue as one of scale:

[D]isagreement with constitutional economics is more than a definitional one. Buchanan and Tullock label a wide range of seemingly voluntary collective choice institutions as 'government' and, admittedly, a reasonable case can be made that, say, a village fire department might make a good example of voluntary government, at least on a relatively small scale [emphasis added]. But the distinguishing characteristic is that in a truly voluntary setting the parties to an agreement have a right to secede from the agreement. (Block & DiLorenzo, 2000, p. 580)

The key words are 'on a relatively small scale.' Of course, the above quote refers to only an element of the state, namely that of 'government' (the other main elements being population and territory), but it still gives a good illustration of the scalar anchor between markets and politics. The right to secede itself can be seen as indicative of a large polity still viable in the event of secession.

The analogy between markets and politics imports another dimension, in addition to the homo economicus and the exchange process. For markets to function properly (i.e. to be Pareto efficient), one needs to ensure a level of competition in the provision of goods and services. An analogy with politics would see this competition reflected in the provision of goods of a public nature, through competing jurisdictions.[7] Such competition, which is discussed in the next section, is salient in Spinoza's sovereignty.

SPINOZISTIC SOVEREIGNTY

Constitutional economics (à la Buchanan) does not accept absolute sovereignty (Brennan & Buchanan, 2000). It sides instead with Spinoza (Buchanan & Tullock, 1962). Spinoza separates the constitutional and operational levels of collective decision-making, hence paving the way for the possibility of a divided sovereignty. His preferred structure follows from this divided sovereignty and results in a polycentric commonwealth between independent cities.

Note that some commentators question whether Spinoza in fact had a conception of sovereignty. Interested readers are referred to Prokhovnik (1997, 2001, 2004) for a detailed analysis on this point. For its purposes, this Chapter starts from the proposition that "Spinoza must by definition have a conception of sovereignty. According to this perspective, sovereignty is a general feature of all political societies across time and place, underlying the diversity of laws and institutions" (Prokhovnik, 2001, p. 290). Spinoza's approach is similar to that of Hobbes, when he was able to use sovereignty to rank different forms of the state. However, while Hobbes reaches a conclusion in favor of the unitary state, Spinoza finds the form of federal polity superior.

Taking Holland as the point of reference for his analysis, Spinoza intended to show that 'the failure of the experiment in Holland was not due to lack of zeal but to lack of theoretical understanding, and that the lack of theoretical understating requires more than mere theoretical understanding to remedy it' (Gross, 1996, p. 123). Hence, on the cover of his Treatise on Politics (TP), Spinoza (1958) declares his objective as '[to show] how a Monarchy and an Aristocracy must be organized if they are not to degenerate into Tyranny, and if the Peace and Freedom of the citizens is to remain intact.' Spinoza declares that his 'objective in applying [his] mind to politics is not to make any new or unheard-of suggestions, but to establish by sound and conclusive reasoning, and to deduce from the real nature of man, nothing save the principles and institutions which accord best with practice' (TP I 4).

For Spinoza, sovereignty is not repugnant to principles of provincial autonomy. In fact, it could be argued that 'Spinoza's notion of sovereignty is crucially designed as an instrument to defend the constitutional tradition, and not as an instrument to unify and strengthen the state. Its purpose is to check the development of centralized government, not to promote it' (Prokhovnik, 2001, p. 297). Spinoza (1958) follows a contractarian approach to sovereignty in which 'breach of the contract [by the sovereign] is not punished by civil right but by the right of war' (TP IV 6).

Spinoza (TP III 10) puts emphasis on understanding human nature and its effect on the obedience demanded of them as subjects. Spinoza sees the 'right of the sovereign … in the fact that it was … the mind of the state by which all its subjects had to be guided … [the sovereign] alone had the right to make laws …' (TP IV 1). He stresses that 'the causes and natural foundations of the state are not to be sought in the precepts of reason, but must be deduced from the common nature or constitution of men' (TP I 7).

According to Spinoza, 'the virtue of a state is stability' (TP I 6). Spinoza was writing in Latin and the word he used for stability is '*securitas*,' which could also be translated as security. Spinoza's stability is akin to the idea of being protected from danger, which suggests an evolutionary connotation. Spinoza sees sovereignty in an evolutionary light: '[M]an, like everything else in nature, does his utmost to preserve his own being' (TP II 7). In this sense, sovereignty guides the analysis for the structural form that best stabilizes the state. Hence, for Spinoza, sovereignty is a logical necessity (Prokhovnik, 2001), a function of evolutionary fitness that prevents the state from collapse, and degeneration into tyranny is the first step into extinction. Accordingly, he states that:

...if a state is to be capable of lasting, its administration must be so organized that it does not matter whether its rulers are led by reason or passion ... In fact it makes no difference to the stability of a state what motive leads men to conduct its affairs properly, provided that they are conducted properly. (TP I 6)

Spinoza then goes on to state that '[t]he best condition of a commonwealth is easily discovered from the purpose of political order: which is simply peace and security of life' (TP V 2).

Spinoza advocates a sovereignty vested in several cities, in which:

...all the cities are joined and bound together, not as allied states, but as constituent parts of one state ... the power of the city constitutes a great part of the power of the state itself, and the larger the city, the greater its contribution to the power of the state; hence the cities cannot all be regarded as equal, but the right of each, like its power, must be determined by its size. (TP IX 4)

Under this arrangement, 'each city must remain in possession of its own right as far as possible, and must have more right in the government in proportion as it exceeds the others in power' (TP IX 6). For Spinoza, this polycentric arrangement in which sovereignty is vested in several cities is superior to one in which a capital city dominates the state. He gives several arguments supporting his position. First, the fact that each city is represented in proportion to its power would increase competition between cities. This competition would lead to cities increasing their populations 'by ruling more by kindness than by fear' (TP IX 14). Moreover, sovereignty vested in several cities 'needs no safeguards to prevent [it] from being overthrown by a sudden attack', since the freedom 'enjoyed by several cities' makes it 'not sufficient for [usurping] sovereignty to seize one city in order to gain control over the rest' (TP IX 15).

Note that this arrangement is different from the arrangements we see today in the United States and Australia. Spinozistic sovereignty provides a model:

...in which powers are shared between sovereign bodies ... which reaffirm their separateness ... In federal systems such as the United States or in Australia, legislative, judicial and executive powers are distributed between

federal and different state governments ... under [Spinozistic sovereignty], however, 'confederal' powers ... were extremely closely restricted ... Rather than attempting to harmonize differences ... [it upholds] the constructiveness of difference ... (Prokhovnik, 2007, p. 228)

Polycentric states are at the center of Spinoza's discourse. Buchanan (1990) echoes Spinoza when he explains his idea of federalism as 'diversity among separate cooperative communities, of shared sovereignty, of effective devolution of political authority and, perhaps most importantly, of the limits on such authority' (Buchanan, 1990, pp. 3–4). Buchanan envisaged a 'federal union within which members of separate units cooperate' (Buchanan, 1990, p. 18) and share sovereignty, in which constitutional requirements guarantee free trade, and with a monetary constitution based on competing national currencies.

CODA

This Chapter argues that sovereignty, as envisaged by Spinoza, is the logical foundation of constitutional economics. Constitutional constructs such as sovereignty weave an evolutionary dialectic between different organizational scales (the local, national, and global). This dialectic continues to wreak havoc at the local scale, and can be interrupted only through explicit constitutional constraints on the size of jurisdictions. The paper argues for more emphasis on constitutional orders in the spirit of Spinoza's understanding of sovereignty. This entails preference for federal policies in which sovereignty is shared between different cities rather states where once capital cities dominate.

Historically, sovereignty succumbed to the concept of 'nation'. This resulted in sovereignty being conceived of as a one-dimensional possibility: a nation state either has it or it does not. It became an absolute quality. Sovereignty as understood today is 'a right of membership, historically determined, in what amounts to a very exclusive political club' (Jackson, 1999, p. 449). This club of nation states is 'the most exclusive political club in the world and has been so for several centuries' (Jackson, 1999, p. 449). A sovereign state is conceived of as an exclusive territorial jurisdiction. Since the signing of the Peace of Westphalia in 1648, and especially in the post-Napoleonic era (after 1815), 'a prominent operating principle regulating the size and shape of states has indeed been that states should be contiguous and non-perforated' (Kurrild-Klitgaard, 2002, p. 146). This should be understood in relation to the observation that 'the Westphalian State is … bound symbiotically to the ideology of nationalism' (Tierney, 2006, p. 245). The relationship between sovereignty and territory is captured by the principle of *uti possidetis juris* (Jackson, 1999). In particular, this principle subordinated the principle of self-determination to boundaries decided by colonial power: juridical territories trumped sociological territories.

It was not until the rise of federal states exemplified by the United States that a shift in the analysis towards the possible divisibility of sovereignty occurred. Today, the political state is 'characterized by polycentric centers of power' (Jayasuriya, 2006, p. 372). These centers of power are an extension of the idea of divisibility of sovereignty. However, using the analogy with the idea of a 'polycentric' legal order (implying a multiplicity of independent centers of decision-making) (Bell, 1991; Hayek, 1983), there is no extensive (economic) evaluation of the need for, or merit of, an analogous 'polycentric' constitutional order (Barnett, 1998). The assumption is usually made that 'there is a state or a commonwealth, without exploring the question of which domain [a scalar construct] this commonwealth or state should actually occupy, and in relation to what other public bodies' (Backhaus 2005, p. 281). While conceding that some literature touches on the structure of the state and its relation to economic structures, emphasis should be on maximizing constitutional options rather than deciding among constraints per se. The 'choice among constraints' does not explain where the total set of available constraints arises in the first place. Constitutional economics seems to treat these constraints as exogenous—a consequence of not engaging sovereignty. The ability to distinguish between different scales (from the global to the local) goes a long way towards explaining how options are limited (and hence constraints created). This in turn results in a dynamic set of constraints from which to choose. However, this is available only when the structure of the state is made the subject of analysis. In particular, when questioning the national scale as the default level of analysis, a very different set of constraints emerges.

Unfortunately, in constitutional economics, a taste of 'Westphalia sovereignty' and its emphasis on the nation state still lingers. Although ideas on sovereignty and jurisdiction are not usually treated explicitly, they can be gleaned from the assumptions typically made by constitutional economics. The central feature here is still the same as it has been since early discourse on political economy, which in fact is the same impetus underlying most theories of sovereignty: legitimization of the nation state. Even when scalar differentiation is engaged, it is never in relation to the state, but rather to government—leaving other elements of the state, especially territory and population, beyond systematic inquiry. Hence, we find discourse on the optimal size of government, but not on the optimal size of states, in which government is understood as only one element of the state, distinct from the latter's territory. There has even been a tendency to treat 'government' and 'state' interchangeably, further disguising the essential issue of territoriality and the ensuing possibilities of divided sovereignty (Hayek 1983, p. 48).

A nuanced reading of Spinozistic sovereignty militates against the existence of colossal jurisdictions. One can trace the logic of limiting the jurisdiction of states within a polycentric constitutional set-up back to Aristotle. Although some pronouncements from constitutional economics echo the same ideas, constitutional economics would not pass muster unless it is understood that the golden principle for constitutional design is the inquiry into how states can be engineered along the lines of Spinoza's federal polity. This aspect of the analysis has not yet received much emphasis when it comes to normative constitutional design. It is submitted that such emphasis would lead to countries as large as Russia and China, and even the United States, being questioned as to their stability in the post-constitutional phase. To be sustainable, such jurisdictional footprints need to be perforated by attractors such as global (and charter) cities.

REFERENCES

Althusius, J. (1965). *The politics of Johannes Althusius* (F. S. Carney, Trans. & Ed.). London: Eyre & Spottiswoode.

Aristotle, . (2013). *Aristotle's politics* (C. Lord, Trans. & Ed.). Chicago: University of Chicago Press.

Backhaus, J. G. (2005). Subsidiarity. In J. G. Backhaus (Ed.), *The Elgar companion to law and economics* (2nd ed., pp. 280–286). Northampton, MA: Edward Elgar. doi:10.4337/9781845425500.00027

Barnett, R. E. (1998). *The structure of liberty: Justice and the rule of law*. Oxford: Clarendon Press.

Beard, C. A. (1935). *The economic basis of politics*. London: George Allen & Unwin.

Bell, T. W. (1991). Polycentric law. *Institute of Humane Studies Review, 7* (1). Retrieved from http://osf1.gmu.edu/~ihs/w91issues.html

Block, W., & DiLorenzo, T. J. (2000). Is voluntary government possible? A critique of constitutional economics. *Journal of Institutional and Theoretical Economics, 156*(4), 567–582.

Bodin, J. (1955). *Six books of the Commonwealth* (M. J. Tooley, Trans.). Oxford: Blackwell.

Brennan, G., & Buchanan, J. A. (2000). *The power to tax*. Indianapolis: Liberty Press.

Buchanan, J. (1990). *Europe's constitutional future*. London: Institute of Economic Affairs.

Buchanan, J. (1991). *The economics and the ethics of constitutional order*. Ann Arbor: The University of Michigan Press. doi:10.3998/mpub.13054

Buchanan, J. (1993). Public choice after socialism. *Public Choice, 77*(1), 67–74. doi:10.1007/BF01049220

Buchanan, J., & Tullock, G. (1962). *The calculus of consent: Logical foundations of constitutional democracy*. Ann Arbor: University of Michigan Press. doi:10.3998/mpub.7687

Calhoun, J. C. (1853). *A disquisition on government and a discourse on the Constitution and Government of the United States*. New York: D. Appleton and Co.

de Tocqueville, A. (1856). *The old regime and the revolution* (J. Bonner, Trans. & Ed.). New York: Harper & Brothers.

Dougherty, K. L. (2011). *The calculus of consent and constitutional design*. New York: Springer. doi:10.1007/978-0-387-98171-0

Foucault, M. (1991). Governmentality. In G. Burchell, C. Gordon, & P. Miller (Eds.), *The Foucault effect: Studies in governmentality* (pp. 87–104). London: Harvester Wheatsheaf.

Foucault, M. (2000). *Power*. New York: New Press.

Gross, G. M. (1996). Spinoza and the federal polity. *Publius, 26*(1), 117–136. doi:10.1093/oxfordjournals.pubjof.a029830

Gussen, B. F. (2013). On the problem of scale: Spinozistic sovereignty as the logical foundation of constitutional economics. *The Journal of Philosophical Economics, 7*(1). Retrieved from http://www.jpe.ro/pdf.php?id=4997

Habermas, J. (1996). *Between facts and norms: Contributions to a discourse theory of law and democracy*. Cambridge: MIT Press.

Halleberg, M. (2011). Fiscal federalism reforms in the European Union and the Greek crisis. *European Union Politics, 12*(1), 127–142. doi:10.1177/1465116510387652

Hamilton, A., Madison, J., & Jay, J. (Eds.). (1852). *The Federalist: On the new Constitution written in 1788; with an appendix containing the letters of Pacificus and Helvidius on the Proclamation of Neutrality of 1793; also the original Articles of Confederation and the Constitution of the United States, with the Amendments made thereto*. Hallowell, ME: Masters & Smith.

Hayek, F. A. (1983). *Law legislation and liberty: A new statement of the liberal principles of justice and political economy* (Vol. 1). Chicago: University of Chicago Press.

Helleiner, E. (2003). *The making of national money: Territorial currencies in historical perspective*. Ithaca: Cornell University Press.

Hinsely, F. H. (1966). *Sovereignty*. London: C. A. Watts & Co.

Hobbes, T. (1982). *Leviathan*. London: Penguin Classics. (Original work published 1651)

Jackson, R. (1999). Sovereignty in world politics: A glance at the conceptual and historical landscape. *Political Studies, 47*(3), 431–456. doi:10.1111/1467-9248.00211

Jayasuriya, K. (2006). Globalization, sovereignty, and the rule of law: From political to economic constitutionalism? In N. Walker (Ed.), *Relocating sovereignty* (pp. 521–550). Aldershot: Dartmouth Ashgate.

Kohr, L. (1978). *The overdeveloped nations: The diseconomies of scale*. New York: Schoken Books.

Kurrild-Klitgaard, P. (2002). Opting-out: The constitutional economics of exit. *Journal of Economics and Sociology*, *61*(1), 123–158. doi:10.1111/1536-7150.00154

Lieber, F. (1861). What is our Constitution: League, pact, or government? New York: Law School of Columbia College, Board of Trustees.

Macdonald, S., & Nielsson, G. (1995). Linkages between the concepts of 'subsidiarity' and sovereignty: The new debate over allocation of authority in the European Union. *Presented at the Fourth European Union Studies Association (EUSA) Biennial Conference.*

Merriam, C. E. (1900). *History of the theory of sovereignty since Rousseau.* New York: Columbia University Press.

Oakeshott, M. (1975). *On human conduct.* Oxford: England Clarendon Press.

Prokhovnik, R. (1997). From democracy to aristocracy: Spinoza, reason and politics. *History of European Ideas*, *23*(2–4), 105–115. doi:10.1016/S0191-6599(96)00012-5

Prokhovnik, R. (2001). Spinozas conception of sovereignty. *History of European Ideas*, *27*(3), 289–306. doi:10.1016/S0191-6599(01)00051-1

Prokhovnik, R. (2004). *Spinoza and republicanism.* Basingstoke: Palgrave Macmillan. doi:10.1057/9780230000902

Prokhovnik, R. (2007). *Sovereignties: Contemporary theory and practice.* New York: Palgrave Macmillan. doi:10.1057/9780230593527

Rabkin, J. A. (2005). *Law without nations? Why constitutional government requires sovereign states.* Princeton: Princeton University Press.

Rousseau, J.-J. (1797). *A dissertation on political economy: To which is added, A treatise on the social compact, or, The principles of politic law.* Albany, NY: Barber & Southwick.

Sinn, H.-W. (2002). *The new systems competition.* Oxford: Blackwell. doi:10.3386/w8747

Smith, A. T. (2011). Archaeologies of sovereignty. *Annual Review of Anthropology*, *40*(1), 415–432. doi:10.1146/annurev-anthro-081309-145754

Smith, D. A., Solinger, D. J., & Topik, S. C. (1999). Introduction. In D. A. Smith, D. J. Solinger, & S. C. Topik (Eds.), *States and sovereignty in the global economy*. London: Routledge.

Sovereign. (2004). In *The Oxford English dictionary*. Oxford University Press.

Spinoza, B. (1958). *The Political Works: The Tractatus Theologico-Politicus in part and the Tractatus Politicus in full* (A. G. Wernham, Trans. & Ed.). Oxford: Clarendon Press.

Tierney, S. (2006). Reframing sovereignty? Sub-state national societies and contemporary challenges to the nation-state. In N. Walker (Ed.), *Relocating Sovereignty* (pp. 239–261). Aldershot: Ashgate Dartmouth.

Veitch, S., Christodoulidis, E. A., & Farmer, L. (2007). *Jurisprudence: Themes and concepts*. London: Routledge-Cavendish.

Walker, R. B. J. (1990). Sovereignty, identity, community: Reflections on the horizons of contemporary political practice. In R.B.J. Walker & S.H. Mendlovitz (Eds.), Contending sovereignties: Redefining political community (pp. 159-185). London: Lynne Rienner Publishers.

Wallerstein, I. (1999). States? Sovereignty? The dilemma of capitalists in an age of transition. In D. A. Smith, D. J. Solinger, & S. C. Topik (Eds.), *States and sovereignty in the global economy* (pp. 20–33). London: Routledge.

Wcbcr, M. (1981). Essay on some categories of interpretive sociology. *The Sociological Quarterly*, *22*(2), 145–150. doi:10.1111/j.1533-8525.1981.tb00654.x

Wicksell, K. (1994). A new principle of just taxation. In R. Musgrave & A. Peacock (Eds.), *Classics in the Theory of Public Finance* (pp. 72–118). New York: Macmillan and Company.

ENDNOTES

1 For the key work on the concept of *universitas*, see Oakeshott (1975).

2 A caveat: Sovereignty, like so many terms that straddle the boundary between law and politics, is a concept denoting a cluster of related ideas rather than one single clearly defined one. Moreover, in nearly all its clustered elements, it is a contested concept, in the sense that different theoretical approaches dispute over its correct explanation or definition, usually also disagreeing about its practical relevance. (Veitch et al., 2007, p. 10–11)

3 For the purposes of this chapter, no distinction needs to be made between contractarian-ism and the original-contract approach.

4 This formulation of a political power exchange has a Foucauldian overtone, in which power is a 'certain type of relation between individuals' (Foucault, 2000, p. 324).

5 For a clearer understanding of the size of population that would constitute a small organization, refer to Kohr (1978).

6 This jurisdictional competition could be linked to what came to be known as systems competition (Sinn, 2002).

Conclusion

FINDINGS

In Chapter II, using the second law of thermodynamics, the concept of 'complex power,' and the principle of equipartition (from statistical mechanics), we developed an analytical model, the ψ model, to investigate the economic efficiency of countries. This efficiency was measured as thermodynamic loss. The economic process was modeled as one of energy transformation, where low entropy is a necessary condition for the existence of economic value. The concept of complex power was used to model capital as a form of apparent or imaginary power that affects the stability (sustainability) of the world-system but does not add (directly) to the real power captured by the inputs (land and people) and the output (produced goods and services). In other words, capital is modeled as real energy from apparent power. More broadly, capital is understood as a form of complex energy. Using per-unit energy-equivalent inputs (area and population) and outputs (GDP), the model identifies the economic efficiency of every country in the world-system.

The model presumes that (in a given time interval) countries are entrusted with a portion of the world's area and population, and are expected to transform energies 'stored' in these inputs into goods and services (output). This expectation provides a normative signal for an output floor (a minimum), as a proportion of the 'world-system' output. For countries to exceed this minimum output, they have to absorb capital from the 'world-system,' and accumulate this capital within their economies. Countries that can do so are efficient. This efficiency is linked to economic complexity and suggests a corresponding level of economic growth and development. These efficient countries were referred to as 'sink' countries because of their ability to attract and absorb capital. On the other hand, countries that are unable to employ capital in their economic process were called 'sources,' because they release their capital to sink countries. These source countries are below the ψ floor output and hence are classified as inefficient. In 2015, according to the model, there were only 70 efficient countries (out of 196). The most efficient countries have small jurisdictional footprints (*qua* area). Such countries include the Holy See, Monaco, Qatar, Lichtenstein, and Luxembourg. We also found efficient countries with large jurisdictional footprints. The quintessential examples are the United States and China. These countries were able to achieve economic efficiency by perforating their jurisdictional footprints with capital attractors. In the case of the United States, these attractors were in the form of global cities, while in the case of China they were in the form of Special Economic Zones (SEZs). Our analysis of G-20 countries confirms these findings. At the sub-national level, the efficiency signatures of the 50 US States and the District of Columbia also confirm the role of small jurisdictional footprints and global cities in attaining economic efficiency.

The analysis suggests that an evolutionary understanding of economics produces specific normative signals as to the structure of the political state. The general theory presented in Chapter II models complexity as a force, similar to gravitation. Evolution is understood as a condition exhibiting an increase in this (morphological) complexity. In the final analysis, economic change is linked to the structure of the political state. Pathologies of economic change, including morphostasis (i.e. reaching a stage where growth and development are anemic due to the system's form and structure becoming static), necessitate a rethinking of political organization. Polycentricity and the principle of hypotaxis (also known as subsidiarity or spheres of sovereignty), with a praxis inspired by global cities, are imperative for the continuous evolution of economies, and hence societies. Our analysis suggests a problematization of scale where the rise of the large nation-state portends a structural collapse. Evading such collapse would require restructuring inter-communal relations away from the epistemological privilege attached to the nation-state. Moving from large to small polities does not necessarily mean secession. Instead, the decision-making process needs to be embedded in the affected localities. This could be achieved by borrowing from one of the pages of the Middle Ages, by resurrecting the idea of charter cities. In this future, nation-states become hypotactic to city-regions. Charter cities replace nation-states on the 'international' stage.

Our analytical journey started with a call for brings localism to the center of any response to (economic) crises—and by doing so surrendering all other scales of social organization (from the national to the global) to hypotaxis. Disembeddedness (or delocalization) is identified as the root cause of crises.

Localism was the leitmotif of the historical (pre-Enlightenment) response. Today, however, the response marginalizes localism through the fiction of 'indigenous peoples,' through the 'universal human rights' paradigm, and above all through the illusion of the 'complexity imperative.' Notwithstanding, there is a growing understanding of the importance of localism, shared by international organizations and the civil society. The principle of hypotaxis was identified as the mechanism through which localism can be actionalized. Hypotaxis is the solution to the economic inefficiency and instability of the current world-system. Hypotaxis is to sustainability what self-organization is to emergence. In highly complex systems, such as world economies, emergence (sustainability) cannot occur without self-organization (hypotaxis). This solution requires embedding the decision-making process at the city-region, and ensuring that central government is hypotactic to this city-centric scale. Hypotaxis leads to a departure from the contiguous-and-non-perforated-state principle. Emphasis shifts towards providing 'polycentric' constitutional orders, where sovereignty is shared in a way not very different from that envisaged by Spinoza in his description of the Dutch Republic (1581-1795). This solution differs from the way sovereignty is divided under federal systems. Federal systems attempt to 'migrate' decision-making to the national (or even supra-national level) to ensure harmonization. Hypotaxis on the other hand envisages so much expertise in the ever-smaller governance units as possible, and as much competence for ever larger governance units as necessary. The current nation-state-centered world-system needs to move to a future where global cities replace nation-states as the privileged modality for social organization.

In summary, small jurisdictional footprints are a necessary but not sufficient condition for economic efficiency. Countries can achieve these footprints by having small areas, roughly at the scale of New York City, which has an area of around 25,000 square kilometers; or by perforating their existing (large) areas with attractors such as global cities and SEZs. A third type of attractors, namely industrial clusters, can be found in highly complex economies such as Germany and Japan. These economies enjoyed a long development trajectory that enables them to achieve economic efficiency through distributed urban systems. Once a small jurisdictional footprint is achieved, countries efficiency can be secured by choice of legal systems, and governance institutions.

LIMITATIONS

It is hoped that the ideas presented in this monograph provide a stimulus for the future development of economic and legal doctrines that embody the drive towards smaller polities. However, there remains questions in relation to the robustness of the findings. Salient among these questions is the choice of variables in the ψ model. Some might suggest that land, people, and capital are not enough to capture the complexity inherent in economic systems. This could well be true, although there is a long pedigree of classical economists that endorse this approach. Richard Cantillon provides an exemplar of such economic analysis. There might however still be a need for more inputs and outputs to ascertain the level of economic efficiency enjoyed by a given country. The choice of the variables in the ψ model (land, people, and capital) could be seen as a starting point towards more accurate models. There is also room for improvement in modeling the variables. Under the veil of ignorance in the 'original position,' we assumed away any differences between countries in terms of their inputs. The justification for this simplification was that any differences would be captured as capital. However, it would be interesting to see how heterogeneous inputs can affect the findings.

Probably, the way capital was modeled, namely as imaginary or apparent power that sums up to zero at the global scale, could also represent some conceptual difficulties. These difficulties are on three fronts. First, there is the unorthodoxy of modeling capital as a form of energy. In simple terms, energy is force applied to distance. In this sense, we can think of capital as related to complexity——even as a synonym for complexity. The ability to attain economic complexity, and hence economic efficiency, is predicated on capital. However, the idea that capital in itself is a form of energy is novel and is not likely to find speedy acceptance. But even if we surpass this hurdle, we then need to contemplate how capital could be, not only a form of energy, but an imaginary one. Many would argue that capital is as real as any other input to the economic process. This is especially so in terms of physical capital, which could also overlap with the inputs to our model (land and people). Using 'imaginary power' was simply a mathematical trick to allow for negative capital, which is the capital exported by source countries. The difference between 'real power' such as that stored in land and people and 'imaginary power,' is that the former is capable of performing work in the form of goods and services, while the latter does not perform work. Capital, however, helps improve the stability of the economic system by increasing its efficiency. While in physics we tend to interpret imaginary power as counter efficiency, capital in the ψ model operates to improve efficiency. Potentially, there could be other ways to account for capital without the need for complex (apparent) power. Whether that would result in better insights as to economic efficiency is something worth investigating.

Another salient question relates to measurement. While area and population do not represent any particular difficulty, measuring GDP could be problematic, especially for countries where there is a large black economy (e.g. India). It is possible to adjust available GDP figures for such measurement issues, but that in itself introduces another set of approximations——and inaccuracies. It would be useful however, to compare the findings with and without such adjustments. If anything, these adjustments would increase the number of efficient countries. On the other hand, the very fact that GDP figure for some countries are not as reliable as those for other countries could suggest institutional deficiencies that have a direct effect on economic efficiency, and should hence be captured in any attempt to measure said efficiency. Only a comparison of findings with and without GDP adjustments will ascertain the impact of these adjustments on the accuracy of the findings.

But even if all these questions are answered, we are still left with lingering doubts as to the practicality of the recommendations. In particular, the idea that countries with large jurisdictional footprints such as China and the United States would be willing to enhance their economic efficiency by expanding the 'privilege' given to global cities and SEZs to a form of constitutional autonomy (as charter cities) is, to many, simply an aspirational ideal. Nation-states have very little incentive for creating such self-organization. This jurisprudence would hence need to find a political voice through a new breed of political parties that emphasize constitutional limits on geopolitical footprints (territories). Probably, the coming collapse of the current world-system (see below) might be the ideal setting for a transition to this charter-city future. We have already seen a similar 'future' in the rise of Venice from the ashes of the Middle Ages, and by doing so ushering the age of Enlightenment and the rise of Europe to an economic power.

PREDICTIONS

A key objective of the analysis is to make predictions as to the state of the world-system in the next few decades. These predictions hinge on the following understanding: economic efficiency is not absolute. A country is efficient (or otherwise) only relative to other countries in the world-system. A stable world-system is then defined as one where these efficiency relativities are constant over time. When these relativities exhibit long positive or negative trends, countries switch from sources to sinks or vice versa. Such reversal leads not only to economic consequences, but also to socio-political ones, and eventually to new superpowers and world-systems. Based on our results from the ψ model, we can look at the nature of the changes in these efficiency relativities over the observation period from 1990 to 2015. Given that over 80 percent of the world's goods and services come from G-20 countries, we can focus our analysis on these (19) countries. Identifying clear trends in relativities in this group of countries would suggest that the current (WTO) world-system is in a phase of transition to a new equilibrium.

In our analysis of the largest world economies (the Group of Twenty, or G-20), we found three types of countries (or six tiers in total). The First, and largest group, are countries that exhibit a Red Queen Effect (RQE): they are able to maintain the same level of economic efficiency over the observation period (1990 to 2015) or (long) parts of it. Classic examples of such economies are the United Kingdom and Germany. However, there are also inefficient countries that also exhibit an RQE. While these countries are inefficient, their level of inefficiency is stable over time. Hence, these countries exhibit constant relativities. In this sub-group we find Australia, Canada, Indonesia, Saudi Arabia, and South Africa. Note that Australia and Canada, which together with Russia form the G-20 Tier 6 countries (the lowest tier), have RQEs at levels of lower efficiency relative to the RQEs seen in Tier 4 countries (Indonesia, Saudi Arabia, and South Africa). Other countries with inefficient RQEs include Argentina, Brazil, and India, which form Tier 5. These countries have constant inefficiency levels between Tier 4 and Tier 6.

In the second type, we find countries like South Korea and China, which are able to exhibit a positive trend in their economic efficiency. South Korea belongs to Tier 1 countries, which exhibit the highest economic efficiency levels, where we also find the United Kingdom and Germany. China on the other hand belongs to Tier 3, together with Mexico and Turkey. These countries have shown a remarkable increase in their efficiency since 1990——interrupted only by the Global Financial Crisis (GFC). South Korea exhibited a strong improvement from 1990 to 1998. However, this improvement was interrupted by the AFC, then again from 2002 to 2004, and from 2007 to 2011. After the GFC, South Korea's efficiency saturates at an RQE that continued until 2015. In the case of China, we see a substantial increase in efficiency between 1995 and 1996, which coincides with the introduction of the WTO, although China became a member only in 2001. Since then, China continued a strong positive trend that was interrupted only by the GFC. After the GFC China continued to improve its efficiency. In 2015 China was able, for the first time, to switch from a source to a sink country. Countries such as China are repositioning their economies within the current world-system to compete more successfully for a larger share of world capital.

In the third group of countries we find economic giants in decline. Members of this group include the United States, France, and Italy. These countries have already started to exhibit 'economic collapse' where their economies are becoming less and less efficient. In the case of the US, the country lost almost 17 percent of its economic efficiency since 1990. In the case of France, the country shed 40 percent of its 1990 economic efficiency level. As to Italy, even though it shows an overall improvement in its efficiency over the observation period (1990 to 2015), after the GFC, Italy shed 21 percent of its efficiency (between 2009 and 2015). These countries are already 'exporting' capital to countries of the second type. By exporting this capital, they are altering the 'efficiency relativities' on which the current (WTO) world-system had been built. *Ceteris paribus*, countries in this third group will continue this economic decline. When this happens, it is inevitable that economic collapse will lead to political, and even existential crises. Given the importance of countries in this third group to the current world-system, especially the leading role played by France in Africa, and by the United States across the globe, it is inevitable that the next few decades will see a transition to leadership roles played by other countries. In fact, we can already see such transition happening, for example through the ever-growing involvement of China in Africa. There has been 'jockeying' for a new world-system since the early 2000s.

The interesting question is whether the efficiency decline in third-type countries will continue, intensify, or be reversed. Our analysis suggests that there will be a clear departure from the current world-system by the 2030s. But we cannot predict which evolutionary path will materialize after this bifurcation. It could be that these countries are able to reverse their decline. But this will have a direct effect on second-type countries——potentially even on first-type countries. Think of a 'water bed.' The analogy here is that a rising West (as exemplified in the G-20) will lead to a falling East, and vice versa. Probably, the correct question to ask is not what evolutionary path will materialize, but what can be done to ensure that a specific path will materialize. An extension of the observation period (to 2020) is likely to provide more insights as to the nature of the coming world-system. This will hopefully be the remit of the next edition of this book.

Appendices

APPENDIX FOR CHAPTER 3: WORLD EFFICIENCY SIGNATURES

This appendix provides the 'efficiency signature' for each of the 196 countries represented in the ψ model. See Figures 1-196. Signatures of sink countries are represented in green (positive efficiency), while those of source countries are represented in red (negative efficiency).

Figure 1. The efficiency signature for Afghanistan

Figure 2. The efficiency signature for Albania

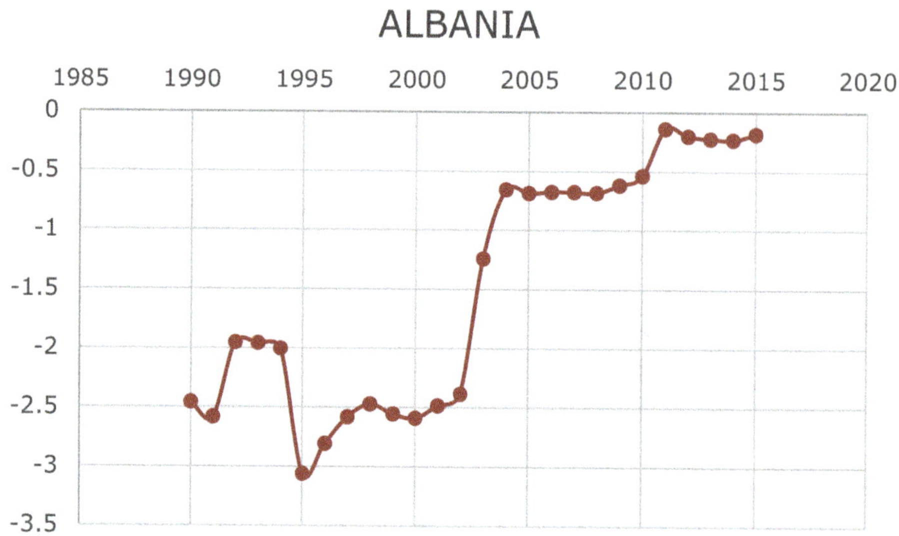

Figure 3. The efficiency signature for Algeria

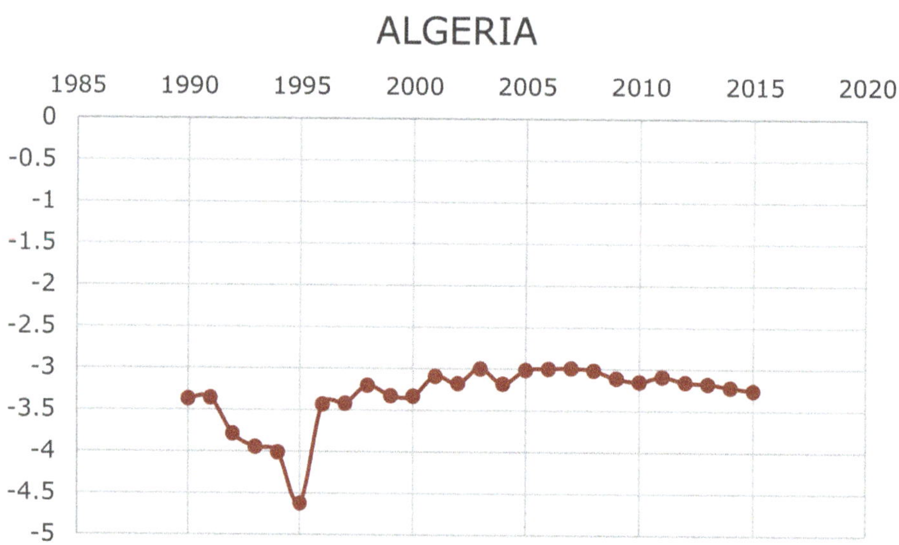

Figure 4. The efficiency signature for Andorra

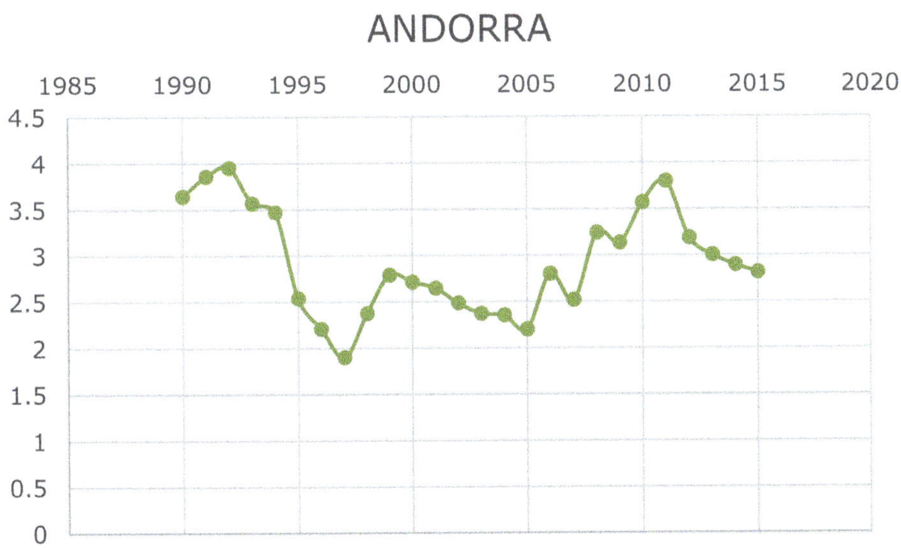

Figure 5. The efficiency signature for Angola

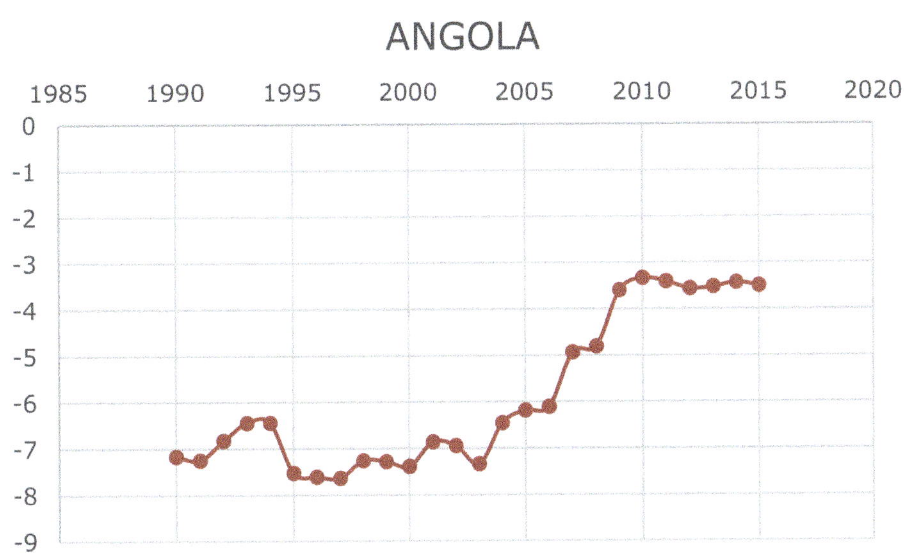

Figure 6. The efficiency signature for Antigua and Barbuda

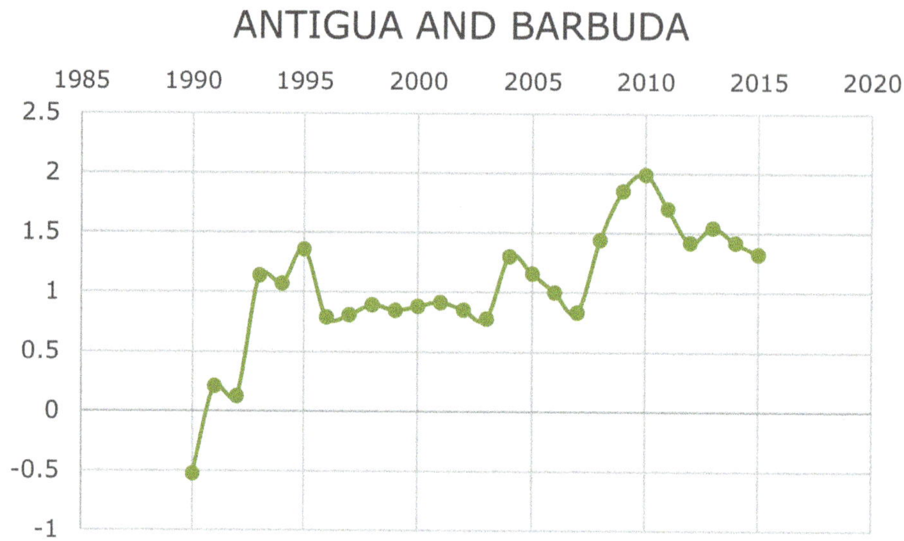

Figure 7. The efficiency signature for Argentina

Figure 8. The efficiency signature for Armenia

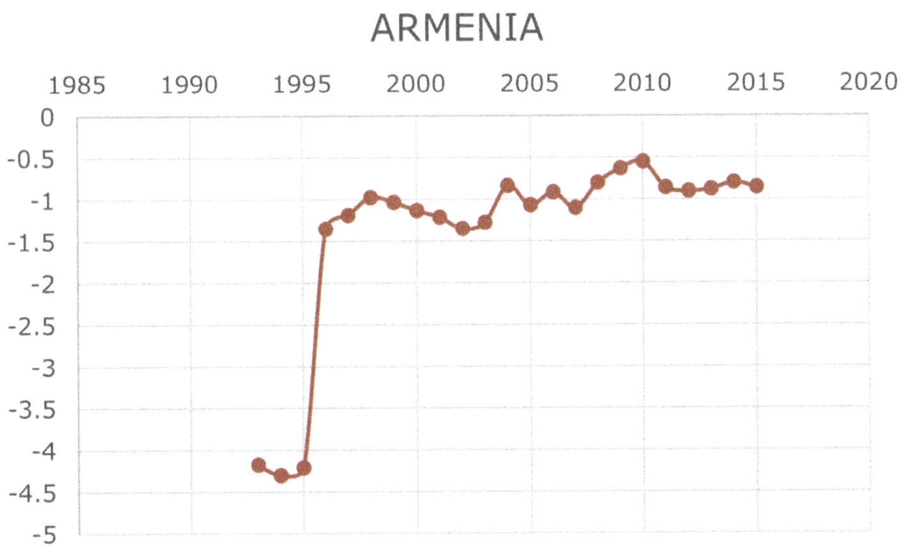

Figure 9. The efficiency signature for Australia

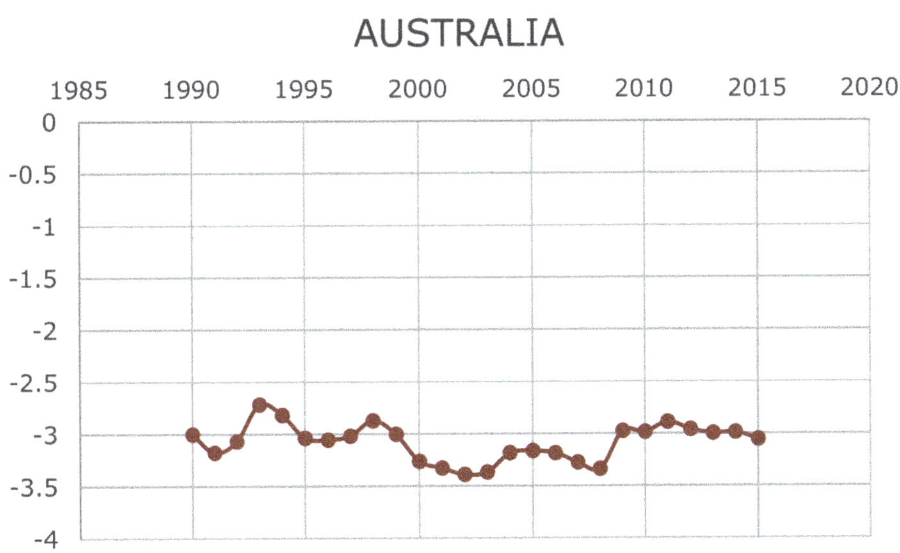

Figure 10. The efficiency signature for Austria

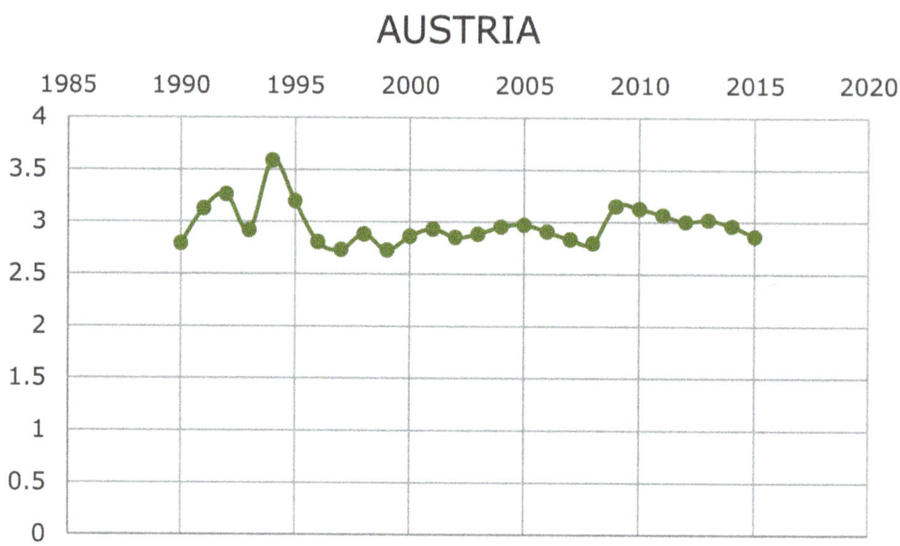

Figure 11. The efficiency signature for Azerbaijan

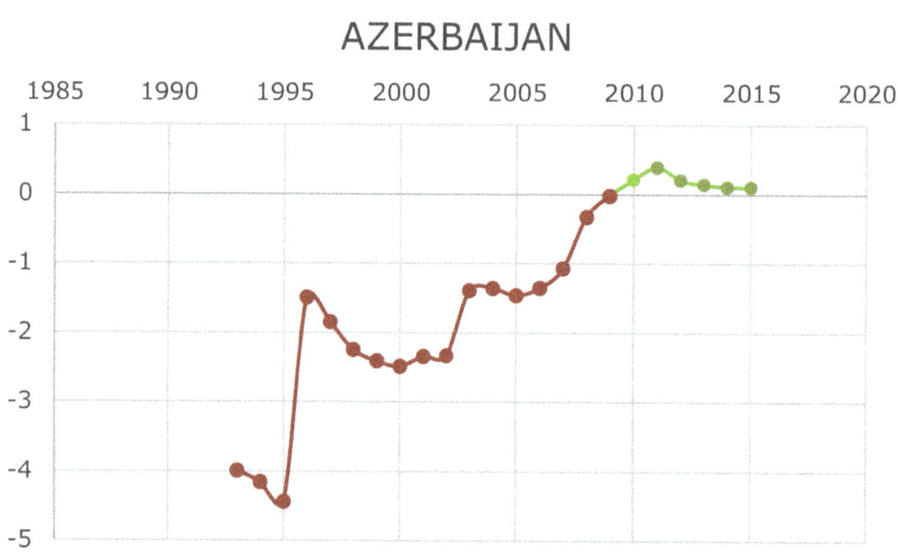

Figure 12. The efficiency signature for the Bahamas

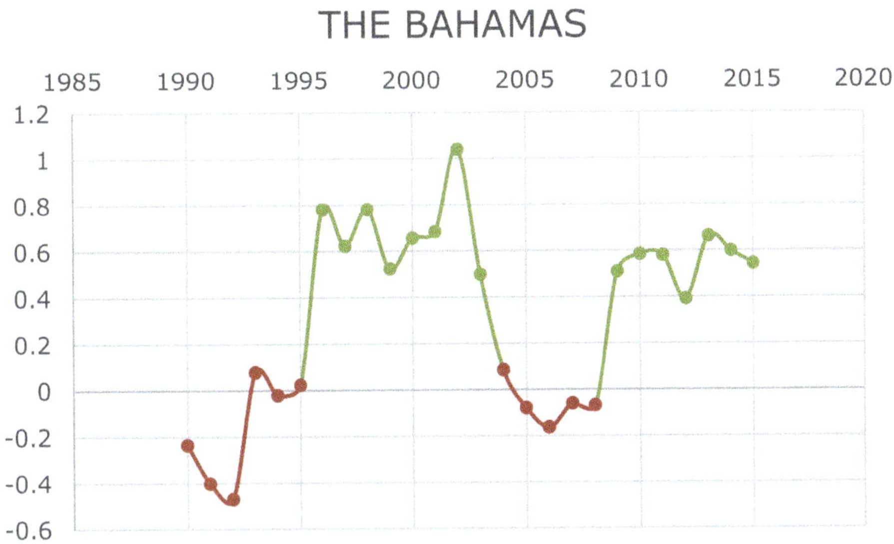

Figure 13. The efficiency signature for Bahrain

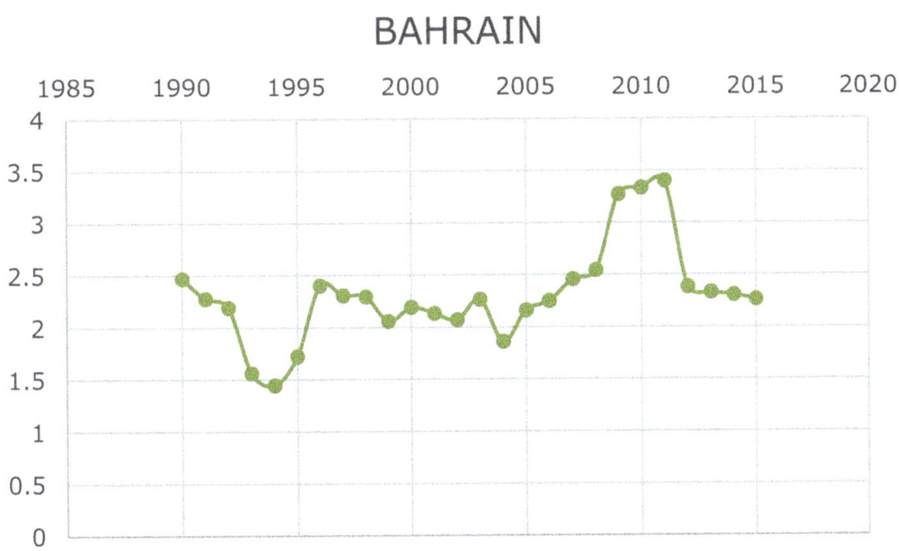

Figure 14. The efficiency signature for Bangladesh

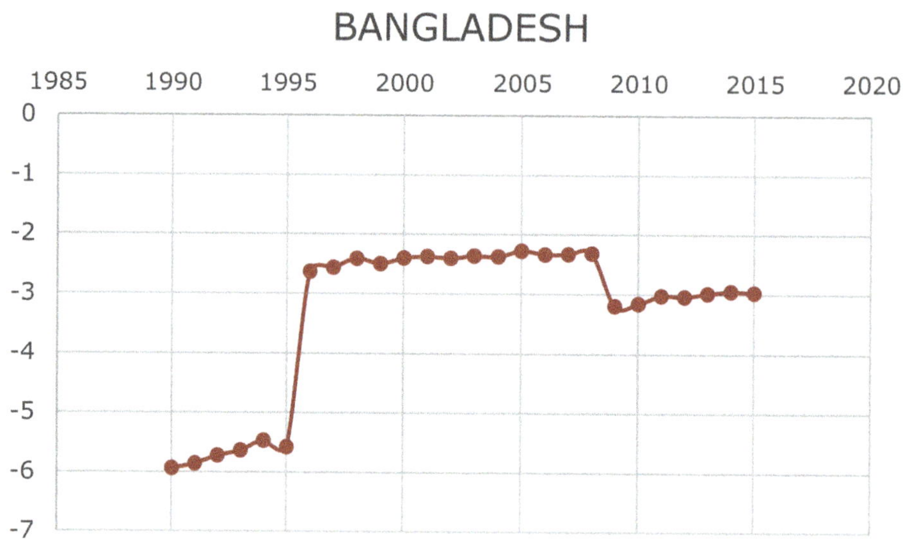

Figure 15. The efficiency signature for Barbados

Figure 16. The efficiency signature for Belarus

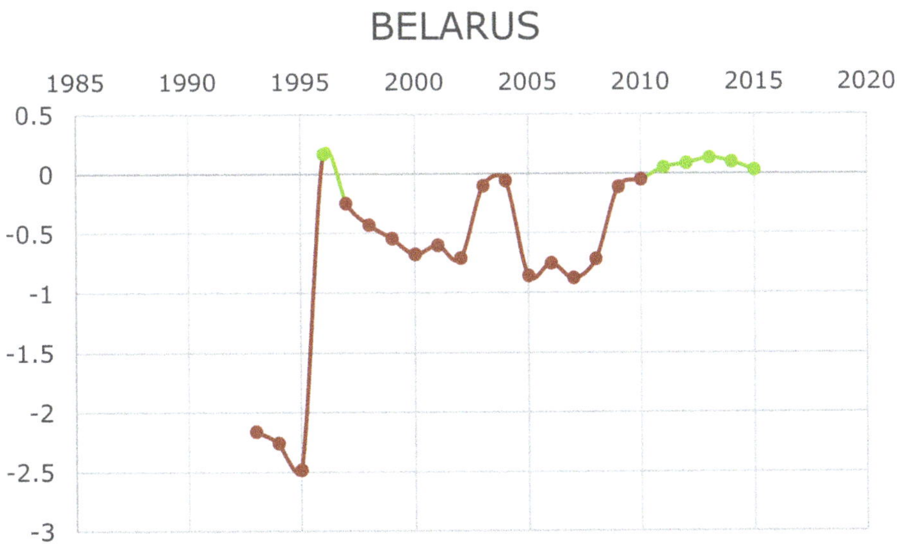

Figure 17. The efficiency signature for Belgium

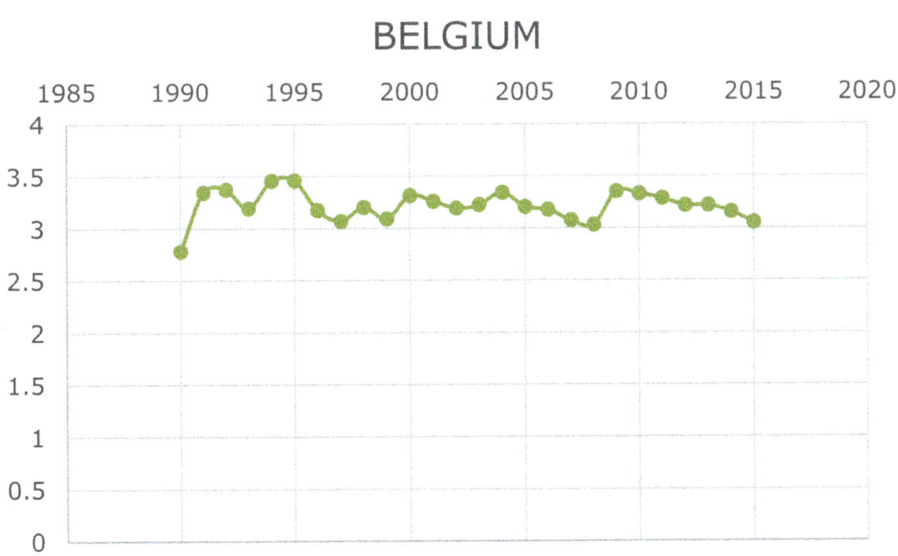

Figure 18. The efficiency signature for Belize

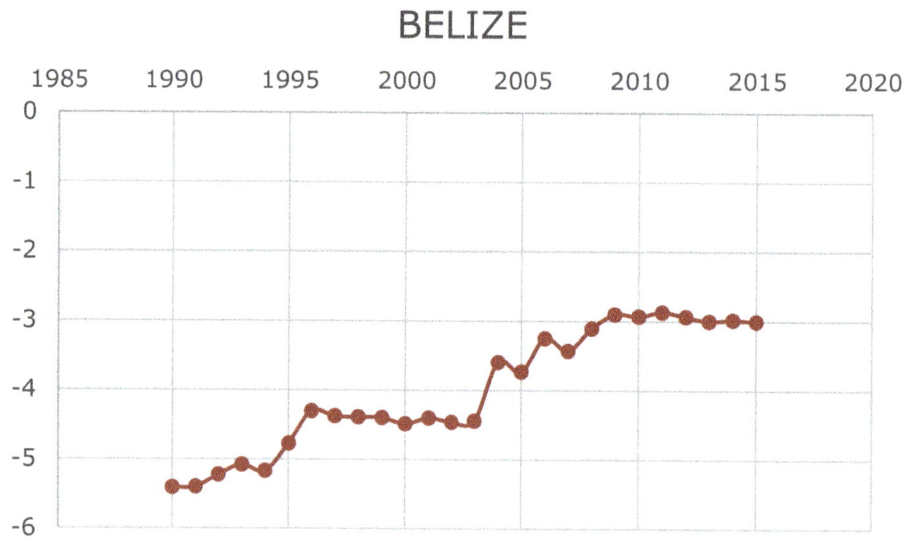

Figure 19. The efficiency signature for Benin

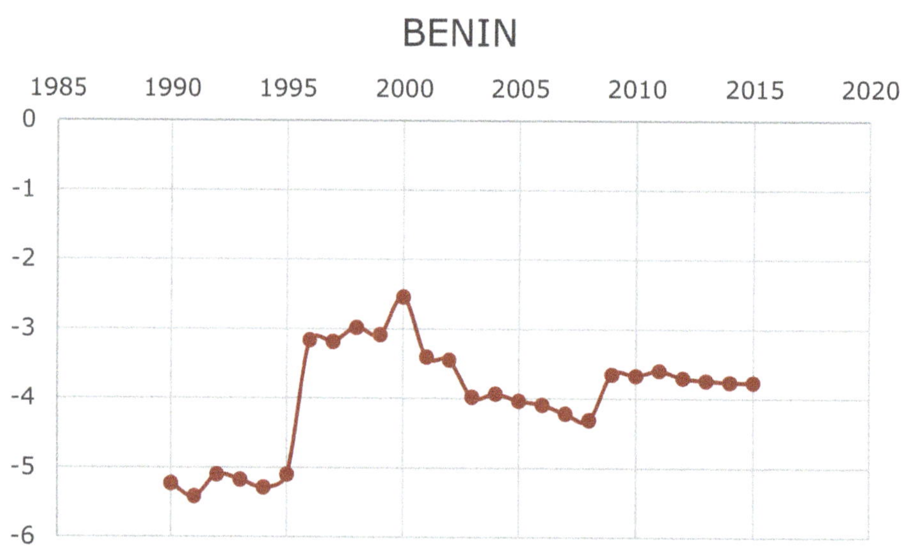

Figure 20. The efficiency signature for Bhutan

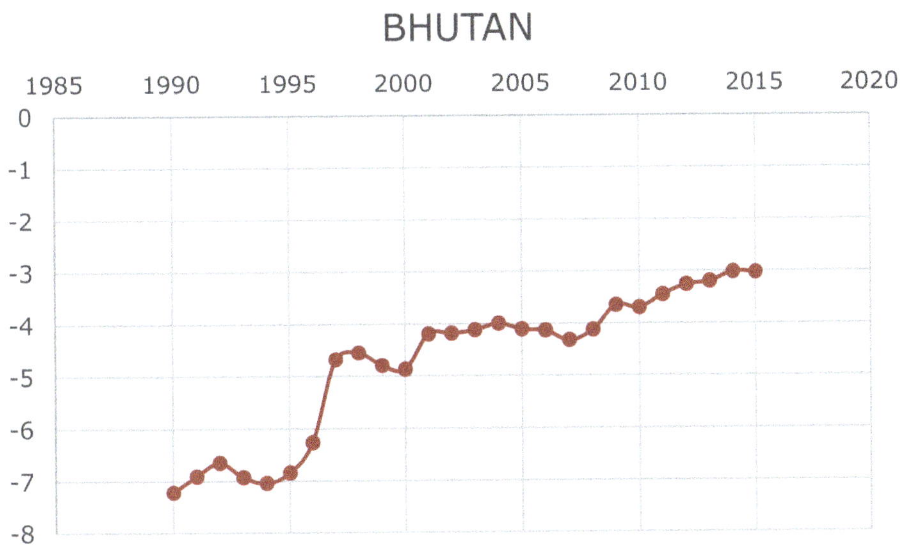

Figure 21. The efficiency signature for Bolivia

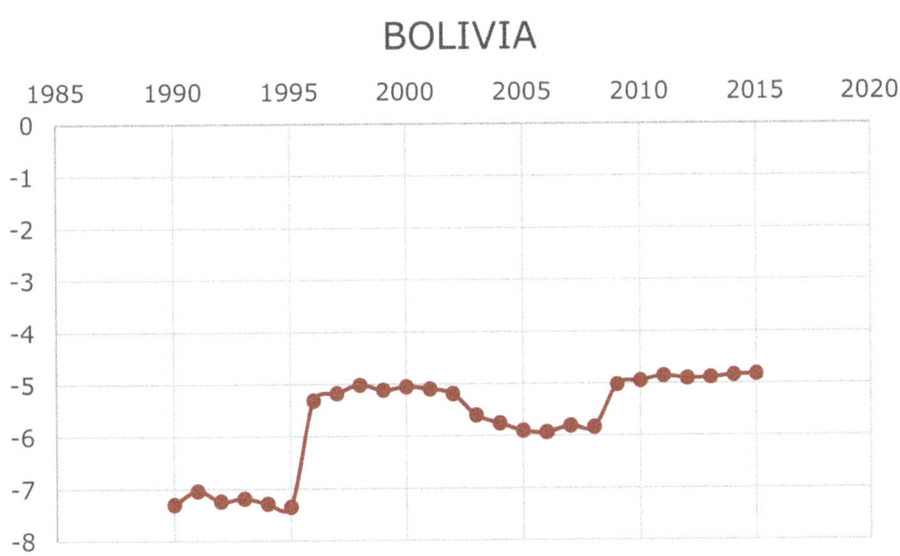

Figure 22. The efficiency signature for Bosnia and Herzegovina

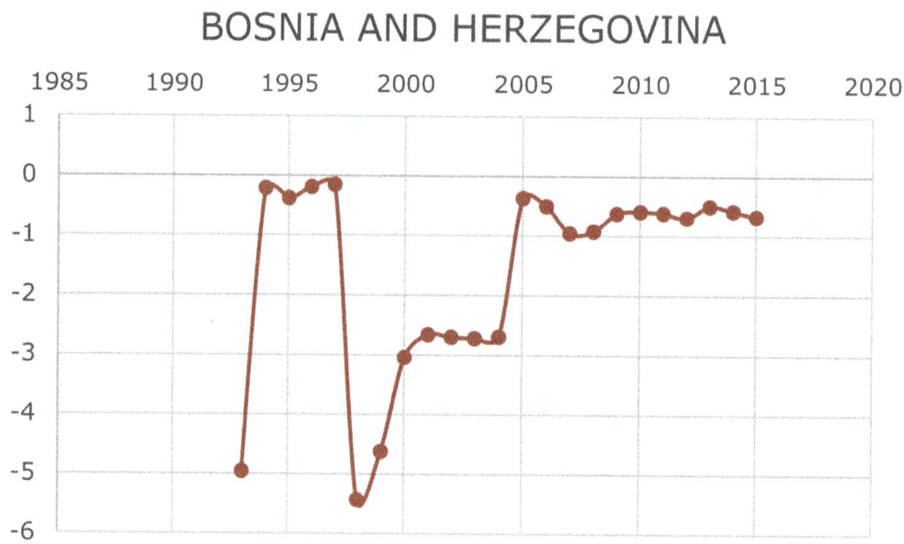

Figure 23. The efficiency signature for Botswana

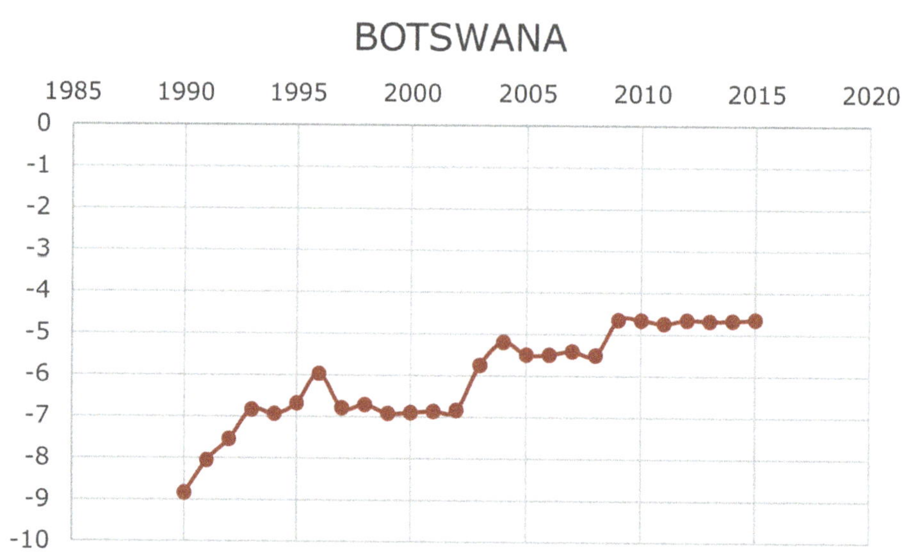

Figure 24. The efficiency signature for Brazil

Figure 25. The efficiency signature for Brunei

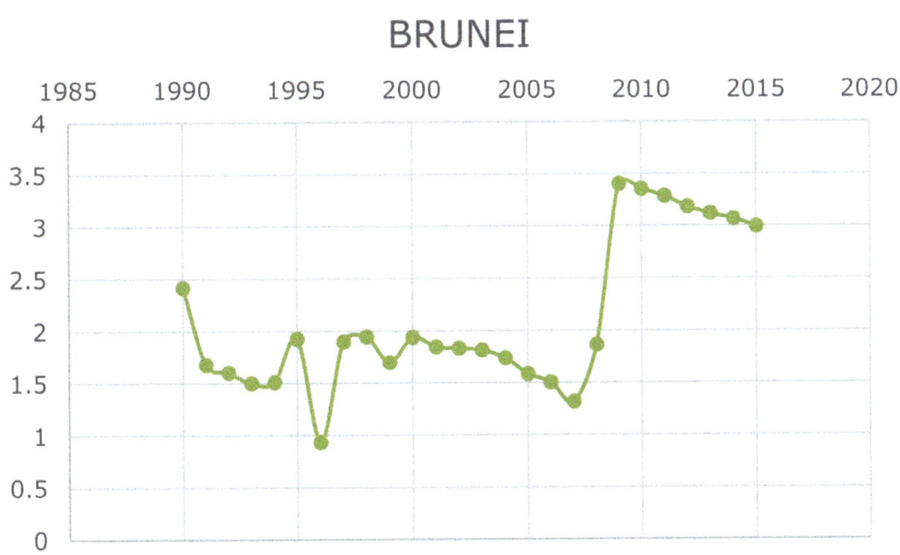

Figure 26. The efficiency signature for Bulgaria

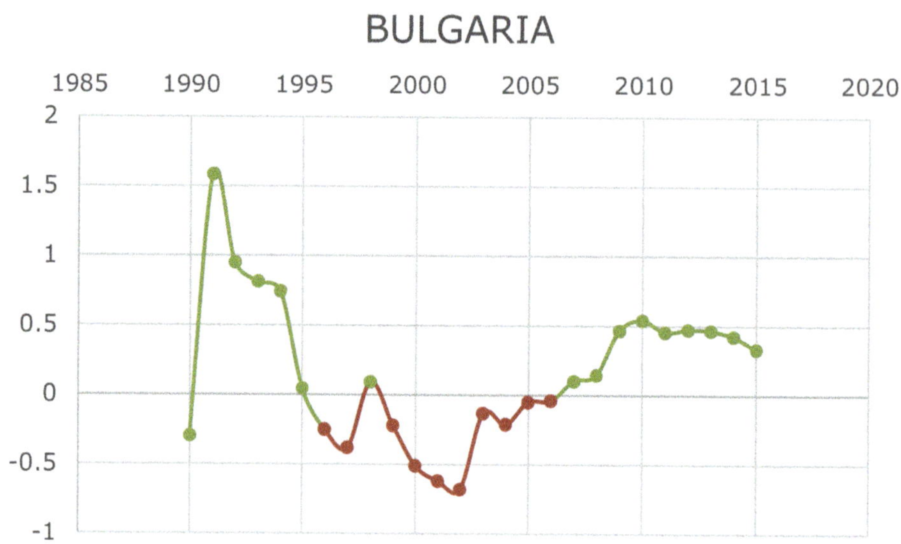

Figure 27. The efficiency signature for Burkina Faso

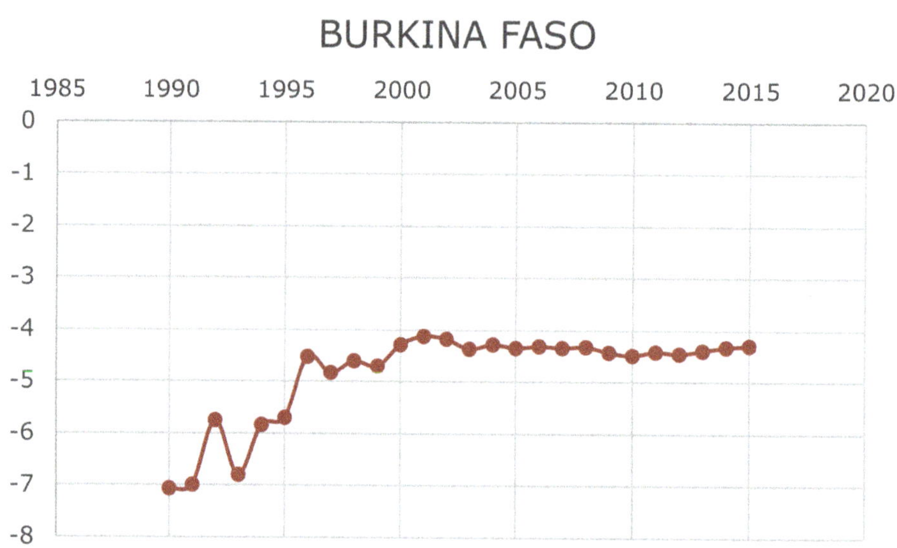

Figure 28. The efficiency signature for Burundi

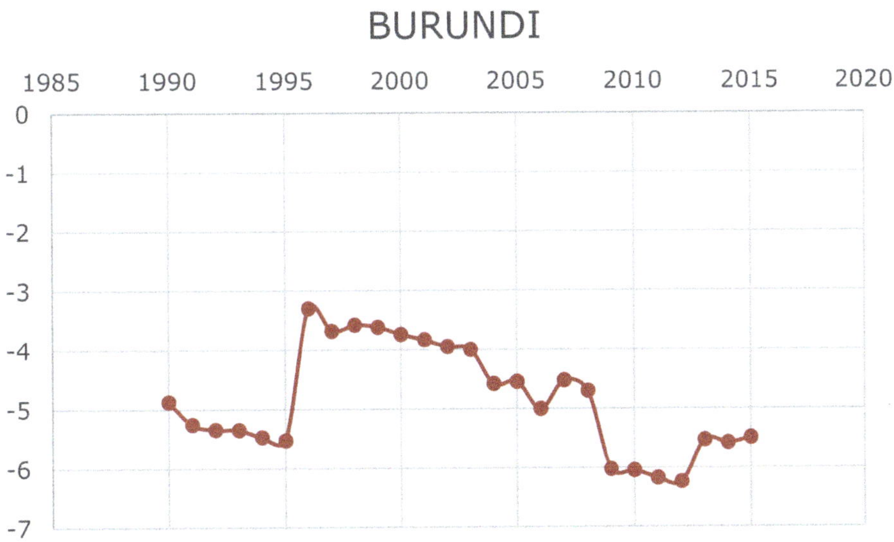

Figure 29. The efficiency signature for Cambodia

Figure 30. The efficiency signature for Cameroon

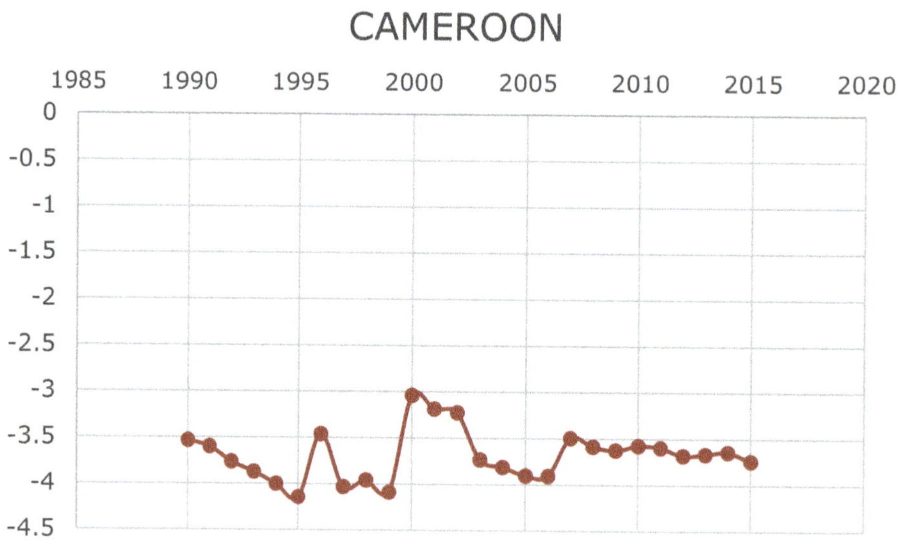

Figure 31. The efficiency signature for Canada

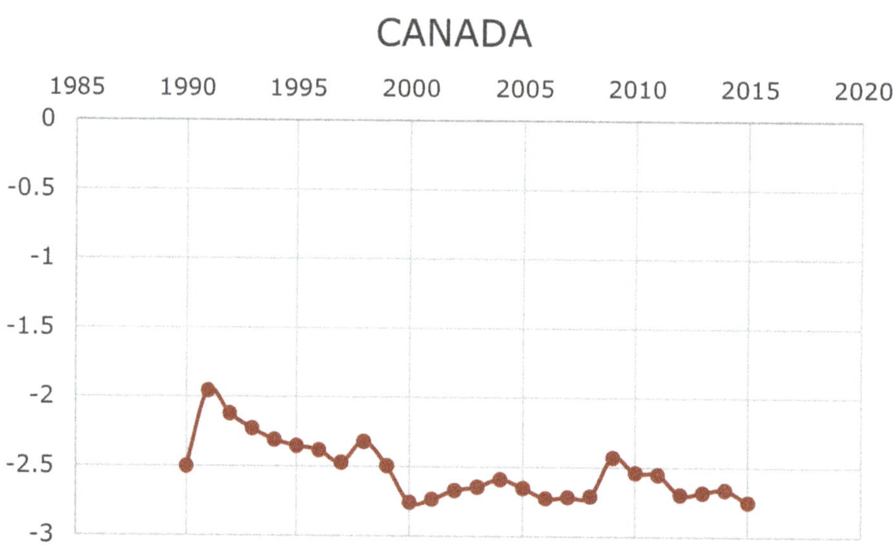

Figure 32. The efficiency signature for Cape Verde

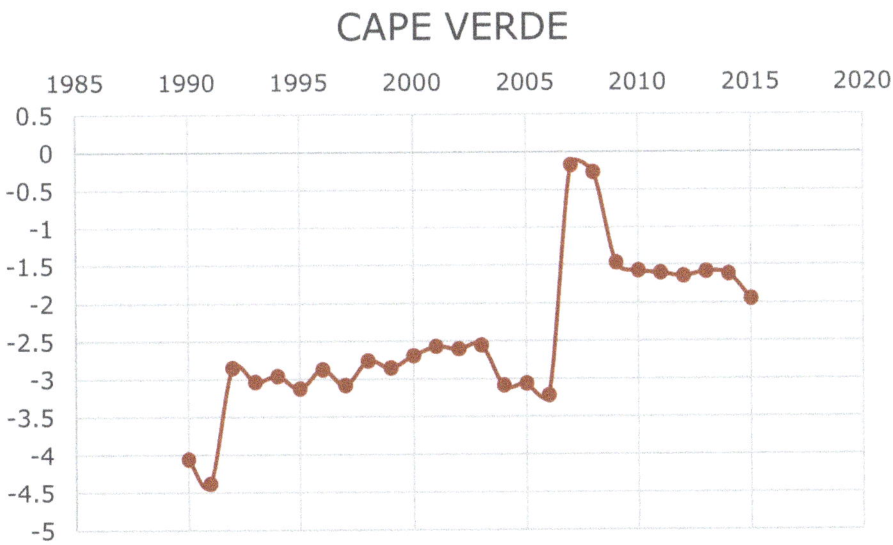

Figure 33. The efficiency signature for the Central African Republic

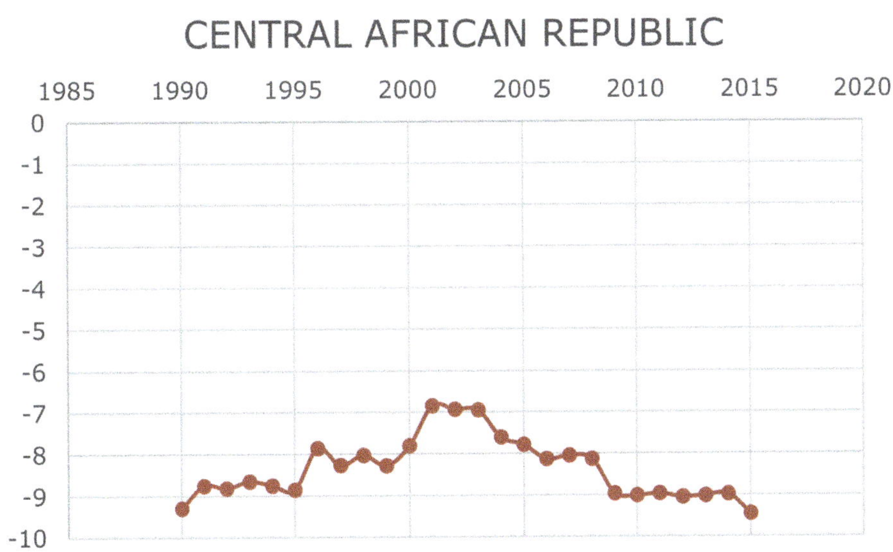

Figure 34. The efficiency signature for Chad

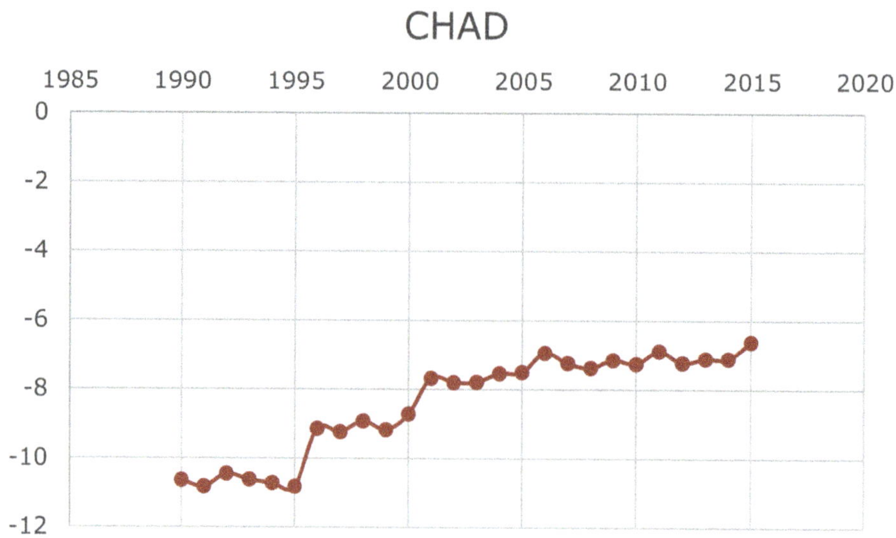

Figure 35. The efficiency signature for Chile

Figure 36. The efficiency signature for the People's Republic of China

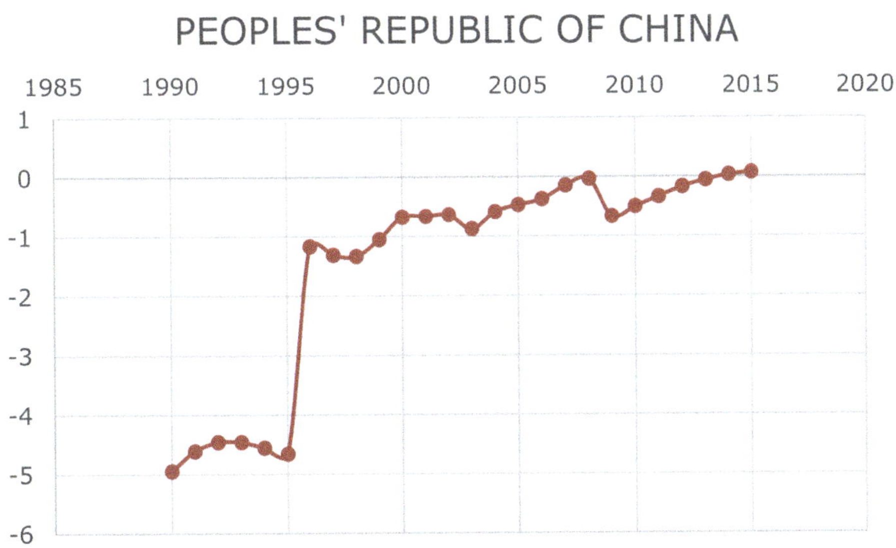

Figure 37. The efficiency signature for Columbia

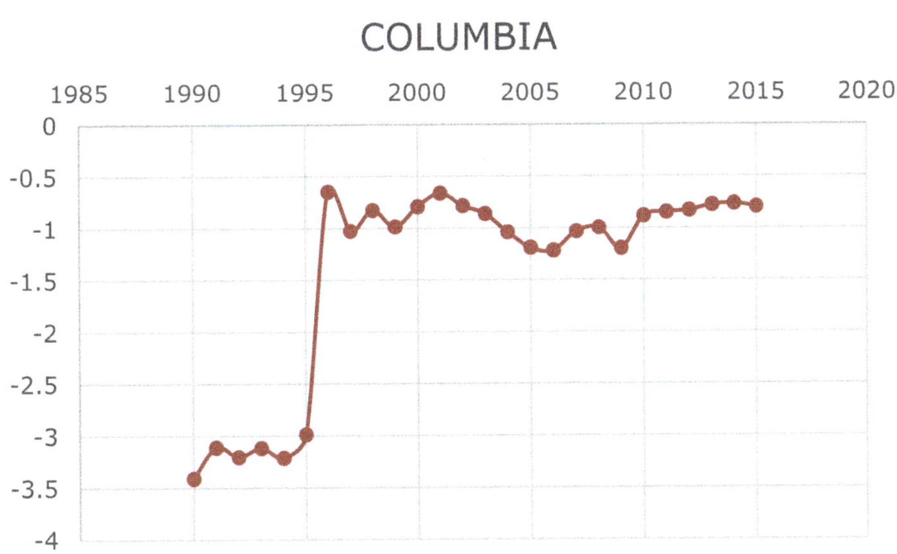

Figure 38. The efficiency signature for Comoros

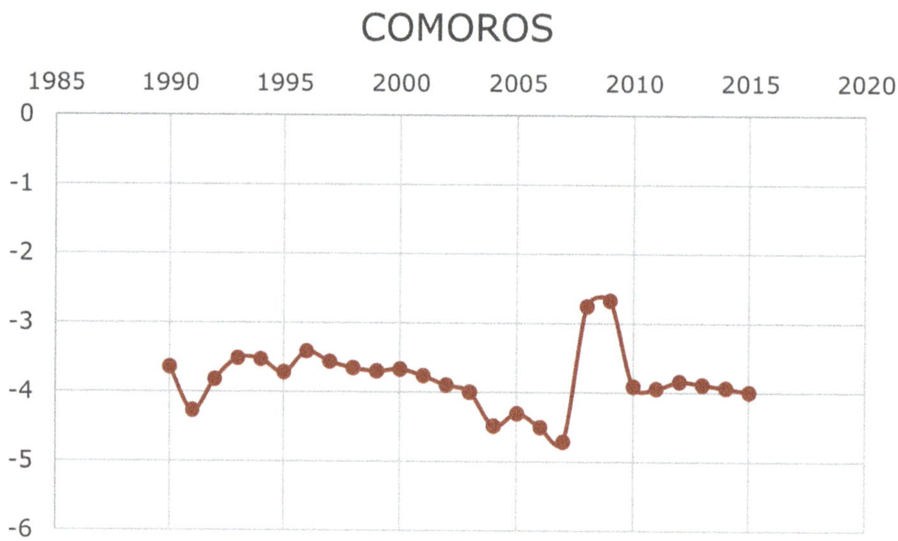

Figure 39. The efficiency signature for the Democratic Republic of Congo

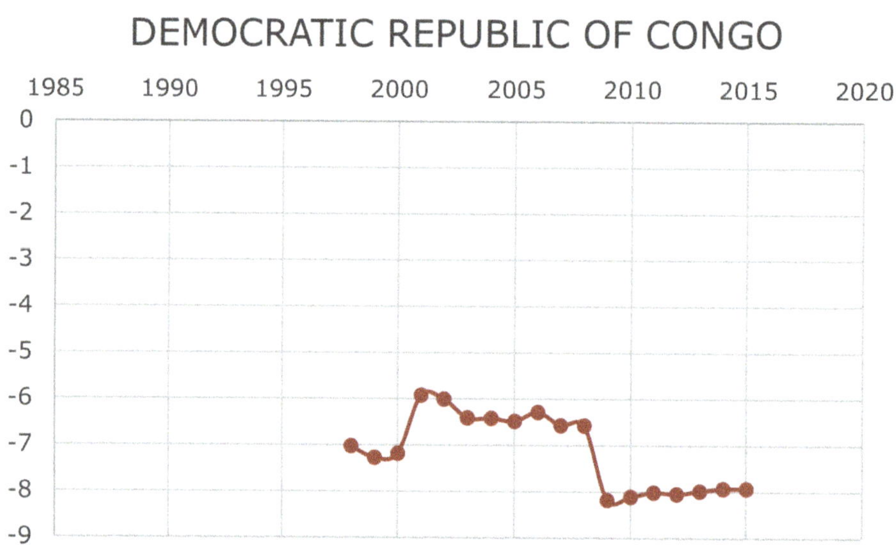

Figure 40. The efficiency signature for the Republic of Congo

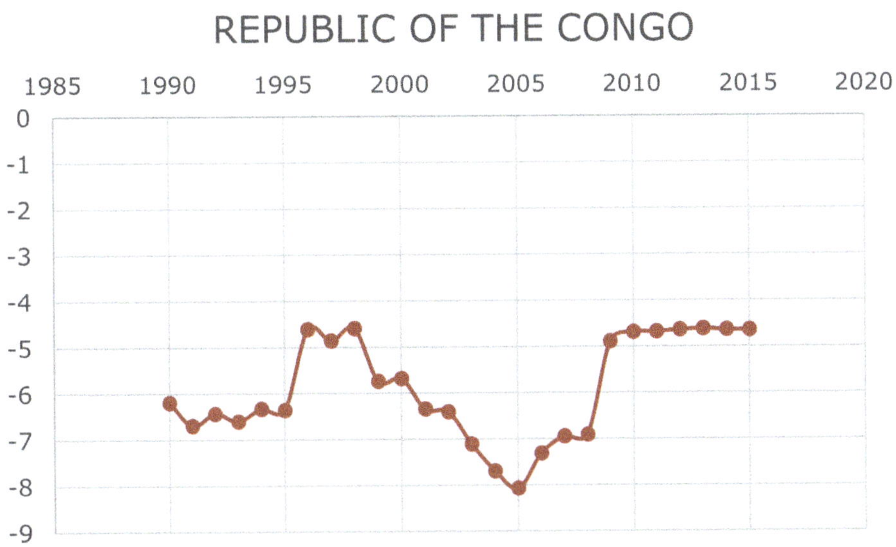

Figure 41. The efficiency signature for Costa Rica

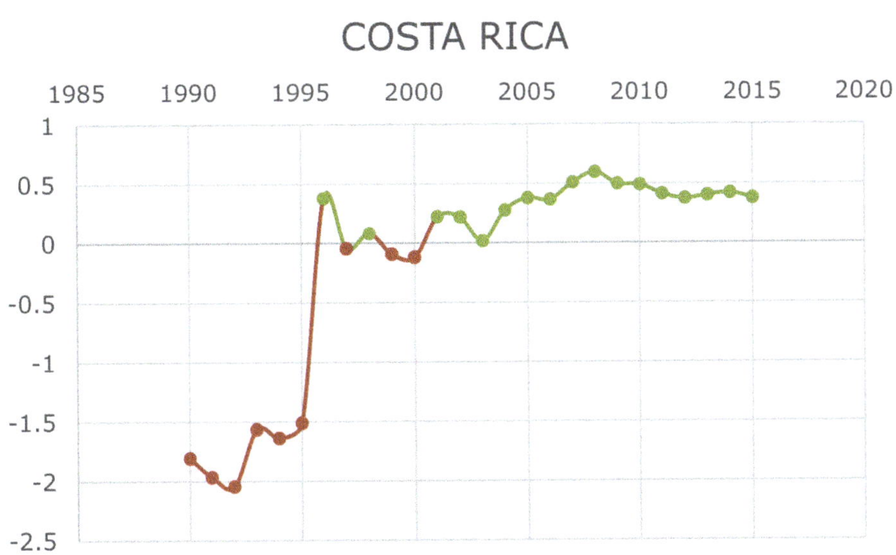

Figure 42. The efficiency signature for Cote d'Ivoire (Ivory Coast)

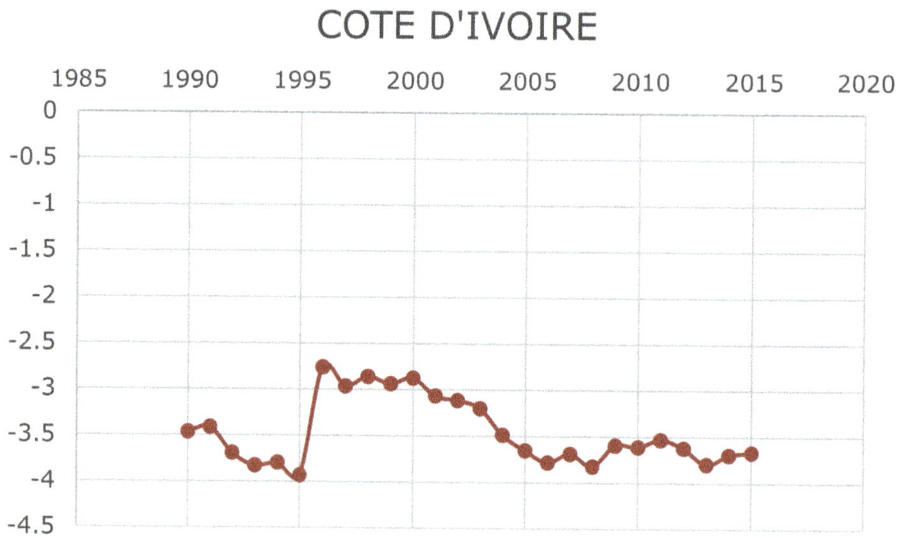

Figure 43. The efficiency signature for Croatia

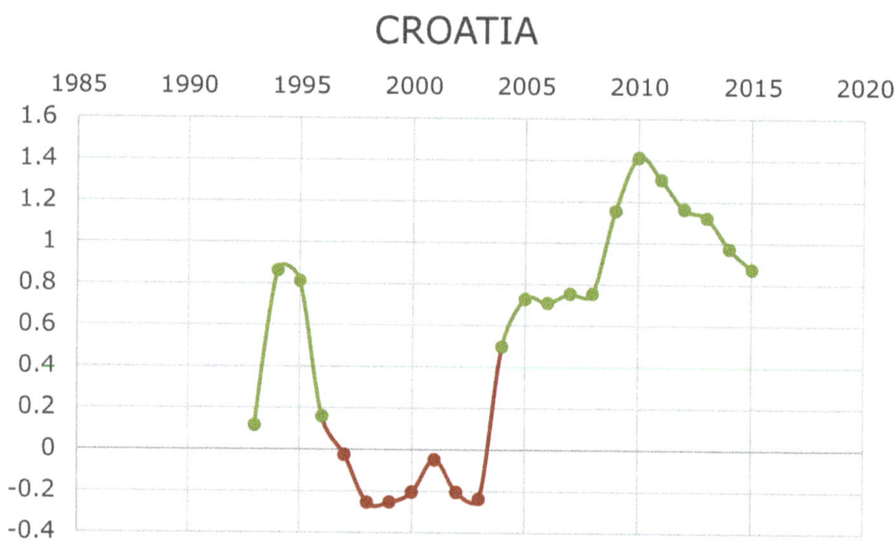

Figure 44. The efficiency signature for Cuba

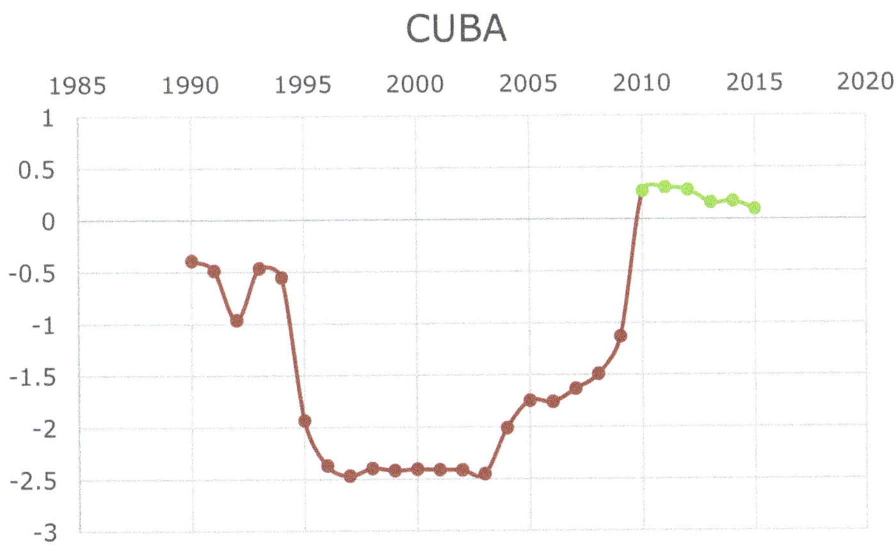

Figure 45. The efficiency signature for Cyprus

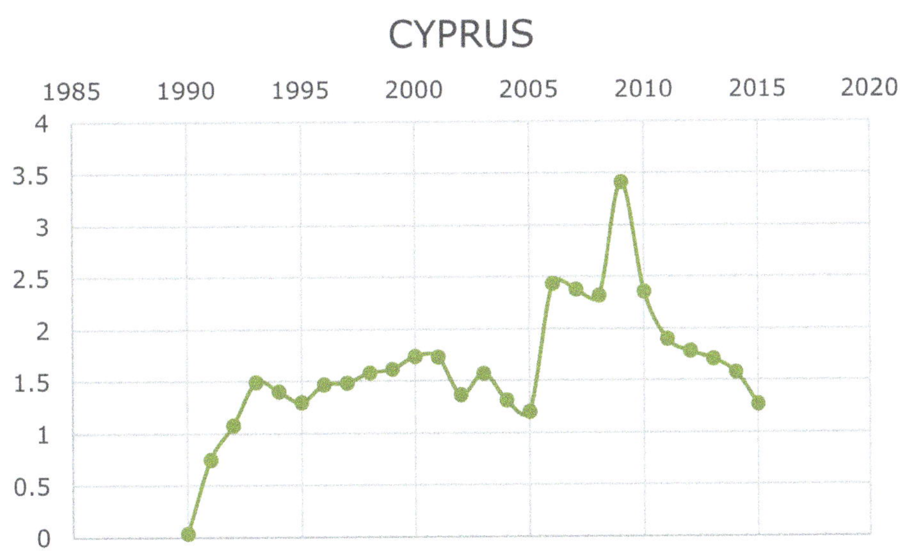

Figure 46. The efficiency signature for the Czech Republic

Figure 47. The efficiency signature for Denmark

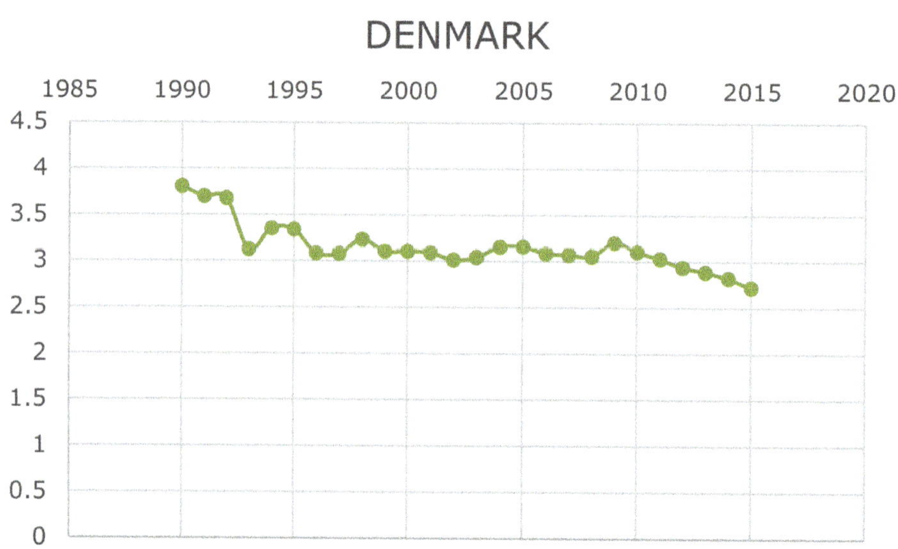

Figure 48. The efficiency signature for Djibouti

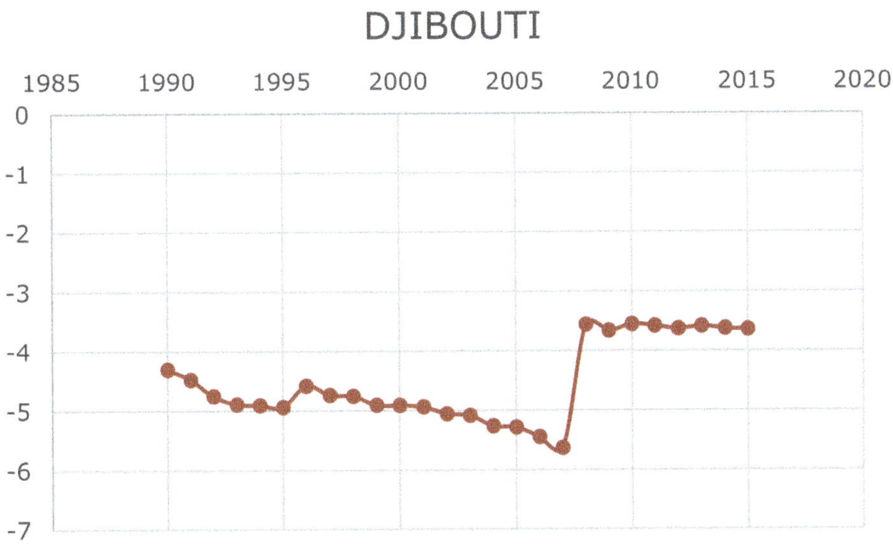

Figure 49. The efficiency signature for Dominica

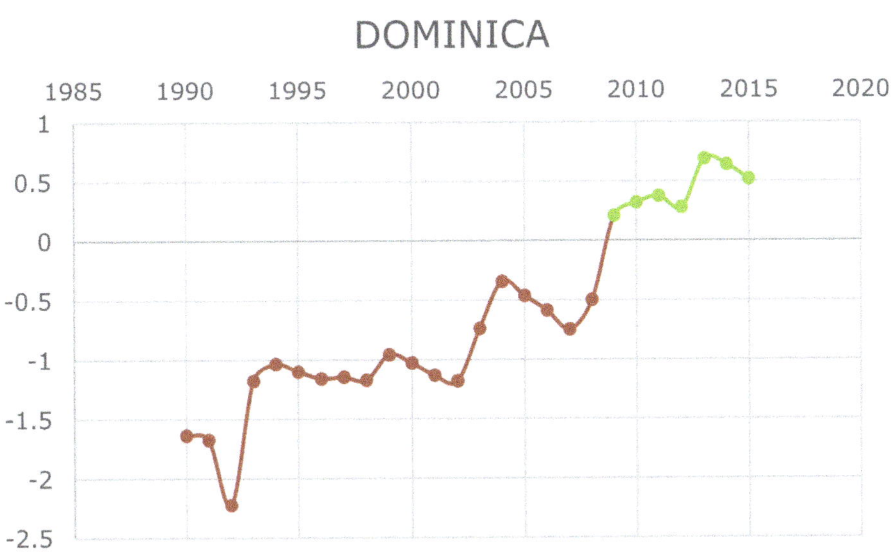

Figure 50. The efficiency signature for the Dominican Republic

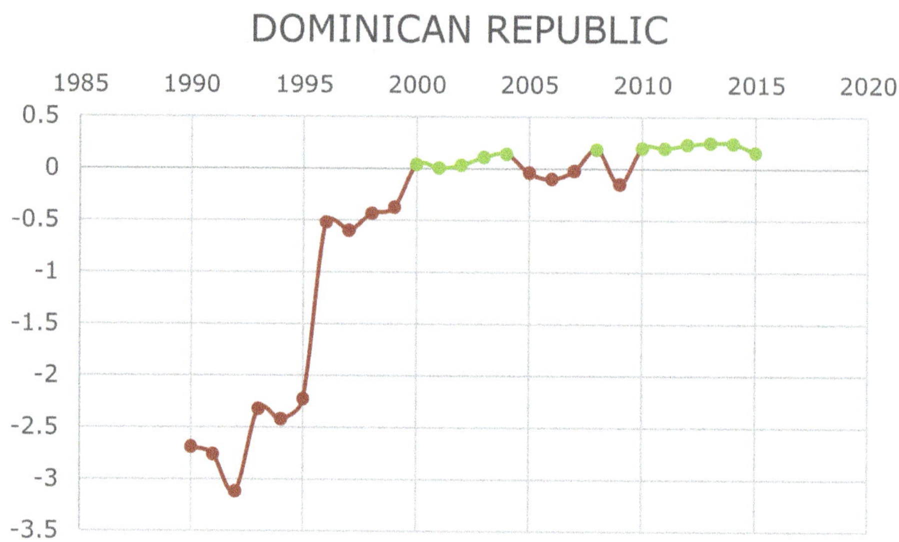

Figure 51. The efficiency signature for Ecuador

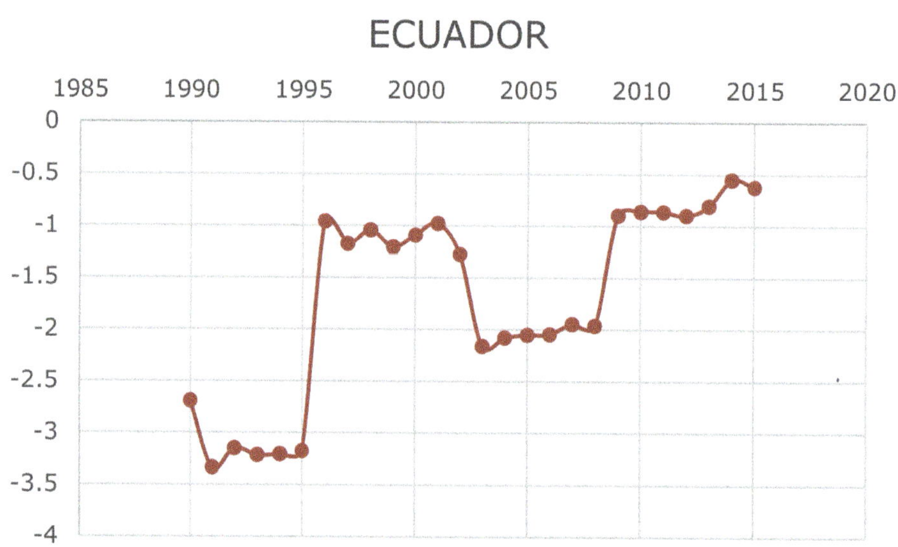

Figure 52. The efficiency signature for Egypt

Figure 53. The efficiency signature for El Salvador

Figure 54. The efficiency signature for Equatorial Guinea

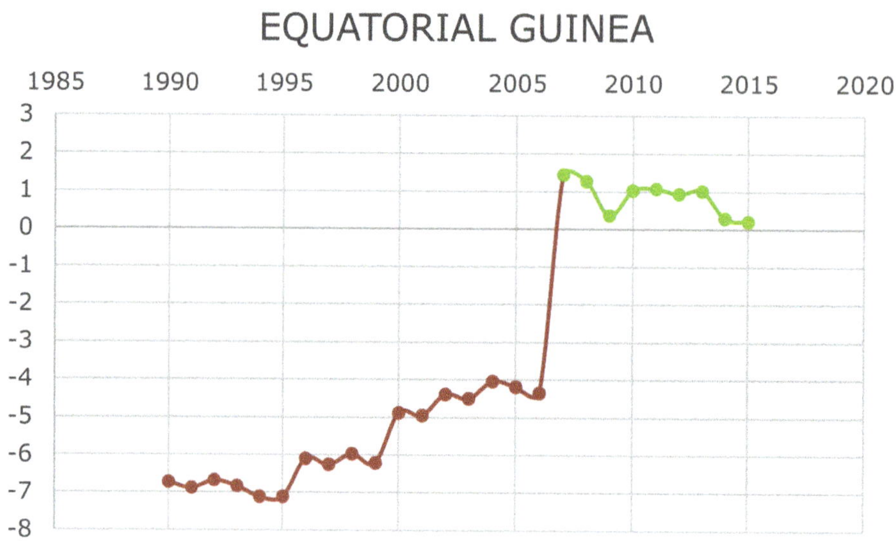

Figure 55. The efficiency signature for Eritrea

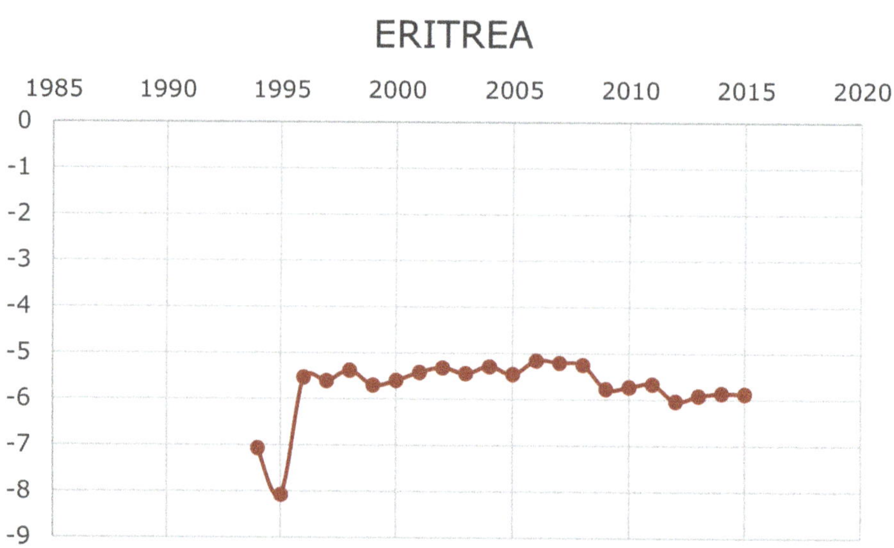

Figure 56. The efficiency signature for Estonia

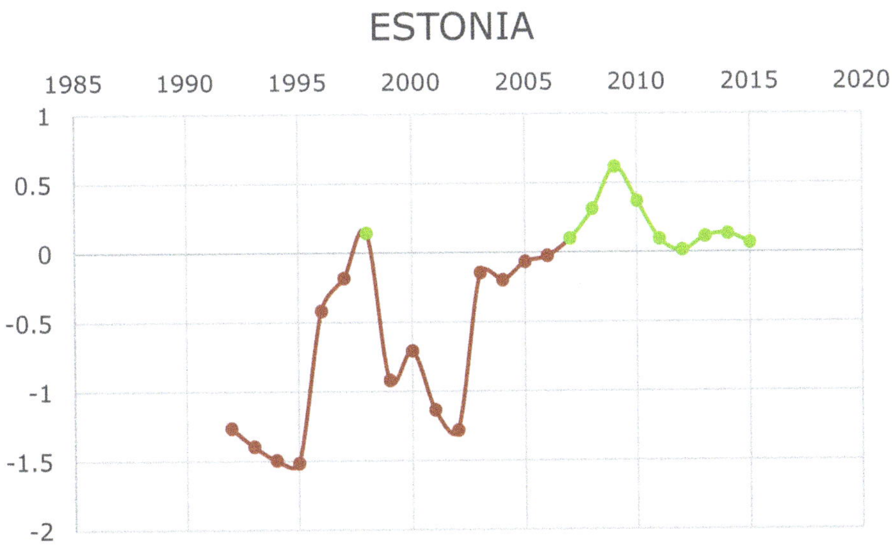

Figure 57. The efficiency signature for Ethiopia

Figure 58. The efficiency signature for Fiji

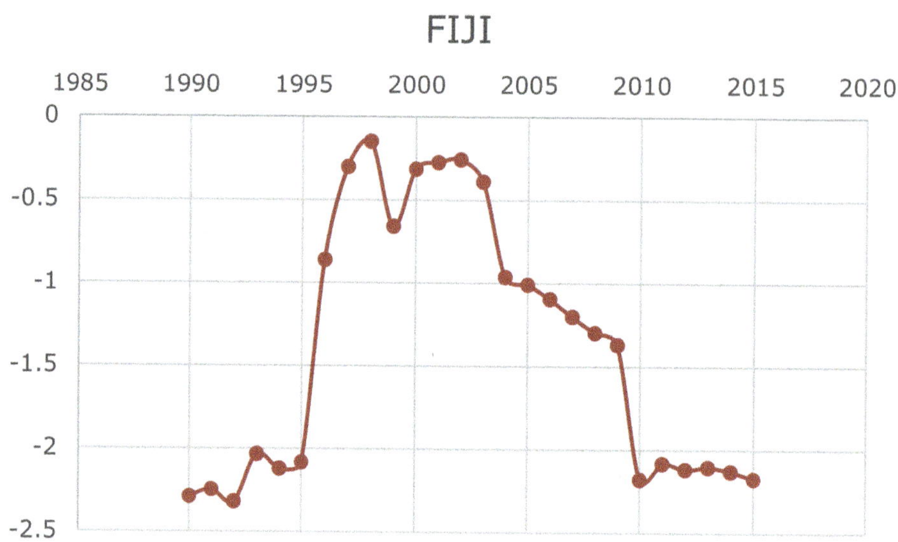

Figure 59. The efficiency signature for Finland

Figure 60. The efficiency signature for France

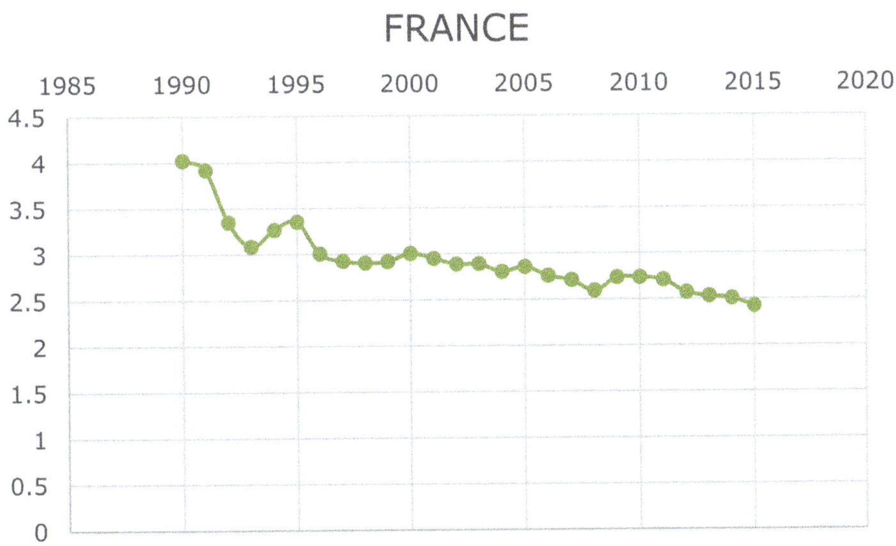

Figure 61. The efficiency signature for Gabon

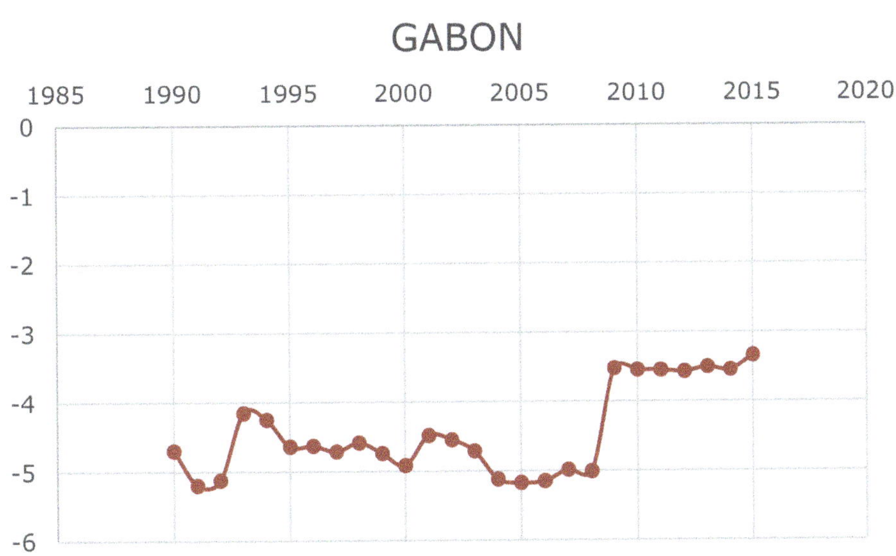

Figure 62. The efficiency signature for the Gambia

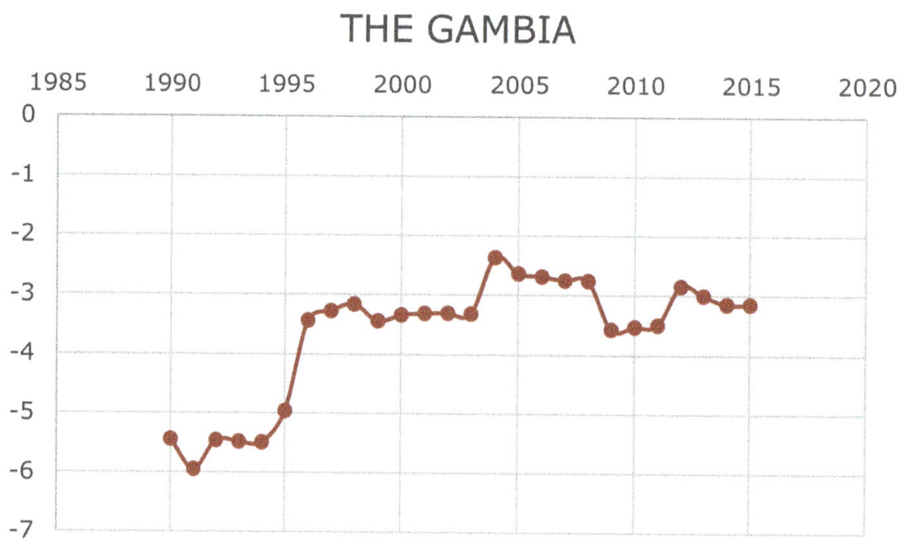

Figure 63. The efficiency signature for Georgia

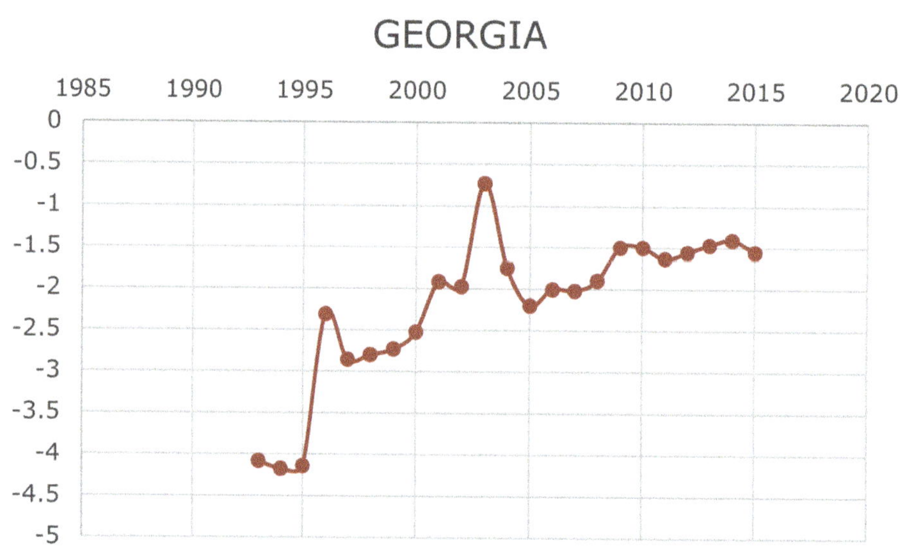

Figure 64. The efficiency signature for Germany

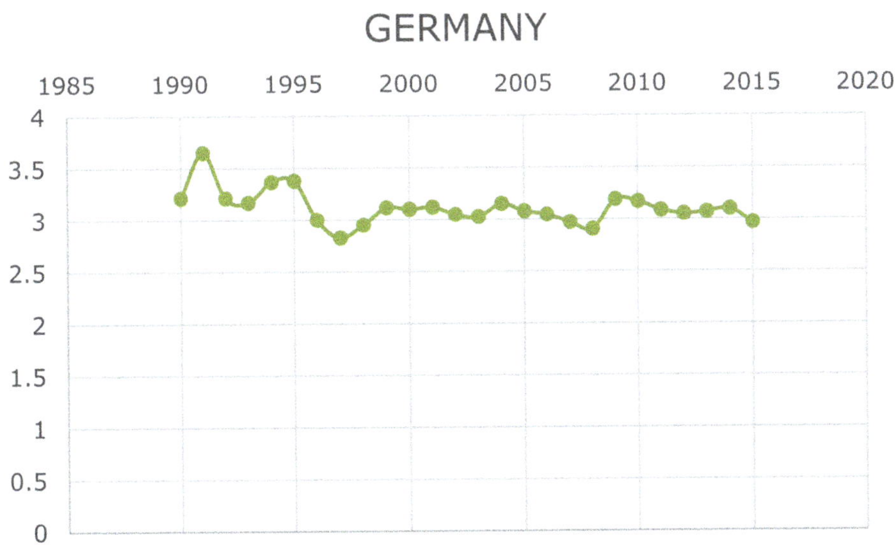

Figure 65. The efficiency signature for Ghana

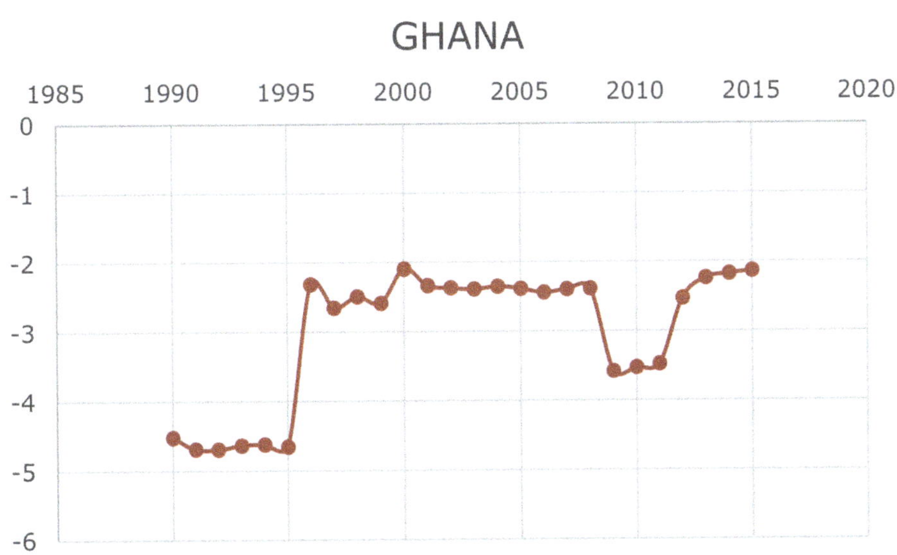

Figure 66. The efficiency signature for Greece

Figure 67. The efficiency signature for Grenada

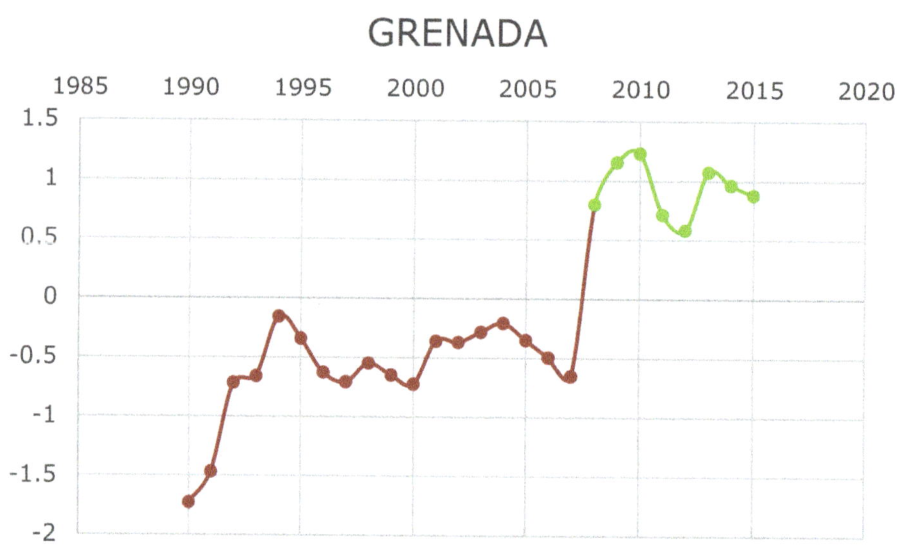

Figure 68. The efficiency signature for Guatemala

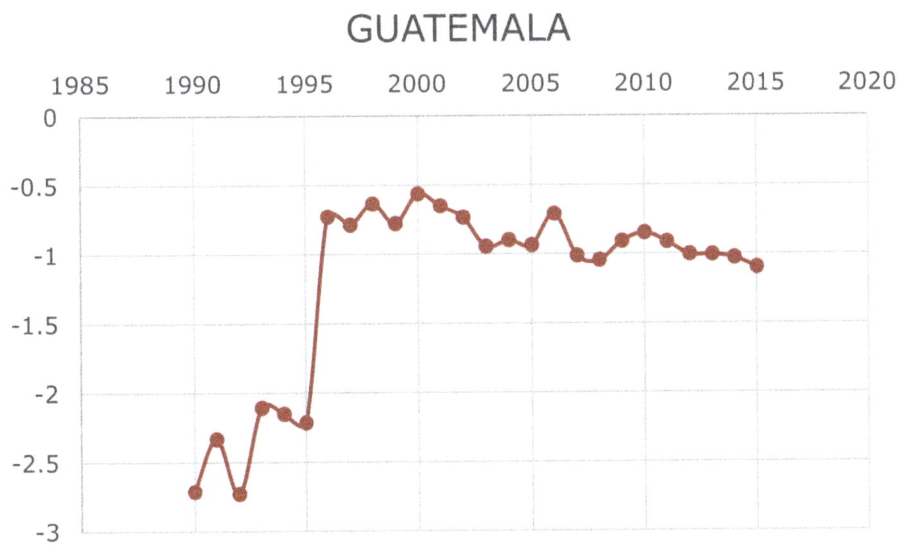

Figure 69. The efficiency signature for Guinea

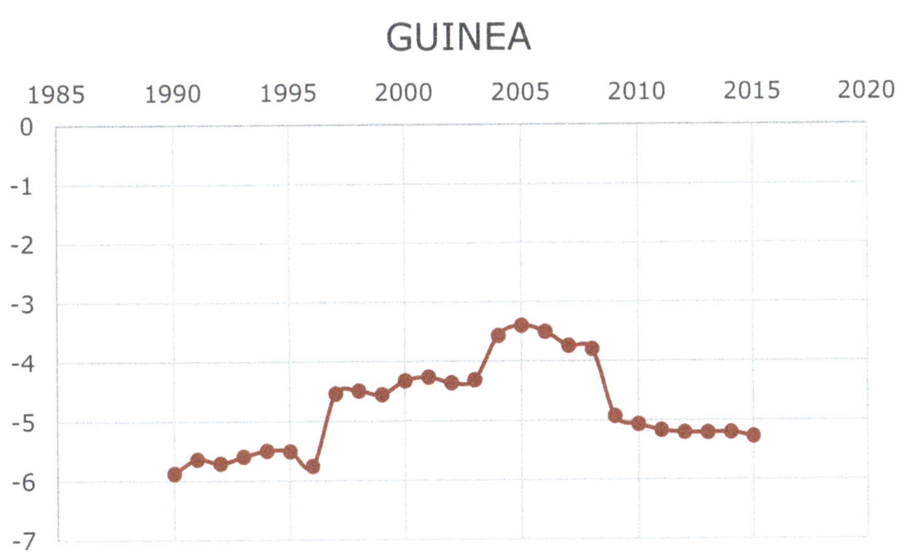

Figure 70. The efficiency signature for Guinea-Bissau

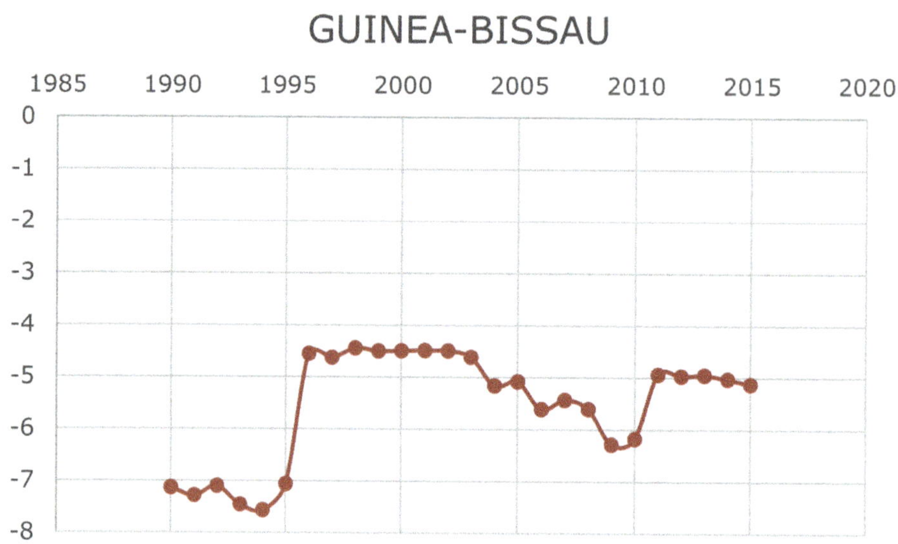

Figure 71. The efficiency signature for Guyana

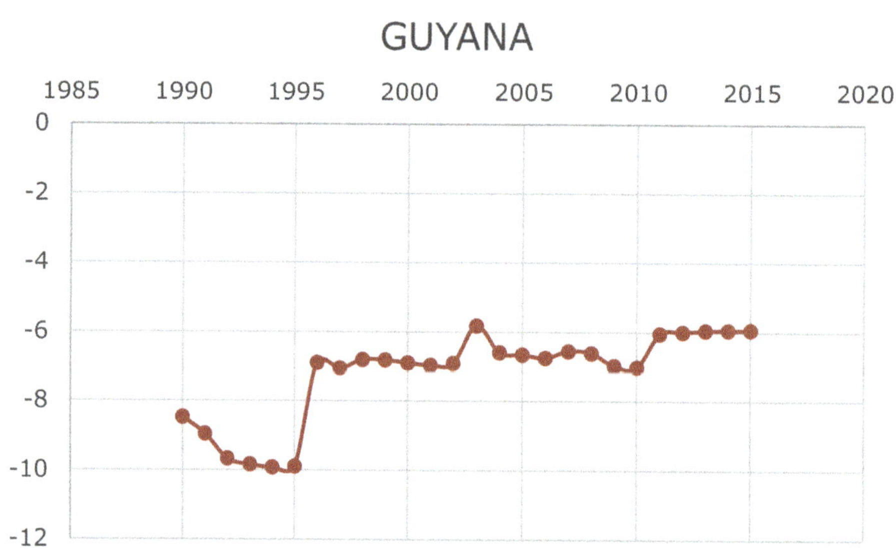

Figure 72. The efficiency signature for Haiti

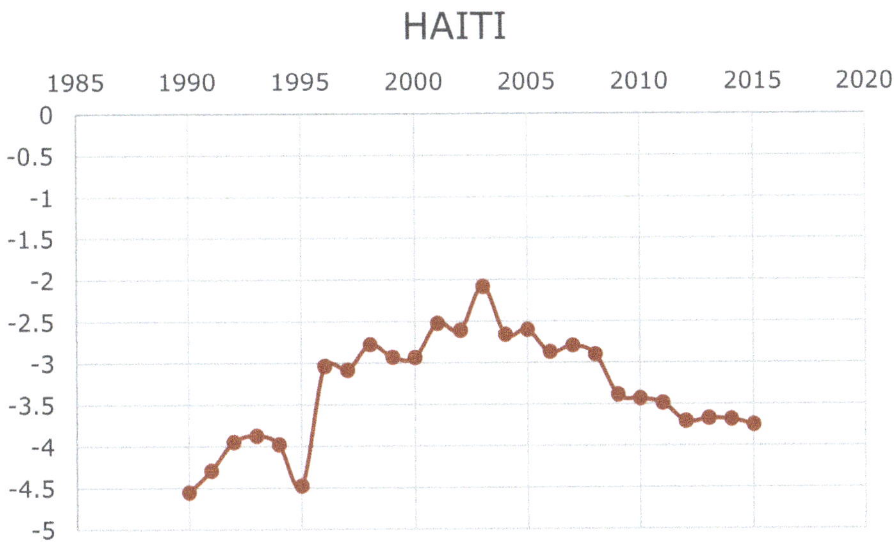

Figure 73. The efficiency signature for Honduras

Figure 74. The efficiency signature for Hungary

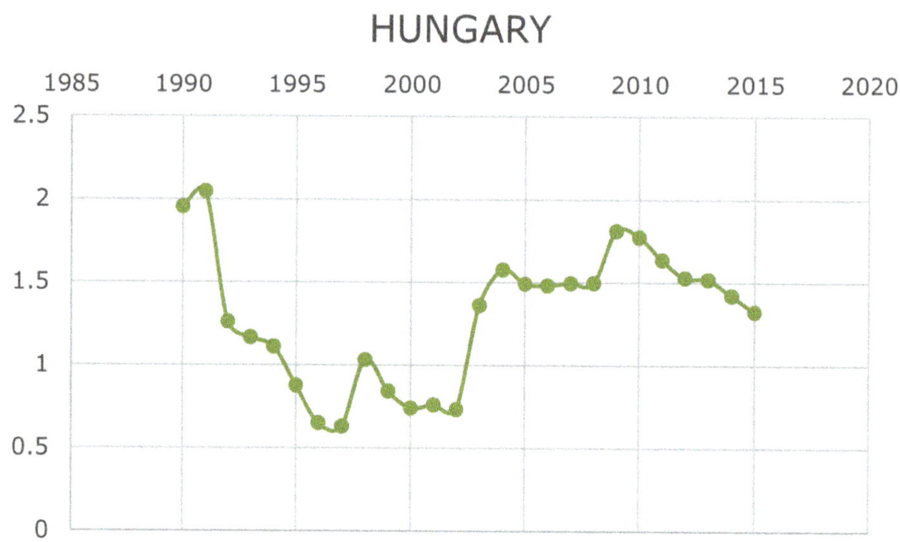

Figure 75. The efficiency signature for Iceland

Figure 76. The efficiency signature for India

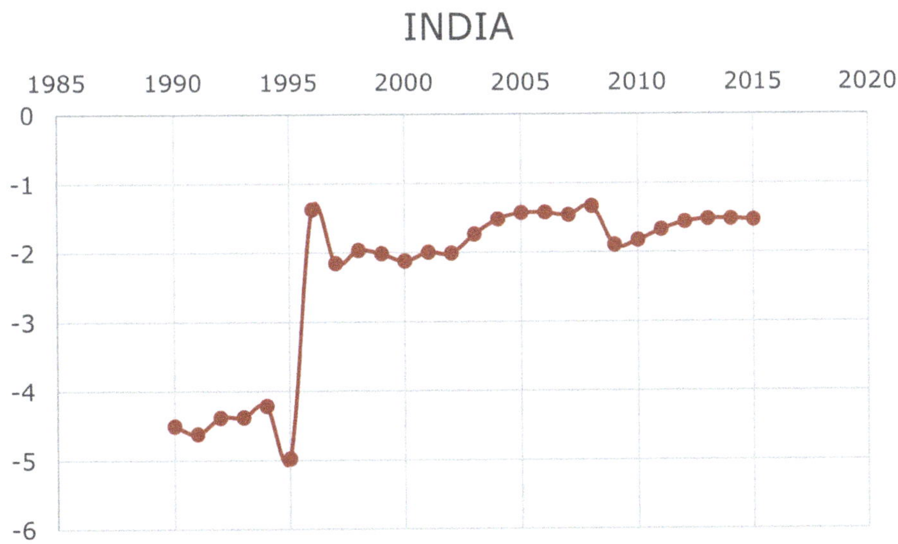

Figure 77. The efficiency signature for Indonesia

Figure 78. The efficiency signature for Iran

Figure 79. The efficiency signature for Iraq

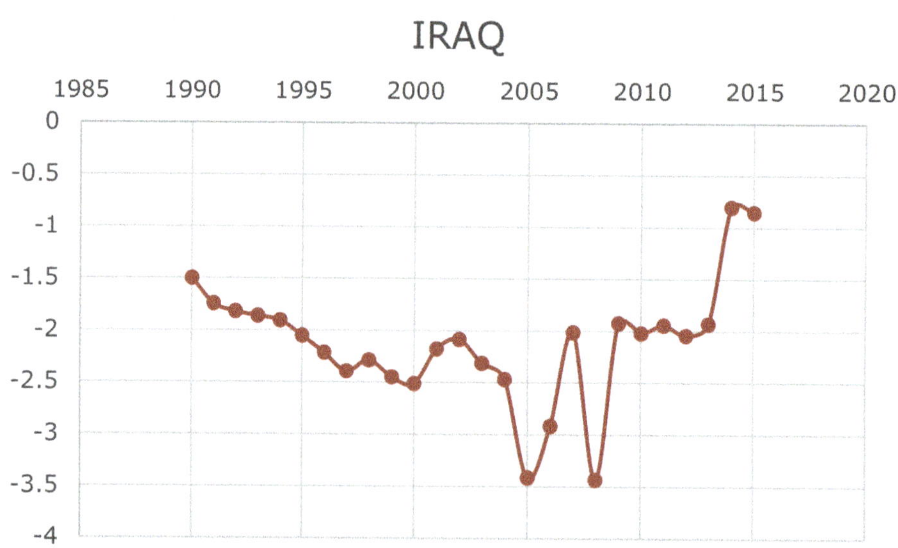

Figure 80. The efficiency signature for Ireland

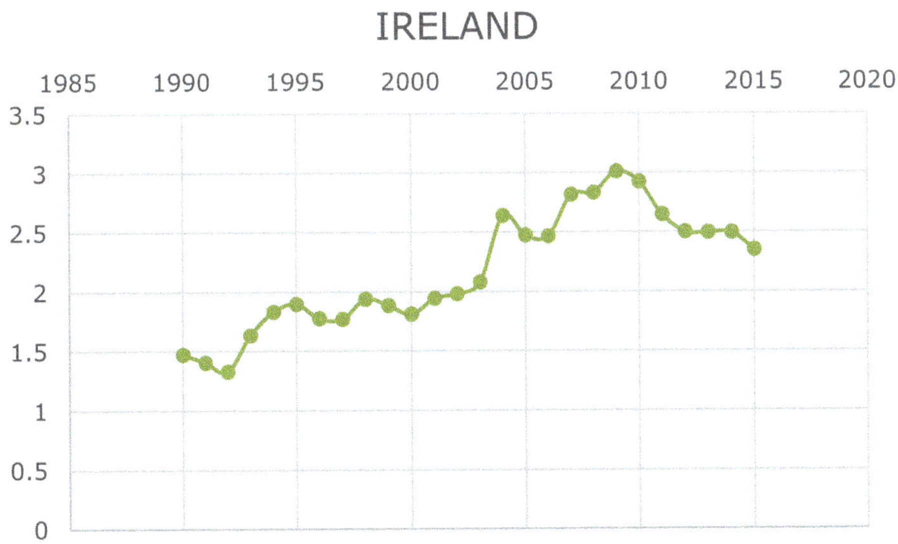

Figure 81. The efficiency signature for Israel

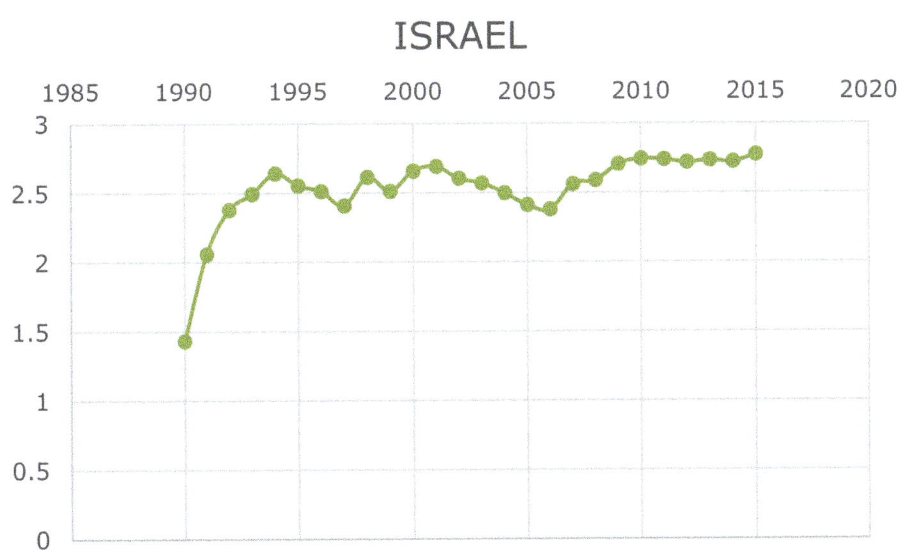

Figure 82. The efficiency signature for Italy

Figure 83. The efficiency signature for Jamaica

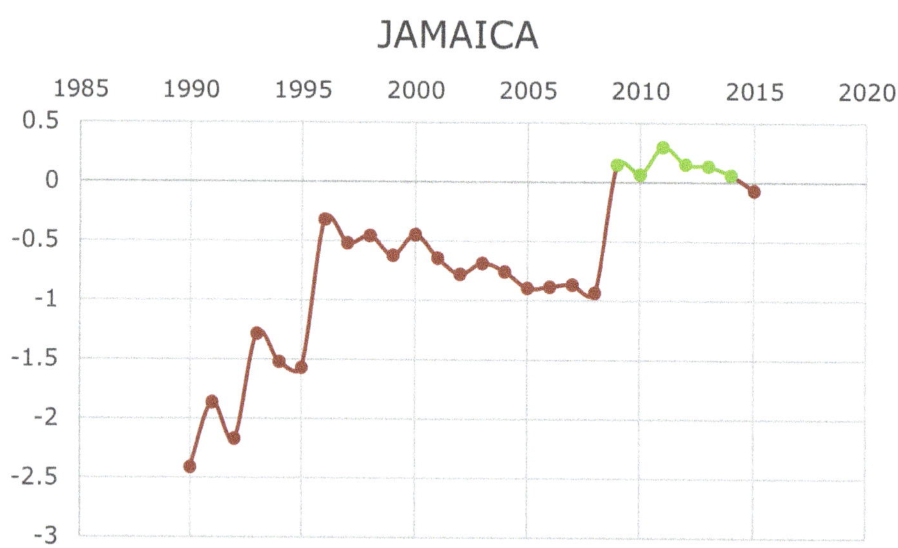

Figure 84. The efficiency signature for Japan

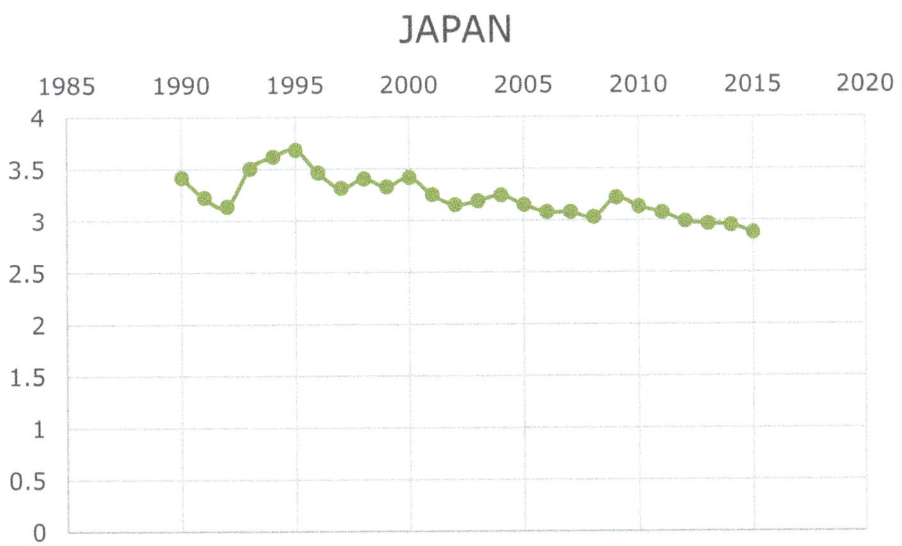

Figure 85. The efficiency signature for Jordan

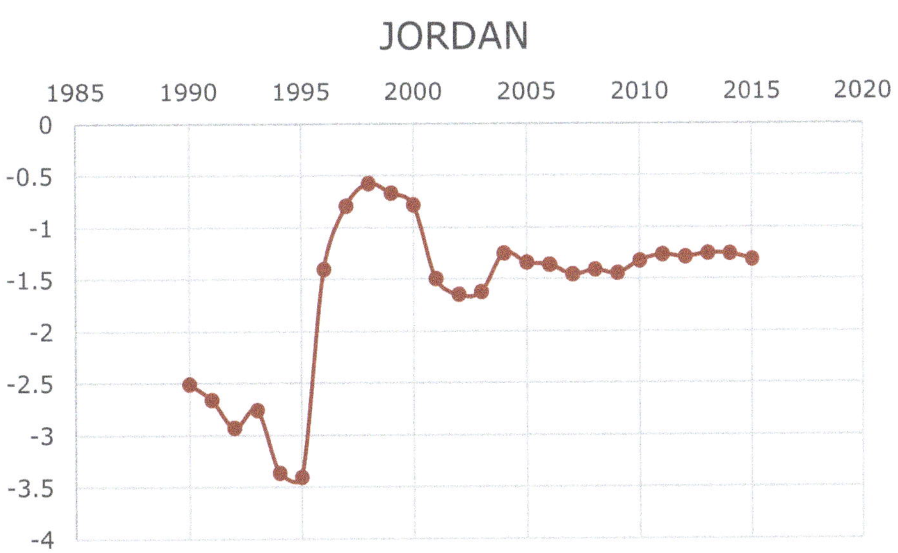

Figure 86. The efficiency signature for Kazakhstan

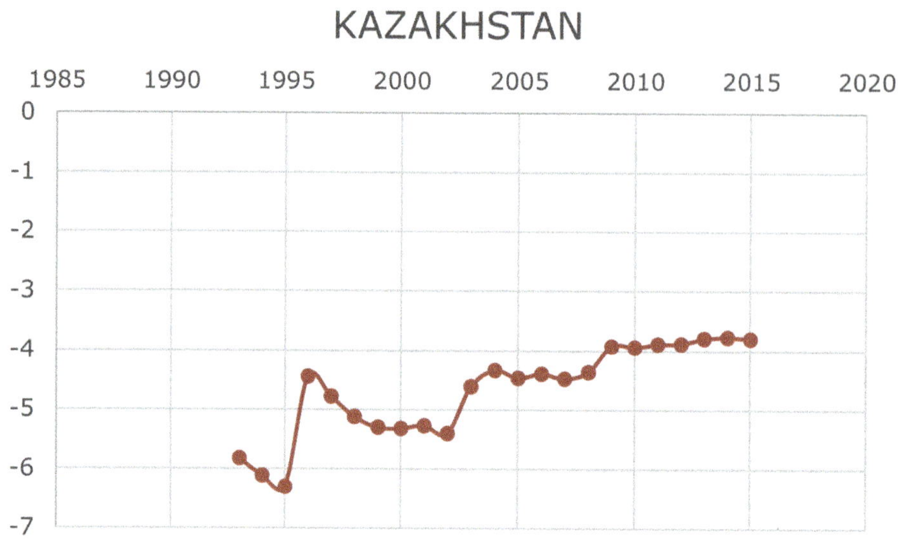

Figure 87. The efficiency signature for Kenya

Figure 88. The efficiency signature for Kiribati

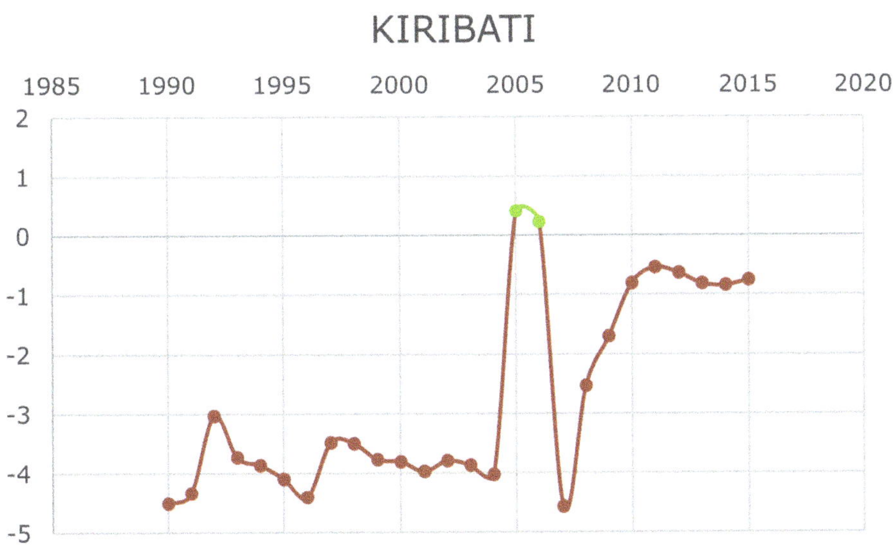

Figure 89. The efficiency signature for North Korea

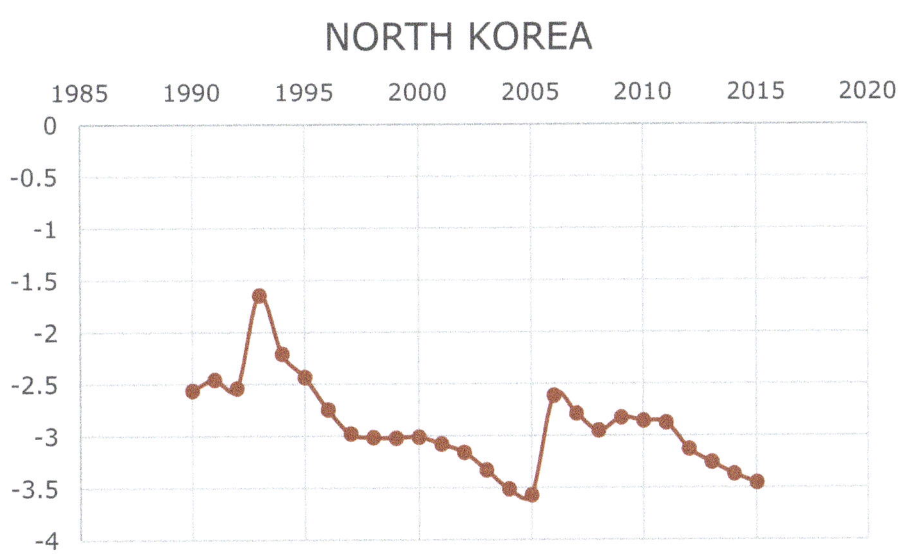

Figure 90. The efficiency signature for South Korea

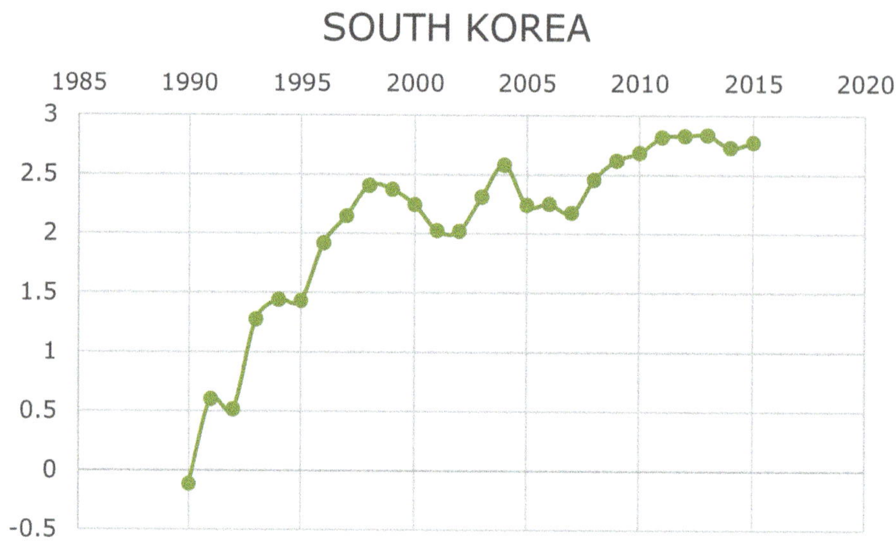

Figure 91. The efficiency signature for Kosovo

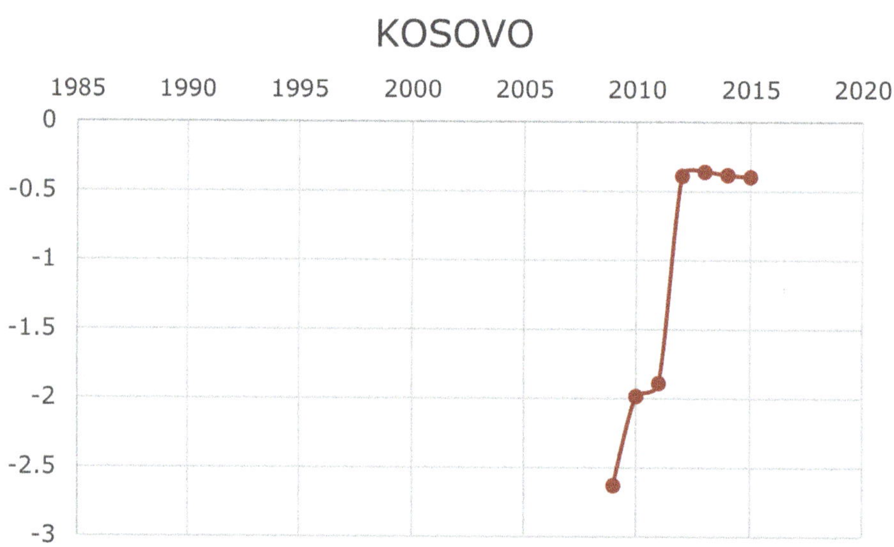

Figure 92. The efficiency signature for Kuwait

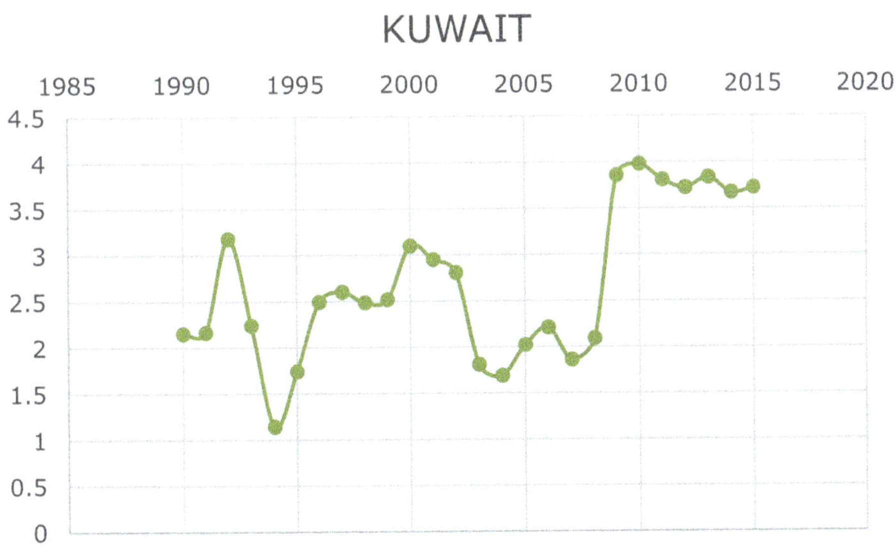

Figure 93. The efficiency signature for Kyrgyzstan

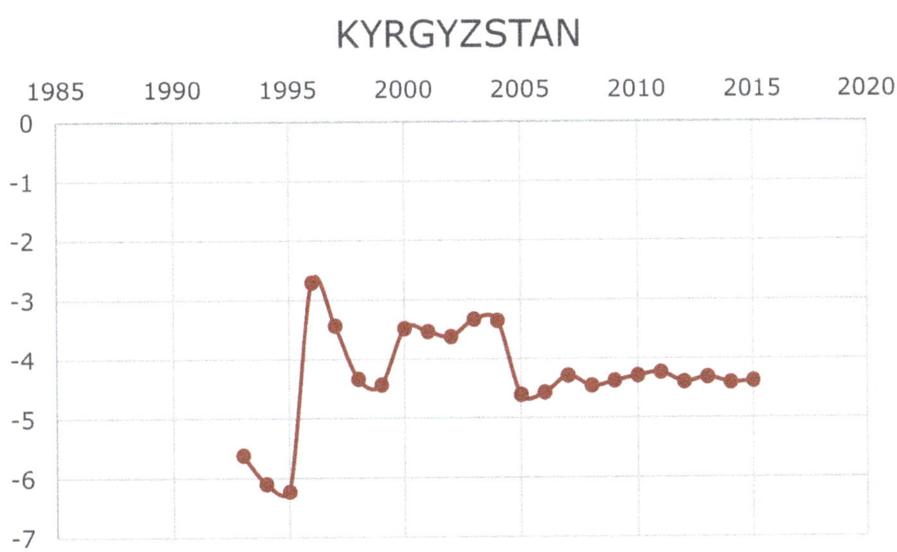

Figure 94. The efficiency signature for Laos

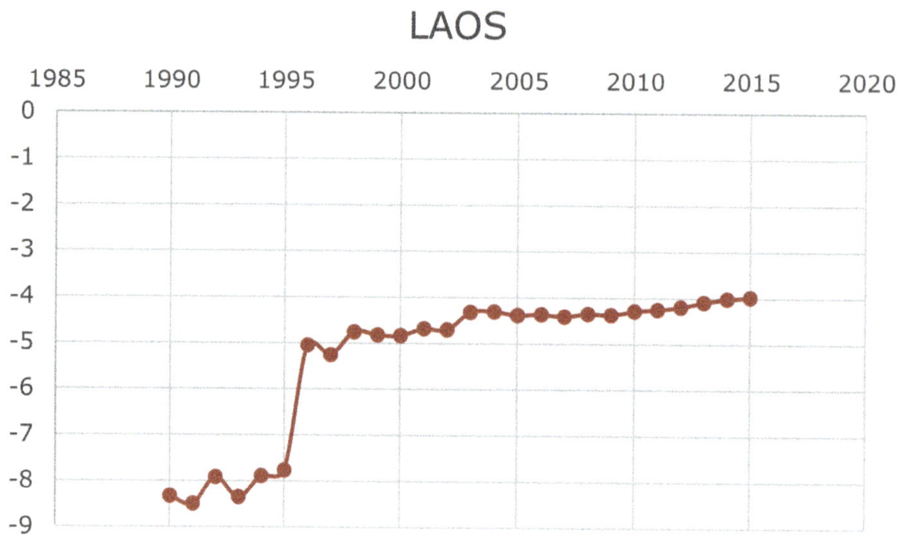

Figure 95. The efficiency signature for Latvia

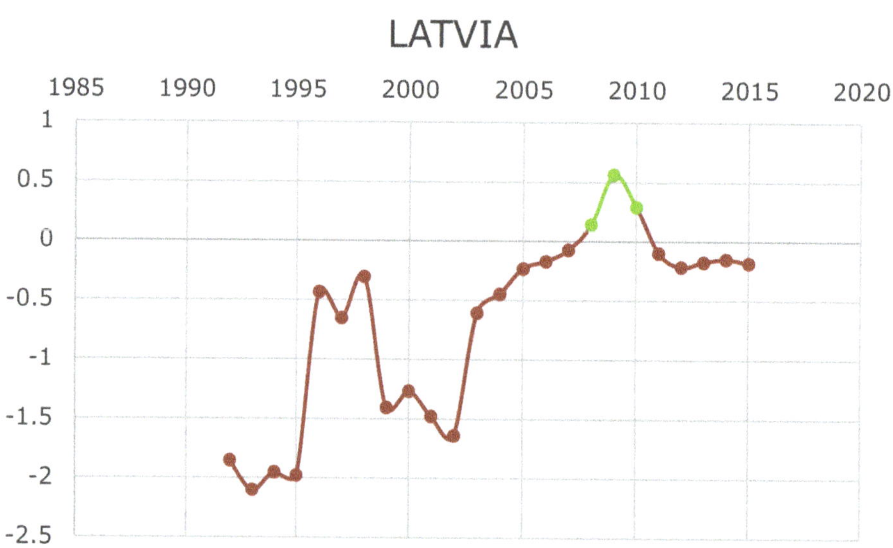

Figure 96. The efficiency signature for Lebanon

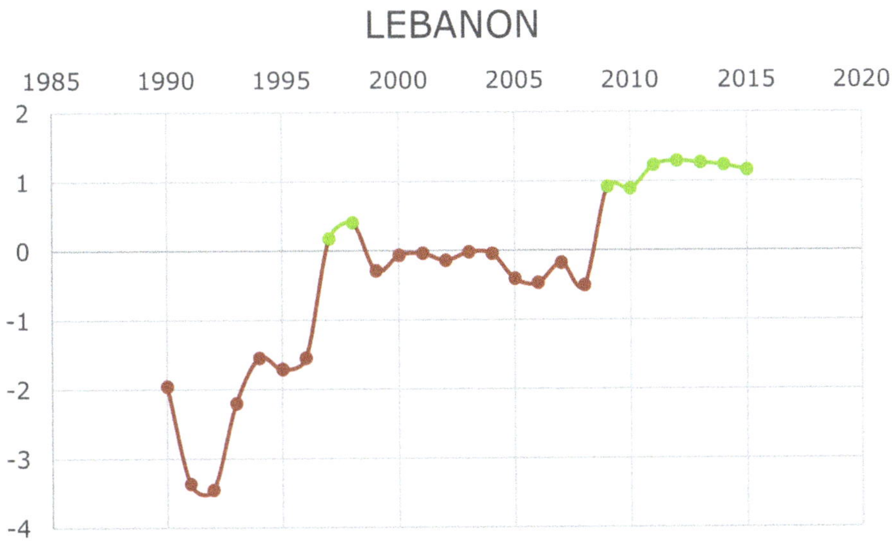

Figure 97. The efficiency signature for Lesotho

Figure 98. The efficiency signature for Liberia

Figure 99. The efficiency signature for Libya

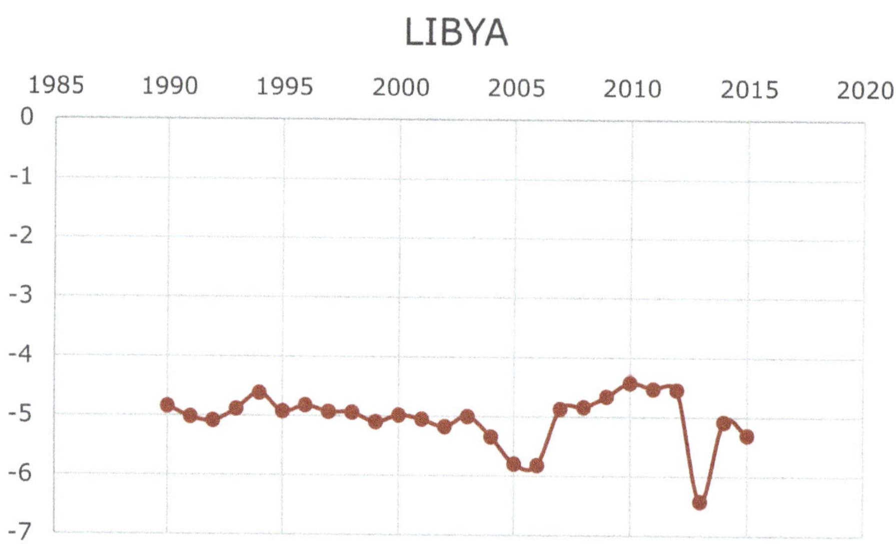

Figure 100. The efficiency signature for Liechtenstein

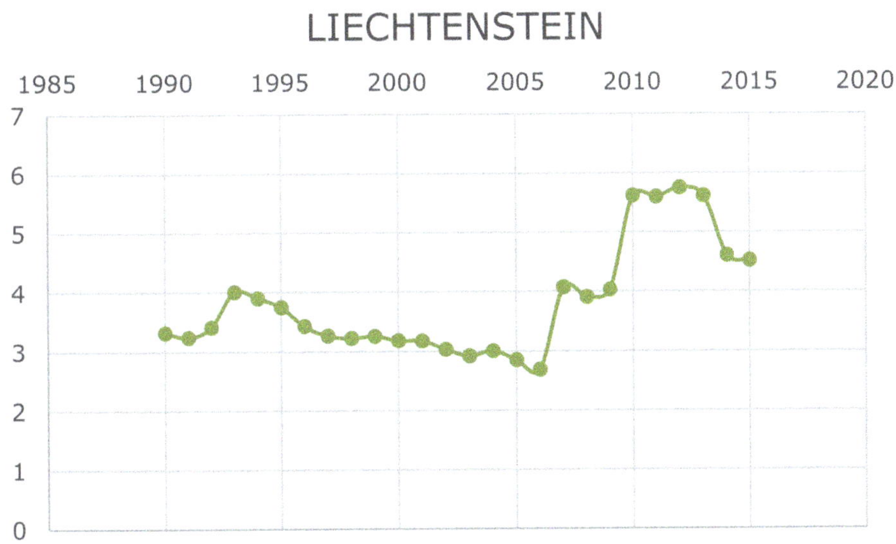

Figure 101. The efficiency signature for Lithuania

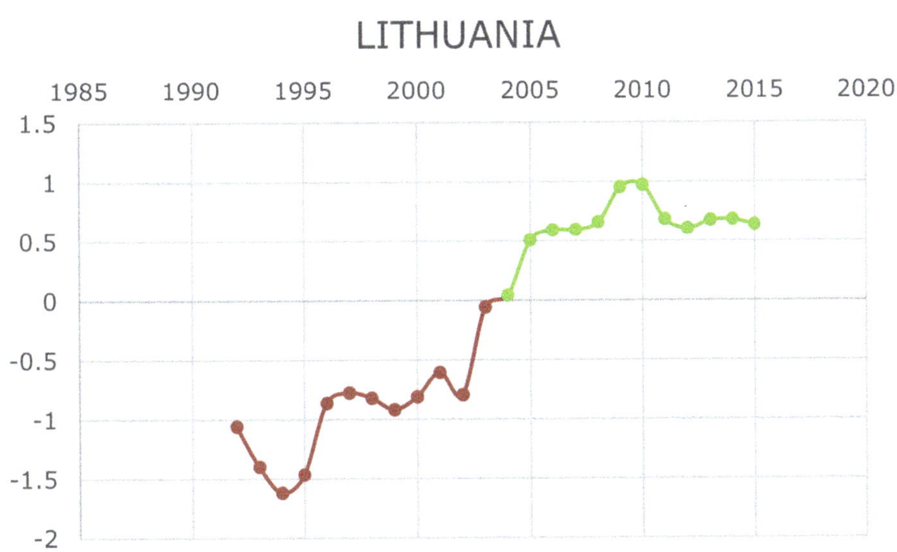

Figure 102. The efficiency signature for Luxembourg

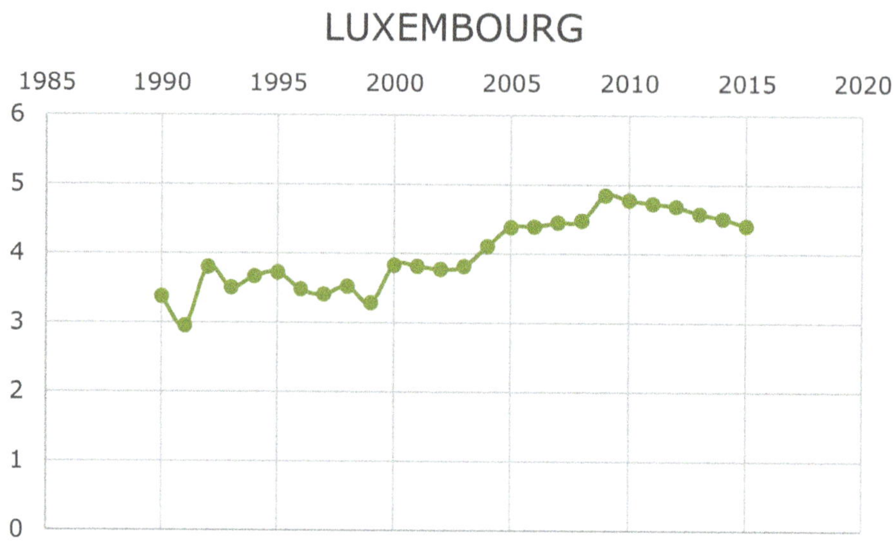

Figure 103. The efficiency signature for Macedonia

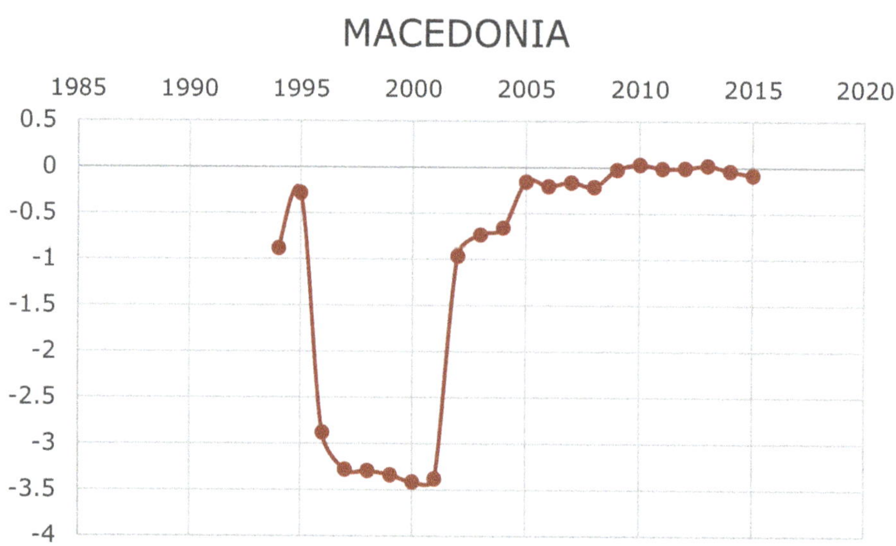

Figure 104. The efficiency signature for Madagascar

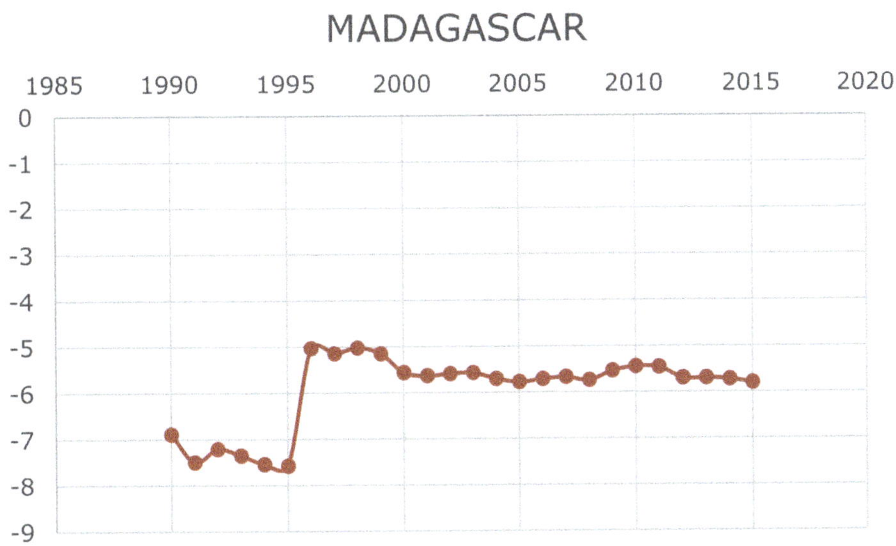

Figure 105. The efficiency signature for Malawi

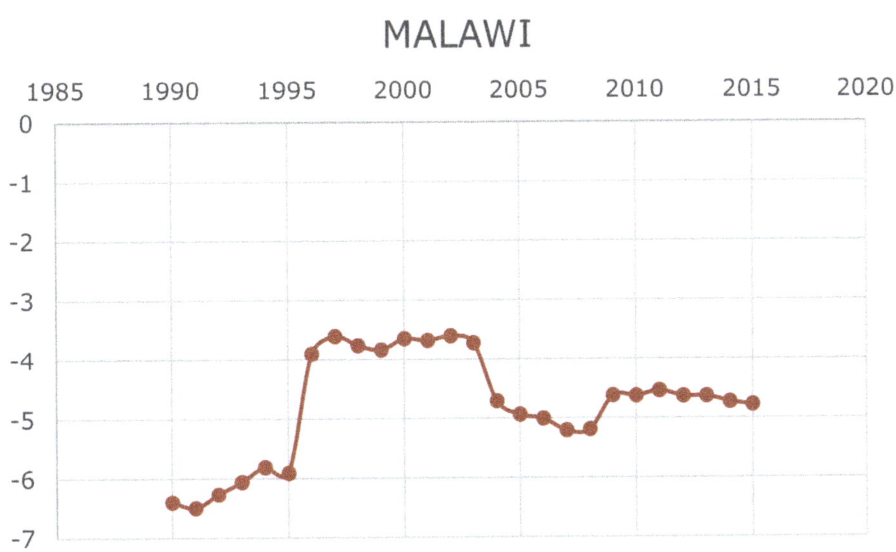

Figure 106. The efficiency signature for Malaysia

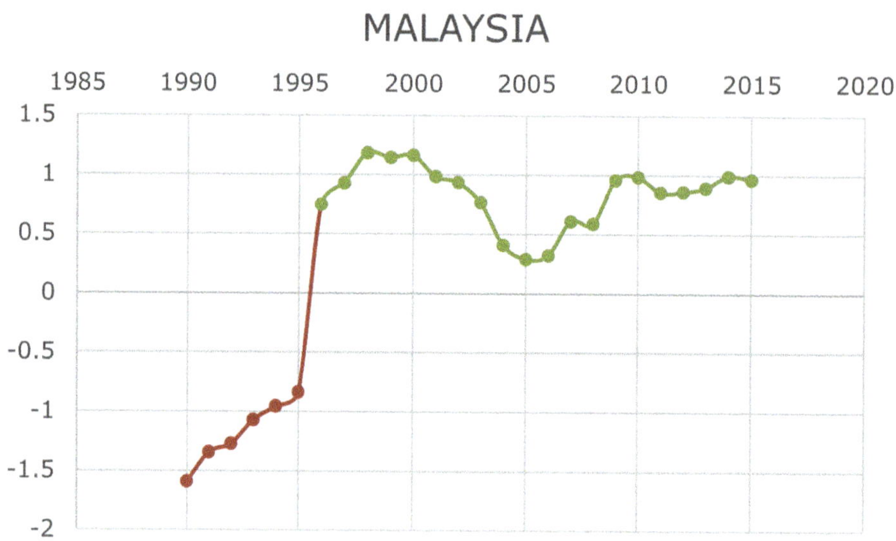

Figure 107. The efficiency signature for Maldives

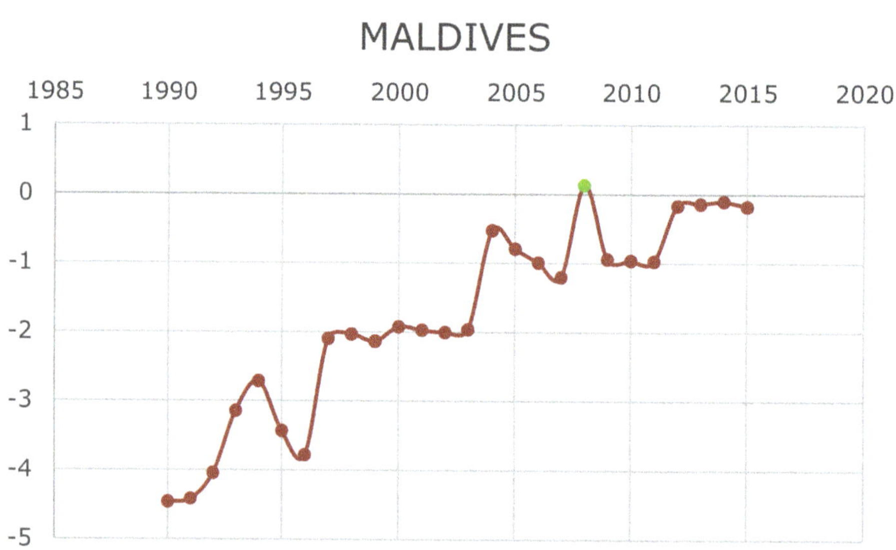

Figure 108. The efficiency signature for Mali

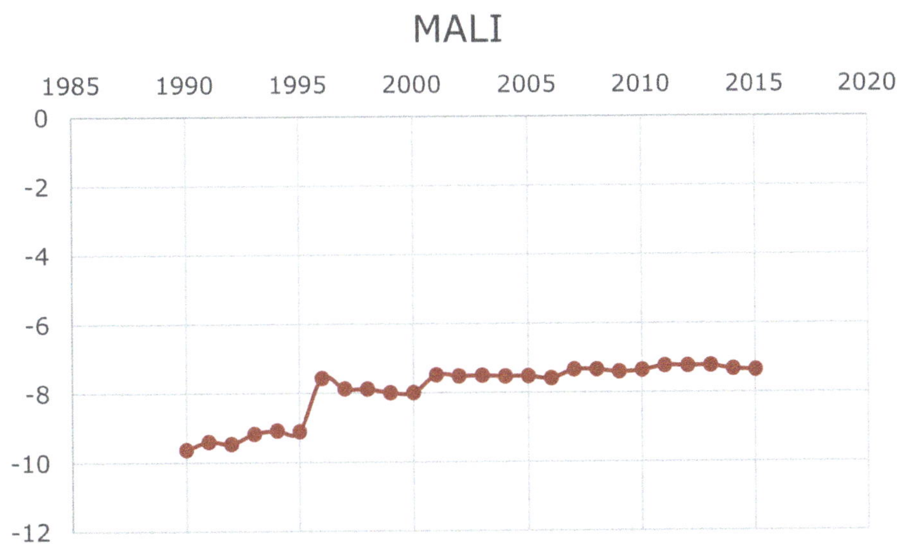

Figure 109. The efficiency signature for Malta

Figure 110. The efficiency signature for Marshall Islands

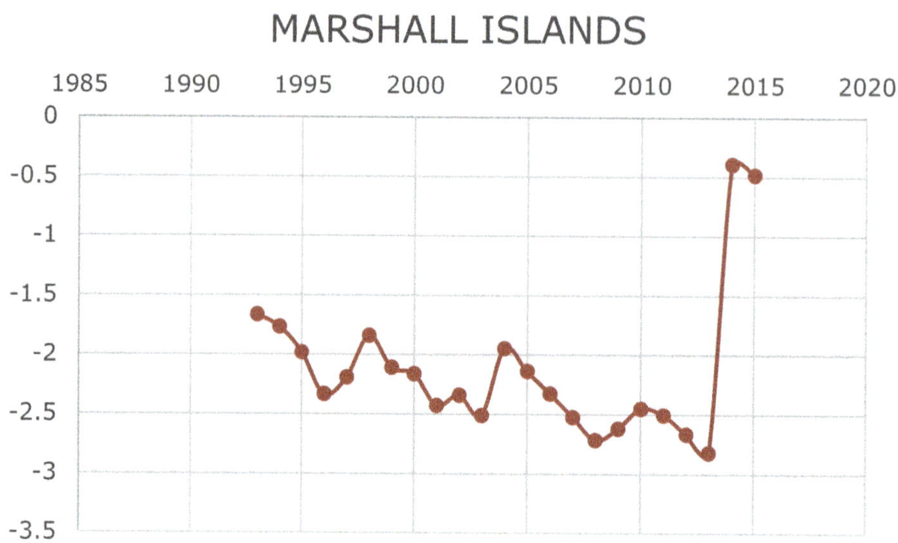

Figure 111. The efficiency signature for Mauritania

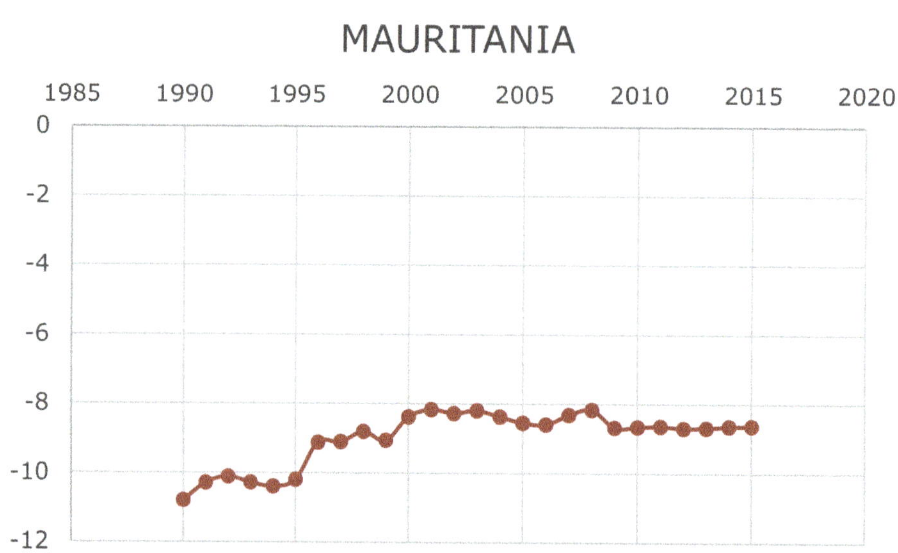

Figure 112. The efficiency signature for Mauritius

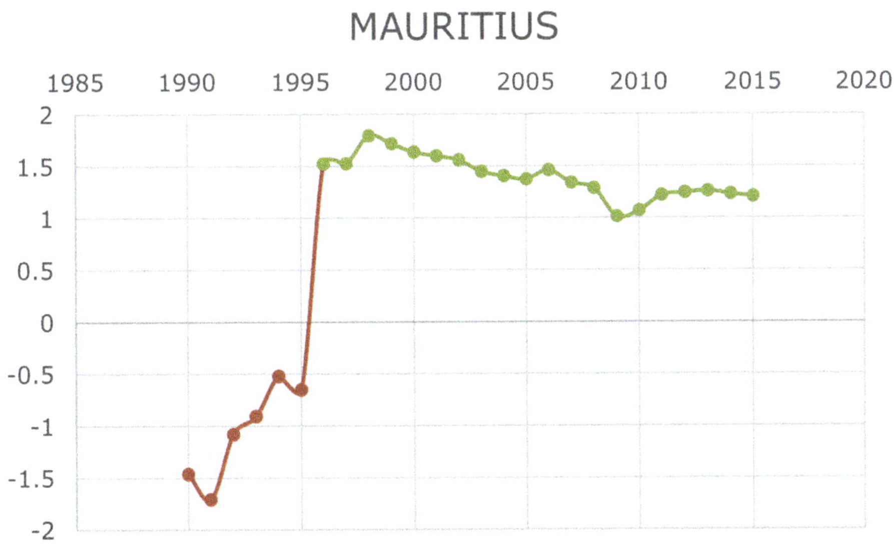

Figure 113. The efficiency signature for Mexico

Figure 114. The efficiency signature for the Federated States of Micronesia

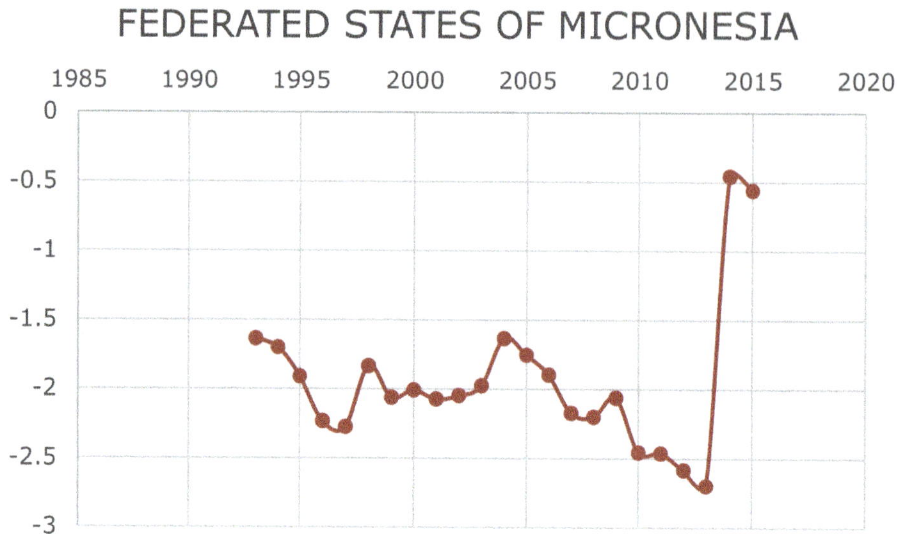

Figure 115. The efficiency signature for Moldova

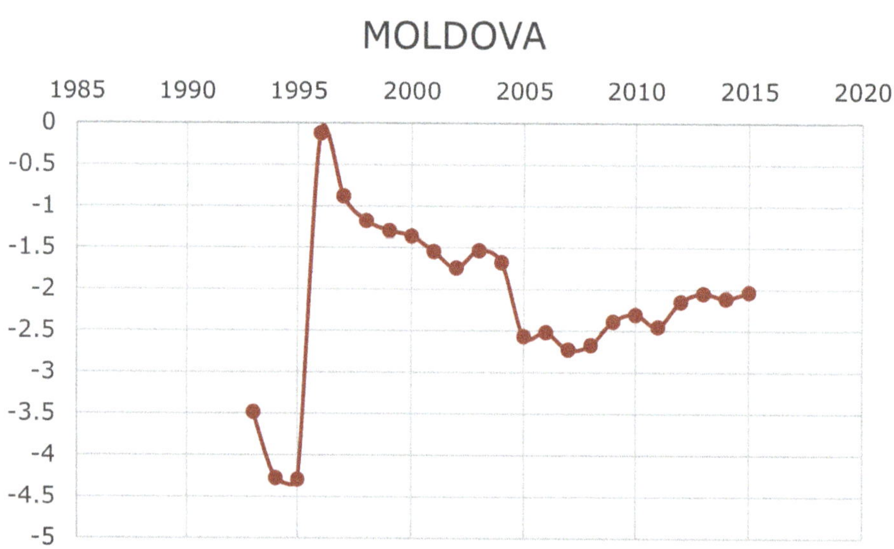

Figure 116. The efficiency signature for Monaco

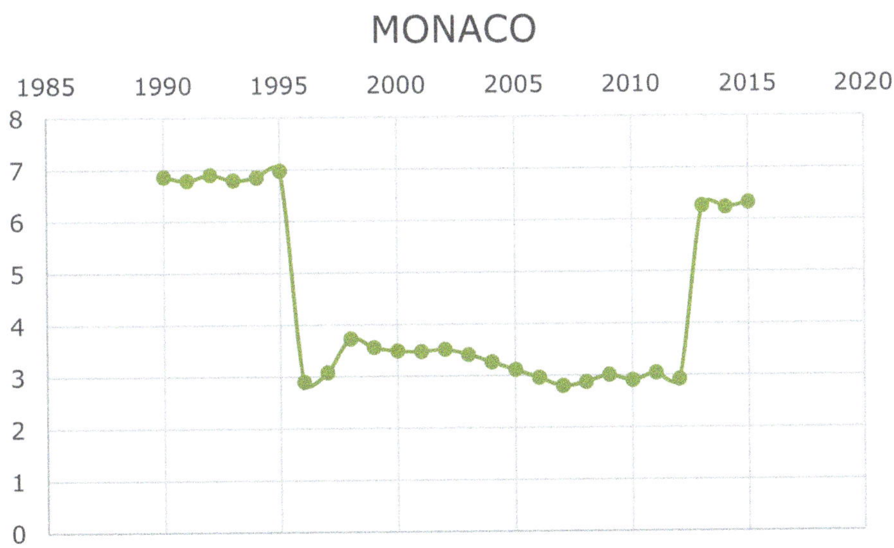

Figure 117. The efficiency signature for Mongolia

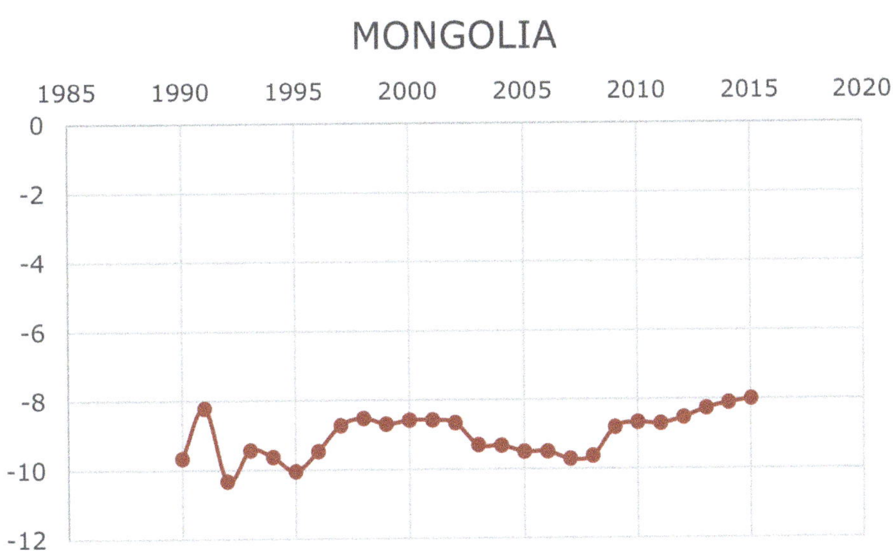

Figure 118. The efficiency signature for Montenegro

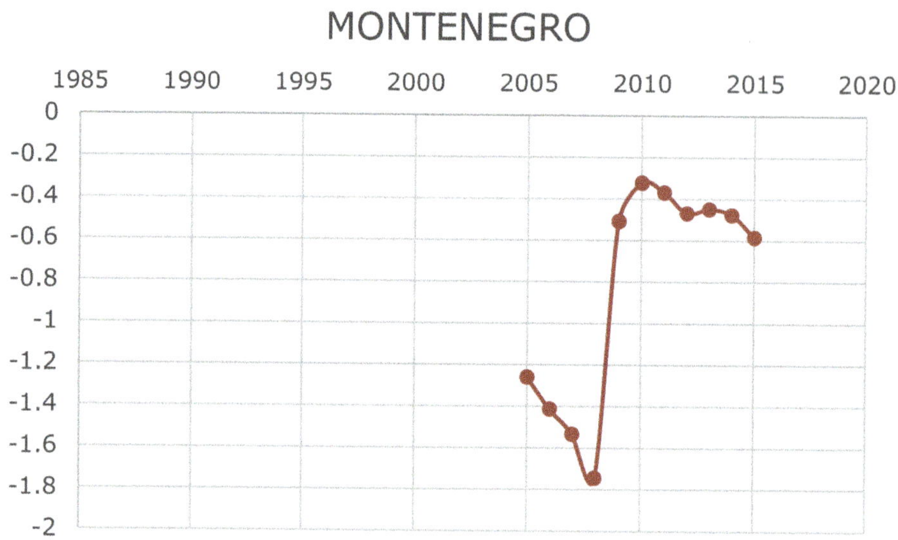

Figure 119. The efficiency signature for Morocco

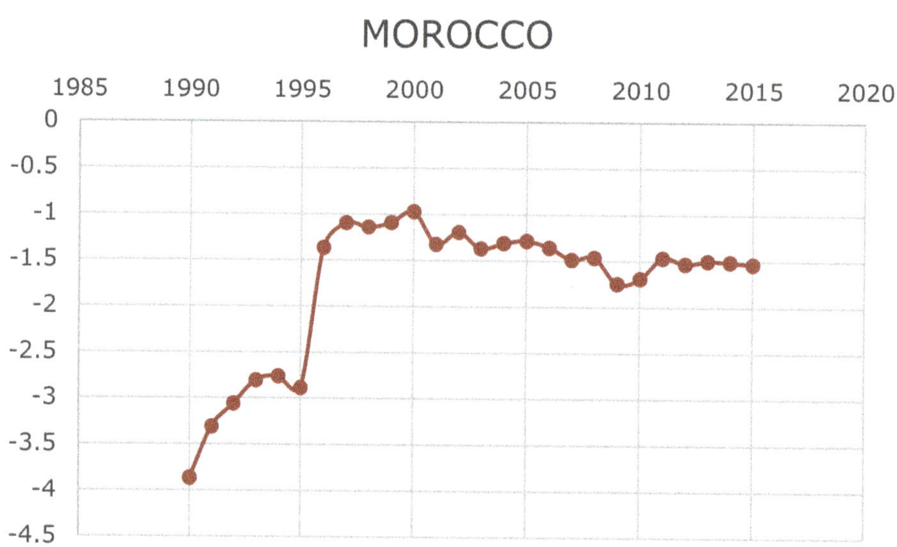

Figure 120. The efficiency signature for Mozambique

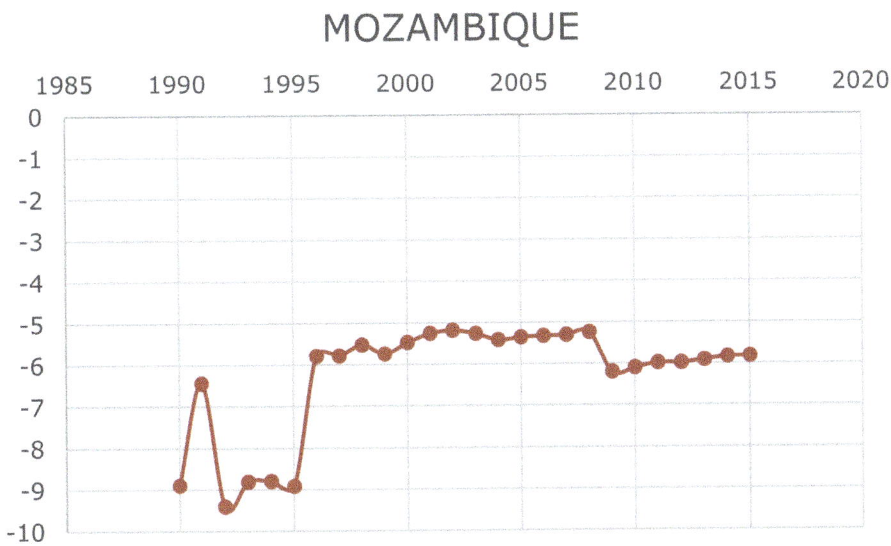

Figure 121. The efficiency signature for Myanmar

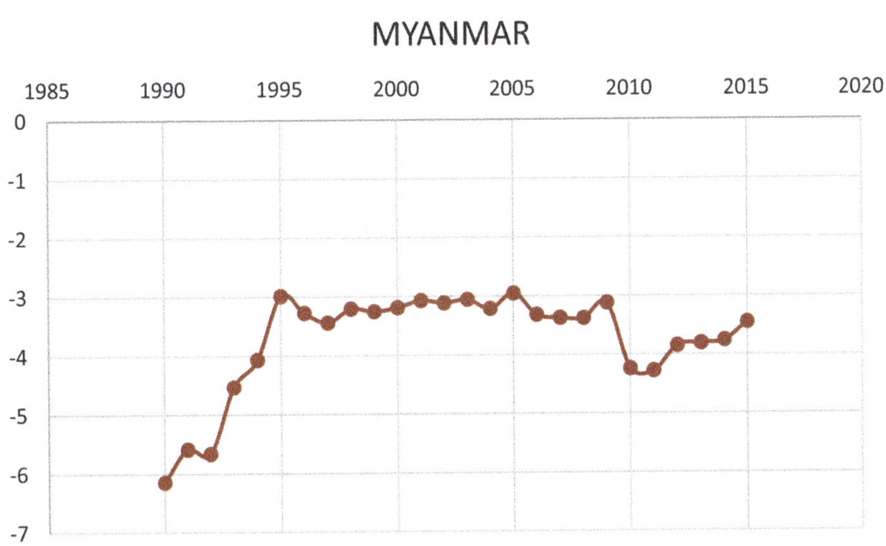

Figure 122. The efficiency signature for Namibia

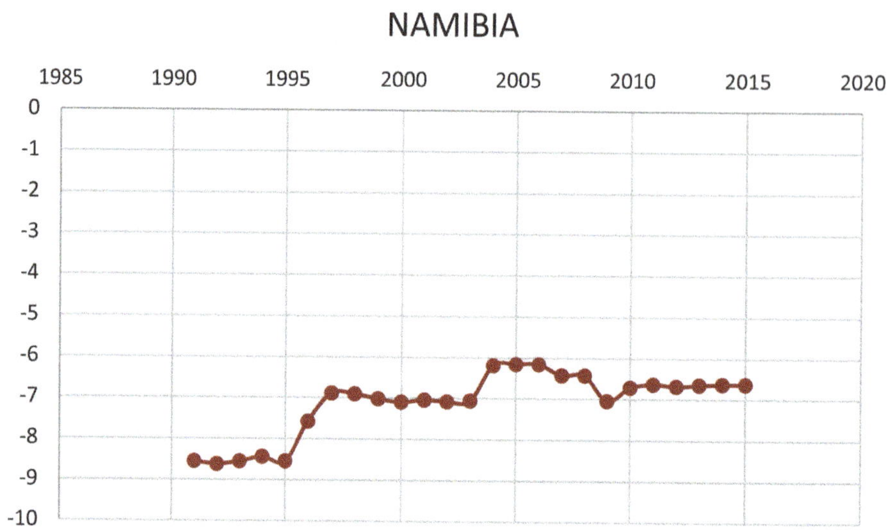

Figure 123. The efficiency signature for Nauru

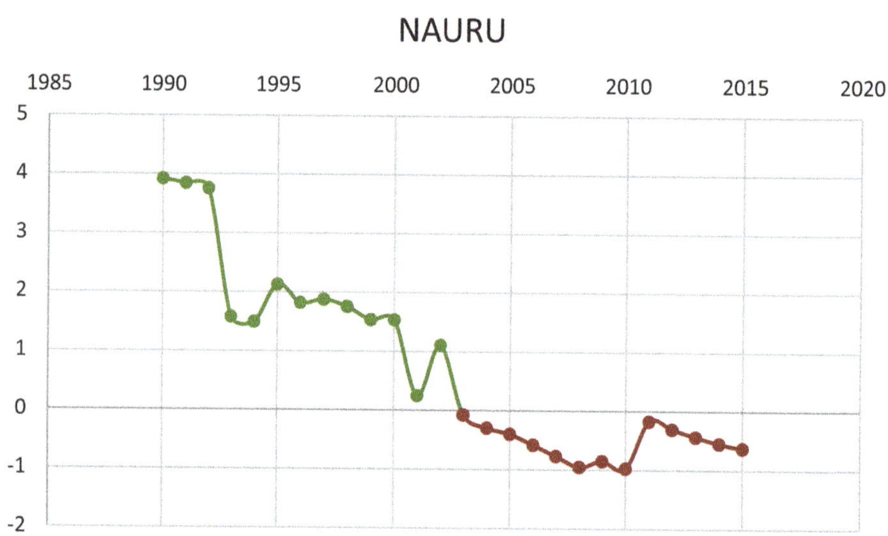

Figure 124. The efficiency signature for Nepal

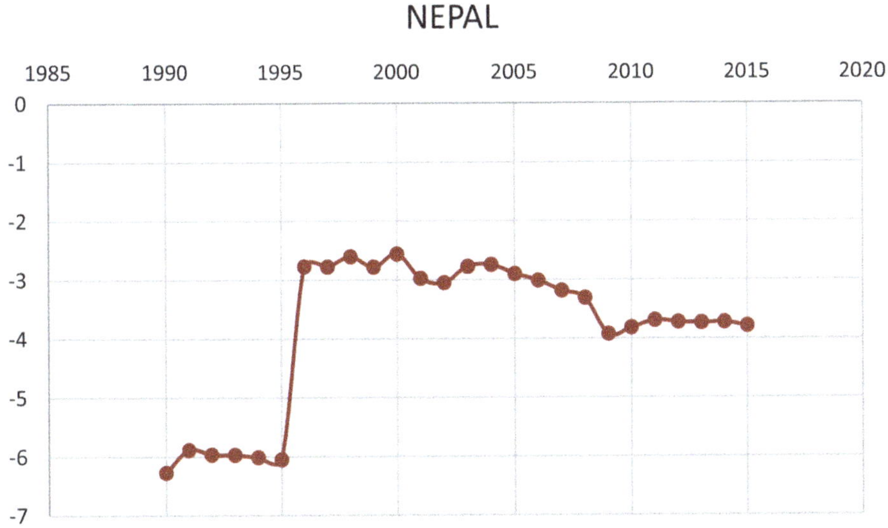

Figure 125. The efficiency signature for the Netherlands

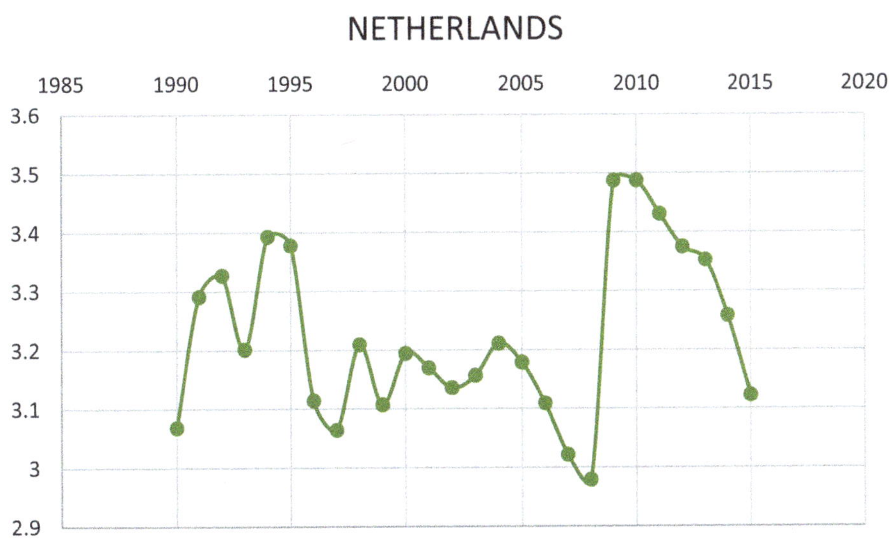

Figure 126. The efficiency signature for New Zealand

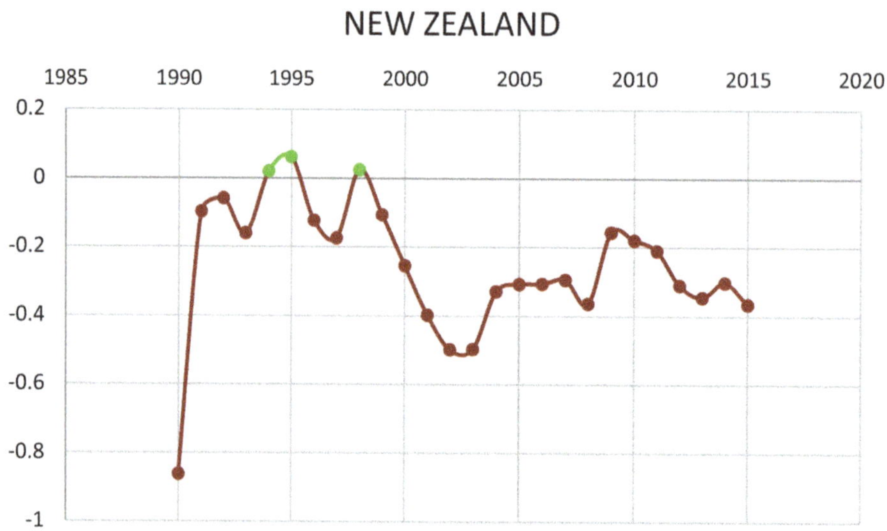

Figure 127. The efficiency signature for Nicaragua

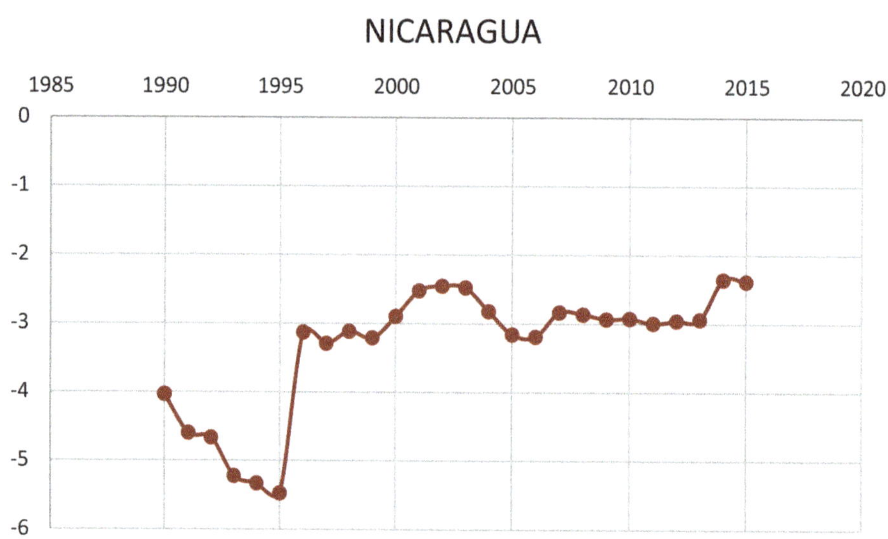

Figure 128. The efficiency signature for Niger

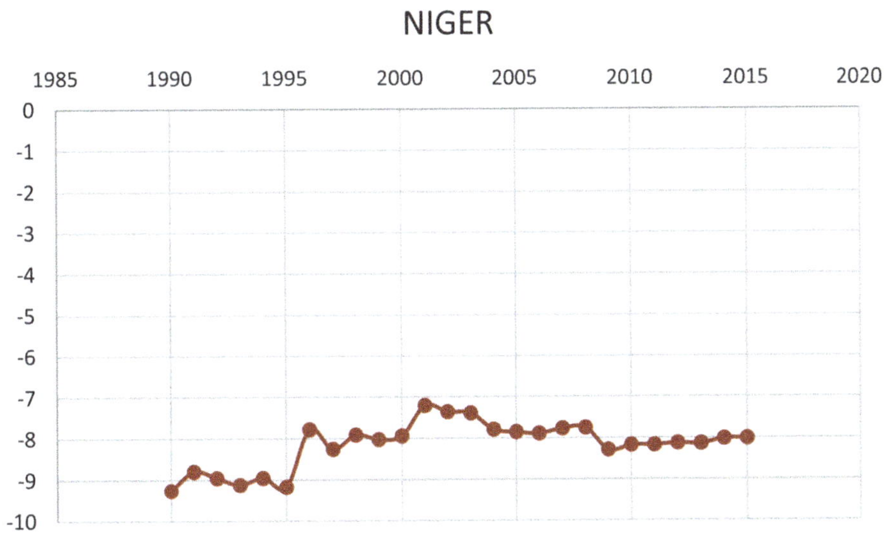

Figure 129. The efficiency signature for Nigeria

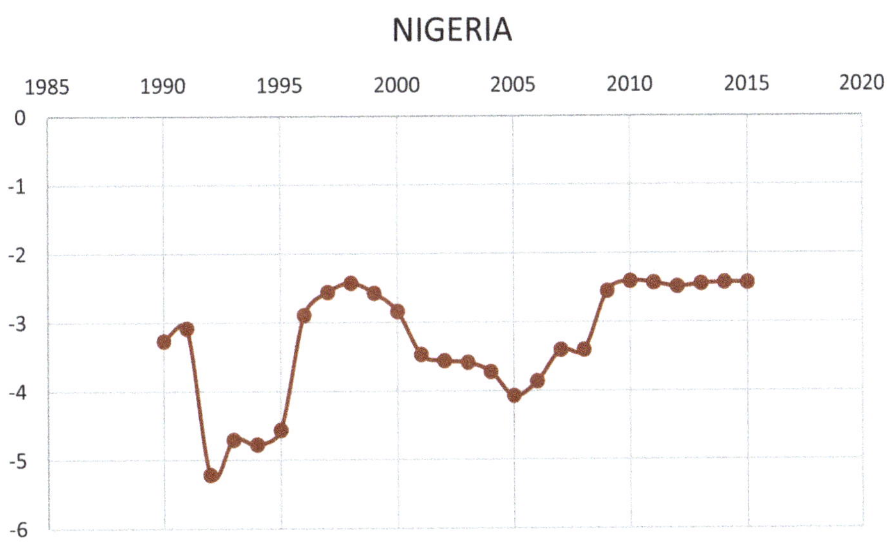

Figure 130. The efficiency signature for Norway

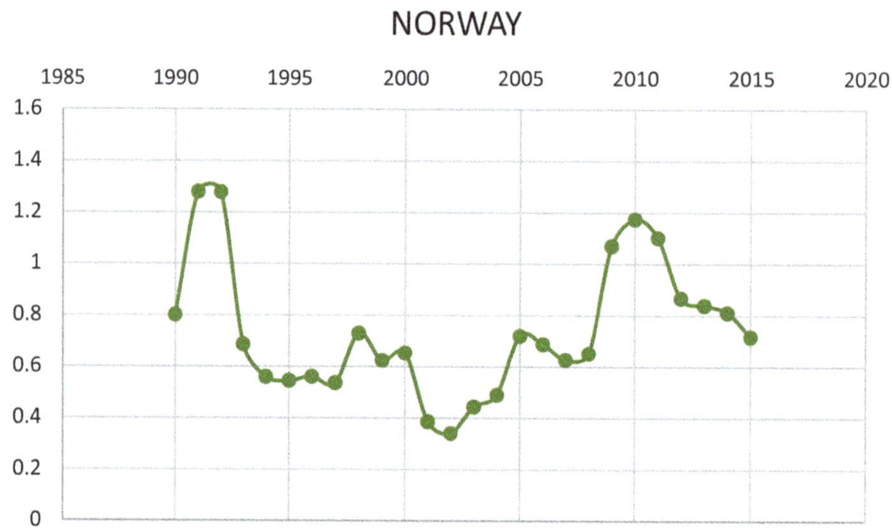

Figure 131. The efficiency signature for Oman

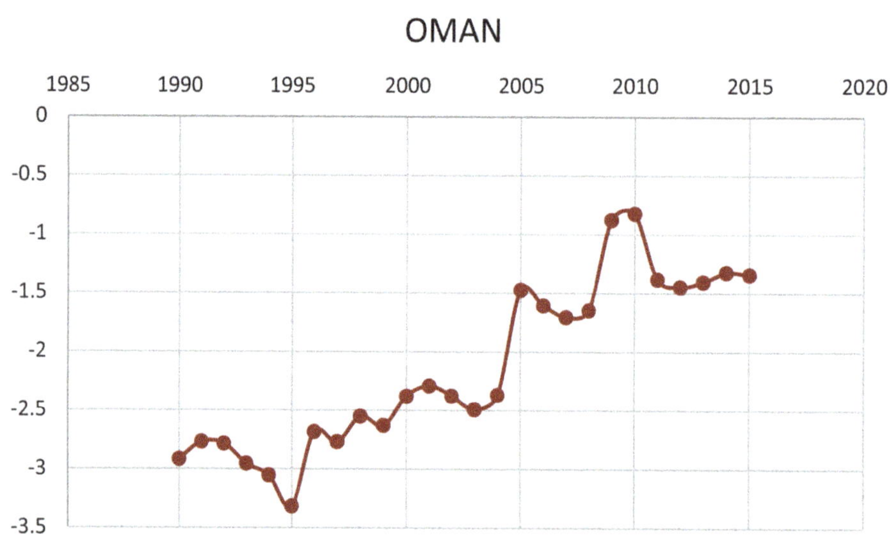

Figure 132. The efficiency signature for Pakistan

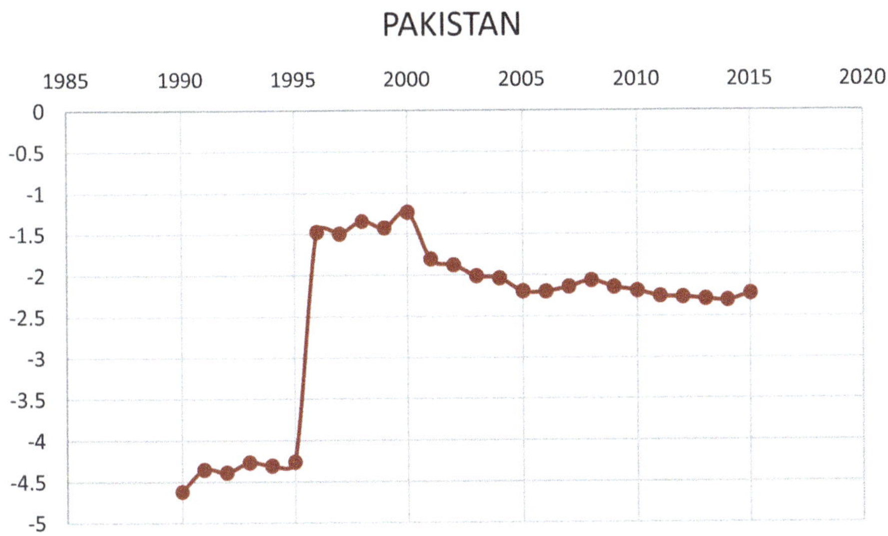

Figure 133. The efficiency signature for Palau

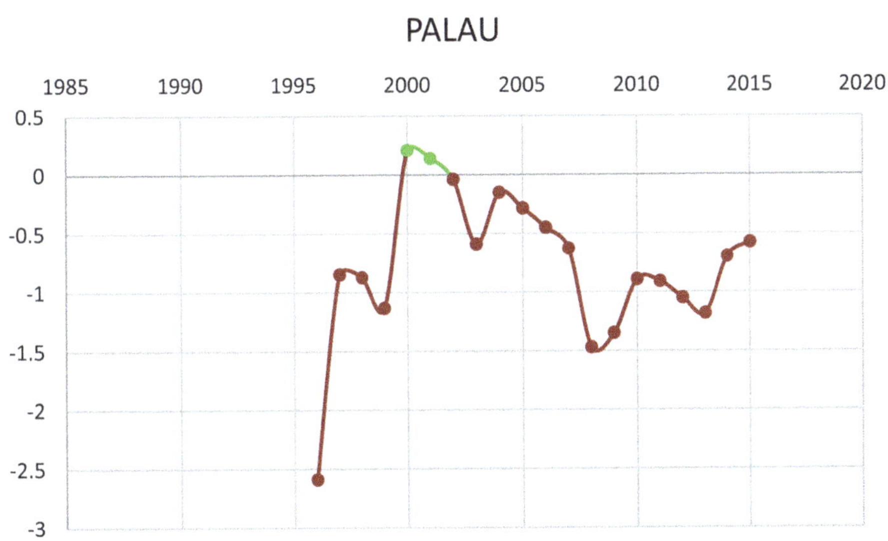

Figure 134. The efficiency signature for Panama

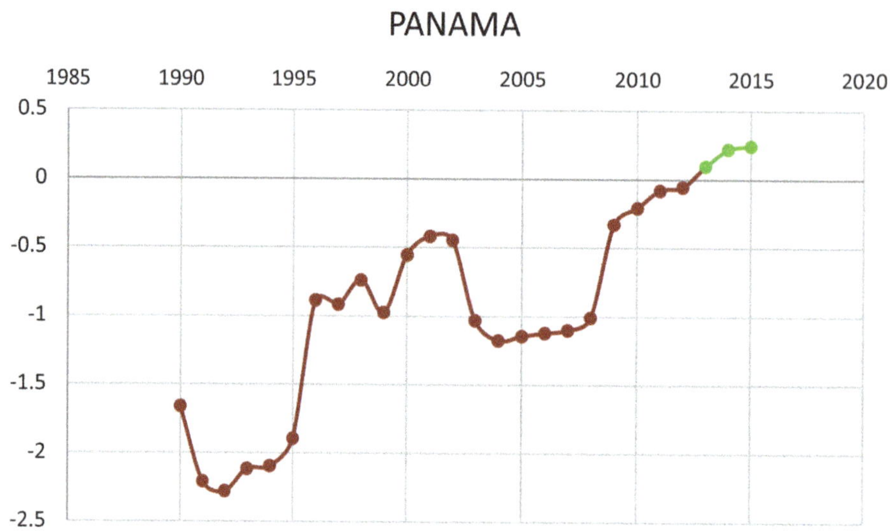

Figure 135. The efficiency signature for Papua New Guinea

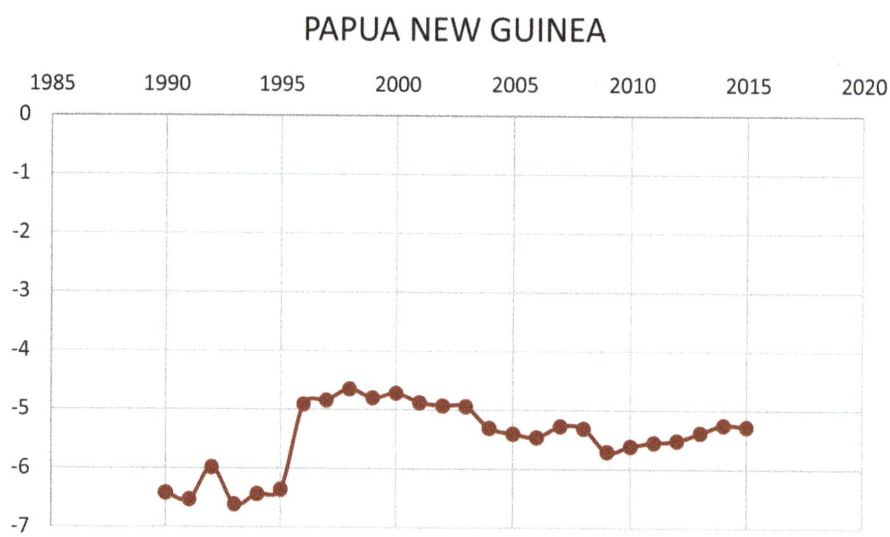

Figure 136. The efficiency signature for Paraguay

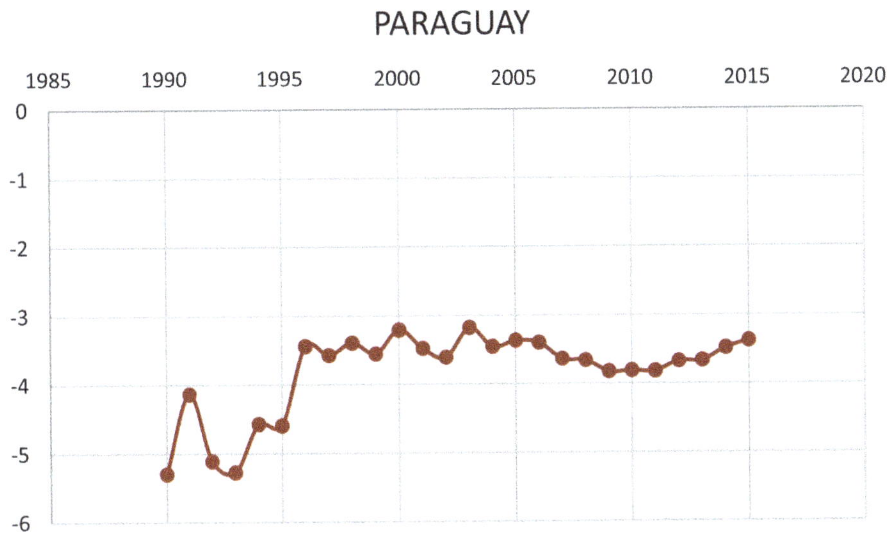

Figure 137. The efficiency signature for Peru

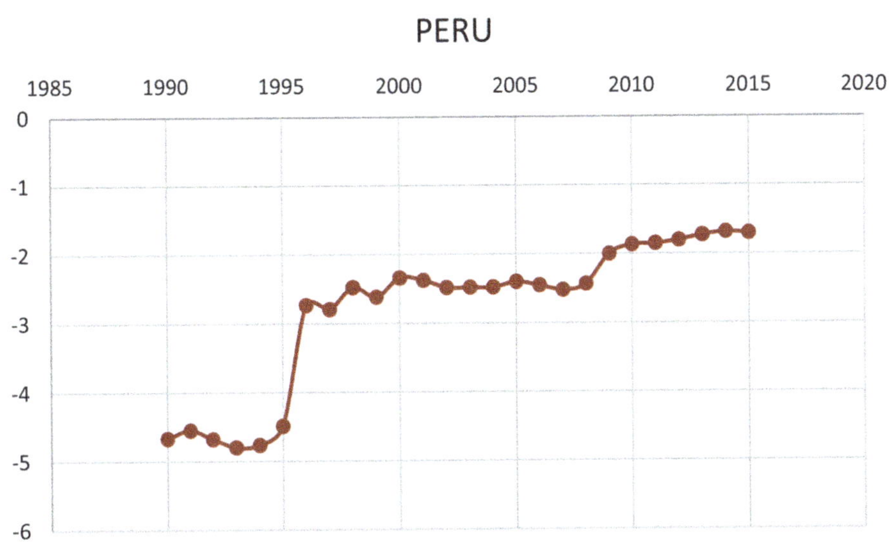

Figure 138. The efficiency signature for the Philippines

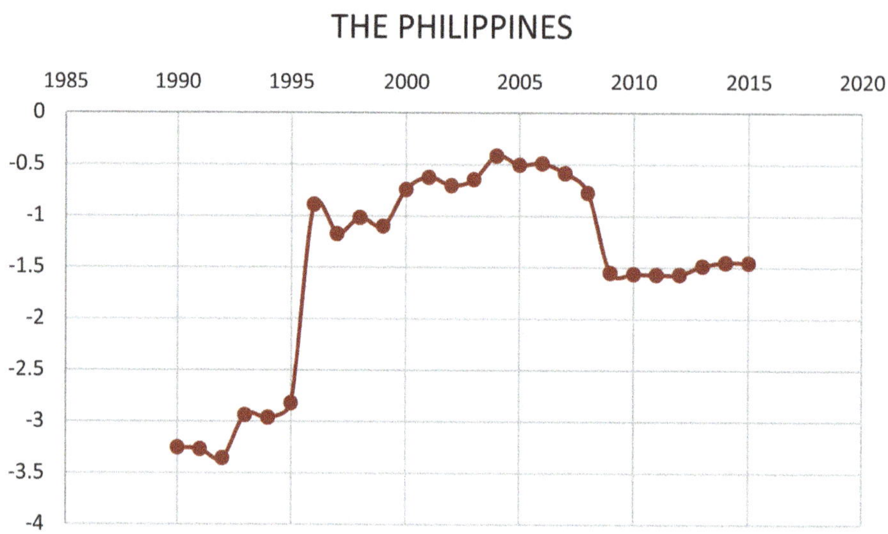

Figure 139. The efficiency signature for Poland

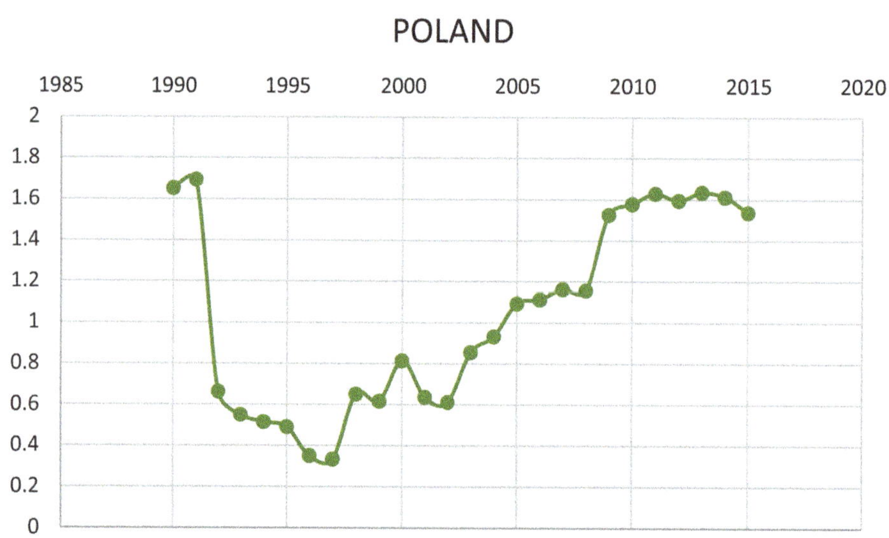

Figure 140. The efficiency signature for Portugal

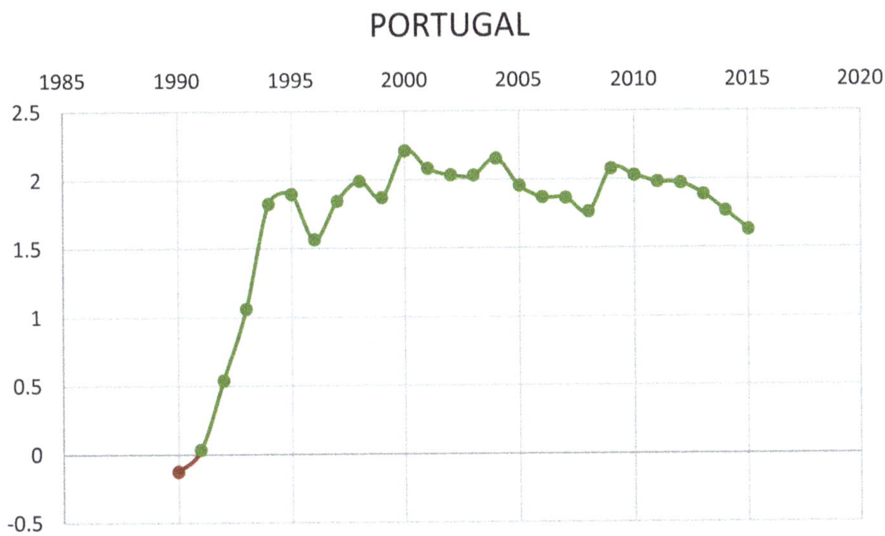

Figure 141. The efficiency signature for Qatar

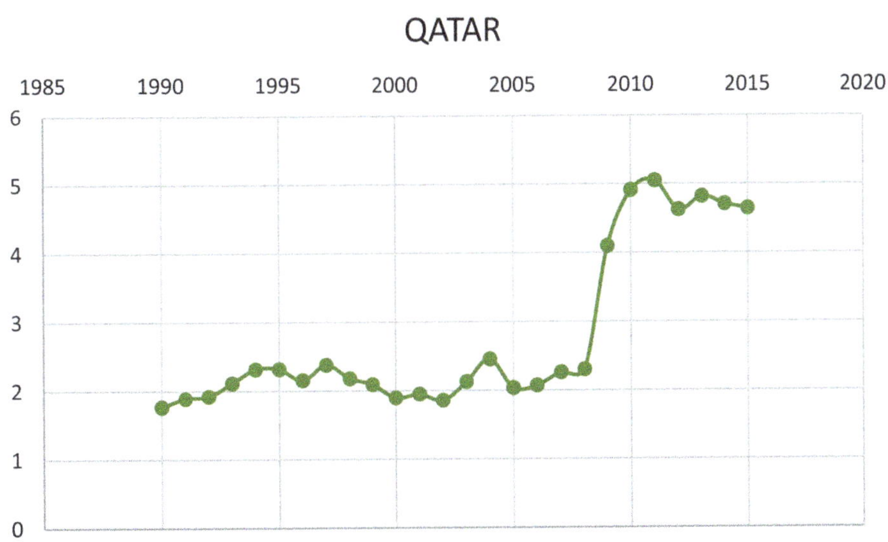

Figure 142. The efficiency signature for Romania

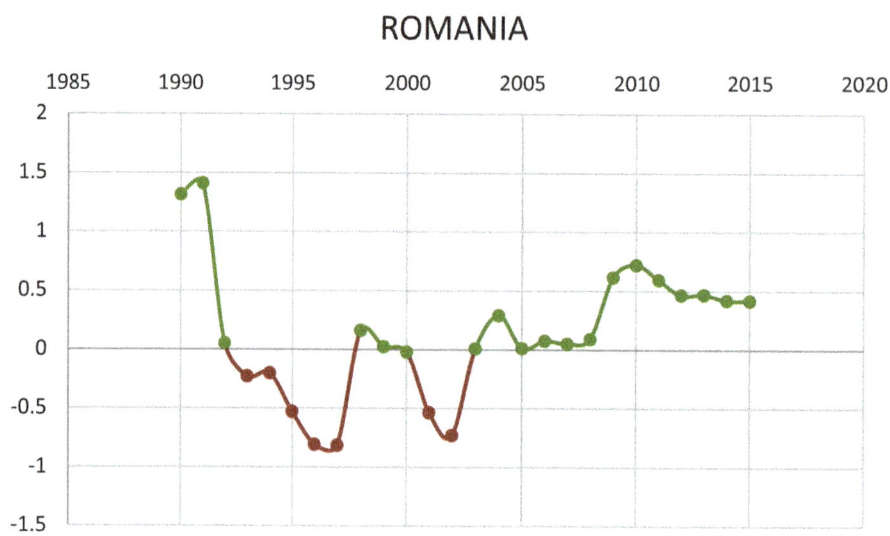

Figure 143. The efficiency signature for Russia (from 1992)

Figure 144. The efficiency signature for Rwanda

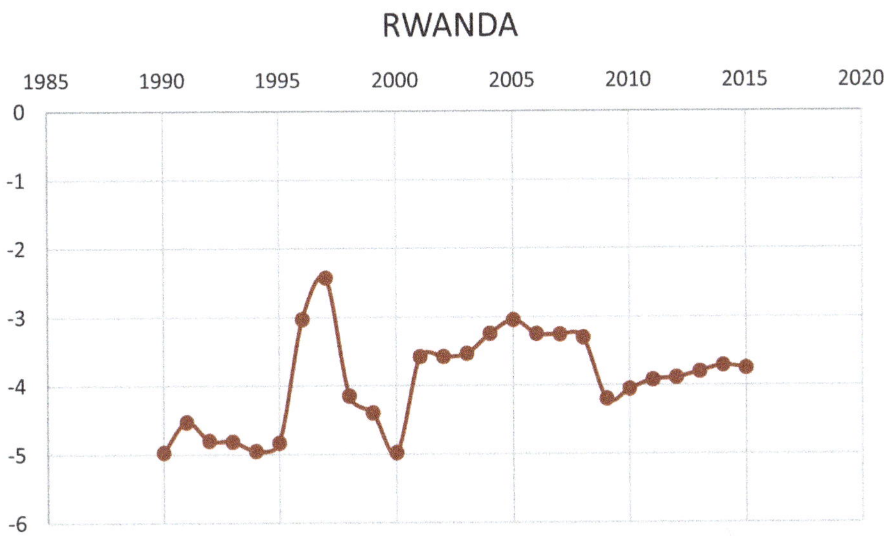

Figure 145. The efficiency signature for Saint Kitts and Nevis

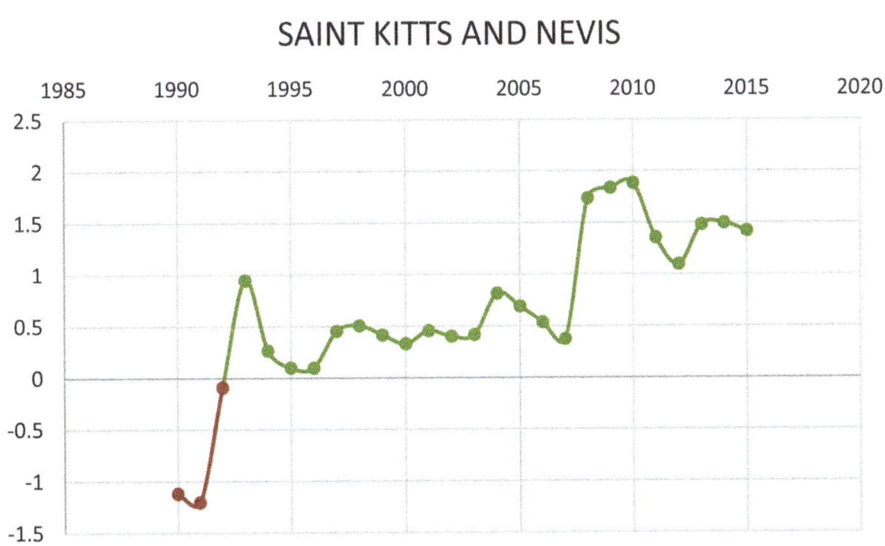

Figure 146. The efficiency signature for Saint Lucia

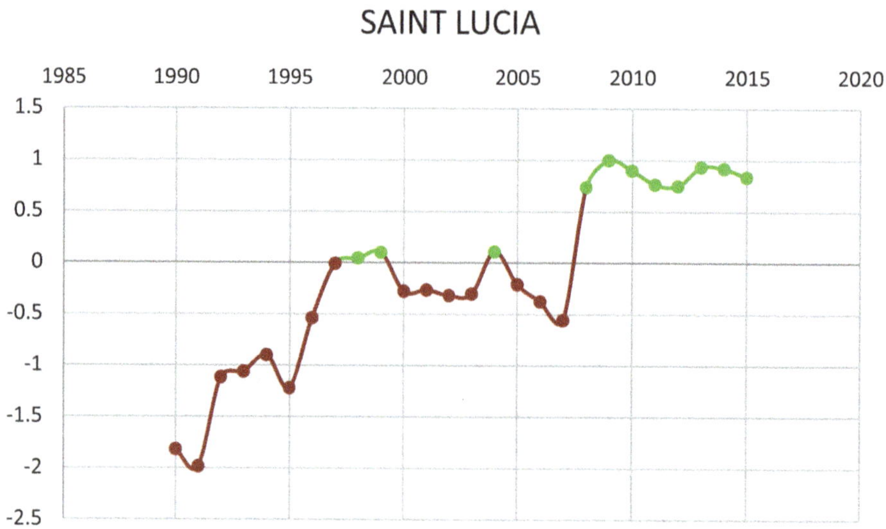

Figure 147. The efficiency signature for Saint Vincent and the Grenadines

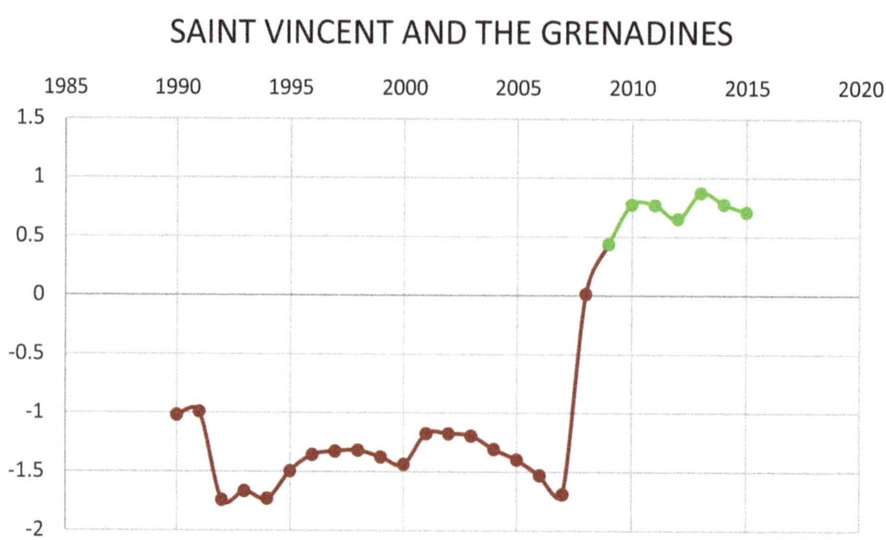

Figure 148. The efficiency signature for Samoa

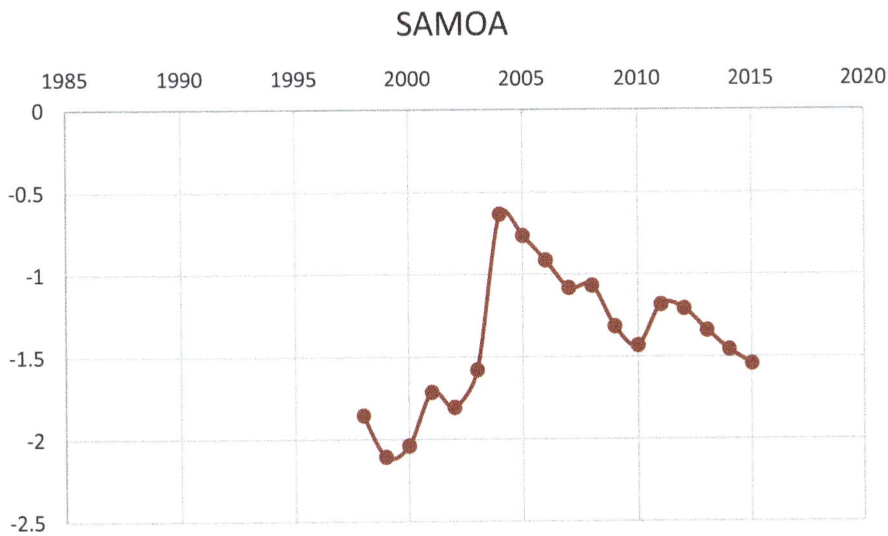

Figure 149. The efficiency signature for San Marino

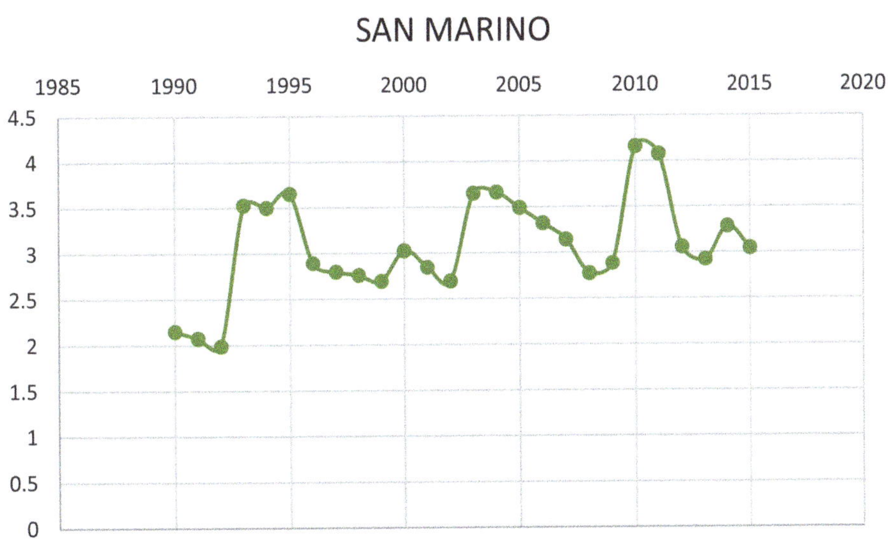

Figure 150. The efficiency signature for Sao Tome and Principe

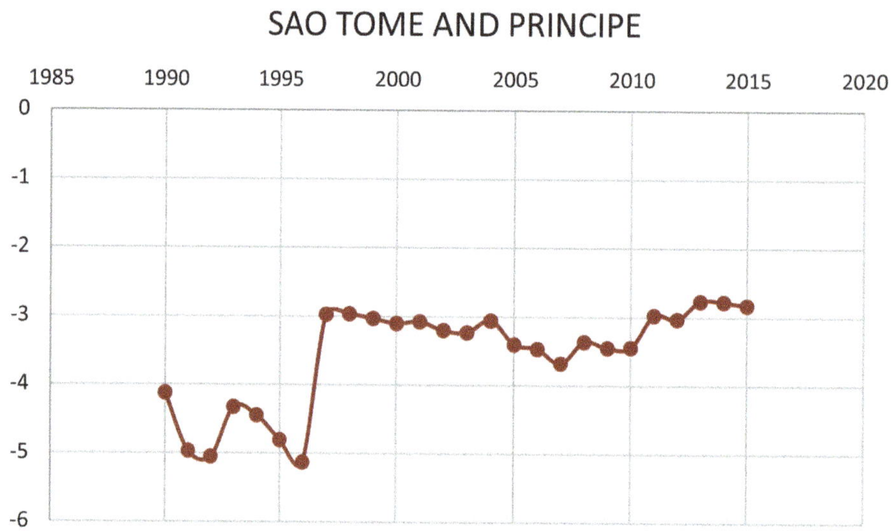

Figure 151. The efficiency signature for Saudi Arabia

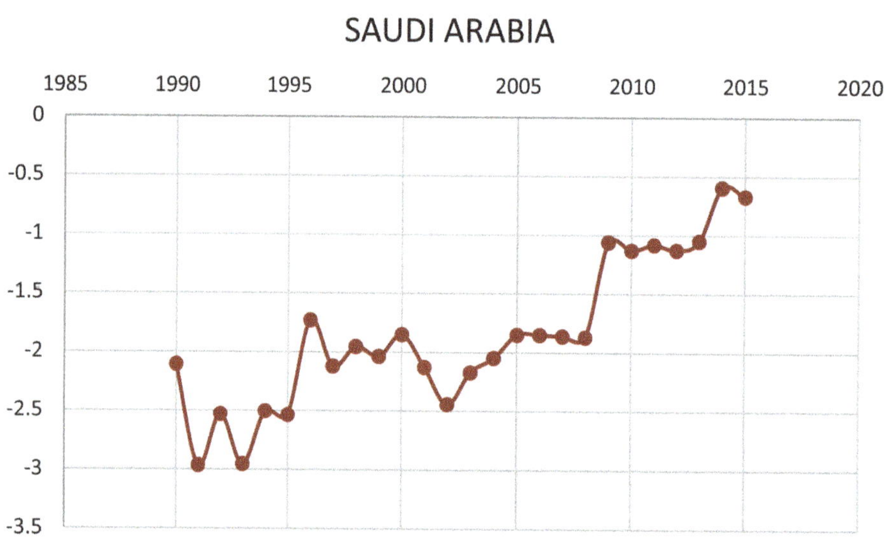

Figure 152. The efficiency signature for Senegal

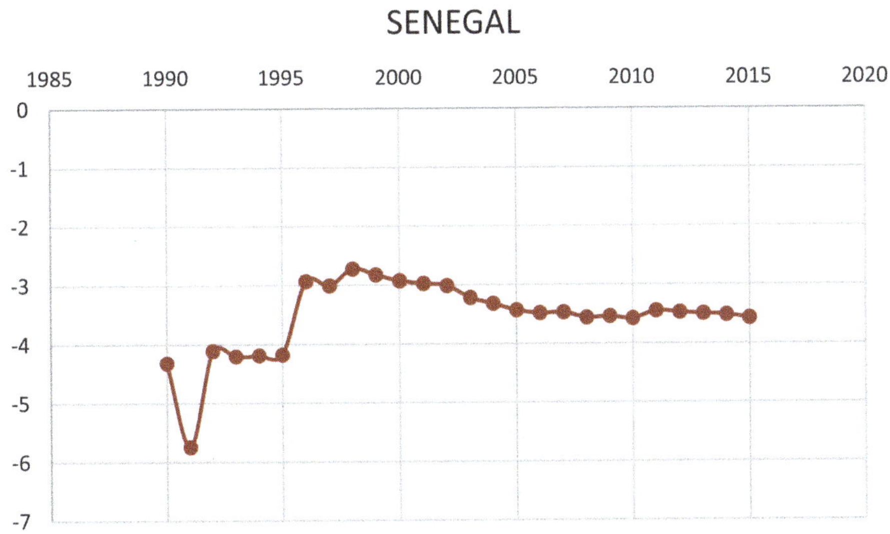

Figure 153. The efficiency signature for Serbia

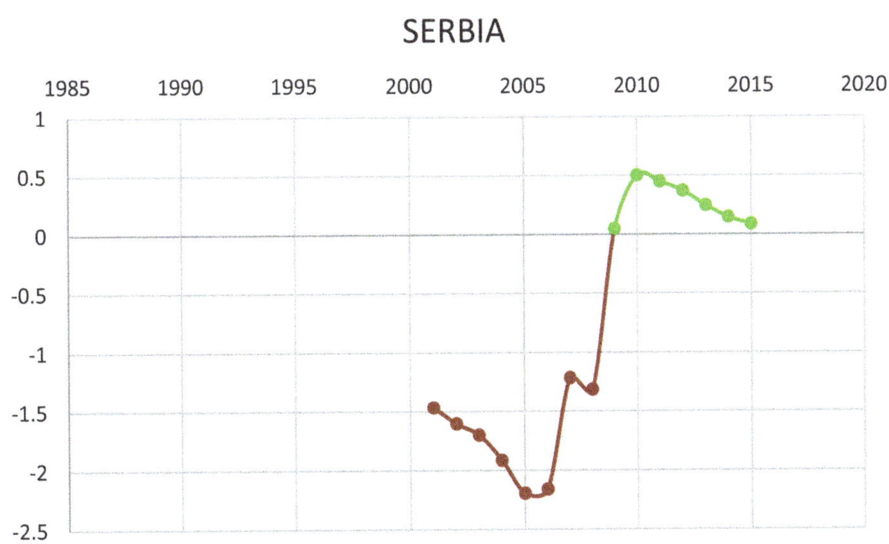

Figure 154. The efficiency signature for Seychelles

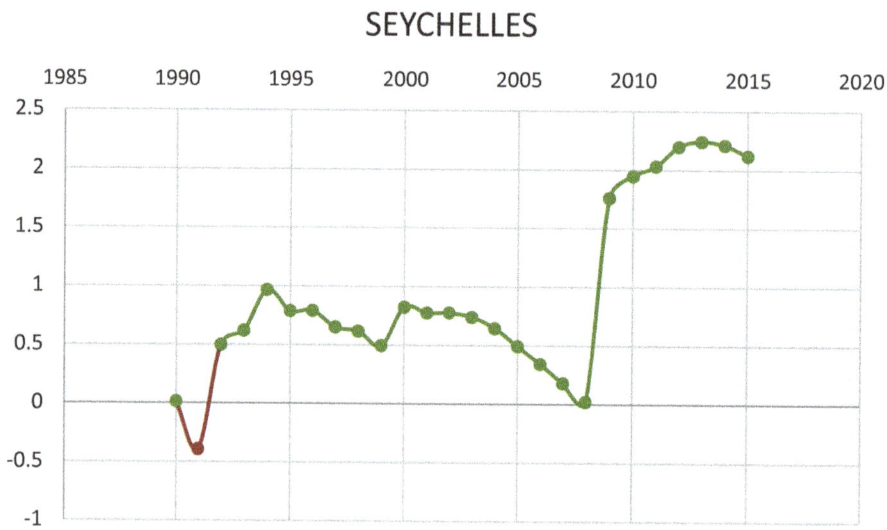

Figure 155. The efficiency signature for Sierra Leone

Figure 156. The efficiency signature for Singapore

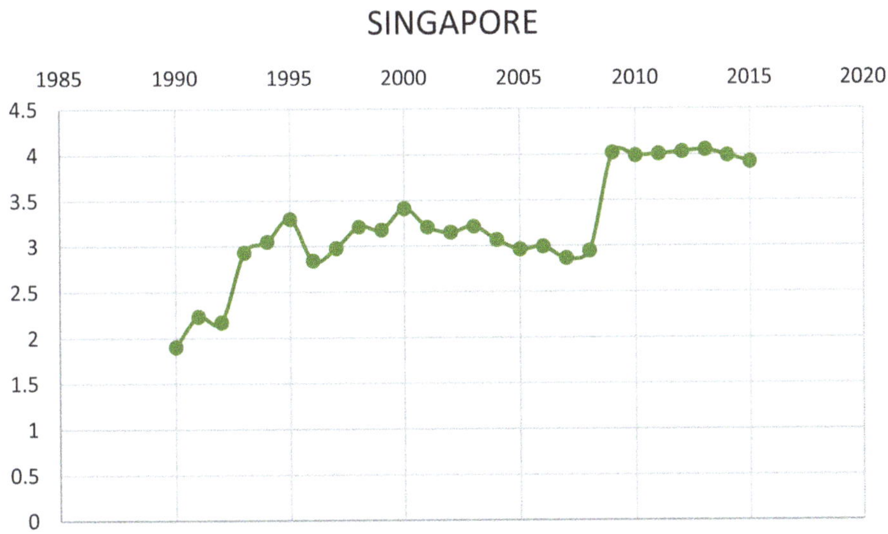

Figure 157. The efficiency signature for Slovakia

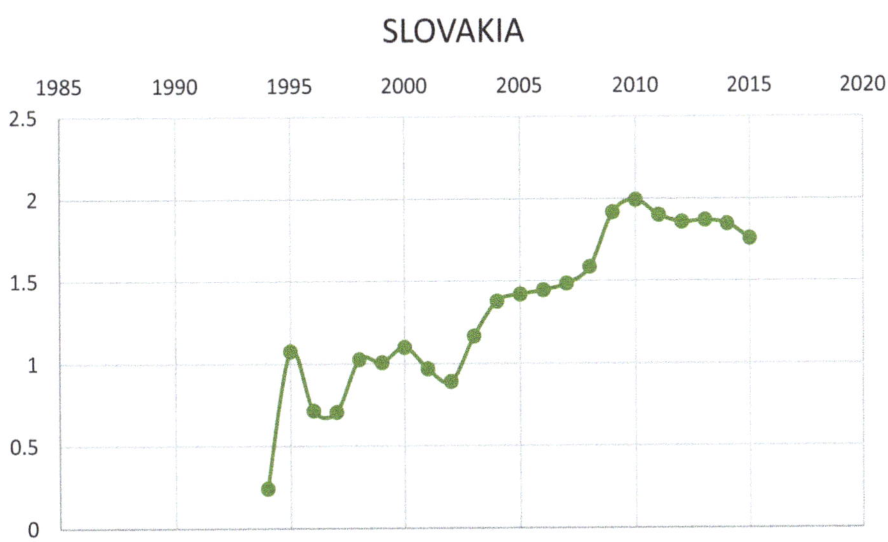

Figure 158. The efficiency signature for Slovenia

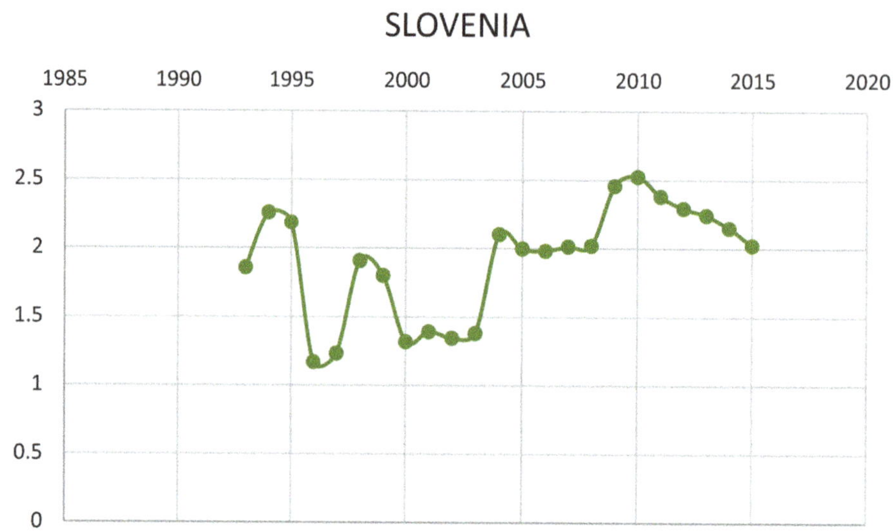

Figure 159. The efficiency signature for the Solomon Islands

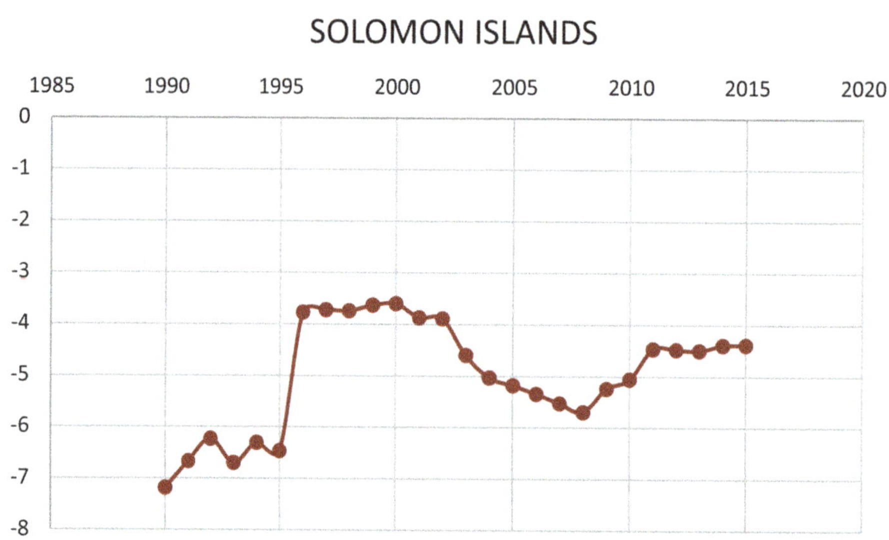

Figure 160. The efficiency signature for Somalia

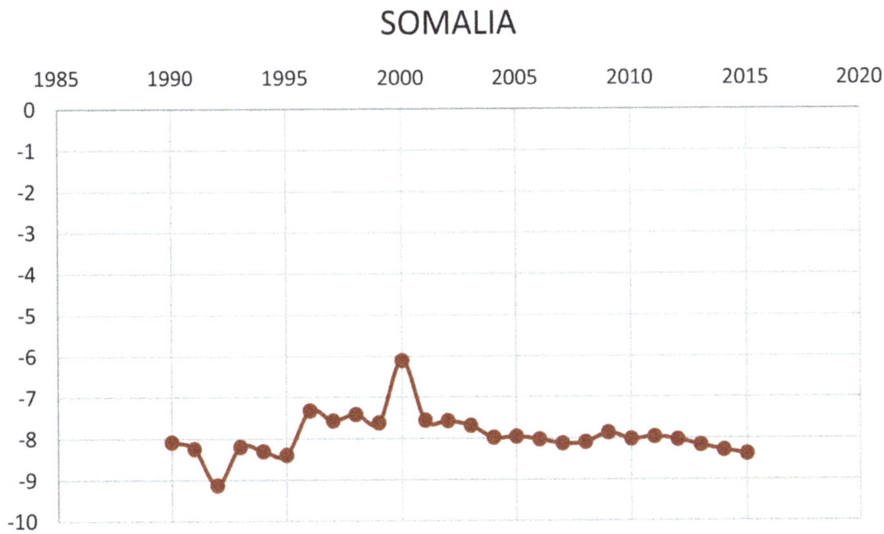

Figure 161. The efficiency signature for South Africa

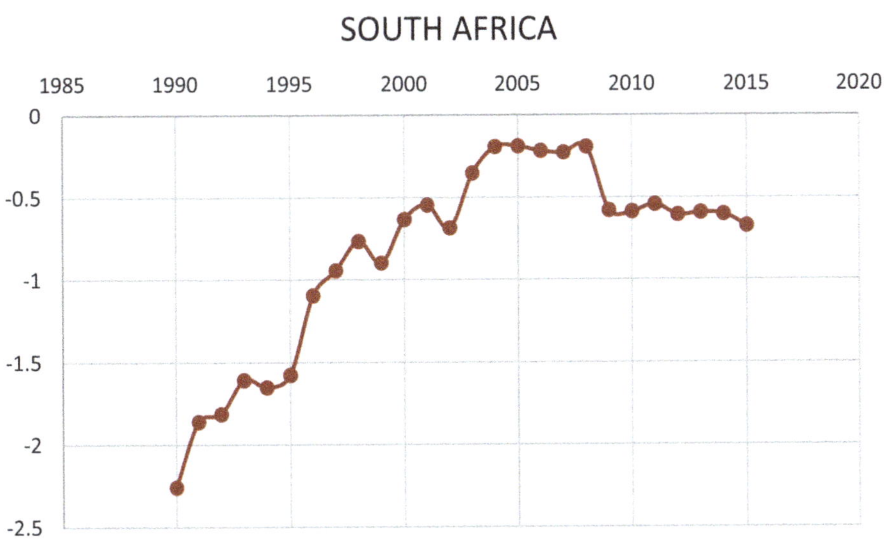

Figure 162. The efficiency signature for South Sudan

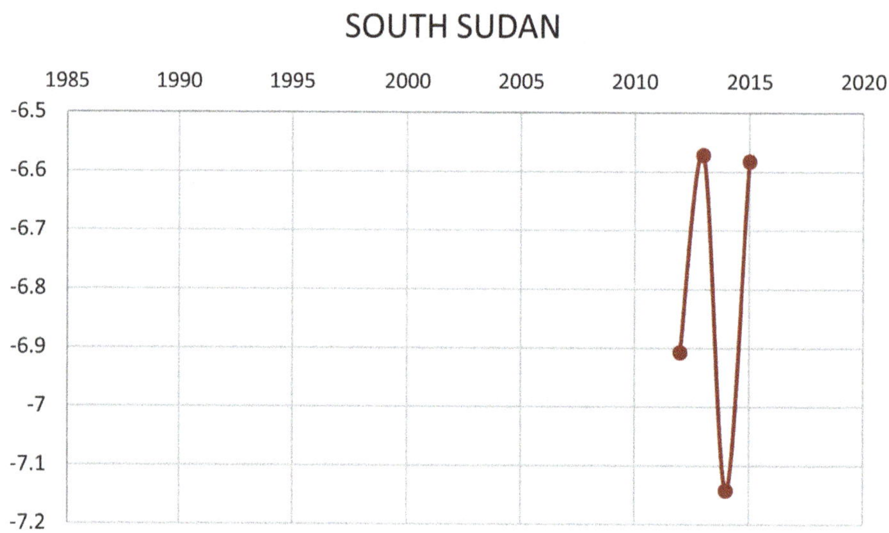

Figure 163. The efficiency signature for Spain

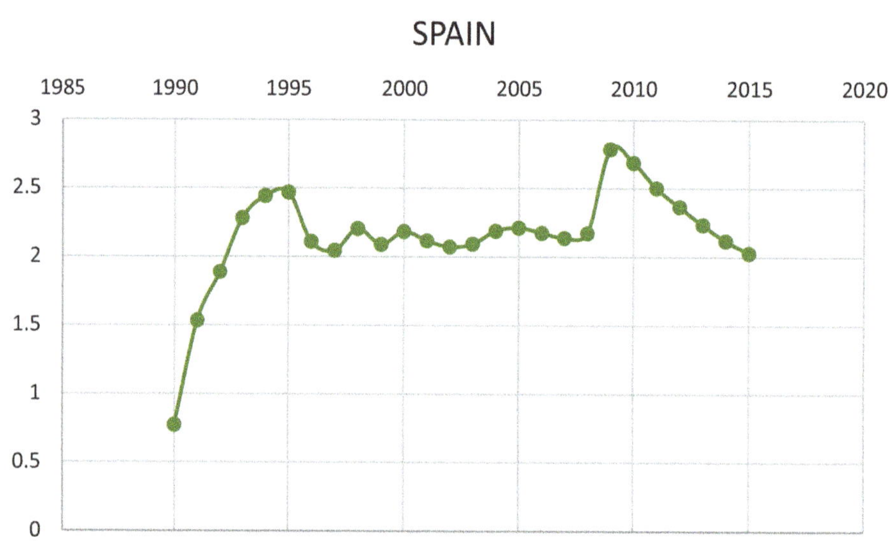

Figure 164. The efficiency signature for Sri Lanka

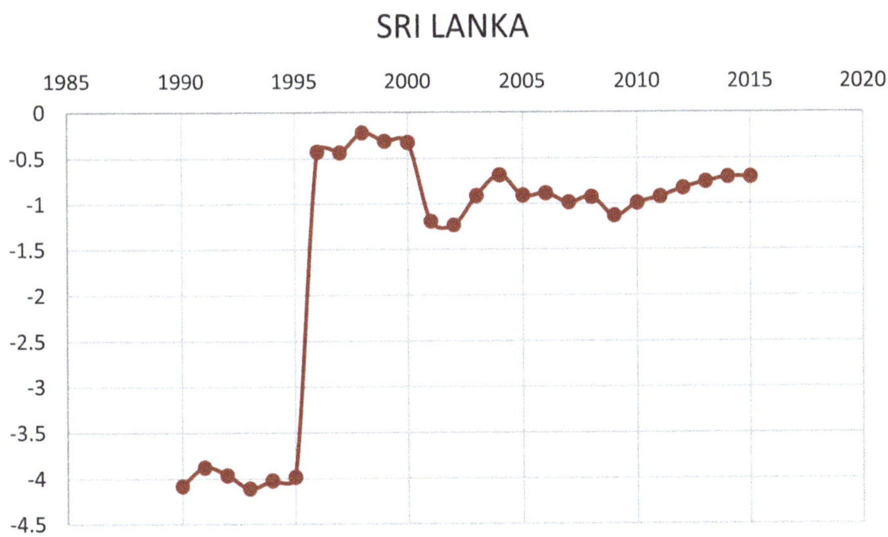

Figure 165. The efficiency signature for Sudan

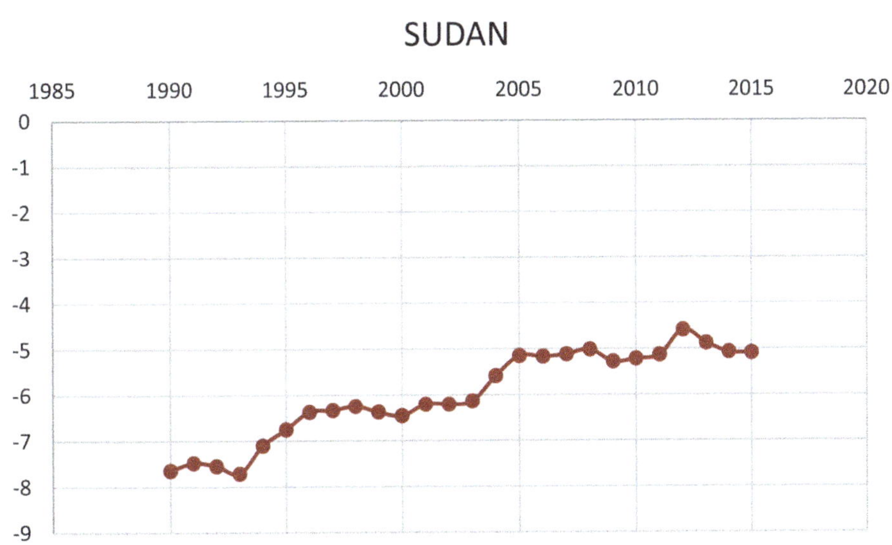

Figure 166. The efficiency signature for Suriname

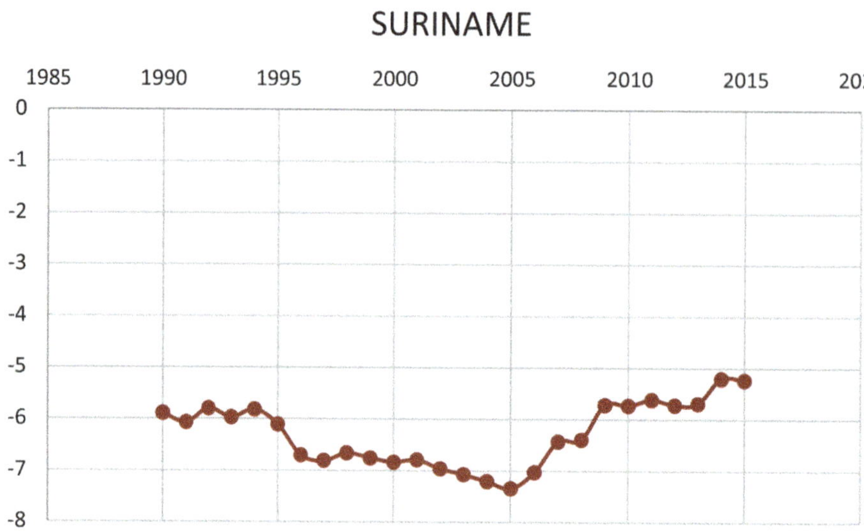

Figure 167. The efficiency signature for Swaziland

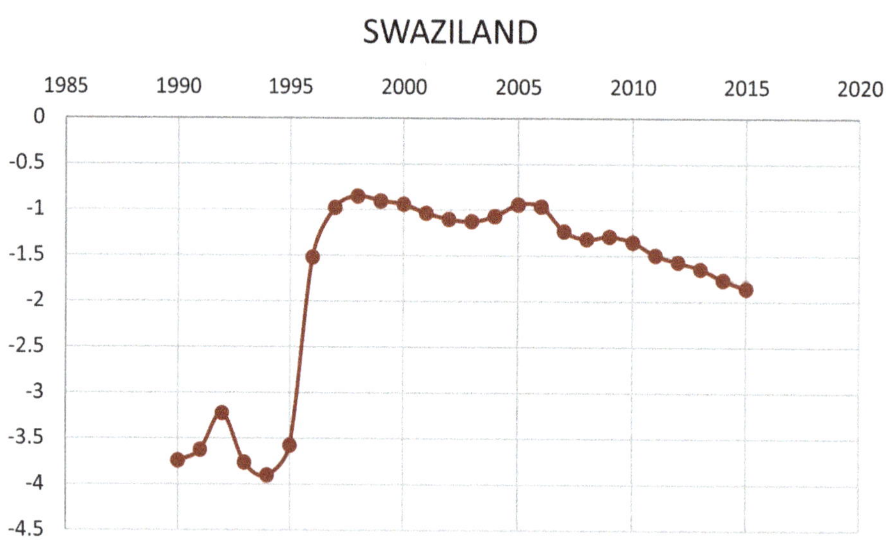

Figure 168. The efficiency signature for Sweden

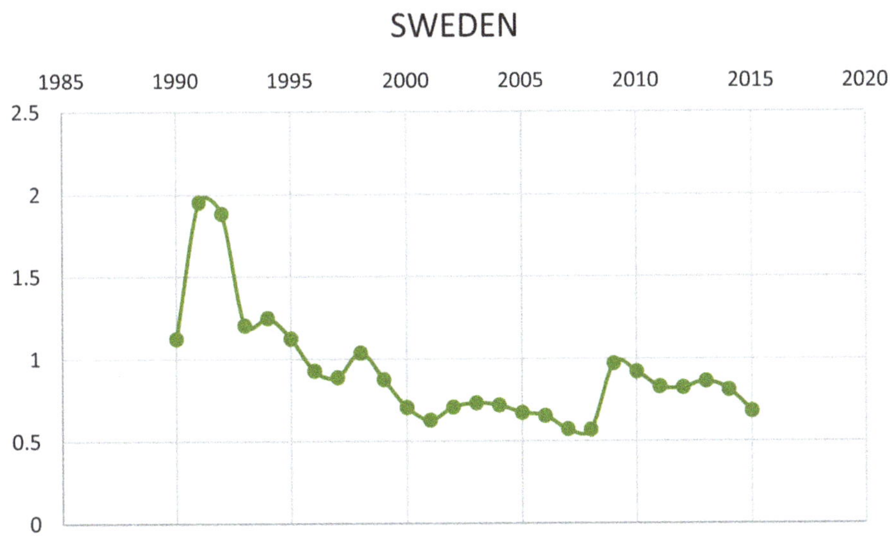

Figure 169. The efficiency signature for Switzerland

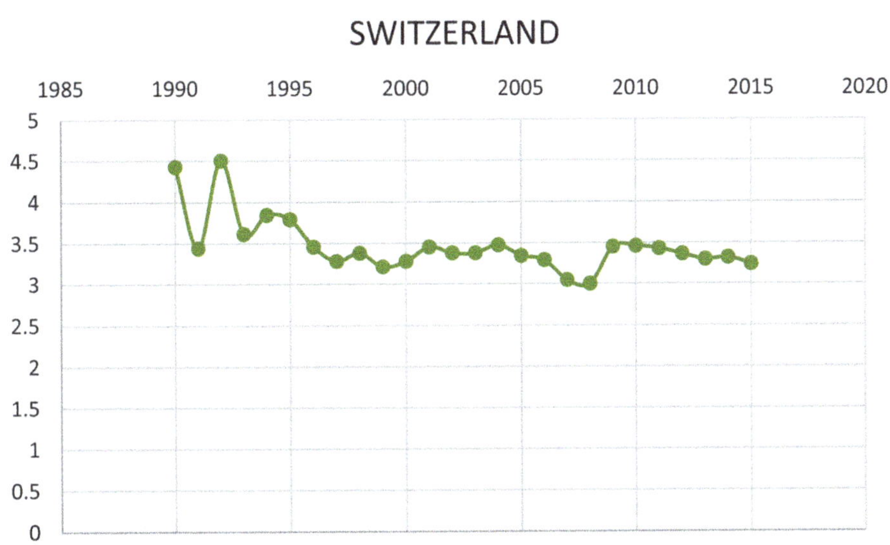

Figure 170. The efficiency signature for Syria

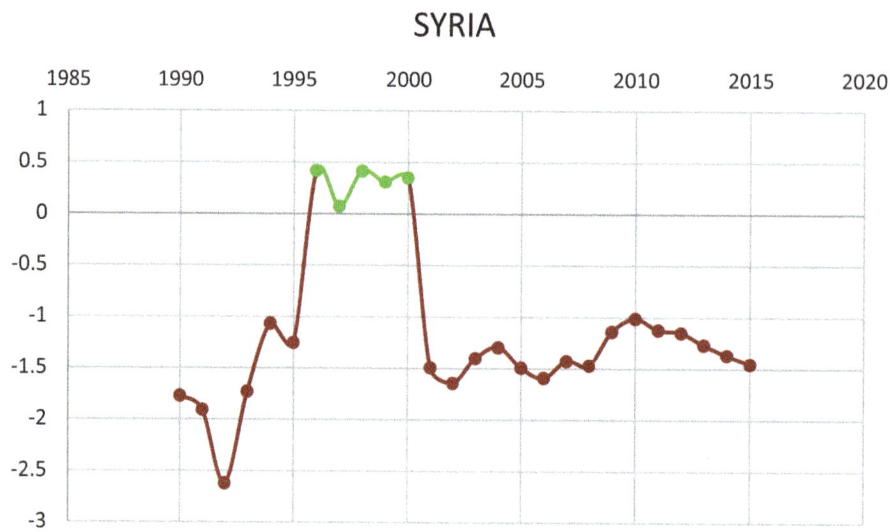

Figure 171. The efficiency signature for Taiwan

Figure 172. The efficiency signature for Tajikistan

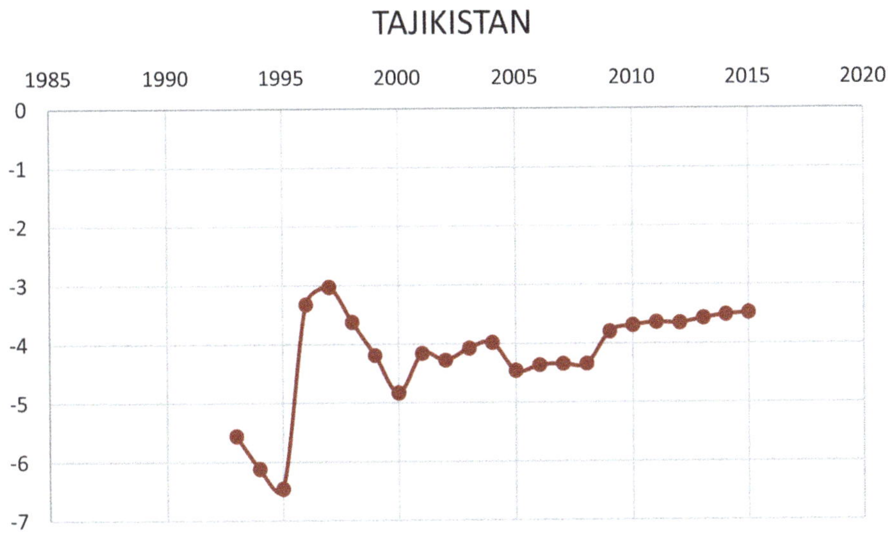

Figure 173. The efficiency signature for Tanzania

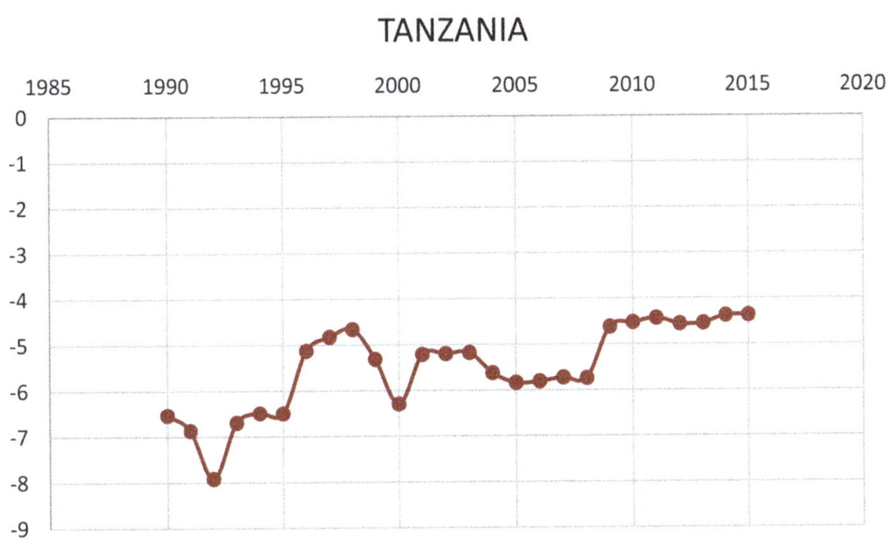

Figure 174. The efficiency signature for Thailand

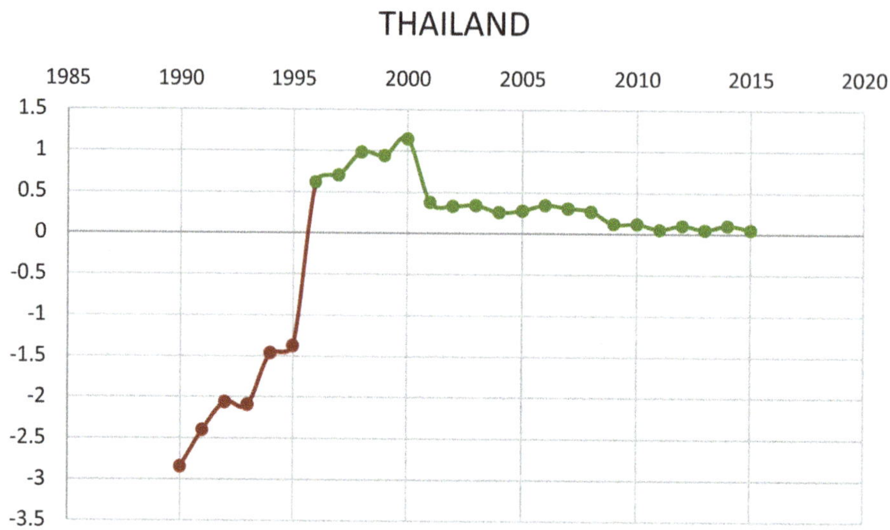

Figure 175. The efficiency signature for Timor-Leste

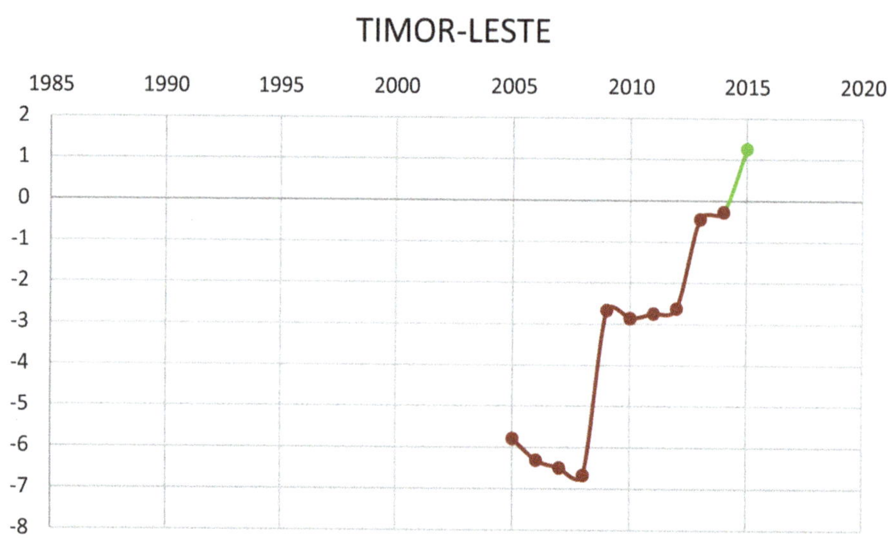

Figure 176. The efficiency signature for Togo

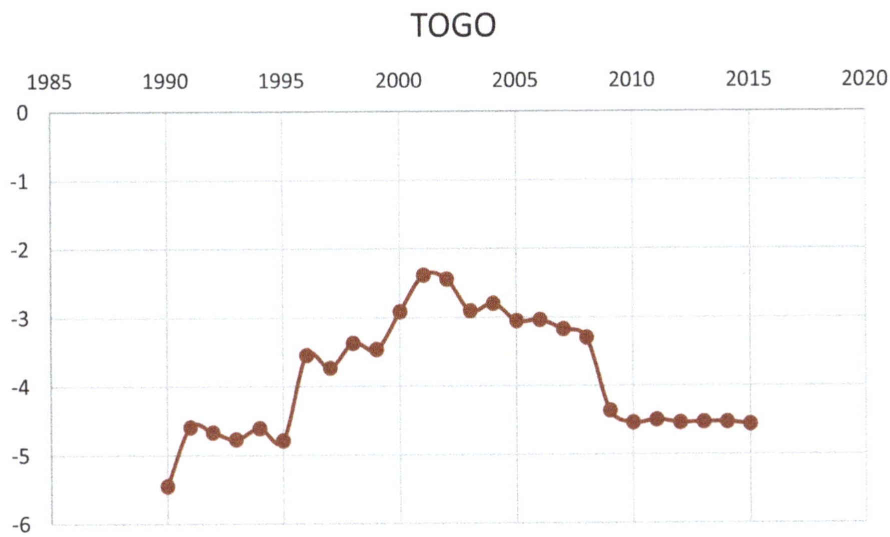

Figure 177. The efficiency signature for Tonga

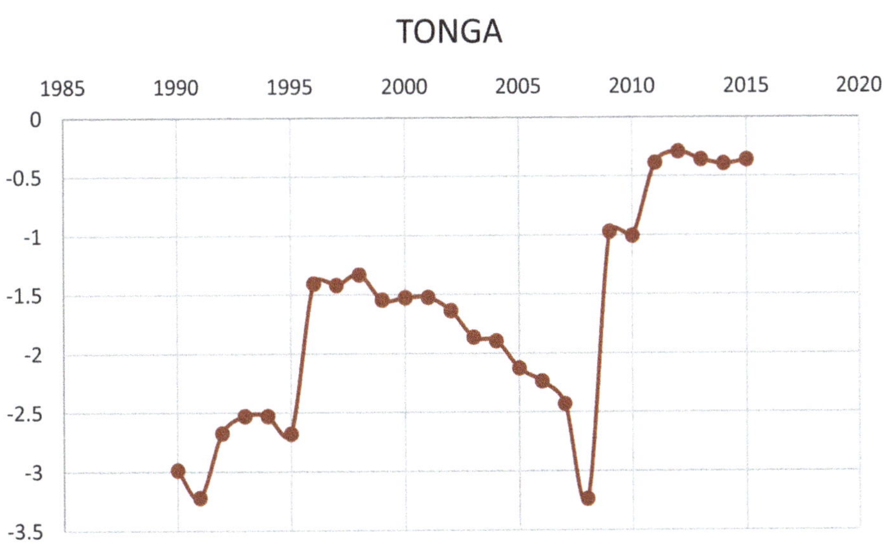

Figure 178. The efficiency signature for Trinidad and Tobago

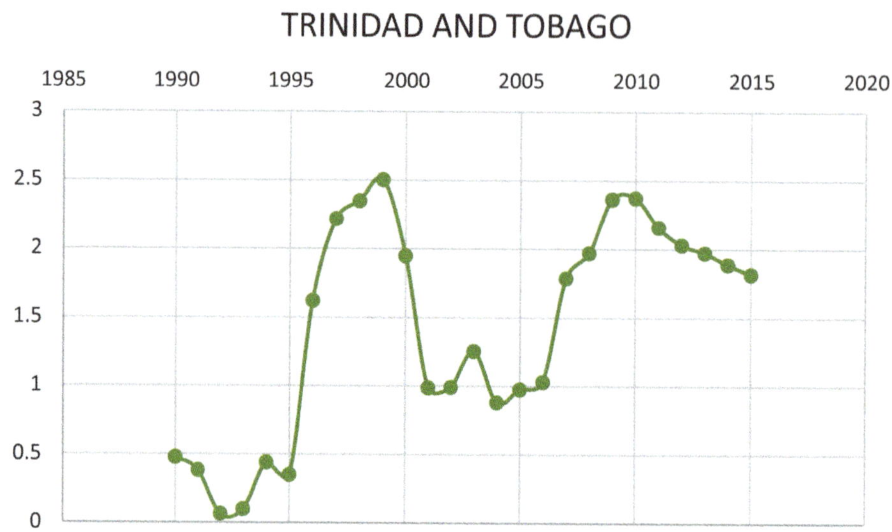

Figure 179. The efficiency signature for Tunisia

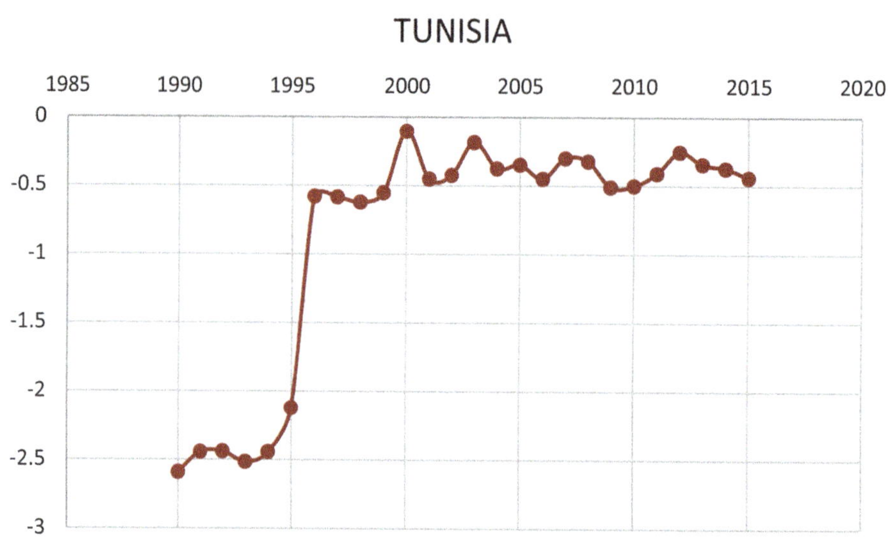

Figure 180. The efficiency signature for Turkey

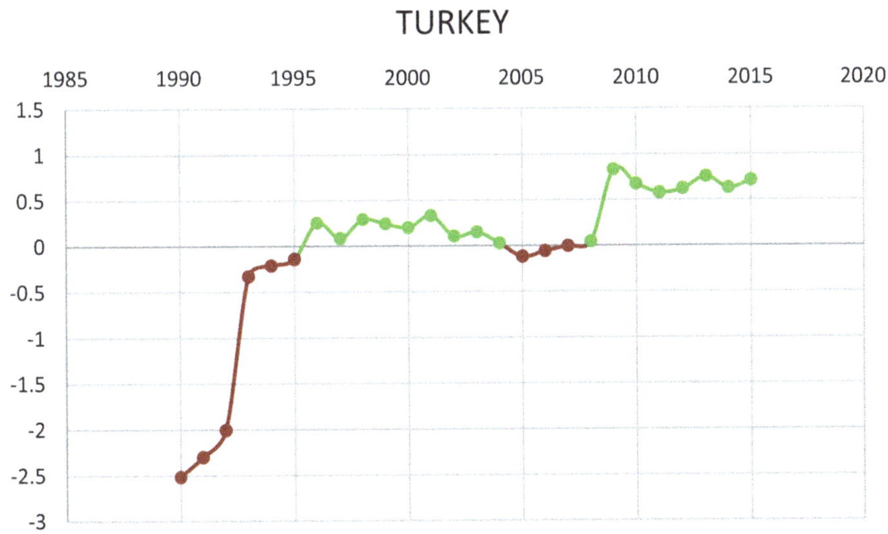

Figure 181. The efficiency signature for Turkmenistan

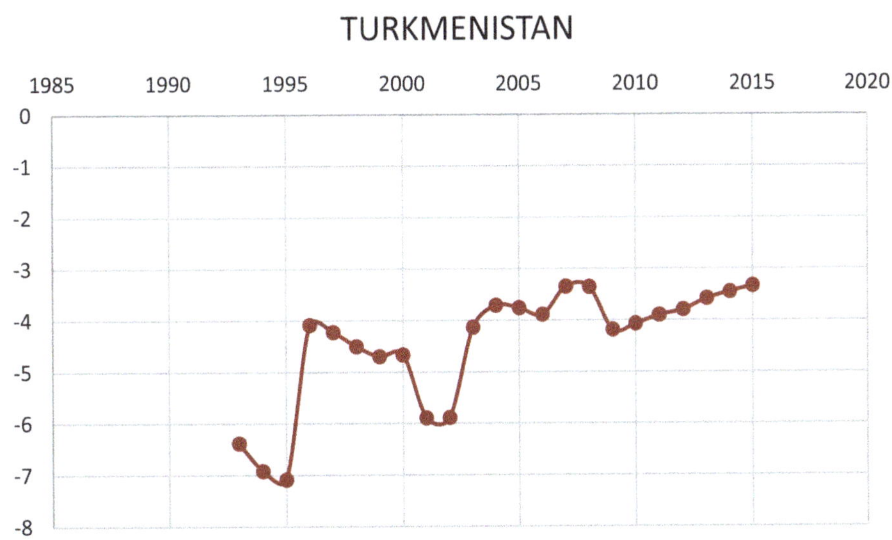

Figure 182. The efficiency signature for Tuvalu

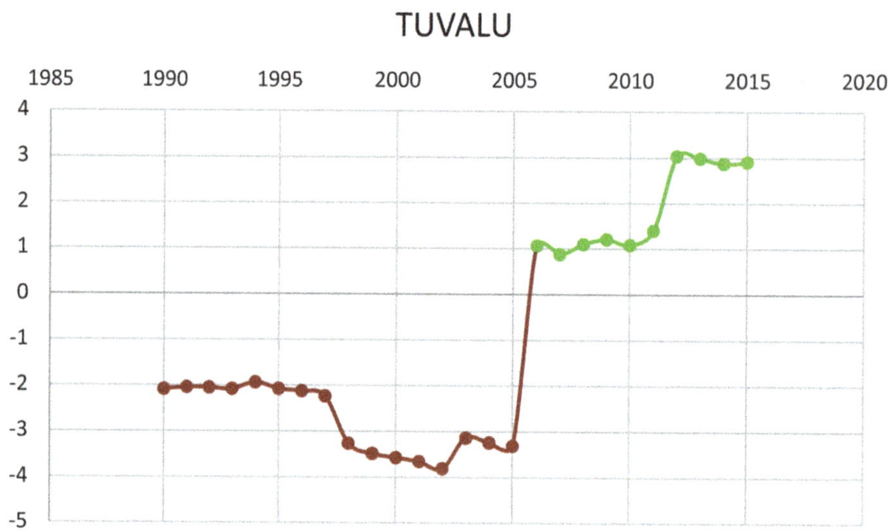

Figure 183. The efficiency signature for Uganda

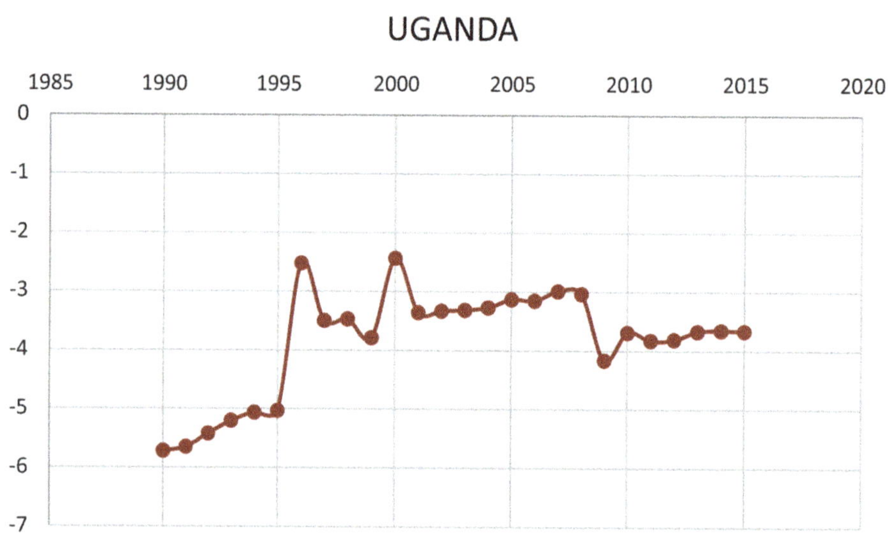

Figure 184. The efficiency signature for Ukraine

Figure 185. The efficiency signature for the United Arab Emirates

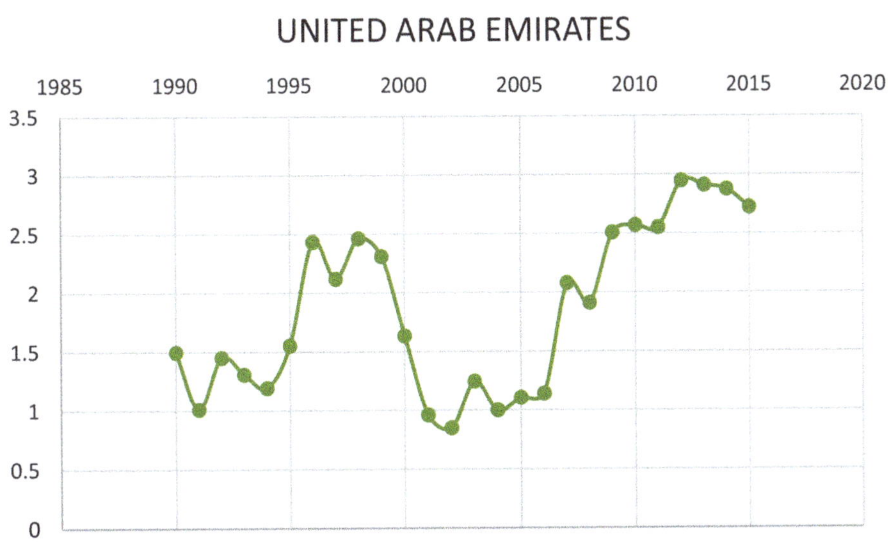

Figure 186. The efficiency signature for the United Kingdom

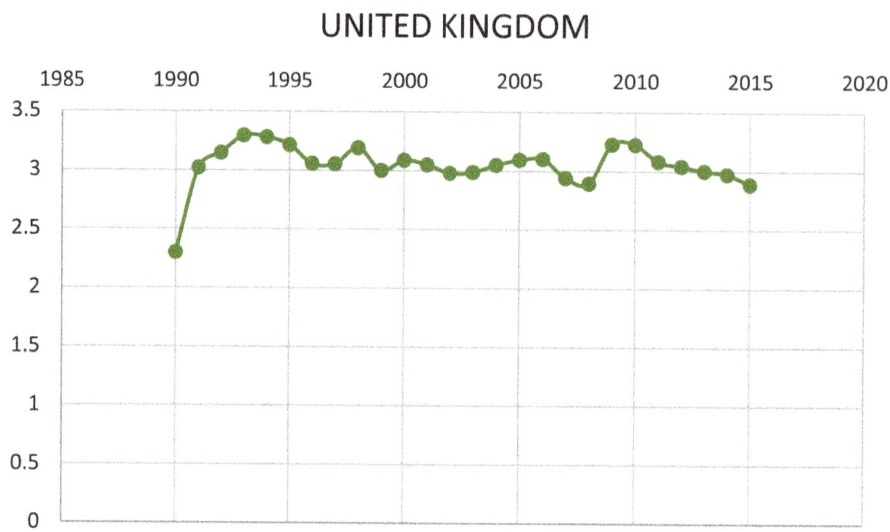

Figure 187. The efficiency signature for the United States

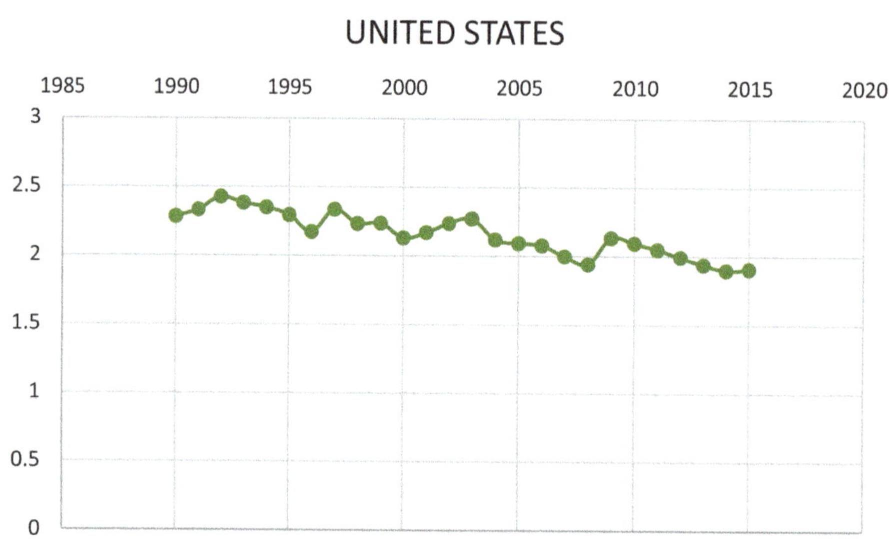

Figure 188. The efficiency signature for Uruguay

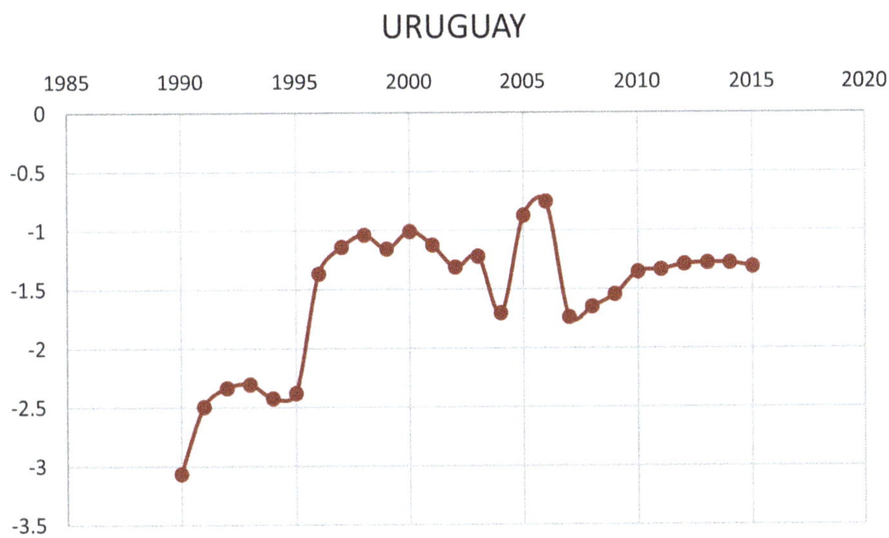

Figure 189. The efficiency signature for Uzbekistan

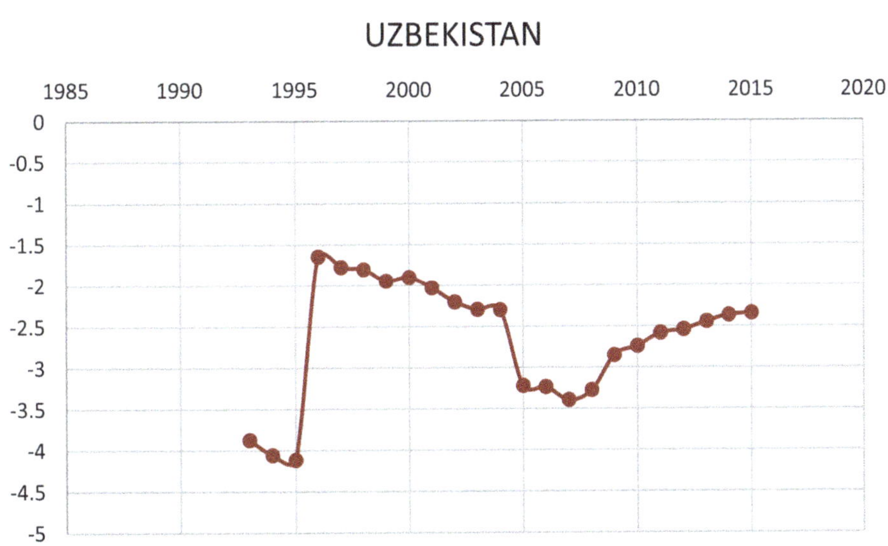

Figure 190. The efficiency signature for Vanuatu

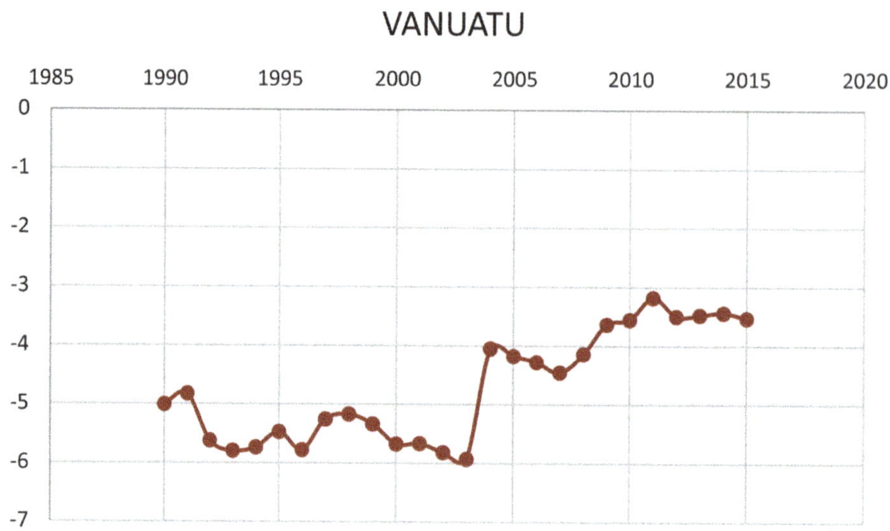

Figure 191. The efficiency signature for Vatican City

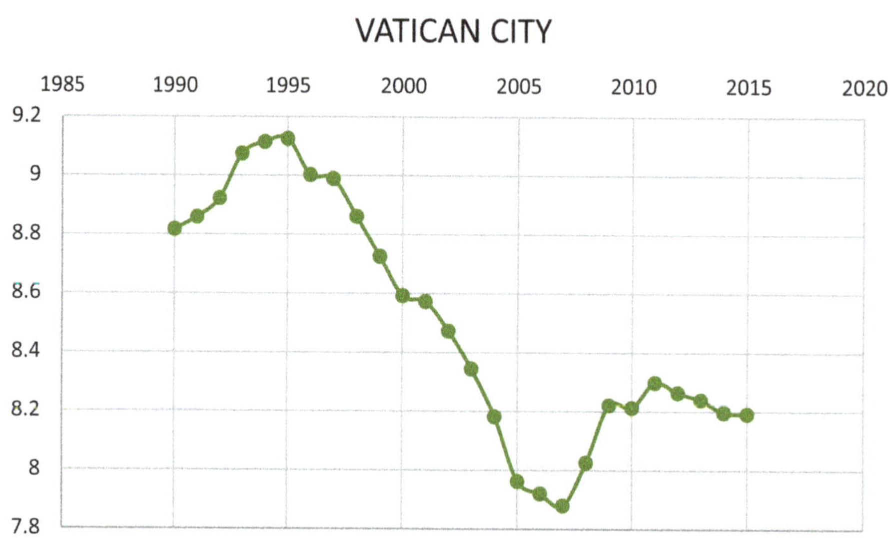

Figure 192. The efficiency signature for Venezuela

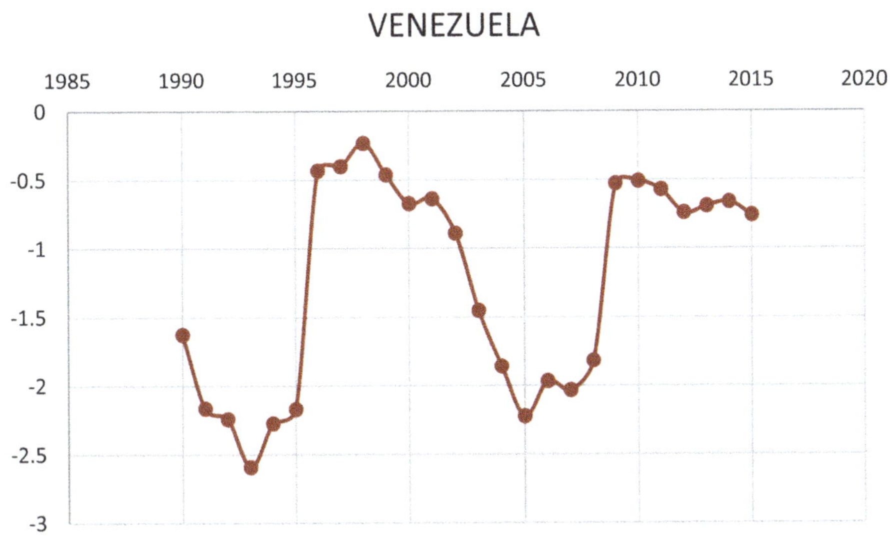

Figure 193. The efficiency signature for Vietnam

Figure 194. The efficiency signature for Yemen

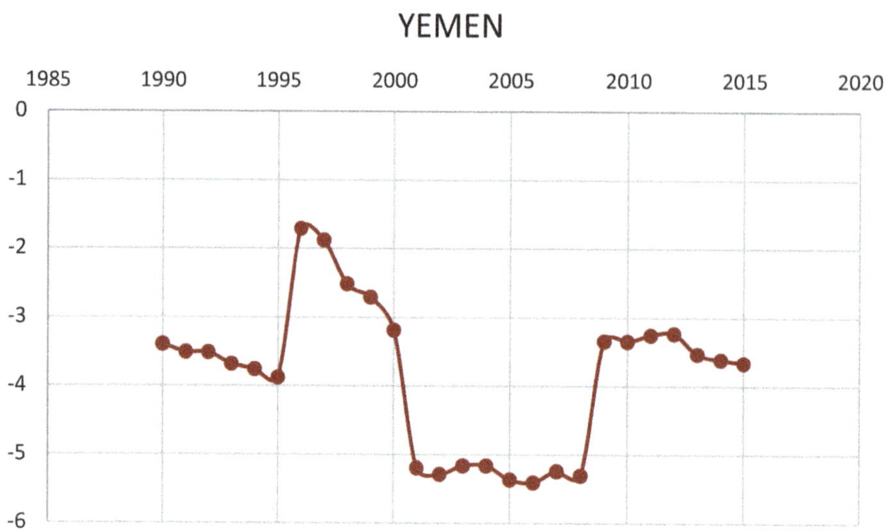

Figure 195. The efficiency signature for Zambia

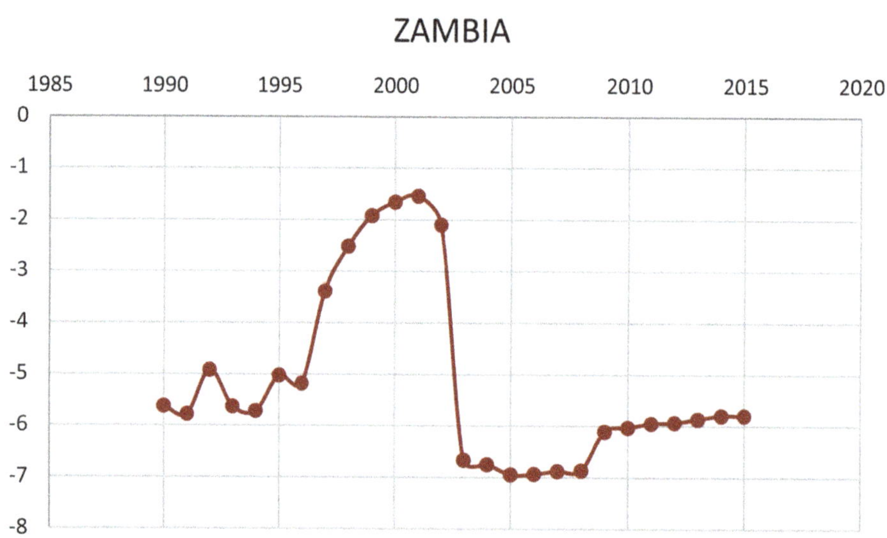

Figure 196. The efficiency signature for Zimbabwe

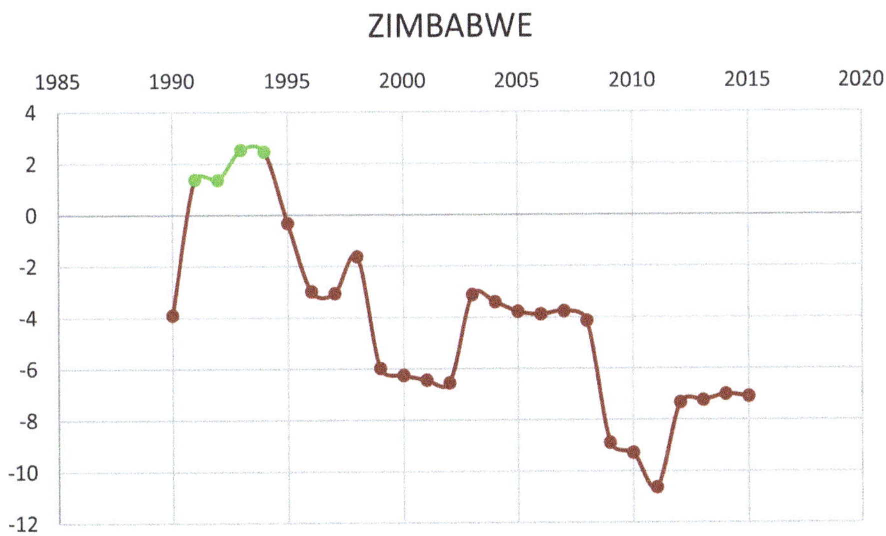

APPENDIX FOR CHAPTER 4: ANALYSIS OF G-20 COUNTRIES

In Chapter 3, we analyzed the nexus between economic efficiency and global cities. Further analysis will be provided in Chapters 6 and 7. This appendix looks in detail at each of the 19 countries in the G-20 group. For each country, a summary 'scorecard' provides its efficiency scores for the beginning (1990) and the end (2015) of the observation period, the difference between these scores, a chart showing the evolution of the country's ψ score over the observation period, its Economic Complexity Index (ECI) ranking, its area ranking, and its global cities ranking by the Globalization and World Cities (GaWC). See Figures 197 – 215.

During the observation period from 1990 to 2015, Argentina consistently exhibited a negative ψ score. It is useful to break the observation period into four intervals: the first from 1990 to 1993, the second from 1994 to 1997, the third from 1998 to 2002, and the last from 2003 to 2015. In the aftermath of hyperinflation in 1989 and 1990, Argentina witnessed a reduction in economic efficiency. During this period, the country's ability to absorb and accumulate capital was deteriorating. This period witnessed an influx of imports aided by

Figure 197. The efficiency scorecard for Argentina

<table>
<tr><td>ARGENTINA</td><td>$\psi_{1990} = (3.22)$</td><td>$\psi_{2015} = (1.57)$</td><td>$\Delta = 1.65$</td></tr>
<tr><td></td><td colspan="3">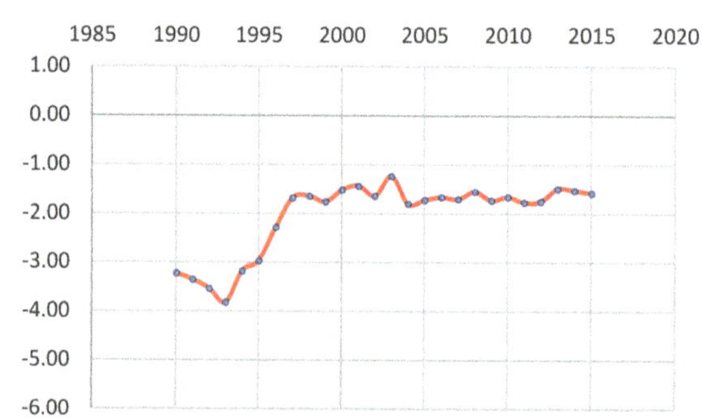
</td></tr>
<tr><td>ECI (2014) = 64</td><td>Area ranking = 8</td><td colspan="2">GaWC (2012): Buenos Aires (Alpha –)</td></tr>
</table>

pegging the exchange rate of the Argentine peso to the US dollar. However, also during this period, there was a push towards more deregulation and privatization, which led to efficiency gains in the following period.

Argentina exhibits a substantial increase in its economic efficiency from 1994 to 1997. The efficiency increase during this period is a characteristic of a number of G-20 countries (see below). This increase could be attributed to improvements in the measurement of output (GDP), but more importantly, to the regulation of international trade by the World Trade Organization (WTO).[1] This period ended with the Argentine great depression from 1998-2002. The influx of foreign investment was not able to service the foreign debt accumulated through the trade deficit from the previous period. This depression finally led to devaluing the peso in 2002. While the GDP shrank during this period, the country was able to improve its efficiency substantially by increasing its trade surplus, with a sharp fall in imports and a steady increase in exports.

While the country shows an improvement in efficiency from 1993 to 1997, it seems to be locked into a 'Red Queen Effect' (RQE) only from 1998 to 2015. Since 1997, Argentina's economic efficiency has a ceiling of $\psi = -1.00$. Although the country has the third largest economy in Latin America, it does not seem able to attract more capital from the world-system. Note that Argentina has only one global city, which also serves as the capital. In the Globalization and World Cities (GaWC) ranking of 2012, Buenos Aires came in as an Alpha – city. In comparison, cities like London and New York were classified as Alpha ++ cities.

Australia exhibits an RQE throughout the observation period. After a slight decrease in efficiency in the early 2000s, the GFC restored the ψ score to its 1990s level. There is effectively an equilibrium at $\psi = -3.00$. Unlike Argentina, Australia does not exhibit huge swings in its efficiency——the WTO does not seem to have had an effect on its efficiency. Nevertheless, just like Argentina, Australia is a source country. In fact, in the last 15 years, Argentina has been able to stabilize its efficiency at a ceiling higher than that in Australia. This suggests that Australia is relatively unable to attract as much capital from the world-system. Note that Australia has an area larger than Argentina, but has a less complex economy. Note also that Australia has five global cities compared to Argentina's one city. Even with these five global cities, Australia is still unable to absorb enough capital to breach the ψ floor. For Australia, the limiting input is population. Australia has a per-unit energy-equivalent population of 0.00013 compared to 0.00048 for

Figure 198. The efficiency scorecard for Australia

<table>
<tr><td>AUSTRALIA</td><td>$\psi_{1990} = (2.99)$</td><td>$\psi_{2015} = (3.05)$</td><td>$\Delta = (0.06)$</td></tr>
<tr><td></td><td colspan="3">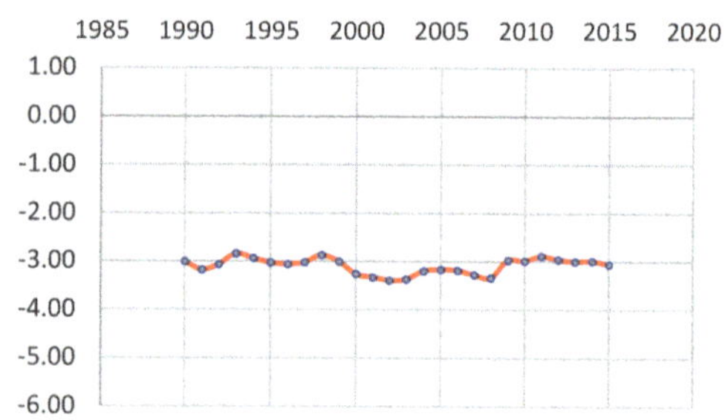</td></tr>
<tr><td>ECI (2014) = 82</td><td>Area ranking = 6</td><td colspan="2">GaWC (2012): Sydney (Alpha), Melbourne (Alpha –), Brisbane (Beta), Perth (Beta –), Adelaide (Gamma +)</td></tr>
</table>

Argentina. Argentina faces a negative residual of 0.0080 compared to Australia's 0.071 (see Chapter 1). For Argentina to return positive efficiency, it requires much less capital than Australia.

In economic terms, Australia is an archipelago rather than a continent (Judah, 2014). Australia is a network of its global cities and their hinterlands, where over 80 percent of the population aggregates. The rest of the continent remains, for all practical purposes, underdeveloped. We will see a similar pattern when we look at Canada (below).

Brazil exhibits an efficiency evolution similar to that seen in Argentina. There was a huge increase in 1995, followed by a 'Red Queen' Ceiling at $\psi = -1.00$. However, the evolution for Brazil from 1990 to 1994 seems to be a mirror image of that seen in Argentina. The years from 1990 to 1992 show an increase in efficiency followed by a decrease from 1992 to 1995. Note that the currency pegging in Argentina occurred in 1991, while in Brazil it occurred in 1994. The reduction of efficiency due to increased imports can be seen to occur from 1992. The collapse of both economies, and the concomitant decrease in imports and the increase of economic efficiency, can be seen from 1995 to 1998. After the transient period from 1990 to 1996,

Figure 199. The efficiency scorecard for Brazil

BRAZIL	$\psi_{1990} = (3.09)$	$\psi_{2015} = (1.60)$	$\Delta = 1.49$
	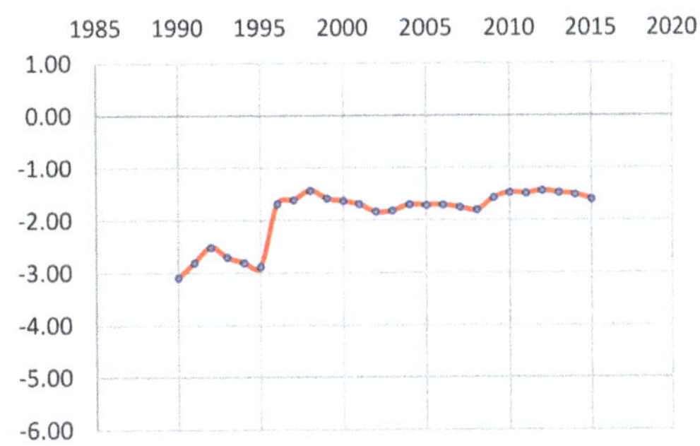		
ECI (2014) = 54	Area ranking = 5	GaWC 2012: Sao Paulo (Alpha), Rio De Janeiro (Beta)	

we see the Brazilian economy stabilizing at an efficiency score with a $\psi_{ceiling} = -1.00$ and a $\psi_{floor} = -2.00$. There was a spike in efficiency in 2003 due to an IMF bailout package that required Brazil to increase its budget surplus in 2003 (by at least 3.75 percent), and to post a similar surplus for 2004 and 2005.

Compared to Argentina, Brazil has a larger area and a larger economy. It also has a more complex economy. Brazil also has two global cities compared to Argentina's one. Notwithstanding these differences, the two countries absorb a similar amount of capital from the world-system. Both countries exhibit the same problem of not having enough attractors (global cities) to reach economic efficiency.

According to the OECD, "Brazil has become one of the world's leading economic powers. Since the achievement of macroeconomic stability in the mid-1990s, the economy's growth has outpaced the OECD area, and unemployment has been low" (OECD, 2015, p. 10). However, "It is crucial to raise productivity, as weak productivity is the main reason why GDP per capita levels are lower than in OECD countries … The industrial sector will play a leading role in this respect due to its large untapped potential for productivity improvements ..." (OECD, 2015, p. 10).

From 1996 onwards, Brazil exhibits a WTO efficiency boost similar to that seen in Argentina.

While Canada's area is the second largest in the world and its economy is the 39th most complex, the country still exhibits a negative efficiency score throughout the observation period. In effect, Canada has an inefficiency band between $\psi_{floor} = -3.00$ and $\psi_{ceiling} = -2.00$. In comparison with Australia, Canada has a higher efficiency band. The reasons for inefficiency in Canada are similar to those in Australia. Canada has a large area served by only four attractors, namely Toronto, Montréal, Vancouver, and Calgary. Given the size of the country, these four attractors cannot achieve a positive efficiency score. Similar to Australia, the economic geography of Canada is represented by an archipelago——a network of these four global cities. The rest of the country remains largely underdeveloped. Similar to Australia, Canada continues to struggle with developing its North (Australia, 2015; Canada, 2009). The Northern regions of both countries exhibit harsh environments, low population densities, and no global cities. For the analysis in this appendix,

Figure 200. The efficiency scorecard for Canada

<table>
<tr><td>CANADA</td><td>$\psi_{1990} = (2.49)$</td><td>$\psi_{2015} = (2.75)$</td><td>$\Delta = (0.26)$</td></tr>
<tr><td></td><td colspan="3">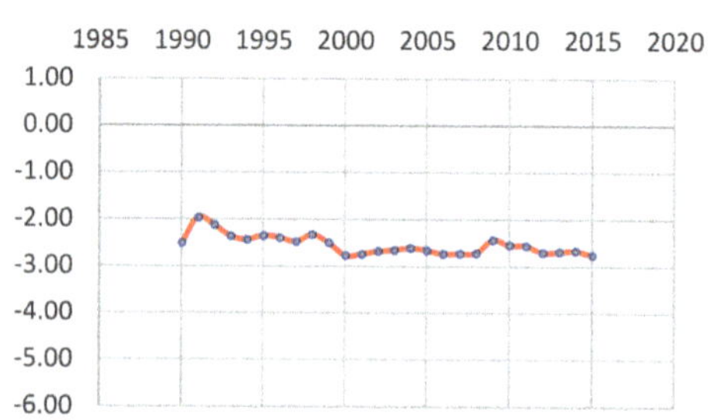
</td></tr>
<tr><td>ECI (2014) = 39</td><td>Area ranking = 2</td><td colspan="2">GaWC (2012): Toronto (Alpha), Montréal (Beta +), Vancouver (Beta), Calgary (Beta –)</td></tr>
</table>

the archipelago or network-like nature of these two countries is emphasized, where most of the population lives in a limited number of global cities.

The efficiency evolution of Canada had a boost in the early 1990s due to an economic recession. Since then, the ψ score slipped deeper into the inefficiency band. However, in contrast to Australia, Canada shows a slow decline of its ψ score since the GFC (OECD, 2016a, p. 16). Similar to Australia, however, the WTO did not have an impact on long-term efficiency in Canada.

For most of the observation period, China exhibited negative economic efficiency. Only in 2014 did China succeed in shifting from a source to a sink country. It seems that the GFC delayed this transition by dragging the 2009 efficiency score downwards to the level seen back in 2004. There was a notable dip in 2009 $\left(\psi_{2009} = -0.67\right)$ due to the GFC. It took China six years to go back to where it were in 2008. Had the GFC not occurred, China would have a ψ_{2015} score of one. The important point is that China registers an upward secular variation in the period from 1995 to 2015. In other words, China does not exhibit an RQE as seen, for example, in Australia and Canada.

Figure 201. The efficiency scorecard for China

CHINA	$\psi_{1990} = (4.94)$	$\psi_{2015} = 0.07$	$\Delta = 5.01$
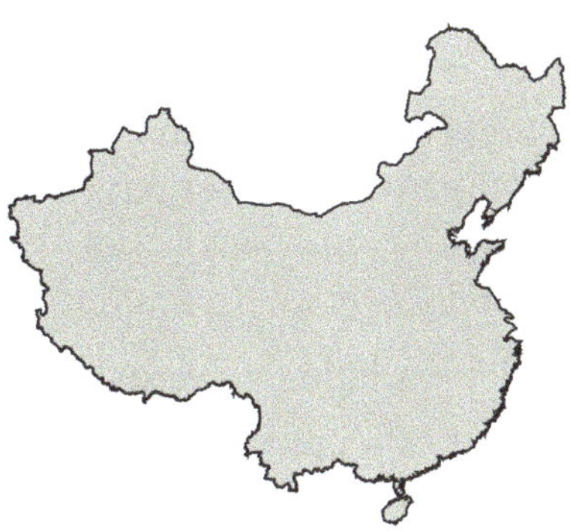	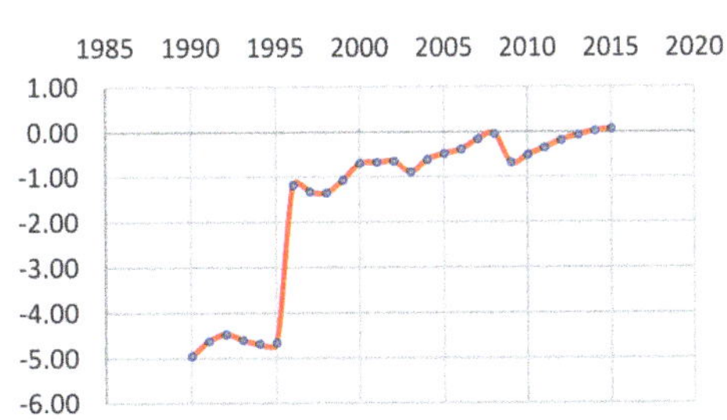		
ECI (2014) = 19	Area ranking = 3	GaWC (2012): Hong Kong (Alpha +), Shanghai (Alpha +), Beijing (Alpha +), Guangzhou (Beta +), Shenzhen (Beta –), Tianjin (Gamma –)	

With only six global cities and an area ranked third in the world, shifting from a source to a sink country is a great achievement. To better understand how this was possible, we also need to point out the Special Economic Zones (SEZs) that China has (Falkenheim, 1985). These SEZs serve a function analogous to industrial clusters in other countries, notably Germany (see below). These are in addition to Special Administrative Regions (SARs) such as Hong Kong and Macau. Since 1980, China has established SEZs in Shenzhen, Zhuhai, and Shantou (in Guangdong Province), Xiamen (in Fujian Province), and designated the entire province of Hainan as an SEZ. Furthermore, in 1984, China opened the following 14 coastal cities to overseas investment: Dalian, Qinhuangdao, Tianjin, Yantai, Qingdao, Lianyungang, Nantong, Shanghai, Ningbo, Wenzhou, Fuzhou, Guangzhou, Zhanjiang, and Beihai. Further expansion of these SEZs can be seen in the 1990s. These zones provide a special tax incentive for foreign investors and greater independence on trade activities. SEZs offer a better explanation of how the country was able to absorb enough capital from the world-economy to switch its status from a source to a sink country.

However, even with these SEZs, the country can still be classified as an economic archipelago. The issues that Australia and Canada face in their Northern regions, China faces in the West (Jie, 2004)—which covers roughly 70 percent of its total area. It is unlikely that China will be able to continue improving its economic efficiency if it does not increase the number of global cities within its jurisdiction. As the country becomes more affluent, it needs to create more global cities, especially in non-coastal areas.

Even though China's accession to the WTO was delayed until December 2001, its economic efficiency exhibits a 1995 WTO boost similar to that seen in Argentina and Brazil. China, however, achieved more efficiency improvement due to the WTO relative to Argentina and Brazil: China had an increase of 3.5 points in its efficiency score, compared to 1.3 for Argentina and 1.2 for Brazil.

While France exhibits an efficiency band between $\psi_{ceiling} = 4.00$ and $\psi_{floor} = 2.00$, it also seems to exhibit a secular variation towards lower efficiency—since 1990. France shed a quarter of its efficiency between 1990 and 1993. The country was able to sustain an RQE from 1996 to 2005. However, since 2006, the economy is on a path of 'extinction.' Even the GFC was not able to arrest this downwards trend. The WTO seems to be draining French efficiency, albeit at a slow rate. This is especially so since 2005. It seems that France will have lost half of its 1990 efficiency level by 2020.

Figure 202. The efficiency scorecard for France

FRANCE	$\psi_{1990} = 4.02$	$\psi_{2015} = 2.42$	$\Delta = (1.60)$
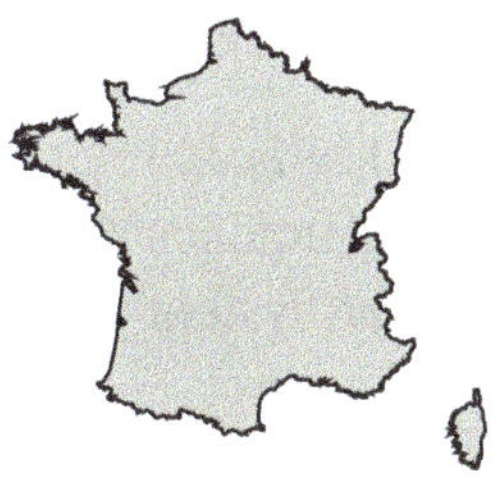			
ECI (2014) = 17	Area ranking = 41	GaWC (2012): Paris (Alpha +), Lyon (Beta –), Marseille (Gamma), Nantes (Gamma)	

The early 1990s reforms to the French agricultural sector appear to have failed to bring more efficiency to the economy as a whole (Naylor, 1995). On the other hand, the creation of the European Economic Community (EEC) in 1993 increased economic efficiency, but only up to 1995. Since the introduction of the WTO, there seems to have been an RQE from 1996 to 2005. Since then, however, French efficiency exhibits a constant decline.

While the area of France is relatively small (compared to other G-20 countries), it also does not have enough (capital) attractors. The country has only four global cities. France's current economic efficiency is the main driver behind the high complexity of its economy. Jump-starting economic efficiency in the Hexagon requires creating new global cities or even SEZs 'à la Chinoise.' The other possible approach is the German model of industrial clusters. France seems to have moved in the German direction with its 'pôles de compétivité' (de Géry, 2014; France, 2011; Hussler, Muller, & Ronde, 2013; Renou & Crague, 2015), but that has not registered an improvement in efficiency. The country requires more attractors to be able to absorb enough capital from the world-economy and to reverse the secular trend. This of course will also entail a more asymmetrical approach to the economic policies within these cities and regions (and outside them). France needs to accommodate a strong free market economy within attractors while maintaining a largely socialist economy outside them.

Germany exhibits stable economic efficiency throughout the period from 1990 to 2015. While the country registers some fluctuations in the early 1990s, mainly due to German reunification, since 1996, its economic efficiency has been roughly equal to 3. In this sense, Germany exhibits a quintessential 'Red Queen Effect' (RQE) where it keeps producing at a level that ensures a stable efficiency. Germany can absorb enough capital from the world-system only to the extent that allows it to maintain this efficiency level.

The country is smaller than many G-20 countries but has one of the most complex economies in the world. This economic complexity is related to Germany's economic efficiency. Both (complexity and efficiency) emerge from industrial clusters that are based on a "polycentric urban system" (Curzio & Fortis, 2002). In other words, German economic efficiency cannot be understood in terms of its global cities. The country has only eight global cities, mainly third-tier cities, although some had a long history as free and Hanseatic cities (such as Hamburg). The effect of German cities on the country's economic performance should be distinguished from that seen in other countries:

Figure 203. The efficiency scorecard for Germany

GERMANY	$\psi_{1990} = 3.21$	$\psi_{2015} = 2.97$	$\Delta = (0.24)$
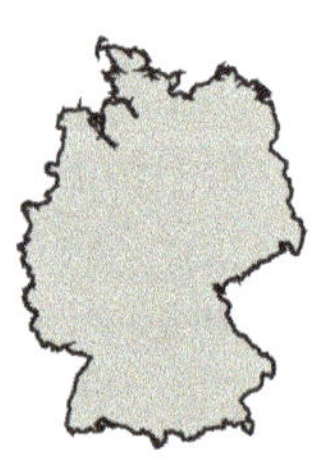	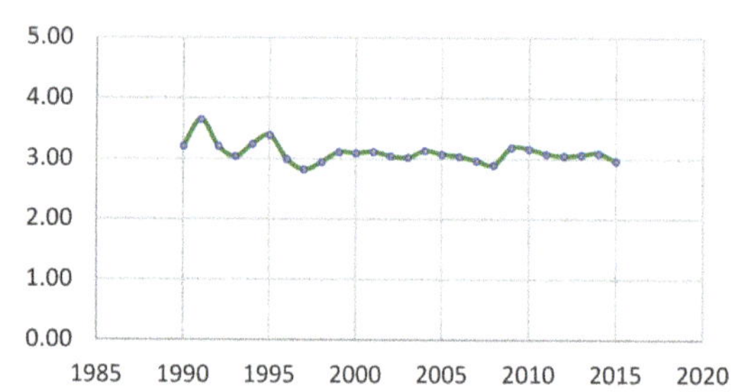		
ECI (2014) = 2	Area ranking = 62	GaWC (2012): Frankfurt (Alpha), Munich (Alpha –), Hamburg (Beta +), Düsseldorf (Beta +), Berlin (Beta +), Stuttgart (Beta), Cologne (Gamma +), Leipzig (Gamma –)	

Germany has been a world export champion for many years, and few economies are as strongly integrated into the world market. Yet despite this, no German city makes it into the top group of global cities. Exceptionally, the Inventory of World Cities classifies Frankfurt – a 'small' city with just 660,000 inhabitants – as an 'alpha world city'. But other German metropolises such as Berlin, Hamburg, Munich, and Düsseldorf only rank as 'gamma world cities' – third-class global cities. Other German cities do not even rate a mention. (Läpple, 2016)

Läpple explains this apparent contradiction by pointing out the *sui generis* nature of German development (Läpple, 2006), and to the fact that:

[T]oday, Germany has a highly polycentric urban system, with its metropolitan functions distributed between Berlin, Hamburg, Munich, Frankfurt (Rhine/ Main), Cologne/ Düsseldorf (Rhine/Ruhr), Stuttgart, and the potential metropolis Halle/Leipzig/Dresden (Saxony Triangle). After reunification Berlin was reinstated as the seat of government, but it is highly unlikely that it will resume its former central economic role. (Läpple, 2016)

This urban polycentricity is attributed to Germany's history—from the Prusso-German Empire and through the rise and fall of the Third Reich. Germany, in essence, provides an alternative model of urbanization, one where "individual metropolises are developing increasing specializations in particular clusters of high value services" (Läpple, 2016). This is in contrast to the approach found in larger countries, such as the United States, as I discuss further below.

India exhibits efficiency fluctuations in the early 1990s similar to those seen in Argentina, Brazil, and China. In terms of their magnitude, these fluctuations are closer to those in China than in the other two countries. Due to the WTO and its impact on international trade, India improved its efficiency score by 3.1 points (compared to China's 3.5). India, China, and Indonesia (see below) appear to have benefited the most from the WTO. Like China, India's efficiency trend was interrupted by the GFC. However, unlike China, India exhibits an RQF in a ψ band between $\psi_{ceiling} = -1.00$ and a $\psi_{floor} = -2.00$. India is still not able to switch to a sink status.

By area, India is much smaller than China. While it has a total of eight global cities, its economy is not as complex as that of China. India also has SEZs, with the same objective of absorbing capital from the world-economy.

Figure 204. The efficiency scorecard for India

<table>
<tr><td>INDIA</td><td>$\psi_{1990} = (4.50)$</td><td>$\psi_{2015} = (1.54)$</td><td>$\Delta = 2.96$</td></tr>
<tr><td></td><td colspan="3">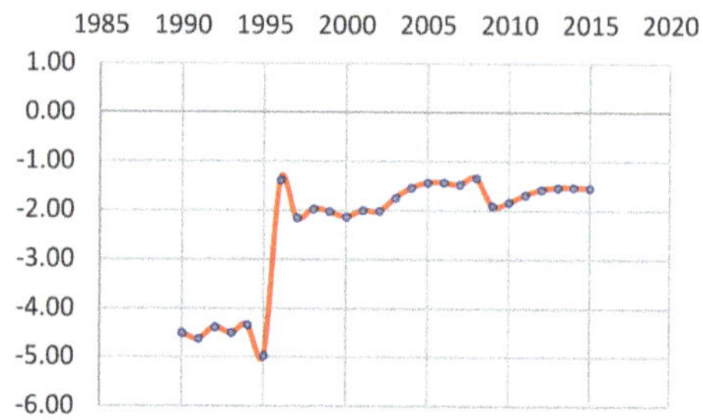
</td></tr>
<tr><td>ECI (2014) = 45</td><td>Area ranking = 7</td><td colspan="2">GaWC (2012): Mumbai (Alpha), New Delhi (Alpha –), Bangalore (Beta +), Chennai (Beta), Calcutta (Beta –), Hyderabad (Beta –), Ahmadabad (Gamma –), Pune (Gamma –)</td></tr>
</table>

However, these SEZs were introduced in the 2000s (Narayanan & Sekar, 2012), much later than those in China. Moreover, in India, the development of SEZs has been met with resistance from disenfranchised groups such as peasants and farmers (Oza, 2011).

India's area is closer to that of Argentina. Both countries have a similar ψ efficiency band (between -1.00 and -2.00). However, Argentina has only one global city, compared to India's eight. To explain why Argentina is able to achieve a ψ score similar to that of India while having only one global city, we need to take into account the difference in their respective populations. In 2015, India had a per-unit population energy equal to 0.397 compared to 0.00048 for Argentina. Argentina is able to register an efficiency similar to that of India as a result of a smaller per-unit portion of (energy-equivalent) population. It can achieve the same level of efficiency as India without needing to absorb the large amount of capital required by India. Hence, in 2015, India's per-unit energy-equivalent GDP output was 0.088, compared to 0.002 for Argentina. This translates into a residual of -0.322 for India compared to -0.008 for Argentina. The key point is that the need for global cities is linked to the size of a given country. Where the per-unit inputs (population and area) are small, the need to absorb capital is reduced. As we also saw in the case of Germany, smaller countries rely on a distributed urban system based on clusters rather than global cities.

Unlike other emerging economies, such as China and India, Indonesia exhibits an overshoot (into sink status) after the commencement of the WTO, with an efficiency increase of 4.4. This increase suggests that Indonesia benefited from the introduction of the WTO more than any other G-20 country—except China, which continues to exhibit a positive efficiency trend. The efficiency increase was driven mainly by foreign investment into a rapidly developing manufacturing sector. This effect was soon dampened by the advent of the Asian Financial Crisis (AFC) in mid-1997. Since 2001, Indonesia settled into an RQF between $\psi_{ceiling} = -1.00$ and $\psi_{floor} = -2.00$. This ψ band is similar to that seem in India, although in India there was a break in a mild upwards trend in 2008. In other words, Indonesia seems to have been less affected by the GFC, mainly due to the weakness of its attractors, and hence the relative isolation of the Indonesian economy from the world-system. Indonesia's lack of global cities acted as a buffer for the economy, but also prevented it from maintaining its sink status from the mid-nineties.

While Indonesia's area is ranked 14th in the world, it has only one global city, which also serves as its capital city. Nevertheless, it was able to attain an efficiency similar to that of India with its eight global cities. To explain

Figure 205. The efficiency scorecard for Indonesia

INDONESIA	$\psi_{1990} = (3.82)$	$\psi_{2015} = (1.27)$	$\Delta = 2.55$
	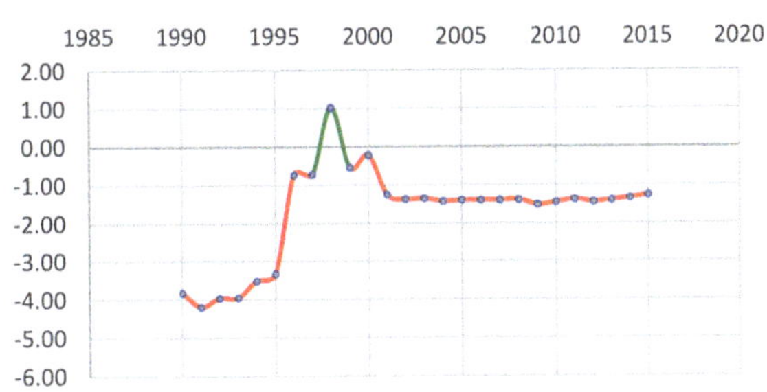		
ECI (2014) = 56	Area ranking = 14	GaWC (2012): Jakarta (Alpha –)	

why, we need to compare the per-unit inputs of the two countries. In 2015, Indonesia had a per-unit (energy-equivalent) population of 0.017 and a per-unit area of 0.0045. It produced a per-unit energy-equivalent GDP of 0.006, which resulted in a negative residual of 0.015. For the same year, India had a per-unit population of 0.37, a per-unit area of 0.013, and a per-unit energy-equivalent GDP output of 0.088. India's negative residual was 0.32. Given the lower per-unit inputs conferred on Indonesia, the country would need to absorb less capital to achieve the level of efficiency registered in India.

Indonesia has been less successful in introducing SEZs. Since the first SEZ in Batam, which has historical roots in the industrial zone created in 1971 (Wong & Ng, 2009), the country announced plans to introduce more SEZs to bring the total number to 25 by 2019 (Vidaurri, 2015). However, even if SEZs prove to be a successful strategy, for Indonesia to attain a higher level of efficiency, it needs to create more global cities. If Indonesia creates two more global cities, it could be in a position similar to that of Mexico, which has an area similar to Indonesia, but only half the population. We will look at Mexico in some more detail later in the chapter.

Italy registers three distinct efficiency phases between 1990 and 2015. The first phase saw a considerable jump in efficiency from 1990 to 1991. The second phase exhibited an RQE from 1991 to 2008. The third phase, from 2009 to 2015, suggests a secular 'extinction' similar to that seen in France.

Figure 206. The efficiency scorecard for Italy

<table>
<tr><td>ITALY</td><td>$\psi_{1990} = 1.62$</td><td>$\psi_{2015} = 2.34$</td><td>$\Delta = 0.72$</td></tr>
<tr><td></td><td colspan="3">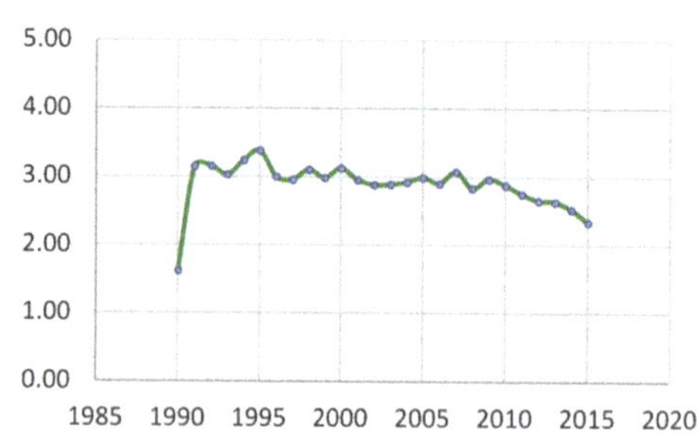
</td></tr>
<tr><td>ECI (2014) = 15</td><td>Area ranking = 71</td><td colspan="2">GaWC (2012): Milan (Alpha), Rome (Beta +), Turin (Gamma –)</td></tr>
</table>

The 1990 jump can be attributed to phenomenal growth in GDP that continued a trend from the late 1980s. This was followed by two decades of RQE at around the $\psi = 3.00$ level, which is similar to that seen in Germany and the United Kingdom (see below). This run seems to come to an end after the GFC. In fact, Italy seems to have been the G-20 country most affected by the GFC, losing almost 25 percent of its efficiency—double what France lost. The period from 2008 to 2015 suggests a secular decline in efficiency. However, compared to France, the decline in that country's efficiency seems to have started from 2005 (see above).

Italy has an ECI ranking much lower than Germany's but is still able to register an efficiency similar to that of Germany. Compared to Germany, Italy has an area 15 percent smaller, and a population 25 percent smaller. It has only three global cities compared to Germany's eight. However, Italy's economic efficiency depends on global cities even less than in the case of Germany. To understand the Italian approach, the scholarship of Robert Putnam is informative. Putnam describes 'social capital' as referring to "features of social organization, such as trust, norms, and networks, that can improve the efficiency of society by facilitating coordinated actions …" (Putnam, Leonardi, & Nonetti, 1994, p. 167). Putnam describes the evolution of social capital through Italian history, and the emergence of industrial clusters, similar to those in Germany. He describes the operation of these clusters in the following terms:

Among the distinguishing features of these decentralized, but integrated industrial districts is a seemingly contradictory combination of competition and cooperation. Firms compete vigorously for innovation in style and efficiency while cooperating in administrative services, raw materials purchases, financing, and research. These networks of small firms combine low vertical integration and high horizontal integration, through extensive subcontracting and "putting out" of extra business to temporarily underemployed competitors. Active industrial associations provide administrative and even financial aid, while local government plays an active role in providing the necessary social infrastructure and services, such as professional training, information on export markets and world fashion trends, and so on. The result is a technologically advanced and highly flexible economic structure, which proved precisely the right recipe for competing in the fast-moving economic world of the 1970s and 1980s. Not surprisingly, these regions of flexible specialization have enjoyed above average prosperity during those two decades. (Putnam et al., 1994, p. 160)

These same networks continued to provide economic efficiency throughout the period from 1995 to 2010. However, after the GFC these networks do not seem to be able to continue their historical contribution to Italian efficiency. The cost of the GFC was born mainly by Small and Medium Sized firms (SMEs) (Di Quirico, 2010). The crisis heightened Italy's poor productivity from 2008 until 2015 (Morsy & Sgherri, 2010).

Italy's ability to attract more capital from the world-economy requires a rethinking of its global cities and their contribution to its economy. For Italy to return to its RQE (from 1996 to 2007), it needs to not only enhance the performance of its current global cities but also create new ones.

Japan is another G-20 country that seems to exhibit secular economic degradation. During the observation period, Japan's ψ score has been between $\psi_{ceiling} = 4.00$ and $\psi_{floor} = 3.00$. However, the GFC seems to have accentuated the downwards trend seen in Japan's economic efficiency (as far back as 1995). To diagnose the reasons for this loss in efficiency, we need to examine the per-unit inputs of land and population, and the architecture of the Japanese urban system.

In 2015, Japan had a land-equivalent of 0.00018 (similar to that of Germany: 0.00016) and a population energy-equivalent of 0.0042. Japan's expected energy-equivalent output was 0.0044. Its residual was 0.074. The output is dominated by the population input. Due to its distributed urban

Figure 207. The efficiency scorecard for Japan

JAPAN	$\psi_{1990} = 3.42$	$\psi_{2015} = 2.88$	$\Delta = (0.54)$
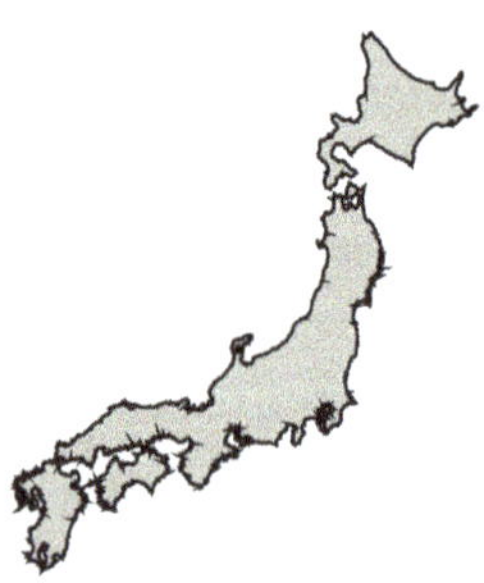	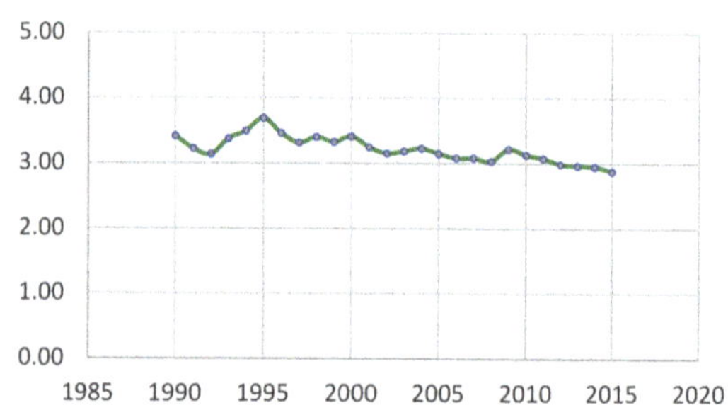		
ECI (2014) = 1	Area ranking = 61	GaWC (2012): Tokyo (Alpha +), Osaka (Gamma +)	

system (Yamawaki, 2002), however, Japan is still able to exhibit positive efficiency with only two global cities. In fact, Japan hosts the largest number of SMEs among industrialized countries. In the late 1990s, Japan had around 550 industrial clusters. These clusters are found in prefectures. Japan has 47 of these administrative divisions. Only one is classified as a metropolis (Tokyo), and only two are classified as urban: Osaka and Kyoto. Clusters can be found in prefectures like Tokyo, Gumma, Fukui and Ishikawa, and Saga. Each cluster specializes in a certain industry. Many of these clusters, similar to the situation in Germany, are historical clusters that date back to the 17th and 18th centuries. Some can even be traced back to the 12th century (such as the Seto Ceramics cluster in the prefecture of Aichi).

However, it seems that Japan's ability to arrest the downturn trend in its efficiency requires a reinvigoration of its urban systems. Japan needs to produce more global cities. The country needs to 'produce space' in the form of new jurisdictions that balance the critical element of land with that of population. Moreover, Japan needs to rethink the 'legal personality' of its existing cities (as part of the prefecture system), and their ability to tap into the world-system.

Mexico is one of the few G-20 countries to switch its efficiency status from a source to a sink. This success was mainly due to the North American Free Trade Agreement (NAFTA), which came into force in January 1994;

Figure 208. The efficiency scorecard for Mexico

MEXICO	$\psi_{1990} = (2.05)$	$\psi_{2015} = 0.29$	$\Delta = 2.34$
	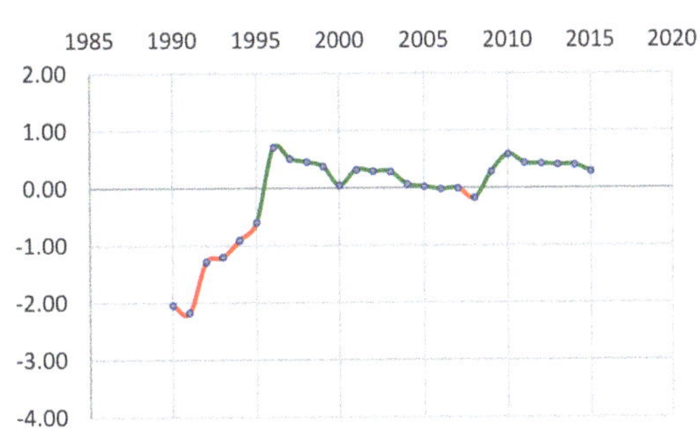		
ECI (2014) = 22	Area ranking = 13	GaWC (2012): Mexico City (Alpha), Guadalajara (Gamma), Monterrey (Beta –)	

the sudden devaluation of the Mexican peso against the US dollar in the same year, and the introduction of the WTO in 1995. Since 1995, the country exhibited a ψ band between $\psi_{ceiling} = 1.00$ and a $\psi_{floor} = 0.00$. However, Mexico is one of the countries that does not exhibit a 'Red Queen Effect' (RQE).

Unlike in the case of India and China, the GFC enhanced Mexico's economic efficiency. In other words, the GFC helped increase Mexico's productivity relative to other countries. According to the IMF, "Mexico entered the global crisis with greatly strengthened public and private sector balance sheets" (IMF, 2010, p. 3). As expected, the country achieved a growth rebound (IMF, 2010, p. 11).

Mexico is similar in area to Indonesia (0.0048 to Indonesia's 0.0045), has half the population (0.0038 to Indonesia's 0.017). However, it has a ψ band higher than that of Indonesia. In 2015, as a result of the population differential, Mexico's expected energy-equivalent per-unit output was 0.0085 compared to Indonesia's 0.021. Mexico needed to surmount a lower hurdle towards becoming a sink country relative to Indonesia. Moreover, Indonesia has only one global city, compared to Mexico's three. Mexico is required to absorb less capital to get to efficiency, and is able to do so with more attractors.

For the period from 1990 to 1992, the data is for the Union of Soviet Socialist Republics. Correcting the data to include only Russia gives a ψ

Figure 209. The efficiency scorecard for Russia

<table>
<tr><td>RUSSIA</td><td>$\psi_{1990} = (0.52)$</td><td>$\psi_{2015} = (2.74)$</td><td>$\Delta = (3.26)$</td></tr>
<tr><td>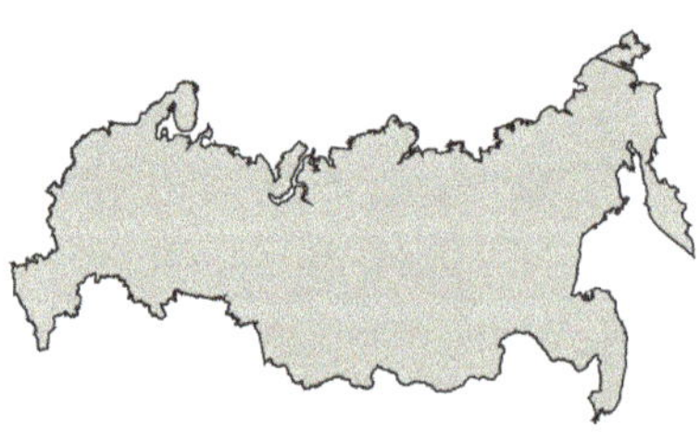</td><td colspan="3">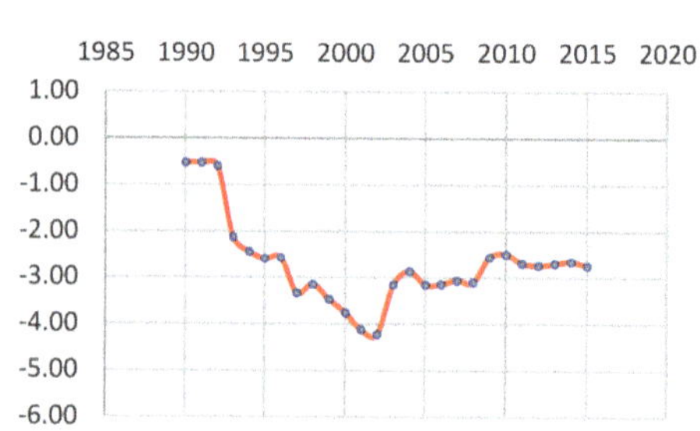
</td></tr>
<tr><td>ECI (2014) = 50</td><td>Area ranking = 1</td><td colspan="2">GaWC (2012): Moscow (Alpha), St Petersburg (Gamma +)</td></tr>
</table>

score of around -2.5. The collapse of the Soviet Union indicates a clear deterioration of economic efficiency. The advent of the WTO and the 1998 Russian Financial Crisis exacerbated the decline of the ψ score. So far, Russia's accession to the WTO in 2012 has not resulted in any improvement in efficiency. In fact, Russia is one of the countries that has been affected negatively by the WTO (since 1994).

Since 2003, Russian efficiency seems to stabilize within a band of $\psi_{ceiling} = -2.00$ and a $\psi_{floor} = -3.00$. Sanctions against Russia in the aftermath of its intervention in the Ukraine in 2014, and the ensuing financial crisis, could see Russia exhibit a downward trend similar to that seen from 1996 to 2002.

Russia is the world's largest country by area. In 2015, it had an energy-equivalent of 0.36, with a population equivalent of 0.005. In the case of Russia, the critical factor is population. With only three global cities, the country does not have enough attractors to achieve economic efficiency. Recent programs to boost the existing industrial clusters and to introduce new ones do not seem to improve Russian economic efficiency (Mindlin, Kolpak, & Gasratova, 2016).

Saudi Arabia is another country that benefited from the introduction of the WTO, even though its accession was delayed until 2005. The country has

Figure 210. The efficiency scorecard for Saudi Arabia

<table>
<tr><td>SAUDI ARABIA</td><td>$\psi_{1990} = (2.11)$</td><td>$\psi_{2015} = (0.66)$</td><td>$\Delta = 1.45$</td></tr>
<tr><td>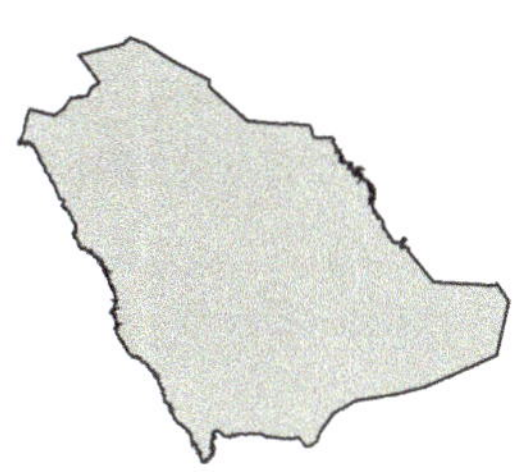</td><td colspan="3">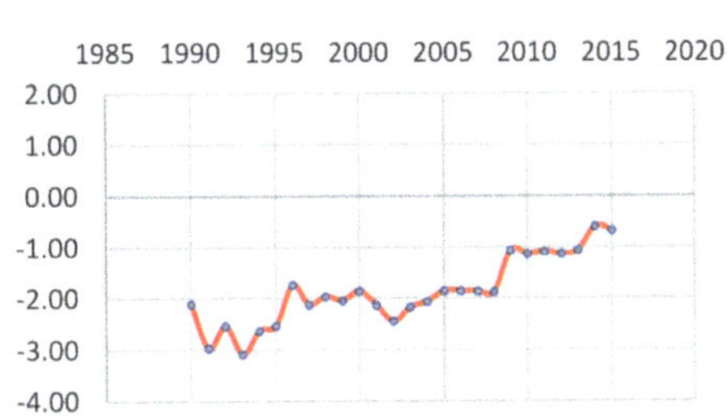
</td></tr>
<tr><td>ECI (2014) = 74</td><td>Area ranking = 12</td><td colspan="2">GaWC (2012): Riyadh (Beta), Jeddah (Gamma +)</td></tr>
</table>

also benefited from the GFC. The country had an RQE between 2005 and 2008, at around a ψ score of -2.00, and again between 2009 and 2013 around a ψ score of -1.00. The Saudi economy registered further improvement in 2013. The IMF explains this improvement as follows:

Saudi Arabia's economy has grown very strongly in recent years, and has been one of the best performing in the G-20 … It has benefitted from high oil prices and output, strong private sector activity, and government spending. Rising oil prices and production have resulted in large external and fiscal surpluses, while government debt has declined to 2.7 percent of GDP. (IMF, 2014, p. 4)

Further efficiency improvements could come from what the IMF calls a "fundamental policy shift to respond to oil prices" (IMF, 2016a, p. 4). If these policy shifts prove to be unsuccessful, the country is likely to see a substantial decrease in its efficiency by 2020, probably back to the 2008 level of -2.00.

Saudi Arabia has an area similar to that of Indonesia, although its economic complexity is much less in comparison. Moreover, the country has a population equivalent of only 0.0002, which is its limiting factor. With only two global cities, the country is unlikely to switch from a source to a sink. Saudi Arabia needs to rethink the global position of its cities in relation to its neighboring countries, especially the UAE. Creating new cities similar to Dubai or Abu Dhabi could see the country switch to a sink status.

South Africa is another G-20 country that exhibits negative efficiency throughout the observation period. Unlike Saudi Arabia, it was affected negatively by the GFC. Its efficiency shows a steady increase from 1990 to 2003, followed by an RQE from 2004 to 2008 and again (at a lower ψ score) from 2009 to 2015. Had the GFC not occurred, South Africa could have switched into a sink country. Given its area and global cities, the country is restricted by its ability to absorb capital. With a 2015 population equivalent of 0.00061 and a land equivalent of 0.002, the country faces a limiting factor in its population.

The reduction in efficiency in South Africa is explained by the IMF in the following terms:

Many countries in sub-Saharan Africa enjoyed robust economic growth in recent years that strengthened their balance sheets. Sound economic policies were an important factor, as was the favorable external environment and increased external support in the form of debt relief and higher inflows. But

Figure 211. The efficiency scorecard for South Africa

SOUTH AFRICA	$\psi_{1990} = (2.26)$	$\psi_{2015} = (0.67)$	$\Delta = 1.59$
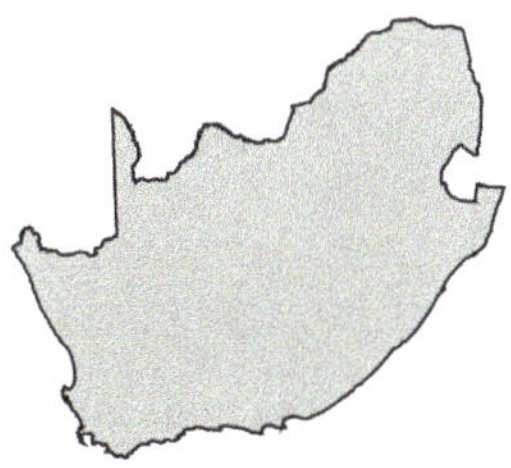	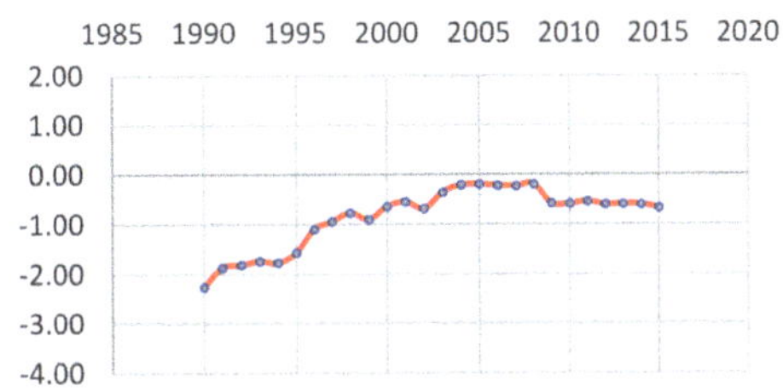		
ECI (2014) = 55	Area ranking = 24	GaWC (2012): Johannesburg (Alpha –), Cape Town (Beta +), Durban (Gamma +)	

the food and fuel price shocks of 2007–08 that preceded the current global financial crisis weakened the external position of net importers of food and fuel, caused inflation to accelerate, and dampened growth prospects. The global financial crisis greatly compounds the policy challenges confronting the region as it strives to consolidate its economic gains ... (IMF, 2009, p. 2)

Given the recent collapse in oil prices, South Africa could move back to the RQE seen before the GFC, and could even switch from a source to a sink country by 2020. However, the country's ability to maintain a positive efficiency cannot be divorced from its ability to augment its current global cities with new ones.

South Korea stands out as the G-20 country that was able to improve its economic efficiency the most. From a marginal position in 1990, the country seems to be settling into an RQE at the same efficiency level seen in Germany and the United Kingdom. However, according to the IMF:

After decades of impressive economic progress, Korea's growth has slowed, and the economy is facing a number of structural headwinds, including: unfavorable demographics; heavy export reliance; pockets of corporate vulnerabilities; labor-market distortions; lagging productivity; a limited

Figure 212. The efficiency scorecard for South Korea

SOUTH KOREA	$\psi_{1990} = (0.11)$	$\psi_{2015} = 2.77$	$\Delta = 2.88$
	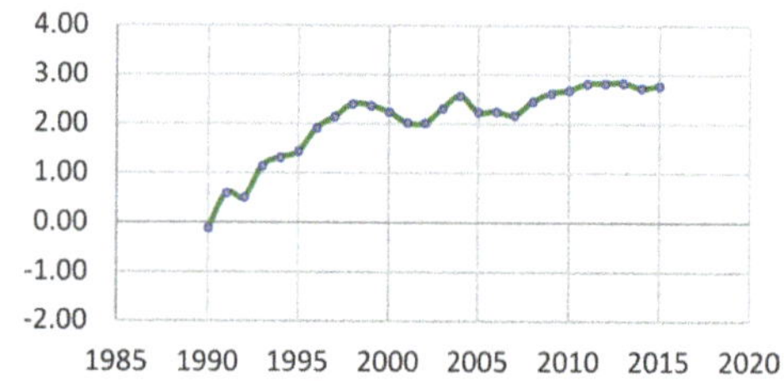		
ECI (2014) = 4	Area ranking = 107	GaWC (2012): Seoul (Alpha –)	

social safety net; and high household debt. Inequality and poverty are also of concern. On the positive side, Korea has considerable fiscal space to manage these challenges.

Growth has been sluggish since 2012, reflecting not only a series of shocks but also a steady decline in the economy's growth potential. The authorities have responded proactively with fiscal and monetary support, along with measures to contain the rapid increase in household debt. Activity started to pick up in the second half of last year but slowed again in the first quarter, reflecting the expiry of the consumption tax cut (which was later extended), weaker fixed investment, and a payback in inventory accumulation. (IMF, 2016b, p. 1)

It will take another decade before ascertaining how successful South Korea is in maintaining its RQE The country started its stellar climb with a positive trend even before the WTO and continued this trend until 1998. This run came to an end due to the AFC of 1997. The GFC had a relatively mild positive effect on South Korea, which saw the country's efficiency stabilize at a ψ score of 3.00.

The country has only one global city. However, it has an area ranking of 107, which makes it the smallest G-20 country by area. South Korea is only one-fourth the size of Japan. Add to this South Korea's history of industrial clusters (Jeong & Lee, 2006), which is similar to what we have seen in Japan, Germany, and Italy. Given its small 'jurisdictional footprint' (as reflected by its area), South Korea was able to absorb much more capital than that required by the ψ model for positive efficiency.

Turkey is another country that seems to have been helped by the GFC. After a long RQE period around a ψ score of 0.00 (from 1995 to 2008), the country's efficiency jumped to a new plateau of around 0.50. Since 1995, Turkey's efficiency benefited also from the WTO and the EU Customs Union. Much of the efficiency in the early 1990s was due to capital inflows from international bond issues.

Turkey has an area close to that of France (0.00076 to 0.00052). Its population equivalent is 0.0017 compared to France's 0.0011. Both are limited by their area input. However, while Turkey has two global cities, France has four. Moreover, French economic complexity at 17 is much higher than that of Turkey. Nevertheless, Turkey is able to achieve positive efficiency. Turkey's small 'jurisdictional footprint' helped the country switch to a sink country. The future trend is explained by the OECD as follows:

Large current account deficits have eroded Turkey's net international investment position. Moreover, between 2007 and 2015, the composition of

Figure 213. The efficiency scorecard for Turkey

TURKEY	$\psi_{1990} = (2.51)$	$\psi_{2015} = 0.71$	$\Delta = 3.22$
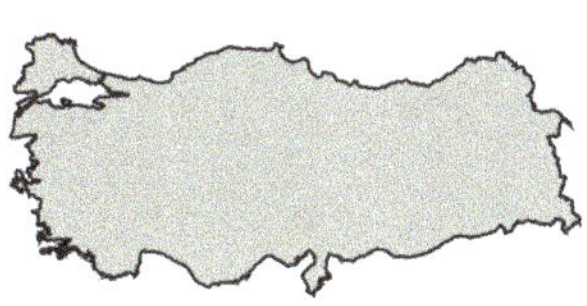	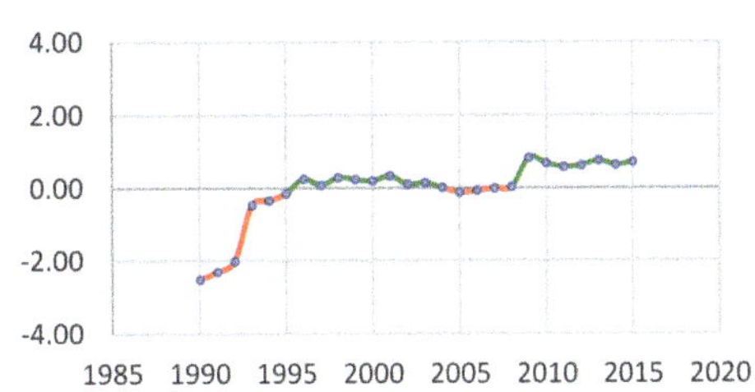 		
ECI (2014) = 42	Area ranking = 36	GaWC (2012): Istanbul (Alpha –), Ankara (Gamma)	

gross external liabilities has shifted towards debt while the share of FDI and equity has declined over the decade—notwithstanding some improvement in 2015 (30% of external liabilities in 2015 against 45% in 2007 and 2010). Over the same period, the share of short-term debt in total external debt has nearly doubled and reached more than 33% in 2013-14, before dropping to about 30% in late 2015 ... As a result, gross external financing needs including the funding of the current account deficit and maturing external debt are projected to reach around 25% of GDP in 2016. Turkey remains vulnerable to volatile international capital flows and erratic exchange rate movements. (OECD, 2016b, p. 19).

While Turkey has industrial clusters (Akküngör, Kumral, & Lenger, 2003), Turkey's ability to move beyond its current level of efficiency will hinge on its ability to create more global cities. Turkey needs to increase its capacity to absorb capital from the world-economy through more connectivity with the world-system through such attractors.

The United Kingdom is one of the most efficient countries in the G-20. It shows an RQE from 1991 to 2015. The GFC resulted in a slight jump in

Figure 214. The efficiency scorecard for the United Kingdom

<table>
<tr><td>UNITED KINGDOM</td><td>$\psi_{1990} = 2.30$</td><td>$\psi_{2015} = 2.89$</td><td>$\Delta = 0.59$</td></tr>
<tr><td></td><td colspan="3">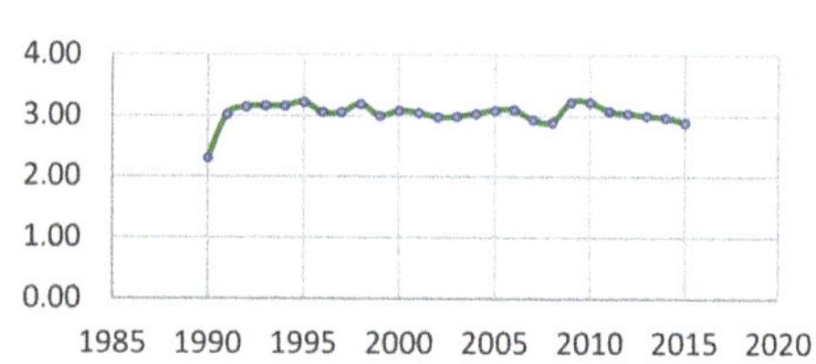
</td></tr>
<tr><td>ECI (2014) = 10</td><td>Area ranking = 78</td><td colspan="2">GaWC (2012): London (Alpha ++), Manchester (Beta), Birmingham (Beta –), Edinburgh (Beta –), Bristol (Gamma +), Glasgow (Gamma), Leeds (Gamma), Belfast (Gamma)</td></tr>
</table>

UK efficiency, but this was followed by a downwards trend towards its secular value of $\psi = 3.00$.

The UK area is one of the smallest in the G-20 group. It is smaller than Germany, Italy, and Japan. Its economic complexity is less than Germany and Japan, but higher than Italy. Given its area and its eight global cities, the UK has been able to absorb enough capital from the world-system to continue its RQE for the last 24 years. However, just like other G-20 Tier 1 countries (see below), the UK is not able to improve its economic efficiency (the exception being South Korea). Although, it has done better than France and Italy (also Tier 1 countries) in that it did not see a downwards pressure on its efficiency as seen in these countries (since 2010).

To improve its economic efficiency, given its area ranking, the UK needs to enhance the ranking of its global cities rather than introduce new cities. This seems to be already occurring, although not necessarily in a way that could ensure boosting economic efficiency. It is useful at this point to provide a synopsis of recent developments on this front.

The *Cities and Local Government Act 2016* (UK) (CLGA, 2016) received the Royal Assent in January 2016. The explanatory note to the Act states its purpose as to make operational the UK Government's objective of boosting economic growth by devolving decision-making powers to local governments in England, similar to the devolution gained previously in Scotland, Wales and Northern Ireland, but on the smaller scale of city-regions. The devolution includes providing city-regions with funding streams through grants but requires these authorities to have balanced budgets for devolved function. To be precise, the objective of the Act is to "devolve far-reaching powers over economic development, transport and social care to large cities which choose to have elected mayors." The local government functions open to devolution are hence limited. They include economic development, urban regeneration, transport, and waste management. Sometimes housing, policing and criminal justice are also added to these functions. The Act comes into force as part of an ongoing devolution process. Before the Act, there has already been devolution in the form of 'City Deals,' such as Greater Manchester, Liverpool City Region, Sheffield City Region, West Midlands, the North East, Tees Valley and Cornwall.

The philosophy behind the CLGA can be gleaned from previous Acts, including the *Local Democracy, Economic Development and Construction Act 2009* (UK) (LDEDCA 2009). Part 6 of the LDEDCA 2009 stipulates for the creation of corporate bodies called 'combined authorities,' which are intended to improve efficiency and effectiveness of transport and economic development by enabling local authorities to work jointly. The LDEDCA 2009 was preceded by the *Local Government Act 2000* (UK) (LGA 2000), which was intended to reform the local government in Wales and England. The LGA 2000 innovation was to give the constituency in a local area the option (through referenda) of electing mayors. The LGA 2000 was followed by the *Local Government Act 2003* (UK) which created the concept of 'business improvement districts' (or BID). These special zones are intended to provide business services supplemental to those provided by municipalities. These added services are funded through additional taxes levied on occupiers within the boundaries of the district.

These Acts were followed by the *Localism Act (2011)* (UK) which aimed to devolve powers to local authorities. The CLGA 2016 operationalizes these objectives through a deal-making approach between the UK government and local governments, which is envisaged to lead to asymmetrical outcomes, based on local preferences. The primary example of such deals so far is the Greater Manchester Combined Authority (GMCA), which from 2017 received new powers and funding streams for economic growth and social care (including health). Similar deals have been struck between the Government and the Cornwall Council, the Sheffield City Region Combined Authority, and the West Yorkshire Combined Authority. Other proposed deals include, for example, the Liverpool City Region.

These devolution deals should be seen through evolutionary lenses. While the dominant current objective of these efforts is efficiency and effectiveness gains through agglomeration, this is only a first step toward making city-regions more competitive on a global stage. As these city-regions gain more competencies in new decision-making areas, it would only be reasonable to expect further devolution to occur. In the long-run, these city-regions will represent charter cities with unique personal identities (through legal systems that cater directly to their local needs).

The United States has an area close to that of China. In 2015, it had a per-unit population of 0.0264 and a per-unit area of 0.12. In comparison, China had a per-unit population of 0.48 and an area of 0.11. However, the US had a ψ_{2015} score of 1.91 compared to 0.07 for China. While the US has its population as a limiting factor, its efficiency can be explained by looking at its global cities. The US has 30 global cities compared to China's six.

Notwithstanding its long-term efficiency, the United States is one of those countries that does not exhibit an RQE. The US has been exhibiting a mild

Figure 215. The efficiency scorecard for the United States

UNITED STATES	$\psi_{1990} = 2.28$	$\psi_{2015} = 1.91$	$\Delta = (0.37)$
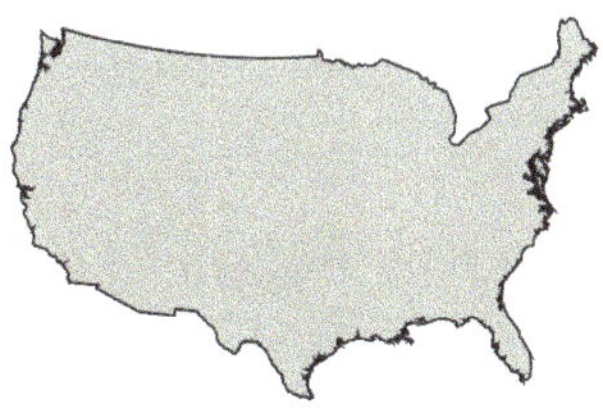	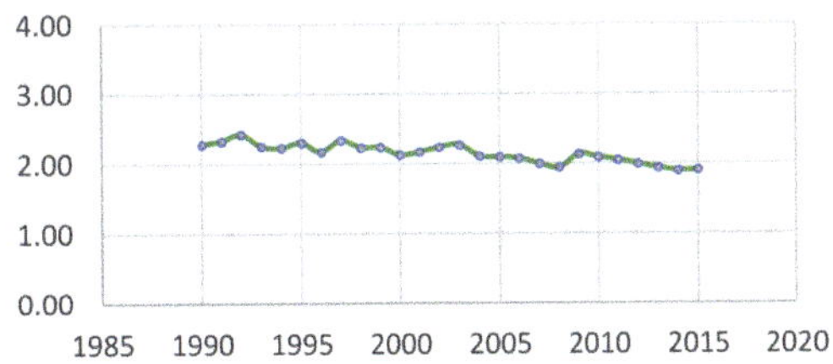		
ECI (2014) = 14	Area ranking = 4	GaWC (2012): New York City (Alpha ++), Chicago and Los Angeles (Alpha), San Francisco, Washington DC, Miami, Boston, and Atlanta (Alpha –), Dallas, Philadelphia and Houston (Beta +), Minneapolis, Cleveland, Seattle, Detroit, Denver, San Diego (Beta –), Baltimore, St Louis, Charlotte, Tampa (Gamma +), San Juan, Raleigh, San Jose, Cincinnati, Milwaukee (Gamma), and Columbus, Orlando, Kansas City, and Portland (Gamma –)	

decline since 2004. The decline was briefly interrupted by the GFC but continued from 2009 to 2015. However, this decline is not as steep as that seen in Italy and France. The country is likely to hover around the $\psi = 2.00$ level. Although a significant reduction could result from the next expected cyclical (efficiency) correction by 2030 (see Chapter 3).

REFERENCES

Akūngör, S., Kumral, N., & Lenger, A. (2003). National industry clusters and regional specializations in Turkey. *European Planning Studies*, *11*(6), 647–669. doi:10.1080/0965431032000108378

Australia, Government of. (2015). Our north, our future: White paper on developing northern Australia.

Canada, Government of. (2009). Canada's northern strategy: Our north, our heritage, our future. Ministry of Indian Affairs and Northern Development.

Curzio, A. Q., & Fortis, M. (Eds.). (2002). *Complexity and industrial clusters: Dynamic models in theory and practice.* New York: Springer. doi:10.1007/978-3-642-50007-7

de Géry, C. (2014). Les pôles de compétitivité français: un nouvel espace participant à la régulation de la relation formation/emploi? *Revue de la Régulation. Capitalisme, Institutions, Pouvoirs, 15.*

Di Quirico, R. (2010). Italy and the global economic crisis. *Bulletin of Italian Politics, 2*(2), 3–19.

Falkenheim, V. C. (1985). The political economy of Chinas SEZs. *The Asian Journal of Public Administration, 7*(2), 144–169. doi:10.1080/02598272.1985.10800163

France, Government of (2011). *Competitiveness clusters in France.* Paris: The Directorate General for Competitiveness, Industry and Services (DGCIS).

Hussler, C., Muller, P., & Ronde, P. (2013). Les pôles de compétitivité: Morphologies et performances. *Gestiòn Internacional, 18*(1), 117–137.

IMF. (2009). *Impact of the Global Financial Crisis on Sub-Saharan Africa.* Washington, D. C.: IMF.

IMF. (2010). *Mexico: Staff report for the 2010 Article IV consultation.* Washington, D. C.: IMF.

IMF. (2014). *Saudi Arabia: Staff report for the 2016 Article IV consultation.* Washington, D. C.: IMF.

IMF. (2016a). *Saudi Arabia: Staff report for the 2016 Article IV consultation.* Washington, D. C.: IMF.

IMF. (2016b). *South Korea: Staff report for the 2016 Article IV consultation.* Washington, D. C.: IMF.

Jeong, J. H., & Lee, J.-M. (2006). Identifying industrial clusters in Korea. Seoul: Korea Institute for Industrial Economics and Trade (KIET).

Jie, F. (2004). Western development policy: Changes, effects and evaluation. In Y. M. Yeung & S. Jianfa (Eds.), *Developing China's West: A critical path to balanced national development* (pp. 79–105). Hong Kong: The Chinese University Press.

Judah, A. (2014). *The Australian century*. Redland Bay, Queensland: Connor Court.

Läpple, D. (2006). The German metropolitan system: An alternative to the global city? Retrieved from https://lsecities.net/media/objects/articles/the-german-metropolitan-system/en-gb/

Läpple, D. (2016). Germany: A global cities system? Retrieved from https://lsecities.net/media/objects/articles/germany-a-global-cities-system/en-gb/

Mindlin, Y. B., Kolpak, E. P., & Gasratova, N. A. (2016). Clusters in system of instruments of territorial development of the Russian Federation. *International Review of Management and Marketing*, *6*(1S).

Morsy, H., & Sgherri, S. (2010). *After the crisis: Assessing the damage in Italy (WP/10/244). International Monetary Fund*. IMF.

Narayanan, T., & Sekar, P. C. (2012). Special economic zones: Performance, resistance, and remedial measures. In M. Soundarapandian (Ed.), *Development of special economic zones in India* (Vol. I, pp. 64–82). New Delhi: Concept Publishing.

Naylor, E. (1995). Agricultural policy reforms in France. *Geography (Sheffield, England)*, *80*(3), 281–283.

OECD. (2015). *OECD economic surveys*. Brazil: OECD.

OECD. (2016a). *OECD economic surveys*. Canada: OECD.

OECD. (2016b). *OECD economic surveys*. Turkey: OECD.

Oza, R. (2011). Special economic zones: Space, law, and dispossession. In W. Ahmed, A. Kundu, & R. Peet (Eds.), *India's new economic policy: A critical analysis* (pp. 240–260). New York: Routledge.

Putnam, R. D., Leonardi, R., & Nonetti, R. Y. (1994). *Making democracy work: Civic traditions in modern Italy*. Princeton: Princeton University Press.

Renou, L., & Crague, G. (2015). Les pôles de compétitivité, des méta-organisations autonomes? Working Paper, n15-05. octobre 2015. Retrieved from https://hal-enpc.archives-ouvertes.fr/hal-01224841/document

Vidaurri, F. (2015). *Indonesia's growing special economic zones – Opportunities and challenges. ASEAN Briefing*. ASEAN.

Wong, P. K., & Ng, K. K. (2009). *Batam, Bintan and Karimun – Past history and current development towards being a SEZ*. Singapore: Lee Kuan Yew School of Public Policy.

Yamawaki, H. (2002). The evolution and structure of industrial clusters in Japan. *Small Business Economics*, *18*(1/3), 121–140. doi:10.1023/A:1015134028335

ENDNOTE

1 As discussed later, the origin of the current world-system can be traced back to the commencement of the WTO on 1 January 1995.

APPENDIX FOR CHAPTER 5: ANALYSIS OF THE UNITED STATES

This appendix provides a scorecard for each of the 50 states and the District of Columbia. These scorecards are similar to the ones used in the appendix to Chapter 5, except that instead of an ECI ranking, which is not available for subnational polities, each scorecard provides the 2015 Gross State Product (GSP) ranking. Similarly, the GaWC 2012 ranking is replaced with major cities. However, where there are global cities, these are highlighted, and their GaWC ranking is provided. See Figures 216 – 266.

Alabama is a second-tier state. It shows a mild improvement in its efficiency score between 1990 and 2015, although it remained an inefficient state throughout the period. At the beginning of the observation period, the State shows an increase in efficiency from 1990 to 1995. This trend tapered off with the introduction of NAFTA and the WTO. The State shows an RQE from 1995 to 2015, with a dip in 2005 (due to Hurricanes Ivan and Katrina).

In 2015, the State had per-unit energy-equivalent inputs as follows: 5.3E-03 population and 3.7E-03 area. Its per-unit energy-equivalent GSP was 3.3E-03, resulting in a negative residual of 5.6E-03. In the same year, Alabama had a population density of only 37 per square kilometer.

Figure 216. The efficiency scorecard for Alabama

ALABAMA	$\psi_{1990} = (1.15)$	$\psi_{2015} = (0.98)$	$\Delta = 0.16$
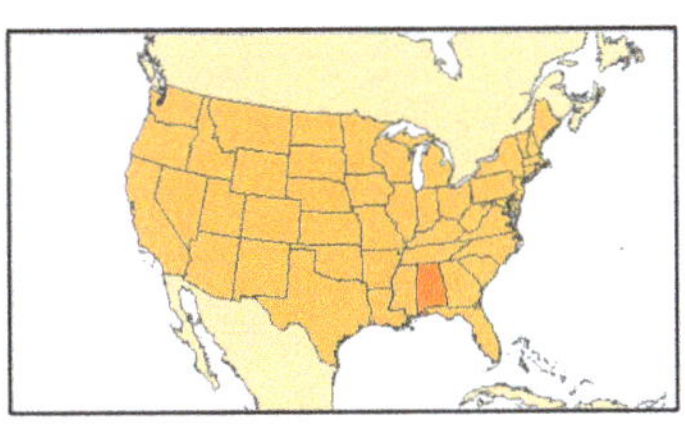	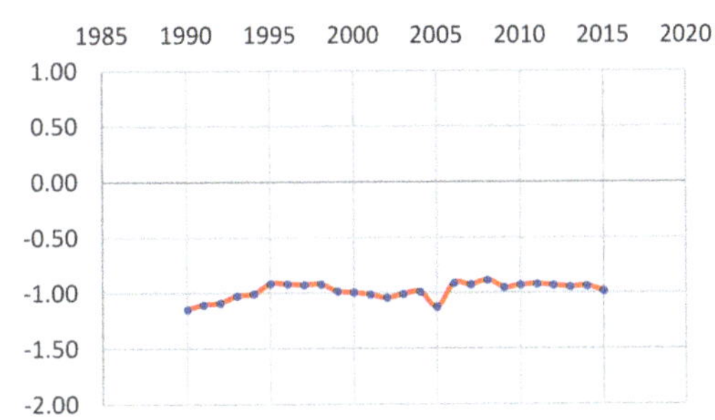		
GSP ranking (2015) = 26	Area ranking = 30	Major cities: Birmingham, Montgomery, Mobile, Huntsville, Tuscaloosa	

Alabama had a 2015 GSP ranking higher than its area ranking. It is relatively small by area (135,765 square kilometers), although none of its major cities are classified as global cities.

Economically, Alaska is one of the worst-performing states, not only regarding its GSP ranking (45th) but also in terms of its economic efficiency (fourth tier). Notwithstanding an improvement of 1.91 points in its ψ score over the observation period, most of this improvement came between 1990 and 1991. Alaska continues to have the lowest ψ score by far. After a jump in its efficiency in 1990 (due to increased oil production), there was downward pressure from 1991 to 2000 (due to lower oil prices). Efficiency showed some improvement from 2000 to 2015. Generally, however, Alaska exhibits an RQE at around $\psi = -8.00$.

The State is ranked number one in terms of area (5.9E-01), but it has a population of 1.2 E-04. With a huge area and a small population, Alaska can generate a GSP per-unit energy-equivalent of only 1.4E-04. This translates to a residual of negative 5.9E-01.

In 2015, the State had a population density of 0.5 per square kilometer. Given its geographic location, Alaska is expected to be economically inefficient. Its geography (location and climate) will always be a constraint on its economy. A similar pattern can also be seen in the Northern parts of

Figure 217. The efficiency scorecard for Alaska

ALASKA	$\psi_{1990} = (10.22)$	$\psi_{2015} = (8.31)$	$\Delta = 1.91$
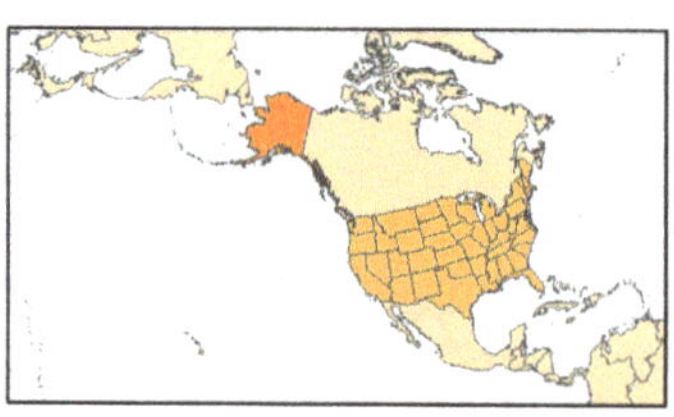	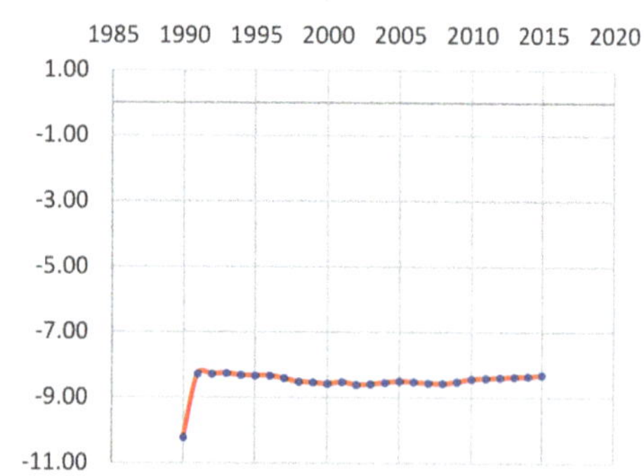		
GSP ranking (2015) = 45	Area ranking = 1	Major cities: Anchorage, Fairbanks, Juneau, Knik-Fairview, College	

Canada and Australia. Nevertheless, the State has abundant natural resources and a strategic location that contribute to the growth of its economy. Still, none of Alaska's major cities has a global ranking. Without such cities, it is hard to see how Alaska can become a sink state.

Arizona, a second-tier state, is one of the few states exhibiting a (continued) positive trend over the observation period. While it increased its efficiency by 0.54 (from 1990 to 2015), it is still inefficient. After an RQE between 1990 and 1994, the State seems to have benefited from the introduction of NAFTA and the WTO. The steady increase in efficiency from 1995 to 2005 appears to have come to an end, however, with the State entering into an RQE around $\psi = -1.50$.

The State had a 2015 per-unit energy-equivalent inputs of 9.9E-03 (population) and 1.73E-02 (area). For the same year, it generated a GSP equivalent of 6.4E-03, which gives a negative residual of 2.1E-02. With only one Gamma + city (Phoenix), the State is unable to absorb enough capital to reach positive efficiency.

Arkansas is another second-tier state that shows a mildly positive trend over the observation period, although it remains in a relatively narrow band. During the period from 1990 and 2015, it registered an increase of 0.22 points. The State seems to have a $\psi_{ceiling} = -1.50$.

Figure 218. The efficiency scorecard for Arizona

<table>
<tr><td>ARIZONA</td><td>$\psi_{1990} = (1.99)$</td><td>$\psi_{2015} = (1.45)$</td><td>$\Delta = 0.54$</td></tr>
<tr><td>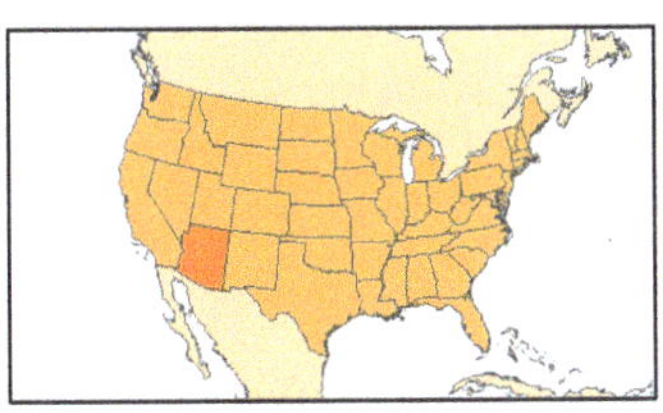</td><td colspan="3">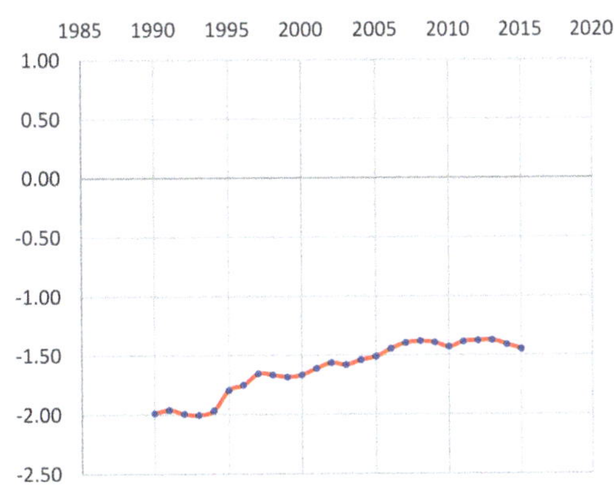
</td></tr>
<tr><td>GSP ranking (2015) = 21</td><td>Area ranking = 6</td><td colspan="2">Major cities: Phoenix (Gamma +), Tucson, Mesa, Chandler, Gilbert</td></tr>
</table>

Figure 219. The efficiency scorecard for Arkansas

ARKANSAS	$\psi_{1990} = (1.82)$	$\psi_{2015} = (1.60)$	$\Delta = 0.22$
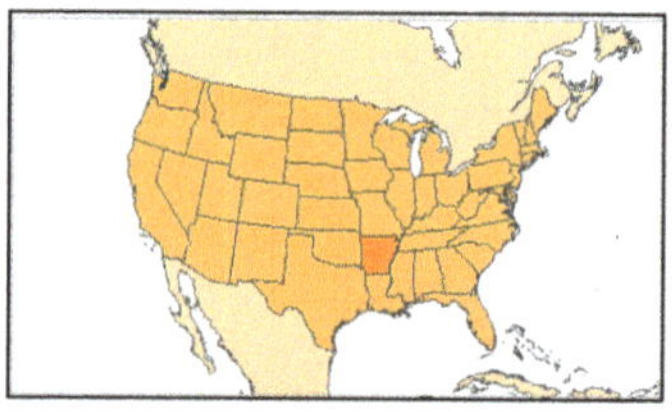	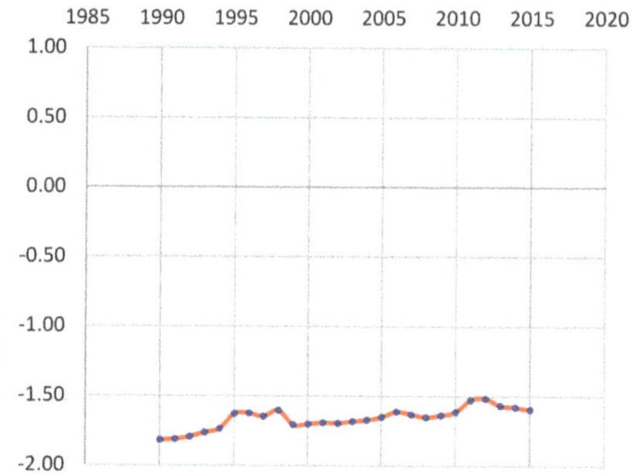		
GSP ranking (2015) = 34	Area ranking = 29	Major cities: Little Rock, Fort Smith, Fayetteville, Springdale, Jonesboro	

In 2015, the State recorded a (per-unit energy-equivalent) population of 2.0E-03 and area of 4.1E-03. For the same year, it generated a (per-unit energy-equivalent) GSP of 1.2E-03, which resulted in a negative residual of 4.8E-03. Arkansas has a GSP ranking (34th) lower than its area ranking (29th).

The State has no global cities.

California, a first-tier state, has shown consistency in its efficiency score throughout the observation period. While it had a marginal positive score in 1990, the State finished the period with a marginal negative score. Since 2002, the State exhibits an RQE at around $\psi = 0$. This RQE was preceded by another lower RQE from 1996 to 2001, which coincides with the introduction of the WTO.

For all practical purposes, California is economically efficient—but only marginally. It can absorb only enough capital to stay efficient. The State is not able to accumulate capital towards a high positive ψ score. The State has the largest economy in the United States, as well as the largest population. Its GSP ranking is higher than its area ranking, although it is also large in terms of area (423,970 square kilometers). In 2015, the State ranked 11th in terms of population density (97 per square kilometer).

The State is home to four global cities, which explains how a State with an area of 3.6E-02 and a population of 3.3E-01 was able to achieve efficiency.

Figure 220. The efficiency scorecard for California

CALIFORNIA	$\psi_{1990} = 0.036$	$\psi_{2015} = (0.038)$	$\Delta = (0.073)$
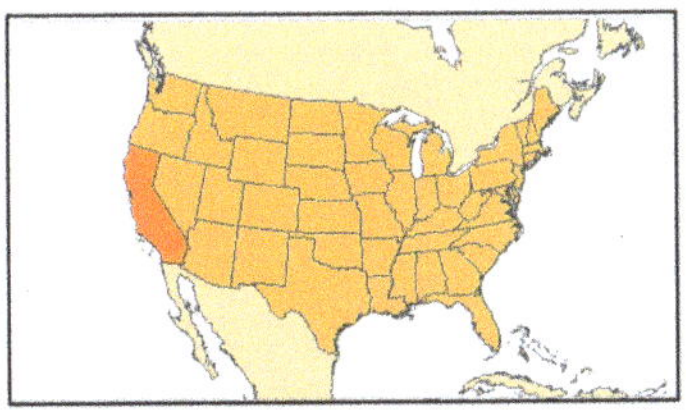	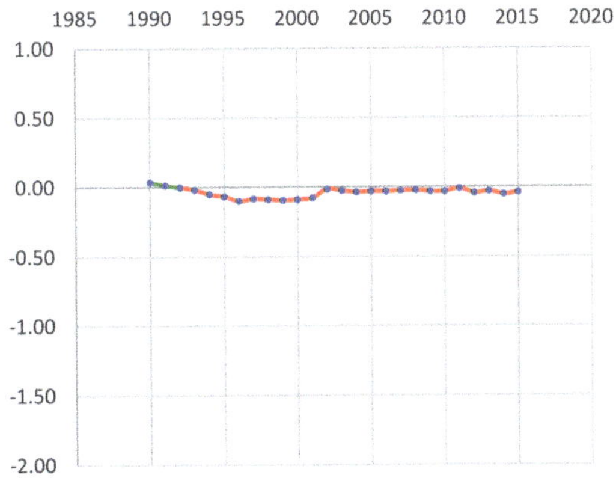		
GSP ranking (2015) = 1	Area ranking = 3	Major cities: **Los Angeles** (Alpha), **San Diego** (Beta –), **San Jose** (Gamma), **San Francisco** (Alpha –), Fresno	

In fact, California had the largest GSP in 2015. California illustrates the rhizomatic causality (see Chapter 6) between economic efficiency and the attractors in a given jurisdiction. Without its global cities, California would not have been able to achieve economic efficiency.

California has also benefited from its industrial clusters as attractors. Clusters such as the San Francisco-San Jose cluster and the San Diego-Tijuana clusters (Alcácer & Zhao, 2016) have also acted as capital attractors.

Colorado has an efficiency 'signature' very similar to that of Arizona (both second-tier states). The State starts with an RQE from 1990 to 1995, followed by a jump in 1995 due to NAFTA and the WTO. A positive trend followed from 1995 to 2003. This period was followed by an RQE $(\psi = -1.15)$ from 2003 to 2015. The State seems to be facing a $\psi_{ceiling} = -1.0$.

At the end of the observation period, Colorado had a per-unit energy-equivalent population of 6.2E-03 and area of 1.4E-02. Its GSP equivalent was 6.5E-03, with a residual of negative 1.4E-02. The State has a GSP ranking (18th) much higher than its area ranking (8th). Nevertheless, it shows negative efficiency due to its limiting factor: population.

Throughout the observation period, Colorado exhibits economic inefficiency, even though it registers an improvement of 0.57 points. The State

Figure 221. The efficiency scorecard for Colorado

COLORADO	$\psi_{1990} = (1.73)$	$\psi_{2015} = (1.16)$	$\Delta = 0.57$
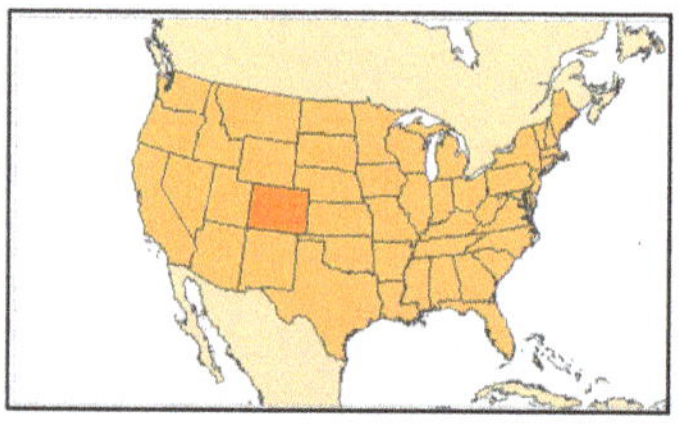	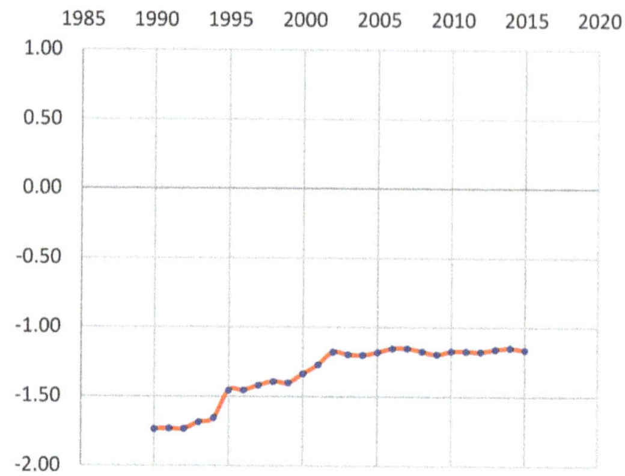		
GSP ranking (2015) = 18	Area ranking = 8	Major cities: **Denver** (Beta –), Colorado Springs, Aurora, Fort Collins, Lakewood	

has only one (Beta –) global city, and this does not appear to be sufficient for it to achieve a positive ψ score.

Connecticut is the most efficient US state, second only to the District of Columbia. The State exhibits an RQE around $\psi = 0.60$ from 1999 to 2015. Before this period, Connecticut had a lower RQE at around $\psi = 0.50$. The State remains in a narrow efficiency band throughout the observation period.

Connecticut is one of the original thirteen colonies, which suggests a longer period of economic evolution. It has a population ranked 29th. Moreover, in 2015, the State had the 4th largest population density among all 50 states (286 per square kilometers). The State has a much higher GSP ranking (23rd) than its area ranking (48th).

To understand why Connecticut is an efficient state, although it has no global cities, we look at its inputs. In 2015, the State had a per-unit energy-equivalent land of 4.1E-05 and population of 2.9E-03. The small 'jurisdictional footprint' gives it a ranking of 48 out of 50 states. With such a small footprint (14,357 square kilometers), the State can exceed the ψ floor without the need for global cities. In other words, attractors in Connecticut come in the form of industry clusters (Jolly, 2005).

Figure 222. The efficiency scorecard for Connecticut

<table>
<tr><td>CONNECTICUT</td><td>$\psi_{1990} = 0.52$</td><td>$\psi_{2015} = 0.55$</td><td>$\Delta = 0.30$</td></tr>
<tr><td>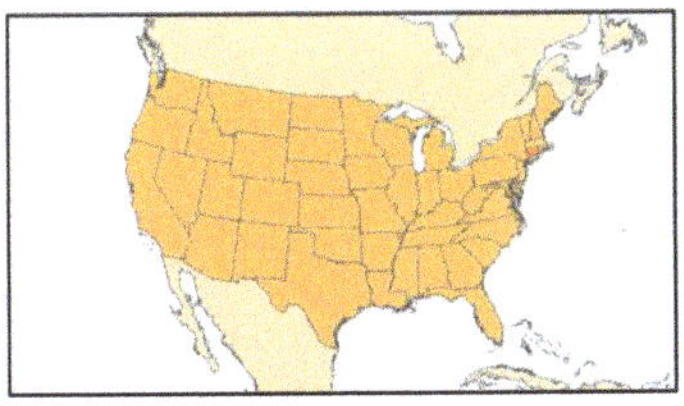</td><td colspan="3">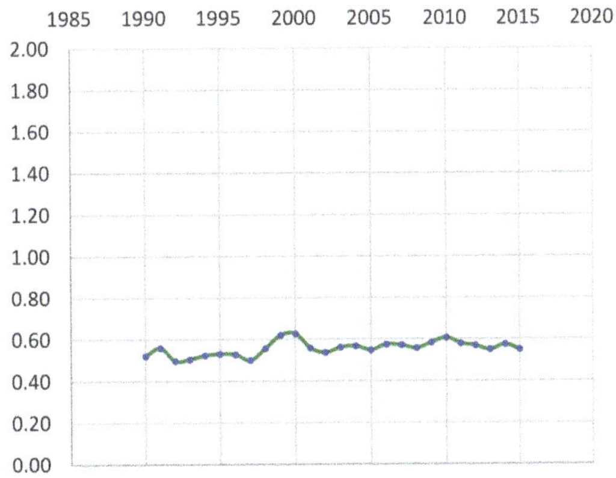
</td></tr>
<tr><td>GSP ranking (2015) = 23</td><td>Area ranking = 48</td><td colspan="2">Major cities: Bridgeport, New Haven, Stamford, Hartford, Waterbury</td></tr>
</table>

It is useful to compare Connecticut with the top sink countries and top global cities from Chapter 3. Table 7 shows that Connecticut has inputs (area and population) larger than that of Qatar, but smaller than that of New York City. Its jurisdictional footprint is at a scale similar to that of Tokyo, although its population is much smaller. Being a state gives Connecticut a margin of legislative autonomy not afforded global cities. The State can achieve economic efficiency due to its small jurisdictional footprint, and an evolutionary process that led to a distributed urban system (and embedded industrial clusters) that can absorb and accumulate capital. For Connecticut to enhance its economic efficiency even further, it has to increase its industrial clusters and increase the density of its distributed urban system.

Delaware is, like California, a marginally efficient state. It exhibits periods of positive scores followed by periods of negative scores, but always within a very narrow band around $\psi = 0$. Delaware seems however to have suffered from the GFC. Since 2008 its ψ score has shown a downward trend, which seems to have troughed in 2013.

In 2015, Delaware had a per-unit energy-equivalent population of 1.9E-04 and an area of 8.2E-06. The per-unit energy-equivalent GSP was 1.9E-04, with a residual of -1.5E-05. In the same year, it had a GSP ranking (41st) lower than its area ranking (49th), which would suggest a high population

Figure 223. The efficiency scorecard for Delaware

<table>
<tr><td>DELAWARE</td><td>$\psi_{1990} = (0.01)$</td><td>$\psi_{2015} = (0.08)$</td><td>$\Delta = (0.07)$</td></tr>
<tr><td>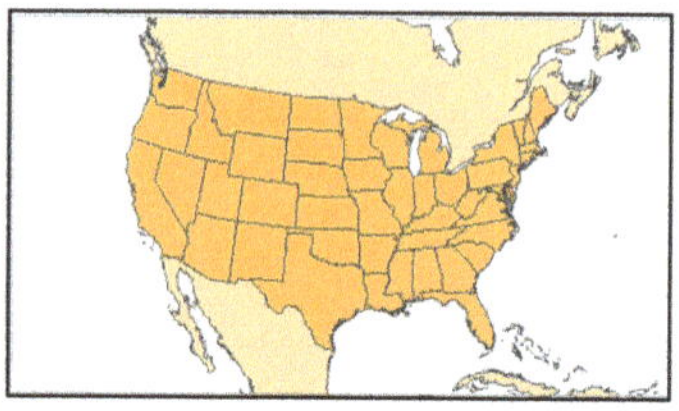</td><td colspan="3">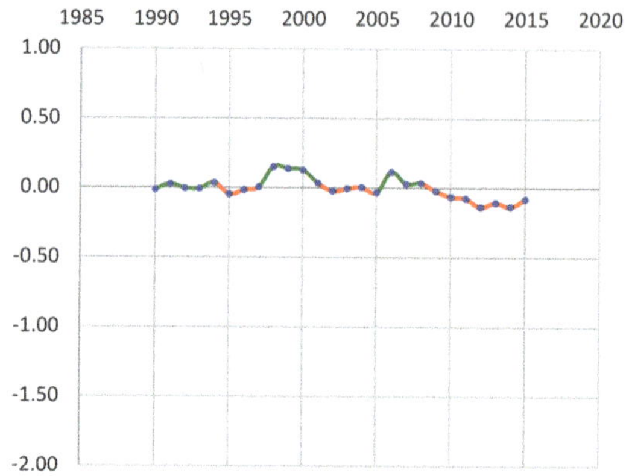
</td></tr>
<tr><td>GSP ranking (2015) = 41</td><td>Area ranking = 49</td><td colspan="2">Major cities: Wilmington, Dover, Newark, Middletown, Bear</td></tr>
</table>

density. Similar to Connecticut, Delaware has a high population density (187 per square kilometer in 2015). It does not have any global cities, but is able to absorb enough capital given its small jurisdictional footprint (5,130 square kilometers).

Florida has exhibited a relatively stable (inefficient) score throughout the observation period. It could be seen as exhibiting an RQE around $\psi = -0.20$. It seems to have a $\psi_{ceiling} = 0$.

In 2015, Florida had a per-unit energy-equivalent population of 8.6E-02 and an area of 5.8E-03. The resulting GSP equivalent was 7.1E-02, or a negative residual of 2.1E-02. Notwithstanding its large area (5.7E-03), Florida has been able to reach this level of efficiency thanks to its three global cities. However, for Florida to move to a sink status, it has to create more global cities.

Florida's GSP ranking is much higher than its area ranking, which would suggest a high population density. The State is in fact ranked 8th in terms of density (146 per square kilometer). However, this density is not enough to bring about agglomeration effects that could lead to economic efficiency. In order to increase this density, Florida has three global cities with the following densities: Miami (4,770 per square kilometer), Tampa (1,147 per

Figure 224. The efficiency scorecard for Florida

FLORIDA	$\psi_{1990} = (0.19)$	$\psi_{2015} = (0.26)$	$\Delta = (0.06)$
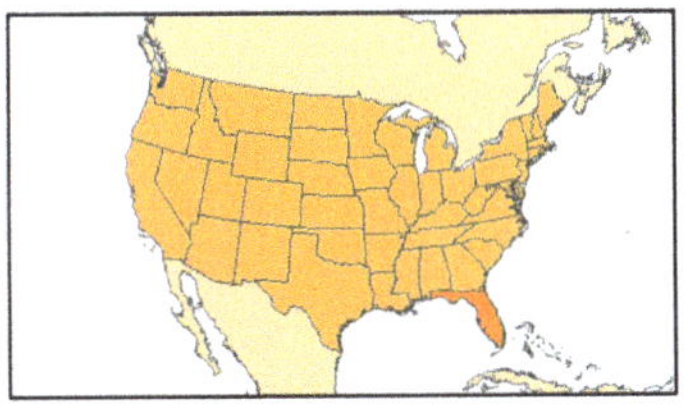	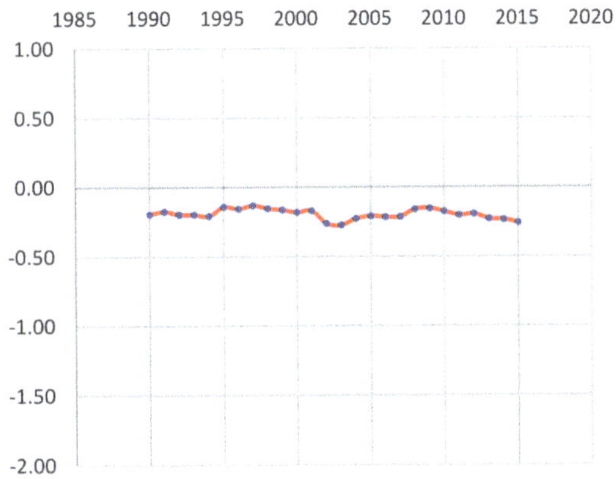		
GSP ranking (2015) = 4	Area ranking = 22	Major cities: Jacksonville, **Miami** (Alpha –), **Tampa** (Gamma +), **Orlando** (Gamma –), Saint Petersburg	

square kilometer), and Orlando (899 per square kilometers). By increasing density, in these cities, Florida was able to absorb enough capital to reach its current RQE efficiency level.

Georgia is similar to Florida in having a relatively consistent score with an RQE around $\psi = -0.50$. There was a mild improvement in efficiency between 1990 and 1995, with a decrease in efficiency between 2005 and 2010. From 2010 to 2015 the State appears to exhibit an efficiency level closer to negative 0.50.

The State has an area equivalent of 4.7E-03 (153,909 square kilometers). In 2015, its population equivalent was 2.3E-02. Its GSP equivalent for that same year was 1.6E-02, with a residual of negative 1.2E-02.

Georgia is one of the thirteen original colonies, which indicates longer economic evolution. It had a 2015 GSP ranking much higher than its area ranking. In 2015, it had a population density of 69 per square kilometer. However, the State has only one global city (with a population density of 1,300 per square kilometer). In order for Georgia to move to a band closer to Florida's and eventually switch into a sink, it needs to grow its other major cities into global ones.

Figure 225. The efficiency scorecard for Georgia

GEORGIA	$\psi_{1990} = (0.60)$	$\psi_{2015} = (0.56)$	$\Delta = (0.05)$
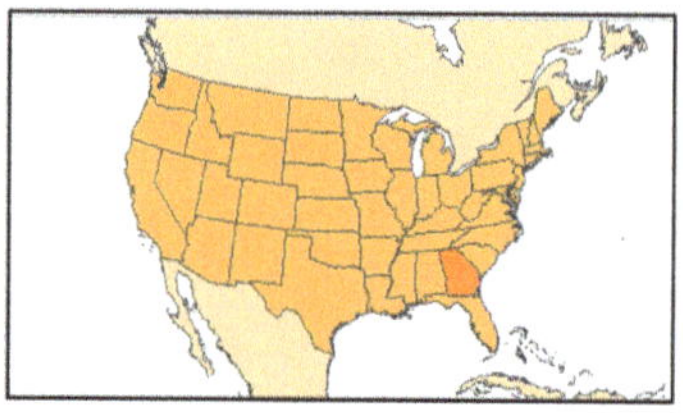	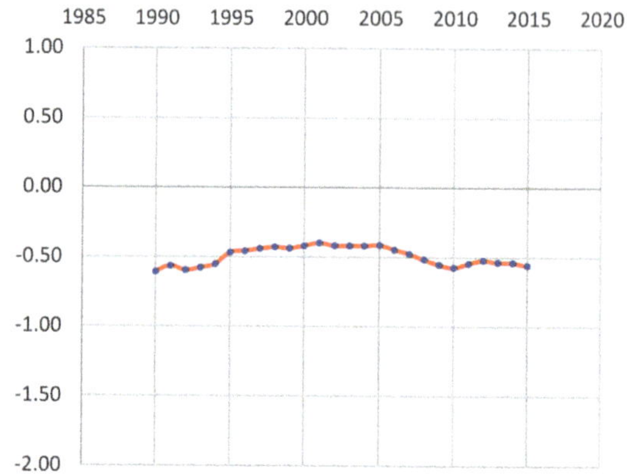		
GSP ranking (2015) = 10	Area ranking = 24	Major cities: **Atlanta** (Alpha –), Augusta, Columbus, Savannah, Athens	

Hawaii, a first-tier state, starts the observation period with a positive increase of 0.20 points (from 1990 to 1993). This improvement in efficiency was followed by a decrease from 1993 to 2002 (a decrease of 0.50 points). From 2003 to 2015 the State shows only minor improvement and remains below its efficiency level in 1990.

The State has an area equivalent of 1.6E-4 and a population equivalent of 4.5E-04. The State GSP equivalent for 2015 was 4.4E-04, with a negative residual of 1.6E-04, which is higher than the residual seen in Delaware in the same year (-1.5E-05), but similar to that observed in Vermont (-1.2E-04). Compared to our equilibrium band analysis in Chapter 4, the State is considered to be a 'break-even' state. It is able to absorb enough capital to reach efficiency, but not enough to accumulate capital.

While the State has a small jurisdictional footprint (28,311 square kilometer), it does not have the same level of efficiency we saw in Connecticut. Hawaii, like Alaska, is remote. While its GSP is higher than its area ranking, it still has negative efficiency. The State does not have any global cities. Hawaii, however, has creative industry clusters, and these are helping improve its efficiency (Bonham, 2016).

Similar to Arizona, Idaho is one of a few states that exhibits a positive trend throughout the observation period, although the period from 2010 to 2015 seems to suggest reaching saturation, and an RQE around $\psi = -3.3$.

Figure 226. The efficiency scorecard for Hawaii

<table>
<tr><td>HAWAII</td><td>$\psi_{1990} = (0.20)$</td><td>$\psi_{2015} = (0.32)$</td><td>$\Delta = (0.12)$</td></tr>
<tr><td>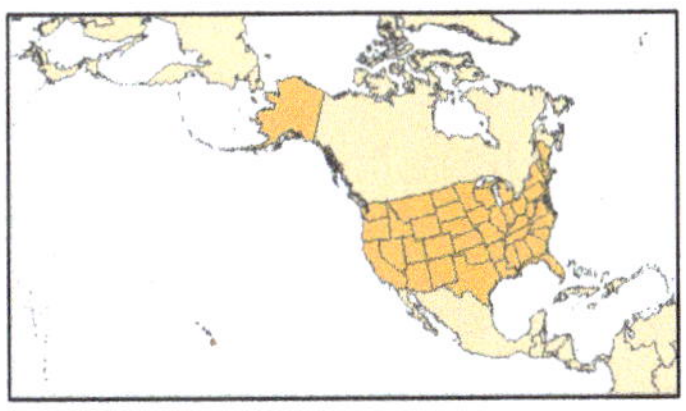</td><td colspan="3">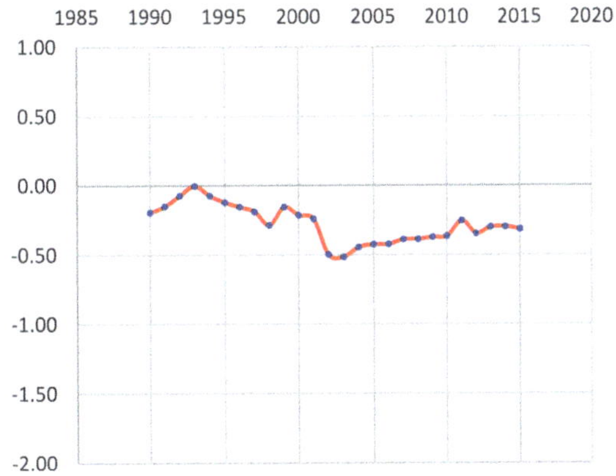
</td></tr>
<tr><td>GSP ranking (2015) = 38</td><td>Area ranking = 43</td><td colspan="2">Major cities: Honolulu, Pear City, Hilo, Waipahu, Kailua</td></tr>
</table>

Figure 227. The efficiency scorecard for Idaho

<table>
<tr><td>IDAHO</td><td>$\psi_{1990} = (4.01)$</td><td>$\psi_{2015} = (3.34)$</td><td>$\Delta = 0.67$</td></tr>
<tr><td>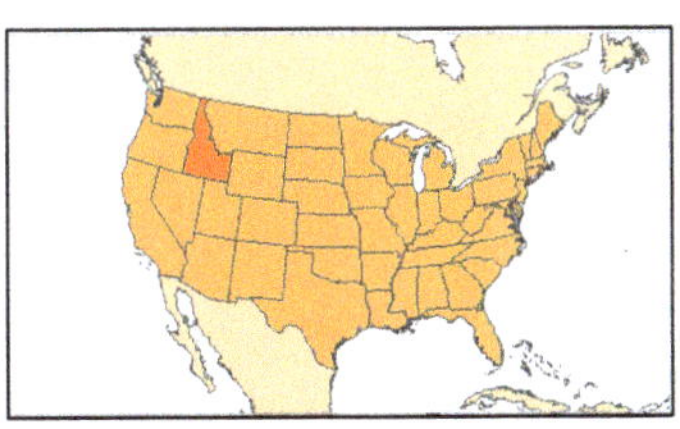</td><td colspan="3">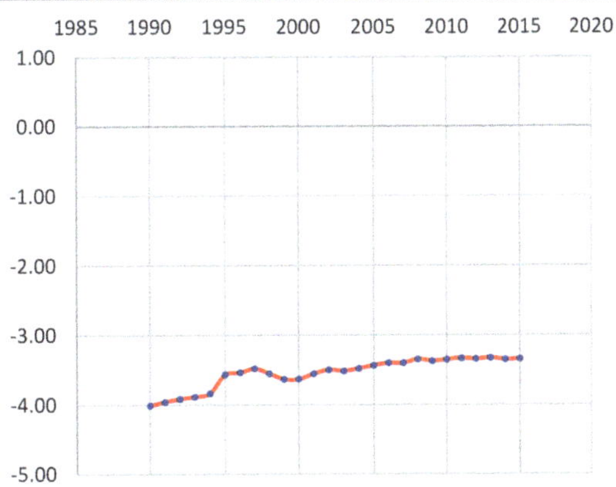
</td></tr>
<tr><td>GSP ranking (2015) = 42</td><td>Area ranking = 14</td><td colspan="2">Major cities: Boise, Nampa, Meridian, Idaho Falls, Pocatello</td></tr>
</table>

However, unlike Arizona, which is a second-tier state, Idaho is still a third-tier state. The State is limited to an efficiency band much lower than Arizona (between $\psi = -4.0$ and $\psi = -3.0$).

Idaho has a large area (9.3E-03) but a small population (5.9E-04). It has a per-unit energy-equivalent GSP of 3.5E-04, with a residual of negative 9.5E-03 (2015). Idaho's footprint (216,900 square kilometers) is still smaller than Arizona's (295,234 square kilometers). However, its population is only 1.7 million, compared to Arizona's 6.9 million. Of course, Idaho became a state only in 1890, compared to 1912 for Arizona. However, Arizona has the advantage of proximity to California and the Mexican border. Idaho's proximity to Washington and the Canadian border has not generated the same level of economic activity.

Unlike Arizona which has a (Gamma +) global city, Idaho has no global cities. If it can elevate one of its major cities into a global status, it could probably move into an efficiency band similar to that seen in Arizona.

As a first-tier state, Illinois exhibits an efficiency signature similar to that seen in California and Pennsylvania. Just like California, Illinois exhibits an RQE around $\psi = 0$. Pennsylvania on the other hand seems to have a $\psi_{ceiling} = 0$. With only one Alpha city (Chicago), Illinois has been able to meet the ψ floor requirements. The small variations in the ψ score over the observation

Figure 228. The efficiency scorecard for Illinois

ILLINOIS	$\psi_{1990} = (0.07)$	$\psi_{2015} = (0.07)$	$\Delta = 0.00$
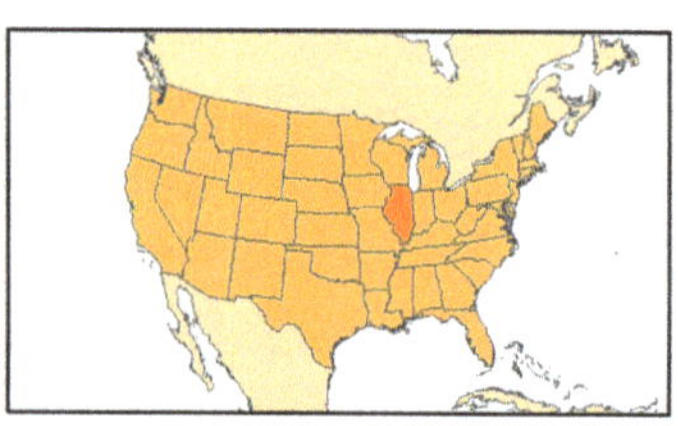	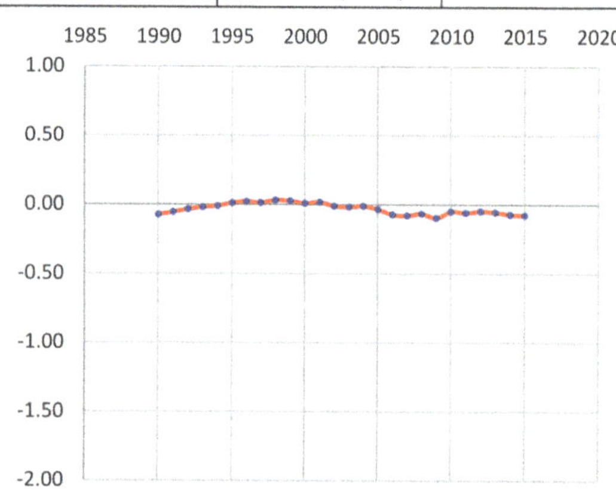		
GSP ranking (2015) = 5	Area ranking = 25	Major cities: **Chicago** (Alpha), Aurora, Rockford, Joliet, Naperville	

period can be attribute to ‘noise’ from the data. Illinois’s efficiency is one of the most robust among the 50 states (and the District of Columbia).

Illinois’s (per-unit energy-equivalent) area and population are 4.5E-03 and 3.7E-02 respectively. This compares to 3.6E-02 and 3.3E-01 for California. California with an area of over 423,000 square kilometers can achieve (marginal) efficiency with four global cities. Illinois with an area just under 150,000 square kilometers can achieve the same efficiency with only one (Alpha) global city. For Illinois, which had a 2015 population density of 89 per square kilometer (compared to 97 per square kilometer for California), the limiting factor of land is easily served by Chicago. However, for Illinois to get to positive efficiency, it needs to have more global cities.

Indiana shows an efficiency level around $\psi = -0.50$ throughout the observation period. The State, a first-tier state, exhibits an efficiency ‘hump’ between 1993 and 2010, which seems to reflect benefit from NAFTA and the WTO. This gain in efficiency seems to have been cancelled out by the GFC. However, the State continues to register an RQE around $\psi = -0.50$.

In 2015, Indiana had a GSP ranking much higher than its area ranking. It had a (per-unit energy-equivalent) population of 9.7E-03 and area of 1.8E-

Figure 229. The efficiency scorecard for Indiana

INDIANA	$\psi_{1990} = (0.50)$	$\psi_{2015} = (0.50)$	$\Delta = 0.00$

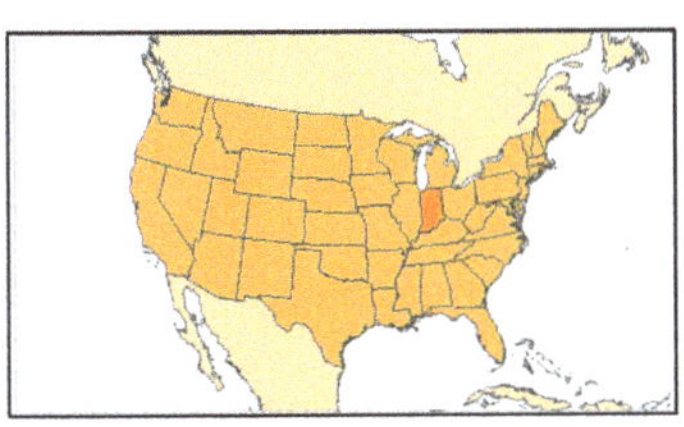

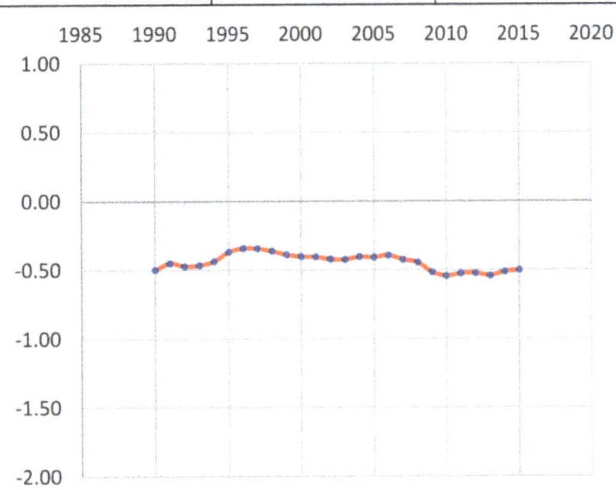

GSP ranking (2015) = 17	Area ranking = 38	Major cities: Indianapolis, Fort Wayne, Evansville, South Bend, Carmel

03. Its GSP equivalent was 7.0E-03, with a negative 4.5E-03 residual. This residual is similar to that seen in Iowa, although Iowa had a lower GDP equivalent which resulted in a lower efficiency score (see below).

Indiana has no global cities and is unlikely to move into a positive score without at least one such city. In its 2012 ranking of global cities, GaWC mentions Indianapolis as a 'high-sufficiency' city, which suggests that with targeted strategic planning it could become a 'Gamma' city in the near future.

Similar to Indiana, Iowa shows a consistent negative efficiency throughout the observation period. Iowa shows a 'dent' in its efficiency after the introduction of NAFTA and the WTO, although it soon settled into an RQE of $\psi = -1.25$. The State seems to have benefited from the GFC, with a positive efficiency trend from 2009 to 2015. Overall, the Sate increased its efficiency by 0.17 points between 1990 and 2015.

In 2015 Iowa had a per-unit energy-equivalent population of 2.2E-03 and an area of 4.2E-03. Its GSP equivalent was 2.1E-03 and its residual was negative 4.3E-03. While Iowa has a similar residual to Indiana, it exhibits much lower efficiency, due to its lower GSP equivalent relative to Indiana. In fact, its GSP ranking is lower than its area ranking.

Just like many other states in the second tier, Iowa does not have any global cities, which makes it difficult for these states to move to positive efficiency.

Figure 230. The efficiency scorecard for Iowa

IOWA	$\psi_{1990} = (1.29)$	$\psi_{2015} = (1.12)$	$\Delta = 0.17$

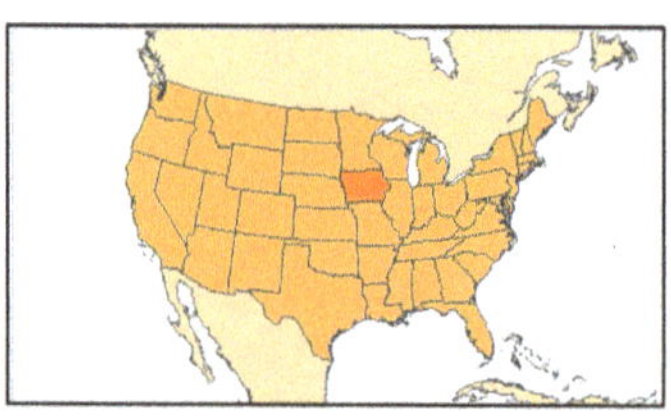

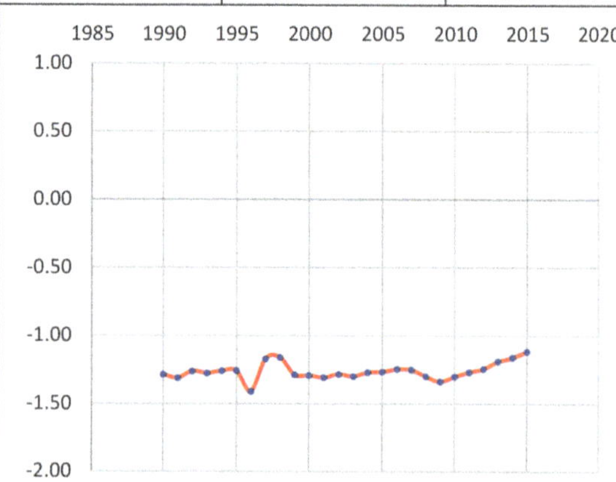

GSP ranking (2015) = 30	Area ranking = 26	Major cities: Des Moines, Cedar Rapids, Davenport, Sioux City, Iowa City

Similar to Iowa, Kansas is another second-tier state. The State exhibits an RQE around $\psi = -1.85$ throughout the observation period. There is a minor increase in efficiency in 1995 (due to NAFTA and the WTO), but it is short-lived. The State seemed to settle at an RQE of $\psi = -1.85$. There was a very small increase in efficiency (0.03) between 1990 and 2015.

In 2015, Kansas had an area and population equivalents of 9.0E-03 and 1.9E-03 respectively. The equivalent GSP was 1.7E-03 with a negative residual of 9.2E-03. The same year, Kansas had a GSP ranking much lower than its area ranking.

Just like Iowa, Kansas does not have any global cities.

Kentucky is another second-tier state with a narrow score band between $\psi_{floor} = -1.0$ and $\psi_{ceiling} = -0.80$. The State maintains an RQE of about $\psi = 0.90$. The State exhibits a stable score throughout the observation period. Kentucky shows improvement in its efficiency from 1990 to 1995, followed by an RQE from 1995 to 2006—roughly at the efficiency level in 1995. A decline occurred from 2006 to 2010. This was then followed by a relatively stable period from 2011 to 2015. Kentucky registers a small improvement in its efficiency (0.13 points) between 1990 and 2015.

Figure 231. The efficiency scorecard for Kansas

KANSAS	$\psi_{1990} = (1.87)$	$\psi_{2015} = (1.84)$	$\Delta = 0.03$
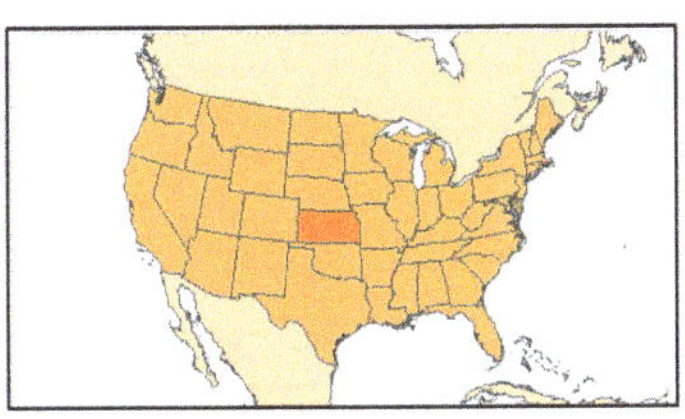	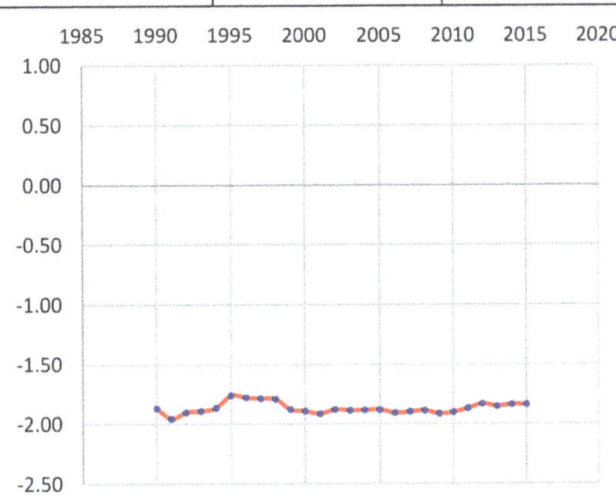		
GSP ranking (2015) = 31	Area ranking = 15	Major cities: Wichita, Overland Park, Kansas City, Olathe, Topeka	

Figure 232. The efficiency scorecard for Kentucky

<table>
<tr><td>KENTUCKY</td><td>$\psi_{1990} = (1.01)$</td><td>$\psi_{2015} = (0.88)$</td><td>$\Delta = 0.13$</td></tr>
<tr><td>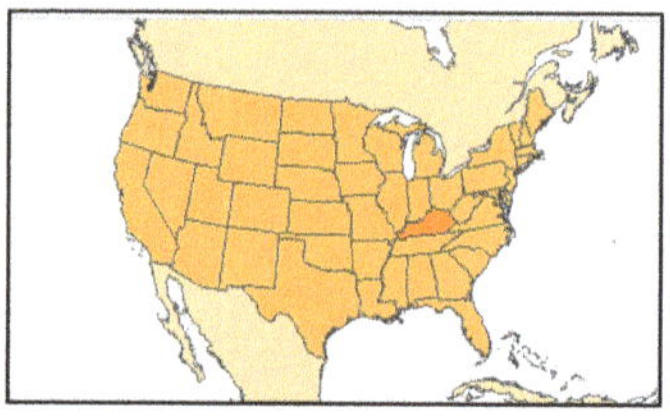</td><td colspan="3">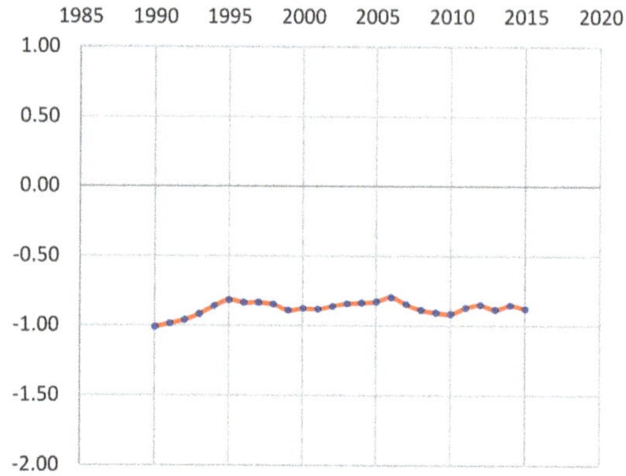
</td></tr>
<tr><td>GSP ranking (2015) = 28</td><td>Area ranking = 37</td><td colspan="2">Major cities: Louisville, Lexington, Bowling Green, Owensboro, Covington</td></tr>
</table>

In 2015, Kentucky had per-unit energy-equivalent area and population of 2.1E-03 and 4.4E-03. These inputs are more balanced than for other states. Its per-unit energy-equivalent GSP output was 2.7E-03, with a residual of negative 3.8E-03. The same year, the State had a GSP ranking higher than its area ranking. The State has an area ranking of 37 (104,659 square kilometers) which makes it a relatively small state. It also had a population density of 43 per square kilometer (in 2015). However, with no global cities, Kentucky is unable to move to economic efficiency.

Louisiana is a second-tier state with a relatively stable efficiency level around $\psi = -1.0$. After a 2007 dip in efficiency (in the aftermath of the 2005 Hurricane Katrina), the State exhibits an improvement from 2008 to 2012, and then a mild decline to 2015. Overall, the State shows an efficiency increase of 0.3 points between 1990 and 2015.

In 2015, Louisiana had a per-unit energy-equivalent of 4.8E-03 (people) and 3.6E-03 (area). Its GSP equivalent was 3.8E-03, with a residual of negative 4.9E-03. The State had a GSP ranking higher than its area ranking and had a population density of 42 per square kilometer (similar to Kentucky).

In 2012, the GaWC global city ranking identified New Orleans as a 'sufficiency' city. In other words, New Orleans shows a level of sufficiency in services (such as accountancy, advertising, banking, and law) so as not

Figure 233. The efficiency scorecard for Louisiana

LOUISIANA	$\psi_{1990} = (1.10)$	$\psi_{2015} = (0.80)$	$\Delta = 0.30$
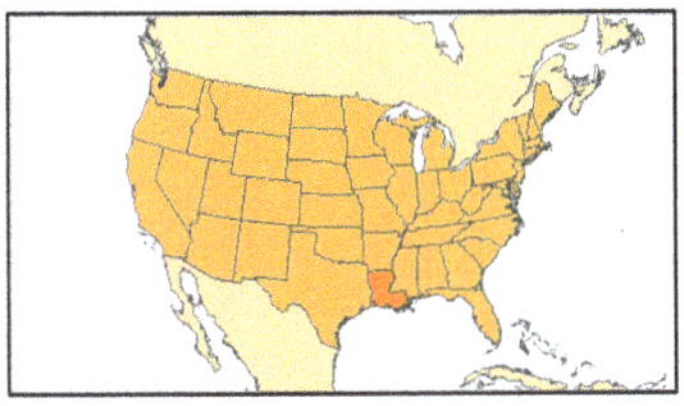	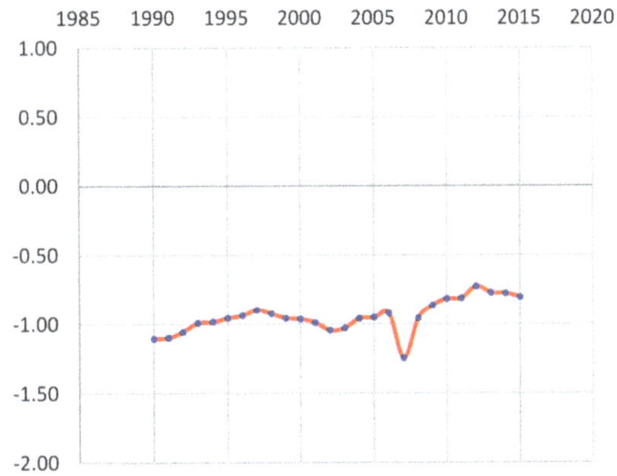		
GSP ranking (2015) = 24	Area ranking = 31	Major cities: New Orleans, Baton Rouge, Shreveport, Metairie, Lafayette	

to be *overly* dependent on world cities (Taylor, 2001). For New Orleans to move into a global ranking, it will have to get, first into 'high sufficiency,' and later into 'Gamma' rankings. Achieving this ranking would see the State lifted into a higher efficiency level.

Maine is a second-tier state that is part of the New England region but is not one of the original states. It voted to secede from Massachusetts in 1820. The State exhibits a stable efficiency signature, although within a negative efficiency band. Maine shed 0.16 efficiency points between 1990 and 2015.

In 2015, Maine has an area equivalent of 1.7E-03 and a population equivalent of 4.0E-04. The 2015 GSP equivalent was 3.2E-04, with a residual of negative 1.7E-03. Maine has an area of 91,646 square kilometers and a low population density (17 per square kilometer). Its GSP ranking in 2015 was higher than its area ranking.

Maine has no global cities.

Maryland is one of only five states with a positive efficiency signature throughout the observation period. From 2000 to 2008, the State exhibited strong efficiency growth. After the GFC, the State seems to settle at an RQE of $\psi = 0.30$.

In 2015, the State had a population equivalent of 8.0E-03 and an area equivalent of 2.0E-04. Its GSP equivalent was 1.1E-02, with a residual of

Figure 234. The efficiency scorecard for Maine

MAINE	$\psi_{1990} = (1.71)$	$\psi_{2015} = (1.87)$	$\Delta = (0.16)$
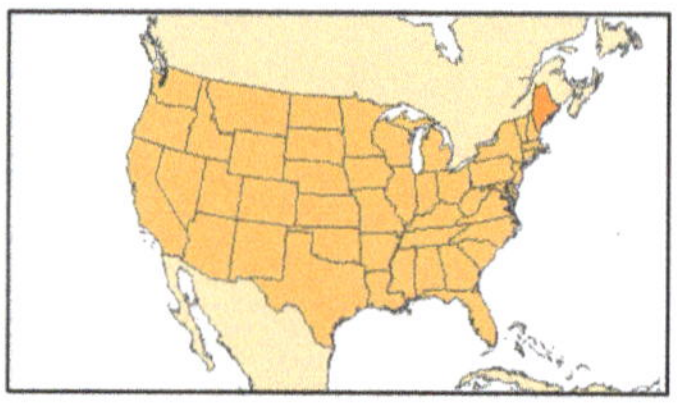	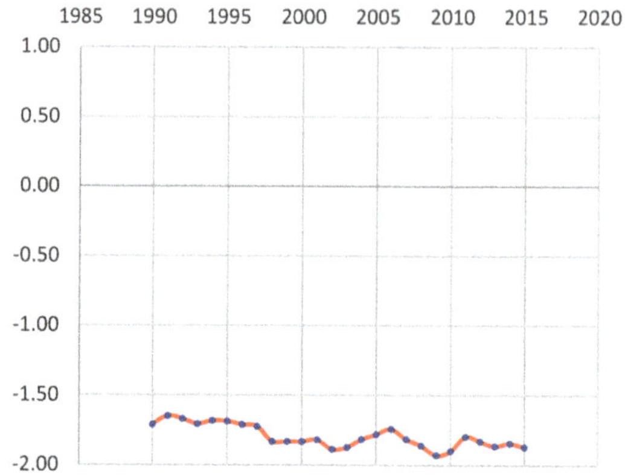		
GSP ranking (2015) = 44	Area ranking = 39	Major cities: Portland, Lewiston, Bangor, South Portland, Auburn	

positive 3.0E-03. Maryland's area is 32,133 square kilometers, twice the size of that of Connecticut. Maryland had a 2015 GSP ranking much higher than the area ranking. It has a Gamma + city (Baltimore) and a large population density (239 per square kilometer), although lower than that of Connecticut (285 per kilometer).

With only one global city, Maryland was able to achieve a positive level of efficiency. Baltimore is in fact one of 41 independent cities in the United States (i.e. cities that are not part of any county).

Massachusetts is another state with a positive efficiency signature throughout the whole observation period. It has a similar signature to that of Maryland in that it moves from a lower to a higher efficiency level towards the end of the period. In the case of Massachusetts, the transition occurs between 1997 and 2002 and resulted in a net gain of 0.08 points. This transition seems to have been triggered by NAFTA and the WTO. In Maryland, the transition occurred between 2001 and 2007 and resulted in a net gain of 0.11 points. Massachusetts has been able to maintain an RQE of $\psi = 0.40$ from 2002 to 2015.

In 2015, the State had a population equivalent of 1.00E-2, an area equivalent of 1.50E-04, and a GSP equivalent of 1.5E-02. The resulting residual was 5.3E-03. The State had a GSP ranking (12th) much higher than its area ranking

Figure 235. The efficiency scorecard for Maryland

MARYLAND	$\psi_{1990} = 0.18$	$\psi_{2015} = 0.31$	$\Delta = 0.11$
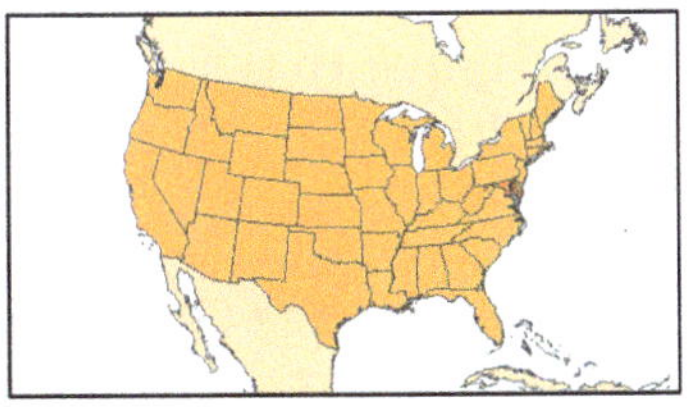	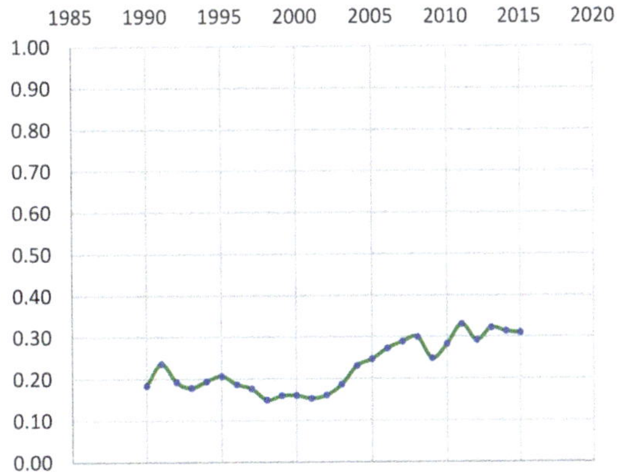		
GSP ranking (2015) = 15	Area ranking = 42	Major cities: **Baltimore** (Gamma +), Columbia, Germantown, Silver Spring, Frederick	

Figure 236. The efficiency scorecard for Massachusetts

MASSACHUSETTS	$\psi_{1990} = 0.33$	$\psi_{2015} = 0.42$	$\Delta = 0.08$
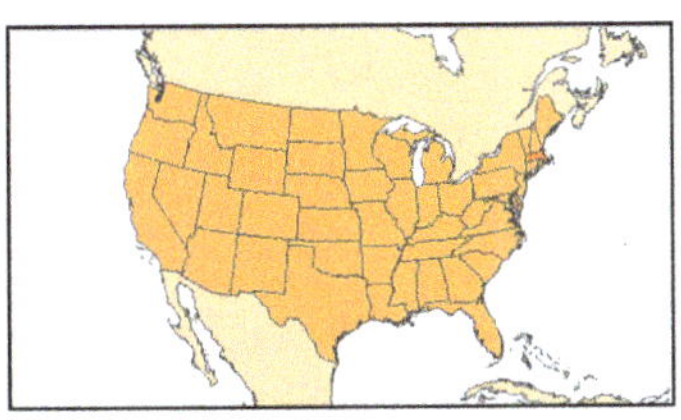	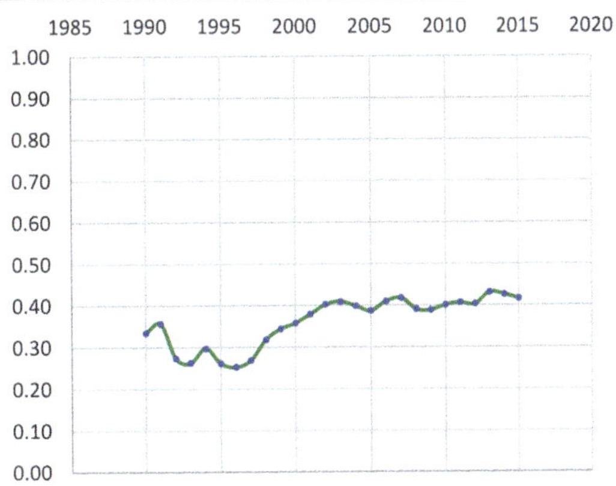		
GSP ranking (2015) = 12	Area ranking = 44	Major cities: **Boston** (Alpha –), Worcester, Springfield, Lowell, Cambridge	

(44th). With an area of 27,336 square kilometers and a population density of 324 per square kilometer, Massachusetts is twice the size of Connecticut (14,357 square kilometers) and has a higher population density (compared to 285 per square kilometer for Connecticut).

Given that Massachusetts has a jurisdictional footprint at the scale of a global city (such as New York), it was able to achieve economic efficiency with one Alpha – city. The State can increase its efficiency substantially if it can boost Boston's ranking into an Alpha ++ city similar to that of New York City (NYC). Boston has an area just under 12,000 square kilometers, one-third that of NYC, and a population density of around 5,344 per square kilometer (compared to 10,831 per square kilometer in NYC). As an Alpha – city, Boston can link major economic regions into the world-economy. To reach an Alpha ++ status, it will have to become more integrated with the world-economy. This does not necessarily mean increased size and density—London achieved this status with less than 10,000 square kilometers and a density similar to that of Boston. What is needed, however, is more integration of services such as accountancy and banking into the world-economy.

Michigan, a second-tier state, shed 0.49 efficiency points during the observation period. NAFTA and the WTO seem to have lowered its efficiency from $\psi = -0.23$ to $\psi = -0.49$. The State entered into an RQE from 2000 to

Figure 237. The efficiency scorecard for Michigan

MICHIGAN	$\psi_{1990} = (0.28)$	$\psi_{2015} = (0.76)$	$\Delta = (0.49)$
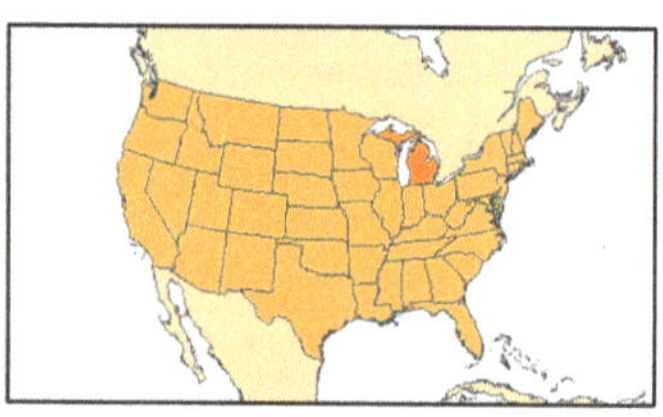	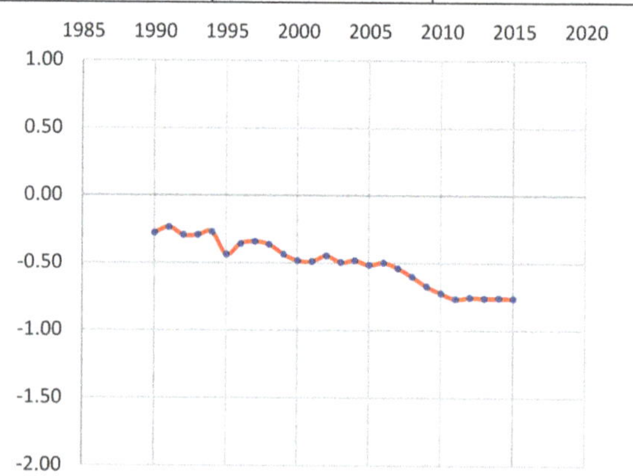		
GSP ranking (2015) = 13	Area ranking = 11	Major cities: **Detroit (Beta –)**, Grand Rapids, Warren, Sterling Heights, Ann Arbor	

2006, but lost another 0.25 efficiency points from 2006 to 2011. It ends the observation period with a lower RQE from 2011 to 2015.

While the State has a GSP ranking (13th) similar to its area ranking (11th), it is unable to (positive) achieve economic efficiency. In 2015, the State had a population equivalent of 2.2E-02 and an area equivalent of 1.2E-02. Its GSP equivalent was 1.6E-02, and its residual was negative 1.8E-02.

Michigan has a significant jurisdictional footprint (250,493 square kilometers), and a low population density of 67 per square kilometer. While it has a Beta – city (Detroit), this attractor on its own is not able to absorb enough capital to achieve efficiency. Michigan needs to add at least one more attractor as well as improving the ranking of Detroit.

Minnesota is a second-tier state with a negative efficiency signature. It shows some improvement over the observation period (0.17 points), mainly due to the introduction of NAFTA and the WTO in 1994-1995. After an RQE from 1990 to 1994, the State moves to a higher RQE around $\psi = -0.80$.

In 2015, Minnesota had a per-unit energy-equivalent population of 6.6E-03 and an area of 1.0E-02. Its GSP equivalent was 7.2E-03, and its residual was negative 9.5E-03. Minnesota's GSP and area ranking are relatively the same. The State area is 225,163 square kilometers, but its population density is only 27 per square kilometer. While it has one Beta – city, that city alone

Figure 238. The efficiency scorecard for Minnesota

MINNESOTA	ψ_{1990} = (1.01)	ψ_{2015} = (0.84)	Δ= 0.17
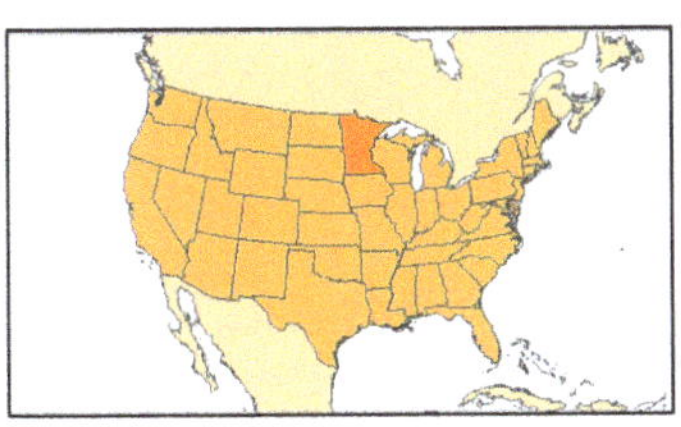	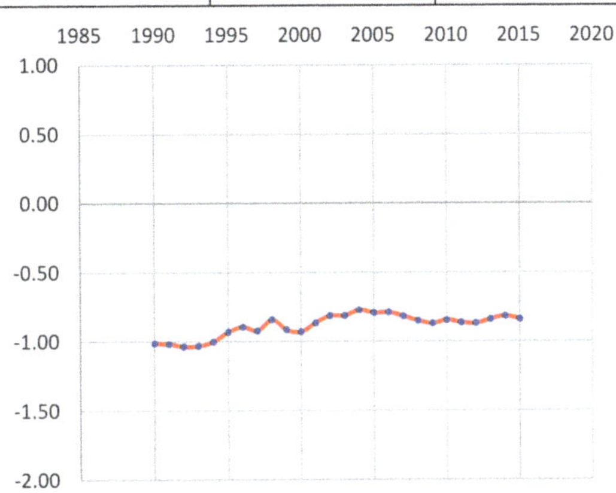		
GSP ranking (2015) = 16	Area ranking = 12	Major cities: **Minneapolis** (Beta –), Saint Paul, Rochester, Bloomington, Duluth	

is unable to absorb enough capital to generate economic efficiency. Note that Beta cities are those that link moderate regions into the world-system. For Minnesota to become a sink state, it will need to enhance the connectivity of Minneapolis to the world system, and by doing so be able to absorb more capital for its economic development.

It is useful to compare Minnesota to Maryland. Both States have one Beta city. Maryland, however, had a 2015 population density of 239 per square kilometer. Given Maryland's city-scale area (32,133 square kilometers), it can achieve efficiency with only one global city. In essence, Maryland as a whole is functioning as a global city. However, this is not the case in Minnesota, given its area. For Minnesota to operate as a network of global cities, it needs to have at least one more global city. A city such as Duluth would provide an ideal candidate for such development. The city forms a metropolitan area with Superior, Wisconsin (Twin Ports), which is the Great Lakes' largest harbor.

Mississippi, another second-tier state, exhibits an improvement in its efficiency score from 1990 to 1995. This improvement was arrested (potentially due to the introduction of NAFTA and the WTO) at a $\psi_{ceiling} = -1.50$. The State exhibits a stable RQE at this ceiling from 2011 to 2015.

Figure 239. The efficiency scorecard for Mississippi

MISSISSIPPI	$\psi_{1990} = (1.77)$	$\psi_{2015} = (1.51)$	$\Delta = 0.27$
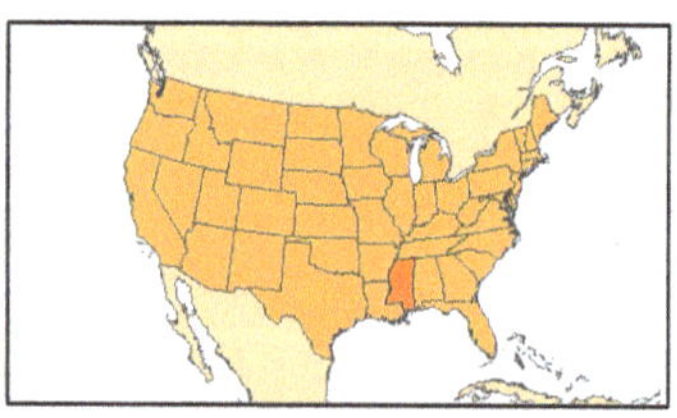	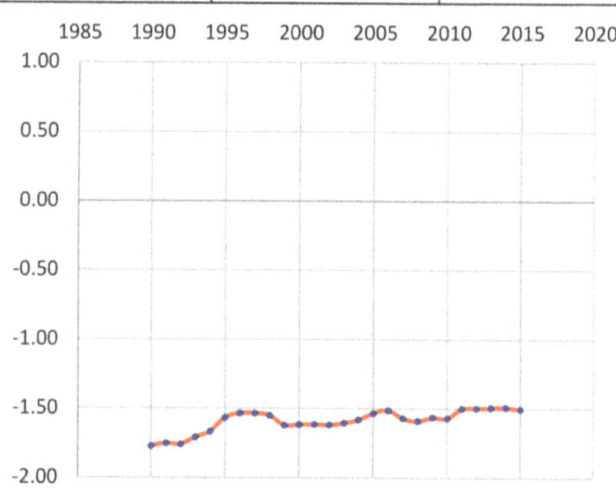		
GSP ranking (2015) = 36	Area ranking = 32	Major cities: Jackson, Gulfport, Southaven, Hattiesburg, Biloxi	

In 2015, Mississippi had a population equivalent of 2.0E-03 and an area equivalent of 3.1E-03. Its GSP equivalent was 1.1E-03, with a residual 4.0E-03. The State GSP and area rankings are similar. It has an area of 125,443 square kilometers but does not have any global cities.

Even though Missouri has two global cities, it exhibited a negative efficiency signature throughout the observation period. The State remained within a narrow ψ band, losing only 0.07 points between 1990 and 2015.

In 2015, the State had a population equivalent of 8.2E-03 and an area equivalent of 6.5E-03. The GSP equivalent was 6.2E-03, with a residual of 8.5E-03. The State's area is 180,533 square kilometers, and its population density is 34 per square kilometer. Its GSP and area rankings are similar. However, even with two Gamma cities, the State is unable to achieve efficiency.

While it has two global cities, one of which is an independent city (from any counties), Missouri is still unable to absorb enough capital to achieve (positive) efficiency. Having more than one Gamma city is not a guarantee of more efficiency. By definition, Gamma cities link smaller economic regions to the world-economy. Two Gamma cities do not produce an Alpha or even a Beta effect. For Missouri to move to positive efficiency, it needs to enhance the global status of its Gamma cities.

Figure 240. The efficiency scorecard for Missouri

<table>
<tr><td>MISSOURI</td><td>$\psi_{1990} = (0.79)$</td><td>$\psi_{2015} = (0.86)$</td><td>$\Delta = (0.07)$</td></tr>
<tr><td>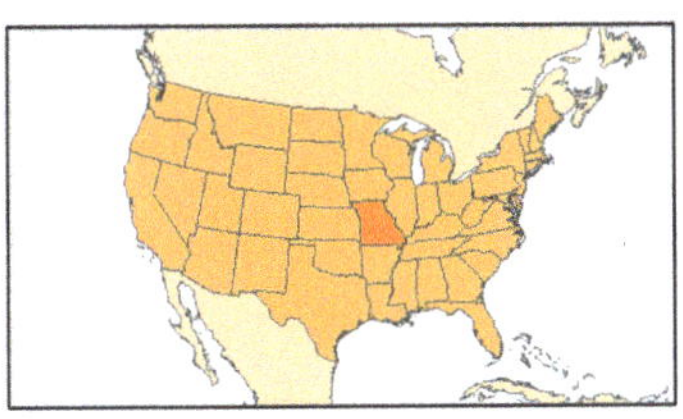</td><td colspan="3">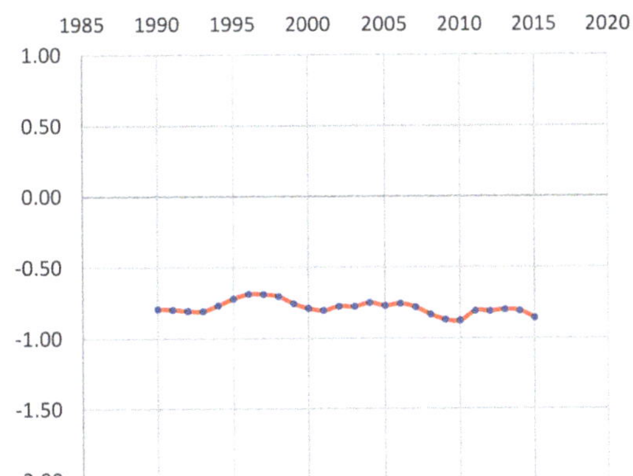
</td></tr>
<tr><td>GSP ranking (2015) = 22</td><td>Area ranking = 21</td><td colspan="2">Major cities: Kansas City (Gamma –), Saint Louis (Gamma +), Springfield, Independence, Columbia</td></tr>
</table>

It is important here to emphasize that the relationship between States and global cities is one of rhizomatic causation, of an 'intermezzo' that is independent of chronological structures. While many would see the evolution of global cities as an outcome of economic efficiency, the proposition is only part of the story. The strategic intent of creating global cities is in itself capable of inducing economic efficiency.

Montana is a third-tier state with a very a negative efficiency signature between $\psi_{floor} = -5.6$ and $\psi_{ceiling} = -5.00$. From 1990 to 2015, I have been able to improve its score by 0.41. From 2012 to 2015 it seems to settle into an RQE equal to -5.15.

The State had a 2015 population and area equivalents of 2.3E-04 and 2.9E-02. Its GSP equivalent was 1.7E-04, with a residual of negative 2.9E-02. The State has a vast area (380,000 square kilometers) with very low population density (2.7 per square kilometer). With no global cities, Montana is not only unable to achieve economic efficiency, but it exhibits a third-tier efficiency signature.

Nebraska is a third-tier state with an RQE of around $\psi = -2.50$. The State has been able to improve its efficiency by 0.22 points over the observation

Figure 241. The efficiency scorecard for Montana

<table>
<tr><td>MONTANA</td><td>$\psi_{1990} = (5.55)$</td><td>$\psi_{2015} = (5.14)$</td><td>$\Delta = 0.41$</td></tr>
<tr><td>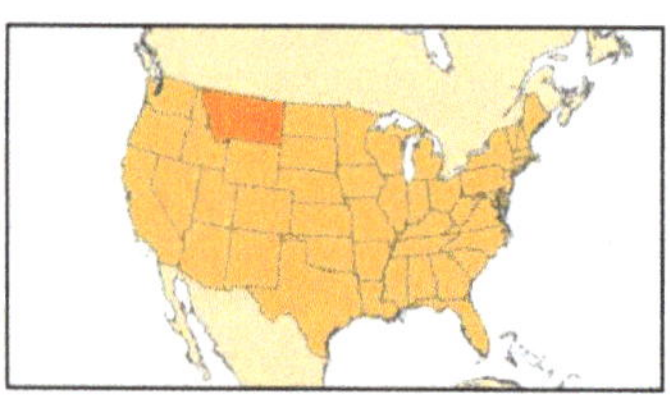</td><td colspan="3">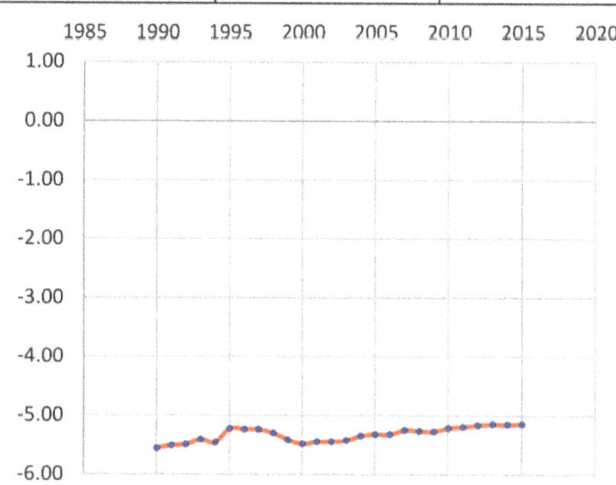
</td></tr>
<tr><td>GSP ranking (2015) = 47</td><td>Area ranking = 4</td><td colspan="2">Major cities: Billings, Missoula, Great Falls, Bozeman, Butte</td></tr>
</table>

Figure 242. The efficiency scorecard for Nebraska

NEBRASKA	ψ_{1990} = (2.62)	ψ_{2015} = (2.40)	Δ= 0.22
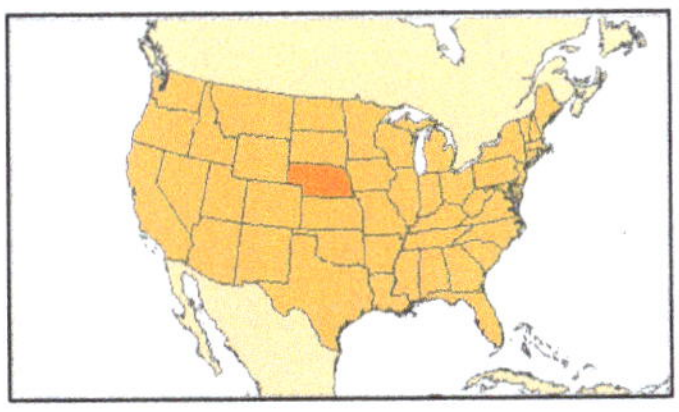	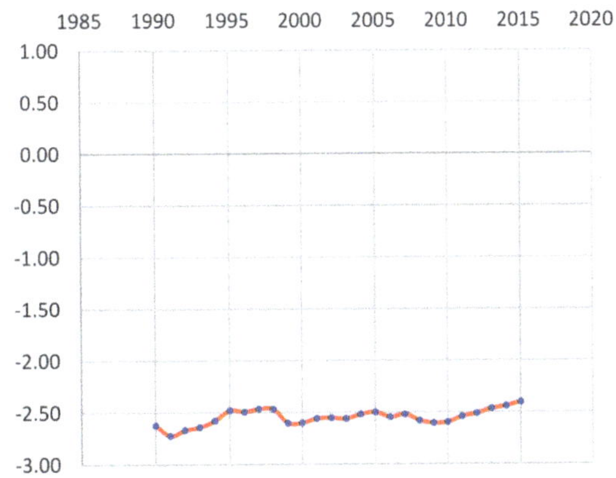		
GSP ranking (2015) = 35	Area ranking = 16	Major cities: Omaha, Lincoln, Bellevue, Grand Island, Kearney	

period. Its efficiency signature, however, does not indicate any positive trends, although there were positive gradients from 1991 to 1995 and from 2010 to 2015.

In 2015, Nebraska had a population and area equivalents of 7.9E-04 and 8.0E-03 respectively. Its GSP equivalent was 7.9E-04 with a residual of negative 7.9E-03 (discrepancy due to rounding).

In 2015, it had a GSP much lower than it area rank. Nebraska has an area of 200,360 square kilometers and a population density of 9.25 per square kilometer. With such a large jurisdictional footprint, low density, and no global cities, the State is unable to absorb enough capital to meet the ψ floor.

Nevada is another third-tier state. It, however, shows a clear positive trend from 1990 to 2009, with a gain of 1.45 points. After this period, the State's efficiency declined by 0.29 points——mainly due to the GFC.

In 2015, the State had a per-unit energy-equivalent population of 1.8E-03 and area of 1.6E-02. It had a GSP equivalent of 1.3E-03 and a residual of 1.7E-02. The State has no global cities, although Las Vegas is classified as a sufficiency city: it has a sufficient degree of services so that it is not dependent on global cities. Further improvement in Nevada's efficiency requires transforming Las Vegas into a global city.

Figure 243. The efficiency scorecard for Nevada

NEVADA	ψ_{1990} = (3.82)	ψ_{2015} = (2.66)	Δ = 1.16
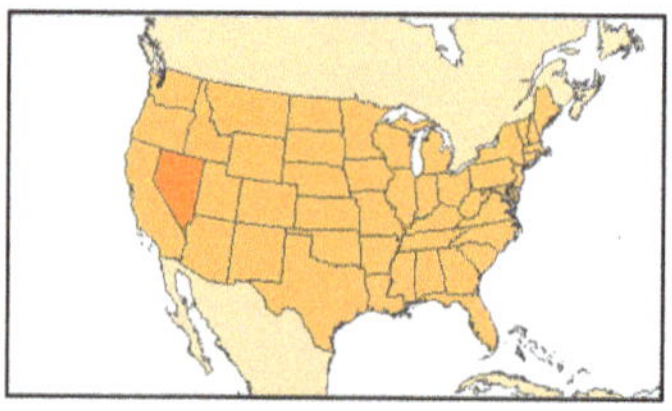	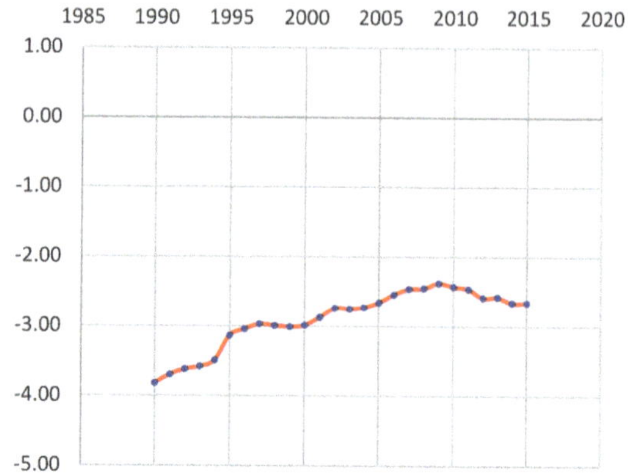		
GSP ranking (2015) = 33	Area ranking = 7	Major cities: Las Vegas, Henderson, Reno, North Las Vegas, Paradise	

New Hampshire is a tier-one state, and one of the thirteen original colonies. In fact, New Hampshire was the first state to establish its own constitution (in 1776). The State exhibits a stable level of efficiency around $\psi = 0.00$, although it is not smooth enough to think of it as an RQE.

The equivalent population and area in 2015 were 4.0E-04 and 1.2E-04 respectively. Its GDP for the same year was 4.7E-04, which resulted in a residual of negative 4.0E-05. The State has an area at the (global) city-scale (24,214 square kilometers) and a population density of 57 square kilometers. New Hampshire's area is similar to that of Massachusetts (27,336 square kilometers), although the latter has a density of 324 per square kilometer. Massachusetts also has Boston (Alpha–), while New Hampshire has no global cities. Even with its industrial clusters (Gurau, 2009), New Hampshire is not able to induce an economic efficiency like that of Massachusetts without a global city.

In terms of economic efficiency, New Jersey is ranked 4th. It is one of the original colonies and, just like New Hampshire, had its first constitution in 1776. It exhibits a relatively stable signature from 1990 to 2015, with a GSP ranking much higher than its area ranking.

Figure 244. The efficiency scorecard for New Hampshire

NEW HAMPSHIRE	$\psi_{1990} = (0.09)$	$\psi_{2015} = (0.08)$	$\Delta = 0.01$
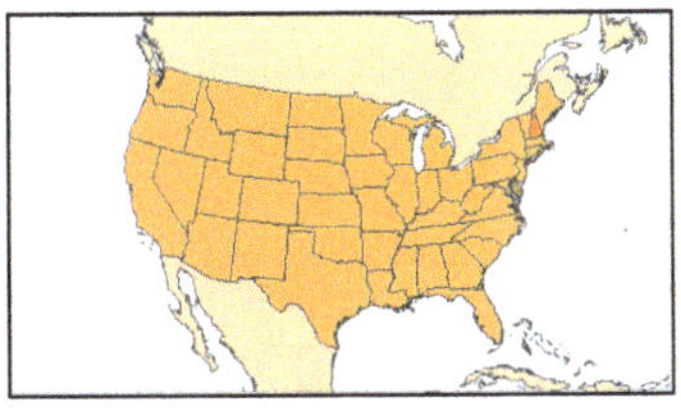	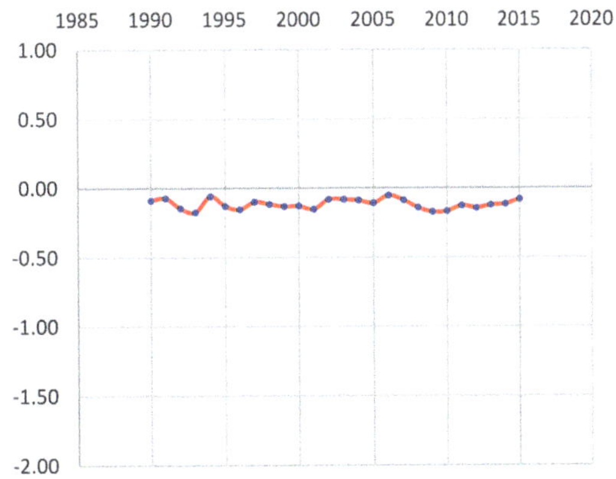		
GSP ranking (2015) = 39	Area ranking = 46	Major cities: Manchester, Nashua, Concord, Dover, Rochester	

Figure 245. The efficiency scorecard for New Jersey

NEW JERSEY	$\psi_{1990} = 0.45$	$\psi_{2015} = 0.39$	$\Delta = (0.06)$
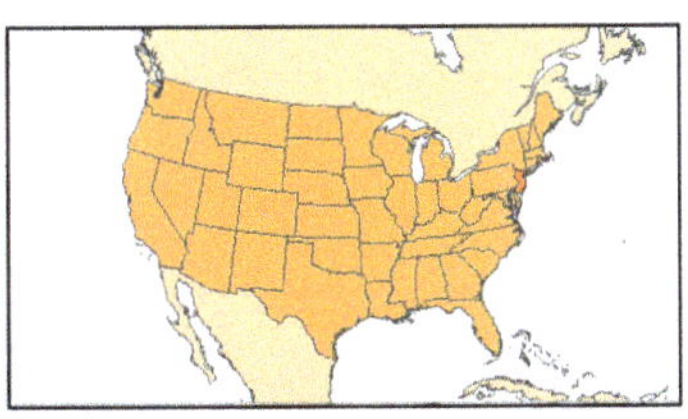	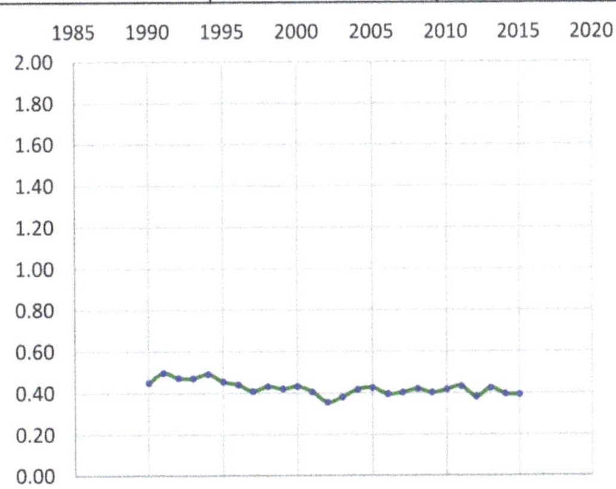		
GSP ranking (2015) = 8	Area ranking = 47	Major cities: Newark, Jersey City, Paterson, Elizabeth, Edison	

In 2015, New Jersey had a population equivalent of 1.8E-02 and an area equivalent of 1.0E-04. Its GSP equivalent was 2.7E-02, with a residual of 8.6E-03.

With an area of 22,591 square kilometers and a population density of 467 per square kilometer, New Jersey is similar to Massachusetts, except that it does not have any global cities. However, unlike New Hampshire, New Jersey was able to produce a level of efficiency similar to Massachusetts. To understand why, we need to recall that the State is 'sandwiched' between two global cities: Philadelphia (Beta +) and New York City (Alpha ++). Even though these global cities are not part of New Jersey, they are close enough to its borders to induce efficiency effects. Moreover, the State has key industry clusters that help it absorb enough capital for economic efficiency (NJLWD, 2010).

New Mexico is a third-tier state with a signature between $\psi_{floor} = -4.00$ and a $\psi_{ceiling} = -3.50$. It shows a weak positive gradient that resulted in an efficiency improvement of 0.46 points over the observation period. However, since 2010, the State seems to saturate its efficiency around $\psi = -3.45$.

New Mexico had 2015 population and area equivalents of 9.8E-04 and 2.0E-02 respectively. Its GSP for the same year was 6.1E-04, and its residual was negative 2.0E-02 (discrepancy due to rounding). The State has a population

Figure 246. The efficiency scorecard for New Mexico

NEW MEXICO	ψ_{1990} = (3.98)	ψ_{2015} = (3.52)	Δ = 0.46

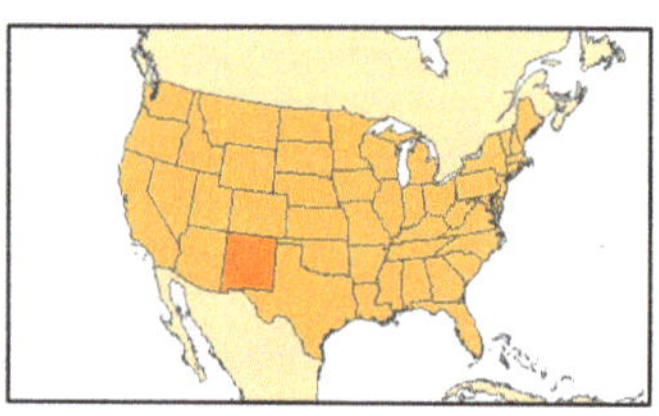

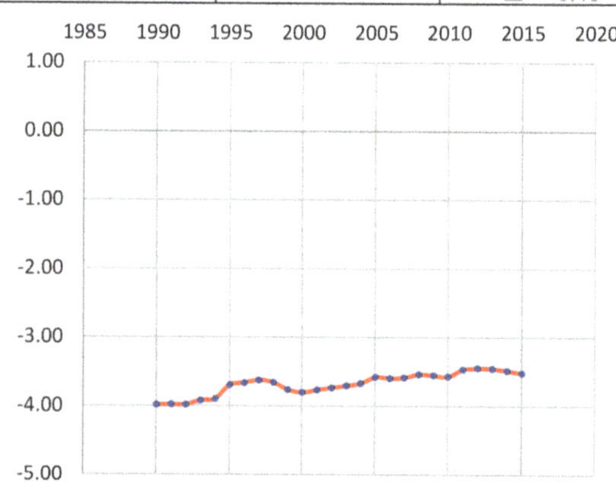

GSP ranking (2015) = 37	Area ranking = 5	Major cities: Albuquerque, Las Cruces, Rio Rancho, Santa Fe, Roswell

density of 7 per square kilometers over an area of 315,194 square kilometers. The State has no global cities, and without such cities, it is unable to achieve economic efficiency.

New York is a first-tier state and one of the original colonies. It shows an efficiency signature around $\psi = 0.20$, with a 0.11 increase between 1990 and 2015. The GFC seems to have improved the States efficiency from 0.20 to an RQE around 0.29.

In 2015, the State had an equivalent population and area of 8.7E-02 and 4.0E-03, respectively. The GSP for the same year was 1.2E-01, with a residual of 3.0E-02. The State's GSP ranking for this year was much higher than its area ranking. The State has an area of 141,300 square kilometers and a population density of 159 per square kilometer (2015 figure). With one Alpha ++ global city, the State can absorb enough capital to maintain economic efficiency.

North Carolina is a first-tier state. The State was one of the original states but shows a consistently negative efficiency signature. After a weak positive slope from 1990 to 1994, NAFTA and the WTO seem to have saturated the State's efficiency. From 1996 to 2015 the State shows an RQE of $\psi = -0.50$.

Figure 247. The efficiency scorecard for New York

NEW YORK	$\psi_{1990} = 0.17$	$\psi_{2015} = 0.28$	$\Delta = 0.11$
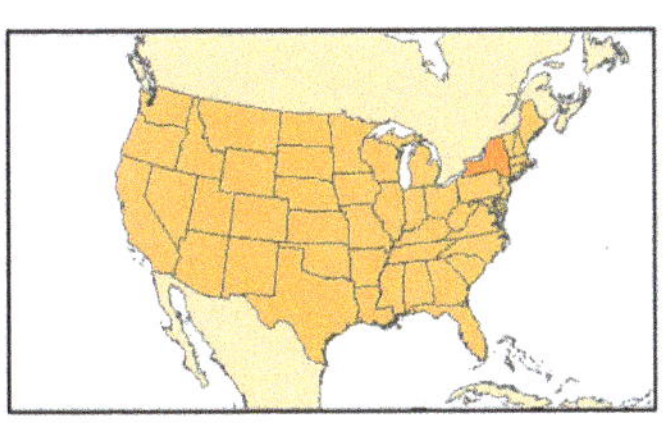	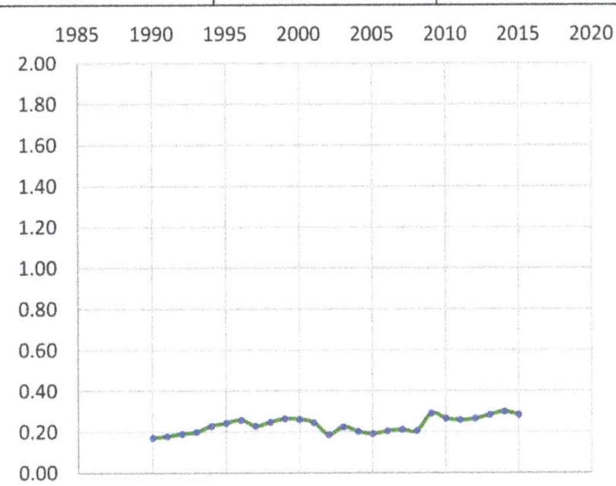		
GSP ranking (2015) = 3	Area ranking = 27	Major cities: **New York City** (Alpha ++), Oyster Bay, Buffalo, North Hempstead, Rochester	

Figure 248. The efficiency scorecard for North Carolina

<table>
<tr><td>NORTH CAROLINA</td><td>$\psi_{1990} = (0.66)$</td><td>$\psi_{2015} = (0.52)$</td><td>$\Delta = 0.14$</td></tr>
<tr><td>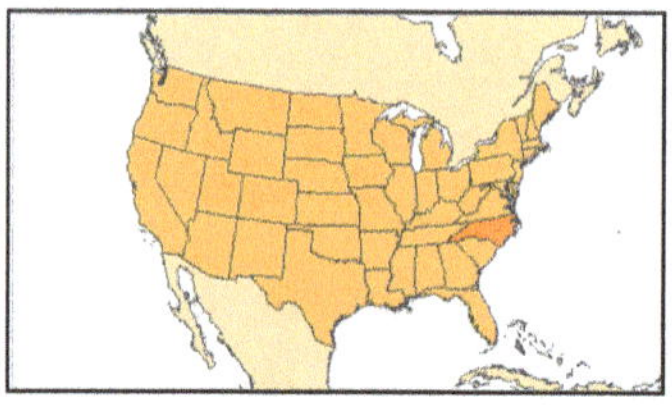</td><td colspan="3">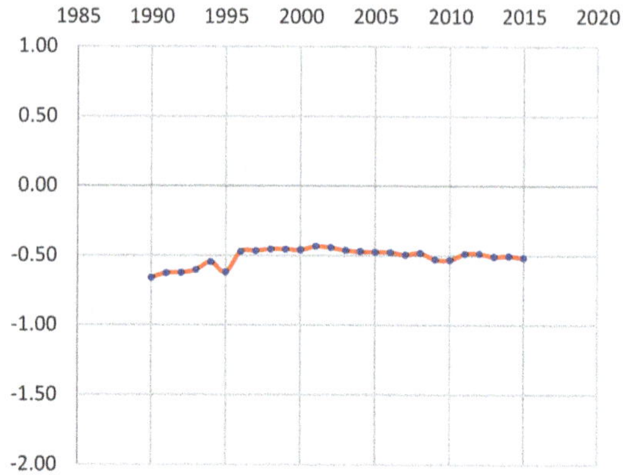</td></tr>
<tr><td>GSP ranking (2015) = 9</td><td>Area ranking = 28</td><td colspan="2">Major cities: Charlotte (Gamma +), Raleigh (Gamma), Greensboro, Durham, Winston-Salem</td></tr>
</table>

In 2015, the State has a GSP ranking much higher than its area ranking. It had a per-unit energy-equivalent population and area of 2.2E-02 and 3.9E-03 respectively. Its 2015 GSP was 1.5E-02, and residual of negative 1.0E-02.

Similar to Missouri (a second-tier state), North Carolina has two Gamma cities, and similar to Missouri these attractors are not enough to achieve economic efficiency. The State has an area of 139,390 square kilometers and a population density of 212 per square kilometer. Missouri is larger (180,533 square kilometers) but has a much lower density (34 per square kilometer). While the smaller jurisdictional footprint and the higher density were able to lift North Carolina to the second-tier, they are not enough to move the Sate to the first-tier. For that to happen, North Carolina will need stronger attractors. Its current global cities will need to go into an Alpha or Beta classification before North Carolina can move into a sink status.

North Dakota is a third-tier state. Its efficiency signature shows a relatively stable RQE from 1990 to 2009. This is followed by a positive trend from 2009 to 2015. The State registered a 0.86 increase in its ψ score from 1990 to 2015.

In 2015, North Dakota had a population equivalent of 1.2E-04 and an area equivalent of 6.6E-03. Its 2015 GSP was 1.8E-04, with a residual of negative 6.6E-03. The State's 2015 ranking was much lower than its area ranking.

Figure 249. The efficiency scorecard for North Dakota

<table>
<tr><td>NORTH DAKOTA</td><td>$\psi_{1990} = (4.47)$</td><td>$\psi_{2015} = (3.61)$</td><td>$\Delta = 0.86$</td></tr>
<tr><td>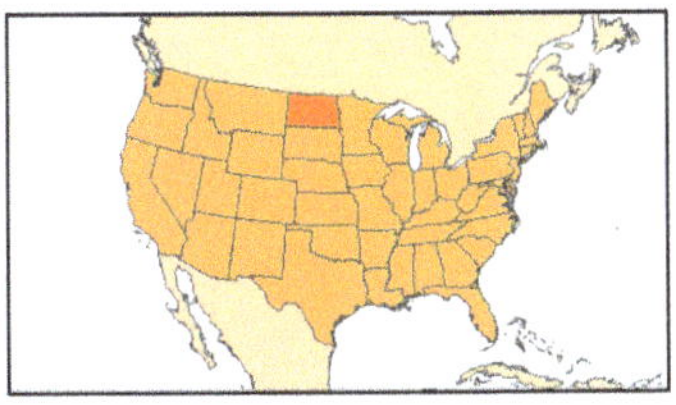</td><td colspan="3">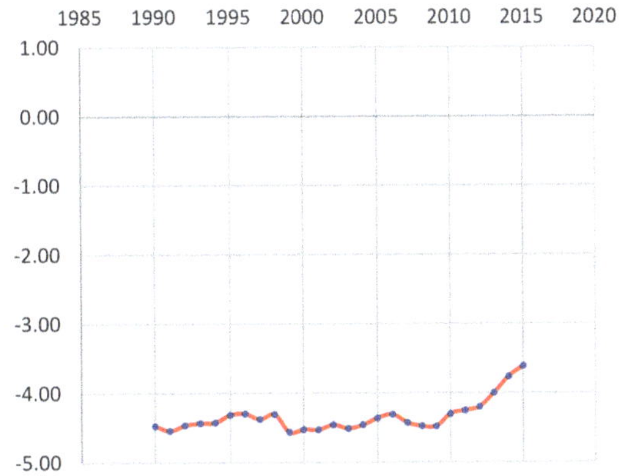
</td></tr>
<tr><td>GSP ranking (2015) = 46</td><td>Area ranking = 19</td><td colspan="2">Major cities: Fargo, Bismarck, Grand Forks, Minot, West Fargo</td></tr>
</table>

The State has an area of 183,108 square kilometers and a population density of 4 per square kilometer. It has no global cities.

Ohio's signature shows a relatively stable RQE at $\psi = 0.30$. The State's efficiency dropped due to NAFTA and the WTO, but recovered in 1996, and continued to register the same level of first-tier inefficiency.

The State has a 2015 GSP ranking much higher than its area ranking. Ohio had a population equivalent of 3.0E-02 and an area equivalent of 2.7E-03. Its GSP equivalent was 2.4E-02, with a residual of negative 9.0E-03.

While the State has three global cities, one Beta and two Gamma, it is still unable to obtain positive efficiency. It has an area of 116,096 square kilometers and a 2015 population density of 109 per square kilometer. However, even with three global cities, it is unable to break through the ψ floor. Ohio's footprint is over 80 percent of New York's (141,300 square kilometers), but its density is only two-thirds that of New York (159 per square kilometers). Unlike Ohio, New York has an Alpha ++ city, and with that city alone it is able to achieve a 0.20 efficiency. Having an Alpha city seems to be a necessary condition for efficiency where the jurisdictional footprint is at a scale greater than that of a global city (around 25,000 square kilometers).

Figure 250. The efficiency scorecard for Ohio

OHIO	$\psi_{1990} = (0.30)$	$\psi_{2015} = (0.32)$	$\Delta =$ (0.02)
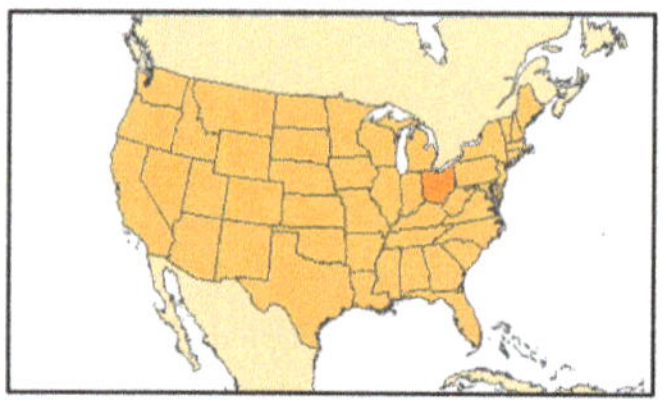	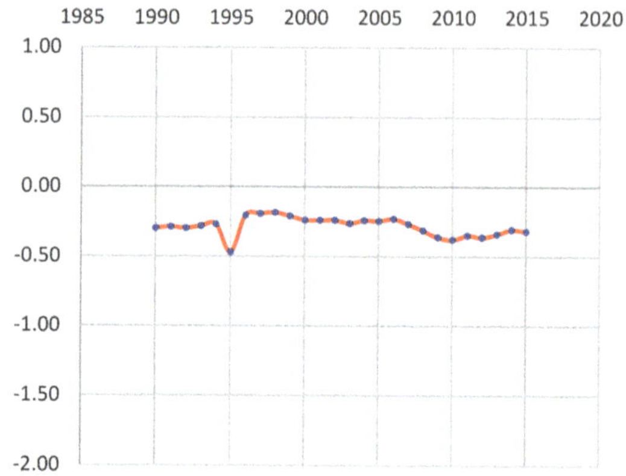		
GSP ranking (2015) = 7	Area ranking = 34	Major cities: **Columbus** (Gamma –), **Cleveland** (Beta –), **Cincinnati** (Gamma), Toledo, Akron	

Oklahoma is a second-tier state with an efficiency signature that registers an improvement from 2000 to 2015. The State ends the observation period with a gain of 0.33 points. The State seems to continue its positive trend as of 2015.

The State had a 2015 population equivalent of 3.3E-03 and an area equivalent of 6.5E-03. The GSP was 2.7E-03, with a residual of negative 7.1E-03. The State had a 2015 GSP ranking similar to its area ranking. It has an area of 181,295 and a 2015 population density of 21 per square kilometers.

Oklahoma does not have any global cities.

Oregon is a second-tier state that registers a stable ψ score from 1995 to 2015. After a positive trend from 1990 to 1995, after NAFTA and the WTO, the State has not been able to improve its score. The State has an area ranking much higher than the GSP ranking.

In 2015, the State had a population equivalent of 3.5E-03 and an area equivalent of 1.3E-02. The GSP for the same period was 2.7E-03, with a residual of negative 1.4E-02.

Oregon has an area of 254,806 square kilometers and a 2015 population density of 15 per square kilometers. It has only one Gamma city. For Oregon to be able to move to the first-tier, it will require elevating Portland to an Alpha city, and the creation of new global cities.

Figure 251. The efficiency scorecard for Oklahoma

OKLAHOMA	$\psi_{1990}=(1.60)$	$\psi_{2015}=(1.28)$	$\Delta=0.33$

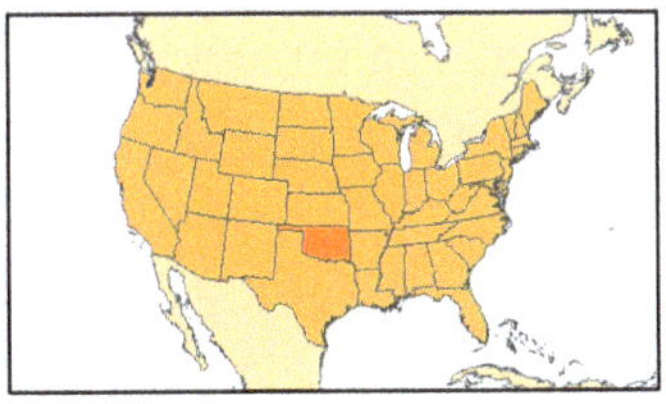

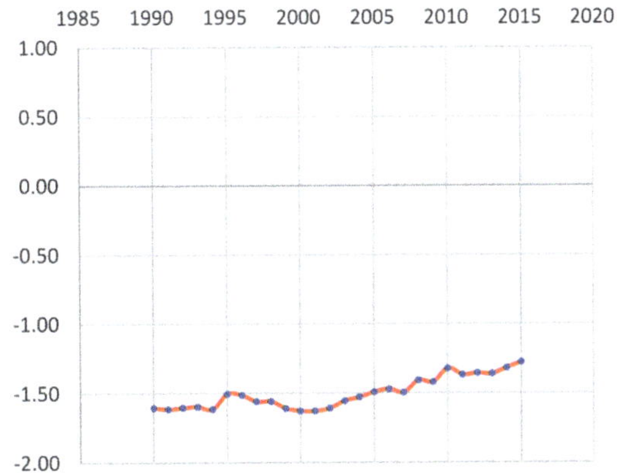

GSP ranking (2015) = 29	Area ranking = 20	Major cities: Oklahoma City, Tulsa, Norman, Broken Arrow, Lawton

Figure 252. The efficiency scorecard for Oregon

OREGON	$\psi_{1990}=(2.09)$	$\psi_{2015}=(1.81)$	$\Delta=0.28$

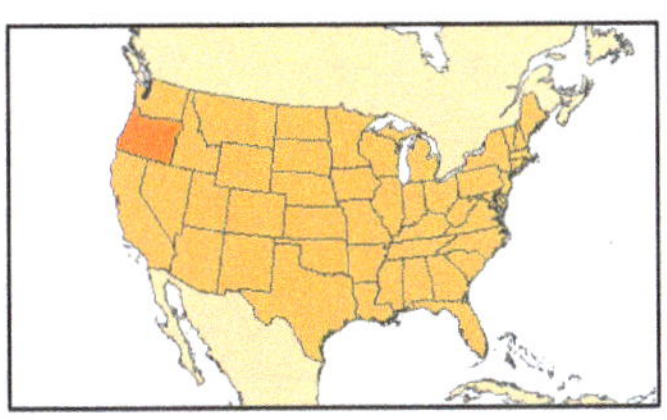

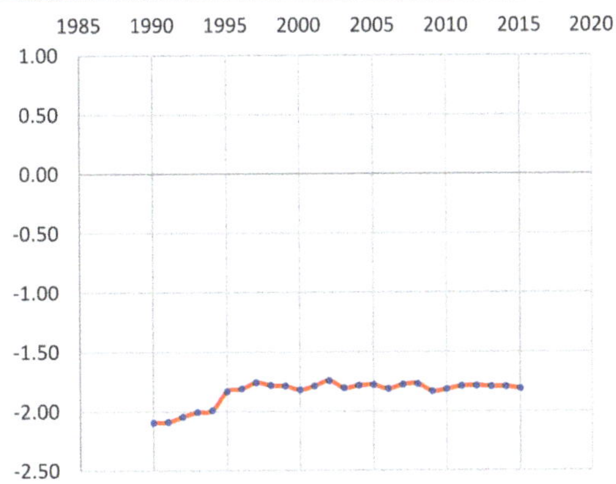

GSP ranking (2015) = 25	Area ranking = 9	Major cities: **Portland** (Gamma –), Salem, Eugene, Gresham, Hillsboro

Pennsylvania is a tier-one state, with a signature that approaches a $\psi_{ceiling} = 0.00$. The State shows a 0.14 increase in efficiency between 1990 and 2015. Given inevitable measurement noise, the State is able to meet the expected output by the ψ model.

In 2015, Pennsylvania had a population equivalent of 3.7E-02 and an area equivalent of 2.8E-03. The 2015 GSP was 3.7E-02, with a negative residual of 2.8E-03. Its 2015 GSP ranking was much higher than its area ranking. The State's area is 119,283 square kilometers, and its 2015 population density was 110 per square kilometer. Pennsylvania has one Beta city (Philadelphia), and one high-sufficiency city (Pittsburg). Pennsylvania was able to achieve 'neutral' efficiency.

Rhode Island is a first-tier state with no global cities, but one sufficiency city (Providence). It shows a consistent score at $\psi = 0.00$. From 1990 to 2015, the State shows a 0.12 point increase in efficiency. It has a GSP ranking slightly higher than its area ranking.

In 2015, the State had a per-unit energy-equivalent population of 2.5E-04 and an area of 3.2E-06. The GSP for that year was 2.6E-04, with a residual of 9.1E-06. The State has an area at the scale of a global city (3,144 square kilometers), and a population density of 388 per square kilometer (in

Figure 253. The efficiency scorecard for Pennsylvania

PENNSYLVANIA	$\psi_{1990} = (0.21)$	$\psi_{2015} = (0.07)$	$\Delta = 0.14$
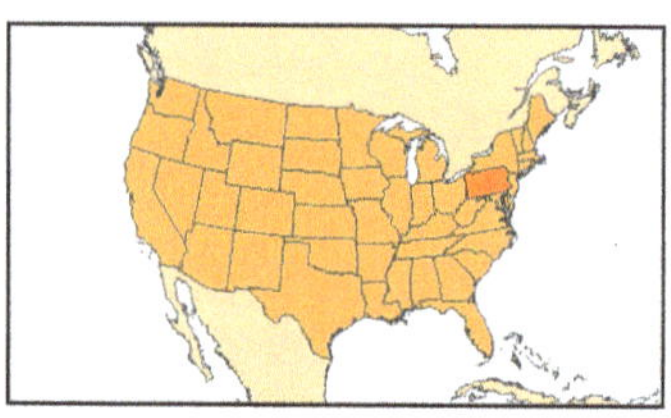	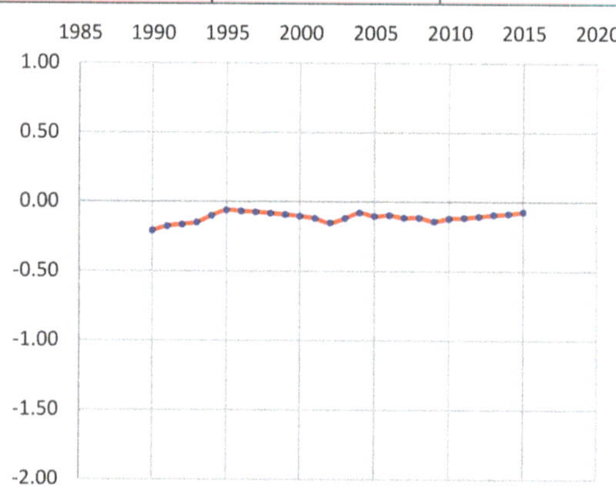		
GSP ranking (2015) = 6	Area ranking = 33	Major cities: **Philadelphia** (Beta +), Pittsburg, Allentown, Erie, Reading	

Figure 254. The efficiency scorecard for Rhode Island

RHODE ISLAND	ψ_{1990} = (0.08)	ψ_{2015} = 0.04	Δ = 0.12
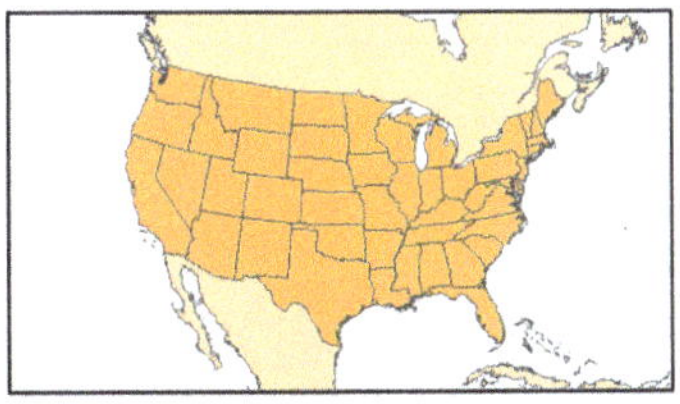	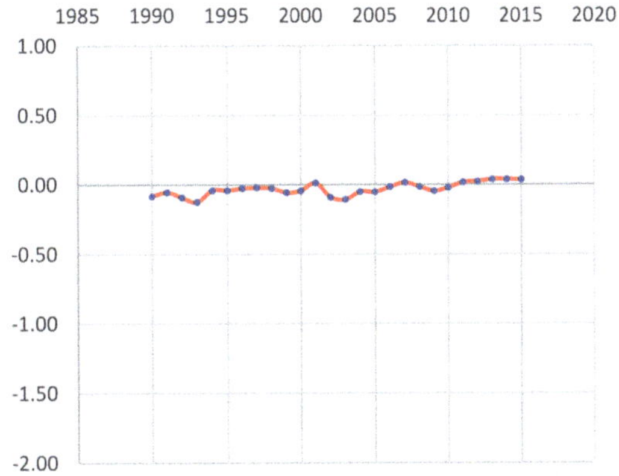		
GSP ranking (2015) = 43	Area ranking = 50	Major cities: Providence, Warwick, Cranston, Pawtucket, East Providence	

2015). This fact reemphasizes the point made earlier. When we start from a jurisdictional footprint smaller than the area of a global city, we can achieve efficiency without the need for global cities. Rhode Island is itself functioning as a global city. On the other hand, if we start from a jurisdictional footprint that is larger than the scale of a global city (New York City providing the benchmark at 25,000 square kilometers), we require Alpha global cities to achieve efficiency.

South Carolina, a second-tier state, was one of the original colonies, and the eighth state to ratify the US Constitution. It was also the first to secede in 1860, and be readmitted into the United States in 1868. The State has a negative efficiency signature throughout the observation period, with a GSP ranking higher than its area ranking. The State registers a gain of 0.15 points between 1990 and 2015.

In 2015, South Carolina had a population equivalent of 5.1E-03 and an area equivalent of 1.4E-03. The GSP for the same year was 3.1E-03, which resulted in a negative residual of 3.4E-03. The State has an area of 82,931 square kilometers and a 2015 population density of 60 per square kilometer.

With no global cities, and given its hyper-city jurisdictional footprint, South Carolina is unable to achieve economic efficiency.

Figure 255. The efficiency scorecard for South Carolina

SOUTH CAROLINA	$\psi_{1990} = (0.91)$	$\psi_{2015} = (0.75)$	$\Delta = 0.15$
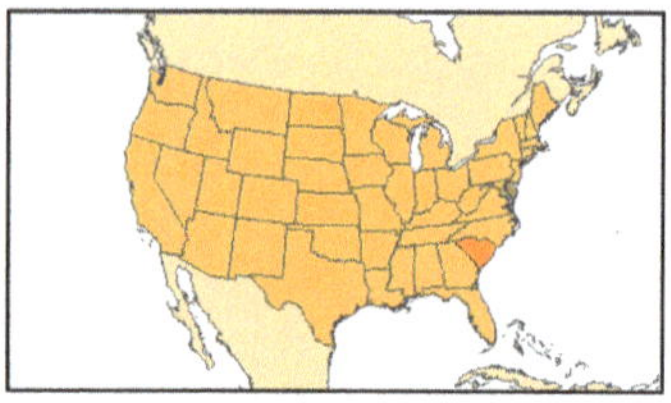	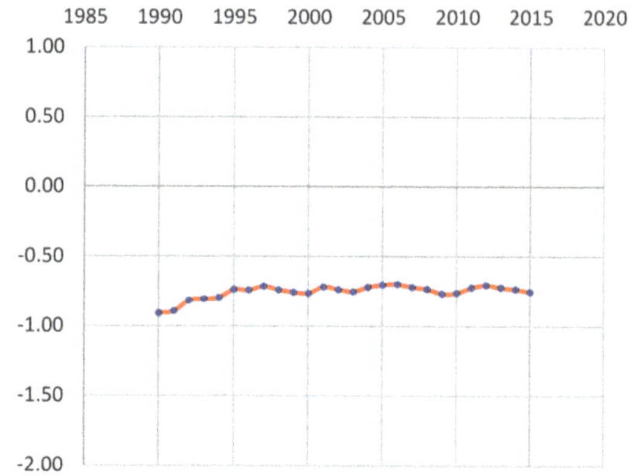		
GSP ranking (2015) = 27	Area ranking = 40	Major cities: Columbia, Charleston, North Charleston, Mount Pleasant, Rock Hill	

South Dakota is a third-tier state. It has a negative efficiency signature throughout the observation period. However, the State has gained 0.62 points between 1990 and 2015. The State has a positive gradient that seems to continue beyond 2015. Notwithstanding, the State is ranked 48th in terms of economic efficiency (see Chapter 5 Table 1).

In 2015, the State had a population and area equivalents of 1.6E-04 and 7.9E-03, and a GSP equivalent of 1.6E-04. The resulting negative residual was 7.9E-03. The State's GSP ranking is much lower than its area ranking.

The State has an area of 199,729 square kilometers, which is much larger than the (global) city-scale (25,000 square kilometers). Its population density is 4.3 per square kilometer.

South Dakota has no global cities.

Tennessee is a first-tier state, ranked 20th overall in terms of economic efficiency (see Chapter 5 Table 1). The State has an efficiency improvement from 1990 to 1995, followed by an RQE from 1996 to 2008 around $\psi = -0.50$. The GFC seems to have resulted in a dip in efficiency, followed by a slow recovery back to a ψ score of -0.50.

Figure 256. The efficiency scorecard for South Dakota

SOUTH DAKOTA	$\psi_{1990} = (4.55)$	$\psi_{2015} = (3.93)$	$\Delta = 0.62$
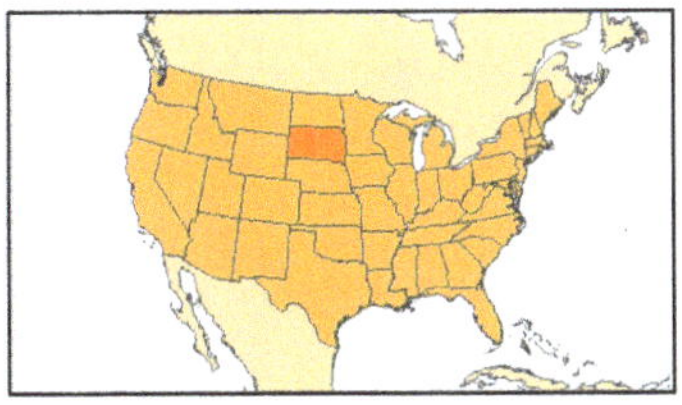	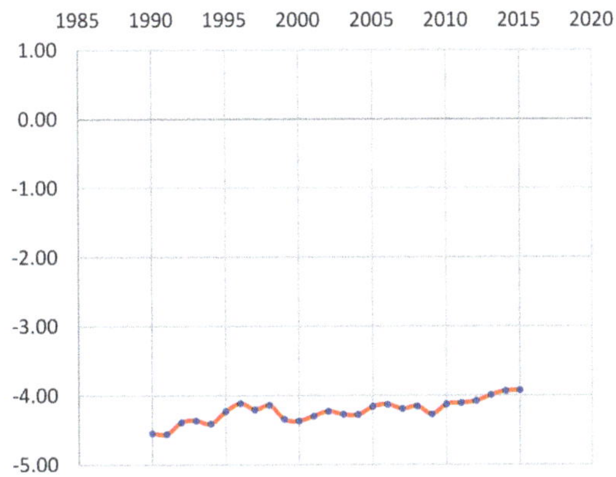		
GSP ranking (2015) = 48	Area ranking = 17	Major cities: Sioux Falls, Rapid City, Aberdeen, Brookings, Watertown	

Figure 257. The efficiency scorecard for Tennessee

TENNESSEE	$\psi_{1990} = (0.75)$	$\psi_{2015} = (0.53)$	$\Delta = 0.22$
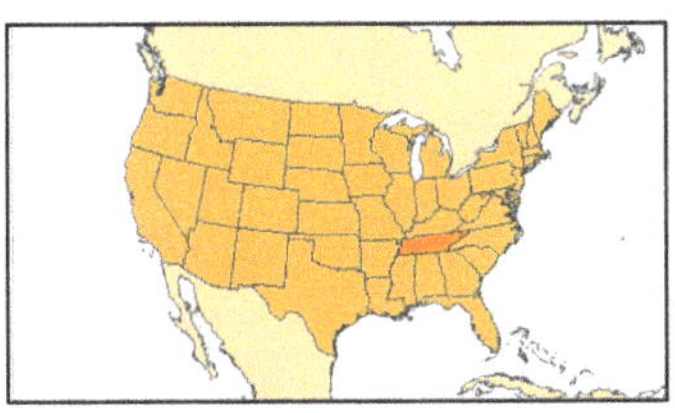	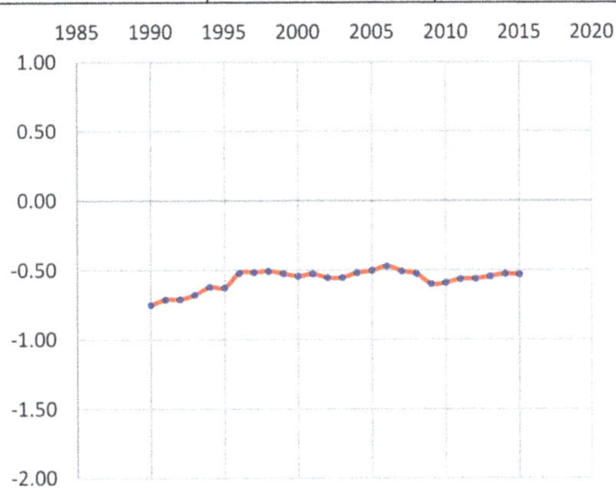		
GSP ranking (2015) = 20	Area ranking = 36	Major cities: Nashville, Memphis, Knoxville, Chattanooga, Clarksville	

The State registers a 2015 population equivalent of 9.5E-03 and an area equivalent of 2.4E-03. The GSP equivalent for the same year was 7.0E-03, with a residual of 4.9E-03. The State has a GSP ranking higher than its area ranking.

The State has an area of 109,247 square kilometers, and a population density of 61 per square kilometer (in 2015). Tennessee has no global cities, but one sufficiency city: Nashville. Given its hyper-city scale, the State needs to enhance Nashville's global status before it can achieve neutral efficiency.

Texas is a second-tier state, although ranked 22nd, just outside the first tier. The State exhibits a stellar improvement of its efficiency from 1990 to 2015: a gain of 0.47. The State has the same ranking on GSP and area.

The State had a 2015 population of 1.6E-01 (equivalent) and an area of 9.6E-02 (equivalent). The GSP equivalent was 1.4E-01 (equivalent), and the resulting residual was a negative 1.1E-01. The State has an area of 696,241 square kilometers and a 2015 population density of 40 per square kilometer.

Texas has two Beta global cities, one high-sufficiency city (Austin), and one sufficiency city (San Antonio). If it can boost the status of these cities, and given its current positive gradient, the State will be able to enter into positive efficiency within the next decade.

Figure 258. The efficiency scorecard for Texas

TEXAS	$\psi_{1990} = (1.05)$	$\psi_{2015} = (0.58)$	$\Delta = 0.47$
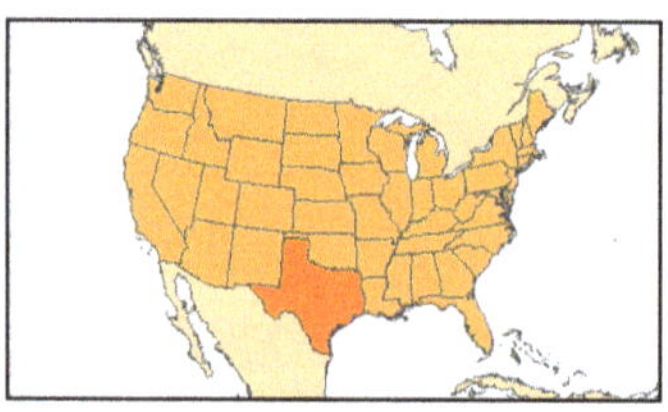	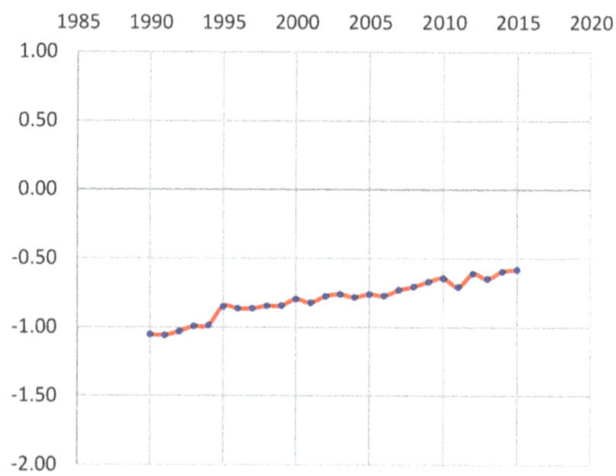		
GSP ranking (2015) = 2	Area ranking = 2	Major cities: **Houston** (Beta +), San Antonio, **Dallas** (Beta +), Austin, Forth Worth	

Utah is a third-tier state, ranked 42nd, just outside the second tier. Just like Texas, Utah shows a strong positive gradient throughout the observation period. In fact, Utah has been able to gain 0.89 points from 1990 to 2015. The State, however, still has a GSP ranking lower than its area ranking.

In 2015, Utah had the following per-unit energy-equivalents: population (1.9E-03), area (9.6E-03), and GSP (1.2E-03). The resulting residual was negative 1.0E-02. The State has an area of 219,653 square kilometers and a 2015 (population) density of 14 per square kilometer.

The State has no global cities, but one high-sufficiency city (Salt Lake City).

Vermont is a second-tier state, ranked 29th. The State shows little improvement in its negative efficiency signature during the observation period. The State's efficiency seems to oscillate around $\psi = -1.00$.

The State has a 2015 population equivalent of 8.9E-05, an area equivalent of 1.2E-04, a GSP equivalent of 8.8E-05, and a residual of negative 1.2E-04. The State has an area of 24,923 square kilometers (at the city-scale), and a (2015) population density of 26 per square kilometer.

Even with a city-scale jurisdictional footprint, the State does not achieve economic efficiency. Compared to Massachusetts, they have the same area, but Massachusetts has a density of 324 per square kilometer (2015). Massachusetts also has an Alpha – city (Boston). For Vermont, the limiting factor is its population.

Figure 259. The efficiency scorecard for Utah

UTAH	$\psi_{1990} = (3.16)$	$\psi_{2015} = (2.27)$	$\Delta = 0.89$
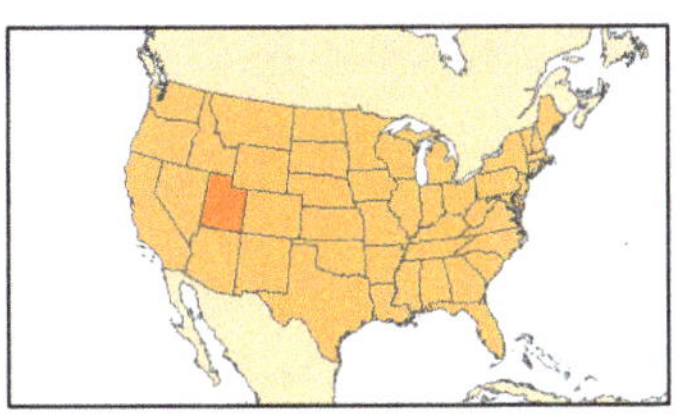	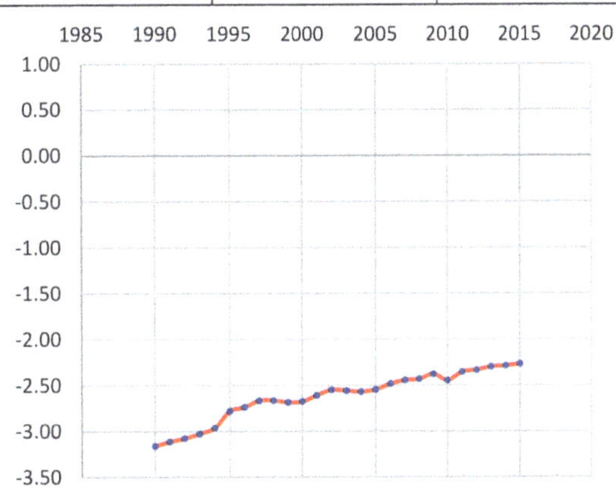		
GSP ranking (2015) = 32	Area ranking = 13	Major cities: Salt Lake City, West Valley City, Provo, West Jordan, Orem	

Figure 260. The efficiency scorecard for Vermont

<table>
<tr><td>VERMONT</td><td>$\psi_{1990} = (1.04)$</td><td>$\psi_{2015} = (0.88)$</td><td>$\Delta = 0.17$</td></tr>
<tr><td>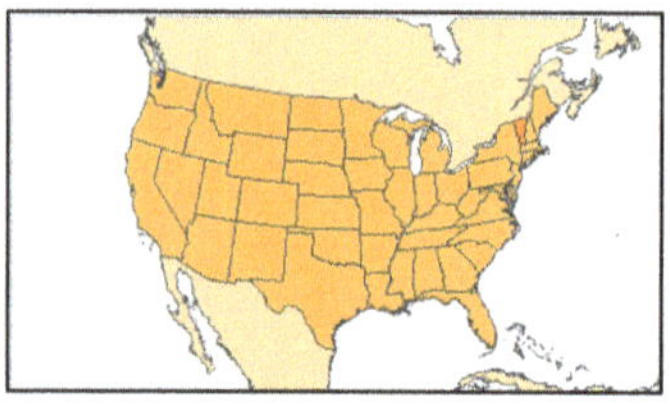</td><td colspan="3">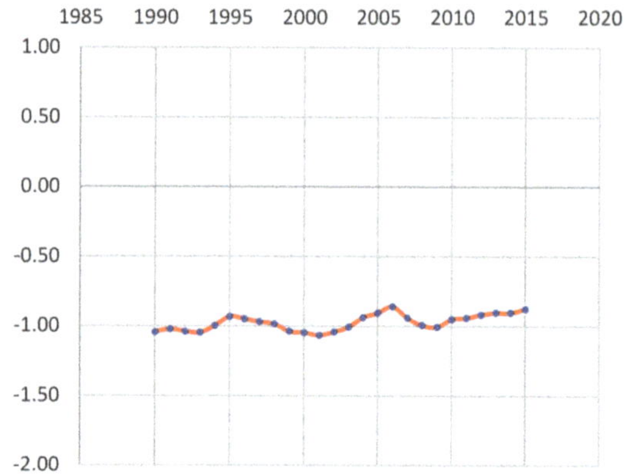
</td></tr>
<tr><td>GSP ranking (2015) = 50</td><td>Area ranking = 45</td><td colspan="2">Major cities: Burlington, Essex, South Burlington, Colchester, Rutland</td></tr>
</table>

Virginia is a first-tier state, and one of the (thirteen) original colonies. During the observation period, the State was able to achieve positive efficiency. It gained a total of 0.12 points from 1990 to 2015. Since 2011, the State has been able to achieve an RQE of $\psi = 0.00$. Except for a dip in efficiency in 1991 (due to a national recession) (Knapp, 1999), the State was able to maintain an RQE of $\psi = 0.15$ from 1992 to 2001. This RQE was followed by an increase of efficiency from 2002 to 2007. The GFC had a negative impact in 2008 and 2009.

In 2015, the State had a per-unit energy-equivalent population of 1.5E-02 and an area of 2.4E-03. Its 2015 GSP equivalent was 1.7E-02, with a residual of negative 4.4E-04. Virginia has a hyper-global city area of 110,785 square kilometers and a population density of 80 per square kilometer. Its 2015 GSP ranking was much higher than its area ranking.

The State has a high-efficiency city (Richmond), and many private-sector industry clusters (Slaper, Harmon, & Rubin, 2016). These attractors were able to elevate the State to neutral efficiency. Similar to Tennessee, Virginia can move to an efficiency level similar to that seen, for example, in New York $\left(\psi_{2015} = 0.28\right)$, if it improves the global status of Richmond. If Virginia can make Richmond a Gamma city within the next decade, it can potentially move into a sink status.

Figure 261. The efficiency scorecard for Virginia

VIRGINIA	$\psi_{1990} = (0.15)$	$\psi_{2015} = (0.05)$	$\Delta = 0.12$
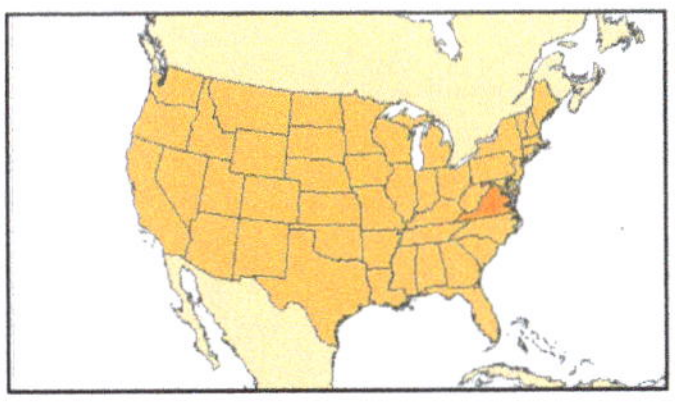	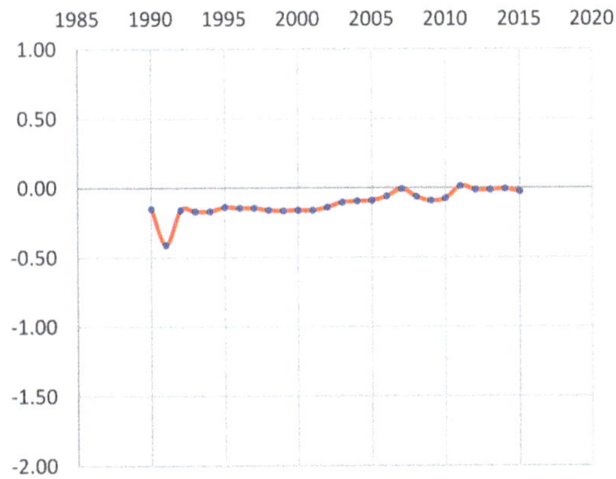		
GSP ranking (2015) = 11	Area ranking = 35	Major cities: Virginia Beach, Norfolk, Chesapeake, Richmond, Arlington	

Washington is a first-tier state, ranked 17th overall (see Chapter 5 Table 1). During the observation period (from 1990 to 2015), the State shows an improvement in efficiency from 1990 to 1995, followed by an RQE from 1995 to 2005. After the GFC, the State had a minor increase in efficiency that seems to saturate at an RQE of 0.42. Between 1990 and 2015, the State increased its efficiency by 0.30 points. Nevertheless, Washington's efficiency signature is always below zero.

Washington had a 2015 population equivalent of 1.1E-02 and an area equivalent of 6.8E-03. Its 2015 GSP was 1.2E-02, which resulted in a residual of 6.2E-03. The State has an area of 184,827 square kilometers and a 2015 population density of 40 per square kilometer. Washington has a hyper-global city area similar to that of North Dakota (183,108 square kilometers) but has a much higher population density (compared to North Dakota's 4 per square kilometer).

The difference between North Dakota and Washington is that the latter has a Beta – city: Seattle. It is not only the higher population density that makes Washington a first-tier state. It is having that higher population density organized into global cities. Out of a total population over seven million, more than half lived in metropolitan Seattle (in 2015). The city (proper) has a density of over 3,000 per square kilometer. It is the ability of states to

Figure 262. The efficiency scorecard for Washington

WASHINGTON	$\psi_{1990} = (0.73)$	$\psi_{2015} = (0.43)$	$\Delta = 0.30$
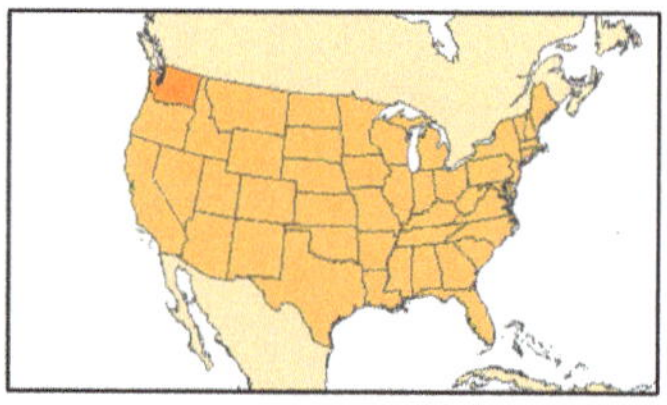	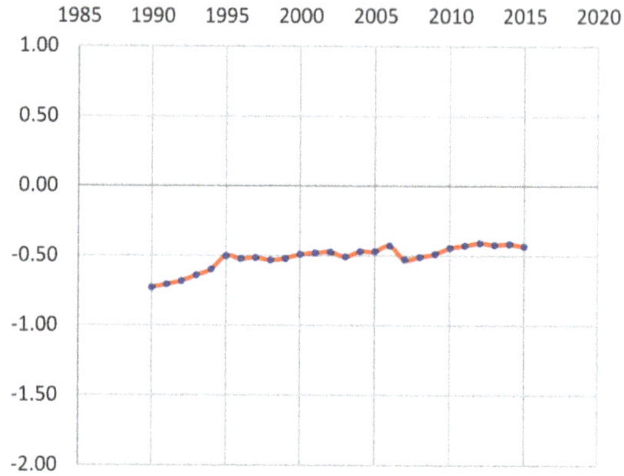		
GSP ranking (2015) = 14	Area ranking = 18	Major cities: **Seattle** (Beta –), Spokane, Tacoma, Vancouver, Bellevue	

generate such high density in global cities that absorbs (and accumulates) capital. However, even for Washington, moving into a sink status $(\psi > 0)$ will require more than just a Beta city.

West Virginia is ranked 34th in terms of economic efficiency (second-tier). Its efficiency signature shows an improvement at the beginning of the observation period (from 1990 to 1995), followed by a 'hump' from 1995 to 1997, and a return to its previous efficiency level. Since 2010, the State has an RQE of $\psi = -1.17$. Overall, the State was able to improve its efficiency by 0.12 points.

In 2015, West Virginia had a population and area equivalents of 7.8E-04 (each). Its GSP for the same year was 4.7E-04, which give a negative residual of 1.1E-03. Its 2015 GSP is almost equal to its area ranking. The State has an area of 62,755 square kilometers and a 2015 population density of 30 per square kilometer.

The State has no global cities.

Wisconsin is a second-tier state, ranked 23rd overall (see Chapter 5 Table 1). The State exhibits a minimal change in its ψ score between 1990 and 2015. Its efficiency signature is 'choppy,' but continues to live in a narrow band around $\psi = -0.65$.

Figure 263. The efficiency scorecard for West Virginia

WEST VIRGINIA	ψ_{1990} = (1.32)	ψ_{2015} = (1.20)	Δ = 0.12

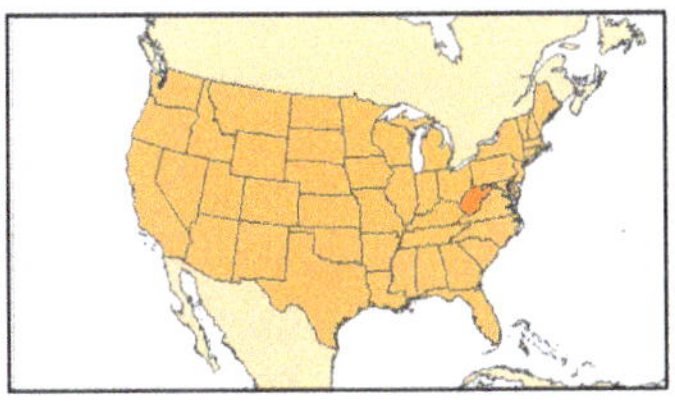
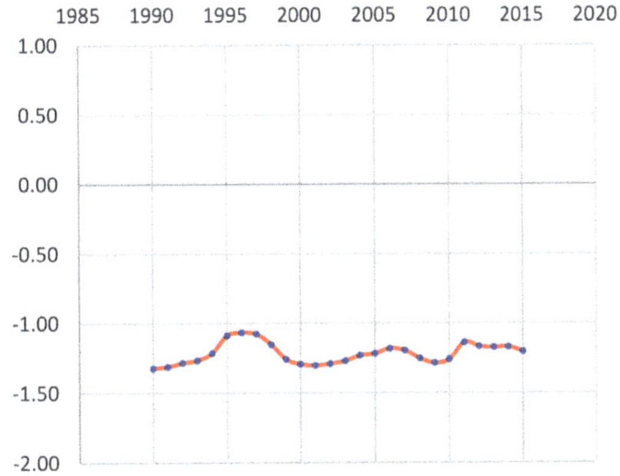

GSP ranking (2015) = 40	Area ranking = 41	Major cities: Charleston, Huntington, Morgantown, Parkersburg, Wheeling

Figure 264. The efficiency scorecard for Wisconsin

WISCONSIN	ψ_{1990} = (0.68)	ψ_{2015} = (0.69)	Δ = (0.02)

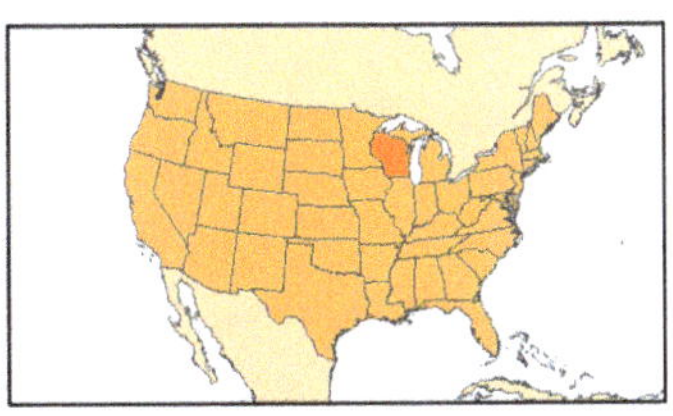
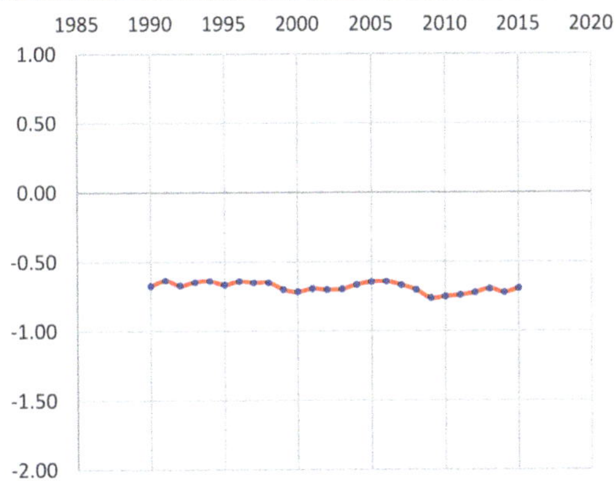

GSP ranking (2015) = 20	Area ranking = 23	Major cities: **Milwaukee** (Gamma), Madison, Green Bay, Kenosha, Racine

Wisconsin's 2015 population equivalent was 7.4E-03, and area equivalent was 5.7E-03. Its 2015 GSP was 6.6E-03, which resulted in a negative residual of 6.6E-03. Wisconsin's GSP ranking in 2015 was slightly higher than its area ranking. The State has an area of 169,640 square kilometers and a density of 41 per square kilometer. Its area is similar to that of Florida (ranked 14th), although Florida $\left(\psi_{2015} = -0.26\right)$ has a much higher density (121 per square kilometer). Moreover, Florida has this density organized into three global cities, one of which an Alpha – city. In contrast, Wisconsin has only one Gamma city.

Wyoming is ranked 49th overall (out of 51) in terms of its economic efficiency. While the State's efficiency signature shows a positive gradient from 1990 to 2010, it has entered into an RQE at $\psi = -5.00$. The State has a GSP ranking much lower than its area ranking.

In 2015, Wyoming had a population equivalent of 7.7E-05 and an area equivalent of 1.3E-02. Its 2015 GSP equivalent was 9.4E-05, with a residual of negative 1.3E-02. The State has an area of 253,600 square kilometers and a density of 2.3 per square kilometer. Wyoming's area is similar to that of Oregon. The latter is ranked 39th in terms of economic efficiency

Figure 265. The efficiency scorecard for Wyoming

WYOMING	$\psi_{1990} = (5.61)$	$\psi_{2015} = (4.91)$	$\Delta = 0.70$
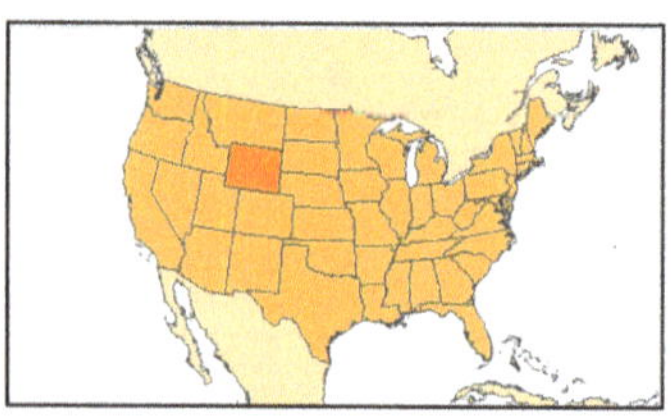	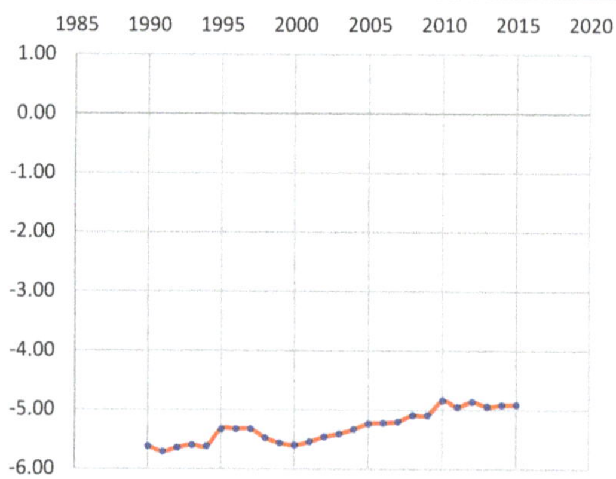		
GSP ranking (2015) = 49	Area ranking = 10	Major cities: Cheyenne, Casper, Laramie, Gillette, Rock Springs	

Figure 266. The efficiency scorecard for the District of Columbia

DISTRICT OF COLUMBIA	$\psi_{1990} = 0.78$	$\psi_{2015} = 0.97$	$\Delta = 0.19$
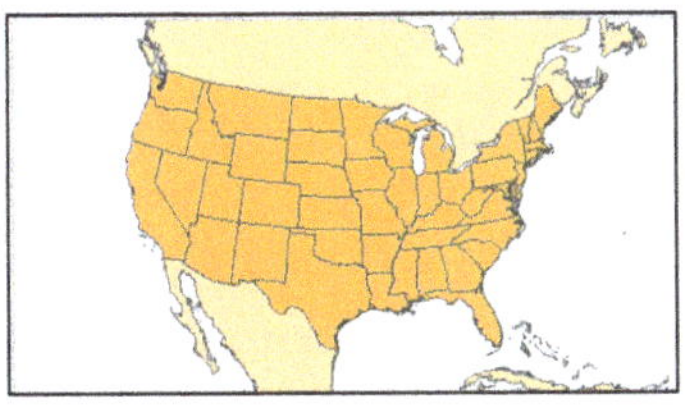	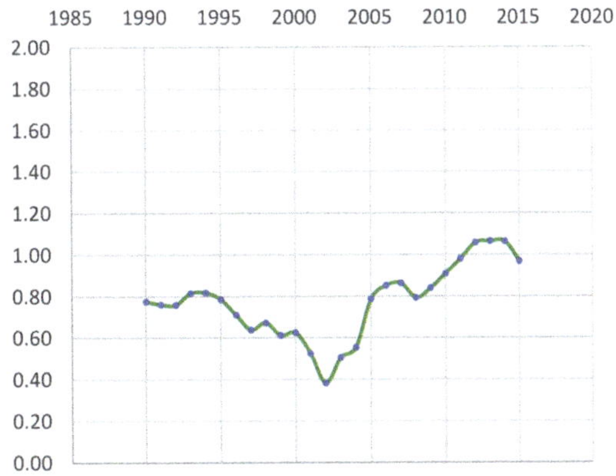		
GSP ranking (2015) = 35	Area ranking = 51	Major cities: **Washington, D.C.** (Alpha –)	

$\left(\psi_{2015} = -1.81\right)$. The difference is that Oregon had a density of 15 per square kilometer. Oregon is also able to organize this density into a Gamma – global city (Portland).

The most efficient sub-national entity in the US turns out to be not a state, but the district of the capital of the US: the District of Columbia. The District had a 2015 GSP ranking much higher than its area ranking. With a $\psi_{2015} = 0.97$, the District has double the efficiency score of Connecticut (2nd ranked), but shows only 0.19 points improvement in its efficiency over the observation period. The distance between the peak and trough of its efficiency signature is the largest of all observed entities (in the US). From a score of 0.78 in 1990, the District had its efficiency drop to 0.38 by 2002, but was able to regain all of that efficiency by 2005, and continued its improvement until 2012. Since then, its efficiency saw another 0.09 drop.

In 2015, the District had a population equivalent of 9.4E-05 and an area equivalent of 6.1E-09. Its GSP equivalent was 2.5E-04, and its residual was 1.5E-04, for the same year. This District has an area of 177 square kilometers, and a density of 4,300 per square kilometer (in 2015). Washington, D.C. is ranked as an Alpha – city. No doubt with such a small jurisdictional footprint, and high density, organized into an Alpha – city that such economic efficiency is possible.

REFERENCES

Alcácer, J., & Zhao, M. (2016). Zooming in: A practical manual for identifying geographic clusters. *Strategic Management Journal*, *37*(1), 10–21. doi:10.1002/smj.2451

Bonham, C. (2016). Clusters of Economic Growth Wailea, Maui The Economic Research Organization at the University of Hawai'i.

Gurau, M. (2009). A stronger New England through industry clusters *Communities & Banking, Fall*, 3-5.

Jolly, N. (2005). Connecticut's Industry Clusters Wethersfield, Conn.: Connecticut Department of labor

Knapp, J. L. (1999). Virginia's economy in the 1990s: Some causation is warranted *The Virginia Newsletter, 75*(2), 1-7.

NJLWD. (2010). New Jersey Key Industry Clusters New Jersey Department of Labor and Workforce Development.

Slaper, T. F., Harmon, K. M., & Rubin, B. (2016). *Industry Clusters and Regional Economic Performance: A Study Across U.S. Metropolitan Statistical Areas* (Research Paper No. 16-15). Kelley School of Business. Retrieved from https://ssrn.com/abstract=2715263

Taylor, P. J. (2001). Specification of the world city network. *Geographical Analysis*, *33*(2), 181–194. doi:10.1111/j.1538-4632.2001.tb00443.x

Glossary

Attractors: The area a dynamical system reaches when in equilibrium. Attractors represent steady states of typical behavior. Cities are the prime example of attractors in nation-states. Global cities play a major role in the current world-system as attractors of capital.

Autocatalytic: An autocatalytic process is one where an output is also an input that acts as a catalyst. This is sometimes also referred to as autoactivation. The process is nonlinear, and this results in a reduction in the entropy of the system through the creation of spontaneous order. An autocatalyzing system results in a positive, self-reinforcing, feedback loop. Biodiversity can be understood as a system of autocatalytic sets.

Charter City: A charter city is a city-region (a city and its hinterland) that is governed according to a charter bestowed on the city through nation-state parliaments. The charter represents an international treaty (under the United Nations) that devolves most functions of governance to the city for an extended period (for example, 100 years), which is open for renewal. This charter would allow the city to have its *sui generis* legal system including currency, immigration laws (e.g. refugee quotas), employment laws, and so forth. The city remains under the sovereignty of its nation-state but could have a separate citizenship that does not lead to any residency rights in the nation-state. In essence, charter cities allow nation-states to leverage the multiplicity of different legal systems.

City: Densely populated urban areas characterized by cosmopolitan diversity. What distinguishes cities from towns and villages is not the size of their population but their ability to attract (all forms of) capital. Cities play the role of attractors in nation-states.

Collapse: The final phase in the life of a dynamical system (such as a nation-state) where it exhibits chaotic behavior that precedes the destruction of system's structure. Collapse is a function of the level of coupling (synchronization) between attractors (such as cities). The higher the coupling (through harmonized legal systems), the higher is the probability of (system-wide) collapse.

Complexity Theory: An analytical paradigm that moves away from reductionist tendencies and accepts the limitations on our ability to fully control or predict the behavior of dynamical systems such as nation-states. Complexity is an attribute of dynamical systems that are evolving, i.e. systems that are adapting (through self-organization) to local variations. The structure of such systems is a complex network of interactions.

Emergence: The appearance in a dynamical system of new structures under self-organization. Emergence introduces higher scales into existing structures, at the lowest possible increase in complexity.

Global City: Also known as 'world cities.' These are large, urbanized regions that are defined by dense patterns of interaction rather than by political-administrative boundaries. Global cities have a direct effect on global affairs.

Hypotaxis: The legal, economic, and ethical principle that decides the scale of social organization based on the following decision rule: as much freedom as possible and as much state as necessary. In Catholic social doctrine, the principle is known as 'subsidiarity,' while in Protestant doctrine it is referred to as 'spheres of sovereignty.'

Jurisdictional Footprint: The legislative monopoly of a given polity over a territory (area). It represents the authority of a country to make law, and hence influence decision-making, over a particular land and its inhabitants.

Rhizomatic Organization: One of two types of organization resulting in (different types of) complexity (the other being hierarchical organization). Rhizomatic causality is neither chronological nor hierarchical. In a rhizomatic organization, causality is diffused (without beginning and end points). History ceases to be a narrative and becomes a map of attractors. A rhizomatic organization of polities favors a non-hierarchical polity based on non-linear self-organization and decentralization. The defining features of such policies are acentricity, heterogeneity, and multiplicity.

Self-Organization: The ability of a dynamical system to acquire a stable structure without external control. Self-organization allows for emergence.

Stability: The ability of a dynamical system to remain within the area of an attractor in the face of sudden changes in its environment. Stability suggests immunity from collapse. This concept is related to resilience, namely the ability to manage change and be able to develop in the long run.

Subsidiarity: A legal, political, and social principle that nests authority structures around constituent powers at the local scale. Under complexity theory, subsidiarity translates into self-organization. See also hypotaxis above.

Sustainability: A response mechanism that prevents complexity from leading to collapse. While sustainability is also a legal principle, it is better understood as an emergent property leading to stability and resulting from self-organization.

World-System: An analytical framework to understand the interaction between world polities. Historically the framework was used to analyze the interaction between nation-states. In this book, it is used to analyze the interaction between (global) cities.

About the Author

Benjamen F. Gussen is a lecturer in law-and-economics at the University of Southern Queensland School of Law and Justice. Benjamen's research interests are focused on comparative law-and-economics. They include the amelioration of Australian federalism, the application of constitutional economics to constitutional designs, the comparative analysis of sub-national constitutions, and the application of complexity theory to the analysis of legal pluralism. He is a Vice President of the Australian Law and Economics Association (AustLEA). Benjamen holds graduate degrees in law, economics, engineering, business administration and education.

Index

P

R

S

T

U

W

www.ingramcontent.com/pod-product-compliance
Lightning Source LLC
LaVergne TN
LVHW081539300926
849161LV00006B/1492